Liberty, Equality, Power

A HISTORY OF THE AMERICAN PEOPLE

COMPACT FIFTH EDITION

Volume II: Since 1863

John M. Murrin
PRINCETON UNIVERSITY, EMERITUS

Paul E. Johnson
UNIVERSITY OF SOUTH CAROLINA, EMERITUS

James M. McPherson
PRINCETON UNIVERSITY, EMERITUS

Alice Fahs
UNIVERSITY OF CALIFORNIA, IRVINE

Gary Gerstle
VANDERBILT UNIVERSITY

Emily S. Rosenberg
UNIVERSITY OF CALIFORNIA, IRVINE

Norman L. Rosenberg
MACALESTER COLLEGE

∿ **WADSWORTH**
CENGAGE Learning™

D0565407

Australia • Brazil • Japan • Korea • Mexico • Singapore • Spain • United Kingdom • United States

WADSWORTH
CENGAGE Learning™

Liberty, Equality, Power: A History of the American People, **Compact Fifth Edition, Volume II: Since 1863**

John M. Murrin, Paul E. Johnson, James M. McPherson, Alice Fahs, Gary Gerstle, Emily S. Rosenberg, and Norman L. Rosenberg

Publisher: Clark Baxter

Senior Acquisitions Editor: Ashley Dodge

Development Editor: Margaret McAndrew Beasley

Assistant Editor: Kristen Tatroe

Editorial Assistant: Ashley Spicer

Senior Marketing Manager: Janise Fry

Marketing Communications Manager: Tami Strang

Senior Content Project Manager: Joshua Allen

Senior Art Director: Cate Rickard Barr

Print/Media Buyer: Barbara Britton

Permissions Editor: Roberta Broyer

Production Service: Lachina Publishing Services

Photo Manager: Sheri Blaney

Photo Researcher: Sarah Evertson

Cover Designer: Cheryl Carrington

Cover Printer: Transcontinental— Louiseville

Compositor: International Typesetting and Composition

Printer: Transcontinental— Louiseville

Cover Art: William Sidney Mount (American, 1807–1868). *The Power of Music.* 1847. Oil on canvas, 43.4 × 53.5 cm. © The Cleveland Museum of Art, 2002. Leonard C. Hanna, Jr. Fund 1991.110

For product information and technology assistance, contact us at **Cengage Learning Academic Resource Center, 1-800-423-0563**

For permission to use material from this text or product, submit all requests online at **www.cengage.com/permissions** Further permissions questions can be emailed to **permissionrequest@cengage.com**

Library of Congress Control Number: 2007924447

Student Edition
ISBN-13: 978-0-495-411031
ISBN-10: 0-495-41103-5

Instructor Edition
ISBN-13: 978-0-495-502456
ISBN-10: 0-495-50245-6

Wadsworth Cengage Learning
10 Davis Drive
Belmont, CA 94002-3098
USA

Cengage Learning products are represented in Canada by Nelson Education, Ltd.

For your course and learning solutions, visit academic.cengage.com

Purchase any of our products at your local college store or at our preferred online store www.ichapters.com

Printed in Canada
4 5 11 10 09

About the Authors

 JOHN M. MURRIN *Princeton University, Emeritus* John M. Murrin is a specialist in American colonial and revolutionary history and the early republic. He has edited one multivolume series and five books, including two co-edited collections, *Colonial America: Essays in Politics and Social Development,* Fifth Edition (2001), and *Saints and Revolutionaries: Essays in Early American History* (1984). His own essays on early American history range from ethnic tensions, the early history of trial by jury, the rise of the legal profession, and the political culture of the colonies and the new nation, to the rise of professional baseball and college football in the 19th century. Professor Murrin served as president of the Society for Historians of the Early American Republic in 1998–99.

 PAUL E. JOHNSON *University of South Carolina, Distinguished Professor Emeritus* A specialist in early national social and cultural history, Paul E. Johnson is also the author of *The Early American Republic, 1789–1829* (2006); *Sam Patch, the Famous Jumper* (2003); *A Shopkeeper's Millennium: Society and Revivals in Rochester, New York, 1815–1837,* 25th Anniversary Edition (2004); co-author (with Sean Wilentz) of *The Kingdom of Matthias: Sex and Salvation in 19th-Century America* (1994); and editor of *African-American Christianity: Essays in History* (1994). He has been awarded the Merle Curti Prize of the Organization of American Historians (1980), the Richard P. McCormack Prize of the New Jersey Historical Association (1989), and fellowships from the National Endowment for the Humanities (1985–86), the John Simon Guggenheim Foundation (1995), and the Gilder Lehrman Institute (2001) and the National Endowment for the Humanities We the People Fellowship (2006–2007).

JAMES M. McPHERSON *Princeton University, Emeritus* James M. McPherson is a distinguished Civil War historian and was president of the American Historical Association in 2003. He won the 1989 Pulitzer Prize for his book *Battle Cry of Freedom: The Civil War Era.* His other publications include *Marching Toward Freedom: Blacks in the Civil War,* Second Edition (1991); *Ordeal by Fire: The Civil War and Reconstruction,* Third Edition (2001); *Abraham Lincoln and the Second American Revolution* (1991); *For Cause and Comrades: Why Men Fought in the Civil War* (1997), which won the Lincoln Prize in 1998; and *Crossroads of Freedom: Antietam* (2002).

ALICE FAHS *University of California, Irvine* Alice Fahs is a specialist in American cultural history of the 19th and 20th centuries. Her 2001 *The Imagined Civil War: Popular Literature of the North and South, 1861–1865* was a finalist in 2002 for the Lincoln Prize. Together with Joan Waugh she published the edited collection *The Memory of the Civil War in American Culture* in 2004; she has also edited Louisa May Alcott's *Hospital Sketches* (2004), an account of Alcott's nursing experiences during the Civil War first published in 1863. Fahs has published on the cultural history of the Civil War and gender in such journals as the *Journal of American History and Civil War History.* Her honors include an American Council of Learned Societies Fellowship and a Gilder Lehrman Fellowship, as well as fellowships from the American Antiquarian Society, the Newberry Library, and the Huntington Library. She is currently at work on a study of popular literary culture in the late 19th and early 20th centuries, focused on the emergence of mass-market newspapers during an age of imperialism.

GARY GERSTLE *Vanderbilt University* Gary Gerstle is a historian of the 20th-century United States. His books include *Working-Class Americanism: The Politics of Labor in a Textile City, 1914–1960* (1989), and *American Crucible: Race and Nation in the Twentieth Century* (2001), winner of the Saloutos Prize for the best work in immigration and ethnic history. He has also published three coedited works: *The Rise and Fall of the New Deal Order, 1930–1980* (1989); *E Pluribus Unum: Immigrants, Civic Culture, and Political Incorporation* (2001); and *Ruling America: Wealth and Power in a Democracy* (2005). His articles have appeared in the *American Historical*

Review, Journal of American History, American Quarterly, and other journals. He has served on the board of editors of both the *Journal of American History* and the *American Historical Review.* His honors include a National Endowment for the Humanities Fellowship and a John Simon Guggenheim Memorial Fellowship.

 EMILY S. ROSENBERG *University of California, Irvine* Emily S. Rosenberg specializes in U.S. foreign relations in the 20th century and is the author of *Spreading the American Dream: American Economic and Cultural Expansion, 1890–1945* (1982); *Financial Missionaries to the World: The Politics and Culture of Dollar Diplomacy* (1999), which won the Ferrell Book Award; and A *Date Which Will Live: Pearl Harbor in American Memory* (2004). Her other publications include (with Norman L. Rosenberg) *In Our Times: America Since 1945,* Seventh Edition (2003), and numerous articles dealing with foreign relations in the context of international finance, American culture, and gender ideology. She has served on the board of the Organization of American Historians, on the board of editors of the *Journal of American History,* and as president of the Society for Historians of American Foreign Relations.

 NORMAN L. ROSENBERG *Macalester College* Norman L. Rosenberg specializes in legal history with a particular interest in legal culture and First Amendment issues. His books include *Protecting the "Best Men": An Interpretive History of the Law of Libel* (1990) and (with Emily S. Rosenberg) *In Our Times: America Since 1945,* Seventh Edition (2003). He has published articles in the *Rutgers Law Review, UCLA Law Review, Constitutional Commentary, Law & History Review,* and many other journals and law-related anthologies.

Contents in Brief

Contents in Detail

Features

Note: Maps with "CI" page numbers appear in Color Inserts.

Maps

History through Film

To the Student: Why Study History?

Why take a course in American history? This is a question that many college and university students ask. In many respects, students today are like the generations of Americans who have gone before them: optimistic and forward looking, far more eager to imagine where we as a nation might be going than to reflect on where we have been. If anything, this tendency has become more pronounced in recent years, as the Internet revolution has accelerated the pace and excitement of change and made even the recent past seem at best quaint, at worst uninteresting and irrelevant.

But it is precisely in these moments of change that a sense of the past can be indispensable in terms of guiding our actions in the present and future. We can find in other periods of American history moments, like our own, of dizzying technological change and economic growth, rapid alterations in the concentration of wealth and power, and basic changes in patterns of work, residence, and play. How did Americans at those times create, embrace, and resist these changes? In earlier periods of American history, the United States was home, as it is today, to a broad array of ethnic and racial groups. How did earlier generations of Americans respond to the cultural conflicts and misunderstandings that often arise from conditions of diversity?

How did immigrants of the early 1900s perceive their new land? How and when did they integrate themselves into American society? To study how ordinary Americans of the past struggled with these issues is to gain perspective on the opportunities and problems that we face today.

History also provides an important guide to affairs of state. What role should America assume in world affairs? Should we participate in international bodies such as the United Nations, or insist on our ability to act autonomously and without the consent of other nations? What is the proper role of government in economic and social life? Should the government regulate the economy? To what extent should the government enforce morality regarding religion, sexual practices, drinking and drugs, movies, TV, and other forms of mass culture? And what are our responsibilities as citizens to each other and to the nation? Americans of past generations have debated these issues with verve and conviction. Learning about these debates and how they were resolved will enrich our understanding of the policy possibilities for today and tomorrow.

History, finally, is about stories—stories that we all tell about ourselves; our families; our communities; our ethnicity, race, region, and religion; and our nation. They are stories of triumph and tragedy, of engagement and flight, and of high ideals and high comedy. When telling these stories, "American history" is often the furthest thing from our minds. But, often, an implicit sense of the past informs what we say about grandparents who immigrated many years ago; the suburb in which we live; the church, synagogue, or mosque at which we worship; or the ethnic or racial group to which we belong. How well, we might ask, do we really understand these individuals, institutions, and groups? Do our stories about them capture their history and complexity? Or do our stories wittingly or unwittingly simplify or alter what these individuals and groups experienced? A study of American history helps us first to ask these questions and then to answer them. In the process, we can embark on a journey of intellectual and personal discovery and situate ourselves more firmly than we had thought possible in relation to those who came before us. We can gain a firmer self-knowledge and a greater appreciation for the richness of our nation and, indeed, of all humanity.

Preface

We are pleased to present the fifth edition of *Liberty, Equality, Power*. Like the first four editions, this one captures the drama and excitement of America's past, from the pre-Columbian era through our own time. It integrates social and cultural history into a political story that is organized around the themes of liberty, equality, and power, and synthesizes the finest historical scholarship to create a narrative that is balanced, lively, and accessible to a broad range of students.

The *Liberty, Equality, Power* Approach

In this book, we tell many small stories, and one large one: how America transformed itself, in a relatively brief period of world history, from a land inhabited by hunter-gatherer and agricultural Native American societies into the most powerful industrial nation on earth. This story has been told many times before, and those who have told it in the past have usually emphasized the political experiment in liberty and equality that took root here in the 18th century. We, too, stress the extraordinary and transformative impact that the ideals of liberty and equality exerted on American politics, society, and economics during the American Revolution and after.

We show how the creation of a free economic environment—one in which entrepreneurial spirit, technological innovation, and industrial production have flourished—underpinned American industrial might. We have also emphasized the successful struggles for freedom that, over the course of the last 230 years, have brought—first to all white men, then to men of color, and finally to women—rights and opportunities that they had not previously known.

But we have also identified a third factor in this pantheon of American ideals—that of power. We examine power in many forms: the accumulation of vast economic fortunes and their influence on the economy and on politics; the dispossession of American Indians from land that they regarded as theirs; the enslavement of millions of Africans and their African American descendants for a period of almost 250 years; the relegation of women and of racial, ethnic, and religious minorities to subordinate places in American society; and the extension of American control over foreign peoples, such as Latin Americans and Filipinos, who would have preferred to have been free and self-governing. We do not mean to suggest that American power has always been turned to these negative purposes. Subordinate groups have also marshaled power to combat oppression, as in the abolitionist and civil-rights crusades, the campaign for woman suffrage, and the labor movement. The government has at times used its power to moderate poverty and to manage the economy in the interests of general prosperity. And it has used its military power to defeat Nazi Germany, World War II Japan, the Cold War Soviet Union, and other enemies of freedom.

The invocation of power as a variable in American history impels us to widen the lens through which we look at the past and to enrich the stories we tell. Ours has been a history of freedom and domination; of progress toward realizing a broadly democratic polity and of delays and reverses; of abundance and poverty; of wars for freedom and justice and for control of foreign markets. In complicating our master narrative in this way, we think we have rendered American history more exciting and intriguing. Progress has not been automatic, but the product of ongoing struggles.

In this book, we have tried to capture the diversity of the American past, both in terms of outcomes and in terms of the variety of groups who have participated in America's making. American Indians are not presented simply as the victims of European aggression but as peoples remarkably diverse in their own ranks, with a variety of systems of social organization and cultural expression. We give equal treatment to the industrial titans of American history—the likes of Andrew Carnegie and John D. Rockefeller—and to those, such as small farmers and poor workers, who resisted the corporate reorganization of economic life. We celebrate the great moments of 1863, when African Americans were freed from slavery, and of 1868, when they were made full citizens of the United States. But we also note how a majority of African Americans had to wait another 100 years, until the civil-rights movement of the 1960s, to gain full access to American freedoms. We tell similarly complex stories about women, Latinos, and other groups of ethnic Americans.

Political issues are only part of America's story. Americans have always loved their leisure and have created the world's most vibrant popular culture. They have embraced technological innovations, especially those promising to make their lives easier and more fun. We have, therefore, devoted considerable space to a discussion of American popular culture, from the founding of the first newspapers in the 18th century and the rise of movies, jazz, and the comics in the early 20th century to the cable television and Internet revolutions in recent years. We have also analyzed how American industry has periodically altered home and personal life by making new products—such as clothing, cars, refrigerators, and computers—available to consumers. In such ways, we hope to give our readers a rich portrait of how Americans lived at various points in our history.

New to This Edition

The biggest change to the fifth edition was our decision to add a new author, Professor Alice Fahs of the University of California, Irvine. This is the first time in 17 years of work on this textbook that we have reached out to a new historian, and we are delighted that Professor Fahs has decided to join us. Professor Fahs is an accomplished historian of the 19th and early 20th centuries, with special expertise in cultural history and the history of gender. She has already contributed significantly to this edition by substantially reworking chapters 18 and 19, bringing to them her extraordinary knowledge of the period and her accessible and evocative writing style. We invite readers to look closely at those two revised and expanded chapters, and we think they will share our enthusiasm about adding Professor Fahs to our team. We expect her to work on this book for many years, and we are excited by the many contributions she will make.

Specific Revisions to Content and Coverage

Chapters 7 to 9 have been substantially reorganized. New titles are chapter 7, "Completing the Revolution, 1789–1815"; chapter 8, "Northern Transformations, 1800–1830"; and chapter 9, "The Old South, 1790–1850."

Chapters 11 and 12 have been reorganized to provide smoother chronology and transitions with surrounding chapters.

Chapter 18 is now titled: "A Transformed Nation: The West and the New South, 1865–1900" and includes a new introduction on experiences of homesteader Mary Abell. New material on "Industrializing West" is added, as well as a new History through Film feature on the musical *Oklahoma!*.

Chapter 19 is now titled: "The Emergence of Corporate America, 1865–1900" and includes new material on economic growth, class distinction, and culture.

Chapter 24 now includes a new History through Film feature on *Inherit the Wind*.

Chapter 26 now includes a new History through Film feature on *Casablanca*.

Chapters 30 to 32 have been revised and reorganized to include the addition of new chapter 32. New titles are chapter 30, "Power and Politics, 1974–1992"; chapter 31, "Economic, Social, and Cultural Change in the Late 20th Century"; and chapter 32, "Politics of Hope and Fear, 1993–2007."

Reconstruction, 1863–1877

From the beginning of the Civil War, the North fought to "reconstruct" the Union. Lincoln first attempted to restore the Union as it had existed before 1861, but once the abolition of slavery became a Northern war aim, the Union could never be reconstructed on its old foundations. Instead, it must experience a "new birth of freedom," as Lincoln had said at the dedication of the military cemetery at Gettysburg.

But precisely what did "a new birth of freedom" mean? At the very least, it meant the end of slavery. The slave states would be reconstructed on a free-labor basis. But what would liberty look like for the 4 million freed slaves? Would they become citizens equal to their former masters in the eyes of the law? Would they have the right to vote? Should Confederate leaders and soldiers be punished for treason? On what terms should the Confederate states return to the Union? What would be the powers of the states and of the national government in a reconstructed Union?

Wartime Reconstruction

Lincoln pondered the problems of Reconstruction long and hard. At first he feared that whites in the South would never extend equal rights to the freed slaves. After all, even most Northern states denied full civil equality to the few black people within their borders. In 1862, Lincoln encouraged freedpeople to emigrate to all-black countries such as Haiti, where they would have a chance to get ahead without having to face the racism of whites. Black leaders, abolitionists, and many Republicans objected to that policy. Black people were Americans, they asserted. Why should they not have the rights of American citizens instead of being urged to leave the country?

Lincoln eventually acknowledged the logic and justice of that view, but in beginning the process of reconstruction, he first reached out to Southern *whites* whose allegiance to the Confederacy was lukewarm. On December 8, 1863, Lincoln issued his Proclamation of Amnesty and Reconstruction, which offered presidential pardon to Southern whites (with the exception of Confederate government officials and high-ranking military officers) who took an oath of allegiance to the United States and accepted the abolition of slavery. In any state where the number of white males aged 21 or older who took this oath equaled 10 percent of the number of voters in 1860, that nucleus could reestablish a state government to which Lincoln promised presidential recognition.

CHRONOLOGY

1863	Lincoln issues Proclamation of Amnesty and Reconstruction
1864	Congress passes Wade-Davis bill; Lincoln kills it by pocket veto
1865	Congress establishes Freedmen's Bureau • Andrew Johnson becomes president, announces his reconstruction plan • Southern states enact Black Codes • Congress refuses to seat Southern congressmen elected under Johnson's plan
1866	Congress passes civil rights bill and expands Freedmen's Bureau over Johnson's vetoes • Race riots in Memphis and New Orleans • Congress approves 14th Amendment • Republicans increase congressional majority in fall elections
1867	Congress passes Reconstruction acts over Johnson's vetoes • Congress passes Tenure of Office Act over Johnson's veto
1868	Most Southern senators and representatives readmitted to Congress under congressional plan of Reconstruction • Andrew Johnson impeached but not convicted • Ulysses S. Grant elected president • 14th Amendment is ratified
1870	15th Amendment is ratified
1871	Congress passes Ku Klux Klan Act
1872	Liberal Republicans defect from party • Grant wins reelection
1873	Economic depression begins with the Panic
1874	Democrats win control of House of Representatives
1875	Democrats implement Mississippi Plan • Congress passes civil rights act
1876	Centennial celebration in Philadelphia • Disputed presidential election causes constitutional crisis
1877	Compromise of 1877 installs Rutherford B. Hayes as president • Hayes withdraws troops from South
1883	Supreme Court declares civil rights act of 1875 unconstitutional

Because the war was still raging, this policy could be carried out only where Union troops controlled substantial portions of a Confederate state: Louisiana, Arkansas, and Tennessee in early 1864. Nevertheless, Lincoln hoped that once the process had begun in those areas, it might snowball as Union military victories convinced more and more Confederates that their cause was hopeless. In the end, those military victories were long delayed, and in most parts of the South, reconstruction did not begin until 1865.

Another problem that slowed the process was growing opposition within Lincoln's own party. Many Republicans believed that white men who had fought *against* the Union should not be rewarded with restoration of their political rights while black men who had fought *for* the Union were denied those rights. The Proclamation of Reconstruction had stated that any provision which may be adopted by [a reconstructed] State government in relation to the freed people of such State, which shall recognize and declare their permanent freedom, provide for their education, and which may yet be consistent, as a temporary arrangement, with their present condition as a laboring, landless, and homeless class, will not be objected to by the national Executive.

This seemed to mean that white landowners and former slaveholders could adopt labor regulations and other measures to control former slaves, so long as they recognized their freedom and made minimal provision for their education.

Radical Republicans and Reconstruction

These changes were radical advances over slavery, but for many Republicans they were not radical enough. Led by Thaddeus Stevens in the House and Charles Sumner in the Senate, the radical Republicans wanted to go much further. If the freedpeople were landless, they said, provide them with land by confiscating the plantations of leading Confederates as punishment for treason. Radical Republicans also distrusted oaths of allegiance sworn by ex-Confederates. Rather than simply restoring the old ruling class to power, asked Charles Sumner, why not give freed slaves the vote, to provide a genuinely loyal nucleus of supporters in the South?

These radical positions did not command a majority of Congress in 1864. Yet the experience of Louisiana, the first state to reorganize under Lincoln's more moderate policy, convinced even nonradical Republicans to block Lincoln's program. With the protection of Union soldiers in the occupied portion of Louisiana (New Orleans and several parishes in the southern half of the state), enough white men took the oath of allegiance to satisfy Lincoln's conditions. They adopted a new state constitution and formed a government that abolished slavery and provided a school system for blacks. But despite Lincoln's private appeal to the new government to grant literate blacks and black Union soldiers the right to vote, the reconstructed Louisiana legislature chose not to do so. It also authorized planters to enforce restrictive labor policies on black plantation workers. Louisiana's actions alienated a majority of congressional Republicans, who refused to admit representatives and senators from the "reconstructed" state.

At the same time, though, Congress failed to enact a reconstruction policy of its own. This was not for lack of trying. In fact, both houses passed the Wade-Davis reconstruction bill (named for Senator Benjamin Wade of Ohio and Representative Henry Winter Davis of Maryland) in July 1864. That bill did not **enfranchise** blacks, but it did impose such stringent loyalty requirements on Southern whites that few of them could take the required oath. Lincoln therefore vetoed it.

Lincoln's action infuriated many Republicans. Wade and Davis published a blistering "manifesto" denouncing the president. This bitter squabble threatened for a time to destroy Lincoln's chances of being reelected. Union military success in fall 1864, however, combined with sober second thoughts about the consequences of a Democratic electoral victory, reunited the Republicans behind Lincoln. The collapse of Confederate military resistance the following spring set the stage for compromise between the president and Congress on a policy for the postwar South. Two days after Appomattox, Lincoln promised that he would soon announce such a policy, which probably would have included voting rights for some blacks and stronger measures to protect their civil rights. But three days later, Lincoln was assassinated.

Andrew Johnson and Reconstruction

Focus Question
What were the positions of Presidents Abraham Lincoln and Andrew Johnson and of the moderate and radical Republicans in Congress on the issues of restoring the South to the Union and protecting the rights of freed slaves?

In 1864, Republicans had adopted the name Union Party to attract the votes of War Democrats and border-state Unionists who could not bring themselves to vote Republican. For the same reason, they also nominated Andrew Johnson of Tennessee as Lincoln's running mate.

Of "poor white" heritage, Johnson had clawed his way up in the rough-and-tumble politics of east Tennessee. This region of small farms and few slaves held little love for the planters who controlled the state. Andrew Johnson denounced the planters as "stuck-up aristocrats" who had no empathy with the Southern yeomen for whom Johnson became a self-appointed spokesman. Johnson, although a Democrat, was the only senator from a seceding state who refused to support the Confederacy. For this stance, the Republicans rewarded him with the vice presidential nomination, hoping to attract the votes of pro-war Democrats and upper-South Unionists.

Booth's bullet therefore elevated to the presidency a man who still thought of himself as primarily a Democrat and a Southerner. The trouble this might cause in a party that was mostly Republican and Northern was not immediately apparent, however. In fact, Johnson's enmity toward the "stuck-up aristocrats" whom he blamed for leading the South into secession prompted him to utter dire threats against "traitors." "Treason is a crime and must be made odious," he said, soon after becoming president. "Traitors must be impoverished. . . . They must not only be punished, but their social power must be destroyed."

Radical Republicans liked the sound of this pronouncement. It seemed to promise the type of reconstruction they favored—one that would deny political power to ex-Confederates and would enfranchise blacks. They envisioned a coalition between these new black voters and the small minority of Southern whites who had never supported the Confederacy. These men could be expected to vote Republican. Republican governments in Southern states would guarantee freedom and would pass laws to provide civil rights and economic opportunity for freed slaves. Not incidentally, they would also strengthen the Republican Party nationally.

Johnson's Policy

From a combination of pragmatic, partisan, and idealistic motives, therefore, Radical Republicans prepared to implement a progressive reconstruction policy. But Johnson unexpectedly refused to cooperate. Instead of calling Congress into special session, he moved ahead on his own. On May 29, 1865, Johnson issued two proclamations. The first provided a blanket **amnesty** for all but the highest-ranking Confederate officials and military officers, and those ex-Confederates with taxable property worth $20,000 or more—the "stuck-up aristocrats." The second named a provisional governor for North Carolina and directed him to call an election of delegates to frame a new state constitution. Only white men who had received amnesty and taken an oath of allegiance could vote. Similar proclamations soon followed for other former Confederate states. Johnson's policy was clear: He would exclude both blacks and upper-class whites from the reconstruction process. The backbone of the new South would be yeomen whites who, like himself, had remained steadfastly loyal to the Union, along with those who now proclaimed themselves loyal.

Although at first many Republicans supported Johnson's policy, the radicals were dismayed. They feared that restricting the vote to whites would lead to oppression of the newly freed slaves and restoration of the old power structure in the South. They began to sense that Johnson (who had owned slaves) was as dedicated to white

Andrew Johnson and Frederick Douglass   By 1866, the president and the leading black spokesman for equal rights represented opposite poles in the debate about Reconstruction. Johnson wanted to bring the South back into the Union on the basis of white suffrage; Douglass wanted black men to be granted the right to vote. Johnson's resistance to this policy as Republicans tried to enact it was a factor in his impeachment two years later.

supremacy as any Confederate. "White men alone must govern the South," he told a Democratic senator. After a tense confrontation with a group of black men led by Frederick Douglass, who had visited the White House to urge black suffrage, Johnson told his private secretary: "Those damned sons of bitches thought they had me in a trap! I know that damned Douglass; he's just like any nigger, and he would sooner cut a white man's throat than not."

Moderate Republicans believed that black men should participate to some degree in the reconstruction process, but in 1865 they were not yet prepared to break with the president. They regarded his policy as an "experiment" that would be modified as time went on. "Loyal negroes must not be put down, while disloyal white men are put up," wrote a moderate Republican. "But I am quite willing to see what will come of Mr. Johnson's experiment." If the new Southern state constitutions failed to enfranchise at least literate blacks and those who had fought in the Union army, said another moderate, "the President then will be at liberty to pursue a sterner policy."

Southern Defiance

As it happened, none of the state conventions enfranchised a single black. Some of them even balked at ratifying the 13th Amendment (which abolished slavery). The rhetoric of some white Southerners began to take on a renewed anti-Yankee tone of defiance that sounded like 1861 all over again. Reports from Unionists and army officers in the South told of neo-Confederate violence against blacks and their white sympathizers. Johnson seemed to encourage such activities by his own rhetoric, which sounded increasingly like that of a Southern Democrat, and by allowing the organization of white militia units in the South. "What can be hatched from such an egg," asked a Republican newspaper, "but another rebellion?"

Then there was the matter of presidential pardons. After talking fiercely about punishing traitors, and after excluding several classes of them from his amnesty proclamation, Johnson began to issue special pardons to many ex-Confederates, restoring to them all property and political rights. Moreover, under the new state constitutions, Southern voters were electing hundreds of ex-Confederates to state offices. Even more alarming to Northerners, who thought they had won the war, was the election to Congress of no fewer than nine ex-Confederate congressmen, seven ex-Confederate state officials, four generals, four colonels, and even the former Confederate vice president, Alexander H. Stephens. To apprehensive Republicans, it appeared that the rebels, unable to capture Washington in war, were about to do so in peace.

Somehow the aristocrats and traitors Johnson had denounced in April had taken over the reconstruction process. Instead of weapons, they had resorted to flattering the presidential ego. Thousands of prominent ex-Confederates or their tearful female relatives applied for pardons, confessing the error of their ways and appealing for presidential mercy. Reveling in his power over these once-haughty aristocrats who had disdained him as a humble tailor, Johnson waxed eloquent on his "love, respect, and confidence" toward

Southern whites, for whom he now felt "forbearing and forgiving." More effective, perhaps, was the praise and support Johnson received from leading Northern Democrats. Although the Republicans had placed him on their presidential ticket in 1864, Johnson was after all a Democrat. That party's leaders enticed Johnson with visions of reelection as a Democrat in 1868 if he could manage to reconstruct the South in a manner that would preserve a Democratic majority there.

The Black Codes

That was just what the Republicans feared. Their concern that state governments devoted to white supremacy would reduce the freedpeople to a condition close to slavery was confirmed in fall 1865, when some of those governments enacted **"Black Codes."**

One of the first tasks of the legislatures of the reconstructed states was to define the rights of 4 million former slaves. The option of treating them exactly like white citizens was scarcely considered. Instead, the states excluded black people from juries and the ballot box, did not permit them to testify against whites in court, banned interracial marriage, and punished blacks more severely than whites for certain crimes. Some states defined any unemployed black person as a vagrant and hired him out to a planter, forbade blacks to lease land, and provided for the apprenticing to whites of black youths who did not have adequate parental support.

These Black Codes aroused anger among Northern Republicans, who saw them as a brazen attempt to reinstate a **quasi-slavery.** "We tell the white men of Mississippi," declared the *Chicago Tribune,* "that the men of the North will convert the State of Mississippi into a frog pond before they will allow such laws to disgrace one foot of the soil in which the bones of our soldiers sleep and over which the flag of freedom waves." And, in fact, the Union army's occupation forces did suspend the implementation of Black Codes that discriminated on racial grounds.

Land and Labor in the Postwar South

The Black Codes, although discriminatory, were designed to address a genuine problem. The end of the war had left black-white relations in the South in a state of limbo. The South's economy was in a shambles. Burned-out plantations, fields growing up in weeds, and railroads without tracks, bridges, or **rolling stock** marked the trail of war. Nearly half of the livestock in the former Confederacy and most other tangible assets except the land had been destroyed. Many people, white as well as black, lived from meal to meal. Law and order broke down in many areas. The war had ended early enough in the spring to allow the planting of at least some food crops, but who would plant and cultivate them? One-quarter of the South's white farmers had been killed in the war; the slaves were slaves no more. "We have nothing left to begin anew with," lamented a South Carolina planter. "I never did a day's work in my life, and I don't know how to begin."

Despite all of this trouble, life went on. Soldiers' widows and their children plowed and planted. Slaveless planters and their wives calloused their hands for the first time. Confederate veterans drifted home and went to work. Former slave owners asked their former slaves to work the land for wages or shares of the crop, and many did so. Others refused, because for them to leave the old place was an essential part of freedom. In slavery times, the only way to become free was to run away, and the impulse to leave the scene of bondage persisted. "You ain't, none o' you, gwinter feel rale free," said a black preacher to his congregation, "till you shakes de dus' ob de Ole Plantashun offen yore feet" (dialect in original source).

Thus the roads were alive with freedpeople who were on the move in summer 1865. Many of them signed on to work at farms just a few miles from their old homes. Others moved into town. Some looked for relatives who had been sold away during slavery or from whom they had been separated during the war. Some wandered aimlessly. Crime increased as people, both blacks and whites, stole food to survive, and as whites organized vigilante groups to discipline blacks and force them to work.

The Freedmen's Bureau

Into this vacuum stepped the U.S. Army and the **Freedmen's Bureau.** Tens of thousands of troops remained in the South as an occupation force until civil government could be restored. The Freedmen's Bureau (its official title was Bureau of Refugees, Freedmen, and Abandoned Lands), created by Congress in March 1865, became the principal agency for overseeing relations between former slaves and owners. Staffed by army officers, the bureau established posts throughout the South to supervise free-labor wage contracts between landowners and freedpeople. The Freedmen's Bureau also issued food rations to 150,000 people daily during 1865, one-third of them to whites. Southern whites viewed the Freedmen's Bureau with hostility. Without it, however, the postwar chaos and devastation in the South would have been much greater—as some whites privately admitted. Bureau agents used their influence with black people to encourage them to sign free-labor contracts and return to work.

In negotiating labor contracts, the bureau tried to establish minimum wages. Lack of money in the South, however, caused many contracts to call for **share wages**—that is, paying workers with shares of the crop. At first, landowners worked their laborers in large groups (called gangs) under direct supervision, but many black workers resented this arrangement as reminiscent of slavery. Thus, a new system evolved, called **sharecropping**, whereby a black family worked a specific piece of land in return for a share of the crop produced on it.

Land for the Landless

Freedpeople, of course, would have preferred to farm their own land. "What's de use of being free if you don't own land enough to be buried in?" asked one black sharecropper. "Might juss as well stay slave all yo' days" (dialect in original). Some black farmers did manage to save up enough money to buy small plots of land. Demobilized black soldiers purchased land with their bounty payments, sometimes pooling their money to buy an

Sharecroppers Working in the Fields   This photograph shows two families of sharecroppers picking cotton. Freed slaves resisted landowners' efforts to work them in gangs as they had in slavery, so the owners rented land to black families in return for a share of the crop. These croppers do not appear to be overjoyed with the new system.

entire plantation on which several black families settled. Northern philanthropists helped some freedmen buy land. Most ex-slaves found the purchase of land impossible. Few of them had money, and even if they did, whites often refused to sell their land because it would mean losing a source of cheap labor and encouraging notions of black independence.

Several Northern radicals proposed legislation to confiscate ex-Confederate land and redistribute it to freedpeople, but those proposals went nowhere. The most promising effort to put thousands of slaves on land of their own also failed. In January 1865, after his march through Georgia, General William T. Sherman had issued a military order setting aside thousands of acres of abandoned plantation land in the Georgia and South Carolina low country for settlement by freed slaves. The army even turned over some of its surplus mules to black farmers. The expectation of **"40 acres and a mule"** excited freedpeople in 1865, but President Johnson's Amnesty Proclamation and his wholesale issuance of pardons restored most of this property to pardoned ex-Confederates. The same thing happened to white-owned land elsewhere in the South. Placed under the temporary care of the Freedmen's Bureau for subsequent possible distribution to freedpeople, by 1866 nearly all of this land had been restored to its former owners by order of President Johnson.

Education

Abolitionists were more successful in helping freedpeople obtain an education. During the war, freedmen's aid societies and missionary societies founded by abolitionists had sent teachers to Union-occupied areas of the South to set up schools for freed slaves. After the war, this effort was expanded with the aid of the Freedmen's Bureau. Two thousand Northern teachers, three-quarters of them women, fanned out into every part of the South. There they trained black teachers to staff first the mission schools and later the public schools established by Reconstruction state governments. After 1870, the missionary societies concentrated more heavily on making higher education available to African Americans. Many of the traditionally black colleges in the South today were founded and supported by their efforts. This education crusade, which the black leader W. E. B. Du Bois described as "the most wonderful peace-battle of the nineteenth century," reduced the Southern black illiteracy rate to 70 percent by 1880 and to 48 percent by 1900.

The Advent of Congressional Reconstruction

Political reconstruction shaped the civil and political rights of freedpeople. By the time Congress met in December 1865, the Republican majority was determined to control the process by which former Confederate states would regain full representation. Congress refused to admit the representatives and senators elected by the former Confederate states under Johnson's reconstruction policy and set up a special committee to formulate new terms. The committee held hearings at which Southern Unionists, freedpeople, and U.S. Army officers testified to abuse and terrorism in the South. Their testimony convinced Republicans of the need for stronger federal intervention to define and protect the civil rights of freedpeople. Many radicals wanted to go further and grant the ballot to black men, who would join with white Unionists and Northern settlers in the South to form a Southern Republican Party.

Most Republicans realized that Northern voters would not support such a radical policy, however. Racism was still strong in the North, where most states denied the right to vote to the few blacks living within their borders. Moderate Republicans feared that Democrats would exploit Northern racism in the congressional elections of 1866 if Congress made black suffrage a cornerstone of Reconstruction. Instead, the special committee decided to draft a constitutional amendment that would encourage Southern states to enfranchise blacks but would not require them to do so.

Schism between President and Congress

Meanwhile, Congress passed two laws to protect the economic and civil rights of freedpeople. The first extended the life of the Freedmen's Bureau and expanded its powers. The second defined freedpeople as citizens with equal legal rights and gave federal courts appellate jurisdiction to enforce those rights. To the dismay of moderates who were trying to heal the widening breach between the president and Congress, Johnson vetoed both measures. He followed this action with an intemperate speech to Democratic supporters in which he denounced Republican leaders as traitors who did not want to restore the Union except on terms that would degrade white Southerners. Democratic newspapers applauded the president for vetoing bills that would "compound our race with niggers, gypsies, and baboons."

The 14th Amendment

Johnson had thrown down the gauntlet to congressional Republicans, and they did not hesitate to take it up. With more than a two-thirds majority in both houses, they passed the Freedmen's Bureau and Civil Rights bills over the president's vetoes. Then, on April 30, 1866, the special committee submitted to Congress its proposed 14th Amendment to the Constitution. After lengthy debate, the amendment received the required two-thirds majority in Congress on June 13 and went to the states for ratification. Section 1 defined all native-born or naturalized persons, including blacks, as American citizens and prohibited the states from abridging the "privileges and immunities" of citizens, from depriving "any person of life, liberty, or property without due process of law," and from denying to any person "the equal protection of the laws." Section 2 gave states the option of either enfranchising black males or losing a proportionate number of congressional seats and electoral votes. Section 3 disqualified a significant number of ex-Confederates from holding federal or state office. Section 4 guaranteed the national debt and repudiated the Confederate debt. Section 5 empowered Congress to enforce the 14th Amendment by "appropriate legislation." The 14th Amendment had far-reaching consequences. Section 1 has become the most important provision in the Constitution for defining and enforcing civil rights.

The 1866 Elections

Republicans entered the 1866 congressional elections campaign with the 14th Amendment as their platform. They made clear that any ex-Confederate state that ratified the amendment would be declared "reconstructed" and that its representatives and senators would be seated in Congress. Tennessee ratified the amendment, but Johnson counseled other Southern legislatures to reject the amendment, which they did. Johnson then prepared for an all-out campaign to gain a friendly Northern majority in the congressional elections.

Johnson began his campaign by creating a National Union Party made up of a few conservative Republicans who disagreed with their party, some border-state Unionists who supported the president, and Democrats. The inclusion of Democrats doomed the effort from the start. Many Northern Democrats still carried the taint of having opposed the war effort, and many Northern voters did not trust them. The National Union Party was further damaged by race riots in Memphis and New Orleans, where white mobs including former Confederate soldiers killed 80 blacks, among them several former Union soldiers. The riots bolstered Republican arguments that national power was necessary to protect "the fruits of victory" in the South. Perhaps the biggest liability of the National Union Party was Johnson. In a whistle-stop tour through the North, he traded insults with hecklers and embarrassed his supporters by comparing himself to Christ and his Republican adversaries to Judas.

Republicans swept the election: They gained a three-to-one majority in the next Congress. Having rejected the Reconstruction terms embodied in the 14th Amendment, Southern Democrats now faced far more stringent terms. "They would not cooperate in rebuilding what they destroyed," wrote an exasperated moderate Republican, so "we must remove the rubbish and rebuild from the bottom. Whether they are willing or not, we must compel obedience to the Union and demand protection for its humblest citizen."

The Reconstruction Acts of 1867

In March 1867, the new Congress enacted over Johnson's vetoes two laws prescribing new procedures for the full restoration of the former Confederate states (except Tennessee, which had already been readmitted) to the Union. These laws represented a complex compromise between radicals and moderates that had been hammered out in a confusing sequence of committee drafts, caucus decisions, all-night debates on the floor, and frayed tempers. The Reconstruction acts of 1867 divided the 10 Southern states into five military districts, directed army officers to register voters for the election of delegates to new constitutional conventions, and enfranchised males aged 21 and older (including blacks) to vote in those elections. The acts also disenfranchised (for these elections only) those ex-Confederates who were disqualified from holding office under the not-yet-ratified 14th Amendment—fewer than 10 percent of all white voters. When a state had adopted a new constitution that granted equal civil and political rights regardless of race and had ratified

NEW YORK, SATURDAY, MAY 26, 1866.

The Burning of a Freedmen's School   Because freedpeople's education symbolized black progress, whites who resented and resisted this progress sometimes attacked and burned freedmen's schools, as in this dramatic illustration of a white mob burning a school during antiblack riots in Memphis in May 1866.

the 14th Amendment, it would be declared reconstructed, and its newly elected congressmen would be seated.

These measures embodied a true revolution. Just a few years earlier, Southern whites had been masters of 4 million slaves and part of an independent Confederate nation. Now they were shorn of political power, with their former slaves not only freed but also politically empowered. To be sure, radical Republicans who warned that the revolution was incomplete as long as the old master class retained economic and social power turned out to be right in the end. In 1867, however, the emancipation and enfranchisement of black Americans seemed, as a sympathetic French journalist described it, "one of the most radical revolutions known in history."

Like most revolutions, the reconstruction process did not go smoothly. Many Southern Democrats breathed defiance and refused to cooperate. The presence of the army minimized anti-black violence, but thousands of white Southerners who were eligible to vote refused to do so, hoping that their nonparticipation would delay the process long enough for Northern voters to come to their senses and elect Democrats to Congress.

Blacks and their white allies organized **Union leagues** to inform and mobilize the new black voters into the Republican Party. Democrats branded Southern white Republicans as "**scalawags**" and Northern settlers as "**carpetbaggers.**" By September 1867, the 10 states had 735,000 black voters and only 635,000 white voters registered. At least one-third of the registered white voters were Republicans.

President Johnson did everything he could to block Reconstruction. He replaced several Republican generals in command of Southern military districts with Democrats. He had his attorney general issue a ruling that interpreted the Reconstruction acts narrowly, thereby forcing a special session of Congress to pass a supplementary act in July 1867. He encouraged Southern whites to obstruct the registration of voters and the election of convention delegates.

Johnson's purpose was to slow the process until 1868 in the hope that Northern voters would repudiate Reconstruction in the presidential election of that year, when Johnson planned to run as the Democratic candidate. Off-year state elections in fall 1867 encouraged that hope. Republicans suffered setbacks in several Northern states, especially where they endorsed referendum measures to enfranchise black men. "I almost pity the radicals," chortled one of President Johnson's aides after the 1867 elections. "After giving ten states to the negroes, to keep the Democrats from getting them, they will have lost the rest."

The Impeachment of Andrew Johnson

Focus Question
Why was Andrew Johnson impeached? Why was he acquitted?

Johnson struck even more boldly against Reconstruction after the 1867 elections, despite warnings that he was risking **impeachment.** "What does Johnson mean to do?" an exasperated Republican asked another. "I am afraid his doings will make us all favor impeachment." In February 1868, Johnson took a fateful step. He removed from office Secretary of War Edwin M. Stanton, who had administered the War Department in support of the congressional Reconstruction policy. This appeared to violate the Tenure of Office Act, passed the year before over Johnson's veto, which required Senate consent for such removals. By a vote of 126 to 47 along party lines, the House impeached Johnson on February 24. The official reason for impeachment was that he had violated the Tenure of Office Act (which Johnson considered unconstitutional). The real reason was Johnson's stubborn defiance of Congress on Reconstruction.

Under the U.S. Constitution, impeachment by the House does not remove an official from office. It is more like a grand jury indictment that must be tried by a petit jury—in this case, the Senate, which sat as a court to try Johnson on the impeachment charges brought by the House. If convicted by a two-thirds majority of the Senate, he would be removed from office.

The impeachment trial proved long and complicated, which worked in Johnson's favor by allowing passions to cool. The Constitution specifies the grounds on which a president can be impeached and removed: "Treason, Bribery, or other high Crimes and Misdemeanors." The issue was whether Johnson was guilty of any of these acts. His able defense counsel exposed technical ambiguities in the Tenure of Office Act that raised doubts about whether Johnson had actually violated it. Several moderate Republicans feared that the precedent of impeachment might upset the delicate balance of powers between the executive branch, Congress, and the judiciary that was an essential element of the Constitution. Behind the scenes, Johnson strengthened his case by promising to appoint the respected General John M. Schofield as secretary of war and to stop obstructing the Reconstruction acts. In the end, seven Republican senators voted for acquittal on May 16, and the final tally fell one vote short of the necessary two-thirds majority.

The Completion of Formal Reconstruction

The impeachment trial's end cleared the poisonous air in Washington, and Johnson quietly served out his term. Constitutional conventions met in the South during winter and spring 1867–68. Hostile whites described them as "Bones and Banjoes Conventions" and the Republican delegates as "ragamuffins and jailbirds." In sober fact, however, the delegates were earnest advocates of a new order, and the constitutions they wrote were among the most progressive in the nation. Three-quarters of the delegates to the 10 conventions were Republicans. About 25 percent of those Republicans were Northern whites who had relocated to the South after the war; 45 percent were native Southern whites who braved the social ostracism of the white majority to cast their lot with the despised Republicans; and 30 percent were blacks. Only in the South Carolina convention were blacks in the majority.

The new state constitutions enacted **universal male suffrage,** putting them ahead of most Northern states on that score. Some of the constitutions disenfranchised certain classes of ex-Confederates for several years, but by 1872, all such disqualifications had been removed. The constitutions mandated statewide public schools for both races for the first time in the South. Most states permitted segregated schools, but schools of any kind for blacks represented a great step forward. Most of the constitutions increased the state's responsibility for social welfare beyond anything previously known in the South.

Violence in some parts of the South marred the voting on ratification of these state constitutions. The **Ku Klux Klan,** a night-riding white terrorist organization, made its first appearance during the elections. Nevertheless, voters in seven states ratified their constitutions and elected new legislatures that ratified the 14th Amendment in spring 1868. That amendment became part of the U.S. Constitution the following summer, and the newly elected representatives and senators from those seven states, nearly all Republicans, took their seats in the House and Senate.

The 15th Amendment

The remaining three Southern states completed the reconstruction process in 1869 and 1870. Congress required them to ratify the 15th as well as the 14th Amendments. The 15th Amendment prohibited states from denying the right to vote on grounds of race, color, or previous condition of servitude. Its purpose was not only to prevent the reconstructed states from any future revocation of black suffrage, but also to extend equal suffrage to the border states and to the North. With final ratification of the 15th Amendment in 1870, the Constitution became truly color blind for the first time in U.S. history.

But the 15th Amendment still left half of the population disenfranchised. Many supporters of woman suffrage were embittered by its failure to ban discrimination on the grounds of gender as well as race. The radical wing of the suffragists, led by Elizabeth Cady Stanton and Susan B. Anthony, therefore opposed the 15th Amendment, causing a split in the woman suffrage movement.

This movement had shared the ideological egalitarianism of abolitionism since the Seneca Falls Convention of 1848. In 1866, male and female abolitionists formed the American Equal Rights Association (AERA) to work for both black and woman suffrage. Although some Republicans sympathized with the suffragists, they knew that no strong constituency among male voters favored granting the vote to women. A woman suffrage amendment to the state constitution of Kansas in 1867 suffered a lopsided defeat in a referendum. Most members of the AERA recognized that although Reconstruction politics made black enfranchisement possible, woman suffrage would have to wait until public opinion could be educated up to the standard of gender equality.

Stanton and Anthony refused to accept this reasoning. Why should illiterate Southern blacks have the right to vote, they asked, when educated Northern women remained shut out from the polls? It was "infinitely more important to secure the rights of 10 million women than to bring a million more men to the polls," declared Stanton. The 15th Amendment would establish "the most odious form of aristocracy the world has ever seen: an aristocracy of sex." When a majority of delegates at the 1869 convention of the AERA voted to endorse the 15th Amendment, several women led by Stanton and Anthony walked out and founded the National Woman Suffrage Association. The remainder reorganized themselves as the American Woman Suffrage Association. For the next two decades, these rival organizations, working for the same cause, remained at odds with each other.

The Election of 1868

Just as the presidential election of 1864 was a referendum on Lincoln's war policies, so the election of 1868 was a referendum on the Reconstruction policy of the Republicans. The Republican nominee was General **Ulysses S. Grant.** Although he had no political experience, Grant commanded greater authority and prestige than anyone else in the country. As general-in-chief of the army, he had opposed Johnson's Reconstruction policy in 1866 and had broken openly with the president in January 1868. That spring, Grant agreed to run for the presidency in order to preserve in peace the victory for Union and liberty he had won in war.

The Democrats turned away from Andrew Johnson, who carried too many political liabilities. They nominated Horatio Seymour, the wartime governor of New York, bestowing on him the dubious privilege of running against Grant. Hoping to put together a majority consisting of the South plus New York and two or three other Northern states, the Democrats adopted a militant platform denouncing the Reconstruction acts as "a flagrant usurpation of power . . . unconstitutional, revolutionary, and void." The platform also demanded "the abolition of the Freedmen's Bureau, and all political instrumentalities designed to secure negro supremacy."

The vice presidential candidate, Frank Blair of Missouri, became the point man for the Democrats. In a public letter, he proclaimed, "There is but one way to restore the Government and the Constitution, and that is for the President-elect to declare these [Reconstruction] acts null and void, compel the army to undo its usurpations at the South, disperse the carpet-bag State Governments, [and] allow the white people to reorganize their own governments."

The only way to achieve this bold counterrevolutionary goal was to suppress Republican voters in the South. This the Ku Klux Klan tried its best to do. Federal troops failed to prevent much of the violence because martial law had been lifted in the states where civilian governments had been restored. In Louisiana, Georgia, Arkansas, and Tennessee, the Klan or Klan-like groups committed dozens of murders and intimidated thousands of black voters. The violence helped the Democratic cause in the South, but probably hurt it in the North, where many voters perceived the Klan as an organization of neo-Confederate paramilitary guerrillas. In fact, many Klansmen were former soldiers, and such famous Confederate generals as Nathan Bedford Forrest and John B. Gordon held high positions in the Klan.

Seymour did well in the South, carrying five former slave states and coming close in others despite the solid Republican vote of the newly enfranchised blacks. Grant, however, swept the electoral vote 214 to 80. Seymour actually won a slight majority of the white voters nationally; without black enfranchisement, Grant would have had a minority of the popular vote.

The Grant Administration

A great military commander, Grant is usually branded a failure as president. That indictment is only partly correct. Grant's inexperience and poor judgment betrayed him into several unwise appointments of officials who were later convicted of corruption, and his back-to-back administrations (1869–77) were plagued by scandals. His secretary of war was impeached for selling appointments to army posts and Indian reservations, and his attorney general and secretary of the interior resigned under suspicion of malfeasance in 1875.

Although he was an honest man, Grant was too trusting of subordinates. He appointed many former members of his military family, as well as several of his wife's relatives, to offices for which they were scarcely qualified. In an era notorious for corruption at all levels of government, many of the scandals were not Grant's fault. The Tammany Hall "Ring" of "Boss" William Marcy Tweed in New York City may have stolen more money from taxpayers than all of the federal agencies combined. It was said that the only thing the Standard Oil Company could not do with the Ohio legislature was to refine it. In Washington, one of the most widely publicized scandals, the **Credit Mobilier** affair, concerned Congress rather than the Grant administration. Several congressmen had accepted stock in the Credit Mobilier, a construction company for the Union Pacific Railroad, which received loans and land grants from the government. In return, the company expected lax congressional supervision, thereby permitting financial manipulations by the company.

What accounted for this explosion of corruption in the postwar decade, which one historian has called "The Era of Good Stealings"? During the war, expansion of government contracts and the bureaucracy had created new opportunities for the unscrupulous. Following the intense sacrifices of the war years came a relaxation of tensions and standards. Rapid postwar economic growth, led by an extraordinary rush of railroad construction, further encouraged greed and get-rich-quick schemes of the kind satirized by Mark Twain and Charles Dudley Warner in their 1873 novel *The Gilded Age,* which gave its name to the era.

Civil Service Reform

Some of the apparent increase in corruption during the Gilded Age was more a matter of perception. During a civil service reform movement to purify the government bureaucracy and make it more efficient, reformers focused a harsh light into the dark corners of corruption hitherto unilluminated because of the nation's preoccupation with war and reconstruction. Thus reformers' publicity may have exaggerated the actual extent of corruption. In reality, during the Grant administration, several government agencies made real progress in eliminating abuses that had flourished in earlier administrations.

The chief target of civil service reform was the **"spoils system."** With the slogan "To the victor belongs the spoils," the victorious party in an election rewarded party workers with appointments as postmasters, customs collectors, and the like. The hope of getting appointed to a government post was the glue that kept the faithful together when a party was out of power. An assessment of 2 or 3 percent on the beneficiaries' government salaries kept party coffers filled when the party was in power. The spoils system politicized the bureaucracy and staffed it with unqualified personnel who spent more time working for their party than for the government. It also plagued every incoming president (and other elected officials) with the "swarm of office seekers" that loom so large in contemporary accounts (including those of the humorist Orpheus C. Kerr, whose nom de plume was pronounced "Office Seeker").

Civil service reformers wanted to separate the bureaucracy from politics by requiring competitive examinations for the appointment of civil servants. This movement gathered steam during the 1870s and finally achieved success in 1883 with the passage of the

Pendleton Act, which established the modern structure of the civil service. When Grant took office, he seemed to share the sentiments of civil service reformers; several of his cabinet officers inaugurated examinations for certain appointments and promotions in their departments. Grant also named a civil service commission headed by George William Curtis, a leading reformer and editor of *Harper's Weekly*. But many congressmen, senators, and other politicians resisted civil service reform. **Patronage** greased the political machines that kept them in office and all too often enriched them and their political chums. They managed to subvert reform, sometimes using Grant as an unwitting ally and thus turning many reformers against the president.

Foreign Policy Issues

A foreign policy controversy added to Grant's woes. The irregular procedures by which his private secretary had negotiated a treaty to annex Santo Domingo (now the Dominican Republic) alienated leading Republican senators, who defeated ratification of the treaty. Politically inexperienced, Grant acted like a general who needed only to give orders rather than as a president who must cultivate supporters. The fallout from the Santo Domingo affair widened the fissure in the Republican Party between "spoilsmen" and "reformers."

The Grant administration had some solid foreign policy achievements to its credit, however. Hamilton Fish, the able secretary of state, negotiated the Treaty of Washington in 1871 to settle the vexing Alabama Claims. These were damage claims against Britain for the destruction of American shipping by the C.S.S. *Alabama* and other Confederate commerce raiders built in British shipyards. The treaty established an international tribunal to arbitrate the U.S. claims, thus creating a precedent for the peaceful settlement of disputes. It resulted in the award of $15.5 million in damages to U.S. shipowners and a British expression of regret.

The events leading to the Treaty of Washington also resolved another long-festering issue between Britain and the United States: the status of Canada. The seven separate British North American colonies were especially vulnerable to U.S. desires for annexation. In fact, many bitter Northerners demanded British cession of Canadian colonies to the United States as fair payment for the wartime depredations of the *Alabama* and other commerce raiders. Such demands tended to strengthen the loyalty of many Canadians to Britain as a counterweight to the aggressive Americans. In 1867, Parliament passed the British North America Act, which united most of the Canadian colonies into a new and largely self-governing Dominion of Canada.

Canadian nationalism was further strengthened by the actions of the Irish American Fenian Brotherhood. A secret society organized during the Civil War, the Fenians believed that an invasion of Canada would strike a blow for the independence of Ireland. Three times from 1866 to 1871, small "armies" of Fenians, composed mainly of Irish American veterans of the Union Army, crossed the border into Canada, only to be driven back after comic-opera skirmishes. The Fenian raids intensified Canadian anti-Americanism and complicated the negotiations leading to the Washington Treaty, but after its signing, Canadian-American tensions cooled. The treaty also helped resolve disputes over American commercial fishing in Canadian waters. U.S. troops prevented further Fenian raids, and American demands for annexation of Canada faded away. These events gave birth to the modern nation of Canada.

Reconstruction in the South

During Grant's two administrations, the "Southern Question" was the most intractable issue. A phrase in Grant's acceptance of the presidential nomination in 1868 had struck a responsive chord in the North: "Let us have peace." With the ratification of the 15th Amendment, many people breathed a sigh of relief at this apparent resolution of "the last great point that remained to be settled of the issues of the war." It was time to deal with other matters that had been long neglected. Ever since the annexation of Texas a quarter-century earlier, the nation had known scarcely a moment's respite from sectional strife. "Let us have done with Reconstruction," pleaded the New York *Tribune* in 1870. "LET US HAVE PEACE." But there was no peace. Reconstruction was not over; it had hardly begun. State governments elected by black and white voters were in place in the South, but Democratic violence against Reconstruction and the instability of the Republican coalition that sustained it portended trouble.

Blacks in Office

Because the Republican Party had no antebellum roots in the South, most Southern whites perceived it as a symbol of conquest and humiliation. In the North, the Republican Party represented the most prosperous, educated, and influential elements of the population, but in the South, most of its adherents were poor, illiterate, and landless.

About 80 percent of Southern Republican voters were black. Although most black leaders were educated and many had been free before the war, most black voters were illiterate ex-slaves. Neither the leaders nor their constituents, however, were as ignorant or as venal as stereotypes have portrayed them. Of 14 black representatives and two black senators elected in the South between 1868 and 1876, all but three had attended secondary school and four had attended college. Several of the blacks elected to state offices were among the best-educated men of their day. Jonathan Gibbs, secretary of state in Florida from 1868 to 1872 and state superintendent of education from 1872 to 1874, was a graduate of Dartmouth College and Princeton Theological Seminary. Francis L. Cardozo, secretary of state in South Carolina for four years and treasurer for another four, was educated at the University of Glasgow and at theological schools in Edinburgh and London.

It is true that some lower-level black officeholders, as well as their constituents, could not read or write, but the fault for that situation lay not with them but with the slave regime that had denied them an education. Illiteracy did not preclude an understanding of political issues for them any more than it did for Irish American voters in the North, some of whom were also illiterate. Southern blacks thirsted for education. Participation in the Union League and the experience of voting were forms of education. Black churches and fraternal organizations proliferated during Reconstruction and tutored African Americans in their rights and responsibilities.

Linked to the myth of black incompetence was the legend of the "Africanization" of Southern governments during Reconstruction. The theme of "Negro rule"— by which the "barbarous African" exercised "unbridled power" in the 10 Southern states—was a staple of Democratic propaganda. It was enshrined in folk memory and in generations of textbooks. In fact, blacks held only 15 to 20 percent of public offices, even at the height of Reconstruction in the early 1870s. No states had black governors (although the black lieutenant governor of Louisiana acted as governor for a month), and only one black man became a state supreme court justice. Nowhere except in South Carolina did blacks hold office in numbers anywhere near their proportion of the population; in that state, they constituted 52 percent of all state and federal elected officials from 1868 to 1876.

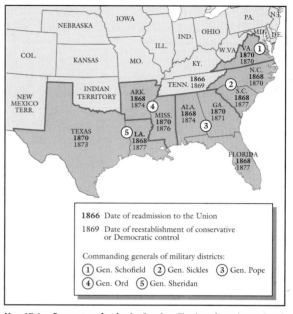

1866 Date of readmission to the Union

1869 Date of reestablishment of conservative or Democratic control

Commanding generals of military districts:

① Gen. Schofield ② Gen. Sickles ③ Gen. Pope
④ Gen. Ord ⑤ Gen. Sheridan

Map 17.1   Reconstruction in the South   The dates for each state listed on this map show how short-lived "Radical Reconstruction" was in most Southern states.

"Carpetbaggers"

Next to "Negro rule," carpetbagger corruption and scalawag rascality have been the prevailing myths of Reconstruction. Carpetbaggers did hold a disproportionate number of high political offices in Southern state governments during Reconstruction. More than half of the Republican governors and nearly half of the congressmen and senators were Northerners. A few did resemble the proverbial adventurer who came south with nothing but a carpetbag in which to stow the loot plundered from a helpless people. Most of the Northerners were Union army officers who stayed on after the war as Freedmen's Bureau agents, teachers in black schools, business investors, pioneers of a new political order—or simply because they liked the climate.

Like others who migrated to the West as a frontier of opportunity, those who settled in the postwar South hoped to rebuild its society in the image of the free-labor North. Many were college graduates at a time when fewer than 2 percent of Americans had attended college. Most brought not empty carpetbags but considerable capital, which they invested in what they hoped would become a new South. They also invested human capital—themselves—in a drive to modernize the region's social structure and democratize its politics. But they underestimated the hostility of Southern whites, most of whom regarded them as agents of an alien culture and leaders of an enemy army—as indeed they had been—in a war that for many Southerners was not yet over.

"Scalawags"

Most of the native-born whites who joined the Southern Republican Party came from the upcountry Unionist areas of western North Carolina and Virginia, eastern Tennessee, and elsewhere. Others were former Whigs who saw an opportunity to rebuild the South's economy in partnership with equally Whiggish Northern Republicans. Republicans, said a North Carolina scalawag, were the "party of progress, of education, of development. . . . Yankees and Yankee notions are just what we want in this country. We want their capital to build factories and work shops, and railroads."

But Yankees and Yankee notions were just what most Southern whites did not want. Democrats saw that the Southern Republican Party they abhorred was a fragile coalition of blacks and whites, Yankees and Southerners, hill-country yeomen and low-country entrepreneurs, illiterates and college graduates. The party was weakest along the seams where these disparate elements joined, especially the racial seam. Democrats attacked that weakness with every weapon at their command, from social ostracism of white Republicans to economic intimidation of black employees and sharecroppers. The most potent Democratic weapon was violence.

The Ku Klux Klan

The generic name for the secret groups that terrorized the Southern countryside was the Ku Klux Klan, but some went by other names (the Knights of the White Camelia in Louisiana, for example). Part of the Klan's purpose was social control of the black population. Sharecroppers who tried to extract better terms from landowners, or black people who were considered too "uppity," were likely to receive a midnight whipping—or worse—from white-sheeted Klansmen. Scores of black schools, perceived as a particular threat to white supremacy, went up in flames.

The Klan's main purpose was political: to destroy the Republican Party by terrorizing its voters and, if necessary, by murdering its leaders. No one knows how many politically motivated killings took place—certainly hundreds, probably thousands. Nearly all of the victims were Republicans; most of them were black. In one notorious incident, the Colfax Massacre in Louisiana (April 18, 1873), a clash between black militia and armed whites left three whites and nearly 100 blacks dead. Half of the blacks were killed in cold blood after they had surrendered. In some places, notably Tennessee and Arkansas, Republican militias formed to suppress and disarm the Klan, but in most areas the militias were outgunned and outmaneuvered by ex-Confederate veteran Klansmen. Some Republican governors were reluctant to use black militia against white guerrillas for fear of sparking a racial bloodbath—as happened at Colfax.

© CORBIS

Two Members of the Ku Klux Klan　Founded in Pulaski, Tennessee, in 1866 as a social organization similar to a college fraternity, the Klan evolved into a terrorist group whose purpose was intimidation of Southern Republicans. The Klan, in which former Confederate soldiers played a prominent part, was responsible for the beating and murder of hundreds of blacks and whites alike from 1868 to 1871.

The answer seemed to be federal troops. In 1870 and 1871, Congress enacted three laws intended to enforce the 14th and 15th Amendments. Interference with voting rights became a federal offense, and any attempt to deprive another person of civil or political rights became a felony. The third law, passed on April 20, 1871, and popularly called the Ku Klux Klan Act, gave the president power to suspend the writ of **habeas corpus** and send in federal troops to suppress armed resistance to federal law.

Armed with these laws, the Grant administration moved against the Klan. Because Grant was sensitive to charges of "military despotism," he used his powers with restraint. He suspended the writ of habeas corpus in only nine South Carolina counties. Nevertheless, there

The Birth of a Nation (1915)

Directed by D. W. Griffith. Starring Lillian Gish (Elsie Stoneman), Henry B. Walthall (Ben Cameron), Ralph Lewis (Austin Stoneman), George Siegmann (Silas Lynch).

Few if any films have had such a pernicious impact on historical understanding and race relations as *Birth of a Nation*. This movie popularized a version of Reconstruction that portrayed predatory carpetbaggers and stupid, brutish blacks plundering a prostrate South and lusting after white women. It perpetuated vicious stereotypes of rapacious black males. It glorified the Ku Klux Klan of the Reconstruction era, inspiring the founding of the "second Klan" in 1915, which became a powerful force in the 1920s (see chapter 24).

The first half of the film offers a conventional Victorian romance of the Civil War. The two sons and daughter of Austin Stoneman (a malevolent radical Republican who is a thinly disguised Thaddeus Stevens) become friends with the three sons and two daughters of the Cameron family of "Piedmont," South Carolina, through the friendship of Ben Cameron and Phil Stoneman at college. The Civil War tragically separates the families. The Stoneman and Cameron boys enlist in the Union and Confederate armies and—predictably—

face each other on the battlefield. Two Camerons and one Stoneman are killed in the war, and Ben Cameron is badly wounded and captured, to be nursed back to health by—you guessed it—Elsie Stoneman. After the war, the younger Camerons and Stonemans renew their friendship. During the Stonemans' visit to South Carolina, Ben Cameron and Elsie Stoneman, and Phil Stoneman and Flora Cameron, fall in love. If the story had stopped there, *Birth of a Nation* would have been just another Hollywood romance. But Austin Stoneman brings south with him Silas Lynch, an ambitious, leering mulatto demagogue who stirs up the animal passions of the ignorant black majority to demand "Equal Rights, Equal Politics, Equal Marriage." A "renegade Negro," Gus, stalks the youngest Cameron daughter, who saves herself from rape by jumping from a cliff to her death. Silas Lynch tries to force Elsie to marry him. "I will build a Black Empire," he tells the beautiful, virginal Elsie (Lillian Gish was the Hollywood beauty queen of silent films),"and you as my queen shall rule by my side."

and elsewhere federal marshals backed by troops arrested thousands of suspected Klansmen. Federal grand juries indicted more than 3,000 members, and several hundred defendants pleaded guilty in return for suspended sentences. To clear clogged court dockets so that the worst offenders could be tried quickly, the Justice Department dropped charges against nearly 2,000 others. About 600 Klansmen were convicted; most of them received fines or light jail sentences, but 65 went to a federal penitentiary for terms of up to five years.

The Election of 1872

These measures broke the back of the Klan in time for the 1872 presidential election. A group of dissident Republicans had emerged to challenge Grant's reelection. They believed

Finally, provoked beyond endurance, white South Carolinians led by Ben Cameron organize the Ku Klux Klan to save "the Aryan race." Riding to the rescue of embattled whites in stirring scenes that anticipated the heroic actions of the cavalry against Indians in later Hollywood Westerns, the Klan executes Gus, saves Elsie, disperses black soldiers and mobs, and carries the next election for white rule by intimidating black voters. The film ends with a double marriage that unites the Camerons and Stonemans in a symbolic rebirth of a nation that joins whites of the North and South in a new union rightfully based on the supremacy of "the Aryan race."

The son of a Confederate lieutenant colonel, David Wark (D. W.) Griffith was the foremost director of the silent movie era. He pioneered many precedent-setting cinematic techniques and profoundly influenced filmmaking throughout the world. *Birth of a Nation* was the first real full-length feature film, technically and artistically superior to anything before it. Apart from its place in the history of cinema, though, why should anyone today watch a movie that perpetuates such wrongheaded history and noxious racist stereotypes? Precisely *because* it reflects and amplifies an interpretation of Reconstruction that prevailed from the 1890s to the 1950s, and thereby shaped not only historical understanding but also contemporary behavior (as in its inspiration for the Klan of the 1920s). Although Birth of a Nation aroused controversy in parts of the North and was picketed by the NAACP, some 200 million people saw the film in the United States and abroad from 1915 to 1946. The story, and director Griffith, demonstrated in dramatic fashion how the South, having lost the Civil War, won the battle for how the war and especially Reconstruction would be remembered for more than half a century.

© Bettmann/CORBIS

Henry B. Walthall (Ben Cameron) kissing the hand of Elsie Stoneman (Lillian Gish) in Birth of a Nation.

that conciliation of Southern whites rather than continued military intervention was the only way to achieve peace in the South. Calling themselves Liberal Republicans, these dissidents nominated Horace Greeley, the famous editor of the New York *Tribune*. Under the slogan "Anything to beat Grant," the Democratic Party also endorsed Greeley's nomination, although he had long been their antagonist. On a platform denouncing "bayonet rule" in the South, Greeley urged his fellow Northerners to put the issues of the Civil War behind them and to "clasp hands across the bloody chasm which has too long divided" North and South.

This phrase would come back to haunt Greeley. Most voters in the North were still not prepared to trust Democrats or Southern whites. Powerful anti-Greeley cartoons by political cartoonist Thomas Nast showed Greeley shaking the hand of a Klansman dripping with the blood of a murdered black Republican. Nast's most famous cartoon portrayed Greeley as a pirate captain bringing his craft alongside the ship of state, while Confederate leaders, armed to the teeth, hid below waiting to board it.

Grant swamped Greeley on election day. Republicans carried every Northern state and 10 of the 16 Southern and border states. Blacks in the South enjoyed more freedom in voting than they would again for a century. This apparent triumph of Republicanism and Reconstruction would soon unravel.

The Panic of 1873

The U.S. economy had grown at an unprecedented pace since recovering from a mild postwar recession. In eight years, 35,000 miles of new railroad track were laid down, equal to all the track laid in the preceding 35 years. The first **transcontinental railroad** had been completed on May 10, 1869, when a golden spike was driven at Promontory Summit, Utah Territory, linking the Union Pacific and the Central Pacific. But the building of a second transcontinental line, the Northern Pacific, precipitated a Wall Street panic in 1873 and plunged the economy into a five-year depression.

Jay Cooke's banking firm, fresh from its triumphant marketing of Union war bonds, took over the Northern Pacific in 1869. Cooke pyramided every conceivable kind of equity and loan financing to raise the money to begin laying rails west from Duluth, Minnesota. Other investment firms did the same as a fever of speculative financing gripped the country. In September 1873, the pyramid of paper collapsed. Cooke's firm was the first to go bankrupt. Like dominoes, thousands of banks and businesses also collapsed. Unemployment rose to 14 percent, and hard times set in.

The Retreat from Reconstruction

Focus Question
Why did a majority of the Northern people and their political leaders turn against continued federal involvement in Southern Reconstruction in the 1870s?

It is an axiom of American politics that the voters will punish the party in power in times of economic depression. That axiom held true in the 1870s. Democrats made large gains in the congressional elections of 1874, winning a majority in the House for the first time in 18 years.

Public opinion also began to turn against Republican policies in the South. The campaign by Liberal Republicans and Democrats against "bayonet rule" and "carpetbag corruption" that left most Northern voters unmoved in 1872 found a growing audience in subsequent years. Intraparty battles among Republicans in Southern states enabled Democrats to regain control of several state governments. Well-publicized corruption scandals also discredited

Republican leaders. Although corruption was probably no worse in Southern states than in many parts of the North, Southern postwar poverty made waste and extravagance seem worse. White Democrats scored propaganda points by claiming that corruption proved the incompetence of "Negro-carpetbag" regimes.

Northerners grew increasingly weary of what seemed to be the endless turmoil of Southern politics. Most of them had never had a strong commitment to racial equality, and they were growing more and more willing to let white supremacy regain sway in the South. "The truth is," confessed a Northern Republican, "our people are tired out with this worn out cry of 'Southern outrages'!!! Hard times & heavy taxes make them wish the 'nigger,' 'everlasting nigger,' were in hell or Africa."

By 1875, only four Southern states remained under Republican control: South Carolina, Florida, Mississippi, and Louisiana. In those states, white Democrats had revived paramilitary organizations under various names: White Leagues (Louisiana), Rifle Clubs (Mississippi), and Red Shirts (South Carolina). Unlike the Klan, these groups operated openly. In Louisiana, they fought pitched battles with Republican militias in which scores were killed. When the Grant

How the Mississippi Plan Worked   This cartoon shows how black counties could report large Democratic majorities in the Mississippi state election of 1875. The black voter holds a Democratic ticket while one of the men, described in the caption as a "Democratic reformer," holds a revolver to his head and says: "You're as free as air, ain't you? Say you are, or I'll blow your black head off!"

administration sent large numbers of federal troops to Louisiana, people in both North and South cried out against military rule. The protests grew even louder when soldiers marched onto the floor of the Louisiana legislature in January 1875 and expelled several Democratic legislators after a contested election. Was this America? asked Republican Senator Carl Schurz in a widely publicized speech: "If this can be done in Louisiana, how long will it be before it can be done in Massachusetts and Ohio? How long before a soldier may stalk into the national House of Representatives, and, pointing to the Speaker's mace, say 'Take away that bauble!'"

The Mississippi Election of 1875

The backlash against the Grant administration affected the Mississippi state election of 1875. Democrats there devised a strategy called the Mississippi Plan. The first step was to "persuade" the 10 to 15 percent of white voters still calling themselves Republicans to switch to the Democrats. Only a handful of carpetbaggers could resist the economic pressures, social ostracism, and threats that made it "too damned hot for [us] to stay out," wrote one white Republican who changed parties. "No white man can live in the South in the future and act with any other than the Democratic Party unless he is willing and prepared to live a life of social isolation and remain in political oblivion."

The second step in the Mississippi Plan was to intimidate black voters because even with all whites voting Democratic, the party could still be defeated by the 55 percent black majority. Economic coercion against black sharecroppers and workers kept some of them away from the polls, but violence was the most effective method. Democratic "rifle clubs" showed up at Republican rallies, provoked riots, and shot down dozens of blacks in the ensuing melees. Governor Adelbert Ames—a native of Maine, a Union general who had won a medal of honor in the war, and one of the ablest of Southern Republicans—called for federal troops to control the violence. Grant intended to comply, but Ohio Republicans warned him that if he sent troops to Mississippi, the Democrats would exploit the issue of "bayonet rule" to carry Ohio in that year's state elections. Grant yielded—in effect giving up Mississippi for Ohio. The U.S. attorney general replied to Ames's request for troops:

> The whole public are tired out with these annual autumnal outbreaks in the South, and the great majority are now ready to condemn any interference on the part of the government. . . . Preserve the peace by the forces in your own state, and let the country see that the citizens of Mississippi, who are . . . largely Republican, have the courage to fight for their rights.

Governor Ames did try to organize a loyal state militia, but that proved difficult—and in any case, he was reluctant to use a black militia for fear of provoking a race war. "No matter if they are going to carry the State," said Ames with weary resignation, "let them carry it, and let us be at peace and have no more killing." The Mississippi Plan worked like a charm. In five of the state's counties with large black majorities, the Republicans polled 12, 7, 4, 2, and 0 votes, respectively. What had been a Republican majority of 30,000 in 1874 became a Democratic majority of 30,000 in 1875.

The Supreme Court and Reconstruction

Even if Grant had been willing to continue intervening in Southern state elections, Congress and the courts would have constricted such efforts. The new Democratic majority in the House threatened to cut any appropriations for the Justice Department and the army intended for use in the South. In 1876, the Supreme Court handed down two decisions that declared parts of the 1870 and 1871 laws for enforcement of the 14th and 15th Amendments unconstitutional. In *U.S.* v. *Cruikshank* and *U.S.* v. *Reese,* the Court ruled on cases from Louisiana and Kentucky. Both cases grew out of provisions in these laws authorizing federal officials to prosecute *individuals* (not states) for violations of the civil and voting rights of blacks. But, the Court pointed out, the 14th and 15th Amendments apply to actions by *states:* "No State shall . . . deprive any person of life, liberty, or property . . . nor deny to any person . . . equal protection of the laws": the right to vote "shall not be denied . . . by any State." Therefore, the portions of these laws that empowered the federal government to prosecute individuals were declared unconstitutional.

The Court did not say what could be done when states were controlled by white-supremacy Democrats who had no intention of enforcing equal rights. (In the mid-20th century, the Supreme Court would reverse itself and interpret the 14th and 15th Amendments much more broadly.) Meanwhile, in another ruling, *Civil Rights Case* (1883), the Court declared unconstitutional a civil rights law passed by Congress in 1875. That law, enacted on the eve of the Democratic takeover of the House elected in 1874, was a crowning achievement of Reconstruction. It banned racial discrimination in all forms of public transportation and public accommodations. If enforced, it would have effected a sweeping transformation of race relations—in the North as well as in the South. Even some of the congressmen who voted for the bill doubted its constitutionality, however, and the Justice Department had made little effort to enforce it. Several cases made their way to the Supreme Court, which in 1883 ruled the law unconstitutional—again on grounds that the 14th Amendment applied only to states, not to individuals. Several states—all in the North—passed their own civil rights laws in the 1870s and 1880s, but less than 10 percent of the black population resided in those states. The mass of African Americans lived a segregated existence.

The Election of 1876

In 1876, the remaining Southern Republican state governments fell victim to the passion for reform. The mounting revelations of corruption at all levels of government ensured that reform would be the leading issue in the presidential election. In this centennial year of the birth of the United States, marked by a great exposition in Philadelphia, Americans wanted to put their best foot forward. Both major parties gave their presidential nominations to governors who had earned reform reputations in their states: Democrat Samuel J. Tilden of New York and Republican Rutherford B. Hayes of Ohio.

Democrats entered the campaign as favorites for the first time in two decades. It seemed likely that they would be able to put together an electoral majority from a "solid South" plus New York and two or three other Northern states. To ensure a solid South, they looked to the lessons of the Mississippi Plan. In 1876, a new word came into use to describe Democratic techniques of intimidation: *bulldozing*. To bulldoze black voters meant to trample them down or keep them away from the polls. In South Carolina and Louisiana, the Red Shirts and the White Leagues mobilized for an all-out bulldozing effort.

The most notorious incident, the Hamburg Massacre, occurred in the village of Hamburg, South Carolina, where a battle between a black militia unit and 200 Red Shirts resulted in the capture of several militiamen, five of whom were shot "while attempting to escape." This time Grant did send in federal troops. He pronounced the Hamburg Massacre "cruel, blood-thirsty, wanton, unprovoked . . . a repetition of the course that has been pursued in other Southern States."

The federal government also put several thousand deputy marshals and election supervisors on duty in the South. Although they kept an uneasy peace at the polls, they could do little to prevent assaults, threats, and economic coercion in backcountry districts, which reduced the potential Republican tally in the former Confederate states by at least 250,000 votes.

Disputed Results

When the results were in, Tilden had carried four Northern states, including New York with its 35 electoral votes. Tilden also carried all of the former slave states except—apparently—Louisiana, South Carolina, and Florida, which produced disputed returns. Because Tilden needed only one of them to win the presidency, while Hayes needed all three, and because Tilden seemed to have carried Louisiana and Florida, it appeared initially that he had won the presidency. But frauds and irregularities reported from several bulldozed districts in the three states clouded the issue. For example, a Louisiana parish that had recorded 1,688 Republican votes in 1874 reported only 1 in 1876. Many other similar discrepancies appeared. The official returns ultimately sent to Washington gave all three states—and therefore the presidency—to Hayes, but the Democrats refused to recognize the results, and they controlled the House.

The country now faced a serious constitutional crisis. Armed Democrats threatened to march on Washington. Many people feared another civil war. The Constitution offered no clear guidance on how to deal with the matter. A count of the state electoral votes required the concurrence of both houses of Congress, but with a Democratic House and a Republican Senate, such concurrence was not forthcoming. To break the deadlock, Congress created a special electoral commission consisting of five representatives, five senators, and five Supreme Court justices split evenly between the two parties, with one member, a Supreme Court justice, supposedly an independent—but in fact a Republican.

Tilden had won a national majority of 252,000 popular votes, and the raw returns gave him a majority in the three disputed states. But an estimated 250,000 Southern Republicans

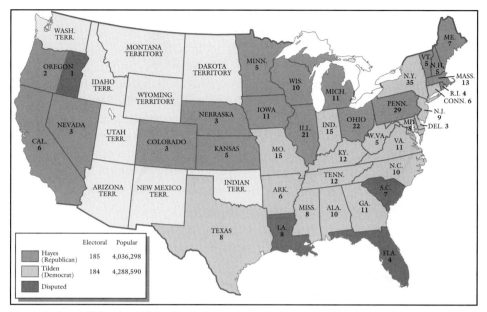

Map 17.2 Hayes-Tilden Disputed Election of 1876 A comparison of this map with those on pp. 523 and 527 shows the persistence of geographical voting patterns once Southern Democrats had overthrown most Republican state governments and effectively disenfranchised many black voters.

had been bulldozed away from the polls. In a genuinely fair and free election, the Republicans might have carried Mississippi and North Carolina as well as the three disputed states. While the commission agonized, Democrats and Republicans in Louisiana and South Carolina each inaugurated their own separate governors and legislatures (Republicans in Florida gave up the fight at the state level). Only federal troops in the capitals at New Orleans and Columbia protected the Republican governments in those states.

The Compromise of 1877

In February 1877, three months after voters had gone to the polls, the electoral commission issued its ruling. By a partisan vote of 8 to 7—with the "independent" justice voting with the Republicans—the commission awarded all of the disputed states to Hayes. The Democrats cried foul and began a **filibuster** in the House to delay the final electoral count beyond the inauguration date of March 4, so as to throw the election to the House of Representatives, an eventuality that threatened to bring total anarchy. But, behind the scenes, a compromise began to take shape. Both Northern Republicans and Southern Democrats of Whig heritage had similar interests in liquidating the sectional rancor and in getting on with the business of economic recovery and development. Among these neo-Whigs were Hayes and his advisers. To wean Southern Whiggish Democrats away from a House filibuster, Hayes promised his support as president for federal appropriations to rebuild war-destroyed **levees** on the lower Mississippi and federal aid for a southern transcontinental railroad. Hayes's lieutenants also hinted at the appointment of a Southerner as postmaster general, who would have a considerable amount of patronage at his disposal—the appointment of thousands of local postmasters.

Most important, Southerners wanted to know what Hayes would do about Louisiana and South Carolina. Would he withdraw the troops and allow the Democrats who already governed those states in fact to do so in law as well? Hayes signaled his intention to end "bayonet rule," which he had for some time considered a bankrupt policy. He believed that the goodwill and influence of Southern moderates would offer better protection for black rights than federal troops could provide. In return for his commitment to withdraw the troops, Hayes asked for—and received—promises of fair treatment of freedpeople and respect for their constitutional rights.

The End of Reconstruction

Such promises were easier to make than to keep, as future years would reveal. In any case, the Democratic filibuster collapsed, and Hayes was inaugurated on March 4. He soon fulfilled his part of the Compromise of 1877: ex-Confederate Democrat David Key of Tennessee became postmaster general; in 1878, the South received more federal money for internal improvements than ever before; and federal troops left the capitals of Louisiana and South Carolina. The last two Republican state governments collapsed. The old abolitionist and radical Republican warhorses denounced Hayes's actions as a sellout of Southern blacks. His was a policy "of weakness, of subserviency, of surrender," in the words of the venerable crusader William Lloyd Garrison, a policy that sustained "might against right . . . the rich and powerful against the poor and unprotected."

Voices of protest could scarcely be heard above the sighs of relief that the crisis was over. Most Americans, including even most Republicans, wanted no more military intervention in state affairs. "I have no sort of faith in a local government which can only be propped up by foreign bayonets," wrote the editor of the New York *Tribune* in April 1877. "If negro suffrage means that as a permanency then negro suffrage is a failure."

Conclusion

Before the Civil War, most Americans had viewed a powerful government as a threat to individual liberties. That is why the first 10 amendments to the Constitution (the Bill of Rights) imposed strict limits on the powers of the federal government. During the Civil War and especially during Reconstruction, however, the national government had to exert an unprecedented amount of power to free the slaves and guarantee their equal rights as free citizens. That is why the 13th, 14th, and 15th Amendments to the Constitution contained clauses stating that "Congress shall have power" to enforce these provisions for liberty and equal rights.

During the post–Civil War decade, Congress passed civil rights laws and enforcement legislation to accomplish this purpose. Federal marshals and troops patrolled the polls to protect black voters, arrested thousands of Klansmen and other violators of black civil rights, and even occupied state capitals to prevent Democratic paramilitary groups from overthrowing legitimately elected Republican state governments.

By 1875, many Northerners had grown tired of or alarmed by this continued use of military power to intervene in the internal affairs of states. The Supreme Court stripped the federal government of much of its authority to enforce certain provisions of the 14th and 15th Amendments. Traditional fears of military power as a threat to individual liberties came to the fore again.

The withdrawal of federal troops from the South in 1877 constituted both a symbolic and a substantive end of the 12-year postwar era known as Reconstruction. Reconstruction had achieved the two great objectives inherited from the Civil War: (1) to reincorporate the former Confederate states into the Union, and (2) to accomplish a transition from slavery to freedom in the South. That transition was marred by the economic inequity of sharecropping and the social injustice of white supremacy. A third goal of Reconstruction, enforcement of the equal civil and political rights promised in the 14th and 15th Amendments, was betrayed by the Compromise of 1877. In subsequent decades, the freed slaves and their descendants suffered repression into segregated, second-class citizenship. Not until another war hero-turned-president sent troops into Little Rock (chapter 28), 80 years after they had been withdrawn from New Orleans and Columbia, did the federal government launch a second Reconstruction to fulfill the promises of the first.

SUGGESTED READINGS

The most comprehensive and incisive history of Reconstruction is **Eric Foner, *Reconstruction: America's Unfinished Revolution 1863–1872*** (1988). For a skillful abridgement of this book, see **Foner, *A Short History of Reconstruction*** (1990). Also valuable is **Kenneth M. Stampp, *The Era of Reconstruction, 1865–1877*** (1965). Important for their insights on Lincoln and the reconstruction question are **Peyton McCrary, *Abraham Lincoln and Reconstruction: The Louisiana Experiment*** (1978) and **LaWanda Cox, *Lincoln and Black Freedom: A Study in Presidential Leadership*** (1981). A superb study of the South Carolina Sea Islands as a laboratory of Reconstruction is **Willie Lee Rose, *Rehearsal for Reconstruction: The Port Royal Experiment*** (1964).

Three important studies of Andrew Johnson and his conflict with Congress over Reconstruction are **Eric L. McKitrick, *Andrew Johnson and Reconstruction*** (1960); **Hans L. Trefousse, *The Radical Republicans: Lincoln's Vanguard for Racial Justice*** (1969); and **Michael Les Benedict, *The Impeachment and Trial of Andrew Johnson*** (1973). Two books by **Michael Perman** connect events in the South and in Washington during Reconstruction: ***Reunion without Compromise: The South and Reconstruction, 1865–1868*** (1973) and ***The Road to Redemption: Southern Politics 1868–1879*** (1984). For counter-Reconstruction violence in the South, see **George C. Rable, *But There Was No Peace: The Role of Violence in the Politics of Reconstruction*** (1984) and **Nicholas Lemann, *Redemption: The Last Battle of the Civil War*** (2006). The evolution of sharecropping and other aspects of the transition from slavery to freedom are treated in **Roger L. Ransom and Richard Sutch,** *One Kind of Freedom: The Economic Consequences of Emancipation* (1977).

Of the many books on African Americans in Reconstruction, the following are perhaps the most valuable: **Thomas Holt,** *Black over White: Negro Political Leadership in South Carolina during Reconstruction* (1977) and **Laura F. Edwards,** *Gendered Strife and Confusion: The Political Culture of Reconstruction* (1997). An excellent collection of essays on the Freedmen's Bureau is **Paul A. Cimbala and Randall Miller, eds.,** *The Freedmen's Bureau and Reconstruction* (1999). Both black and white churches are the subject of **Daniel Stowell,** *Rebuilding Zion: The Religious Reconstruction of the South, 1863–1877* (1998).

Visit the Liberty Equality Power Companion Web site for resources specific to this textbook: http://www.thomsonedu.com/history/murrin

Also find self-tests and additional resources at ThomsonNOW. ThomsonNOW is an integrated online suite of services and resources with proven ease of use and efficient paths to success, delivering the results you want—NOW!

www.thomsonedu.com/login/

A Transformed Nation: The West and the New South, 1865–1900

"**H**ow I do wish you could all come out here," the new Kansas homesteader Mary Abell wrote to her family back east in 1871. "It is such a beautiful country—I did not know there was any thing so beautiful in the whole world as the country we passed over in coming here." Just arrived from New York with her husband, Abell was clearly excited about the prospect of a new life in the West: "Robert has got a piece of land that suits him," she told her sister. "It seems so fortunate." She knew there was much to do in the days ahead—"There is a house to be built fences to make—a well to be dug and a cow to be got." But Abell didn't seem to mind: "I should never be content to live East now," she said. "Things there would look very little."

Abell was part of a great wave of settlement in the post–Civil War era that would transform the West. From 1865 to 1890, the white population in the trans-Mississippi west increased some 400 percent to 8,628,000—a figure that includes both native-born and white immigrants. The dream of western lands also inspired many African Americans, whose cherished hopes for liberty led hundreds of thousands to leave the South for points west from 1880 to 1910. At the same time, immigrants from China, Mexico, and other countries were drawn to the economic opportunities of the West as part of a global movement of peoples in this period.

All of these men and women were driven by desires for a better life, but their desires often conflicted with the rights and desires of the diverse peoples who already inhabited the West, including a variety of Indian cultures and societies; borderlands villages of Spanish-speaking peoples; settlements of Chinese miners and laborers; and Mexicans in California, among others. Settlement set in motion conflict and resistance in numerous places. Who would gain power over Western lands? Whose liberty would be respected? What efforts would be made to achieve equality—or deny equality—to all of these peoples? This chapter explores the transformation of the West and the South during the late 19th century, part of a larger process of industrialization in this period.

The Homestead Act

Mary Abell and her husband were able to become homesteaders because of a remarkable piece of legislation that took effect on January 1, 1863—the same day that the Emancipation Proclamation became law. Meant to provide free land for western settlers, the **Homestead Act** was

CHRONOLOGY

1862	Sioux uprising in Minnesota; 38 Sioux executed
1864	Colorado militia massacres Cheyenne in village at Sand Creek, Colorado
1866	Cowboys conduct first cattle drive north from Texas
1869	President Grant announces his "peace policy" toward Indians
1876	Sioux and Cheyenne defeat Custer at Little Big Horn
1880	James A. Garfield elected president
1881	Garfield assassinated; Chester A. Arthur becomes president
1883	Pendleton Act begins reform of civil service
1884	Grover Cleveland elected president
1887	Dawes Severalty Act dissolves Indian tribal units and implements individual ownership of tribal lands
1888	Benjamin Harrison elected president
1889	Government opens Indian Territory (Oklahoma) to white settlement
1890	Wounded Knee massacre • New Mississippi constitution pioneers black disenfranchisement in South • Republicans try but fail to enact federal elections bill to protect black voting rights • Congress enacts McKinley Tariff
1892	Grover Cleveland again elected president
1895	Booker T. Washington makes his Atlanta Compromise address
1896	*Plessy* v. *Ferguson* legalizes "separate but equal" state racial segregation laws
1898	*Williams* v. *Mississippi* condones use of literacy tests and similar measures to restrict voting rights

the result of a dream that stretched back decades. "Go West, young man!" had been a famous saying during the 1850s, associated with an extended campaign for a homestead law by newspaper editor Horace Greeley. The saying embodied a cherished American ideal: the belief that individual ownership of land by farmers was at the heart of a virtuous citizenry and a sound democratic republic. That ideal had fueled Jeffersonian agrarianism, too.

In the 1850s, many people believed that a western "safety valve" was necessary to ward off the potential evils of industrialization, urbanization, and capitalist expansion. Free land in the West would help prevent a system of perpetual wage labor, or "wage slavery," by allowing individual farmers to support themselves. Thus free land would ultimately help preserve American values of democratic individualism.

In fact, the provisions of the Homestead Act were remarkably egalitarian for their day—at least up to a point. Both men and unmarried women were eligible to file for up to 160 acres of surveyed land in the public domain, as long as they were over the age of 21. (Married women were assumed to be dependents of their homesteading husbands.) Immigrants who affirmed their intention to become citizens were also eligible. As long as homesteaders lived on the land for five years, not only cultivating it but also "improving" it by building a house or barn, they could receive full title for a fee of only $10. Utilizing these provisions, white homesteaders ultimately claimed some 285 million acres of land, a remarkable redistribution of public acreage by the government.

But we need to consider the Act's costs as well. Despite a surface egalitarianism, the Homestead Act privileged white farmers over African Americans and Hispanics, who rarely had the resources necessary to homestead. After all, even free land required tools, seed, plus often costly transportation to a far-away place: experts in the Agriculture Department estimated such needs at $1,000, an unimaginably large amount for most Americans at the time. The act denied access to Chinese laborers, who could not become U.S. citizens and had few property rights. It made no provisions for the truly poor in eastern cities.

But the Act's most obvious cost was its severe impact on such groups as New Mexico sheepherders or Native Americans for whom such settlement did not open up land but instead took it away. The Homestead Act was in fact part of a larger process of conquest, driven by the twin pressures of industrialization and white settlement, through which Indians were irrevocably stripped of their lands.

A final problem with the Act was extensive corruption in its implementation. Those who agitated for a Homestead Act in the antebellum period had been fueled by a sense of idealism. Ironically, however, through chicanery, outright fraud, and government give-aways, more public land actually fell into the hands of railroads and other corporations, as well as speculators, than into the hands of individual farmers during this period. Clearly, this result was not the intention of the Homestead Act's framers, but it did reflect the new power of an emerging corporate order (see chapter 19).

Was the Homestead Act a success or failure in American life? To younger sons in Norwegian or German farm families who could expect to inherit no land at home, the opportunity to obtain 160 acres in Minnesota or Nebraska seemed miraculous. But that perspective was not shared by Native Americans. This chapter explores the complex answers to that seemingly simple question as part of a broader examination of the industrialization of the West, a process that went into high gear after the Civil War.

An Industrializing West

Focus Question
How did the industrialization of the West affect Americans in different ways?

Traditionally, historians have associated industrialization with the East in the post–Civil War era, but in fact the West also industrialized in this period. That industrialization had many linked components: settlement of the West, including the creation of farms, communities, and western cities; production of commodities such as cattle and timber that could be shipped east; the creation of western consumers and thus the demand for manufactured goods; the extensive extraction of resources through mining and logging; and the ability to ship commodities efficiently using a nationally linked transportation network. These western processes of resource extraction may have looked different from the factory-centered industrialization that developed in the East and Midwest at this time (see chapter 19), but they still involved the transformation of an agrarian economy to an industrial society. Like eastern industrialization, western industrialization also had global reach, pulling immigrants from China, Peru, Chile, Hawaii, European countries, and Mexico to the already diverse West.

Railroads

Nothing was more important to the industrialization of the West than the railroad. Just as free land for homesteaders was a long-held dream for many Americans, so, too, was the creation of a transcontinental railroad that would link East and West and allow the transportation of people and commodities over long distances. The two dreams were connected: the settlement of the West would be greatly facilitated by the extension of the railroad into far-flung territory. Thus it was no accident that in 1862, the year the government passed the Homestead Act, it also passed the **Pacific Railroad Bill,** which provided large loans and extremely generous subsidies of land to two railroad companies, the **Union Pacific** (working west) and the **Central Pacific** (working east), in order to enable them to build a transcontinental line stretching from Omaha, Nebraska, to Sacramento, California. (Railroad lines already existed from Omaha to the East.) Two years later, the government also provided a substantial monetary subsidy for each mile of track laid in the West. Ultimately, the government would give away 131 million acres of land to support transcontinental railroads, including huge land subsidies to three additional railroads: the Atchison, Topeka, and Santa Fe (following the Santa Fe Trail between Missouri and the Southwest); the Southern Pacific (from Southern California to New Orleans); and the Northern Pacific (from the Great Lakes to the Columbia River).

These lavish subsidies set off a frenzy of railroad building; they also made a few individuals very rich, including **the "Big Four" of the Central Pacific:** Leland Stanford, Collis P. Huntington, Mark Hopkins, and Charles Crocker. Big in every way (they collectively weighed 860 pounds), the four men had come to California during the Gold Rush and had shrewdly sized up its entrepreneurial opportunities. They now avidly seized the historic opportunity at hand and formed a partnership that effectively split up the work necessary in such a giant task, including the work of influencing lawmakers. Like so many others involved in the notoriously corrupt postwar railway boom, they were not shy about using bribery or graft to achieve their aims. The leader of the Union Pacific, Thomas C. Durant, was not shy either, having been the chief architect of the scandalous Crédit Mobilier scheme (see chapter 17).

Having provided generous subsidies, the government expected the railroads to obtain their own financing, and so various railroads sold millions of dollars of stocks or bonds, many selling as much stock as the market would bear without much relationship to the actual value of the railroads. This "watered" stock was part of the runaway corruption that surrounded financing railroads. The Big Four participated wholeheartedly in this corruption, creating construction contracts, for instance, that paid them $90 million for work that only cost them $32.2 million.

Once financing had been arranged for this complex venture, the Union Pacific and Central Pacific embarked on a daunting task that would engage some 20,000 workers at a time. From 1865 on, the two railroads raced against one another, as whoever laid the most track stood to gain in government subsidies as well as later commerce. The Union Pacific employed primarily Irish laborers, while the Central Pacific employed a workforce that was by 1867 almost 90 percent Chinese. All worked almost constantly.

Chinese Laborers and the Railroads

A global economy had drawn thousands of **Chinese laborers** to California during the Gold Rush, beginning in 1849. Mostly peasants emigrating from the Pearl River delta of Guangdong Province in southeast China, they were pushed from home by poverty and unstable political conditions related to China's defeat in the British Opium Wars; they were pulled to America by their hope to make a better living in "Gold Mountain." While only a few hundred men emigrated in 1849 and 1850, by the mid-1850s, thousands of Chinese immigrants arrived annually. By 1870, there were some 63,000 Chinese in the United States, with over three-quarters settled in California.

Almost entirely men, Chinese immigrants intended to be sojourners, not permanent settlers: they planned to take their hard-earned savings home to the wives and families they had left behind. At first they worked as independent prospectors panning for gold, but as gold profits dwindled, they moved into other areas of work. In the 1860s, labor contractors in China actively recruited young men to come to America to build the transcontinental railroad, as well as to work as agricultural laborers, to develop fisheries and vineyards, and to help reclaim California swamplands. Some 12,000 Chinese laborers ultimately built the Central Pacific Railroad, often under exceptionally harsh conditions, and with substantially less pay than white laborers.

Even before they began working on the railroads, Chinese miners and laborers faced extremes of prejudice from white nativists. In 1850, the California State legislature responded to anti-foreigner agitation with a Foreign Miners' Tax aimed at all foreigners; two years later, the legislature specifically targeted Chinese immigrants. Western labor leaders, particularly Dennis Kearney of the Workingman's Party of California, inflamed nativist crowds of white workers with anti-Chinese rhetoric: in 1877, during the national Great Railway Strike (see chapter 19), mobs of white workers rioted against Chinese workers in San Francisco's Chinatown. Violence against Chinese workers occurred in numerous places in the West during the 1870s and 1880s, including a massacre in Rock Springs, Colorado, after the Union Pacific Railroad decided to hire Chinese workers. Twenty-eight Chinese died in an attack that included burning down Chinese homes; similar attacks soon occurred throughout the West.

At the local level, Chinese immigrants faced a host of discriminatory ordinances specifically targeting them, from queue ordinances regulating the length of men's hair (and thus targeting the distinctive braid worn by Chinese men); to sidewalk ordinances preventing the carrying of baskets on shoulders. At the state level, California laws denied Chinese the right to own land, to testify in court, to intermarry with whites, and to immigrate. Under these conditions, Chinese workers created communities of their own against stiff odds. Yet by 1850, a thriving Chinatown had emerged in San Francisco, and Chinese sections emerged in numerous communities throughout the West.

In 1882, the federal government weighed in with its first discriminatory law targeting a specific immigrant group. The **Chinese Exclusion Act** suspended Chinese immigration for 10 years with the exception of a few job categories such as merchants. Interest in trade with China dictated against preventing immigration by wealthy businessmen, but the virulent white **nativism** that had taken hold throughout the West encouraged Congress to outlaw Chinese laborers, who supposedly endangered "the good order of certain localities." The Chinese Exclusion Act was renewed in 1892. That the Exclusion Act achieved its aim can be seen in the declining population of Chinese in this period: from 105,465 in 1880 to 89,863 in 1900, during a period in which immigration swelled for other groups (for more on Chinese immigrants, see chapter 20).

The Golden Spike

By the early spring of 1869, what one commentator called the "irrepressible railroad" was almost an accomplished fact. The only question was where East and West would meet. In the final stages of track-laying, the two railroads—which would receive money, after all, based on miles of track built—actually built some track parallel to one another before finally being instructed by no less than President Grant to determine a meeting point.

The result, on May 10, 1869, was the historic driving of a "**golden spike**" in Promontory, Utah, to mark the merging of the two lines. Present that day, we know from the historical record, were "men of every color, creed, and nationality," including the Chinese laborers who had built the railroad and laid the very last track. But official photographs of the event leave them out—a silence that speaks volumes about racial prejudice at the time.

This first transcontinental railroad was soon followed by others, although there were numerous difficulties and abortive attempts. The Northern Pacific ran out of capital in 1873 and went into receivership; the Santa Fe fell short of its goal. Still, by 1893, a total of five trans-continental railroads would be in service, and track mileage west of the Mississippi would increase from 3,272 miles at the end of the Civil War to 72,473 miles. No single factor was as important to the industrialization of the West as the building of railroads, which provided an internal infrastructure for the western economy as well as connection to eastern markets.

© Bettmann/CORBIS

The Golden Spike   This carefully posed scene records the merging of the Central Pacific and Union Pacific Railroads at Promontory Point, Utah, on May 10, 1869, to create the nation's first transcontinental railroad. A celebration of the industrialization of the American West, the photograph includes hundreds of white laborers, but reflects the racial prejudice of the time in excluding Chinese railroad workers who also played a central role in building the railroad.

Railroads and Borderlands Communities

Railroads also changed ordinary people's lives across the West. The arrival of the railroads, as well as the Anglo settlers who followed swiftly in their wake, dramatically changed established patterns of life in the borderlands communities of northern New Mexico and southern Colorado. In the 1870s, Hispanic villagers living communally in this area maintained an economy that included grazing sheep and cattle on the open range, as well as freighting—the transportation of goods by wagons. That way of life had not changed much even in the wake of the conquest and annexation of the northern provinces of Mexico by the United States in 1848.

But the coming of the railroads in the 1880s put new pressure on Hispanic village life. In places like Rio Arriba County, New Mexico, Hispanic villagers who had done a thriving trade hauling goods found their livelihood replaced by the railroads. As a result, communities that had combined trade with grazing and farming were now forced to go back only to farming and grazing, even though this combination had never produced quite enough for their needs. Even worse, in a pattern repeated throughout the West, Hispanic villagers found that Anglo settlement and fencing of once-open lands reduced the available range for grazing.

As Anglo-owned livestock companies moved in, bringing in better breeds and buying up grazing land, they began to squeeze out the Hispanic farmers. With fewer sources of income, by the 1890s, villagers were starting to depend on credit for the first time, borrowing money from an Anglo merchant to fund their grazing, and in the turbulent economy of that decade, many of them were unable to pay their debts. The end result was the loss of their sheep—and livelihood—to Anglo businessmen who had extended credit to them. Many ended up working for livestock companies, sometimes caring for herds they had once owned themselves. Eventually others ended up as miners, forced to become wage laborers.

Resentment became active resistance in the 1880s, when a secret organization, **las Gorras Blancas (White caps),** rode mostly at night to cut fences, tear up railroad track, and burn bridges. "Our purpose is to protect the rights of the people in general and especially those of the helpless classes," the group declared in its platform. But the group had only limited success in achieving these goals. There was no question that industrialization had transformed lives in the borderlands, making many formerly independent producers newly dependent on corporations.

Mining

A similar process held true in mining. The California Gold Rush of 1849 and the early 1850s had drawn miners from across the United States—and from Mexico, Europe, China, Chile, and other countries, as well—to pan for gold. After the Civil War, mining continued to be part of a global industrial economy, but the image of the individual prospector striking it rich on his own claim became increasingly quaint. By the 1870s, the majority of miners were wage laborers who worked for corporations, not for themselves. Mining was big business, with groups of investors consolidating holdings in some of the richest mines. **George Hearst,** for instance, began by investing in 1859 in the legendary Comstock Lode in Nevada—the richest vein of silver in America. "If you're ever inclined to think that there's no such thing as luck," Hearst remarked, "just think of me." In 1877, Hearst and business partners bought the Homestake Mine in the Black Hills, and then enriched their holdings still further by buying up the claims of surrounding miners. Other financiers invested in the industries related to mining, including railroads, lumber companies, and smelters.

Gold Rush miners had worked the surface of the earth with picks, shovels, and tin pans, but as this placer mining gave out, miners and mining companies developed new technologies to extract ore, whether on the surface of the earth or underground. **Hydraulic mining,** used as early as the 1850s, employed high-pressure jets of water to wash away banks of earth and even mountains in order to extract gold. By the 1880s, hydraulic mining produced 90 percent of California's gold, but it also ravaged the environment, tearing away indiscriminately at earth, boulders, and trees, and leaving desolate landscapes in its wake. The debris (tailings) from hydraulic mining clogged rivers and caused floods, ruining farms with muddy waste. Other types of mining destroyed landscapes as well, with copper mining in particular creating strip-mining moonscapes.

¶ Railroads played a central role in the development of industrial mining. It wasn't just that they allowed access to mines; they also made it possible to perform a new kind of mining late in the century. Gold discoveries had propelled the first waves of western settlement, but by the 1870s, silver eclipsed gold in volume and some years even in value. Mining of copper became profitable with the arrival of the railroads, as they for the first time allowed transportation of huge quantities of ore. In the mining town of Butte, Montana, mining had centered around diminishing supplies of silver up until 1881, but the arrival of railroads that year made it possible to extract Butte's rich lode of copper, known as the "richest hill on earth." The same held true for large-scale copper mining in southern Arizona, which was also catalyzed by the arrival of the railroads in the 1880s. Such large-scale resource extraction was at the heart of western industrialization. (**See Map 18.1, Mining and Cattle Frontiers, 1870s, in the color insert following page 816.**)

Miners' working conditions grew steadily worse by the end of the century in the heavily mechanized hard-rock mines. Mining on the Comstock Lode involved work in mines with temperatures of well over 100 degrees—sometimes as much as 150 degrees deep underground. Miners died of the heat, of poor ventilation, of the release of toxic gases, and of accidents with mining equipment. Accidents disabled one out of every 30 miners in the 1870s. By the end of the 19th century, mining was the most dangerous industry in the country.

Unions struggled with varying degrees of success to gain a foothold in the 1870s and 1880s, but with wage cuts in the early 1890s, there was a new burst of labor radicalism and resistance. A violent confrontation between miners and the National Guard occurred at Coeur d'Alene, Idaho, in 1892; the next year, individual mining unions met at Butte, Montana, to form the **Western Federation of Miners (WFM),** whose radical politics included a call to transform the American economic system. In 1893, a violent strike at Cripple Creek, Colorado, centered around mine owners' attempts to move from an eight-hour to a ten-hour day. These strikes were part of nationwide labor activism and resistance in the 1890s (see chapter 19). The WFM would ultimately be important in helping to found the 20th-century Industrial Workers of the World (IWW) (see chapter 20). The IWW's leader, William "Big Bill" Haywood, remembered being approached by a WFM organizer as a young man in Idaho. "I had never heard of the need of workingmen organizing for mutual protection," Haywood said, but he soon became a leader of the WFM himself. The industrialization of the West became a radicalizing political experience for many.

Ranching

It wasn't just miners who went on strike: by the 1880s, even some cowboys attempted strikes for better pay and better working conditions. The idea of a striking cowboy initially goes against the grain: this mythic figure in American life symbolizes solitary, rugged individualism, after all. But cowboys were also employees; and increasingly in the late 19th century,

Oklahoma! (1955)

Directed by Fred Zinnemann. Starring Gordon MacRae (Curly); Shirley Jones (Laurey); and Rod Steiger (Jud).

Only a history textbook would ask you to connect the great Rodgers & Hammerstein musical *Oklahoma!* to the range wars of the late-19th-century West. But think about it: when the cast sings "The Farmer and the Cowman" during a square dance, right before launching into a colorful fistfight, they express the different worldviews of farmers and cattle ranchers. "Whyn't those dirtscratchers stay in Missouri where they belong?" asks a cowman, and another protests, the farmer "come out west and built a lot of fences! And built 'em right acrost our cattle ranges!" It's up to the song's refrain to tell us how to resolve this dispute:

> The farmer and the cowman should be friends,
> Oh, the farmer and the cowman should be friends.
> One man likes to push a plow,
> The other likes to chase a cow,
> But that's no reason why they cain't be friends.

The song is every bit as campy as these lyrics indicate, and if you never got a chance to see (or be in) a school production in high school, then you could do worse than to rush out and rent a copy of the 1955 movie *Oklahoma!*, based on the extraordinarily popular Broadway musical of 1943. The dancing cowboys alone are worth the price of admission.

But don't be fooled: *Oklahoma!* isn't really about Oklahoma, even if it is set in 1907 right before the territory became a state. It's really about a mythic Western space in Americans' imagination, where Americans come together in harmony at square dances and box suppers and where a cowboy like the masculine hero Curly is no wage laborer for life, but instead is about to become a prosperous farmer. *Oklahoma!* may be set in Indian Territory, but there are no Native Americans here. It is an entirely white, native-born world except for the peddler Ali Hakim, and he is clearly just passing through. There's certainly no indication of Oklahoma's arid climate and the devastating drought of the Great Depression, which would have been in recent memory when the musical was written in 1943. In fact, some of the people associated with the musical were uneasy about the title "Oklahoma," precisely because they were afraid it would remind audiences of the "Okies," the poverty-stricken they were employees of large industrial corporations. Contrary to most Hollywood images, they were also a diverse group: among trail cowboys, approximately one-third were African American, Mexican, or Indian.

Cattle Drives and the Open Range

A postwar boom in the range cattle industry had its beginnings in southern Texas. The Spaniards had introduced longhorn cattle there in the 18th century. This hardy breed multiplied rapidly; by the 1850s, millions of them roamed freely on the Texas plains. The market for them was limited in this sparsely settled region; the nearest railhead was usually too far distant to make shipping them north and east economically feasible.

farmers forced to flee the arid plains during the Depression. Instead, this is a world of green abundance where "the corn is as high as an elephant's eye." The only shadow in this sunlit world with its "bright golden haze on the meadow" is Jud, the hired hand.

And perhaps that's why Jud is the most interesting character in this movie musical. Played with a heavy, menacing scowl by no less than Rod Steiger, Jud is the dark side of the Western dream, a man with a deep violent streak (unlike the boys-will-be-boys scuffling of the cowboys) and an unhealthy liking for "girly pictures." All of these negative qualities are loaded onto his status as the "hired hand"; he provides an uneasy reminder that class did exist in the West and that not everyone was on the brink of becoming prosperous. Jud is the only real problem in the mythic world of *Oklahoma!*, and the musical blithely dispatches him by having him fall on his own knife in a fight with Curly.

A huge hit right in the midst of World War II, the show's determined American exuberance and confidence struck deep chords. The show's brilliant choreographer Agnes DeMille remembered that soldiers and sailors would stand weeping at the back of the theater, so deeply did *Oklahoma!* evoke what they considered the essence of America. "Oh, what a beautiful mornin'," sings Curly at the beginning, and it reassured Americans that having grown up on that mythic frontier, they were at the dawn of a new era.

Vibrant movie posters for the 1955 movie musical *Oklahoma!* emphasized the fresh-faced, homespun appeal of romantic leads Gordon MacRae (Curly) and Shirley Jones (Laurey), who began her movie career with this role.

The Civil War changed all that. Beef supplies in the older states dropped drastically, and prices rose to the unheard-of sum of $40 per head. The postwar explosion of population and railroads westward brought markets and railheads ever closer to western cattle that were free to anyone who rounded them up and branded them.

Astute Texans quickly saw that the longhorns represented a fortune on the hoof—if they could be driven northward the 800 miles to the railhead at Sedalia, Missouri. In spring 1866, cowboys hit the trail with 260,000 cattle in the first of the great drives. Disease, stampedes, bad weather, Indians, and irate farmers in Missouri (who were afraid that the Texas fever carried by some of the longhorns would infect their own stock) killed or ran off most of the cattle.

Only a few thousand head made it to Sedalia, but the prices they fetched convinced ranchers that the system would work, if only they could find a better route. By 1867, the rails of the Kansas Pacific had reached Abilene, Kansas, 150 miles closer to Texas, making it possible to drive the herds through a sparsely occupied portion of Indian Territory. About 35,000 longhorns reached Abilene that summer, where they were loaded onto cattle cars for the trip to Kansas City or Chicago. This success resulted in the interlocking institutions of the cattle drive and the Chicago stockyards. The development of refrigerated rail cars in the 1870s enabled Chicago to ship dressed beef all over the country. Abilene mushroomed overnight from a sleepy village whose one bartender spent his spare time catching prairie dogs into a boomtown where 25 saloons stayed open all night, and the railroad made almost as much money shipping liquor into town as it did shipping cattle out.

More than a million longhorns bellowed their way north on the **Chisholm Trail** to Abilene over the next four years, while the railhead crept westward to other Kansas towns, chiefly Dodge City, which became the most wide-open and famous of the cow towns. As **buffalo** and Indians disappeared from the grasslands north of Texas, ranches moved northward to take their place. Cattle drives grew shorter as railroads inched forward. Ranchers grazed their cattle for free on millions of acres of open, unfenced government land. But clashes with **"grangers"** (the ranchers' contemptuous term for farmers), on the one hand, and with a growing army of sheep ranchers on the other—not to mention rustlers—led to several "range wars." Most notable was the Johnson County War in Wyoming in 1892. Grangers and small ranchers there (who had sometimes gotten their start by rustling) defeated the hired guns of the Stock Growers' Association, which represented larger ranchers.

By that time, however, the classic form of **open-range grazing** was already in decline. The boom years of the early 1880s had overstocked the range and driven down prices. Then came record cold and blizzards on the southern range in winter 1884–85, followed by even worse weather on the northern plains two years later. Hundreds of thousands of cattle froze or starved to death. These catastrophes spurred reforms that ended open-range grazing. The ranchers who survived turned to growing hay and supplemental feed for the winter. They reduced the size of their herds, started buying or leasing land and fencing in their cattle, and invested in scientific breeding that crossed longhorns with higher-quality stock to produce a better grade of beef.

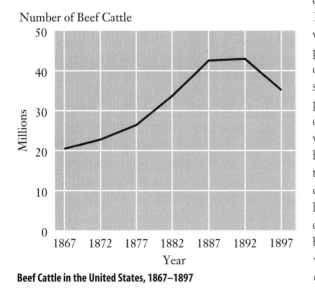

Number of Beef Cattle

Beef Cattle in the United States, 1867–1897

The Industrialization of Ranching

As open-range grazing declined, more industrialized ranching expanded. We don't usually think of ranching as an industrial process—industrialization tends to conjure up images of eastern factories belching smoke—but in fact major ranching companies operated as big businesses by the end of the century. As historian David Igler has shown, by 1900, the California corporation Miller & Lux was one of the largest industrial enterprises in the country, having integrated raising cattle on vast landholdings together with meatpacking in San Francisco. Its two founding partners were both ambitious German immigrants who had started out working as butchers in San Francisco but quickly moved into ownership of their own shops: despite their remarkably similar backgrounds—or perhaps because of them—they never liked each other much. Still, they were enormously successful business partners, building a corporation that shared many similarities with other large companies in the late 19th century. Mobilizing large amounts of capital, they employed over a thousand laborers in extensive operations that tightly connected ranchlands with the city.

Industrial Cowboys

Cowboys did not just ride the open range in the Texan cattle drives that have became the stuff of legend; they also rode the extensive Miller & Lux landholdings. Before the 1870s, the most valuable of the firm's cowboys were **vaqueros,** Mexican cowboys who rounded up cattle, branded them, and drove them to San Francisco. The tradition of *vaqueros* had arrived in the New World with the Spanish, who introduced herding by men on horseback. By the late 19th century, the raising of cattle herds by *vaqueros* had been practiced for centuries in California.

Not surprisingly, the head *vaquero* at Miller & Lux was a Mexican American, **Rafael Cuen.** His was a position of skill, and he was given a great deal of respect. Yet his salary was not as high as that of the white workers in the corporation who occupied parallel positions of authority, reflecting prevalent discrimination against Mexicans; it's possible this carried an especially sharp sting given the fact that his father had once owned (and lost) a piece of the Miller & Lux land. After the 1870s, the arrival of railroads took a toll on the positions of *vaqueros* like Cuen: cattle were shipped to market by rail.

Mexican Americans

Throughout the late 19th century, Mexican Americans, many of whom had owned their land for generations, lost both property and political influence to the incoming Anglo-American settlers. Many elite *Californios* who were ranchers in southern California, for instance, had to sell their lands to pay outstanding debts after devastating droughts in the 1860s virtually destroyed the ranching industry. But even as early as 1849 in the northern California goldfields, resentment of "foreigners" provoked violence against Mexican American miners—and the Foreign Miners' Tax of 1850 effectively forced Mexican Americans out of the goldfields (even though they were not "foreigners"). As the 19th century progressed, hordes of

Anglo-American "squatters" invaded the expansive holdings of the Mexican American elite, *Californios* who were forced to seek relief in the courts. Although their claims were generally upheld, these legal proceedings often stretched on for years. After exorbitant legal fees and other expenses were taken into account, a legal triumph was often a Pyrrhic victory. In the end, most Mexican American landholders in northern California, like those in southern California, had to sell the very lands they had fought to keep in order to pay their mounting debts.

Elsewhere, the migration of Anglos into eastern Texas had played a role in fomenting the war for Texas independence and in bringing about the war with Mexico (see chapter 13). By the latter half of the 19th century, eastern Texas was overwhelmingly Anglo; most *Tejanos* (people of Mexican origin or descent) were concentrated in the Rio Grande Valley of southern Texas. As in California, Anglos in Texas used force and intimidation, coupled with exploitative legal maneuvering, to disenfranchise the *Tejanos*. The **Texas Rangers** often acted as an Anglo vigilante force that exacted retribution for the real or imagined crimes of Mexican Americans. Eventually, Mexican Americans in Texas were reduced to a state of peonage, dependent on their Anglo protectors for political and economic security.

Similar patterns prevailed in New Mexico, but the effects were mitigated somewhat because New Mexicans continued to outnumber Anglo-American settlers. Earlier in the 19th century, international trade along the Santa Fe Trail had strengthened the political and economic status of the New Mexican elites. Now these same elites consolidated their position by acting as power brokers between poorer New Mexicans and wealthy Anglos. Despite such difficult conditions, Spanish-speaking peoples maintained their cultural traditions in the face of Anglo settlement, with the Roman Catholic Church serving as an important center of community life. An influx of immigrants from Mexico toward the end of the century created a new basis for community as well.

Itinerant Laborers

The *vaquero* Rafael Cuen was a highly skilled worker of great value to his employer; he was one of the lucky employees who had long-term employment. But for many workers in the West, itineracy was the norm; a virtual army of workers and wanderers traveled the western countryside. Most low-level jobs in ranching were seasonal, meaning that workers were forced to move from place to place periodically in search of work. And as western industrialization uprooted many workers from their traditional lives, more and more people took to the road. As Henry George said in his bestselling 1879 book *Progress and Poverty,* a scathing indictment of the current economic system, "the 'tramp' comes with the locomotive." For George, who had been a prospector before becoming a newspaper editor in California, the fault lay in a system of "land monopoly" that allowed control of land and resources by the few at the expense of the many.

At Miller & Lux, **itinerant laborers** were Chinese, Portuguese, Italian, Mexican, and Mexican American, in addition to white, native-born Americans. One of the itinerant laborers who hired on to an irrigation crew was a man named Joseph Warren Matthews, a farmer who had heavy debts. To pay these debts, he had taken on a series of grueling temporary jobs, including wage labor for a lumber company in the Pacific Northwest, work in the Alaskan goldfields, pipe laying for a water company, ore smelting, and digging ditches. His situation underlined the precariousness of many lives in the industrializing West.

Homesteading and Farming

Many homesteaders and farmers shared that precariousness: not only were 49 percent of all homesteaders unable to "prove up" their claims, but many were ultimately forced off their homesteads by the unforgiving climate of the Great Plains.

For much of the antebellum period, the Great Plains were known as the Great American Desert and assumed to be uninhabitable. By the 1850s, however, many boosters of western expansion promoted the idea that the Great Plains were a potentially lush American garden perfect for settlement. In this view, aridity was not a problem; the folk belief that "rainfall follows the plow"—that settlement would somehow prevent droughts—even gained credence among some geologists and other experts.

A great wave of settlement of the Great Plains occurred during the late 1870s to the mid-1880s, when rainfall was in fact relatively abundant. But the truth was that the average normal rainfall on the plains west of the 98th meridian (a line running roughly from the center of the Dakotas through the center of Texas) was scarcely enough to support farming except in certain river valleys. Years of drought inevitably followed, beginning in 1886 and lasting through the mid-1890s—and fueling farmers' discontent and protests (see chapter 19). Homesteaders and farmers in Minnesota, Iowa, and parts of Kansas and Nebraska were relatively lucky because those areas offered rich soil and adequate rainfall. In Iowa, for instance, farmers had great success with a "corn and hog" farm economy. But other land was arid and unproductive, producing heartbreak for homesteaders and farmers. Between 1888 and 1892, half the population of Kansas and Nebraska was forced to give up and move back east to Illinois or Iowa.

The Experience of Homesteading

Homesteading families on the Great Plains literally built their houses from the ground up: in an environment without trees, they cut the dense prairie sod into blocks and stacked them up to form walls, providing a small window and a door in a "soddy" of around 18 by 24 feet. **Soddies** were a practical solution to a difficult problem on the plains, but they were also dark, dank, and claustrophobic.

As Kansas homesteader Mary Abell (an excerpt from one of her letters opens this chapter) explained to her sister: "Imagine living in a place dug out of the side of a hill (one side to the weather with door and window—top covered with dirt and you have our place of abode). No one east would think of putting pigs in such a place." Abell's letters from 1871 to 1875 made clear the hard labor involved in homesteading: in addition to caring for five

A Nebraska Soddy   This appealing young family stands proudly in front of their Nebraska soddy in 1884 or 1885, during a time when rainfall was abundant on the Great Plains. A long-term drought began in 1886, however, making us wonder whether this family was able to hang on to its homestead through the coming difficult times.

Library of Congress, Prints and Photographs Division

children, in the fall of 1873, she had been her husband's "sole help in getting up and stacking at least 25 tons of hay and oats." Less than a week later, "one of those dreadful prairie fires" swept through the Abells' land, and they lost not only their hay and oats but also chickens and farm equipment. In 1874, she faced both drought and grasshoppers, and wrote her family that "none of you have the least conception" of "actual want, destitution." In 1875, Abell died at the age of 29.

Of course, not all homesteaders faced the same dire straits. Many of the 4 million immigrants who came from Germany, the Czech region of the Austro-Hungarian empire, and the Scandinavian countries from 1865 to 1890 settled in the upper Midwest and northern plains and became successful farmers. The northern plains region had the highest proportion of foreign-born residents in the nation during the last quarter of the century. These European immigrants formed homogenous ethnic enclaves that maintained the distinctive culture and traditions of their homelands. Swedish immigrants in Minnesota, for instance, spoke Swedish with one another and centered their lives around the Swedish Lutheran church; their children attended Swedish schools and learned to read the Swedish bible, sing Swedish songs, and recite Swedish history; and both men and women wore traditional Swedish dress on holidays. By the end of the century, there were also homogenous ethnic communities of Germans, Czechs, Poles, Hungarians, and Norwegians dotting the northern landscape.

Gender and Western Settlement

The Homestead Act was unusual in allowing unmarried women to make claims; between 5 percent and 15 percent of homestead entries in different locales went to women in the late 19th century. Many of these women probably "proved up" only to immediately sell their land, rather than farm it themselves: but still, the existence of women homesteaders reminds us that in some ways, gender arrangements were different in the West than in other regions of the country.

The most pronounced difference was a gender-divided society in mining camps and towns, which were overwhelmingly masculine. During the Gold Rush, California was up to 93 percent male, and many ranches, including Miller & Lux holdings, were exclusively male as well. Mining towns were known as violent places, and many observers were anxious to establish a more respectable family life there.

Prostitutes from all over the world were drawn to mining towns throughout the late 19th century, but nowhere except in San Francisco were women systematically forced into sexual slavery. There, the situation of Chinese laborers encouraged an exploitative world trade in women. While by the last decades of the century, Chinese merchants were allowed to bring their wives and daughters to America, laborers had no such rights. By custom, as well, respectable Chinese women were expected to stay home. The numbers of Chinese women in America remained extremely low in the 19th century, never rising above 5,000.

The difficulty in bringing Chinese women to America encouraged a brutal international trade in prostitution. Chinese women who were kidnapped or purchased from poor parents were sold into indentured servitude or slavery and unknowingly shipped to America to become prostitutes. In San Francisco, an estimated 85 percent to 97 percent of Chinese women were prostitutes in 1860; around 72 percent in 1870; and between 21 percent to 50 percent in 1880. They faced a singularly harsh existence. However, some women managed to escape prostitution. Some women married men who had saved up enough money to purchase the contracts that bound them; Protestant missionaries worked to rescue prostitutes, as well.

As these few examples show, settlement patterns of the West produced—at least for a short period of time—societies with unequal numbers of men and women, with different results in different places. The impact of these disparities continues to intrigue historians, who still puzzle, for instance, over the reasons why several western states were the first to grant woman suffrage (see chapter 21). In the realm of Western myth, one obvious legacy of the West's early gender arrangements is the enduring place in American culture of the white cowboy as an icon of rugged masculinity.

Conquest and Resistance: American Indians in the Trans-Mississippi West

Focus Question
How did the Indian peoples of the trans-Mississippi West respond to white settlement and U.S. government policies?

The westward expansion of ranching and farming after 1865 doomed the free range of the Plains Indians and the buffalo. In the 1830s, eastern tribes had been forcibly moved to pre-serves west of the Mississippi so as permanently to separate whites and Indians. In scarcely a decade, white settlers had penetrated these lands via the overland trails to the Pacific Coast. In the 1850s, when the Kansas and Nebraska territories opened to white settlement, the government forced a dozen tribes living there to cede 15 million acres, leaving them on reservations totaling less than 1.5 million acres. Thus began what historian Philip Weeks has called the "policy of concentration": No longer were Indians to be pushed west onto the arid plains that early white explorers had christened The Great American Desert. Rather, as white settlers moved onto and through the plains and mountains, they began to covet these large spaces, which earlier treaties had assigned to the Indians for "as long as waters shall run and the grass shall grow."

Even before the Civil War, the nomadic Plains Indians, whose culture and economy were based on the buffalo, faced pressure not only from the advancing tide of white set-tlement but also from the forced migration of eastern tribes into their domain. In the after-math of the Civil War, the process of concentrating Indian tribes on reservations acceler-ated. Chiefs of the five **"civilized tribes"**—Cherokees, Creeks, Choctaws, Chickasaws, and Seminoles—had signed treaties of alliance with the Confederacy. At that time, they were living in Indian Territory (most of present-day Oklahoma), where their economy was linked to the South. Many of them, especially members of the mixed-blood upper class, were slaveholders. Bitter toward the United States, the tribal leaders cast their lot with the Confederacy on the principle that "the enemy of my enemy is my friend." The Cherokee leader Stand Watie rose to brigadier general in the Confederate army and was the last Con-federate commander to surrender, on June 23, 1865. **(See Map 18.2, Indian Reservations, 1875 and 1900, in the color insert following page 816.)**

Siding with the Confederacy proved to be a costly mistake for these tribes. The U.S. government "reconstructed" Indian Territory more quickly and with less contention than it reconstructed the former Confederate states. Treaties with the five tribes in 1866 required them to grant tribal citizenship to their freed slaves and reduced tribal lands by half. The government then settled Indians who had been dispossessed from other areas on the land it had taken from these tribes.

Conflict with the Sioux

The Civil War had set in motion a generation of Indian warfare that was more violent and widespread than anything since the 17th century. During the war, the Union army was forced to pull many units out of frontier posts to fight the Confederacy. Moreover, the drain on the Union treasury to finance the war compounded the usual corruption of Indian agents and delayed annuity payments to tribes that had sold their land to the government. These events had dire consequences on the northern plains.

Herded onto reservations along the Minnesota River by the **Treaty of Traverse des Sioux** in 1851, the Santee Sioux were angry when late annuity payments in summer

1862 threatened starvation. Warriors began to speak openly of reclaiming ancestral hunting grounds. Then on August 17, a robbery in which five white settlers were murdered seemed to open the floodgates. The warriors persuaded Chief Little Crow to take them on the warpath, and over the next few weeks, at least 500 white Minnesotans were massacred.

Hastily mobilized militia and army units finally suppressed the uprising. A military court convicted 319 Indians of murder and atrocities and sentenced 303 of them to death. Appalled by this ferocious retaliation, Lincoln personally reviewed the trial transcripts and reduced the number of executions to 38—the largest act of executive clemency in American history. Even so, the hanging of 38 Sioux on December 26, 1862, was the largest mass execution the country has ever witnessed. The government evicted the remaining Sioux from Minnesota to Dakota Territory.

In the meantime, the army's pursuit of fleeing Santee Sioux provoked other Sioux tribes farther west. By 1864, and for a decade afterward, fighting flared between the army and the Sioux across the northern plains. It reached a climax in 1874 and 1875 after gold-seekers poured into the Black Hills of western Dakota, a sacred place to the Sioux. At the **battle of Little Bighorn** in Montana Territory on June 25, 1876, Sioux warriors led by **Sitting Bull** and **Crazy Horse,** along with their Cheyenne allies, wiped out **George A. Custer** and the 225 men with him in the Seventh Cavalry. In retaliation, General Philip Sheridan carried out a winter campaign in which the Sioux and Cheyenne were crushed.

Largest and most warlike of the Plains tribes, the Sioux were confined to a reservation in Dakota Territory where poverty, disease, apathy, and alcoholism reduced this once-proud people to desperation.

Suppression of Other Plains Indians

Just as the Sioux uprising in Minnesota had triggered war on the northern plains in 1862, a massacre of Cheyennes in Colorado in 1864 sparked a decade of conflict on the southern plains. The discovery of gold near Pike's Peak set off a rush to Colorado in 1858–59. The government responded by calling several Cheyenne and Arapaho chiefs to a council, and with a combination of threats and promises, the agents persuaded the chiefs to sign a treaty giving up all claims to land in this region (guaranteed by an earlier treaty of 1851) in exchange for a reservation at Sand Creek in southeast Colorado.

In 1864, hunger and resentment on the reservation prompted many warriors to return to their old hunting grounds and to raid white settlements. Skirmishes soon erupted into open warfare. In the fall, Cheyenne Chief Black Kettle, believing that he had concluded peace with the Colorado settlers, returned to the reservation. There, at dawn on November 29, militia commanded by Colonel John Chivington surrounded and attacked Black Kettle's unsuspecting camp, killing 200 Indians, half of them women and children.

The notorious **Sand Creek massacre** set a pattern for several similar attacks on Indian villages in subsequent years. Ever since the earliest battles between colonists and Indians in the

17th century, whites had followed the strategy of burning Indian crops and villages as a means of destroying or driving off the Indians. Sherman and Sheridan had adopted a similar strategy against the Confederates and followed it again as military commanders responsible for subduing the Plains Indians. Their purpose was to corral all of the Indians onto the reservations that were being created throughout the West. In addition to trying to defeat the Indians in battle, which proved to be difficult against the mounted Plains Indians, the army encouraged the extermination of the buffalo herds. Professional hunters slaughtered the large, clumsy animals by the millions for their hides, thus depriving Plains Indians of both physical and spiritual sustenance. When the buffalo became nearly extinct in 1883, the Plains Indians understood that their old way of life was gone forever. "Nothing happened after that," recalled one Crow warrior. "We just lived. There were no more war parties, no capturing horses from the Piegan and the Sioux, no buffalo to hunt. There is nothing more to tell."

The Indians were left with no alternative but to come into the reservations, and by the 1880s, nearly all of them had done so. Chief Joseph of the Nez Percé pronounced the epitaph for their way of life when federal troops blocked the escape of his band from Montana to Canada in 1877:

> I am tired of fighting. Our chiefs are killed. The old men are all dead. It is cold and we have no blankets . . . no food. . . . The little children are freezing to death. . . . Hear me, my chiefs; I am tired; my heart is sick and sad. From where the sun now stands, I will fight no more forever.

The "Peace Policy"

Many Eastern reformers condemned America's violent repression of the Indians. The most prominent was **Helen Hunt Jackson,** whose 1881 book *A Century of Dishonor* was an outraged indictment of anti-Indian violence, exploitation, and broken treaties. Yet as sympathetic as Jackson was to the Indians' plight, she was not sympathetic to Indian culture; like other white Protestant reformers of her day, she believed that Indians must be stripped of their culture in order to assimilate productively to American society.

In this view she was in alignment with the government: in 1869, President Grant had announced a new **"peace policy"** toward Indians, urging "their civilization and ultimate citizenship." "Civilization" meant acceptance of white culture, including the English language, Christianity, and individual ownership of property. It also meant allegiance to the United States rather than to a tribe. In 1869, Grant established a Board of Indian Commissioners and staffed it with humanitarian reformers. In 1871, the century-long policy of negotiating treaties with Indian "nations" came to an end. From then on, Indians became "wards of the nation," to be civilized and prepared for citizenship, first on reservations and eventually on individually owned parcels of land that were carved out of the reservations. Most Indians acquiesced in the "reconstruction" that offered them citizenship by the 1880s; they had little choice.

The Dawes Severalty Act and Indian Boarding Schools

In order to further the goal of Indian ownership of private property, Protestant reformers in the 1880s found themselves in a strange alliance with land-hungry westerners, who greedily eyed the 155 million acres of land tied up in reservations. If part of that land could be allotted directly to individual ownership by Indian families, the remainder would become available for purchase by whites. The 1887 **Dawes Severalty Act** combined these impulses toward greed and reform. This landmark legislation called for the dissolution of Indian tribes as legal entities, offered Indians the opportunity to become citizens, and allotted each head of family 160 acres of farmland or 320 acres of grazing land as long as they were "severed" from their tribe.

For whites who were eager to seize reservation land, the Dawes Act brought a bonanza. At noon on April 22, 1889, the government threw open specified parts of the Indian Territory to "Boomers," who descended on the region like locusts and by nightfall had staked claim to nearly 2 million acres. Indians did not just lose the lands legally opened for white settlement: many Indians who received individual land titles through the Dawes Act also lost these lands to unscrupulous whites through fraud and misrepresentation. Eventually, whites gained title to 108 million acres of former reservation land.

For Indians, the Dawes Severalty Act was a disaster. Private ownership of land was an alien concept to most tribes, yet Indians received little training for a transition to farming, much less appropriate tools or supplies. Moreover, the poor quality of their land allotments made farming difficult, if not impossible. In addition the Dawes Act directly attacked Indian culture by forbidding Indian religions, the telling of Indian myths and legends, and the practices of medicine men.

Indian boarding schools established beginning in the late 1870s were another attempt to strip Indians of their culture. Children were taken from their families to the Hampton Institute in Virginia and the Carlisle Institute in Pennsylvania, among other schools. There they were forbidden to speak Indian languages or wear Indian clothing: as one 1890 set of instructions from the U.S. Bureau of Indian Affairs put it, "Pupils must be compelled to converse with each other in English, and should be properly rebuked or punished for persistent violation of this rule." The writer Zitkala-Sa, a Yankton Sioux, later remembered her life in an Indian school: "the melancholy of those black days has left so long a shadow that it darkens the path of years that have since gone by."

Indian schools may have had assimilation to white culture as a goal, but they also had a very narrow vision of the place Indians would hold in a white world. Girls were taught domestic science but little more and were educated for menial jobs as servants; many spent long hours working in school laundries as virtual servants of the schools that were supposed to teach them. Students resisted as best they could by running away, often only to be caught and returned to school again; many adults later resisted the training they had received by returning to Indian traditions. This was the case with Zitkala-Sa: after graduation from an Indian boarding school, Zitkala-Sa taught at the Carlisle School and became a much-praised writer in New York. But later she would undergo a spiritual crisis: she compared herself to a "slender tree" that had been "uprooted from my mother, nature, and God," and lamented that she had "forgotten the healing in trees and brooks." Eventually she left New York, married a Sioux, and became an activist for Native American rights.

The Ghost Dance

At a time of despair for many Indians, a new visionary religious movement swept through Indian peoples in 1890, offering a different kind of resistance to white domination. The **Ghost Dance** began with the visions of the Paiute shaman Wovoka, who counseled Indians that if they gave up alcohol, lived a simple life, and devoted themselves to prayer, white men would disappear from the earth, Indian lands would be restored, and dead Indians would rejoin the living. This message of hope was embodied in the Ghost Dance ritual, involving days of worship expressed in part through dance.

When the Ghost Dance religion spread to those Sioux led by Sitting Bull and they began days of ecstatic dancing, Indian agents grew alarmed: as one agent telegraphed authorities, "Indians are dancing in the snow and are wild and crazy. *We need protection and we need it now.*" The results of the ensuing confrontations between Indians and authorities were tragic: first Sitting Bull and his grandson were killed in a skirmish with reservation author-ities; then a few days later, a trigger-happy military—members of the Seventh Cavalry, Custer's old regiment—opened fire on Sioux men, women, and children at **Wounded Knee** in the Pine Ridge Reservation, killing 146 Indians, including 44 women and 18 chil-dren, as well as 25 soldiers. For many, the massacre at Wounded Knee symbolized the death of 19th-century Plains Indian culture. While Indians throughout the West would adapt to a new world with great resilience, working to preserve their cultural practices, there was no question that their old world had been demolished.

Sitting Bull and Buffalo Bill: Popular Myths of the West

Only a few years before he was killed, Sitting Bull had been one of the chief attractions in the entertainment extravaganza known as **Buffalo Bill Cody's Wild West Show.** No mere vic-tim of white exploitation, Sitting Bull had been a canny negotiator of fees for his appearances in 1885; he required an interpreter, several attendants, and a salary that came to half the annual salary of the typical Indian agent. He also used press interviews while on the Wild West tour to ask the U.S. government to live up to its promises to Indians. If Sitting Bull was being used by Cody, he was certainly using Cody right back.

Having "real" Indians in his show was of vital importance to Cody, who capitalized on the public's hunger for "authentic" spectacular entertainments in his popular Wild West shows. Cody was an extraordinary mix of the new industrializing West, the frontier West, and an emerging culture of mass entertainment. Having begun his career as a soldier in the Civil War, Cody then worked for one of the transcontinental railroad lines (where he gained the nickname "Buffalo Bill" for slaughtering buffalo) before becoming a scout for the Fifth Cavalry. When Cody became the subject of a popular dime Western novel, the

Sitting Bull and Buffalo Bill   Before he was killed in 1890 during the Ghost Dance movement, the renowned Sioux leader Sitting Bull became an important part of Buffalo Bill's Wild West Show, negotiating shrewdly for his salary. In this remarkable 1885 staged image, the elaborately costumed Buffalo Bill and Sitting Bull appear as virtual equals, both resting a hand on the same rifle.

most improbable turn in Cody's career occurred: he decided to dramatize his own life in a series of theatrical entertainments. By the year Sitting Bull joined Buffalo Bill's Wild West Show with its band of trick riders and sharpshooters, it required 18 railroad cars to transport performers (including a number of Indians), work crews, animals, and equipment.

The Wild West Show celebrated the white conquest of the West in a series of acts called "The Drama of Civilization," which showed scenes of an emigrant train crossing the prairie, Buffalo Bill rescuing a pioneer family from Indians, and a mining camp. Billed as

"America's National Entertainment," these shows revealed just how tightly linked industrialization and conquest were in Americans' thinking—and even in their entertainment.

Industrialization and the New South

Focus Question
How did industrialization shape African American experience in the post-Reconstruction South?

Like the West, the South underwent a surge of industrialization in the last decades of the 19th century. Boosters like the energetic and influential Henry Grady, editor of the Atlanta *Constitution,* proclaimed that a **New South** had emerged, one hospitable to industry and to Northern investment.

Some people scoffed at such promotional talk in a world that was still decidedly rural, but in fact the pace of industrialization quickened in the last decades of the century, with textiles leading the way. In 1880, the South had only 5 percent of the country's textile-producing capacity; by 1900, it had 23 percent and was well on its way to surpassing New England a generation later. Tobacco also industrialized, with James B. Duke of North Carolina transforming the industry with his installation of cigarette-making machines at Durham in 1885. In 1890, he created the American Tobacco Company, which controlled 90 percent of the market.

Railroads and iron also saw a surge in growth. Between 1877 and 1900, the South built railroads faster than any other region in the country. In 1880, the former slave states produced only 9 percent of the nation's pig iron; by 1890, after a decade of extraordinary expansion for the industry nationwide, that proportion had doubled. Most of the growth was concentrated in northern Alabama, where the proximity of coal, limestone, and ore made the new city of Birmingham the "Pittsburgh of the South."

But there were limits to Southern industrialization. It was difficult to catch up with well-established Northern industries. Thus Southerners competed in the few areas in which they could find markets for local crops and resources: textiles produced from their own cotton; cigarettes manufactured from Southern tobacco; as well as lumber, sugar, and iron.

Not all of the wealth from the new industries went into the pockets of Southerners, though. Over the late 19th century, Southern industry attracted more and more Northern capital in a pattern that held true across industries. At first, for instance, Southerners supplied most of the capital in the expansion of the textile industry. But after 1893, an increasing amount came from the North, as New England mill owners began to recognize the benefits of relocating to the low-wage, nonunion South. In the tobacco industry, too, initial Southern capital gave way to Northern financing, especially after James Duke moved to New York in the 1880s. But most dependent on Northern capital were the railroads and iron industries. When in 1886 Southern railroads switched their tracks from the regional gauge to the national standard, the symbolic domination of the North seemed complete.

Heavy Northern investment in Southern industry meant that the South had less control over economic decisions that affected its welfare. Some historians have referred to the South's "colonial" relationship to the North in the late 19th century. One result was that the low wages prevailing in the South made for inequitable distribution of the economic benefits of industrial growth. Average Southern per capita income remained only two-fifths of the average in the rest of the country well into the 20th century.

Race and Industrialization

Even those low wages were unequally distributed, as the politics of race influenced the structuring of industrial jobs. Along the piedmont from Virginia to Alabama, new cotton mills sprang up for a white labor force drawn from farm families on the worn-out red clay soil of this region. About 40 percent of the workers were women, and 25 percent were children aged 16 and younger. Living in company towns, they labored long hours for wages about half the level prevailing in New England's mills, with their cheap labor giving mill owners a competitive advantage.

At first many African Americans confidently assumed that there would be jobs for them in this new textile industry. And why not? Blacks had worked before the Civil War in mills, and they continued to work in tobacco factories in the postwar era, albeit in the lowest-paid jobs and performing the dirtiest work. There seemed no reason why such a large and inexpensive workforce might not become a mainstay of the mills.

But industrialization did not mean progress for blacks in most places. Instead, it went hand in hand with segregation in the increasingly white supremacist world of the 1880s and 1890s. To attract white workers, mill owners promised them segregated environments. The bargain offered was this: mill workers might not earn very much, but they would gain what one historian has called the **"wages of whiteness,"** a sense of racial superiority that could serve as compensation for their low economic status. Thus the New South was built around the politics of race, and many African Americans lost ground in the emerging industrial economy. For most African Americans, agricultural work was thus the only option.

Southern Agriculture

A major success story, however, was increasing black ownership of land in the post-Reconstruction period, with almost 200,000 farmers achieving that cherished goal. Most black landowners in the South were in the Upper South or coastal areas; others were in the trans-Mississippi West.

Still, most blacks were tenants rather than landowners, and many blacks and whites faced lives of grinding rural poverty. Those who owned land risked sliding into tenantry; those who did not own land found it impossible to make the leap to land ownership. One-crop specialization, overproduction, declining prices, and an exploitative credit system all contributed to the problem. The basic institution of the Southern rural economy was the crop lien system, which came into being because of the shortage of money and credit in the war-ravaged South. Few banks had survived the war, and land values had plummeted, which left farmers unable to secure a bank loan with their land as collateral. Instead, merchants in the crossroads country stores that sprang up across the South provided farmers with supplies and groceries in return for a lien on their next crop.

This system might have worked well if the merchants had charged reasonable interest rates and if cotton and tobacco prices had remained high enough for the farmer to pay off his debts after harvest with a little left over. But the country storekeeper charged a credit price 50 or 60 percent above the cash price, partly because he had no competition and partly because of the high risk of loss on his loans. And crop prices, especially for cotton, were dropping steadily. Cotton prices declined from an average of 12 cents per pound in the 1870s to 6 cents in the 1890s. As prices fell, many farmers went deeper and deeper into debt to the merchants. **Sharecroppers** and tenants incurred a double indebtedness: to the landowner whose land they sharecropped or rented, and to the merchant who furnished them supplies on credit. Because many landowners became merchants, and vice versa, that indebtedness was often to the same man.

One reason cotton prices fell was overproduction. Britain had encouraged the expansion of cotton growing in Egypt and India during the Civil War to make up for the loss of American cotton. After the war, Southern growers had to face international competition. By 1878, the Southern crop had reached the output of the best antebellum year, and during the next 20 years, output doubled. This overproduction drove prices ever lower. To obtain credit, farmers had to plant every acre with the most marketable cash crop—cotton. This practice exhausted the soil and required ever-increasing amounts of expensive fertilizer, which fed the cycle of overproduction and declining prices.

It also reduced the amount of land that could be used to grow food crops. Farmers who might otherwise have produced their own cornmeal and raised their own hogs for bacon became dependent on merchants for these supplies. Before the Civil War, the cotton states had been nearly self-sufficient in food; by the 1890s, they had to import nearly half their food at a price 50 percent higher than it would have cost to grow their own. Many Southerners recognized that only diversification could break this dependency, but the crop lien system locked them into it. "We ought to plant less [cotton and tobacco] and more of grain and grasses," said a North Carolina farmer in 1887, "but how are we to do it; the man who furnishes us rations at 50 percent interest won't let us; he wants money crop planted. . . . It is cotton! cotton! cotton! Buy everything and make cotton pay for it." Many sharecroppers, particularly blacks, fell into virtual peonage.

Exodusters and Emigrationists

Given the multiple difficulties rural African Americans faced—from persistent poverty to dependence on white owners to racial discrimination and violence—it is not surprising that many dreamed of leaving the South entirely. In the late 1870s, a movement called Exodus gained momentum among African Americans who believed that they might have to "repeat the history of the Israelites" and "seek new homes beyond the reign and rule of Pharaoh." Most pinned their hopes on internal emigration to the West, although some explored the possibility of emigration to Liberia as well. In 1875, Benjamin Singleton, a former Tennessee slave, helped a group of African Americans establish new lives in an agrarian colony in western Kansas; three years later, he circulated an alluring advertisement picturing prairie abundance in the hopes of enticing a few hundred more settlers. Instead, in the spring of 1879, some 20,000 African Americans began an exodus to Kansas from all over the Southwest—drawn not just by the advertisement but also by rumors that there was free land available for settlers as well as free supplies from the government. The rumors were false, but many of these **Exodusters** stayed on in Kansas anyway, although not as homesteaders amidst the prairie abundance but as domestics and laborers in Kansan towns, including towns they founded such as Nicodemus.

Race Relations in the New South

The desire to emigrate for better jobs, autonomy, and a place where African Americans could be truly free did not end with the Exodusters. "The disposition among the colored people to migrate now is strong, and is increasing," commented a white Southerner in 1889. There was a net loss of 537,000 African Americans in the South between 1880 and 1910. Economic reasons were important, but so too was the worsening world of white supremacy that arose in that period.

Adherence to the industrial ideology behind the New South, with its emphasis on racial cooperation, was shallow at best among broad classes of whites. Instead, many refused to let go of the legacy of the defeated plantation South. They celebrated the Lost Cause by organizing fraternal and sororal organizations such as the **United Daughters of the Confederacy (UDC).** The UDC, like the Daughters of the American Revolution (DAR) on which it was modeled, was open only to whites who could prove their relation to the "first families" of the South. Its members decorated the graves of Confederate soldiers, funded public statues of Confederate heroes, and sought to preserve a romanticized history of the slavery era. Several white Southern authors became famous writing stories about this fabled South. Thomas Nelson Page's racist sentimental story "Marse Chan" created a national craze for Southern literature in the 1880s. Published in a Northern magazine, the story was written in what Page claimed to be authentic black dialect, with an aging freedman telling of the glorious days before the war when slaves supposedly had little work to do. Such stories romanticized the Southern plantation, cleansing it of the horrors of slavery.

The national appeal of such stories made it clear that anti-black racism was not just a Southern phenomenon. Certainly, there was shockingly little Northern reaction to the wave of **lynchings** of black men in the South in the 1890s. Lynchings rose to an all-time high, averaging 188 per year, while the viciousness of racist propaganda reached an all-time low. At a time when many professional middle-class African American men and women were steadily gaining economically, even as a downward spiral in the rural economy frustrated whites, lynchings of black men were not just extraordinarily violent acts. They were also clear symbolic messages to entire black communities to keep their "place" in a white-dominated society. Ritualized expressions of white power, lynchings were not secret or furtive events, but often well-orchestrated community affairs advertised in advance and sometimes even including men, women, and children as spectators.

In 1892, three respected African American businessmen who owned a grocery store in Memphis, Tennessee, were taken from the jail where they awaited trial and lynched by a white mob. Their ostensible crime was attempted murder—firing on three white intruders who had burst into their store—but their real offense was successfully challenging the dominance of a white grocery store in their area.

In response to the lynching, the African American journalist **Ida B. Wells** embarked on an extensive anti-lynching campaign involving an economic boycott as well as a series of fiery editorials in her newspaper, *Free Speech,* that called into question the usual white rationale for lynching: the supposed rape or molestation of a white woman. Correctly exposing this common trumped-up charge as "the old racket," Wells ignited the wrath of white Memphis residents and was forced to flee for her life to the North. But there her anti-lynching campaign met with indifference from Northerners until Wells traveled to England on a speaking tour. She received widespread publicity as she called into question how civilized America could be if it tolerated a barbaric practice like lynching; she also touched a nerve back home. Upperclass white Northerners indifferent to the murder of blacks but sensitive to English opinion finally sat up and began to notice her campaign. Her English travels were a brilliant strategy to shake up Northern complacency and challenge Northern complicity in lynching.

The Emergence of an African American Middle Class

Wells was part of an extensive African American middle class that came of age in the 1880s and 1890s. These men and women, educated in the emerging black colleges, became teachers, doctors, lawyers, ministers, and business owners. They formed numerous civic organizations, such as the 1896 National Association of Colored Women, which was part of the women's club movement of the late 19th century (see chapter 19). Echoing the moral reform activities of white middle-class women, its president, Mary Church Terrell, called on middle-class black women to work with "the masses of our women" and to "uplift and claim them."

Such institution building, combined with increasing prosperity, gave middle-class blacks great optimism that "racial uplift" might reduce or even eliminate racism in American society. "We as a race are enjoying the brightest rays of Christian civilization," wrote one bishop in the African Methodist Episcopal (AME) Church. Middle-class blacks believed that through education and self-improvement, they could become "best men" and "best women," seen as equals by middle-class whites. These were not naïve hopes, as black entry into the middle class surged in the 1880s and early 1890s.

The Rise of Jim Crow

But these visible successes of middle-class African Americans enraged white supremacists, who denied any possibility of class solidarity across racial lines. Serious anti-black riots broke out in Wilmington, North Carolina, in 1898 and in Atlanta in 1906. Several states adopted new constitutions that disenfranchised most black voters by means of literacy or property

© The Granger Collection, New York

Ida B. Wells A passionate crusader for justice, the renowned journalist Ida B. Wells received death threats after she began a campaign against lynching in her Memphis, Tennessee newspaper, *Free Speech*, in 1892. Forced to leave Memphis, Wells moved to Chicago and continued her anti-lynching crusade in pamphlets, newspaper columns, and public lectures delivered both in the U.S. and in England. Together with Booker T. Washington, Wells was one of the most prominent African American leaders of the 1890s.

qualifications (or both), poll taxes, and other clauses implicitly aimed at black voters. The new constitutions contained "understanding clauses" or "grandfather clauses" that enabled registrars to register white voters who were unable to meet the new requirements. In *Williams* v. *Mississippi* (1898), the U.S. Supreme Court upheld these disenfranchisement clauses on the grounds that they did not discriminate "on their face" against blacks. Most blacks lost the right to vote, and the Republican Party almost disappeared from most southern states. State Democratic parties then established primary elections in which only whites could vote. For the next 60 years, the primary was the only meaningful election in the South.

During these same years, most southern states passed **Jim Crow laws** (the name came from blackface minstrelsy; see chapter 10) mandating racial segregation in public facilities of all kinds. Many African Americans resisted: in 1884, Ida B. Wells, at the time a young schoolteacher, refused to give up her seat in a railway "ladies' car." The conductor "tried to drag me out of the seat," she remembered, "but the moment he caught hold of my arm I fastened my teeth in the back of his hand. I had braced my feet against the seat in front and was holding to the back, and as he had already been badly bitten he didn't try it again by himself. He went forward and got the baggageman and another man to help him and of course they succeeded in dragging me out." Wells sued the railroad, winning her case in a lower court before losing it on appeal.

In 1896 came a tremendous setback for American equality. In the landmark case of **Plessy v. Ferguson** (1896), the Supreme Court sanctioned Jim Crow laws so long as the separate facilities for blacks were equal to those for whites—which, in practice, they never were. At this "nadir" of the black experience in freedom, as one historian has called the 1890s, a new black leader emerged as successor of the abolitionists and Reconstruction politicians who were fading from the scene. **Booker T. Washington,** a 39-year-old educator who had founded Tuskegee Institute in Alabama, gave a speech at the 1895 Atlanta Exposition that made him famous—and has been controversial ever since.

Speaking to a white audience at this celebration of Southern industry and progress, Washington was introduced as "a representative of Negro enterprise and civilization." Assuring his audience that he wanted to "cement the friendship of the races," Washington talked of the "new era of industrial progress" and told the industrialists before him that they should hire African Americans rather than immigrants. "Cast down your bucket where you are," he told them, "among the eight million of Negroes whose habits you know." If they did so, Washington said, they would not only find people to "run your factories," but could also be assured that they would be surrounded by a "faithful, law-abiding, and unresentful" people. In the most famous sentence of the speech, Washington then promised that "in all things that are purely social we can be as separate as the fingers, yet one as the hand in all things essential to mutual progress." In effect, Washington accepted segregation as a temporary accommodation between the races in return for white support of black efforts for education, social uplift, and economic progress.

It was a complex, canny speech, much like the man himself, and Washington's listeners came away with very different impressions. Many African Americans applauded his appeal for black inclusion in the new industrial order; many white audience members simply took away the idea that Washington approved of segregation, vocational training for blacks, and a permanent, second-class status. An eloquent response to Washington came from the emerging African American leader **W. E. B. Du Bois** in his 1903 masterpiece, *The Souls of Black Folk,* a set of essays written between 1897 and 1903. Criticizing Washington for a policy of conciliation and submission, Du Bois reminded his audience that "only a firm adherence to their higher ideals and aspirations will ever keep those ideals within the realm of possibility."

The Politics of Stalemate

Focus Question
Why did politicians fail to address many of the most serious economic and social issues facing the nation in the post-Reconstruction world?

During the 20 years between the Panic of 1873 and the Panic of 1893, serious economic and social issues beset the American polity. As described in the next chapter, the strains of rapid industrialization, an inadequate monetary system, agricultural distress, and labor protest built up to potentially explosive force. The two mainstream political parties, however, seemed indifferent to these problems. Paralysis gripped the national government as the Civil War continued to cast its shadow, preventing political leaders from grappling with new issues facing the country because they remained mired in the passionate partisanship of the past.

The Republican Party did not disappear from the South after 1877. Nor was the black vote immediately and totally suppressed. Republican presidential candidates won about 40 percent of the votes in former slave states throughout the 1880s, and some blacks continued to win elections to state legislatures until the 1890s. Until 1901, every U.S. Congress but one had at least one black representative from the South. Independent parties occasionally formed coalitions with Republicans to win local or state elections, especially in Virginia.

Even so, "bulldozing" of black voters (chapter 17) continued to keep the southern states solid for the Democrats. In 1880, the Democratic Party hoped to build on this foundation to win the presidency for the first time in a generation. Taking their cue from the Republicans, the Democrats nominated a Civil War hero, General Winfield Scott Hancock. His opponent was another Civil War general, **James A. Garfield,** who had served in Congress since the war. In an election with the closest popular vote in American history (Garfield had a plurality of only 10,000 votes out of 9 million cast), Hancock carried every southern state, while Garfield won all but three northern states—and the election.

Knife-Edge Electoral Balance

The five presidential elections from 1876 through 1892, taken together, were the most closely contested elections in American history. No more than 1 percent separated the popular vote of the two major candidates in any of these contests except 1892, when the margin was 3 percent. The Democratic candidate won twice (**Grover Cleveland** in 1884 and 1892), and in two other elections carried a tiny plurality of popular votes (Tilden in 1876 and Cleveland in 1888) but lost narrowly in the Electoral College. During the 20 years covered by these five administrations, the Democrats controlled the House of Representatives in seven Congresses to the Republicans' three, while the Republicans controlled the Senate in eight Congresses to the Democrats' two. During only 6 of those 20 years did the same party control the presidency and both houses, and then by razor-thin margins.

The few pieces of major legislation during these years—the Pendleton Civil Service Act of 1883, the Interstate Commerce Act of 1887, and the Sherman Antitrust Act of 1890—could be enacted only by bipartisan majorities, and only after they had been watered down by numerous compromises. Politicians often debated the tariff, but the tariff laws they passed had little real impact on the economy. Tariffs were still the principal source of federal tax revenue, but because the federal budget amounted to less than 3 percent of the gross national product (compared with 20 percent today), federal fiscal policies played only a marginal role in the economy.

Divided government and the even balance between the two major parties accounted for the political stalemate. Neither party had the power to enact a bold legislative program; both parties avoided taking firm stands on controversial issues. Both parties practiced the politics of the past rather than the politics of the present. Individuals voted Republican or Democratic in the 1880s because they or their fathers had done so during the passionate years of the 1860s. Every Republican president from 1869 to 1901 had fought in the Union army; the one Democratic president, Grover Cleveland, had not. At election time, Republican candidates "waved the bloody shirt" to keep alive the memory of the Civil War. They castigated Democrats as former rebels or Copperheads who could not be trusted with the nation's destiny. Democrats, in turn, especially in the South, denounced racial equality and branded Republicans as the party of "Negro rule"—a charge that took on added intensity in 1890 when Republicans tried (and failed by one vote in the Senate) to enact a federal elections law to protect the voting rights of African Americans. From 1876 almost into the 20th century, scarcely anyone but a Confederate veteran could be elected governor or senator in the South.

Availability rather than ability or a strong stand on issues became the prime requisite for presidential and vice presidential nominees. Geographical availability was particularly important. The solid Democratic South and the rather less solid Republican North gave each party a firm bloc of electoral votes in every election. But in three large northern states—New York, Ohio, and Indiana—the two parties were so closely balanced that the shift of a few thousand votes would determine the margin of victory for one or the other party in the state's electoral votes. These three states alone represented 74 electoral votes, fully one-third of the total necessary for victory. The party that carried New York (36 electoral votes) and either of the other two won the presidency.

It is not surprising that of 20 nominees for president and vice president by the two parties in five elections, 16 were from these three states. Only once did each party nominate a presidential candidate from outside these three states: Democrat Winfield Scott Hancock of Pennsylvania in 1880 and Republican James G. Blaine of Maine in 1884—both lost.

Civil Service Reform

The most salient issue of national politics in the early 1880s was civil service reform. Old-guard factions in both parties opposed it. Republicans split into three factions known in the colorful parlance of the time as **Mugwumps** (the reformers), **Stalwarts** (who opposed reform), and

Half-Breeds (who supported halfway reforms). Mugwumps and Half-Breeds combined to nominate James A. Garfield for president in 1880. Stalwarts received a consolation prize with the nomination of **Chester A. Arthur** for vice president. Four months after Garfield took office, a man named Charles Guiteau approached the president at the railroad station in Washington and shot him. Garfield lingered for two months before dying on September 19, 1881.

Described by psychiatrists as a paranoid schizophrenic, Guiteau was viewed by the public as a symbol of the spoils system at its worst. He had been a government clerk and a supporter of the Stalwart faction of the Republican Party but had lost his job under the new administration. As he shot Garfield, he shouted, "I am a Stalwart and Arthur is president now!" This tragedy gave a final impetus to civil service reform. If the spoils system could cause the assassination of a president, it was time to get rid of it.

Although a Stalwart, President Arthur supported reform. In 1883, Congress passed the Pendleton Act, which established a category of civil service jobs that were to be filled by competitive examinations. At first, only one-tenth of government positions fell within that category, but a succession of presidential orders gradually expanded the list to about half by 1897. State and local governments began to emulate federal civil service reform in the 1880s and 1890s.

Like the other vice presidents who had succeeded presidents who died in office (John Tyler, Millard Fillmore, and Andrew Johnson), Arthur failed to achieve nomination for president in his own right. The Republicans turned in 1884 instead to their most charismatic figure, James G. Blaine of Maine. His 18 years in the House and Senate had included six years (1869–75) as Speaker of the House. He had made enemies over the years, however, especially among Mugwumps, who believed that his cozy relationship with railroad lobbyists while Speaker and rumors of other shady dealings disqualified him for the presidency.

The Mugwumps, heirs of the old Conscience Whig element of the Republican Party, had a tendency toward elitism and self-righteousness in their self-appointed role as spokesmen for political probity. They were small in number but large in influence. Many were editors, authors, lawyers, college professors, or clergymen. Concentrated in the Northeast, particularly in New York, they admired the Democratic governor of that state, Grover Cleveland, who had gained a reputation as an advocate of reform and "good government." When Blaine won the Republican nomination, the Mugwumps defected to Cleveland.

In such a closely balanced state as New York, that shift could make a decisive difference, but Blaine hoped to neutralize it by shaving a few percentage points from the normal Democratic majority of the Irish vote. He made the most of his Irish ancestry on the maternal side, but that effort was rendered futile late in the campaign when a Protestant clergyman characterized the Democrats as the party of "Rum, Romanism, and Rebellion." Although Blaine was present when the Reverend Samuel Burchard made this remark, he failed to repudiate it. When the incident hit the newspapers, Blaine's hope for Irish support went glimmering. Cleveland carried New York State by 1,149 votes (a margin of one-tenth of 1 percent) and thus became the first Democrat to be elected president in 28 years.

The Tariff Issue

Ignoring a rising tide of farmer and labor discontent, Cleveland decided to make or break his presidency on the tariff issue. He devoted his annual State of the Union message in December 1887 entirely to the tariff, maintaining that lower duties would help all Americans by reducing the cost of consumer goods and by expanding American exports through reciprocal agreements with other nations. Republicans responded that low tariffs would flood the country with products from low-wage industries abroad, forcing American factories to close and throwing American workers out on the streets. The following year, the Republican nominee for president, Benjamin Harrison, pledged to retain the protective tariff. To reduce the budget surplus that had built up during the 1880s, the Republicans also promised more generous pensions for Union veterans.

The voters' response was ambiguous. Cleveland's popular-vote plurality actually increased from 29,000 in 1884 to 90,000 in 1888 (out of more than 10 million votes cast). Even so, a shift of six-tenths of 1 percent put New York in the Republican column and Harrison in the White House. Republicans also gained control of both houses of Congress. They promptly made good on their campaign pledges by passing legislation that almost doubled Union pensions and by enacting the **McKinley Tariff of 1890.** Named for Congressman William McKinley of Ohio, this law raised duties on a large range of products to an average of almost 50 percent, the highest since the infamous Tariff of Abominations in 1828.

The voters reacted convincingly—and negatively. They handed the Republicans a decisive defeat in midterm congressional elections, converting a House Republican majority of 6 to a Democratic majority of 147, and a Senate Republican majority of eight to a Democratic majority of six. Nominated for a third time in 1892, Cleveland built on this momentum to win the presidency by the largest margin in 20 years, but this outcome was deceptive. On March 4, 1893, when Cleveland took the oath of office for the second time, he stood atop a social and economic volcano that would soon erupt. When the ashes settled and the lava cooled, the political landscape would be forever altered.

Conclusion

In 1890, the superintendent of the U.S. Census made a sober announcement of dramatic import: "Up to and including 1880 the country had a frontier of settlement, but at present the unsettled area has been so broken into by isolated bodies of settlement that there can hardly be said to be a frontier line . . . any longer."

This statement prompted a young historian at the University of Wisconsin, Frederick Jackson Turner, to deliver a paper in 1893 that became the single most influential essay ever published by an American historian. For nearly 300 years, said Turner, the existence of a frontier of European-American settlement advancing relentlessly westward had shaped American character. To the frontier Americans owed their upward mobility, their high standard of living, and the rough equality of opportunity that made liberty and democracy possible. "American social development has been continually beginning over again on the frontier," declared Turner. He continued:

> This perennial rebirth, this fluidity of American life, this expansion westward with its new opportunities . . . furnish the forces dominating American character. . . . Frontier individualism has from the beginning promoted democracy [and] that restless, nervous energy, that dominant individualism . . . and withal that buoyancy and exuberance which comes with freedom—these are traits of the frontier, or traits called out elsewhere because of the existence of the frontier.

For many decades, Turner's insight dominated Americans' perceptions of themselves and their history. Today, however, the Turner thesis is largely discredited as failing to explain the experiences of the great majority of people throughout most of American history who lived and worked in older cities and towns or on farms or plantations hundreds of miles from any frontier, and whose culture and institutions were molded more by their place of origin than by a frontier. The whole concept of a frontier as a line of white settlement beyond which lay empty land has been discredited because other peoples had lived on that land for millennia.

The Turner thesis also ignored the environmental consequences of the westward movement. The virtual destruction of the bison, the hunting almost to extinction of other forms of wildlife, the ravaging of virgin forests by indiscriminate logging, and the plowing of semi-arid grasslands on the plains drastically changed the ecological balance in the West. These ecological changes stored up trouble for the future in the form of soil erosion, dust bowls, and diminished biodiversity. Thoughtful Americans began to express concern about these problems in the 1890s, foreshadowing the launching of a conservation movement in the following decade.

The significance of the Turner thesis, however, is not whether he got everything right; in the 1890s, he expressed a widely shared belief among white Americans. They believed that liberty and equality were at least partly the product of the frontier, of the chance to go west and start a new life. And now that opportunity seemed to be ending. In fact, to many Americans it seemed that a new and worrisome power had overtaken American life, threatening American liberty: the power of the corporation.

SUGGESTED READINGS

For general histories of the West, see **Robert V. Hine and John Mack Faragher**, *The American West: A New Interpretive History* (2000); **Richard White**, *"It's Your Misfortune and None of My Own": A New History of the American West* (1991); **William Deverell, ed.**, *A Companion to the American West* (2004); and **Patricia Nelson Limerick**, *The Legacy of Conquest: The Unbroken Past of the American West* (1987). For one of the "classics" of Western history, see **Henry Nash Smith**, *Virgin Land: The American West as Symbol and Myth* (1950).

On industrial ranching, see especially **David Igler**, *Industrial Cowboys: Miller & Lux and the Transformation of the Far West, 1850–1920* (2001). Influential and useful treatments of the industrial transformation of the West are **William Cronon**, *Nature's Metropolis: Chicago and the Great West* (1991), and **William G. Robbins**, *Colony and Empire: The Capitalist Transformation of the American West* (1994).

Histories that explore the Chinese in America include **Ronald Takaki,** *Strangers from a Different Shore: A History of Asian Americans* (1989, rev. 1998); **Yong Chen,** *Chinese San Francisco, 1850–1943: A Trans-Pacific Community* (2000); **Judy Yung,** *Unbound Feet: A Social History of Chinese Women in San Francisco* (1995); **Erika Lee,** *At America's Gates: Chinese Immigration during the Exclusion Era, 1882–1943* (2003); and **Sucheng Chan,** *This Bittersweet Soil: The Chinese in California Agriculture, 1860–1910* (1986). For a discussion of Southwest borderlands, see **Sarah Deutsch,** *No Separate Refuge: Culture, Class, and Gender on an Anglo-Hispanic Frontier in the American Southwest, 1880–1940* (1987). On mining, see **Elizabeth Jameson,** *All That Glitters: Class, Conflict, and Community in Cripple Creek* (1998). On women, see **Rebecca J. Mead,** *How the Vote Was Won: Woman Suffrage in the Western United States, 1868–1914* (2004); **Peggy Pascoe,** *Relations of Rescue: The Search for Female Moral Authority in the American West, 1974–1939* (1990); and **Sandra Myres,** *Western Women and the Frontier Experience, 1880–1915* (1982).

On the 19th- and 20th-century myths of the frontier, see **Richard White and Patricia Nelson Limerick,** *The Frontier in American Culture* (1994). The Indians' response to the reservation system after the 1860s is discussed in **Frederick Hoxie, Peter C. Mancall, and James H. Merrill, eds.,** *American Nations: Encounters in Indian Country, 1850 to the Present* (2001) and **Robert M. Utley,** *The Indian Frontier of the American West, 1846–1890* (1984). For a fascinating discussion of Buffalo Bill, see **Joy S. Kasson,** *Buffalo Bill's West: Celebrity, Memory, and Popular History* (2000).

On the New South, see especially **Edward I. Ayers,** *The Promise of the New South: Life after Reconstruction* (1992) and the classic **C. Vann Woodward,** *Origins of the New South, 1877–1913* (1951). The Lost Cause ideology is examined in **Gaines M. Foster,** *Ghosts of the Confederacy: Defeat, the Lost Cause, and the Emergence of the New South* (1987). The rising tide of white racism is chronicled by **Joel Williamson,** *The Crucible of Race: Black-White Relations in the American South Since Emancipation* (1984), which was also published in an abridged edition with the title *A Rage for Order: Black-White Relations in the American South Since Emancipation* (1986).

On African American political action after the war, the best book is **Steven Hahn,** *A Nation under Our Feet: Black Political Struggles in the Rural South from Slavery to the Great Migration* (2003). On black experience after Reconstruction, see **Glenda Elizabeth Gilmore,** *Gender and Jim Crow: Women and the Politics of White Supremacy in North Carolina, 1896–1920* (1996); **Leon Litwack,** *Trouble in Mind: Black Southerners in the Age of Jim Crow* (1998); and **Michele Mitchell,** *Righteous Propagation: African Americans and the Politics of Racial Destiny after Reconstruction* (2004). On Ida B. Wells' anti-lynching campaign, a good place to start is **Gail Bederman,** *Manliness and Civilization: A Cultural History of Gender and Race in the United States, 1880–1917* (1995).

Visit the Liberty Equality Power Companion Web site for resources specific to this textbook: http://www.thomsonedu.com/history/murrin

Also find self-tests and additional resources at ThomsonNOW. ThomsonNOW is an integrated online suite of services and resources with proven ease of use and efficient paths to success, delivering the results you want—NOW!

www.thomsonedu.com/login/

The Emergence of Corporate America, 1865–1900

In the summer of 1877, the same year that President Rutherford B. Hayes withdrew federal troops from the South and effectively ended Reconstruction, he called out the military to suppress the most serious labor uprising in the nation's history. The Great Railroad Strike was no local, isolated disturbance: it was a national event that ultimately involved hundreds of thousands of people across America; claimed at least 100 lives; resulted in injuries to hundreds more; and caused the destruction of millions of dollars of property. It also caught many onlookers by surprise: "Sudden as a thunderburst from a clear sky," one journalist wrote, "the crisis came upon the country. It seemed as if the whole social and political structure was on the very brink of ruin."

But the strike was not so sudden as it seemed to shocked middle-class observers: the truth was that tensions between capital and labor had been building for years. The end of the Civil War had inaugurated an era of economic expansion such as America had never seen before, but it also fueled a process of industrialization that left many workers as permanent wage-earners, with little hope of the independence that had been a cherished part of antebellum free-labor ideology. As a roller-coaster economy also subjected employers to boom-and-bust cycles, many resorted to periodic price-cutting and wage-cutting, even while demanding longer hours. As a result, capital and labor had never been more at odds with one another.

A wage cut triggered the Great Railway Strike. In July, the Baltimore and Ohio Railroad cut wages by 10 percent—its third recent wage reduction. B & O workers had seen their wages drop steadily ever since 1873, a depression year. A brakeman earning $70 per month in 1873 earned only $30 by 1877; conductors' earnings slipped from $90 to $50. A small decline in the price of goods during this period was not enough to make up for such punitive cuts, and so when workers in Martinsburg, West Virginia, received news of the wage cuts, they walked out in protest. Soon workers up and down the B & O line joined them. "At the present state of wages," one group of railroad workers said, "we cannot live and provide our wives and children with the necessities of life."

The strike touched a nerve nationally and spread rapidly; within a few days, what had begun as a local protest had traveled to Baltimore, Philadelphia, Pittsburgh, New York, Louisville, Chicago, St. Louis, Kansas City, and San Francisco. Women as well as men

CHRONOLOGY

1869	Knights of Labor founded
1873	"Crime of 1873" demonetizes silver • Financial panic begins economic depression
1877	Railroad strikes cost 100 lives and millions of dollars in damage
1878	Bland-Allison Act to remonetize silver passed over Hayes's vetos
1883	Railroads establish four standard time zones
1886	Knights of Labor membership crests at 700,000 • Haymarket riot causes antilabor backlash • American Federation of Labor founded
1887	Interstate Commerce Act creates the first federal regulatory agency
1888	Edward Bellamy publishes *Looking Backward*
1890	Congress passes Sherman Antitrust Act • Congress passes Sherman Silver Purchase Act
1892	Homestead strike fails • Populists organize the People's Party
1893	Financial panic begins economic depression • Congress repeals Sherman Silver Purchase Act
1894	"Coxey's army" of the unemployed marches on Washington • Pullman strike paralyzes the railroads and provokes federal intervention
1896	William McKinley defeats William Jennings Bryan for the presidency

joined angry crowds in the streets; workers from a variety of industries walked out in sympathy; and in some places the strike crossed both gender and racial lines—as in Galveston, Texas, where black laundresses struck for higher wages. Strikers and militia in a number of cities fired on each other, and workers set fire to railroad cars and depots. Alarmed at the possibility of a "national insurrection," President Hayes called in the army.

The strike finally ended in early August— "The strikers have been put down by *force*," Hayes noted in his diary—but it left troubling questions in its wake: Had America become a permanently unequal society? Who held power in the emerging corporate order? How was liberty now defined, and whose liberty would the government uphold?

This chapter examines the emergence of a new corporate order in American life in the last decades of the 19th century. It explores the expansive, boom-and-bust economy of post–Civil War America, the rise of "robber barons," and the consolidation of middle-class culture within an emerging national culture of consumption. It explores working-class culture in cities and looks closely at the rise of national labor organizations, as well as a series of violent altercations between labor and capital. Finally, it examines farmers' protests and the political crisis of the 1890s.

America's preoccupation with sectional issues before the Civil War and the gnawing problems of Reconstruction after the war had diverted attention from the economic and social problems associated with industrialization. But in 1877, those problems burst spectacularly into view. For a time, economic growth promised to deflect class conflict. By the 1890s, however, a new corporate society had created opportunity but also inequality for many Americans.

An Expansive and Volatile Economy

The decades following the Civil War saw an unprecedented surge of growth in the economy. Statistics give us a snapshot of this extraordinary rise in American production: the **gross national product** was $9 billion for the five-year period from 1869–73; it was $37 billion for the period from 1897–1901. What's more, in the 1880s, manufacturing began to outstrip agriculture as a source of new value added to the economy, underlining America's ongoing transformation to an industrial society. In the period from 1878 to 1893, for instance, manufacturing increased by 180 percent, compared to a 26 percent increase for agriculture. America moved from fourth in the world in production in 1865

Library of Congress, Prints and Photographs Division

The Great Railway Strike   On August 11, 1877, the national magazine *Harper's Weekly* printed this illustration with the caption, "The Great Strike—the Sixth Maryland Regiment Fighting Its Way Through Baltimore." At first glance the illustration seems sympathetic to the strikers being fired upon in the foreground. The article accompanying this illustration, however, talked of the "reign of terror inaugurated by the railroad strikers" and "scenes of riot and bloodshed" such as "we have never before witnessed in the uprising of labor against capital."

to first in 1900; its industrial production now outstripped the combined output of France, Germany, and Great Britain. It was a stunning economic coming of age.

But this tremendous economic growth was also accompanied by spectacular volatility. The two, in fact, were closely connected in an unregulated economy. Cycles of overexpansion and overproduction were followed by inevitable cycles of contraction. The boom years right after the Civil War were followed by a crash in 1873 and a depression lasting through 1878, and there were additional depressions from 1882–85 and from 1893–97.

Not surprisingly, significant labor uprisings correlated with economic downturns, as employers and businesses sought to cut their losses by cutting wages or laying workers off. **The Great Railroad Strike of 1877** occurred during an extended depression; 1886, another depression year, saw 1,400 strikes involving half a million workers. The great Homestead Strike of 1892 followed the announcement of a wage cut of 18 percent.

Just as workers struggled to eke out a living, many business owners also periodically faced the threat of failure. The American economy may have grown enormously in this period, but expansion often meant saturation of markets followed by price-cutting of products, lower profits, and the inevitable layoffs. As the president of the stovemaker's association lamented in 1888, "It is a chronic case of too many stoves and not enough people to buy them." Around 10 percent of businesses failed each year, many of these small enterprises. During the depression years of the 1870s, bankruptcies rose from 5,000 in 1873 to more than 10,000 in 1878. The rate of collapse was even greater during the depression years of the 1890s.

Still, the enormous growth of the economy in this period meant great opportunity and increased prosperity for many Americans. Titans of industry piled up previously unimaginable fortunes. A flourishing middle class achieved new power, establishing a variety of public institutions such as libraries, symphonies, and museums. The working class, however, shared unequally in this rising prosperity.

Engines of Economic Growth

Focus Question
What were the main engines of American economic growth in the last third of the 19th century?

What fueled the dynamic economy of the post–Civil War era? We can start with railroads, the largest single employer of labor in this period. An important spur to economic growth, railroads increased greatly in miles of track—from 30,000 in 1860 to some 200,000 in 1900. Railroad expansion meant a greater need for coal and iron, then steel, to build railroad cars and lay track: steel production soared from 732,000 tons in 1878 to 10,188,000 tons by 1900. The steel industry in turn was a catalyst for a host of other industries, in a pattern repeated across the American industrial landscape.

As a result, manufacturing expanded dramatically in this period. Again, statistics help tell the story: In 1859, the value of American manufactured goods was $1.9 billion, but by 1899, it had risen to $13 billion. Likewise, just before the Civil War, there were 140,000 factories and manufacturing shops across the country; this figure had risen to 512,000 in 1899, and included the rise of industrial giants such as Carnegie Steel.

Technological Innovation and Celebrations of the Machine

Technological innovation and increased manufacturing fed one another. Growth in manufacturing spurred invention, and invention in turn spurred increased and more efficient manufacturing. Railroads, for instance, ran on a promise of reliability and efficiency, but poorly constructed tracks and rails were a significant hindrance to delivering on that promise. Technological advances like automatic signals, air brakes, and knuckle couplers all improved the efficiency and thus potentially contributed to the profitability of railroads; similarly, the switch from iron to steel tracks, combined with the use of the Bessemer and then the open-hearth process in steel mills, not only aided efficient production of railroad tracks but also promoted the tremendous growth of the new steel industry.

Technological innovations were related to market needs. No one understood this better than **Thomas Alva Edison,** who invented an astonishing array of devices in this period, from a patented vote-recording machine before he was 21 to the phonograph, the incandescent light bulb, and the kinetoscope (or movie camera). "The Wizard of Menlo Park" is often assumed to have been a solitary genius working in a quiet lab far from the hustle and bustle of business. Nothing could be further from the truth. While Edison was certainly a genius, he was also a savvy businessman and self-promoter who kept a sharp

Value Added by Economic Sector, 1869–1899 (in 1879 Prices)

eye on the market. "I have always kept," he once told a reporter, "strictly within the lines of commercially useful inventions." In 1876, Edison moved a group of workers to Menlo Park, New Jersey, to set up an "invention factory" that deliberately mimicked the world of manufacturing. Incorporating the Edison Electric Light Company in 1878, he worked closely with financiers, and when he decided to produce a spectacular display of his new Edison lamps in 1882, he carefully chose Wall Street as the site of his demonstration.

Technological innovation was central to the creation of corporate America. In addition to Edison's wizardry, there were numerous other inventions in this period, from Kodak cameras to the Otis elevator to the gasoline engine to Alexander Graham Bell's telephone, which he demonstrated at the 1876 Philadelphia Centennial Exhibtion to astonished onlookers (characteristically, Edison would greatly improve upon Bell's telephone transmitter the next year). An international fair trumpeting American industrial progress to the world, the Centennial Exhibition displayed inventions and innovations ranging from the Westinghouse air brake to the typewriter to Fleischmanns' yeast. Underlining America's romance with technology, its most prominent exhibition was the colossal Corliss steam engine, the world's largest power generator. Visitors were agreeably awed by its size; the poet Walt Whitman, one of the 10 million visitors to the fair, insisted on sitting in silent contemplation of this mechanical marvel. The antebellum Market Revolution had become a full-fledged Industrial Revolution, and many Americans embraced the new technological order with a sense of pride and wonder.

Changes in Business Organization and Practice

Before the Civil War, most American businesses were local, family-run affairs that received little or no aid from the government and did not sell stock to raise capital. But railroad companies inaugurated a new era of big business that had profound effects on business practice. Many businesses now organized as corporations rather than single proprietorships: this mode of organization provided a flexible means of raising capital by allowing shares in a company to be sold directly to the public. New, expanded corporations used boards of directors as a management tool, allowing for shared responsibility and promoting a new scale and complexity of enterprise.

Railroads were big business in every way, requiring huge tracts of land as well as enormous amounts of capital. In order to encourage railroad building, between 1862 and 1871 the government stepped in with extremely generous land subsidies—over 100 million acres of federal lands—as well as monetary subsidies based on miles of track built. This largesse signaled the beginning of a close relationship between government and business in the postwar period—so much so that throughout the late 19th century, government supported the rights of corporations rather than the rights of workers in a series of legal cases as well as major strikes.

Even with government support, railroad companies still faced something of a catch-22: they stood to gain greatly if they managed to build enough miles of track, but in order to build, they first needed often staggering sums of money. The answer to this dilemma came in the form of financiers, bankers, and a wealthy elite—many of whom seized a golden opportunity to obtain power in the new industrial order. The savvy young banker **J. P. Morgan,** for instance, not only helped finance the Albany & Susquehanna Railroad in upstate New York but joined its board in 1870. Morgan would become the most celebrated and powerful banker of the late 19th century, in large part through his shrewd investing in a variety of industries, including Edison's first electric power plant in 1882. By the turn of the century, Morgan's banking firm had built an empire of leveraged financing and corporate directorates. Numerous other bankers would also gain new power through providing the finance capital needed by industry.

But there were financial losers as well as winners in the railroad-building frenzy of the post–Civil War era. More than 300 companies, most of them railroads, were listed on a greatly expanded New York Stock Exchange right after the war. But not all of these companies were sound; in fact, shaky financing characterized much of the railway boom, which was accompanied by a speculative fever reminiscent of the Gold Rush. The most notorious speculator was the secretive Jay Gould, who built a railroad empire using bribery, trickery, and manipulation. Ordinary investors who hoped to make their fortunes by investing in the railroads often lost their shirts instead when rickety financial scaffoldings collapsed.

The most spectacular and far-reaching downfall of the postwar years was that of **Jay Cooke,** the legendary financial genius behind the sale of Union bonds during the Civil War. Cooke was undone by his attempts to finance the Northern Pacific Railroad: he ran out of capital in 1873 after selling risky bonds and mortgaging government property. When the Northern Pacific went into receivership, Cooke was forced to close his powerful Philadelphia banking house. Within hours, his closure triggered the crash of the New York Stock Exchange, which in turn began the Panic of 1873. In the severe depression that followed, 18,000 businesses went under.

But it wasn't only Jay Cooke or Jay Gould who participated in the late 19th-century culture of speculation. A wider culture of speculation prevailed in the new corporate society. During periods when the economy was hot, many ordinary people also engaged in speculation—only to lose everything when the economy suddenly cooled off again. The reporter Elizabeth Garver Jordan remembered that after the panic of 1893, her meager earnings suddenly became vital to her middle-class Milwaukee family. Her father, a real estate dealer, had bought up "huge tracts of land in and around Milwaukee" on speculation. But when "every bank in the city failed," her father "went down in the debacle with most of Milwaukee's other business men." The "shock and strain" were "too much for him," she recalled, and "his health broke." Speculation clearly meant turmoil in many individuals' lives.

One prominent industrialist who announced his disdain for speculation was **Andrew Carnegie,** the industrial titan who built giant Carnegie Steel after the Civil War. "I have never bought or sold a share of stock speculatively in my life," Carnegie somewhat self-righteously asserted in his autobiography. "I have adhered to the rule never to purchase what I did not pay for, and never to sell what I did not own." An immigrant from Scotland in 1848 at the age of 12, Carnegie began his career—like so many in this period—with the railroads. Cutting his teeth in industry by working as an errand boy on the Pennsylvania

Railroad, Carnegie spent 12 years in positions of increasing authority before striking out on his own—as he said, "determined to make a fortune." First forming a rail-making concern in 1862 and then a locomotive factory in 1866, Carnegie turned to steel in 1872, employing the new Bessemer process that allowed efficient production of steel from pig iron.

"Watch the pennies, and the pounds will take care of themselves," Carnegie was famous for saying, and he kept close track of expenses, paying punitively low wages to workers and forcing them to work long hours. He also developed a system of cost analysis that allowed him to undercut competitors. One of Carnegie's major strengths was an important innovation in 19th-century business organization: vertical integration. Carnegie steadily took control of all parts of the steel-making process, starting with the mining of the raw material of iron ore and ending with the transportation and marketing of the final product. Vertical integration was a powerful new form of business organization that allowed for unprecedented consolidation and the building of business on a previously unimagined scale.

Another titan, **John D. Rockefeller** of Standard Oil, also innovated with business structure. A legendarily ruthless competitor who led a private life of quiet, prim rectitude, Rockefeller either bought out or ruined his rivals through practices such as "predatory pricing" (selling below cost until he bankrupted a competitor) and demanding secret **rebates** from railroads that wanted his business. Having invested in oil during the Civil War, Rockefeller incorporated in 1870, and then in the 1880s pioneered a new form of corporate structure, the **trust,** as a way of making a determined assault on competitors in the oil refinery business. As a congressional investigating committee commented in 1886, it was well known that "the Standard Oil Company brooks no competition; that its settled policy and firm determination is to crush out all who may be rash enough to enter the field against it; that it hesitates at nothing in the accomplishment of this purpose."

A vehicle for the creation of a monopoly (a term Rockefeller avoided later in life, preferring to talk of "cooperation" among businesses), a trust was initially used by Rockefeller to gain control over the oil refining industry and create the horizontal integration of one aspect of his business. Soon, like Carnegie, he engaged in vertical integration as well in order to gain control over every aspect of the oil industry, from extraction of crude oil to marketing. By the 1890s, Rockefeller controlled an astonishing 90 percent of the oil business, with Standard Oil a major force on the world stage.

It might seem obvious that monopolies were a violation of fair trade, but a weak federal government and a conservative Supreme Court set few limits on corporations in this period, despite significant antitrust agitation in the 1880s and 1890s. By then, many Americans feared the power wielded by tycoons who had established monopolies or monopoly market shares not only in oil and steel, but also in sugar, tobacco, and transportation, among other industries. The Sherman Antitrust Act of 1890 was an attempt to declare any form of **"restraint of trade"** illegal, but it was so vague as to be almost useless in the actual prosecution of corporations. Several states passed antitrust legislation, but other states virtually negated this legislation by passing laws favorable to trusts. Numerous corporations, for instance, rushed to set up headquarters in New Jersey after it passed an 1889 law allowing holding companies. In 1895, the Supreme Court dealt a crippling blow to the already weak Sherman Antitrust Act when it ruled in *U.S.* v. *E.C. Knight Company* that the federal government did not have authority over manufacturing because it was not commerce—a form of semantic hair-splitting that revealed the conservative Court's unwillingness to curtail the power of big business. As a result, the American Sugar Refining Company, which had driven out competitors, including the plaintiff, E.C. Knight, retained its 98 percent share of the national market. Only in the 20th century would the Supreme Court begin seriously to tackle the questions raised by the consolidation of giant businesses and the concentration of power in the hands of a wealthy few.

Wealth and Society

Both Rockefeller and Carnegie justified their business practices, as well as their right to wealth, with an emerging post–Civil War vocabulary of **social Darwinism.** "The growth of a large business," Rockefeller wrote, "is merely a survival of the fittest, the working out of a law of nature and a law of God." In assuming that market forces were in fact laws of nature, both Rockefeller and Carnegie drew upon the influential work of the English author Herbert Spencer, who had coined the phrase "survival of the fittest" in applying the evolutionary theories of Charles Darwin to human society. Social Darwinism was popular among both white intellectuals and a wider middle-class reading public to explain existing racial and class hierarchies in society: according to its tenets, human history could be understood in terms of an ongoing struggle among races, with the strongest and the fittest invariably triumphing. The wealth and power of the Anglo-Saxon race were ample testimony, in this view, to its superior fitness.

Social Darwinism reflected a widely shared belief that human society operated according to principles that were every bit as scientific as those governing the natural world. The ability of 19th-century biologists, chemists, and physicists to penetrate the mysteries of the natural world generated confidence in science, in people's ability to know and control their physical environment. That confidence, in turn, prompted intellectuals to apply the scientific method to the human world. The social sciences—economics, political science, anthropology, sociology, psychology—took shape in the late 19th century, each trying to discover the scientific laws governing individual and group behavior. Awed by the accomplishments of natural scientists, social scientists were prone to exaggerate the degree to which social life mimicked natural life; hence the appeal of Social Darwinism, a philosophy that allegedly showed how closely the history of human beings resembled the history of animal evolution.

At first popular mostly among intellectuals, Social Darwinism was quickly adopted as a way of explaining social and racial hierarchy by a broader public, with "survival of the fittest" becoming a popular catchphrase. There was no question that such theory provided a comfortable way of understanding the glaring social inequality of the post–Civil War era: workers were doomed to be permanent wage laborers not because of some fault in the emerging corporate system, but because they were not "fit." The rich, meanwhile, were entitled to every dollar that came their way.

The estimated number of *millionaires* (a word that came into use during this era) in 1860 was 300; by 1892, the number was 4,000. While this was not a large proportion of the population, it was nevertheless a highly visible group. Many practiced what the economist Thorstein Veblen described in *The Theory of the Leisure Class* (1899) as "conspicuous consumption." They sent agents to Europe to buy paintings and tapestries from impoverished aristocrats. In their mansions on Fifth Avenue and their summer homes at Newport, Rhode Island, they entertained lavishly, sometimes spending on a single party an amount that would have supported a tenement full of immigrant families for a year. At one famous costume ball in New York in 1897, guests in satin gowns sewn with jewels impersonated aristocrats: 50 women came dressed as Marie Antoinette, one wearing $250,000 worth of jewels. Such aristocratic pretensions extended to marriage: between 1874 and 1911, 72 American heiresses married British peers. The extravagant habits of a wealthy elite gave substance to Mark Twain's labeling of this era as the Gilded Age.

Class Distinction and Cultural Hierarchy

The well-publicized activities of the wealthy sharpened a growing sense of class distinction in this era. "No observing person can help being aware of an increasing tendency toward a strong *demarcation of classes* in this country," the antebellum abolitionist Lydia Maria Child wrote to a friend in 1877. Different classes "are as much strangers to each other, as if they live in different countries." Throughout the late 19th century, many Americans worried over the class distinctions they saw emerging around them as part of the corporate reordering of American life. The existence of classes was not new in American society, of course—the middle class itself had emerged in the antebellum era with its own distinctive culture—but now class distinctions seemed sharper, class divides more difficult to cross. Was this acceptable in a republican society that promised equality for all? A source of uneasiness at first, class distinctions became a source of alarm among numerous observers in the 1880s and especially the 1890s, when widespread labor activism challenged the existing social order.

But members of different classes would emerge with strikingly different proposed solutions to the problems of corporate America. By the 1890s, many members of the middle class sought not so much to reduce class distinction as to create additional barriers between classes. Fearing working-class violence in the 1880s and 1890s, the middle class erected fortress-like armories in numerous cities. No better symbol existed of the great gulf that had grown up between the classes in the post–Civil War era.

The Consolidation of Middle-class Culture

Focus Question
How did American middle-class culture change in response to the rise of corporations?

A broad middle class consolidated and extended its social and cultural power during the late 19th century. The corporate reordering of American society catalyzed the creation of new institutions of middle-class life, as well as changes in individuals' lives. But race and class went hand in hand: while a thriving African American middle class emerged in African American communities in the post–Civil War era (see chapter 18), its existence was barely acknowledged by the dominant white middle class. Immersed in a world of goods produced by the new corporate economy, the new white middle class also engaged in distinctive styles of consumption that marked a significant change from antebellum middle-class life.

White-Collar Workers

The new corporate order produced a need for salaried managers, professionals, office workers, and retail clerks. The expansion of this "white-collar" work—a term that entered

© Bettmann/CORBIS

Urban Fortresses   In the 1880s and 1890s, numerous armories were built in cities across the country to protect against a perceived threat from the "dangerous classes"—workers and the poor. This immense, castle-like 1894 armory in Brooklyn, New York, was meant to inspire awe.

common usage during the late 19th century and referred to detachable, starched white collars for shirts—marked a change from the antebellum period. Agricultural labor dropped from 53 percent of the gainfully employed in 1870, to 35 percent in 1900, and to 21 percent in 1930; clerical work in the same period rose from less than 1 percent to over 8 percent. By 1900, there were 235,000 bank tellers nationwide, 232,000 salesmen and clerks, and 34,000 real estate agents. The profession of engineer, directly related to the expansion of manufacturing, leapt by an astonishing 586 percent, between 1870 and 1900. In other words, men entered white-collar professions, including management, in large numbers in the post–Civil War decades. By the 1880s, the term "business man" had replaced the antebellum term "merchant."

The Middle-class Home

As was true in the antebellum period, the center of middle-class life was the home and family. But domesticity took on a more consumer-oriented tinge, as the Victorian parlor grew ever more cluttered with doilies, cushions, statuary, clocks, paintings, pianos, and bric-a-brac. Styles of decorating grew more elaborate, reflecting the impact of an expanded world of manufactured consumer goods. When novelist Harriet Beecher Stowe and her sister Catharine Beecher published a revised edition of their antebellum guide *The American Woman's Home* in 1869, they offered humble advice that reflected the prewar reverence for the natural: bring some ivy indoors, they counseled their readers, offering suggestions for making an inexpensive indoor garden that would "gladden the heart." But such advice was already a throwback in the consumption-oriented postwar world. By the 1880s, many women of means not only filled their homes with expensive objects from domestic manufacturers, but also drew upon an international marketplace and vocabulary of decorating, as well. The 1882 Chicago mansion of Bertha Palmer, for instance, featured a Spanish music room, an English dining room, a Moorish ballroom, a Flemish library, and French and Chinese drawing rooms. This "cosmopolitan domesticity" not only shored up status but also marked an imperialist relationship to a wider world of consumption. By the turn of the 20th century, the profession of interior decorator was well-established among a wealthy elite, part of the larger trend of professionalization and the emergence of experts in this period.

Department Stores as Middle-class Communities of Taste

At the center of the new consuming culture, these glittering new "palaces of consumption" dramatically changed the experience of buying goods in cities. Stores such as Marshall Field & Co. in Chicago (1865) and R.H. Macy's in New York (1866) sold a wide variety of items—from perfume to shoes to hats to clothing to household goods—all under one roof. Organizing such an extensive variety of items in different departments rather than different stores was a major retailing innovation. But department stores also changed the experience of shopping in other ways. Customers strolled down carpeted aisles—arranged to mimic city streets—and gazed at a dazzling array of goods arrayed in glass cases. Ornate interiors with mirrors and lights added to a sensory experience of profusion, color, and excitement. Theodore Dreiser captured the desire that experience created in his novel *Sister Carrie*, as his main character Carrie "passed along the busy aisles, much affected by the remarkable displays of trinkets, dress goods, stationery, and jewelry. Each separate counter was a show place of dazzling interest and attraction." As Carrie left the store, she "longed for dress and beauty with a whole heart."

The stores sought to appeal to middle-class women with an elaborate variety of services and amenities, including restaurants, ladies' parlors, check rooms, "retiring rooms," libraries, information bureaus, free wrapping, and free delivery. The new Otis elevator took customers from floor to floor in what were some of the earliest "skyscrapers" of up to 10 stories. Store tearooms quickly became popular places for middle-class women to meet in an urban public space—a novelty at the time.

Domesticity vs. Work

Many middle-class women continued to adhere to the ideology of domesticity, assuming that their place was in the home. Yet an increasing number of women began to explore the world of work—whether out of necessity in the turbulent economy of the late 19th century, or because they chose to enter a wider sphere of life. Historians are not sure how many middle-class women went to work: statistics of the period do not separate out working-class and middle-class women. By 1900, however, 21 percent of all women were in the workforce, as opposed to 9.7 percent of women in 1860. After the Civil War, women moved into nursing and office work in large numbers, while continuing to be a mainstay in teaching. By the end of the 19th century, middle-class women were also becoming editors, literary agents, and journalists in larger numbers, while also entering the professions of medicine and law in small numbers. College women moved to cities to take up work in increasing numbers by the turn of the 20th century, living in apartments on their own as "bachelor girls" and as the subject of numerous newspaper articles.

The increased interest in work was reflected in literature of the period. Louisa May Alcott's 1873 novel *Work*, for instance, imagined an ideal cross-class, cross-race world of supportive female workers, while Elizabeth Stuart Phelps spoke for many discontented middle-class women in her 1877 novel *The Story of Avis*, in which the despairing heroine ultimately gave up being an artist for her marriage. But it was writer and economist Charlotte Perkins Gilman's 1892 biting novella *The Yellow Wallpaper* that spoke most powerfully of a new domestic claustrophobia. In that brief work, the unnamed heroine desires to write after the birth of a child but is told by her husband and doctor that she must rest instead. As a result she becomes virtually imprisoned in her home. Drawing upon Gilman's own experiences, the novel is a bitter indictment of an unequal society.

Few middle-class observers—men or women—were able to imagine women combining work with family. And yet many women had to do so: the nationally known journalist Jane Croly, for instance, who wrote columns under the name "Jenny June," supported her sick husband and four children as an editor and author during the 1880s before becoming the first female professor of journalism at Rutgers University.

The Women's Club Movement and Public Lives

Jane Croly began one of the most important movements among middle-class women in the late 19th century: the women's club movement. In 1868, the New York Press Club decided to bar women journalists from a celebratory dinner for the great novelist Charles Dickens, who was touring the United States. Croly was insulted and furious, but turned that fury toward a positive purpose: forming the women's club Sorosis (the name was chosen to suggest sisterhood). Composed primarily of professional women writers, Sorosis met regularly to discuss topics of the day and to exchange professional advice.

Sorosis inaugurated a movement of women's clubs among working and nonworking middle-class women in communities across the nation. Distinct from antebellum moral reform societies, the new women's clubs were secular and had a variety of different purposes, from intellectual discussion to civic reform. Providing sociability for women without male involvement or supervision, women's clubs also offered leadership opportunities and provided a bridge to middle-class women's activism during the Progressive era. While many clubs in the 1860s and 1870s did not support woman suffrage, by the turn of the 20th century, the women's club movement was an important source of support for the revived suffrage movement. What's more, by 1900, women had used the women's club movement to move into and even take over a variety of civic organizations—a way of practicing politics by other means in an era before women had the vote.

This was especially important in the Jim Crow South, where black men were disfranchised in the 1890s (see chapter 21). Middle-class black women drew on their extensive experiences in church organizations and Republican aid societies to create effective new networks of public civic organizations. African American women also joined the largest women's social organization of the late 19th century, the Woman's Christian Temperance Union (WCTU). Under the leadership of Frances Willard beginning in 1879, the WCTU engaged in a variety of social reform activities nationally and endorsed woman suffrage in 1884.

The New Woman

A clear indication that white middle-class women's positions in society were changing by the turn of the 20th century was the ubiquitous discussion of **the "New Woman"** in the 1890s. A cultural icon of cartoons, illustrations, paintings, short stories, and essays, the New Woman was depicted as a public figure who was athletic, self-confident, young, and independent: she wore the new, less confining fashion of shirtwaists and skirts; rode a bicycle; and even smoked in some images. The painter John Singer Sargent captured this dawning moment of confidence for women in several compelling portraits of strong women.

But to some observers, the New Woman was a fearsome thing, threatening the sanctity of the home and traditional gender roles. A backlash against middle-class women's new roles took different shapes but was often rooted in new "scientific" expertise. Arguing against women's higher education, for instance, the Harvard Medical School professor Edward H. Clarke asserted in 1873 that intellectual work damaged women's reproductive organs. "A girl could study and learn," he warned, "but she could not do all this and retain uninjured health, and a future secure from neuralgia, uterine disease, hysteria, and other derangements of the nervous system."

The Comstock Law (1872) made it illegal to send reproductive literature or devices through the mails on the grounds that they were "obscene," eroding women's already-limited control of reproduction. As women took to bicycles during the bicycle craze of the 1890s, experts warned that it would be unhealthy for women to expend so much strength in physical activity. Women actively resisted these attacks in articles, lectures, and through their own actions, both large and small. Frances Willard of the WCTU, for instance, took up bicycling at age 53 in part, she said, because she knew her example would "help women to a wider world."

Higher Education and Professional Organizations

That wider world included education. Women moved into higher education in large numbers in the late 19th century. In the Midwest and the West, public universities as well as land-grant universities (a result of the 1862 Morrill Act) expanded and began to admit women in the 1860s. In the East there were fewer coeducational institutions, but the founding of women's colleges—with Vassar leading the way in 1865—meant that by 1890, women were approximately 40 percent of all college graduates nationally.

Oddly enough, this move into higher education did not translate into greater ease of access to professional education. Women had broken into medical training in 1849 with the admission of Elizabeth Blackwell to Geneva Medical College in upstate New York. But as separate medical colleges gave way to medical schools within universities in the late 19th century, women began to lose ground in medical education. Professional organizations often excluded women as well; at the turn of the 20th century, the American Medical Association, a gatekeeper to the profession, was an all-white, all-male organization. As other national professional organizations were founded in the 1870s and 1880s—including the American Bar Association, the American Historical Association, and the American Economic Association—they too erected barriers to the entry of women and blacks. Professionalization was thus a double-edged sword: while new professional organizations established much-needed uniform standards and training in a variety of professions and disciplines, they also closed ranks against women and minorities.

Middle-class Cultural Institutions

A politics of exclusion and distinction often characterized new middle-class cultural institutions. In the decades after the Civil War, a significant achievement of the middle class was the creation of new and imposing cultural institutions in American cities. Symphonies, opera companies, museums, and public libraries were housed in imposing buildings that transformed the city landscape. The American museum evolved from a warehouse of curiosities to an ornate space for the display of fine art and scientific artifacts. Newly rich art patrons donated collections to establish museums such as the Metropolitan and Natural History museums in New York, the Field Museum and the Art Institute in Chicago, and the Fine Arts Museum in Boston.

Museums served as markers of class identity as well as repositories of art. In New York, founders of the Metropolitan Museum of Art made the paternalistic claim in 1880 that they sought to "diffuse knowledge of art in its higher forms of beauty" so as to "educate and refine a practical and laborious people." Yet the museum was remarkably ambivalent about those same "laborious people," closing its doors to the public on Sundays—the one day when many workers might have visited—and articulating a fastidious set of rules for behavior within the museum. At one point the museum even evicted a patron because he was wearing overalls, which caused a brief newspaper scandal. The museum spent far more energy courting wealthy art collectors with private receptions. For the newly wealthy in the emerging corporate order, the museum offered a form of alchemy: as one museum leader said, it would "convert pork into porcelain, grain and produce into priceless pottery, the rude ores of commerce into sculptured marble, and railroad shares and mining stocks . . . into the glorified canvas of the world's masters." Donations to museums by the newly wealthy could magically transform social status upward.

The attempt to create cultural hierarchy—and physical distance from the working class—was everywhere an aspect of middle-class institution building. In the antebellum period, for instance, performances of Shakespeare had often been rowdy, participatory, cross-class events. Shakespeare was a beloved part of popular culture. By the end of the century, however, the middle class had not only claimed Shakespeare as an icon of high culture, but had succeeded in imposing a new set of standards for audience behavior at the theater. Vocal audience participation gave way to an expectation of total silence during performances as a marker of gentility.

That gentility could also be found in a new art movement: American Impressionism. Influenced by French Impressionism, artists such as William Merrit Chase and Childe Hassam painted light-flecked landscapes or flower-filled urban parks, recording middle-class pleasures in cities strikingly devoid of workers. Yet some painters, such as Thomas Eakins or Thomas Anshutz, were already pioneering a style that would develop into the "realism" of the early 20th century, with its grittier view of city life and less idealized vision of the human form.

Within literary magazines and books, critics sought to create permanent genteel standards and decried the vulgarity of an extensive popular "low" literature of dime novels and westerns. *Century* and *Harper's New Monthly* published serial novels by great authors and a variety of articles and "tasteful" fiction, including an emerging literature of nostalgia for slavery with virulently racist portrayals of blacks. This white nostalgia for black subordination paralleled growing middle-class alarm over the "insubordination" of the working class in late 19th-century labor strife.

Yet increasingly over the late 19th century, mere gentility began to seem arid to some middle-class writers. The dean of American letters, William Dean Howells, called for a new "realism" based on close observation of and engagement with life. His novels explored issues that had rarely been touched by American authors, including divorce, the moral bankruptcy of capitalism, and interracial marriage. Discouraged by the widening gulf between the classes, in 1886 Howells even broke with most of his class in his plea for clemency for the defendants in the **Haymarket** affair (see later section).

The gulf between the classes also alarmed Edward Bellamy, whose 1888 utopian novel, *Looking Backward,* imagined a world in the year 2000 in which "labor troubles" and social inequities had been eradicated through a form of socialism called Nationalism. Bellamy's powerful fictional indictment of Gilded Age society resonated with half a million readers, making his novel one of the most popular of the 19th century. More than 160 Nationalist clubs sprang up in which members of the middle class mulled over the possibilities of government ownership of industry. For some authors and artists in the 1880s and 1890s, a pull away from genteel standards was inspired by a broader understanding of the considerable social costs of the new corporate order.

Yet the drive for class differentiation continued unabated for most in the middle class. One important spatial realization of this drive was the post–Civil War suburbanization movement. As early as 1873, *Scribner's* magazine noted that "the middle class, who cannot live among the rich, and will not live among the poor . . . go out of the city to find their houses." By the end of the 19th century, suburban communities of detached houses, surrounded by lawns, were markers of the middle-class status of businessmen and professionals who worked by day in cities and traveled back and forth by train or streetcar to their homes. Embracing a rural aesthetic, these suburbanites nevertheless needed the transportation powered by the new industrial order. Ironically, many children of those who fled cities by the end of the century would return in the early 20th century, finding vitality in the very parts of the city—immigrant and working-class communities—their parents had left behind.

Racial Hierarchy and the City: The 1893 Columbian Exhibition

A pernicious assumption of racial superiority was threaded throughout white middle-class institutions in the late 19th century. We can see this clearly in the 1893 Columbian Exposition in Chicago, a world's fair displaying American achievements to the nation and to the world. At the heart of this enormously successful fair was a monumental set of gleaming buildings called the "White City," meant to evoke the classical grandeur of Greece and Rome and to trumpet the maturation of American civilization. With its broad, open courts studded with statuary and interspersed with lagoons, canals, fountains, and parks, the White City was an exemplar of the new City Beautiful movement, whose advocates hoped to impose a new and more refined cultural order on what they saw as a chaotic urban environment.

With paid admissions at 21,480,141 in a nation with a population of 63 million, this was by far the most successful fair in American history, and Americans from all over the country flocked to see its astonishing array of exhibitions, from an Agricultural Hall displaying American farm machinery to the Woman's Building to the many state buildings to international exhibitions. The fair celebrated both technological innovations and high cultural achievements, and many fairgoers dutifully recorded their impressions in special printed books that thoughtfully guided them through the fair, beginning with the category "My first day in the 'White City.'"

The World's Columbian Exposition   The opening day of this Chicago World's Fair on May 1, 1893, drew well over 100,000 visitors.

But by far the most popular part of the Fair was an amusement strip called the Midway Plaisance, located at some distance from the White City, which included "ethnographic" displays of life in "primitive" villages in Africa, Morocco, China, and other locations. It was hard to miss the implication that civilization occurred in America and Europe, while primitivism belonged to people of color from Africa, the Middle East, and Asia.

The very structure of the fair thus embodied and reinforced a racial hierarchy that posited the superiority of white, middle-class civilization. Moreover, the fair denied African Americans a voice, refusing their repeated requests to display black achievements. Outraged, the anti-lynching crusader Ida B. Wells (see chapter 18) published a pamphlet, with contributions from several black leaders, titled "The Reason Why the Colored American Is Not in the World's Columbian Exposition." Exploring the intertwined histories of American slavery and racism, this pamphlet offered a detailed accounting of the refusal by the fair to include African Americans. "Theoretically open to all Americans, the Exposition practically is, literally and figuratively, a 'White City'," the pamphlet asserted. Wells boycotted the Fair on "Colored American Day," but former abolitionist Frederick Douglass attended in order to give a stirring speech. "Men talk of the Negro problem," he said. "There is no Negro problem. The problem is whether the American people have honesty enough, loyalty enough, honor enough, patriotism enough to live up to their own Constitution."

The City and Working-class Culture

As much as the white middle class attempted to impose a genteel order on city life, the city's vitality escaped such bounds. Cities grew rapidly after the Civil War. From 1870 to 1880, for instance, New York grew to over 1 million in population, a 25 percent rate of increase in just one decade. Chicago's growth was even more startling: from 30,000 residents in 1850 to 500,000 in 1880 to 1,700,000 by 1900. While San Francisco was a much smaller city, with fewer than 250,000 inhabitants, it, too, grew at a dramatic rate of 163 percent in the 1870s. In 1860, about one in five Americans lived in cities; by 1900, this number had doubled to two in five.

A fast-growing industrial economy created new jobs at an astonishing rate: between 1870 and 1910, jobs in iron and steel grew by 1,200 percent; in the oil, rubber, and chemical industries, by 1,900 percent. This tremendous job growth drew workers from a number of countries, with 85 percent of immigrants before 1880 from Germany, Ireland, England, and the Scandinavian countries; and with 80 percent from eastern and southern Europe after 1880. By 1900, more than one-third of the U.S. population worked as industrial workers, and most lived in cities.

Working-class Women and Men

For men, large as well as smaller cities often offered a variety of job possibilities—at least in flush times. Cincinnati, for instance, boasted firms that manufactured or processed beer, tobacco, lumber, meat, liquor, clothing, books, carriages, clothes, tools, and baked goods. Women had many fewer opportunities for work; in 1900, only 18.3 percent of the workforce was female. Most working-class families were in agreement with the middle class that married women's place was in the home. But young, single working-class women often worked outside the home before marriage: both young men and women were expected to supplement the family's earnings. In 1900, around one-third of all single women living in cities worked for wages in the garment trade and other industries. Young, single workers helped fuel a lively culture of urban entertainments at the turn of the 20th century.

Commercial Amusements

While the poorest workers could not afford commercial amusements, most workers shared in a new culture of leisure that included dance halls, music halls, vaudeville houses, nickelodeons (early storefront movie theaters), and amusement parks. Storefront vaudeville theaters, for instance, began to advertise "cheap amusements" to a broad working public in the 1880s. With roots in such antebellum entertainments as minstrelsy, circuses, and dime museums, vaudeville shows offered a variety of miscellaneous short acts for only a dime: a typical show might include sentimental ballads, acrobats, soft-shoe dances, magicians, mind readers, one-act plays, blackface minstrelsy, sports stars from baseball or boxing, puppeteers, jugglers, and dancing bears. Not considered respectable middle-class fare at first, vaudeville became increasingly popular, and eventually became a cross-class, national phenomenon.

Amusement parks such as Steeplechase Park at Coney Island, built in 1895, attracted a large working-class audience of men and women while soon also appealing to middle-class youth. Older middle-class commentators found the unchaperoned mingling of young men and women in an urban public space troubling, even shocking, but that loosening of restraint was what made Coney Island so pleasurable and exciting. A new kind of institution in American life, Coney Island was a structured world promoting gaiety and play, with dozens of rides and titillating attractions such as the "Blowhole Theater," whose jets of air blew women's skirts up. "Will she throw her arms around your neck and yell?" asked a sign for the "Cannon Coaster," providing its own answer: "Well, I guess, yes!"

The rides at Coney Island offered young men and women a temporary escape from their industrial working lives, yet ironically enough many of the rides themselves imitated the industrial workplace. The 1884 Switchback Railroad, for instance, an early precursor to the roller coaster, was directly inspired by the operation of gravity-powered coal cars in the shafts of coal mines. New innovations in technology and transportation found a pleasurable mirror at Coney Island and at the other amusement parks around the country that quickly sprang up in imitation.

While vaudeville theaters and amusement parks at first attracted a primarily working-class crowd of pleasure-seekers, they eventually crossed class lines by appealing to large middle-class audiences, as well. Both the working class and the middle class sometimes pushed at the boundaries between them. In the 1880s, for instance, labor unions in New York City resisted middle-class control by demanding that trustees open the Metropolitan and Natural History museums on their free day, Sunday. More than 100 labor organizations, representing some 50,000 workers, petitioned the museums. After a lengthy campaign, both museums capitulated in 1892.

Popular Literature

Just as in the antebellum period, urban workers read a wide variety of dime novels (cheap paperbacks that sold for a dime; see chapter 10) and newspapers. Beginning in the 1860s and 1870s, a flourishing cheap literature reflected the presence of working women in the new industrial order: the popular 1871 story "Bertha the Sewing Machine Girl; or, Death at the Wheel," inspired many imitators and was staged as a popular play in New York City. Its author, Laura Jane Libbey, published more than 60 novels in the 1880s appealing to a working-class audience. Working women read a variety of romances as well, purchasing dime novels from newsstands and pushcarts in large cities. Featuring wealthy heroines or working women who discovered that by birth they were actually aristocrats, these romantic tales offered fantasies that—in imagination, at least—closed the gulf between the classes.

Dime novels appealing to working-class men often told heroic stories of working-class manhood in which men overcame numerous obstacles to become the foremen or owners of factories. Such stories allowed a form of imagined compensation for the loss of independence men actually experienced as permanent wage earners.

Emergence of a National Culture

The rise of a corporate society may have created a gulf between classes in post–Civil War America, but paradoxically it also created a shared national culture. New technological innovations as well as an emerging consumer culture reshaped almost all Americans' lives. Electricity, streetcars, and elevators were just a few of the industrial innovations that changed urban dwellers' everyday relationship to physical space. Even people's relationship to time changed. Before the post–Civil War boom in railroads, there was no such thing as "standard" time: instead, many localities and cities kept their own time, derived from the sun's meridian in each locality. If the clock read noon in Chicago, for instance, it read 11:50 in St. Louis, 11:38 in St. Paul, and 11:27 in Omaha, with many other local times in between. This situation played havoc with railroad timetables.

In a sign of corporations' power over American life, in 1883 a consortium of railroad companies agreed to standardize North American time with the creation of four different time zones—much as they exist today—in which all clocks would be set to exactly the same time. This was a corporate act, not an official government act, and some grumbling followed about the arrogance of railroad presidents changing "God's time." The U.S. attorney general even ruled that government agencies need not change their clocks until authorized to do so by Congress; the next day, he missed a train by eight minutes because he had not reset his watch to the new Eastern Standard Time. "Railroad time" was quickly adopted by people everywhere, although Congress did not officially sanction standard time zones until 1918.

Advertising

A plethora of consumer goods also standardized experience as manufacturers produced national brands such as Ivory soap, Quaker oats, and Jell-O. Advertising firms such as J. Walter Thompson (founded in 1878) and N.W. Ayer & Son (founded in 1869) became an important part of corporate culture, working hand in hand with manufacturers to create national marketing campaigns. In 1899, for instance, N.W. Ayer & Son worked closely with the National Biscuit Company to create a national campaign for a new biscuit (what we would call a cracker today). First the name "Uneeda Biscuit" was carefully chosen, beating out such alternatives as "Taka Cracker," "Hava Cracker," and "Wanta Cracker." Next a distinctive shape was chosen for the cracker and special packaging was created. A national advertising campaign was devised with trademarks and popular catch phrases ("Do You Know Uneeda Biscuit?" and "Lest you forget, we say it yet, Uneeda Biscuit"). Finally, ads were placed in numerous newspapers and magazines, as well as on outdoor signs and streetcars. The results were spectacular: within one year, the National Biscuit Company was selling 10 million packages of Uneeda Biscuits per month, with an annual profit of $3 million. N.W. Ayer crowed that it had produced the "advertising success of the century."

Not surprisingly, expenditures on advertising increased enormously: from some $50 million in 1867 to $500 million by 1900. But national advertising did not just affect what people chose to buy; it sometimes reflected and spread dominant racial stereotypes. Several national brands—including Aunt Jemima mixes and Cream of Wheat, with its portrayal of the character Rastus—created trademark images that hearkened back to blackface minstrelsy (a racist entertainment popular in the antebellum period; see chapter 10) and to mythic images of supposedly happy slaves. At the 1893 Columbian Exposition, the manufacturer of Aunt Jemima mixes even hired an African American woman to play the part of Aunt Jemima, asking her to tell nostalgic tales of plantation life in her new corporate role as a plantation "mammy." Thus a nostalgia for slavery could be found in corporate advertising culture as well as in literature of the period.

A Shared Visual Culture

With their bright, colorful images, advertisements changed daily visual experience. Advertising featured little visual imagery before the 1880s, but with multicolor advertising trade cards (including baseball cards from cigarette companies) a fad in the 1880s, followed by increased visual imagery in ads in the 1890s, advertising helped create a shared national visual culture.

Technological improvements in lithography and the half-tone process in the 1880s and 1890s lay behind this shared visual culture. Picture postcards became popular in the 1890s, as did stereographs that allowed people to become vicarious travelers by viewing the wonders of the world through stereoscopes. The Kodak camera allowed people to take snapshots for the first time, creating a visual record of ordinary life. The most popular magazines and newspapers of the 1890s also created a new shared visual culture. *Ladies' Home Journal*, for instance, a socially conservative magazine founded in 1893 that argued women's place was in the home, achieved enormous success with its profusion of illustrations, photographs, and advertisements. It reached an impressive circulation of 500,000 within only a few years. Cheap new popular magazines such as *Munsey's* reached audiences of hundreds of thousands of national readers with a steady diet of racy stories and photographs of celebrities and chorus girls. Such magazines dwarfed the circulation figures of their more staid literary cousins like the *Atlantic Monthly*.

Urban newspapers also created a shared visual culture. The new sensational or "yellow" newspapers (so-called because of the popularity of the *New York World*'s first color comic, "The Yellow Kid") of the late 1880s and early 1890s responded to the demands of an expanded culture of consumption by adding illustrated women's pages, Sunday sections, society pages, and sports pages. On those sports pages, readers could follow the standings of the first national teams in baseball.

Mail-order Catalogues

How did people outside of cities participate nationally in the new culture of consumption? It was the brilliant idea of A. Montgomery Ward, who had worked at Marshall Field's firm in Chicago, to create a mail-order business reaching out to rural consumers. Starting with a single price sheet of items in 1872, Ward expanded to an 8-page-booket within two years, then a 72-page catalogue, and by 1884 was producing a thick, 240-page catalogue that listed close to 1,000 items for sale—everything from women's underclothing to entire houses.

Ward attempted to reproduce the face-to-face experience of going to a country store as much as possible within the imaginative realm of the catalogue, and customers responded as though Ward was an old friend. "As you advertise everything for sale that a person wants," one man wrote, "I thought I would write you, as I am in need of a wife, and see what you could do for me." Montgomery Ward and Sears, Roebuck used the nation's rapidly expanding rail system to speed goods across the country. Similarly, chain stores such as the Great Atlantic and Pacific Tea Company (A&P) and Woolworth's developed extensive national systems of food and dry goods stores, bringing a national consumer culture to localities across the nation.

The department stores, mail-order houses, and chain stores would not have been possible without the standardization of the goods they sold. Standardization had long been central to the American system of manufactures. Already in the 1850s, the American system had allowed for the mass production of many items built with interchangeable parts. Numerous entrepreneurs after the Civil War adapted these basic techniques to the production of additional consumer goods. Fashionable items of clothing and housewares, once obtainable only by the wealthy, could now be made relatively cheaply and quickly. After 1885, the ready-made clothing industry grew two to three times faster than any other industry. By 1915, it was the nation's third largest industry, ranking just behind steel and oil.

A national culture of consumption had grown up in the last decades of the 19th century, but not everyone had equal access to it. Wages that did not keep pace with the booming economy meant less money to spend, not to mention a struggle to put food on the table. "Eight hours for work, eight hours for rest, eight hours for what we will" was a famous slogan of the labor movement in the post–Civil War era. In the demand for "eight hours for what we will," workers voiced their belief that they had a right to leisure time under their own control. As one worker told a Senate committee in 1883, "a workingman wants something besides food and clothes in this country. . . . He wants recreation. Why should not a workingman have it as well as other people?"

Why not indeed? While some alarmed middle-class observers believed that all workers were revolutionaries who wanted to overturn the American government, only a small percentage were political radicals, much less revolutionaries. The truth was more prosaic: workers wanted fair wages and fair conditions in the workplace. They wanted equality in a system in which power had been systematically stripped from them, and liberty legally defined as the right of corporations. Broad-based workers' movements throughout the late 19th century attempted to rectify a situation in which equal opportunities no longer seemed to be available to all.

Workers' Resistance to the New Corporate Order

Focus Question
How did post–Civil War economic changes affect working people? How did they respond?

Although the average per capita income of all Americans increased by 35 percent from 1878 to 1893, **real wages** advanced only 20 percent. That advance masked sharp inequalities of wages by skill, region, race, and gender. Many unskilled and semiskilled workers made barely enough to support themselves, much less a family; many families, especially recent immigrants (who formed a large part of the blue-collar workforce), needed two or three wage earners to survive.

Conditions in the industrial workplace were often dangerous. The drive for even greater speed and productivity on railroads and in factories gave the United States the unhappy distinction of having the world's highest rate of industrial accidents. The railroads were particularly hazardous, with over 72,000 deaths of employees on the tracks between 1890 and 1917. What one historian has called "mechanized violence" characterized other industries as well: coal mines threatened underground collapses, explosions, and the release of toxic gases; iron mills and steel mills required work with molten metals at open hearths; textile mills threatened mutilation and dismemberment.

Yet there was little government regulation of industrial safety, and workmen's compensation did not appear until the 1930s. As a result, many families were impoverished by workplace accidents that killed or maimed their chief breadwinner. This was one source of a rising tide of labor discontent. Another was the erosion of worker autonomy in factories, where new machinery took over tasks once performed by skilled workers and where managers made decisions about the procedures and pace of operations once made by workers. Many crafts that had once been a source of pride to those who practiced them became just a job that could be performed by anyone. Labor increasingly became a commodity bartered for wages rather than a craft whereby the worker sold the product of his labor rather than the labor itself. For the first time in American history, the census of 1870 reported that a majority of employed persons worked for wages paid by others rather than working for themselves.

Skilled artisans considered this an alarming trend. Their efforts to preserve or recapture independence from bosses and robber barons fueled much of the labor unrest in the 1870s and 1880s. In 1866, the leaders of several craft unions had formed the National Labor Union, which advocated for an eight-hour day at a time when many industries required workers to work for 10 or even 12 hours daily. Labor parties sprang up in several states; the Labor Reform candidate for governor of Massachusetts in 1870 won 13 percent of the vote. While the advocacy of an eight-hour day would remain a central demand of the postwar labor movement, the National Labor Union would fade in the 1870s. During the depression that followed the Panic of 1873, workers were virtually powerless to push their agenda.

The National Labor Union withered away in the depression of the 1870s, but industrial violence escalated. In the anthracite coal fields of eastern Pennsylvania, the Molly Maguires (an amalgam of a labor union and a secret order of Irish Americans) carried out guerrilla warfare against mine owners. In the later 1870s, the Greenbackers (a group that urged currency expansion to end **deflation**) and labor reformers formed a coalition that elected several local and state officials plus 14 congressmen in 1878. In 1880, the Greenback-Labor candidate for president won 3 percent of the popular vote.

The Great Railroad Strike of 1877

The Great Railroad Strike of 1877 (see previous discussion), the worst labor violence in U.S. history up to that time, underscored the deep discontent of workers nationwide. But this spontaneous, unorganized labor upheaval did not produce solutions to workers' dilemmas. On the contrary, fears of a workers' "insurrection" led to a new cohesion in the middle class, which began to talk of a "war" between capital and labor. Not only did the middle class strongly support military intervention in the wake of 1877, but it supported the construction of armories in the nation's largest cities.

The Knights of Labor

Many workers in the wake of 1877 looked to a new labor organization for inspiration. **The Knights of Labor** had been founded in 1869 in Philadelphia as a secret fraternal organization, one of many such artisan societies in eastern cities. Under the leadership of Terence Powderly, a machinist by trade, it became public in 1879 and then expanded rapidly in the wake of the Great Railroad Strike, finally achieving hundreds of thousands of members nationally in the 1880s.

The Knights of Labor offered workers an inspiring vision of an alternative to competitive corporate society. Rooted in the artisan republicanism of the antebellum era (see chapter 7), with even its name suggesting a nostalgic look backward, the Knights opposed the wage labor system, declaring "an inevitable and irresistible conflict between the wage-system of labor and republican system of government." Instead it offered an inclusive vision of a "cooperative commonwealth" that would include both men and women and would not discriminate by race. In its platform it called for an eight-hour day, equal pay for women, public ownership of railroads, abolition of child labor, and a **graduated income tax.**

By the late 1870s, the Knights were a potent national federation of unions—or "assemblies," as they were officially known—and departed in several respects from the norm of labor organization at that time. Most of its assemblies were organized by industry rather than by craft, giving many unskilled and semiskilled workers union representation for the first time. It was also a more inclusive labor organization than most, although in local practice the Knights did not live up to its lofty ideals. Only some assemblies admitted women or blacks. Tendencies toward exclusivity of craft, gender, and race divided and weakened many assemblies.

A paradox of purpose also plagued the Knights. Most members wanted to improve their lot within the existing system through higher wages, shorter hours, better working conditions—the bread-and-butter goals of working people. This meant **collective bargaining** with employers; it also meant strikes. The assemblies won some strikes and lost some. Powderly and the Knights' national leadership discouraged strikes, however, partly out of practicality: a losing strike often destroyed an assembly, as employers replaced strikes with strikebreakers, or **"scabs."**

Another reason for Powderly's antistrike stance was philosophical. Strikes constituted a tacit recognition of the legitimacy of the wage system. In Powderly's view, wages siphoned off to capital a part of the wealth created by labor. The Knights, he said, intended "to secure to the workers the full enjoyment of the wealth they create." This was a goal grounded both in the past independence of skilled workers and in a radical vision of the future, in which workers' **cooperatives** would own the means of production. "There is no reason," said Powderly, "why labor cannot, through cooperation, own and operate mines, factories, and railroads."

The Knights did sponsor several modest workers' cooperatives. Their success was limited, though, partly from lack of capital and of management experience and partly because even the most skilled craftsmen found it difficult to compete with machines in a mass-production economy. Ironically, the Knights gained their greatest triumphs through strikes. In 1884 and 1885, successful strikes against the Union Pacific and Missouri Pacific railroads won prestige and a rush of new members, which by 1886 totaled 700,000. Expectations ran high, but defeat in a second strike against the Missouri Pacific in spring 1886 was a serious blow. Then came the Haymarket bombing in Chicago.

Haymarket

Chicago was a hotbed of labor radicalism. In 1878, the newly formed Socialist Labor Party won 14 percent of the vote in the city, electing five aldermen and four members of the Illinois legislature. With recovery from the depression after 1878, the Socialist Labor Party fell onto lean times. Four-fifths of its members were foreign-born, mostly Germans. Internal squabbles generated several offshoots of the party in the 1880s. One of these embraced anarchism and called for the violent destruction of the capitalist system so that a new socialist order could be built on its ashes. **Anarchists** infiltrated some trade unions in Chicago and leaped aboard the bandwagon of a national movement centered in that city for a general strike on May 1, 1886, to achieve the eight-hour workday. Chicago police were notoriously hostile to labor organizers and strikers, so the scene was set for a violent confrontation.

The May 1 showdown coincided with a strike at the McCormick farm machinery plant in Chicago. A fight outside the gates on May 3 brought a police attack on the strikers in which four people were killed. Anarchists then organized a protest meeting at Haymarket

Square on May 4. Toward the end of the meeting, when the rain-soaked crowd was already dispersing, the police suddenly arrived in force. When someone threw a bomb into their midst, the police opened fire. When the wild melee was over, 50 people lay wounded and 10 dead, 6 of them policemen.

This affair set off a wave of hysteria against labor radicals. Police in Chicago rounded up hundreds of labor leaders. Eight anarchists (seven of them German-born) went on trial for conspiracy to commit murder, although no evidence turned up to prove that any of them had thrown the bomb. All eight were convicted; seven were sentenced to hang. One of the men committed suicide; the governor commuted the sentences of two others to life imprisonment; the remaining four were hanged on November 11, 1887. The case became a cause célèbre that bitterly divided the country. Many workers, civil libertarians, and middle-class citizens who were troubled by the events branded the verdicts judicial murder, but most Americans applauded the summary repression of un-American radicalism.

The Knights of Labor were caught in this anti-labor backlash. Although the Knights had nothing to do with the Haymarket affair and Powderly had repeatedly denounced anarchism, his opposition to the wage system sounded suspiciously like socialism, perhaps even anarchism, to many Americans. Membership in the Knights plummeted from 700,000 in spring 1886 to fewer than 100,000 by 1890.

As the Knights of Labor waned, a new national labor organization waxed. Founded in 1886, the American Federation of Labor (AFL) was a loosely affiliated association of unions organized by trade or craft: cigar-makers, machinists, carpenters, and so on. Under the leadership of Samuel Gompers, an immigrant cigar-maker, the AFL accepted capitalism and the wage system, and worked for better conditions, higher wages, shorter hours, and occupational safety within the system— "pure and simple unionism," as Gompers called it. Most AFL members were skilled workers, and few were women or blacks—a strategy that enabled the AFL to survive and even to prosper in a difficult climate (see chapter 20).

The Homestead Strike

During the 1890s, strikes occurred with a frequency and a fierceness that made 1877 and 1886 look like mere preludes to the main event. The most dramatic confrontation took place in 1892 at the **Homestead** plant (near Pittsburgh) of the Carnegie Steel Company. Carnegie and his plant manager, Henry Clay Frick, were determined to break the power of the country's strongest union, the Amalgamated Association of Iron, Steel, and Tin Workers. Frick used a dispute over wages and work rules as an opportunity to close the plant (a **"lockout"**), preparatory to reopening it with nonunion workers. When the union called a strike and refused to leave the plant, Frick called in 300 Pinkerton guards to oust them. (The Pinkerton detective agency had evolved since the Civil War era into a private security force that specialized in antiunion activities.) A full-scale gun battle between strikers and Pinkertons erupted on July 6, leaving nine strikers and seven Pinkertons dead and scores wounded. Frick persuaded the governor to send in 8,000 militia to protect the

North Wind Picture Archive

Pennsylvania Militia at Carnegie's Homestead Steel Mill, 1892   After the shoot-out between striking workers and Pinkerton guards, the Pennsylvania militia reopened the mills and protected strikebreakers from striking workers. This photograph shows the militia using steel beams manufactured by the mill as a makeshift barricade.

strikebreakers, and the plant reopened. Public sympathy, much of it pro-union at first, shifted when an anarchist tried to murder Frick on July 23. The failed Homestead strike crippled the Amalgamated Association; another strike against U.S. Steel (successor of Carnegie Steel) in 1901 destroyed it.

The Depression of 1893–1897

By the 1890s, the use of state militias to protect strikebreakers had become common. Events after 1893 brought an escalation of conflict. The most serious economic crisis since the 1873–78 depression was triggered by the Panic of 1893, a collapse of the stock market that plunged the economy into a severe four-year depression. Its complex origins included an economic slowdown abroad, which caused British banks to call some of their American loans, thereby draining gold from the United States at a time of political controversy about the American monetary system and nervousness in financial circles. Other causes included declining farm prices and attendant rural unrest and the overly rapid expansion of railroad construction and manufacturing capacity after 1885. The bankruptcy of the Reading Railroad and the National Cordage Company in early 1893 set off a process that by the end of the year had caused 491 banks and 15,000 other businesses to fail. By mid-1894, the unemployment rate had risen to more than 15 percent.

An Ohio reformer named Jacob Coxey conceived the idea of sending Congress a "living petition" of unemployed workers to press for appropriations to put them to work on road building and other public works. "Coxey's army," as the press dubbed it, inspired other groups to hit the road and ride the rails to Washington during 1894. This descent of the unemployed on the capital provoked arrests by federal marshals and troops, and ended in anticlimax when Coxey and others were arrested for trespassing on the Capitol grounds. Coxey's idea for using public works to relieve unemployment turned out to be 40 years ahead of its time.

The Pullman Strike

The explosive tensions between capital and labor fueled the Pullman strike of 1894. George M. Pullman had made a fortune in the manufacture of sleeping cars and other rolling stock for railroads. Workers in his large factory complex lived in the company town of Pullman just south of Chicago, with paved streets, clean parks, and decent houses rented from the company. But Pullman controlled many aspects of their lives, including banning liquor from the town and punishing workers whose behavior did not suit his ideas of decorum. When the Panic of 1893 caused a sharp drop in orders for Pullman cars, the company laid off one-third of its workforce and cut wages for the rest by 30 percent, but did not reduce company house rents or company store prices. Pullman refused to negotiate with a workers' committee, which called a strike and appealed to the American Railway Union (ARU) for help.

The ARU had been founded the year before by Eugene V. Debs. A native of Indiana, Debs had been elected secretary of the Brotherhood of Locomotive Firemen in 1875 at the age of 20. By 1893, he had become convinced that the conservative stance of the various craft unions in railroading (firemen, engineers, brakemen, and so forth) was divisive and contrary to the best interests of labor. He formed the ARU to include all railroad workers in one union. With 150,000 members, the union won a strike against the Great Northern Railroad in spring 1894. When George Pullman refused the ARU's offer to arbitrate the strike of Pullman workers, Debs launched a boycott by which ARU members would refuse to run any trains that included Pullman cars. When the railroads attempted to fire the ARU sympathizers, whole train crews went on strike and quickly paralyzed rail traffic.

Over the protests of Illinois Governor John P. Altgeld, who sympathized with the strikers, President Grover Cleveland sent in federal troops. That action inflamed violence instead of containing it. The U.S. attorney general (a former railroad lawyer) obtained a federal injunction against Debs under the Sherman Antitrust Act on grounds that the boycott and the strike were a conspiracy in restraint of trade. This creative use of the Sherman Act, whose purpose had been to curb corporations, was upheld by the Supreme Court in 1895 and became a powerful weapon against labor unions in the hands of conservative judges.

For a week in July 1894, the Chicago railroad yards resembled a war zone. Millions of dollars of equipment went up in smoke. Thirty-four people, mostly workers, were killed. Finally, 14,000 state militia and federal troops restored order and broke the strike. Debs went to jail (for violation of the federal injunction) for six months. He emerged from prison a socialist.

To many Americans, 1894 was the worst year of crisis since the Civil War. The Pullman strike was only the most dramatic event of a year in which 750,000 workers went on strike and another 3 million were unemployed. But it was a surge of discontent from farmers that wrenched American politics off its foundations in the 1890s.

Farmers' Movements

Focus Question
What provoked the farmer protest movements in the last third of the 19th century?

Between 1870 and 1890, America's soaring grain production increased three times as fast as the American population. Only rising exports could sustain such expansion in farm production. But by the 1880s, the improved efficiency of large farms in Eastern Europe brought intensifying competition and consequent price declines, especially for wheat, just as competition from Egypt and India had eroded prices for American cotton. Prices on the world market for these two staples of American agriculture—wheat and cotton—fell about 60 percent from 1870 to 1895, while the wholesale price index for all commodities (including other farm products) declined by 45 percent during the same period. Not surprisingly, distress was greatest and protest loudest in the wheat-producing West and the cotton-producing South.

Victims of a world market largely beyond their control, farmers lashed out at targets nearer home: railroads, banks, commission merchants, and the monetary system. In truth, these institutions did victimize farmers, although not always intentionally.

Resistance to Railroads

The power wielded by the railroad companies inevitably aroused hostility. Companies often charged less for long hauls than for short hauls in areas with little or no competition. The rapid proliferation of tracks produced overcapacity in some areas, which led to rate-cutting wars that benefited some shippers at the expense of others—usually large shippers at the expense of small ones. To avoid "ruinous competition" (as the railroads viewed it), companies formed **"pools"** by which they divided traffic and fixed their rates. Some of these practices made sound economic sense, but others appeared discriminatory and exploitative. Railroads gave credence to farmers' charges of monopoly exploitation by keeping rates higher in areas with no competition (most farmers lived in areas served by only one line) than in regions with competition. Grain elevators, many of which were owned by railroad companies, came under attack for cheating farmers by rigging the classification of their grain.

Farmers responded by organizing cooperatives to sell crops and buy supplies. The umbrella organization for many of these cooperatives was the Patrons of Husbandry, known as the Grange, founded in 1867. But because farmers could not build their own railroads, they organized "antimonopoly" parties and elected state legislators who enacted "Granger laws" in several states. These laws established railroad commissions that fixed maximum freight rates and warehouse charges. Railroads challenged the laws in court. Eight challenges made their way to the U.S. Supreme Court, which in *Munn* v. *Illinois* (1877) ruled that states could regulate businesses clothed with a "public interest"— railroads and other common carriers, millers, innkeepers, and the like. It was a landmark decision.

The welter of different and sometimes conflicting state laws, plus rulings by the U.S. Supreme Court in the 1880s that states could not regulate interstate railroad traffic, brought a drive for federal regulation. After years of discussion, Congress passed the Interstate Commerce Act in 1887. This law, like most such laws, reflected compromise between the varying viewpoints of shippers, railroads, and other pressure groups. It outlawed pools, discriminatory rates, long-haul versus short-haul differentials, and rebates to favored shippers. It required that freight and passenger rates must be "reasonable and just." What that meant was not entirely clear, but the law created the Interstate Commerce

The Kansas State Historical Society Topeka, Kansas

Returning to Illinois, 1894 This photograph shows one of the thousands of farm families who had moved into Kansas, Nebraska, and other plains states in the wet years of the 1870s and 1880s, only to give up during the dry years of the 1890s. Their plight added fuel to the fire of rural unrest and protest during those years.

Commission (ICC) to define the requirement on a case-by-case basis. Because the ICC had minimal enforcement powers, however, federal courts frequently refused to issue the orders the ICC requested. Staffed by men who were knowledgeable about railroading, the ICC often sympathized with the viewpoint of the industry it was supposed to regulate. Nevertheless, its powers of publicity had some effect on railroad practices, and freight rates continued to decline during this period as railroad operating efficiency improved.

Credit and Money

Focus Question

What issues were at stake in the contest between "free silver" and the "gold bugs"?

The long period of price deflation from 1865 to 1897, unique in American history, made credit even more costly for farmers. When the price of wheat or cotton declined, farmers had even less money to pay back loans from country-store merchants. Thus it was not surprising that angry farmers who denounced banks or country-store merchants for gouging them also attacked a monetary system that brought deflation.

The federal government's monetary policies worsened deflation problems. The 1862 emergency wartime issuance of treasury **"greenback"** notes (see chapter 15) had created a dual currency—gold and greenbacks—with the greenback dollar's value relative to gold rising and falling according to Union military fortunes. After the war, the Treasury moved to bring the greenback dollar to par with gold by reducing the amount of greenbacks in circulation. This limitation of the money supply produced deflationary pressures. To complicate matters further, national banknotes backed by the banks' holding of government bonds continued to circulate as money. Because national banks were concentrated in the Northeast, the South and West suffered from downward pressures on prices they received for their crops because of money scarcity. Western farmers were particularly vociferous in their protests against this situation, which introduced a new sectional conflict into politics—not North against South, but East against West.

Because parity between greenbacks and gold would not be reached until 1879, a controversy arose in the postwar years over whether Union war bonds should be paid off in greenbacks or in gold. Congress resolved this issue in 1869 by passing the Public Credit Act, which required payment in gold. Because little silver had been coined into money for years, Congress enacted a law in 1873 that ended the coinage of silver dollars, thus putting the United States on the road to joining the international gold standard. In 1874, President Grant vetoed a bill sponsored by anti-deflation western congressmen to increase the number of greenbacks in circulation, setting the stage for enactment of the important Specie Resumption Act in 1875. When the provisions of this act went fully into effect on January 1, 1879, the U.S. dollar reached par with the gold dollar on the international market.

Grant's role in bringing about these steps toward "sound money" is more important than is generally recognized, but the benefits of his achievement were sharply debated then and remain controversial today. On the one hand, they strengthened the dollar, placed government credit on a firm footing, and helped create a financial structure for the remarkable economic growth that tripled the GNP during the last quarter of the 19th century. On the other hand, the restraints on money supply hurt the rural economy in the South and West; they hurt debtors who found that deflation enlarged their debts by increasing the value of greenbacks; and they probably worsened the two major depressions of the era (1873–78 and 1893–97) by constraining credit.

The Greenback and Silver Movements

Many farmers in 1876 and 1880 supported the Greenback Party, whose platform called for the issuance of more U.S. Treasury notes (greenbacks). Even more popular was the movement for **"free silver."** Until 1873, government mints had coined both silver and gold dollars at a ratio of 16 to 1—that is, 16 ounces of silver were equal in value to one ounce of gold. However, when new discoveries of gold in the West after 1848 placed more gold in circulation relative to silver, that ratio undervalued silver, so that little was being sold for coinage. This was the principal reason for the law of 1873 demonetizing silver, except for small coins. Anti-deflationists later branded this law as "the Crime of 1873"—a conspiracy to destroy silver, the people's money, in favor of gold, the bankers' money.

Ironically, just when the law of 1873 was enacted, the production of new silver mines began to increase dramatically, which soon brought the price of silver below the old ratio of 16 to 1. Silver miners joined with farmers to demand a return to silver dollars. In 1878, Congress responded by passing, over President Hayes's veto, the Bland-Allison Act requiring the Treasury to purchase and coin not less than $2 million nor more than $4 million of silver monthly. Once again, silver dollars flowed from the mint, but those amounts failed to absorb the increasing production of silver and did little, if anything, to slow deflation. The market price of silver dropped to a ratio of 20 to 1.

Pressure for "free silver"—that is, for government purchase of all silver offered for sale at a price of 16 to 1 and its coinage into silver dollars—continued through the 1880s. The admission of five new western states in 1889 and 1890 contributed to the passage of the Sherman Silver Purchase Act in 1890. That act increased the amount of silver coinage, but not at the 16-to-1 ratio. Even so, it went too far to suit **"gold bugs,"** who wanted to keep the United States on the international gold standard.

President Cleveland blamed the Panic of 1893 on the Sherman Silver Purchase Act, which caused a run on the Treasury's gold reserves triggered by uncertainty over the future of the gold standard. Cleveland called a special session of Congress in 1893 and persuaded it to repeal the Sherman Silver Purchase Act, setting the stage for the most bitter political contest in a generation.

Grangers and the Farmers' Alliance

Agrarian reformers supported the free silver movement, but many had additional grievances concerning problems of credit, railroad rates, and the exploitation of workers and farmers by the "money power." Both the Grange and the Farmers' Alliance, a new farmers' organization that expanded rapidly in the 1880s, addressed these political concerns. Both also addressed farm families' social and cultural needs, providing them with a sense of community that helped reduce rural isolation. The Grange sponsored picnics and cultural events, actively encouraging the participation of women. Local chapters were required to have female members, and women took up positions of leadership at the local level and also attended national meetings. The Grangers were not anti-consumption, but they desired to avoid middlemen: this made them a good audience for the new mail-order catalogues. Indeed, the innovative retailer Montgomery Ward first gained a foothold in the mail-order business by styling himself the official supply house for the Grange and including signed testimonials from Grange members in his early catalogues.

The Farmers' Alliance also provided a sense of community for farmers. Starting in Texas as the Southern Farmers' Alliance, it expanded into other southern states and the North. By 1890, the movement had evolved into the National Farmers' Alliance and Industrial Union, which was affiliated with the Knights of Labor. It was also affiliated with a separate Colored Farmers' Alliance, formed by African Americans who recognized the utility of the Farmers' Alliance but were not welcome in the larger whites-only organization. Reaching out to 2 million farm families, the Farmers' Alliance set up marketing cooperatives to eliminate the middlemen who profited as "parasites" on the backs of farmers. Like the Grange, the Alliance served the social needs of farm families as well as their economic needs, organizing picnics and educational institutes in addition to camp meetings. Appealing to women as well as men, the Alliance created what one historian has called a "movement culture" that helped farmers to overcome their isolation, especially in the sparsely settled regions of the West. The Alliance also gave farmers a sense of pride and solidarity to counter the image of "hick" and "hayseed" being purveyed by an increasingly urban American culture.

The Farmers' Alliance developed a comprehensive political agenda. At a national convention in Ocala, Florida, in December 1890, it set forth these objectives: (1) a graduated income tax; (2) direct election of U.S. senators (instead of election by state legislatures); (3) free and unlimited coinage of silver at a ratio of 16 to 1; (4) effective government control and, if necessary, ownership of railroad, telegraph, and telephone companies; and (5) the establishment of **"subtreasuries"** (federal warehouses) for the storage of crops, with government loans at 2 percent interest on those crops. The most important of these goals, especially for southern farmers, was the subtreasuries. Government storage would allow farmers to hold their crops until market prices were more favorable. Low-interest government loans on the value of these crops would enable farmers to pay their annual debts and thus escape the ruinous interest rates of the crop lien system in the South and bank mortgages in the West.

These were radical demands for the time. Nevertheless, most of them eventually became law: the income tax and the **direct election of senators** by constitutional amendments in 1913; government control of transportation and communications by various laws in the 20th century; and the subtreasuries in the form of the Commodity Credit Corporation in the 1930s.

Anticipating that the Republicans and the Democrats would resist these demands, many Alliancemen were eager to form a third party. In Kansas they had already done so, launching the People's Party, whose members were known as Populists, in summer 1890. White Southerners, mostly Democrats, opposed the idea of a third party for fear that it might open the way for the return of the Republican Party, and African Americans, to power.

In 1890, farmers helped elect numerous state legislators and congressmen who pledged to support their cause, but the legislative results were thin. By 1892, many Alliance members were ready to take the third-party plunge. The two-party system seemed fossilized and unable to respond to the explosive problems of the 1890s.

The Rise and Fall of the People's Party

Enthusiasm for a third party was particularly strong in the plains and mountain states, five of which had been admitted since the last presidential election: North and South Dakota, Montana, Wyoming, and Idaho. The most prominent leader of the Farmers' Alliance was Leonidas L. Polk of North Carolina. A Confederate veteran, Polk commanded support in the West as well as in the South. He undoubtedly would have been nominated for president by the newly organized People's Party had not death cut short his career at the age of 55 in June 1892.

The first nominating convention of the People's Party met at Omaha a month later. The preamble of their platform expressed the grim mood of delegates. "We meet in the midst of a nation brought to the verge of moral, political, and material ruin," it declared. "The fruits of the toil of millions are boldly stolen to build up colossal fortunes for a few. . . . From the same prolific womb of governmental injustice we breed the two great classes—tramps and millionaires." The platform called for unlimited coinage of silver at 16 to 1; creation of the subtreasury program for crop storage and farm loans; government ownership of railroad, telegraph, and telephone companies; a graduated income tax; direct election of senators; and laws to protect labor unions against prosecution for strikes and boycotts. To ease the lingering tension between southern and western farmers, the party nominated Union veteran James B. Weaver of Iowa for president and Confederate veteran James G. Field of Virginia for vice president.

Despite winning 9 percent of the popular vote and 22 electoral votes, Populist leaders were shaken by the outcome. In the South, most of the black farmers who were allowed to vote stayed with the Republicans. Democratic bosses in several southern states dusted off the racial demagoguery and intimidation machinery of Reconstruction days to keep white farmers in line for the party of white supremacy. Only in Alabama and Texas, among southern states, did the Populists get more than 20 percent of the vote. They did even worse in the older agricultural states of the Midwest, where their share of the vote ranged from 11 percent in Minnesota down to 2 percent in Ohio. Only in distressed wheat states such as Kansas, Nebraska, and the Dakotas and in the silver states of the West did the Populists do well, carrying Kansas, Colorado, Idaho, and Nevada.

The party remained alive, however, and the anguish caused by the Panic of 1893 seemed to boost its prospects. In several western states, Populists or a Populist-Democratic coalition controlled state governments for a time, and a Populist-Republican coalition won the state elections of 1894 in North Carolina. Women as well as men campaigned for the Populists: Mary Lease, a former homesteader and one of the few women practicing law in Kansas, became famous for her impassioned speeches against corporate power. "We endured hardships, dangers and privations, hours of loneliness, fear and sorrow," she said of the homesteading years. "Yet after all our years of toil and privations, dangers and hardship on the Western frontier, monopoly is taking our homes from us."

In 1893, President Cleveland's success in getting the Sherman Silver Purchase Act repealed drove a wedge into the Democratic Party. Southern and western Democrats turned against Cleveland. In what was surely the most abusive attack on a president ever delivered by a member of his own party, Senator Benjamin Tillman of South Carolina told his constituents in 1894: "When Judas betrayed Christ, his heart was not blacker than this scoundrel, Cleveland, in deceiving the Democracy. He is an old bag of beef and I am going to Washington with a pitchfork and prod him in his fat ribs."

The Silver Issue

Clearly the silver issue stirred deep emotions. For many people silver meant far more than a mere change in monetary policy: it also represented a widespread yearning for a more equitable society in which corporations and banks held less power. Thus when Democratic dissidents stood poised to take over the party in 1896, they adopted free silver as the centerpiece of their program. This stand raised possibilities for a fusion with the Populists, who hoped the Democrats would adopt other features of their platform as well. Meanwhile, out of the West came a new and charismatic figure, a silver-tongued orator named **William Jennings Bryan,** whose shadow would loom large across the political landscape for the next generation. A one-term congressman from Nebraska, Bryan had taken up the cause of free silver. He came to the Democratic convention in 1896 as a young delegate— only 36 years old. Given the opportunity to make the closing speech in the debate on the silver plank in the party's platform, Bryan brought the house to its feet in a frenzy of cheering with his peroration: "You shall not press down upon the brow of labor this crown of thorns, you shall not crucify mankind upon a cross of gold."

This speech catapulted Bryan into the presidential nomination. He ran on a platform that not only endorsed free silver but also embraced the idea of an income tax, condemned trusts, and opposed the use of injunctions against labor. Bryan's nomination created turmoil in the People's Party. Although some Populists wanted to continue as a third party, most of them saw fusion with silver Democrats as the road to victory. At the Populist convention, the fusionists got their way and endorsed Bryan's nomination. In effect, the Democratic whale swallowed the Populist fish in 1896.

The Election of 1896

The Republicans nominated **William McKinley,** who would have preferred to campaign on his specialty, the tariff. Bryan made that impossible. Crisscrossing the country in an unprecedented whistle-stop campaign covering 18,000 miles, Bryan gave as many as 30 speeches a day, focusing almost exclusively on the free silver issue. Republicans responded by denouncing the Democrats as irresponsible inflationists. Free silver, they said, would mean a 57-cent dollar and would demolish the workingman's gains in real wages achieved over the preceding 30 years.

Under the skillful leadership of Ohio businessman Mark Hanna, chairman of the Republican National Committee, McKinley waged a "front-porch campaign" in which various delegations visited his home in Canton, Ohio, to hear carefully crafted speeches that were widely publicized in the mostly Republican press. Hanna sent out an army of speakers and printed pamphlets in more than a dozen languages to reach immigrant voters. His propaganda portrayed Bryan as a wild man from the prairie whose monetary schemes

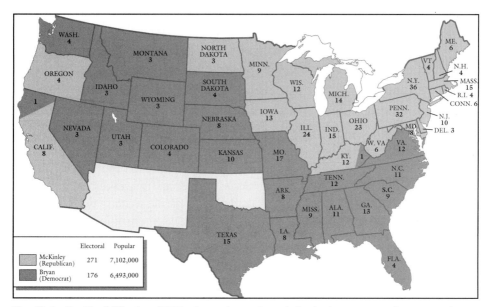

Map 19.1   Presidential Election of 1896   Once again, note the continuity of voting patterns over the two generations from the 1850s to the 1890s by comparing this map with Map 14.1 on page 532 and Map 15.1, Election of 1860, Southern Secession, in the color insert following page 624.

would further wreck an economy that had been plunged into depression during a Democratic administration. McKinley's election, by contrast, would maintain the gold standard, revive business confidence, and end the depression.

The 1896 election was the most impassioned and exciting in a generation. Many Americans believed that the fate of the nation hinged on the outcome. The number of voters jumped by 15 percent over the 1892 election. The sectional pattern of South and West versus Northeast and North Central was almost as pronounced as the North–South split of 1860. Republicans won a substantial share of the urban, immigrant, and labor vote by arousing fear about the Democratic 57-cent dollar and by inspiring hope with the slogan of McKinley as "the advance agent of prosperity." McKinley rode to a convincing victory by carrying every state in the northeast quadrant of the country. Bryan carried most of the rest. Republicans won decisive control of Congress as well as the presidency. They would maintain control for the next 14 years. The election of 1896 marked a crucial turning point in American political history away from the stalemate of the preceding two decades.

Whether by luck or by design, McKinley did prove to be the advance agent of prosperity. The economy pulled out of the depression during his first year in office and entered into a long period of growth—not because of anything the new administration did (except perhaps to encourage a revival of confidence) but because of the mysterious workings of the business cycle. With the discovery of rich new goldfields in the Yukon, in Alaska, and in South Africa, the silver issue lost potency, and a cascade of gold poured into the world economy. The long deflationary trend since 1865 reversed itself in 1897. Farmers entered a new—and unfamiliar—era of prosperity. Bryan ran against McKinley again in 1900 but lost even more emphatically. The nation seemed embarked on a placid sea of plenty. But below the surface, the currents of protest and reform that had boiled up in the 1890s still ran strong. They would soon surface again.

Conclusion

The 1890s were a major watershed in American history. In the past lay a largely rural society and agricultural economy; in the future lay cities and a commercial-industrial economy. Before the 1890s, most immigrants had come from northern and western Europe, and many became farmers. Later immigrants largely came from eastern and southern Europe, and nearly all settled in cities. Before the 1890s, the old sectional issues associated with slavery, the Civil War, and Reconstruction remained important forces in American politics; after 1900, racial issues would not play an important part in national politics for another 60 years. The election of 1896 ended 20 years of even balance between the two major parties and led to more than a generation of Republican dominance.

Most important, the social and political upheavals of the 1890s shocked many people into recognition that the liberty and equality they had taken for granted as part of the American dream was in danger of disappearing before the onslaught of wrenching economic changes that had widened and deepened the gulf between classes. The strikes and violence and third-party protests of the decade were a wake-up call. As the forces of urbanization and industrialism increased during the ensuing two decades, many middle-class Americans supported greater government power to carry out progressive reforms to cure the ills of an industrializing society.

SUGGESTED READINGS

General histories of the Gilded Age include Rebecca Edwards, *New Spirits: Americans in the Gilded Age, 1865–1905* (2006) and **Alan Trachtenberg,** *The Incorporation of America: Culture and Society in the Gilded Age* (1982). For the impact of the railroad on the Gilded Age economy and culture, see **George R. Taylor and Irene D. Neu,** *The American Railroad Network, 1861–1890* (2003). For the rise of industry and "big business," the following are useful: **Walter Licht,** *Industrializing America* (1995); **Glenn Porter,** *The Rise of Big Business, 1860–1910,* rev. ed. (1992); and **Harold G. Vatter,** *The Drive to Industrial Maturity: The U.S. Economy, 1865–1914* (1975). The best biography of Rockefeller is **Ron Chernow,** *Titan* (1998).

On the middle class and class hierarchy see **Sven Beckert,** *The Monied Metropolis: New York City and the Consolidation of the American Bourgeoisie, 1850–1896* (2001); **Stuart Blumin,** *The Emergence of the Middle Class: Social Experience in the American City, 1760–1900* (1989); and **Lawrence W. Levine,** *Highbrow/Lowbrow: the Emergence of Cultural Hierarchy in America* (1988). Several interesting essays on late 19th-century middle-class culture appear in **Burton J. Bledstein and Robert D. Johnston, eds.,** *The Middling Sorts: Explorations in the History of the American Middle Class* (2001).

For discussions of the relation of class hierarchy to race, see **Gail Bederman,** *Manliness and Civilization: A Cultural History of Gender and Race in the United States, 1880–1917* (1995) and **Matthew Frye Jacobson,** *Barbarian Virtues: The United States Encounters Foreign Peoples at Home and Abroad, 1876–1917* (2000). The effects of white-collar work on men and women are detailed in **Olivier Zunz,** *Making America Corporate, 1870–1920* (1990) and **Susan Porter Benson,** *Counter Cultures: Saleswomen, Managers, and Customers in American Department Stores, 1890–1940* (1986).

The rise of the department store is examined in **William Leach,** *Land of Desire: Merchants, Power, and the Rise of a New American Culture* (1993) and **Elaine S. Abelson,** *When Ladies Go A-Thieving: Middle-Class Shoplifters in the Victorian Department Store* (1989). Middle-class consumer culture is also discussed in **Ellen Gruber Garvey,** *The Adman in the Parlor: Magazines and the Gendering of Consumer Culture, 1880s to 1910s* (1996), while the cultural development of American museums is the subject of **Steven Conn,** *Museums and American Intellectual Life, 1876–1926* (1998).

Conflicting visions of the Chicago World's Fair can be found in **Robert W. Rydell,** *All the World's a Fair: Visions of Empire at the American International Expositions, 1876–1916* (1984); **James Gilbert,** *Perfect Cities: Chicago's Utopias of 1893* (1991); and **Christopher Robert Reed,** *"All the World Is Here": The Black Presence at the White City* (2000).

On working-class and popular culture in cities, see **Nan Enstad,** *Ladies of Labor, Girls of Adventure: Working Women, Popular Culture, and Labor Politics at the Turn of the Century* (1999); **John F. Kasson,** *Amusing the Million: Coney Island at the Turn of the Century* (1978); **David Nasaw,** *Going Out: The Rise and Fall of Public Amusements* (1993); **Kathy Peiss,** *Cheap Amusements: Working Women and Leisure in Turn-of-the-Century New York* (1986); and **Roy Rosenzweig and Elizabeth Blackmar,** *The Park and the People: A History of Central Park* (1992).

The labor movement is treated in **David Montgomery**, *The Fall of the House of Labor: The Workplace, the State, and American Labor Activism* (1987) and **Melvin Dubofsky**, *Industrialism and The American Worker, 1865–1920*, rev. ed. (1985). For the Knights of Labor, see **Leon Fink**, *Workingman's Democracy: The Knights of Labor and American Politics* (1983) and **Robert E. Weir**, *Beyond Labor's Veil: The Culture of the Knights of Labor* (1996). Two of the spectacular labor conflicts of the era are described in **Philip S. Foner**, *The Great Labor Uprising of 1877* (1977) and **Paul Krause**, *The Battle for Homestead, 1880–1892* (1992). For Haymarket and Pullman, see **Carl Smith**, *Urban Disorder and the Shape of Belief: The Great Chicago Fire, the Haymarket Bomb, and the Model Town of Pullman* (1995).

On the legacies of Populism, see **Elizabeth Sanders**, *Roots of Reform: Farmers, Workers and the American State, 1877–1917* (1999). A fresh interpretation of several populist movements in American history is **Michael Kazin**, *The Populist Persuasion: An American History* (1995). The best survey of the Populist movement is **Lawrence Goodwyn**, *Democratic Promise: The Populist Moment in America* (1976), which was published in an abridged edition with the title *The Populist Moment* (1978). The politics of the 1890s culminating in the climactic election of 1896 are treated in **J. Rogers Hollingsworth**, *The Whirligig of Politics: The Democracy of Cleveland and Bryan* (1963) and **Paul W. Glad**, *McKinley, Bryan, and the People* (1964). For the beginnings of Progressive reform during this era, see the early chapters of **Michael McGerr**, *A Fierce Discontent: Rise and Fall of the Progressive Movement in America, 1870–1920* (2003).

Visit the Liberty Equality Power Companion Web site for resources specific to this textbook: http://www.thomsonedu.com/history/murrin

Also find self-tests and additional resources at ThomsonNOW. ThomsonNOW is an integrated online suite of services and resources with proven ease of use and efficient paths to success, delivering the results you want—NOW!

www.thomsonedu.com/login/

An Industrial Society, 1900–1920

With the collapse of populism in 1896 and the end of the depression in 1897, the American economy embarked on a remarkable stretch of growth. By 1910, the United States had secured its status as the world's greatest industrial power.

Corporations were changing the face of America. Their railroad and telegraph lines crisscrossed the country. Their factories employed millions. Their production and management techniques became the envy of the industrialized world. A new kind of building—the skyscraper—came to symbolize America's corporate power. These modern towers were made possible by the use of steel rather than stone framework and by the invention of electrically powered elevators.

Impelled upward by rising real estate values, they were intended to evoke the same sense of grandeur as Europe's medieval cathedrals. But these monuments celebrated man, not God; material wealth, not spiritual riches; science, not faith; corporations, not the commonweal. Reaching into the sky, dwarfing Europe's cathedrals, they were convincing embodiments of America's worldly might.

This chapter continues the story begun in the last chapter about how the newly powerful corporations transformed America: how they intensified their search for new forms of production and management; how the jobs they generated attracted millions of immigrants, southern blacks, and young single women to northern cities; and how they triggered an urban cultural revolution that made amusement parks, dance halls, vaudeville theater, and movies integral features of American life.

The power of the corporations dwarfed that of individual wage earners, but wage earners sought to limit the power of corporations through labor unions and strikes and by organizing institutions of collective self-help within their own ethnic or racial communities. Many found opportunities and liberties they had not known before. Immigrant entrepreneurs invented ways to make money through legal and illegal enterprise; young, single, working-class women pioneered a sexual revolution; and radicals dared to imagine building a new society where no one suffered from poverty, inequality, and powerlessness. The power of the new corporations, in other words, did not go unchallenged. Even so, a more egalitarian society would prove difficult to attain.

CHRONOLOGY

1897	Depression ends; prosperity returns
1899	Theodore Roosevelt urges Americans to live the "strenuous life"
1900–14	Immigration averages more than 1 million per year
1901	U.S. Steel is formed from 200 separate companies • Andrew Carnegie devotes himself to philanthropic pursuits • 1 of every 400 railroad workers dies on the job
1904	20 percent of the North's urban population lives below poverty line
1905	*Lochner* v. *New York:* Supreme Court declares unconstitutional a New York state law limiting the workday of bakery employees • Industrial Workers of the World (IWW) founded
1907–11	An average of 73 of every 100 Italian immigrants return to Italy
1909	Henry Ford unveils his Model T • Immigrants and their children constitute more than 96 percent of labor force building and maintaining railroads
1910	Black skilled tradesmen in northern cities reduced to 10 percent of total skilled trades workforce • 20,000 nickelodeons dot northern cities
1911	Triangle Shirtwaist Company fire kills 146 workers • Frederick Winslow Taylor publishes *The Principles of Scientific Management*
1913	Henry Ford introduces the first moving assembly line • 66 men, women, and children killed in "Ludlow massacre" • John D. Rockefeller establishes Rockefeller Foundation
1914	Henry Ford introduces the $5-per-day wage • Theda Bara, movies' first sex symbol, debuts • *The Masses,* a radical journal, begins publication
1919	Japanese farmers in California sell $67 million in agricultural goods, 10 percent of state's total
1920	Nation's urban population outstrips rural population for first time
1921	1,250,000 Model Ts sold, a 16-fold increase over 1912

Sources of Economic Growth

Focus Question

How did corporations respond to the economic opportunities and turmoil of the late 19th century?

A series of technological innovations in the late 19th century fired up the nation's economic engine, but technological breakthroughs alone do not fully explain the nation's spectacular economic boom. New corporate structures and new management techniques—in combination with the new technology—created the conditions that powered economic growth.

Technology

Two of the most important new technologies were the harnessing of electric power and the invention of the gasoline-powered internal combustion engine. Scientists had long been fascinated by electricity, but only in the late 19th century did they find ways to make it practically useful. The work of Thomas Edison, George Westinghouse, and Nikola Tesla produced the incandescent bulb that brought electric lighting into homes and offices and the alternating current (AC) that made electric transmission possible over long distances. From 1890 to 1920, the proportion of American industry powered by electricity rose from virtually nil to almost one-third. Older industries switched from expensive and cumbersome steam power to more efficient and cleaner electrical power. New sectors of the metalworking and machine-tool industries arose in response to the demand for electric generators and related equipment. Between 1900 and 1920, virtually every major city built electric-powered transit systems to replace horse-drawn trolleys and carriages. By 1912, some 40,000 miles of electric railway and trolley track had been laid. In New York City, electricity made possible the construction of the first subways. Electric lighting—on city streets, in department store windows, in brilliantly lit amusement parks such as New York's Coney Island—gave cities a new allure. The public also fell in love with the movies, which depended on electricity to project images onto a screen. Electric power, in short, stimulated capital investment and accelerated economic growth.

Surf Avenue and Luna Park, Coney Island, 1913   With its 1 million lights, Surf Avenue in Brooklyn, New York, advertised itself as the most brilliantly lit thoroughfare in the world. The avenue included the entrance to Luna Park, one of Coney Island's most popular attractions.

The first gasoline engine was patented in the United States in 1878, and the first "horse-less carriages" began appearing on European and American roads in the 1890s, but few thought of them as serious rivals to trains and horses. Rather, they were seen as playthings for the wealthy, who liked to race them along country roads.

In 1900, Henry Ford was an eccentric 37-year-old mechanic who built race cars in Michigan. In 1909, Ford unveiled his Model T: an unadorned, even homely car, but reliable enough to travel hundreds of miles without servicing and cheap enough to be affordable to most working Americans. Ford had dreamed of creating an automobile civilization with his Model T, and Americans began buying his car by the millions. The stimulus this insatiable demand gave to the economy can scarcely be exaggerated. Millions of cars required millions of pounds of steel alloys, glass, rubber, petroleum, and other material. Millions of jobs in coal and iron-ore mining, oil refining and rubber manufacturing, steel-making and machine tooling, road construction, and service stations came to depend on automobile manufacturing.

Corporate Growth

Successful inventions such as the automobile required more than the mechanical ingenuity and social vision of inventors such as Henry Ford. They relied on corporations with sophisticated organizational and technical know-how to mass-produce and mass-distribute the newly invented products. Corporations had played an important role in the nation's economic life since the 1840s, but in the late 19th and early 20th centuries, they underwent significant changes. The most obvious change was in their size. Employment in Chicago's International Harvester factory, where agricultural implements were built, nearly quadrupled from 4,000 in 1900 to 15,000 in 1916. Delaware's DuPont Corporation, a munitions and chemical manufacturer, employed 1,500 workers in 1902 and 31,000 workers in 1920. Founded with a few hundred employees in 1903, the Ford Motor Company employed 33,000 at its Detroit Highland Park plant by 1916 and 42,000 by 1924. That same year, the 68,000 workers employed at Ford's River Rouge plant (just outside Detroit) made it the largest factory in the world.

This growth in scale was in part a response to the enormous domestic market. By 1900, railroads provided the country with an efficient transportation system that allowed corporations to ship goods virtually anywhere in the United States. A national network of telegraph lines allowed constant communication between buyers and sellers separated by thousands of miles. And the population, which was expanding rapidly, demonstrated an ever-growing appetite for goods and services.

Mass Production and Distribution

Manufacturers responded to this burgeoning domestic market by developing **mass-production** techniques that increased production speed and lowered unit costs. Mass production often meant replacing skilled workers with machines that were coordinated to permit high-speed, uninterrupted production at every stage of the manufacturing process. Mass-production techniques had become widespread in basic steel manufacturing and sugar refining by the 1890s, and they spread to the machine-tool industry and automobile manufacturing in the first two decades of the 20th century.

Such production techniques were profitable only if large quantities of output could be sold. Although the domestic market offered a vast potential for sales, manufacturers often found distribution systems inadequate. This was the case with North Carolina smoking tobacco manufacturer James Buchanan Duke, who almost single-handedly transformed the cigarette into one of the best-selling commodities in American history. In 1885, at a time when relatively few Americans smoked, Duke invested in several Bonsack cigarette machines, each of which manufactured 120,000 cigarettes per day. To create a market for the millions of cigarettes he was producing, Duke advertised his product aggressively throughout the country. He also established regional sales offices so that his sales representatives could keep in touch with local jobbers and retailers. As cigarette sales skyrocketed, more corporations sought to emulate Duke's techniques. Over the course of the next 20 years, those corporations that integrated mass production and mass distribution, as Duke did in the 1880s and 1890s, came to define American "big business." (**See Map 20.1, Industrial America, 1900–1920, in the color insert following p. 816.**)

Corporate Consolidation

Corporate expansion also reflected a desire to avoid market instability. The rapid industrial growth of the late 19th century had unsettled industrialists. As promising economic opportunities arose, more industrialists sought to take advantage of them, but overexpansion and increasingly furious competition often turned rosy prospects into less-than-rosy results. Bankrupting busts quickly followed buoyant booms. Soon, corporations began looking for ways to insulate themselves from harrowing downturns in the business cycle.

The railroads led the way in tackling this problem. Rather than engaging in ruinous rate wars, railroads began cooperating. They shared information on costs and profits, established standardized rates, and allocated discrete portions of the freight business among themselves. These cooperative arrangements were variously called "pools," "cartels," or "trusts." The 1890 Sherman Antitrust Act declared such cartel-like practices illegal, but the law's enforcement proved to be short-lived (see chapter 19). Still, the railroads' efforts rarely succeeded for long because they depended heavily on voluntary compliance. During difficult economic times, the temptation to lower freight rates and exceed one's market share could become too strong to resist.

Corporations' efforts to restrain competition and inject order into the economic environment continued unabated, however. Mergers now emerged as the favored instrument of control. By the 1890s, investment bankers, such as J. P. Morgan, possessed both the capital and the financial skills to engineer the complicated stock transfers and ownership renegotiations that mergers required. James Duke again led the way in 1890 when he and four competitors merged to form the American Tobacco Company. Over the next eight years, the quantity of cigarettes produced by Duke-controlled companies quadrupled, from 1 billion to almost 4 billion per year. Moreover, American Tobacco used its powerful position in cigarette manufacture to achieve dominance in pipe tobacco, chewing tobacco, and snuff manufacture as well.

The **merger movement** intensified as the depression of the 1890s lifted. In the years from 1898 to 1904, many of the corporations that would dominate American business throughout most of the 20th century acquired their modern form: Armour and Swift in meatpacking, Standard Oil in petroleum, General Electric and Westinghouse in electrical manufacture, American Telephone and Telegraph (AT&T) in communications, International Harvester in the manufacture of agricultural implements, and DuPont in munitions and chemical processing. The largest merger occurred in steel in 1901, when Andrew Carnegie and J. P. Morgan together fashioned the U.S. Steel Corporation from 200 separate iron and steel companies. U.S. Steel, with its 112 blast furnaces and 170,000 steelworkers, controlled 60 percent of the country's steelmaking capacity. Moreover, its 78 iron-ore boats and 1,000 miles of railroad gave it substantial control over procuring raw materials and distributing finished steel products.

Revolution in Management

The growth in the number and size of corporations revolutionized corporate management. The ranks of managers mushroomed, as elaborate corporate hierarchies defined both the status and the duties of individual managers. Increasingly, senior managers took over from owners the responsibility for long-term planning. Day-to-day operations fell to middle managers who oversaw particular departments (e.g., purchasing, research, production, labor) in corporate headquarters or who supervised regional sales offices or directed particular factories. Middle managers also managed the people—accountants, clerks, foremen, engineers, salesmen—in these departments, offices, or factories. The rapid expansion within corporate managerial ranks created a new middle class, whose members were intensely loyal to their employers but at odds both with blue-collar workers and with the older middle class of shopkeepers, small businessmen, and independent craftsmen.

As management techniques grew in importance, companies tried to make them more scientific. Firms introduced cost-accounting methods into purchasing and other departments charged with controlling the inflow of materials and the outflow of goods. Many corporations began requiring college or university training in science, engineering, or accounting for entry into middle management. Corporations that had built their success on a profitable invention or discovery sought to maintain their competitive edge by creating research departments and hiring professional scientists—those with doctorates from American or European universities—to come up with new technological and scientific breakthroughs. Such departments were modeled on the industrial research laboratory set up by the inventor-entrepreneur Thomas Edison in Menlo Park, New Jersey, in 1876 (see chapter 19).

Scientific Management on the Factory Floor

The most controversial and, in some respects, the most ambitious effort to introduce scientific practices into management occurred in production. Managers understood that improvements in factory organization as well as technological innovation could enhance the speed and efficiency of mass production. So, in league with engineers, they sought optimal arrangements of machines and deployments of workers that would achieve the highest speed in production with the fewest human or mechanical interruptions. Some of these managers, such as Frederick Winslow Taylor, the chief engineer at Philadelphia's Midvale Steel Company in the 1880s, styled themselves as the architects of **scientific management.** They examined every human task and mechanical movement involved in each production process. In "time-and-motion studies," they recorded every distinct movement a worker made in performing his or her job, how long it took, and how often it was performed. They hoped thereby to identify and eliminate wasted human energy. Eliminating waste might mean reorganizing a floor of machinery so as to reduce "down time" between production steps; it might mean instructing workers to perform their tasks differently; or it might mean replacing uncooperative skilled workers with machines tended by unskilled, low-wage laborers. Regardless of the method chosen, the goal was the same: to make human labor emulate the smooth and apparently effortless operation of an automatic, perfectly calibrated piece of machinery.

Taylor publicized his vision, first through speeches to fellow engineers and managers, and then through his writings. By the time he published *The Principles of Scientific Management* (1911), his ideas had already captivated countless corporate managers and engineers, many of whom sought to introduce "Taylorism" into their own production systems.

Introducing scientific management practices rarely proceeded easily. Time-and-motion studies were costly, and Taylor's formulas for increasing efficiency and reducing waste often were less scientific than he claimed. Taylor also overestimated workers' willingness to play the mechanical role he assigned them. Skilled workers and general foremen whom Taylor sought to eliminate often resisted his schemes. In the end, managers and engineers who persisted in their efforts to apply scientific management usually modified Taylor's principles.

Henry Ford's engineers initially adopted Taylorism and with apparent success. By 1910, they had broken down automobile manufacturing into a series of simple, sequential tasks. Each worker performed only one task: adding a carburetor to an engine, inserting a windshield, mounting tires onto wheels. Then, in 1913, Ford's engineers introduced the first moving assembly line, a continuously moving conveyor belt that carried cars in production through each workstation. This innovation eliminated precious time previously wasted in transporting car parts (or partially built cars) by crane or truck from one work area to another. It also limited the time available to workers to perform their assigned tasks. Only the foreman, not the workers, could stop the line or change its speed.

The World's First Automobile Assembly Line   Introduced at his Highland Park plant in 1913, this innovation cut production time on Model Ts by 90 percent, allowing Ford to reduce the price of his cars by more than half and to double the hourly wages of his employees.

By 1913, the continuous assembly line made Ford Motor Company's new Highland Park plant the most tightly integrated and continuously moving production system in American industry. The pace of production exceeded all expectations. Between 1910 and 1914, production time on Ford Model Ts dropped by 90 percent, from an average of more than 12 hours per car to 1.5 hours. A thousand Model Ts began rolling off the assembly line each day. This striking increase in the rate of production enabled Ford to slash the price of a Model T from $950 in 1909 to only $295 in 1923, a reduction of 70 percent. The number of Model Ts purchased by Americans increased 16-fold between 1912 and 1921, from 79,000 to 1,250,000. The assembly line quickly became the most admired—and most feared—symbol of American mass production.

Problems immediately beset the system, however. Repeating a single motion all day long induced mental stupor, and managerial efforts to speed up the line produced physical exhaustion—both of which increased the incidence of error and injury. Some workers tried to organize a union to gain a voice in production matters, but most Ford workers expressed their dissatisfaction simply by quitting. By 1913, employee turnover at Highland Park had reached the astounding rate of 370 percent per year. At that rate, Ford had to hire 51,800 workers every year just to keep his factory fully staffed at 14,000.

A problem of that magnitude demanded a dramatic solution. Ford provided it in 1914 by raising the wage he paid his assembly-line workers to $5 per day, double the average manufacturing wage then prevalent in American industry. The result: Workers, especially young and single men, flocked to Detroit. Highland Park's high productivity rate permitted Ford to absorb the wage increase without cutting substantially into profits.

Taylor had believed that improved efficiency would lead to dramatic wage gains. With his decision to raise wages, Ford was being true to Taylor's principles. Ford went even further, however, in his innovations. He set up a sociology department, forerunner of the personnel department, to collect job, family, and other information about his employees. He sent social workers into workers' homes to inquire into (and "improve") their personal lives. For the foreign-born, he instituted Americanization classes. He offered his employees housing subsidies, medical care, and other benefits. In short, Ford recognized that workers were more complex than Taylor had allowed and that high wages alone would not transform them into the perfectly functioning parts of the mass-production system Taylor had envisioned.

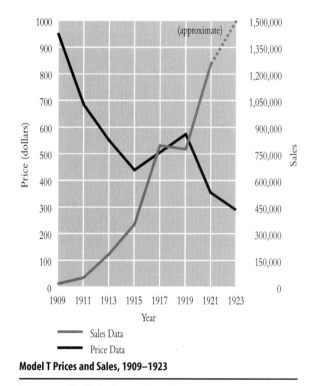

Model T Prices and Sales, 1909–1923

Source: From Alfred D. Chandler, Jr., ed., *Giant Enterprise: Ford, General Motors, and the Automobile Industry* (New York: Harcourt, Brace and World, 1964), pp. 32–33.

Although Ford's success impelled others to move in his direction, it would take time for modern management to come of age. Not until the 1920s did a substantial number of corporations establish personnel departments, institute welfare and recreational programs for employees, and hire psychologists to improve human relations in the workplace.

"Robber Barons" No More

Focus Question
How and why did American elites seek to alter their robber baron image in the late 19th and early 20th centuries?

Innovations in corporate management were part of a broader effort among elite industrialists to shed their "robber baron" image. The swashbuckling entrepreneurs of the 19th century—men such as Cornelius Vanderbilt, Jay Gould, Jay Cooke, and Leland Stanford—had wielded their economic power brashly and ruthlessly, while lavishing money on European-style palaces, private yachts, personal art collections, and extravagant entertainments. But the depression of the 1890s—along with the populist political movement and labor protests such as the Homestead and Pullman strikes—shook the confidence of members of this elite. Industrialists were terrified when in 1892 anarchist Alexander Berkman marched into the office of Henry Clay Frick, **Andrew Carnegie's** right-hand man, and shot him at point-blank range (Frick survived). Although such physical assaults were rare, anger over ill-gotten and ill-spent wealth was widespread. In the 1890s, popular rage forced Mrs. Bradley Martin and her husband to flee to England after she spent $370,000 (roughly $3.5 million in 2007 dollars) on one evening of entertainment for her friends in New York's high society.

Seeking a more favorable image, some industrialists began to restrain their displays of wealth and use their private fortunes to advance the public welfare. As early as 1889, Andrew Carnegie had advocated a "gospel of wealth." The wealthy, he believed, should consider all income in excess of their needs as a "trust fund" for their communities. In 1901, the year in which he formed U.S. Steel, Carnegie withdrew from industry and devoted himself to philanthropic pursuits, especially in art and education. By the time he died in 1919, he had given away or entrusted to several Carnegie foundations 90 percent of his fortune. Among the projects he funded were New York's Carnegie Hall, Pittsburgh's Carnegie Institute (now Carnegie-Mellon University), and 2,500 public libraries throughout the country.

Other industrialists, including John D. Rockefeller, soon followed Carnegie's lead. A devout Baptist with an ascetic bent, Rockefeller had never flaunted his wealth (unlike the Vanderbilts and others), but his ruthless business methods in assembling the Standard Oil Company and in crushing his competition made him one of the most reviled of the robber barons. In the wake of journalist Ida Tarbell's stinging 1904 exposé of Standard Oil's business practices, and of the federal government's subsequent prosecution of Standard Oil for monopolistic practices in 1906, Rockefeller transformed himself into a public-spirited philanthropist. Between 1913 and 1919, his Rockefeller Foundation dispersed an estimated $500 million. His most significant gifts included money to establish the University of Chicago and the Rockefeller Institute for Medical Research (later renamed Rockefeller University). His charitable efforts did not escape criticism, however; many Americans interpreted them as an attempt to establish control over American universities, scientific research, and public policy. Still, Rockefeller's largesse helped build for the Rockefeller family a reputation for public-spiritedness and good works, one that grew even stronger in the 1920s and 1930s. Many other business leaders, such as Julius Rosenwald of Sears Roebuck and Daniel and Simon Guggenheim of the American Smelting and Refining Company, also dedicated themselves to philanthropy during this time.

Obsession with Physical and Racial Fitness

The fractious events of the 1890s also induced many wealthy Americans to engage in what Theodore Roosevelt dubbed "the strenuous life." In an 1899 essay with that title, Roosevelt exhorted Americans to live vigorously, to test their physical strength and endurance in competitive athletics, and to experience nature through hiking, hunting, and mountain climbing. He articulated a way of life that influenced countless Americans from a variety of classes and cultures.

The 1890s were a time of heightened enthusiasm for competitive sports, physical fitness, and outdoor recreation. Millions of Americans began riding bicycles and eating healthier foods. A passion for athletic competition gripped American universities. The power and violence of football helped make it the sport of choice at the nation's elite campuses, and, for 20 years, Ivy League schools were the nation's football powerhouses. In athletic competition, as in nature, one could discover and recapture one's manhood, one's virility. The words "sissy" and "pussyfoot" entered common usage in the 1890s as insults hurled at men whose masculinity was found wanting.

In the vigorous new climate of the 1890s, young women began to engage in sports and other activities. They put away their corsets and long dresses and began wearing simple skirts, shirtwaists, and other clothing that gave them more comfort and freedom of movement. By the standards of the 1920s, these changes would seem mild, but in the 1890s, they were radical.

In the country at large, the new enthusiasm for athletics and the outdoor life reflected a widespread dissatisfaction with the growing regimentation of industrial society. Among wealthy Americans, the quest for physical superiority reflected a deeper and more ambiguous anxiety: their *racial* fitness. Most of them were native-born Americans whose families had lived in the United States for several generations and whose ancestors had come from the British Isles, the Netherlands, or some other region of northwestern Europe. Having embraced the principles of Social Darwinism (see chapter 19), they liked to attribute their success and good fortune to their "racial superiority." They saw themselves as "natural" leaders, members of a noble Anglo-Saxon race endowed with uncommon intelligence, imagination, and discipline. But events of the 1890s had challenged the legitimacy of the elite's wealth and authority, and the ensuing depression mocked their ability to exert economic leadership. The immigrant masses laboring in factories, despite their poverty and alleged racial inferiority, seemed to possess a vitality that the "superior" Anglo-Saxons lacked. Immigrant families were overflowing with children. The city neighborhoods where these families lived exhibited social and cultural energy (especially apparent in popular entertainments—vaudeville, amusement parks, nickelodeons, and dance halls) that were missing in the sedate environs of the wealthy.

Some rich Americans, such as Henry Adams, Henry Cabot Lodge, and other members of Boston's declining political elite, reacted to the immigrants' vigor and industry by calling for a halt to further immigration, but not the ebullient Roosevelt; he argued instead for American men to live the strenuous life and to test themselves unceasingly at work and at play. Through such struggles, the dominance of the "English-speaking peoples" would reassert itself and allow them to enjoy the rewards that racial superiority and racial fitness had put within their grasp: power, prosperity, civilization, and liberty. Roosevelt called on each married American woman, meanwhile, to have at least four children—an absolute necessity, he declared, in order to reproduce the "race" in numbers sufficient to maintain its vigor and dominance.

Immigration

Focus Question
What hardships and successes did immigrants experience in the United States?

A key factor causing this racial consternation among American elites was the extraordinarily large numbers of immigrants in America. The United States had always been a nation of immigrants, but never had so many come in so short a time. Between 1880 and 1920, some 23 million immigrants came to a country that numbered only 76 million in 1900. From 1900 to 1914, an average of 1 million immigrants arrived each year. In many cities of the Northeast and Midwest, immigrants and their children constituted a majority of the population. In 1920s Boston, New York City, Chicago, and Milwaukee, immigrants accounted for more than 70 percent of the total population; in Buffalo, Detroit, and Minneapolis, more than 60 percent; and in Philadelphia, Pittsburgh, and Seattle, more than 50 percent. Everywhere in the country, except in the South, the working class was overwhelmingly ethnic.

European immigration accounted for approximately three-fourths of the total. Some states received significant numbers of non-European immigrants—Chinese, Japanese, and Filipinos in California; Mexicans in California and the Southwest; and French Canadians in New England. Although their presence profoundly affected regional economies, politics, and culture, their numbers, relative to the number of European immigrants, were small. Immigrants from Latin America were free to enter the United States throughout this period, but few did until 1910, when the social disorder caused by the Mexican Revolution propelled a stream of refugees to southwestern parts of the United States. One-half million French Canadians had migrated to New England and the upper Midwest between 1867 and 1901. After that, the rate slowed as the pace of industrialization in their Quebec homeland quickened.

European Immigration

Most of the European immigrants who arrived between 1880 and 1914 came from Eastern and Southern Europe. Among them were 3 to 4 million Italians, 2 million Russian and Polish Jews, 2 million Hungarians, and an estimated 5 million Slavs and other peoples from eastern and southeastern Europe (Poles, Bohemians, Slovaks, Russians, Ukrainians, Lithuanians, Serbians, Croatians, Slovenians, Montenegrins, Bulgarians, Macedonians, and Greeks). Hundreds of thousands came as well from Turkey, Armenia, Lebanon, Syria, and other Near Eastern lands abutting the European continent.

These post-1880 arrivals were called "new immigrants" to underscore the cultural gap separating them from the "old immigrants," who had come from northwestern Europe— Great Britain, Scandinavia, and Germany. Old immigrants were regarded as racially fit,

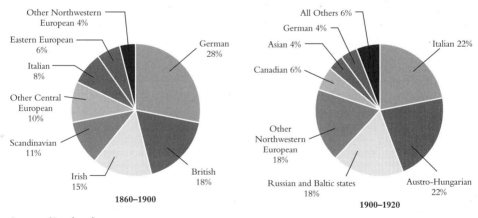

Sources of Immigration

Source: Data from *Historical Statistics of the United States, Colonial Times to 1970* (White Plains, NY: Kraus International, 1989), pp. 105–109.

culturally sophisticated, and politically mature. The new immigrants, by contrast, were often regarded as racially inferior, culturally impoverished, and incapable of assimilating American values and traditions. This negative view of the new immigrants reflected in part a fear of their alien languages, religions, and economic backgrounds. Few spoke English, and most adhered to Catholicism, Orthodoxy, or Judaism rather than Protestantism. Most, with the exception of Jewish immigrants, were peasants, unaccustomed to urban industrial life, but they were not as different from the old immigrants as the label implied. For example, many of the earlier-arriving Catholic peasants from Ireland and Germany had had no more familiarity with American values and traditions than did the Italians and Slavs who arrived later.

In fact, the old and new European immigrants were more similar than different. Both came to America for the same reasons: either to flee religious or political persecution or to escape economic hardship. The United States attracted a small but steady stream of political refugees throughout the 19th century: labor militants from England; nationalists from Ireland; socialists and anarchists from Germany, Russia, Finland, and Italy. Many of these people possessed talents as skilled workers, labor organizers, political agitators, and newspaper editors and thus exercised influence in their ethnic communities. However, only the anti-Semitic policies of Russia in the late 19th and early 20th centuries triggered a mass emigration (in this case Jewish) of political refugees.

Most mass immigration was propelled instead by economic hardship. Europe's rural population was growing faster than the land could support. European factories absorbed some, but not all, of the rural surplus. Industrialization and urbanization were affecting the European countryside in ways that disrupted rural ways of life. As railroads penetrated rural areas, village artisans found themselves unable to compete with the cheap manufactured goods that arrived from city factories. These handicraftsmen were among the first to emigrate. Meanwhile, rising demand for food in the cities accelerated the growth of commercial agriculture in the hinterland. Some peasant families lost their land. Others turned to producing crops for the market, only to discover that they could not compete with larger, more efficient producers. In addition, by the last third of the 19th century, peasants faced competition from North American farmers. Prices for agricultural commodities plummeted everywhere. The economic squeeze that spread distress among American farmers in the 1880s and 1890s caused even more hardship among Europe's peasantry, and many of them decided to try their luck in the New World.

An individual's or family's decision to emigrate often depended on having a contact—a family member, relative, or fellow villager—already established in an American city. These people provided immigrants with a destination, inspiration (they were examples of success in America), advice about jobs, and financial aid. Sometimes whole villages in southern Italy or western Russia—or at least all of the young men—seemed to disappear, only to reappear in a certain section of Chicago, Pittsburgh, or New York. Villages without contacts in the United States were relatively unaffected by the emigration mania.

Most immigrants viewed their trip to the United States as a temporary sojourn. They came not in search of permanent settlement but in search of high wages that would enable them to improve their economic standing in their homeland. For them, America was a land of economic opportunity, not a land to call home. This attitude explains why men vastly outnumbered women and children in the migration stream. From 1899 to 1910, three-fourths of the immigrants from Southern and Eastern Europe were adult men. Some had left wives and children behind; more were single. Most wanted merely to make enough money to buy a farm in their native land. True to their dream, many did return home. For every 100 Italian immigrants who arrived in the United States between 1907 and 1911, for example, 73 returned to Italy. Before the First World War, an estimated 60 percent to 80 percent of all Slavic immigrants eventually returned to the land of their birth.

The rate of return was negligible among certain groups, however. Jews had little desire to return to the religious persecution they had fled, and only 5 percent returned to Europe. The rate of return was also low among the Irish, who saw few opportunities in their long-suffering (although much-loved) Emerald Isle. In the early 20th century, however, such groups were exceptional. Most immigrants looked forward to returning to Europe. Not until the First World War shut down transatlantic travel did most immigrants begin to regard their presence in the United States as permanent.

Immigration tended to move in rhythm with the U.S. business cycle. It rose in boom years and fell off during depressions. It remained high during the first 14 years of the new century when the U.S. economy experienced sustained growth, broken only briefly by the Panic of 1907–08.

Chinese and Japanese Immigration

The relatively small numbers of Chinese and Japanese immigrants who came to the United States in the late 19th and early 20th centuries reflected the efforts of native-born Americans and their allies to keep them out. As many as 300,000 Chinese immigrants arrived in the United States between 1851 and 1882, and more than 200,000 Japanese immigrants journeyed to Hawaii and the western continental United States between 1891 and 1907. They contributed in major ways to the development of two of the West's major industries: railroad building and commercial agriculture. These two immigrant groups might have formed two of America's largest, each numbering in the millions, but the U.S. government began to exclude Chinese immigrant laborers in 1882 (The Chinese Exclusion Act) and Japanese immigrant laborers in 1907 (see chapter 22). The government also interpreted a 1790 law to mean that Chinese, Japanese, and other East Asian immigrants were ineligible for citizenship. These exclusions remained in force until the 1940s and 1950s. They expressed the racial prejudice felt by most native-born white Americans toward nonwhite Asian immigrants, and they also revealed how determined America was to remain a nation of European immigrants and their descendants.

The factors propelling Chinese and Japanese immigrants were similar to those motivating their European counterparts. The rural population in those countries was increasing at a rate faster than the rural economies could support. Chinese and Japanese rural peasants were being integrated into an international market for agriculture, contributing to the global oversupply of agricultural goods and depressing prices. Many Chinese and Japanese immigrants, like their European counterparts, conceived of their movement beyond their countries' borders as temporary. They intended to move abroad just long enough to make enough money to establish themselves economically in their homelands. Thus the early streams of Chinese and Japanese migration to the United States were overwhelmingly composed of men looking for work. Similar to the European immigrants, the Chinese and Japanese sojourners tended to follow precise migratory paths—from one region or village in China or Japan to one city or region in the United States.

Conditions in China were more desperate than those in Japan, where industrialization had begun to generate new wealth and absorb some of the rural population. Chinese immigrants, as a result, often suffered greater hardship than did their Japanese counterparts. In the 19th century, many were forced to sign contracts with suppliers of overseas laborers that subjected them to slave-like conditions: They were herded onto boats for the transpacific voyage, bound to particular employers for years on end, thrust into dangerous working conditions, and paid paltry wages. The conditions of their labor in the western states where they tended to settle inflamed the sentiments of white working men, who saw the Asian migration as a threat to their own wages and livelihoods. These white workers might have made common cause with Asian immigrant workers, but the racial prejudice they harbored toward the "yellow hordes" was simply too great. White workers became leaders of the movements in the western states to keep these immigrants out.

Significant numbers of Chinese and Japanese immigrants continued to try to enter the United States during the period of Asian immigrant exclusion—after 1882 in the case of the Chinese and 1907 in the case of the Japanese. Some were desperate to reunite themselves with family members already living in the United States, while others were driven by deteriorating economic circumstances in their homeland. Many attempted to enter the United States with forged papers declaring them to be merchants (a permitted class of Chinese and Japanese immigrants) when they were not, or to have been resident in the United States before the exclusion laws had gone into effect (and thus entitled to return). San Francisco was their principal port of entry, and Angel Island, in San Francisco harbor, became the counterpart of Ellis Island in New York harbor: the place where inspectors for the U.S. Bureau of Immigration interrogated them and scrutinized their documents and, more often than not, sent them back to Asia.

Other East Asian immigrants attempted to enter the United States through Canada or Mexico, hoping to find an unpatrolled part of the land border and to cross into the United States undetected. They became, in effect, America's first illegal aliens. That a certain percentage of East Asian immigrants were illegals subject to deportation generated considerable fear among the Asian immigrant populations resident in the United States, deepening tendencies within these communities to secrecy and to separation from mainstream American culture and society. Despite these considerable hardships, Asian immigrants would prove to be resourceful and to find ways to build homes and livelihoods in America.

Immigrant Labor

In the first decade of the 20th century, immigrant men and their male children constituted 70 percent of the workforce in 15 of the 19 leading U.S. industries. They concentrated in industries where work was the most backbreaking. Immigrants built the nation's railroads and tunnels; mined its coal, iron ore, and other minerals; stoked its hot and sometimes deadly steel furnaces; and slaughtered and packed its meat in Chicago's putrid packinghouses. In 1909, first- and second-generation immigrants—especially Greeks, Italians, Japanese, and Mexicans—constituted more than 96 percent of the labor force that built and

© Bettmann/CORBIS

Immigrant Japanese Children Arrive at Angel Island, San Francisco Harbor, 1905 Beginning in 1907, as a result of the "gentlemen's agreement" between the United States and Japanese governments, it would no longer be possible for Japanese immigrants such as these children to come to the United States.

maintained the nation's railroads. Of the 750,000 Slovaks who arrived in America before 1913, at least 600,000 headed for the coal mines and steel mills of western Pennsylvania. The steel mills of Pittsburgh, Buffalo, Cleveland, and Chicago also attracted disproportionately large numbers of Poles and other Slavs.

Immigrants also performed "lighter" but no less arduous work. Jews and Italians predominated in the garment manufacturing shops of New York City, Chicago, Philadelphia, Baltimore, and Boston. In 1900, French-Canadian immigrants and their children held one of every two jobs in New England's cotton textile industry. By 1920, the prosperity of California's rapidly growing agricultural industry depended primarily on Mexican and Filipino labor. In these industries, immigrant women and children, who worked for lower wages than men, formed a large part of the labor force. Few states restricted child labor. More than 25 percent of boys and 10 percent of girls aged 10 to 15 were "gainfully employed."

Immigrants were as essential as fossil fuels to the smooth operation of the American economic machine. Sometimes, however, the machine consumed workers as well as coal and oil. Those who worked in heavy industry, mining, or railroading were especially vulnerable to accident and injury. In 1901, for instance, 1 in every 400 railroad workers died on the job and 1 in every 26 suffered injury. Between the years 1906 and 1911, almost one-quarter of the recent immigrants employed at the U.S. Steel Corporation's South Works (Pittsburgh) were injured or killed on the job. Lax attention to safety rendered even light industry hazardous and sometimes fatal. In 1911, a fire broke out on an upper floor of the **Triangle Shirtwaist Company,** a New York City garment factory. The building had no fire escapes. The owners of the factory, moreover, had locked the entrances to each floor as a way of keeping their employees at work. A total of 146 workers, mostly young Jewish and Italian women, perished in the fire or from desperate nine-story leaps to the pavement below.

Chronic fatigue and inadequate nourishment increased the risk of accident and injury. Workweeks averaged 60 hours—10 hours every day except Sunday. Workers who were granted Saturday afternoons off, thus reducing their workweek to a mere 55 hours, considered themselves fortunate. Steelworkers were not so lucky. They labored from 72 to 89 hours per week and were required to work one 24-hour shift every two weeks.

Most workers had to labor long hours simply to eke out a meager living. In 1900, the annual earnings of American manufacturing workers averaged only $400 to $500 per year. Skilled jobs offered immigrants far more (as much as $1,500 to $2,000 per year), but most of them were held by Yankees and by the Germans, Irish, Welsh, and other Europeans who had come as part of the old immigration. Through their unions, workers of Northern European extraction also controlled access to new jobs that opened up and usually managed to fill them with a son, relative, or fellow countryman. Consequently, relatively few of the new immigrants rose into the prosperous ranks of skilled labor. In any case, employers were replacing many skilled workers with machines operated by cheaply paid operatives.

From the 1870s to 1910, real wages paid to factory workers and common laborers did rise, but not steadily. Wages fell sharply during depressions, and the hope for increases during periods of recovery often collapsed under the weight of renewed mass immigration, which brought hundreds of thousands of new job seekers into the labor market. One of every five industrial workers was unemployed, even during the boom years of the early 20th century.

Most working families required two or three wage earners to survive. If a mother could not go out to work because she had small children at home, she might rent rooms to some of the many single men who had recently immigrated. But economic security was difficult to attain. In his 1904 book, *Poverty,* social investigator Robert Hunter conservatively estimated that 20 percent of the industrial population of the North lived in poverty.

Living Conditions

Strained economic circumstances confined many working-class families to cramped and dilapidated living quarters. Many of them lived in two- or three-room apartments, with several people sleeping in each room. To make ends meet, one immigrant New York City family of eight living in a two-room apartment took in six boarders. Some boarders considered themselves lucky to have their own bed. That luxury was denied the 14 Slovaks who shared eight beds in a small Pittsburgh apartment and the New York City printer who slept on a door he unhinged every night and balanced across two chairs. The lack of windows in city tenements allowed little light or air into these apartments, and few had their own toilets or running water. Crowding was endemic. The population density of New York City's Lower East Side—where most of the city's Jewish immigrants settled—reached 700 per acre in 1900, a density greater than that of the poorest sections of Mumbai (formerly Bombay), India. Overcrowding and poor sanitation resulted in high rates of infectious diseases, especially diphtheria, typhoid fever, and pneumonia.

By 1900, this crisis in urban living had begun to yield to the insistence of urban reformers that cities adopt housing codes and improve sanitation. Between 1880 and 1900, housing inspectors condemned the worst of the tenements and ordered landlords to make improvements. City governments built reservoirs, pipes, and sewers to carry clean water to the tenements and to carry away human waste. Newly paved roads lessened the dirt, mud, and stagnant pools of water and thus further curtailed the spread of disease. As a result, urban mortality rates fell in the 1880s and 1890s.

Nevertheless, improvements came far more slowly to the urban poor than they did to the middle and upper classes. Cities such as Pittsburgh built extensive systems of paved roads in wealthy districts but not in working-class areas. Water supplies and pressures were far better in prosperous than in poor neighborhoods. At the outbreak of the First World War, many working-class families still lacked running water in their homes.

Building Ethnic Communities

The immigrants may have been poor, but they were not helpless. Migration had required a good deal of resourcefulness, self-help, and mutual aid—assets that survived in the new surroundings of American cities.

A Network of Institutions

Each ethnic group quickly established a network of institutions that supplied a sense of community and multiplied sources of communal assistance. Some immigrants simply reproduced those institutions that had been important to them in the Old Country. The devout established churches and synagogues. Lithuanian, Jewish, and Italian radicals reestablished Old World socialist and anarchist organizations. Irish nationalists set up clandestine chapters of the Clan Na Gael to keep alive the struggle to free Ireland from the English. Germans felt at home in their traditional *Turnevereins* (athletic clubs) and musical societies.

Immigrants developed new institutions as well. In the larger cities, foreign-language newspapers disseminated news, advice, and culture. Each ethnic group created fraternal societies to bring together immigrants who had known each other in the Old Country, or who shared the same craft, or who had come from the same town or region. Most of these societies provided members with a death benefit (ranging from a few hundred to a thousand dollars) that guaranteed the deceased a decent burial and the family a bit of cash. Some fraternal societies made small loans as well. Among those ethnic groups that prized home ownership, especially the Slavic groups, the fraternal societies also provided mortgage money. And all of them served as centers of sociability—places to have a drink, play cards, or simply relax with fellow countrymen. The joy, solace, and solidarity these groups generated helped countless immigrants adjust to American life.

The Emergence of an Ethnic Middle Class

Within each ethnic group, a sizable minority directed their talents and ambitions toward economic gain. Some of these entrepreneurs first addressed their communities' needs for basic goods and services. Immigrants preferred to buy from fellow countrymen with whom they shared a language, a history, and presumably a bond of trust. Enterprising individuals responded by opening dry-goods stores, food shops, butcher shops, and saloons in their ethnic neighborhoods. Those who could not afford to rent a store hawked their fruit, clothing, or dry goods from portable stands, wagons, or sacks carried on their backs. The work was endless and the competition tough. Men often enlisted the entire family—wife, older children, younger children—in their undertakings. Few family members were ever paid for their labor, no matter how long or hard they worked. Although many of these small businesses failed, enough survived to give some immigrants and their children a toehold in the middle class.

Other immigrants turned to small industry, particularly garment manufacture, truck farming, and construction. A clothing manufacturer needed only a few sewing machines to become competitive. Many Jewish immigrants, having been tailors in Russia and Poland, opened such facilities. If a rented space proved beyond their means, they set up shop in their own apartments. Competition among these small manufacturers was fierce, and work environments were condemned by critics as "sweatshops." Workers suffered from inadequate lighting, heat, and ventilation; 12-hour workdays and 70-hour work-weeks during peak seasons, with every hour spent bent over a sewing machine; and poor pay and no employment security, especially for the women and children who made up a large part of this labor force. Even at this level of exploitation, many small manufacturers failed, but over time, significant numbers of them managed to firm up their position as manufacturers and to evolve into stable, responsible employers. Their success contributed to the emergence of a Jewish middle class.

The story was much the same in urban construction, where Italians who had established themselves as labor contractors, or *padroni,* went into business for themselves to take advantage of the rapid expansion of American cities. Although few became general contractors on major downtown projects, many of them did well building family residences or serving as subcontractors on larger buildings.

One who did make the leap from small to big business was Amadeo P. Giannini, the son of Italian immigrants, who used his savings from a San Francisco fruit and vegetable stand to launch a career in banking. Determined to make bank loans available and affordable to people of ordinary means, Giannini generated a huge business in small loans. Expanding on his ethnic base of small depositors, he eventually made his bank—the Bank of America—into the country's largest financial institution.

In southern California, Japanese immigrants chose agriculture as their route to the middle class. Working as agricultural laborers in the 1890s, they began to acquire their own land in the early years of the 20th century. Altogether, they owned only 1 percent of California's total farm acreage. Their specialization in fresh vegetables and fruits (particularly strawberries), combined with their family-labor-intensive agricultural methods, was yielding $67 million in annual revenues by 1919—one-tenth of the total California agriculture revenue that year. Japanese farmers sold their produce to Japanese fruit and vegetable wholesalers in Los Angeles, who had chosen a mercantile route to middle-class status. The success of Japanese farmers was all the more impressive given that the state of California had passed the Alien Land Law in 1913, prohibiting Japanese and other Asian aliens from owning property in the state. Japanese immigrant farmers thus depended on their native-born children or friendly whites to acquire land for them, arrangements that made them more vulnerable to losing the land—or control of it—than if they had been able to own it outright themselves.

Each ethnic group created its own history of economic success and social mobility. From the emerging middle classes came leaders who would provide their ethnic groups with identity, legitimacy, and power and would lead the way toward Americanization and assimilation. Their children tended to do better in school than the children of working-class ethnics, and academic success served as a ticket to upward social mobility in a society that increasingly depended on university-trained engineers, managers, lawyers, doctors, and other professionals.

Political Machines and Organized Crime

The underside of this success story was the rise of government corruption and organized crime. Many ethnic entrepreneurs operated on the margins of economic failure and bankruptcy, and some accepted the help of those who promised financial assistance. Sometimes the help came from honest unions and upright government officials, but other times it did not. Unions were generally weak, and some government officials, lacking experience and economic security, were susceptible to bribery. Economic necessity became a breeding ground for government corruption and greed. A contractor who was eager to win a city contract—to build a trolley system, a sewer line, or a new city hall, for example—would find it necessary to pay off government officials who could throw the contract his way. By 1900, such payments, referred to as "graft," had become essential to the day-to-day operation of government in most large cities. Graft, in turn, made local officeholding a source of economic gain. Politicians began building political organizations called machines to guarantee their success in municipal elections. The machine "bosses" used a variety of legal and illegal means to bring victory on election day. They won the loyalty of urban voters—especially immigrants—by providing poor neighborhoods with paved roads and sewer systems. They helped newly arrived immigrants find jobs (often on city payrolls) and occasionally provided food, fuel, or clothing to families in dire need. Many of their clients were grateful for these services in an age when government provided little public assistance.

The bosses who ran the political machines—including "King Richard" Croker in New York, James Michael Curley in Boston, Tom Pendergast in Kansas City, Martin Behrman in New Orleans, and Abe Ruef in San Francisco—served their own needs first. They saw to it that construction contracts went to those who offered the most graft, not to those who were likely to do the best job. They protected gamblers, pimps, and other purveyors of urban vice who contributed large amounts to their machine coffers. They often required city employees to contribute to their campaign chests, to solicit political contributions, and to get out the vote on election day. And they engaged in widespread election fraud by rounding up truckloads of newly arrived immigrants and paying them to vote a certain way; having their supporters vote two or three times; and stuffing ballot boxes with the votes of phantom citizens who had died, moved away, or never been born.

Big-city machines, then, were both positive and negative forces in urban life. Reformers despised them for disregarding election laws and encouraging vice, but many immigrants valued them for providing social welfare services and for creating opportunities for upward mobility.

The history of President John F. Kennedy's family offers one example of the economic and political opportunities opened up by machine politics. Both of Kennedy's grandfathers, John Francis Fitzgerald ("Honey Fitz") and Patrick Joseph Kennedy, were the children of penniless Irish immigrants who arrived in Boston in the 1840s. Fitzgerald excelled at academics and won a coveted place in Harvard's Medical School, but left Harvard that same year, choosing a career in politics instead. Between 1891 and 1905, Fitzgerald served as a Boston city councilor, Massachusetts state congressman and senator, U.S. congressman, and mayor of Boston. For much of this period, he derived considerable income and power from his position as the North End ward boss, where he supervised the trading of jobs for votes and favors for cash in his section of Boston's Democratic and Irish-dominated political machine.

Patrick Kennedy, an East Boston tavern owner and liquor merchant, became an equally important figure in Boston city politics. In addition to running the Democratic Party's affairs in Ward Two, he served on the Strategy Board, a secret council of Boston's machine politicians that met regularly to devise policies, settle disputes, and divide up graft. Both Fitzgerald and Kennedy derived a substantial income from their political work and used it to lift their families into middle-class prosperity. Kennedy's son (and the future president's father), Joseph P. Kennedy, would go on to make a fortune as a Wall Street speculator and liquor distributor and to groom his sons for Harvard and the highest political offices in the land. But his rapid economic and social ascent had been made possible by his father's and father-in-law's earlier success in Boston machine politics.

Underworld figures, too, influenced urban life. In the early years of the 20th century, gangsterism was a scourge of Italian neighborhoods, where Sicilian immigrants had established outposts of the notorious Mafia, and in Irish, Jewish, Chinese, and other ethnic communities as well. Favorite targets of these gangsters were small-scale manufacturers and contractors, who were threatened with violence and economic ruin if they did not pay a gang for "protection." Gangsters enforced their demands with physical force, beating up or killing those who failed to abide by the "rules." In Chinese communities, secret societies originating in China, or *tongs,* and initially set up in America to strengthen communal life among the immigrants, occasionally crossed the line into crime. Sometimes this transition resulted from good intentions—for example, tong members might smuggle into the United States the wife and children of an immigrant Chinese man who had no legal way of reuniting his family—but other times, tongs enmeshed themselves in far more damaging criminal activities such as the opium trade, prostitution, and gambling.

Greedy for money, power, and fame, and willing to use any means necessary, many immigrant and ethnic criminals considered themselves authentic entrepreneurs cut from the American mold. By the 1920s, petty extortion had escalated in urban areas, and underworld crime had become big business. Al Capone, the ruthless Chicago mobster who made a fortune from gambling, prostitution, and bootleg liquor during Prohibition, once claimed: "Prohibition is a business. All I do is to supply a public demand. I do it in the best and least harmful way I can." New York City's Arnold Rothstein, whose financial sophistication won him a gambling empire and the power to fix the 1919 World Series, nurtured his reputation as "the J. P. Morgan of the underworld." Mobsters like Rothstein and Capone were charismatic figures, both in their ethnic communities and in the nation at large. Few immigrants, however, followed their criminal path to economic success.

African American Labor and Community

Focus Question
What were the similarities and differences between the immigrant and African American experiences in the early 20th century?

Unlike immigrants, African Americans remained a predominantly rural and southern people in the early 20th century. Most blacks were sharecroppers and tenant farmers. The markets for cotton and other southern crops had stabilized in the early 20th century, but black farmers remained vulnerable to exploitation. Landowners, most of whom were white, often forced sharecroppers to accept artificially low prices for their crops. At the same time, they charged high prices for seed, tools, and groceries at the local stores they controlled. Few rural areas generated enough business to support more than one store or to create a competitive climate that might force prices down. Those sharecroppers who traveled elsewhere to sell their crops or purchase their necessities risked retaliation— either physical assaults by white vigilantes or eviction from their land. Thus most remained beholden to their landowners, mired in poverty and debt.

Some African Americans sought a better life by migrating to industrial areas of the South and the North. In the South, they worked in iron and coal mines, in furniture and cigarette manufacture, as railroad track layers and longshoremen, and as laborers in the steel mills of Birmingham, Alabama. By the early 20th century, their presence was growing in the urban North as well, where they worked on the fringes of industry as janitors, elevator operators, teamsters, longshoremen, and servants of various kinds. Altogether, about 200,000 blacks left the South for the North and West between 1890 and 1910.

In southern industries, blacks were subjected to hardships and indignities that even the newest immigrants were not expected to endure. Railroad contractors in the South, for example, treated their black track layers like prisoners. Armed guards marched them to work in the morning and back at night. Track layers were paid only once a month and forced to purchase food at the company commissary, where the high prices claimed most of what they earned. Their belongings were locked up to discourage them from running away. Although other southern employers of black workers did not engage in labor practices as harsh as those of the railroad contractors, they still confined blacks to the dirtiest and most grueling jobs. The "Jim Crow" laws passed by every southern state legislature in the 1890s legalized this rigid separation of the black and white races (see chapter 18).

The nation's worsening racial climate adversely affected southern blacks who came north, even though these migrants had moved to states that generally did not have Jim Crow laws. Northern industrialists generally refused to hire black migrants for manufacturing jobs, preferring the labor of European immigrants. Only when those immigrants went on strike did employers turn to African Americans. Black workers first gained a foothold in the Chicago meatpacking industry in 1904, when 28,000 immigrant packinghouse workers walked off their jobs. Employers hoped that the use of black strike-breakers would inflame racial tensions between white and black workers and thus undermine labor unity and strength.

African Americans who had long resided in northern urban areas also experienced intensifying discrimination in the late 19th and early 20th centuries. In 1870, about one-third of the black men in many northern cities had been skilled tradesmen: blacksmiths, painters, shoemakers, and carpenters. Serving both black and white clients, these men enjoyed steady work and good pay, but by 1910 only 10 percent of black men made a living in this way. In many cities, the number of barber shops and food catering businesses owned by blacks also went into sharp decline, as did black representation in the ranks of restaurant and hotel waiters. These barbers, food caterers, and waiters had formed a black middle class whose livelihood depended on the patronage of white clients. By the early 20th century, this middle class was in decline, the victim of growing racism. Whites were no longer willing to engage the services of blacks, preferring to have their hair cut, beards shaved, and food prepared and served by European immigrants. The residential segregation of northern blacks also rose in these years, as whites excluded them from growing numbers of urban neighborhoods.

African Americans did not lack for resourcefulness. In urban areas of settlement, they laced their communities with the same array of institutions—churches, fraternal insurance societies, political organizations—that solidified ethnic neighborhoods. A new black middle class arose, consisting of ministers, professionals, and businesspeople who serviced the needs of their racial group. Black-owned real estate agencies, funeral homes, doctors' offices, newspapers, groceries, restaurants, and bars opened for business on the commercial thoroughfares of African American neighborhoods. Many businessmen had been inspired by the words of black educator Booker T. Washington, and specifically by his argument that blacks should devote themselves to self-help and self-sufficiency. **Madame C. J. Walker** offers one example of a black woman who built a lucrative business from the hair and skin lotions she devised and sold to black customers throughout the country. In many cities, African American real estate agents achieved significant wealth and power.

THE JAZZ SINGER (1927)

Directed by Alan Crosland. Starring Al Jolson (Jake Rabinowitz/Jack Robin), May McAvoy (Mary Dale), and Warner Oland (Cantor Rabinowitz).

The *Jazz Singer* was a sensation when it opened because it was the first movie to use sound (although relatively few words of dialogue were actually spoken). It also starred Al Jolson, the era's most popular Broadway entertainer, and bravely explored an issue that the film industry usually avoided—the religious culture and generational dynamics of a "new immigrant" family.

The movie focuses on Jake Rabinowitz and his immigrant parents, who are Jewish and devout. Jake's father is a fifth-generation cantor whose job it is to fill his New York City synagogue with ancient and uplifting melodies on the Sabbath and Jewish holidays. Cantor Rabinowitz looks upon his work as sacred, and he expects Jake to take his place one day. But Jake has other ideas. He loves music but is drawn to the new rhythmic ragtime and sensual jazz melodies emerging from his American surroundings. In an early scene, we encounter Jake at a dance hall, absorbed in playing and singing ragtime tunes and forgetting that he should be at home preparing for Yom Kippur, the holiest day in the Jewish calendar. His distraught father finds him and whips him, and Jake, in anger and pain, runs away. These early scenes allow us to glimpse important themes in the immigrant experience of the early 20th century: the deep attraction among the children of immigrants to the energy and vitality of American popular culture and the strains that this attraction often caused between these children and parents desperate to maintain the traditions they had brought with them from Europe.

Jake's estrangement from his family and community gives him the space to reinvent himself as Jack Robin, the jazz singer. His love relationship with a prominent (and non-Jewish) stage actress, Mary Dale, brings him the big break he needs, a starring role in a Broadway show. Jack hopes to use his return to New York to reconcile with his father. This eventually happens when Jake, on the eve of Yom Kippur once again, agrees to skip his show's premiere in order to take his ailing father's place as cantor in the synagogue. Jake's melodies soar and reach his bedridden father who, thinking that his son has succeeded him as cantor and thus fulfilled his (the father's) deepest wish, peacefully dies.

His father is deceived, for Jake returns to his Broadway show as soon as Yom Kippur ends to deliver an outstanding performance as the "Jazz Singer." His

---

Nevertheless, entrepreneurial success remained a tougher task among African Americans than among immigrants. Black communities were often smaller and poorer than their white ethnic ones; economic opportunities were fewer, and black businessmen found it more difficult than their white ethnic counterparts to cultivate customers outside of their core community. Racial prejudice stood as an obstacle to black business future lies with Broadway rather than with a synagogue, and with the gentile Mary. The movie, however, makes it seem as though everything will work out: Jake's mother is in the audience for the Broadway show, enjoying her son's success and, in effect, blessing him for the career and woman he has chosen. That this resolution requires misleading the father reminds us, however, that the strains between immigrant parents and their American-born children could be deep and sometimes not resolvable.

The movie also allows us to ask questions about the relationship between immigrants and African Americans. As part of his Broadway performance, Jake does a blackface routine, using burnt cork to turn his face and neck black and thus to appear to audiences as a "black" entertainer. From the early 19th to the early 20th centuries, "blacking up" was a performance style popular among white entertainers who wanted both to appropriate and ridicule expressive aspects of black culture. What did it mean for a child of Jewish immigrants, himself vulnerable to being stigmatized as an outsider in America, to "black up"? Jake may have been expressing in part his desire to draw closer to rich elements in black musical culture. But Jake may also have been signaling his desire to distance himself from African

A billboard in New York City advertising *The Jazz Singer*. Al Jolson is shown in blackface.

Americans by participating in tradition popular among white American entertainers. Ironically, "blacking up" may have been a way for an entertainer to embrace not black but white America, and for someone like Jake to be accepted by non-Jewish white Americans as one of their own.

success. Meanwhile, blacks were so marginalized in politics that they had little opportunity to gain power or wealth through holding political office or controlling a political machine. Thus the African American middle class remained smaller and more precarious than did its counterpart in ethnic communities, less able to lead the way toward affluence and assimilation.

A'Lelia Bundles/Walker Family Collection/www.madamcjwalker.com

Madame C. J. Walker   This prominent African American entrepreneur, pictured here behind the wheel of her car, built a successful business selling hair and skin lotions to black customers throughout the country.

Workers and Unions

Middle-class success eluded most immigrants and blacks in the years before the First World War. Even among Jews, whose rate of social mobility was rapid, most immigrants were working class. For most workers, the path toward a better life lay in improving their working conditions, not in escape from the working class. Henry Ford's $5-per-day wage, double the average manufacturing wage, raised the hopes of many. Young immigrant men, in particular, flocked to Detroit to work for Ford. But in the early decades of the 20th century, few other manufacturers were prepared to follow Ford's lead, and most factory workers remained in a fragile economic state.

Samuel F. Gompers and the AFL

For those workers, the only hope for economic improvement lay in organizing unions powerful enough to wrest wage concessions from reluctant employers. This was not an easy task. The charged, often violent, labor protests of the Gilded Age had been put down. Labor organizations, such as the Knights of Labor, that had unified workers had been defeated. Federal and state governments had shown themselves ready to use military force to break strikes. The courts, following the lead of the U.S. Supreme Court, repeatedly found unions in violation of the Sherman Antitrust Act, even though that act had been intended to control corporations, not unions. Judges in most states usually granted employer requests for injunctions—court orders that barred striking workers from picketing their place of employment (and thus from obstructing employer efforts to hire replacement workers). Before 1916, no federal laws protected workers' right to organize or required employers to bargain with the unions to which their workers belonged.

This hostile legal environment retarded the growth of unions from the 1890s through the 1920s. It also made the major labor organization of those years, the American Federation of Labor (AFL), more timid and conservative than it had been before the depression of the 1890s. In the aftermath of that depression, the AFL focused on organizing craft, or skilled, workers such as carpenters, typographers, plumbers, painters, and machinists. Because of their skills, these workers commanded more respect from employers than did the unskilled laborers. Employers negotiated contracts, or trade agreements, with craft unions that stipulated the wages workers were to be paid, the hours they were to work, and the rules under which new workers would be accepted into the trade. These agreements were accorded the same legal protection that American law bestowed on other commercial contracts.

As the AFL emphasized these bread-and-butter issues, it withdrew from the political activism that had once occupied its attention. It no longer agitated for governmental regulation of the economy and the workplace. The AFL had concluded that labor's powerful opponents in the legislatures and the courts would find ways to undermine whatever governmental gains organized labor managed to achieve. That conclusion was reinforced by a 1905 ruling, *Lochner* v. *New York,* in which the U.S. Supreme Court declared unconstitutional a seemingly innocent New York state law limiting bakery employees to a 10-hour day.

The AFL's "business" unionism took its most forceful expression from its president, **Samuel F. Gompers.** A onetime Marxist and cigarmaker who had helped found the AFL in 1886, Gompers was reelected to the AFL presidency every year from 1896 until his death in 1924. The AFL showed considerable vitality under his leadership, especially in the early years when its membership quadrupled from less than a half million in 1897 to more than 2 million in 1904. Aware of the AFL's growing significance and conservatism, the National Civic Federation, a newly formed council of corporate executives, agreed to meet periodically with the organization's leaders to discuss the nation's industrial and labor problems.

Nevertheless, the AFL had limited success. Its 2 million members represented only a small portion of the industrial workforce. Its concentration among craft workers, moreover, distanced it from most workers, who were not skilled. Unskilled and semiskilled workers could only be organized into an industrial union that offered membership to all workers in a particular industry. Gompers understood the importance of such unions and allowed several of them, including the United Mine Workers (UMW) and the International Ladies Garment Workers Union (ILGWU), to participate in the AFL. But AFL ranks remained dominated by skilled workers who looked down upon the unskilled. Ethnic background intensified these craftsmen's sense of superiority over the unskilled. Most skilled workers were from old immigrant stock—particularly English, Scottish, German, and Irish—and they shared the common prejudice against immigrants from Southern and Eastern Europe.

AFL members demonstrated even worse prejudice toward black workers. In the early 20th century, more than 10 AFL unions excluded African Americans from membership. The AFL's racist policies partially account for the shrinking numbers of black tradesmen between 1870 and 1910. White and black workers sometimes managed to set aside their suspicions of each other and cooperate. The UMW allowed black workers to join and to rise to positions of leadership. In New Orleans, black and white dockworkers constructed a remarkable experiment in biracial unionism that flourished from the 1890s through the early 1920s. But these moments of cooperation were rare.

Although blacks made up too small a percentage of the working class to build alternative labor organizations that would counteract the influence of the AFL, the new immigrants from Eastern and Southern Europe were too numerous to be ignored. Their participation in the UMW enabled that union to grow from only 14,000 in 1897 to more than 300,000 in 1914. In 1909, a strike of 20,000 women workers against the owners of New York City's garment factories inspired tens of thousands of workers, male and female, to join the ILGWU.

"Big Bill" Haywood and the IWW

When the AFL failed to help them organize, immigrants turned to other unions. The most important was the Industrial Workers of the World (IWW), founded by western miners in 1905 and led by William "Big Bill" Haywood. The IWW rejected the AFL principle of craft organization, hoping instead to organize all workers into "one big union." It scorned the notion that only a conservative union could survive in American society, declaring its commitment to revolution instead.

The IWW refused to sign collective bargaining agreements with employers, arguing that such agreements only trapped workers in capitalist property relations. Capitalism had to be overthrown through struggles between workers and their employers at the point of production. Although hundreds of thousands of workers passed through its ranks or participated in its strikes, the IWW's membership rarely exceeded 20,000. Nevertheless, few labor organizations inspired as much fear. The IWW organized the poorest and most isolated workers—lumbermen, miners, and trackmen in the West, textile workers and longshoremen in the East. Emboldened by IWW leaders, these workers waged strikes against employers who were unaccustomed to having their authority challenged. Violence lurked beneath the surface of these strikes and occasionally erupted in bloody skirmishes between strikers and police, National Guardsmen, or the private security forces hired by employers. Some blamed the IWW for the violence, seeing it as a direct outgrowth of calls for a "class war." Others understood that the IWW was not solely responsible. Employers had shown themselves quite willing to resort to violence to

Underwood Photo Archives

Men at Work   This photo of male workers stoking a boiler conveys some of the grime and heat associated with much early-1900s blue-collar work as well as the strength and concentration required of workmen.

enforce their will on employees. In 1913, for example, at Ludlow, Colorado, the Colorado Fuel and Iron Company, a subsidiary of Rockefeller's Standard Oil Company, brought in a private security force and the local militia (which it controlled) to break up a UMW strike. When the company evicted strikers and their families from their homes, the union set up 13 tent colonies to obstruct the entrances to the mines. The standoff came to a bloody conclusion in April 1914 when company police, firing into one colony of tents, killed 66 men, women, and children.

The **"Ludlow massacre"** outraged the nation. At hearings held by the U.S. Commission on Industrial Relations, John D. Rockefeller, Jr., was humiliated by Commissioner Frank Walsh's disclosure that the industrialist had been complicit in the events leading up to the violence. The massacre revealed yet again what the IWW strikes had already demonstrated: that many American workers resented their low wages and poor working conditions; that neither the government nor employers offered workers a mechanism for airing and peacefully resolving their grievances; and that workers, as a result, felt compelled to protest through joining unions and waging strikes, even if it meant risking their lives. On the eve of the First World War, almost 40 years after the Great Railroad Strike of 1877 (chapter 19), industrial conflict still plagued the nation.

Nickelodeons in Major American Cities, 1910

Cities	Population	Nickelodeons (estimate)	Seating Capacity	Population per Seat
New York	4,338,322	450	150,000	29
Chicago	2,000,000	310	93,000	22
Philadelphia	1,491,082	160	57,000	26
St. Louis	824,000	142	50,410	16
Cleveland	600,000	75	22,500	27
Baltimore	600,000	83	24,900	24
San Francisco	400,000	68	32,400	12
Cincinnati	350,000	75	22,500	16
New Orleans	325,000	28	5,600	58

Source: Garth Jowett, *Film: The Democratic Art* (Boston: Little, Brown, 1976), p. 46.

The Joys of the City

Industrial workers might be missing their fair share of the nation's prosperity, but they were crowding the dance halls, vaudeville theaters, amusement parks, and ballparks offered by the new world of commercial entertainment. Above all, they were embracing a new technological marvel, the movies.

Movies were well suited to poor city dwellers with little money, little free time, and little command of the English language. Initially, the movies cost only a nickel. The **"nickelodeons"** where they were shown were usually converted storefronts in working-class neighborhoods. Movies required little leisure time because at first they lasted only 15 minutes on average. Viewers with more time on their hands could stay for a cycle of two or three films (or for several cycles). And even non-English-speakers could understand what was happening on the "silent screen." By 1910, at least 20,000 nickelodeons dotted northern cities.

These early "moving pictures" were primitive by today's standards, but they were thrilling just the same. The figures appearing on the screen were "larger than life." Moviegoers could transport themselves to parts of the world they would otherwise never see, encounter people they would otherwise never meet, and watch boxing matches they could otherwise not afford to attend. The darkened theater provided a setting in which secret desires, especially sexual ones, could be explored. As one newspaper innocently commented in 1899: "For the first time in the history of the world it is possible to see what a kiss looks like."

No easy generalizations are possible about the content of these early films, more than half of which came from France, Germany, and Italy. American-made films tended toward slapstick comedies, adventure stories, and romances. Producers did not yet shy away, as they soon would, from the lustier or seedier sides of American life. The Hollywood formula of happy endings had yet to be worked out. In fact, the industry, centered in New

York City and Fort Lee, New Jersey, had yet to locate itself in cheery southern California. In 1914, the movies' first sex symbol, Theda Bara, debuted in a movie that showed her tempting an upstanding American ambassador into infidelity and ruin. She would be the first of the big screen's vamps, so-called because the characters they portrayed, like vampires, thrived on the blood (and death) of men.

The New Sexuality and the Rise of Feminism

The appearance of the vamp was one sign that popular culture had become an arena in which Americans were beginning to experiment with more open expressions of sexuality. Another sign was the growing numbers of women who began insisting that they be accorded the same sexual freedom long enjoyed by men. This impulse was strongest among young, single, working-class women who were entering the workforce in large numbers and mixing at workplaces, in loosely supervised ways, with men their own age. The associations between young men and women that sprang up at work carried over into their leisure. Young people of both sexes flocked to the dance halls that were opening in every major city. They rejected the stiff formality of earlier ballroom dances such as the cotillion or the waltz for the freedom and intimacy of newer forms, such as the fox trot, tango, and bunny-hug. They went to movies and to amusement parks together, and they engaged, far more than their parents had, in premarital sex. It is estimated that the proportion of women having sex before marriage rose from 10 percent to 25 percent in the generation that was coming of age between 1910 and 1920.

Feminism

This movement toward sexual freedom was one expression of women's dissatisfaction with the restrictions that had been imposed on them by earlier generations. By the second decade of the 20th century, eloquent spokeswomen had emerged to make the case for full female freedom and equality. The author Charlotte Perkins Gilman called for the release of women from domestic chores through the collectivization of housekeeping. Social activist Margaret Sanger insisted, in her lectures on birth control, that women should be free to enjoy sexual relations without having to worry about unwanted motherhood. The anarchist Emma Goldman denounced marriage as a kind of prostitution and embraced the ideal of "free love"— love unburdened by contractual commitment. Alice Paul, founder of the National Women's Party, brought a new militancy to the campaign for woman suffrage (see chapter 21).

These women were among the first to use the term *feminism* to describe their desire for complete equality with men. Some of them came together in Greenwich Village, a community of radical artists and writers in lower Manhattan, where they found a supportive environment in which to express and live by their feminist ideals. Crystal Eastman, a leader of the feminist **Greenwich Village** group called Heterodoxy, defined the feminist challenge as "how to arrange the world so that women can be human beings, with a chance to exercise their infinitely varied gifts in infinitely varied ways, instead of being destined by the accident of their sex to one field of activity."

© Bettmann/CORBIS

Margaret Sanger on Trial, 1916   Feminist Margaret Sanger, left, was put on trial for using the U.S. mail service to circulate her book *The Woman Rebel,* which advocated birth control. A federal law barred the use of the mails to spread birth control advice or techniques.

The movement for sexual and gender equality aroused considerable anxiety. Parents worried about the promiscuity of their children. Conservatives were certain that sexual assertiveness among women would transform American cities into dens of iniquity. Vice commissions sprang up in every major city to clamp down on prostitution, drunkenness, and pornography. The campaign for prohibition—a ban on the sale of alcoholic beverages—gathered steam. Movie theater owners were pressured into excluding "indecent" films from their screens. Many believed the lurid tales of international vice lords scouring foreign lands for innocent girls who could be delivered to American brothel owners. This "white slave trade" inspired passage of the 1910 Mann Act, which made the transportation of women across state lines for immoral purposes a federal crime.

Nor did it escape the attention of conservatives that Greenwich Village was home not only to the dangerous exponents of "free love" but also to equally dangerous advocates of class warfare. Prominent IWW organizer Elizabeth Gurley Flynn was a member of Heterodoxy; her lover, Carlo Tresca, was an IWW theoretician. "Big Bill" Haywood also frequented Greenwich Village, where he was lionized as a working-class hero. When Greenwich Village radicals began publishing an avant-garde artistic journal in 1914, they called it *The Masses;* its editor was Max Eastman, the brother of Crystal. This convergence of labor and feminist militancy intensified conservative feeling that the nation had strayed too far from its roots.

Cultural conservatism was strongest in those areas of the country that were least involved in the ongoing industrial and sexual revolutions: in farming communities and small towns; in the South, where industrialization and urbanization were proceeding at a slower rate than elsewhere; and among old social elites, who felt pushed aside by the new corporate men of power.

Conservatives and radicals alike shared a conviction that the country could not afford to ignore its social problems—the power of the corporations; the poverty and powerlessness of wage earners; the role of women and African Americans. Conservatives were as determined to restore 19th-century moral standards as radicals were determined to achieve working-class emancipation and women's equality. But in politics, neither would become the dominant force. That role would fall to the so-called progressives, a diverse group of reformers who confidently and optimistically believed they could bring order and justice to the new society.

Conclusion

Between 1900 and 1920, corporate power, innovation, and demands had stimulated the growth of cities, attracted millions of immigrants, enhanced commercial opportunities, and created the conditions for a vibrant urban culture. Many Americans thrived in this new environment, taking advantage of business opportunities or, as in the case of women, discovering liberties in dress, employment, dating, and sex that they had not known. Millions of Americans, however, remained impoverished, unable to rise in the social order or to earn enough in wages to support their families. African Americans who had migrated to the North in search of economic opportunity suffered more than any other single group, as they found themselves shut out of most industrial and commercial employment.

Henry Ford, whose generous $5-per-day wage drew tens of thousands to his Detroit factories, was an exceptional employer. Although other employers had learned to restrain their crass displays of wealth and had turned toward philanthropy in search of a better public image, they remained reluctant to follow Ford's lead in improving the conditions in which their employees labored.

Working-class Americans proved resourceful in creating self-help institutions to serve their own and each other's needs. In some cities, they gained a measure of power through the establishment of **political machines.** Labor unions arose and fought for a variety of reforms, but their success was limited. How to inject greater equality and opportunity into an industrial society in which the gap between rich and poor had reached alarming proportions remained a daunting challenge.

SUGGESTED READINGS

For a general overview of the period, see **Alan Dawley,** *Struggles for Justice: Social Responsibility and the Liberal State* (1991) and **Nell Irvin Painter,** *Standing at Armageddon: The United States, 1877–1919* (1987). On economic growth and corporate development, see **Harold G. Vatter,**

The Drive to Industrial Maturity: The United States Economy, 1860–1914 (1975); **Glenn Porter,** *The Rise of Big Business, 1860–1910* (1973); and **Robert Kanigel,** *The One Best Way: Frederick Winslow Taylor and the Enigma of Efficiency* (1997). For a discussion of Ford's labor policies and their impact on immigrant workers, see **Stephen Meyer III,** *The Five Dollar Day: Labor Management and Social Control in the Ford Motor Company, 1908–1921* (1981).

On the changing character of American elites, see **Steve Fraser and Gary Gerstle, eds.,** *Ruling America: Wealth and Power in a Democracy* (2005). For an excellent overview concerning immigration, consult **Roger Daniels,** *Coming to America: A History of Immigration and Ethnicity in American Life* (2002). The best single-volume history of eastern and southern European immigrants during this period is **John Bodnar,** *The Transplanted: A History of Immigration* (1985). For an innovative account of European immigrants' encounters with racial patterns in the United States, see **Matthew Frye Jacobson,** *Whiteness of a Different Color: European Americans and the Alchemy of Race* (1998).

The experience of Chinese immigrants during the period of American exclusion is discussed in **Erika Lee,** *At America's Gates: Chinese Immigration During the Exclusion Era, 1882–1943* (2003), while **Steven P. Erie,** *Rainbow's End: Irish Americans and the Dilemmas of Urban Machine Politics, 1840–1945* (1988), insightfully examines the benefits and costs of big-city machines. **David Montgomery,** *The Fall of the House of Labor, 1865–1925* (1987) and **Herbert Gutman,** *Work, Culture, and Society in Industrializing America* (1976) are essential sources on both immigrant and nonimmigrant labor during this period.

John Hope Franklin and Alfred A. Moss Jr., *From Slavery to Freedom: A History of Negro Americans,* 8th ed. (2000) offers a comprehensive account of African American life, while an important account of black female workers can be found in **Jacqueline Jones,** *Labor of Love, Labor of Sorrow: Black Women, Work and the Family from Slavery to the Present* (1985). On the rise of mass culture, see **David Nasaw,** *Going Out: The Rise and Fall of Public Amusements* (1993) and **Warren I. Susman,** *Culture as History: The Transformation of American Society in the Twentieth Century* (1984). On the new woman and feminism, consult **Nancy F. Cott,** *The Grounding of Modern Feminism* (1987) and **Christine Stansell,** *American Moderns: Bohemian New York and the Creation of a New Century* (2000).

Visit the Liberty Equality Power Companion Web site for resources specific to this textbook: http://www.thomsonedu.com/history/murrin

Also find self-tests and additional resources at ThomsonNOW. ThomsonNOW is an integrated online suite of services and resources with proven ease of use and efficient paths to success, delivering the results you want—NOW!

www.thomsonedu.com/login/

21

Progressivism

Progressivism was a reform movement that took its name from individuals who left the Republican Party in 1912 to join Theodore Roosevelt's new party, the Progressive Party. The term *progressive,* however, refers to a much larger and more varied group of reformers than those who gathered around Roosevelt in 1912.

As early as 1900, these reformers had set out to cleanse and reinvigorate an America whose politics and society they considered in decline. Progressives wanted to rid politics of corruption, tame the power of the "trusts," and, in the process, inject more liberty into American life. They fought against prostitution, gambling, drinking, and other forms of vice. They first appeared in municipal politics, organizing movements to oust crooked mayors and to break up local gas or streetcar monopolies. They carried their fights to the states and finally to the nation. Two presidents, Theodore Roosevelt and Woodrow Wilson, placed themselves at the head of this movement.

Progressivism was popular among a variety of groups who brought to the movement distinct, and often conflicting, aims. On one issue, however, most progressives agreed: the need for an activist government to right political, economic, and social wrongs. Some progressives wanted government to become active only long enough to clean up the political process, root out vice, upgrade the electorate, and break up trusts. These problems were so difficult to solve that many other progressives endorsed the notion of a permanently active government—with the power to tax income, regulate industry, protect consumers from fraud, empower workers, safeguard the environment, and provide social welfare. Many progressives, in other words, came to see the federal government as the institution best equipped to solve social problems.

Such positive attitudes toward government power marked an important change in American politics. Americans had long been suspicious of centralized government, viewing it as the enemy of liberty. The Populists had broken with that view (see chapter 19), but they had been defeated. The progressives had to build a new case for strong government as the protector of liberty and equality.

Progressivism and the Protestant Spirit

Focus Question
Which groups of Americans spearheaded the progressive movement?

CHRONOLOGY

1889	Hull House established
1890–1904	All ex-Confederate states pass laws designed to disenfranchise black voters • Virtually all states adopt the Australian (secret) ballot
1900	La Follette elected governor of Wisconsin • City commission plan introduced in Galveston, Texas
1901–14	More than 1,000 African Americans lynched
1901	Johnson elected reform mayor of Cleveland • McKinley assassinated; Roosevelt becomes president
1902	Direct primary introduced in Mississippi • Initiative and referendum introduced in Oregon • Roosevelt sides with workers in coal strike
1903	*McClure's Magazine* publishes Standard Oil exposé • Federal court dissolves Northern Security Company
1904	Roosevelt defeats Alton B. Parker for presidency
1905	National Forest Service established
1906	La Follette elected to U.S. Senate • Congress passes Hepburn Act • Upton Sinclair publishes *The Jungle* • Congress passes Pure Food and Drug Act and Meat Inspection Act
1907	Reformer Hughes elected New York governor • Financial panic shakes economy
1908	Taft defeats Bryan for presidency
1909	Congress passes Payne-Aldrich tariff bill
1910	Ballinger-Pinchot controversy • NAACP founded • Wilson elected governor of New Jersey
1911	National Urban League founded • City manager plan introduced in Sumter, South Carolina • Wisconsin Industrial Commission established
1912	Roosevelt forms Progressive Party • Wilson defeats Roosevelt, Taft, and Debs for presidency
1913	16th and 17th Amendments ratified • Congress passes Underwood-Simmons Tariff • Congress establishes Federal Reserve
1914	Congress establishes Federal Trade Commission • Congress passes Clayton Antitrust Act
1916	Louis Brandeis appointed to Supreme Court • Kern-McGillicuddy Act, Keating-Owen Act, and Adamson Act passed • National Park Service formed • National Women's Party founded
1919	18th Amendment ratified
1920	19th Amendment ratified

Progressivism emerged first and most strongly among young, mainly Protestant, middle-class Americans who felt alienated from their society. Many had been raised in devout Protestant homes in which religious conviction had often been a spur to social action. They were expected to become ministers or missionaries or to serve their church in some other way. They had abandoned this path, but they never lost their zeal for righting moral wrongs and for uplifting the human spirit. They were distressed by the immorality and corruption in American politics and by the gap that separated rich from poor. They became, in the words of one historian, "ministers of reform."

Other Protestant reformers retained their faith. This was true of William Jennings Bryan, the former Populist leader who became an ardent progressive and evangelical. Throughout his political career, Bryan always insisted that Christian piety and American democracy were integrally related. Billy Sunday, a former major league baseball player who became the most theatrical evangelical preacher of his day, elevated opposition to saloons and the "liquor trust" into a righteous crusade. And Walter Rauschenbusch led a movement known as the Social Gospel, which emphasized the duty of Christians to work for the social good.

Protestants formed a large and diverse population, sizable sections of which showed little interest in reform. Thus it is important to identify smaller and more cohesive groups of reformers. Of the many that arose, three were of particular importance, especially in the early years: investigative journalists, who were called **"muckrakers"**; the founders and supporters of settlement houses; and socialists.

Muckrakers, Magazines, and the Turn toward "Realism"

The term *muckraker* was coined by Theodore Roosevelt, who had intended it as a criticism of newspaper and magazine reporters who, for no purpose other than monetary reward, wrote stories about scandalous situations. But the label became a badge of honor among journalists who were committed to exposing repugnant aspects of American life. During the first decade of the 20th century, they presented the public with one startling revelation after another. Ida Tarbell revealed the shady practices by which John D. Rockefeller had transformed his Standard Oil Company into a monopoly. Lincoln Steffens unraveled the webs of bribery and corruption that were strangling local governments in the nation's cities. George Kibbe Turner documented the extent of prostitution and family disintegration in the ethnic ghettos of those cities. These muckrakers wanted to shock the public into recognizing the shameful state of political, economic, and social affairs and to prompt "the people" to take action.

The tradition of investigative journalism reached back at least to the 1870s, when newspaper and magazine writers exposed the corrupt practices of New York City's Boss Tweed and his Tammany Hall machine. The 20th-century rise of the muckrakers reflected two factors, one economic—expanded newspaper and magazine circulation—and the other intellectual—increased interest in **"realism."** Together they transformed investigative reporting into something of national importance.

From 1870 to 1909, daily newspapers rose in number from 574 to 2,600, and their circulation increased from less than 3 million to more than 24 million. During the first decade of the 20th century, the magazine revolution of the 1880s and 1890s (see chapter 19) accelerated. Cheap, 10-cent periodicals such as *McClure's Magazine* and *Ladies' Home Journal,* with circulations of 400,000 to 1 million, began to displace genteel and relatively

Culver Pictures

Pioneering Investigative Journalism   This Christmas 1903 issue of *McClure's Magazine* featured the second part of Ida Tarbell's exposé of John D. Rockefeller's business practices. Tarbell's revelations were regarded as sensational, and they convinced many middle-class Americans of the need for economic and political reform.

expensive 35-cent publications such as *Harper's* and *The Atlantic Monthly*. The expanded readership brought journalists considerably more money and prestige and attracted many talented and ambitious men and women to the profession. Wider circulation also made magazine publishers more receptive to stories—particularly sensational ones about ill-gotten economic power, government corruption, and urban vice—that might appeal to their expanded readership.

The American middle class's growing intellectual interest in "realism" also favored the muckrakers. "Realism" was a way of thinking that prized detachment, objectivity, and skepticism. Those who embraced it pointed out that constitutional theory, with its emphasis on citizenship, elections, and democratic procedures, had little to do with the way government in the United States actually worked. What could one learn about bosses, machines, and graft from studying the Constitution? There was also a sense that the nation's glorification of the "self-made man" and of "individualism" was preventing Americans from coping effectively with large-scale organizations—corporations, banks, labor unions—and their sudden centrality to the nation's economy and to society. The realists, finally, criticized the tendency, which was prevalent among American writers and artists, to emulate European styles, and they called on them to pioneer new styles that would be better able to capture American life and thought.

By the first decade of the 20th century, intellectuals and artists of all sorts—philosophers John Dewey and William James; social scientists Thorstein Veblen and Charles Beard; novelists Frank Norris, Theodore Dreiser, and Upton Sinclair; painters John Sloan, George Bellows, and other members of the "Ashcan School"; photographers Jacob Riis and Lewis Hine; architects Louis Sullivan and Frank Lloyd Wright; jurists Oliver Wendell Holmes and Louis Brandeis—were attempting to create truer, more realistic ways of representing and analyzing American society. Many of them were inspired by the work of investigative journalists, and some had been newspapermen. Years of firsthand observation enabled them to describe American society as it "truly was." They brought shadowy figures vividly to life. They pictured for Americans the captain of industry who ruthlessly destroyed his competitors; the con artist who tricked young people new to city life; the innocent immigrant girl who fell prey to the white slave traders; the corrupt policeman under whose protection urban vice flourished.

A large middle class, uneasy about the state of American society, applauded the muckrakers for telling these stories and became interested in reform. Members of this class pressured city and state governments to send crooked government officials to jail and to stamp out the sources of corruption and vice. Between 1902 and 1916, more than 100 cities launched investigations of the prostitution trade. At the federal level, all three branches of government felt compelled to address the question of "the trusts"—the concentration of power in the hands of a few industrialists and financiers. Progressivism began to crystallize into a political movement centered on the abuses the muckrakers had exposed.

Settlement Houses and Women's Activism

Established by middle-class reformers, settlement houses were intended to help the largely immigrant urban poor cope with the harsh conditions of city life. Much of the inspiration for settlement houses came from young, college-educated, Protestant women who were from comfortable but not particularly wealthy backgrounds. Some had imbibed a commitment to social justice from parents and grandparents who had fought to abolish slavery. Highly educated, talented, and sensitive to social injustice, they rebelled against being relegated solely to the roles of wife and mother and sought to assert their independence in socially useful ways.

Women Enrolled in Institutions of Higher Education, 1870–1930

Year	Women's Colleges (thousands of students)	Coed Institutions (thousands of students)	Total (thousands of students)	Percentage of All Students Enrolled
1870	6.5	4.6	11.1	21.0%
1880	15.7	23.9	39.6	33.4
1890	16.8	39.5	56.3	35.9
1900	24.4	61.0	85.4	36.8
1910	34.1	106.5	140.6	39.6
1920	52.9	230.0	282.9	47.3
1930	82.1	398.7	480.8	43.7

Source: From Mabel Newcomer, *A Century of Higher Education for American Women* (New York: Harper and Row, 1959), p. 46.

Hull House

Jane Addams and Ellen Gates Starr established the nation's first settlement house, in Chicago, in 1889. The two women had been inspired by a visit the year before to London's Toynbee Hall, where a small group of middle-class men had been living and working with that city's poor since 1884. Addams and Starr bought a decaying mansion that had once been the country home of a prominent Chicagoan, Charles J. Hull. By 1889, "**Hull House**" stood amidst factories, churches, saloons, and tenements inhabited by poor, largely foreign-born working-class families.

Addams quickly emerged as the guiding spirit of Hull House. She moved into the building and demanded that all who worked there do the same. She and Starr enlisted extraordinary women such as Florence Kelley, Alice Hamilton, and Julia Lathrop. They set up a nursery for the children of working mothers, a penny savings bank, and an employment bureau, soon followed by a baby clinic, a neighborhood playground, and social clubs. Determined to minister to cultural as well as economic needs, Hull House sponsored an orchestra, reading groups, and a lecture series. Members of Chicago's widening circle of reform-minded intellectuals, artists, and politicians contributed their energies to the enterprise. John Dewey taught philosophy and Frank Lloyd Wright lectured on architecture. Clarence Darrow, the workingman's lawyer, and Henry Demarest Lloyd, Chicago's radical muckraker, spent considerable time at Hull House. In 1893, Illinois Governor John P. Altgeld named Hull House worker Florence Kelley as the state's chief factory inspector. Her investigations led to Illinois's first factory law, which prohibited child labor, limited the employment of women to eight hours a day, and authorized the state to hire inspectors to enforce the law.

The Hull House activists seemed to have unlimited energy, imagination, and commitment. Julia Lathrop used her appointment to the State Board of Charities to agitate for

Brown Brothers

Jane Addams   The founder of the settlement house movement, Addams was the most famous woman reformer of the progressive era. This photograph dates from the 1890s or 1900s, Hull House's formative period.

improvements in the care of the poor, the handicapped, and the delinquent. With Edith Abbott and Sophonisba Breckinridge, she established the Department of Social Research at the University of Chicago (which would evolve into the nation's first school of social work). Alice Hamilton, who had overcome gender discrimination to become a doctor, pioneered in the field of public health.

The Hull House leaders did not command the instant fame accorded the muckrakers. Nevertheless, they were steadily drawn into the public arena. Thousands of women across the country were inspired to build their own settlement houses on the Hull House model (eventually more than 400 settlement houses would open nationwide). By 1910, Jane Addams had become one of the nation's most famous women. She and other settlement house workers played a critical role in fashioning the progressive agenda and in drafting pieces of progressive legislation.

The Cultural Conservatism of Progressive Reformers

In general, settlement house workers were more sympathetic toward the poor, the illiterate, and the downtrodden than the muckrakers were. Although she disapproved of machine politics, Jane Addams saw firsthand the benefits that machine politicians delivered to their constituents. She respected the cultural inheritance of the immigrants and admired their resourcefulness. Although she wanted them to become Americans, she encouraged them to integrate their "immigrant gifts" into their new identities. Those attitudes were more liberal than those of other reformers, who considered many immigrants to be culturally, even racially, inferior.

But there were limits even to Addams's sympathy for the immigrants. In particular, she disapproved of the new working-class entertainments that gave adolescents extensive and unregulated opportunities for intimate association. She was also troubled by the emerging sexual revolution (see chapter 20). Addams tended to equate female sexuality with prostitution, and she joined many other women reformers in a campaign to suppress both. Addams and others had identified a serious problem in American cities, where significant numbers of immigrant and rural women new to urban life were lured into prostitution or chose it as a job preferable to 65 poorly paid hours per week in a sweatshop.

The reformers' zeal on this matter, however, exaggerated the dimensions of the problem and led to some questionable legislation, such as the Mann Act (1910), which made it illegal to transport a woman across state lines "for immoral purposes." If this law permitted the prosecution of true traffickers in women, it also allowed the government to interfere in the private sexual relations of consenting adults. This is what happened in the case of Jack Johnson, the African American heavyweight boxing champion, who was arrested and convicted for "transporting" his white secretary, Lucy Cameron, across state lines. That Johnson's and Cameron's relationship was consensual and would culminate in marriage did not deter the authorities, who wanted to punish Johnson for his dominance of white boxers and his relationship with a white woman.

The cultural conservatism evident in the attitudes of Jane Addams and others on female sexuality also emerged in their attitudes toward alcohol. Drinking rivaled prostitution as a problem in poor, working-class areas. Many men wasted their hard-earned money on drinks at the local saloon, a drain on meager family resources that created tension between these men and their wives. Domestic fights and family violence sometimes ensued. Settlement house workers were well aware of the ill effects of alcoholism (250 saloons did business in Chicago's 19th Ward alone) and sought to combat it. They called on working people to

Jack Johnson, Heavyweight Boxing Champion   Johnson angered whites in America both for defeating white boxers in the ring and for dating and marrying white women. The identity of Johnson's female companion in this photograph is not known.

refrain from drink and pushed legislation that would shut down the saloons. The progressives joined forces with the Women's Christian Temperance Union (245,000 members strong by 1911) and the Anti-Saloon League. By 1916, through their collective efforts, these groups had won prohibition of the sale and manufacture of alcoholic beverages in 16 states. In 1919, their crowning achievement was the 18th Amendment to the U.S. Constitution, making prohibition the law of the land (see chapter 23).

In depicting alcohol and saloons as unmitigated evils, however, the prohibition movement ignored the role saloons played in ethnic, working-class communities. On Chicago's South Side, for example, saloons provided thousands of workers with the only decent place to eat lunch. The meatpacking plants where they labored had no cafeterias, and few workers could stomach eating their lunch where animals were slaughtered, dressed, and packed. Some saloons catered to particular ethnic groups: They served traditional foods and drinks, provided meeting space for fraternal organizations, and offered camaraderie to men longing to speak in their native tongue. Saloonkeepers sometimes functioned as informal bankers, cashing checks and making small loans. Not surprisingly, many immigrants shunned the prohibition movement. They had no interest in being "uplifted" and "reformed" in this way. Here was a gulf separating the immigrant masses from the Protestant middle class that even compassionate reformers such as Jane Addams could not bridge.

A Nation of Clubwomen

Settlement house workers comprised only one part of a vast network of female reformers. Hundreds of thousands of women belonged to local women's clubs. Conceived in the 1860s and 1870s as self-help organizations in which women would be encouraged to sharpen their minds, refine their domestic skills, and strengthen their moral faculties (see chapter 19), these clubs, by 1900, began taking on tasks of social reform. Clubwomen typically focused their energies on improving schools, building libraries and playgrounds, expanding educational and vocational opportunities for girls, and securing fire and sanitation codes for tenement houses. In so doing, they made traditional female concerns—the nurturing and education of children, the care of the home—questions of public policy.

Clubwomen rose to prominence in black communities, too, and addressed similar sorts of issues; on matters of sexuality and alcohol, they often shared the conservative sentiments of their white counterparts. Some groups of black clubwomen ventured into community affairs more boldly than their white counterparts, however, especially in southern states, where black men were being stripped of the right to vote, to serve on juries, and to hold political office. Whites were prepared to punish any African American, male or female, who showed too much initiative or was thought to be challenging the principles of white supremacy. Even so, many black female activists persevered in the face of such threats, determined to provide leadership in their communities and voice their people's concerns.

Socialism and Progressivism

Issues such as women's sexuality and men's alcoholism drew progressives in a conservative direction, but other issues drew them to socialism. In the early 20th century, socialism stood for the transfer of control over big businesses from the capitalists who owned them to the laboring masses who worked in them. Socialists believed that such a transfer, usually defined in terms of government ownership and operation of corporations, would make it impossible for wealthy elites to control society.

The Socialist Party of America, founded in 1901, became a political force during the first 16 years of the century, and socialist ideas influenced progressivism. In 1912, at the peak of its influence, the Socialist Party enrolled more than 115,000 members. Its presidential candidate, the charismatic **Eugene Victor Debs** of Terre Haute, Indiana, attracted almost a million votes—6 percent of the total votes cast that year. In that same year, 1,200 Socialists held elective office in 340 different municipalities. Of these, 79 were mayors of cities as geographically and demographically diverse as Schenectady, New York; Milwaukee, Wisconsin; Butte, Montana; and Berkeley, California. More than 300 newspapers and periodicals, with a combined circulation exceeding 2 million, spread the socialist gospel. The most important socialist publication was *Appeal to Reason,* published by Julius Wayland from Kansas and sent out each week to 750,000 subscribers. In 1905, Wayland published, in serial form, a novel by an obscure muckraker named Upton Sinclair, which depicted the scandalous working conditions in Chicago's meatpacking industry. When it was later published in book form in 1906, *The Jungle* created such an outcry that the federal government was forced to regulate the meat industry.

The Many Faces of Socialism

Socialists came in many varieties. In Milwaukee, they consisted of predominantly German working-class immigrants and their descendants; in New York City, their numbers were strongest among Jewish immigrants from Eastern Europe. In the Southwest, tens of thousands of disgruntled native-born farmers who had been Populists in the 1890s now flocked to the socialist banner. In Oklahoma alone, these erstwhile Populists were numerous enough by 1912 to support 11 socialist weeklies. In that same year, Oklahoma voters gave a higher percentage of their votes, more than 16 percent, to the Socialist candidate Debs than did the voters of any other state. In the West, socialism was popular among miners, timber cutters, and others who labored in isolated areas where industrialists possessed extraordinary power over work, politics, and community life. These radicals gravitated to the militant labor union, the Industrial Workers of the World (IWW) (see chapter 20), which found a home in the Socialist Party from 1905 to 1913.

Socialists differed from each other not only in their occupations and ethnic origins but also in their politics. The IWW was the most radical socialist group, with its incessant calls for revolution. By contrast, mainstream socialism, as articulated by Debs, was more respectful of American political, cultural, and religious traditions. Mainstream socialists saw themselves as the saviors rather than the destroyers of the American republic—as the true heirs of Thomas Jefferson. Their confidence that the nation could be redeemed through conventional politics—through the election of Debs as president—is evidence of their affection for American democracy. And their faith in redemption reveals the degree to which Protestant religious beliefs underlay their quest for social justice and what they called a "cooperative commonwealth." Evolutionary socialists, led by Victor Berger of Milwaukee, abandoned talk of revolution altogether and chose instead an aggressive brand of reform politics. They were dubbed **"gas and water socialists"** because of their interest in improving city services.

These differences would, after 1912, fragment the socialist movement. For a decade or so, however, these divergent groups managed to coexist in a single political party, thanks, largely, to the leadership of Debs. When he was released from a Chicago jail in 1895 after serving time for his role in the strike against the Pullman Company (see chapter 19), Debs declared to a gathering of 100,000 admirers: "Manifestly the spirit of '76 still survives. The fires of liberty and noble aspirations are not yet extinguished. . . . The vindication and glorification of American principles of government, as proclaimed to the world in the Declaration of Independence, is the high purpose of this convocation."

Socialists and Progressives

Debs's speeches both attracted and disturbed progressives. On the one hand, he spoke compellingly about the dangers of unregulated capitalism and excessively concentrated wealth, both progressive concerns. His confidence that a strong state could bring the economic system under control mirrored the progressives' own faith in the positive uses of government. Progressives often worked hand-in-hand with socialists to win economic and political reforms, especially at the municipal and state levels, and many intellectuals and reformers easily moved back and forth between socialism and progressivism. Florence Kelley, Hull House reformer and Illinois factory inspector, was one such person; Clarence Darrow, a Chicago trial lawyer who successfully defended the IWW's William Haywood in 1907 against charges that he had murdered a former Idaho governor, was another. Walter Lippmann, who would become a close adviser to President Wilson during the First World War, began his political career in 1912 as an assistant to the Socialist mayor of Schenectady. Several of the era's most prominent intellectuals, including John Dewey, Richard Ely, and Thorstein Veblen, also traveled back and forth between the socialist and progressive camps. So did Helen Keller, the country's leading spokesperson for the disabled.

On the other hand, Debs's talk of revolution scared progressives, as did his efforts to organize a working-class political movement independent of middle-class involvement or control. Although progressives wanted to tame capitalism, they stopped short of wanting to eliminate it. They wanted to improve working and living conditions for the masses but not cede political control to them. The progressives hoped to offer a political program with enough socialist elements to counter the appeal of Debs's more radical movement. In this, they were successful.

Municipal Reform

Progressive-era reform battles first erupted over control of municipal transportation networks and utilities. Private corporations typically owned and operated street railways and electrical and gas systems. Many of the corporations used their monopoly power to charge exorbitant fares and rates, and they often won that power by bribing city officials who belonged to one of the political machines. Corporations achieved generous reductions in real estate taxes in the same way.

The attack on private utilities and their protectors in city government gained momentum in the mid-1890s. In Detroit, reform-minded Mayor Hazen S. Pingree led successful fights to control the city's gas, telephone, and trolley companies. In Chicago in 1896 and 1897, a group of middle-class reformers ousted a corrupt city council and elected a mayor, Carter Harrison, Jr., who promised to protect Chicago's streetcar riders from exploitation. In Cleveland, the crusading reformer Tom Johnson won election as mayor in 1901, curbed the power of the streetcar interests, and brought honest and efficient government to the city.

Occasionally, a reform politician of Johnson's caliber would rise to power through one of the regular political parties. But this path to power was a difficult one, especially in cities where the political parties were controlled by machines. Consequently, progressives worked for reforms that would strip the parties of their power. Two of their favorite reforms were the city commission and the city manager forms of government.

The City Commission Plan

First introduced in Galveston, Texas, in 1900, in the wake of a devastating tidal wave, the city commission shifted municipal power from the mayor and his aldermen to five city commissioners, each responsible for a different department of city government. In Galveston and elsewhere, the impetus for this reform came from civic-minded businessmen who were determined to rebuild government on the same principles of efficient and scientific management that had energized the private sector. The results were often impressive. The Galveston commissioners restored the city's credit after a brush with bankruptcy, improved the city's harbor, and built a massive seawall to protect the city from future floods. They accomplished all of this on budgets that had been cut by one-third. In Houston, Texas; Des Moines, Iowa; Dayton, Ohio; Oakland, California; and elsewhere, city commissioners similarly improved urban infrastructures, expanded city services, and strengthened the financial health of the cities. Many commissions established publicly owned utilities. By 1913, more than 300 cities, most of them small to middling in size, had adopted the city commission plan.

The City Manager Plan

The city commission system did not always work to perfection, however. Sometimes the commissioners used their position to reward electoral supporters with jobs and contracts; other times, they pursued power and prestige for their respective departments. The city manager plan was meant to overcome such problems. Under this plan, the commissioners continued to set policy, but policy implementation now rested with a "chief executive." This official, who was not elected but appointed by the commissioners, would curtail rivalries among commissioners and ensure that no outside influences interfered with the impartial, businesslike management of the city. The job of city manager was explicitly modeled after that of a corporation executive. First introduced in Sumter, South Carolina, in 1911 and then in Dayton, Ohio, in 1913, by 1919 the city manager plan had spread to 130 cities.

The Costs of Reform

Although these reforms limited corruption and improved services, they were not universally popular. Poor and minority voters, in particular, found that their influence in local affairs was weakened by the shift to city commissioners and city managers. Previously, candidates for municipal office (other than the mayor) competed in ward elections rather than in citywide elections. Voters in working-class wards commonly elected workingmen to represent them, and voters in immigrant wards made sure that fellow ethnics represented their interests on city councils. Citywide elections diluted the strength of these constituencies. Candidates from poor districts often lacked the money needed to mount a citywide campaign, and they were further hampered by the nonpartisan nature of such elections. Denied the support of a political party or platform, they had to make themselves personally known to voters throughout the city. That was a much easier task for the city's "leading citizens"—manufacturers, merchants, and lawyers—than it was for workingmen. In Dayton, the percentage of citizens voting Socialist rose from 25 percent to 44 percent in the years following the introduction of the commission manager system, but the number of Socialists elected to office declined from five to zero. Progressive political reforms thus frequently reduced the influence of radicals, minorities, and the poor in elections.

Political Reform in the States

Focus Question
How did progressive reformers hope to create a "responsible" and "virtuous" electorate? What were the consequences of their reforms?

As at the local level, political parties at the state level were often dominated by corrupt politicians who did the bidding of powerful private lobbies. In New Jersey in 1903, for example, industrial and financial interests, working through the Republican Party machine, controlled numerous appointments to state government, including the chief justice of the state supreme court, the attorney general, and the commissioner of banking and insurance. Such webs of influence ensured that New Jersey would provide large corporations such as the railroads with favorable political and economic legislation.

Restoring Sovereignty to "the People"

Progressives introduced reforms designed to undermine the power of party bosses, restore sovereignty to "the people," and encourage honest, talented individuals to enter politics. One such reform was the direct primary, a mechanism that enabled voters, rather than party bosses, to choose party candidates. Mississippi introduced this reform in 1902 and Wisconsin in 1903. By 1916, all but three states had adopted the direct primary. Closely related was a movement to strip state legislatures of their power to choose U.S. senators. State after state enacted legislation that permitted voters to choose Senate candidates in primary elections. In 1912, a reluctant U.S. Senate was obliged to approve the 17th Amendment to the Constitution, mandating the direct election of senators. The state legislatures ratified this amendment in 1913.

Populists had first proposed direct election of U.S. senators in the 1890s; they also proposed the **initiative** and the **referendum,** both of which were adopted first by Oregon in 1902 and then by 18 other states between 1902 and 1915. The initiative allowed reformers to put legislative proposals before voters in general elections without having to wait for state legislatures to act. The referendum gave voters the right in general elections to repeal an unpopular act that a state legislature had passed. Less widely adopted but important nevertheless was the **recall,** a device that allowed voters to remove from office any public servant who had betrayed his trust. As a further control over the behavior of elected officials, numerous states enacted laws that regulated corporate campaign contributions and restricted lobbying activities in state legislatures. These laws neither eliminated corporate privilege nor destroyed the power of machine politicians. Nevertheless, they made politics more honest and strengthened the influence of ordinary voters.

Creating a Virtuous Electorate

Progressive reformers focused as well on creating a responsible electorate that understood the importance of the vote and that resisted efforts to manipulate elections. To create this ideal electorate, reformers had to see to it that all of those citizens who were deemed virtuous could cast their votes free of coercion and intimidation. At the same time, reformers sought to disenfranchise citizens who were considered irresponsible and corruptible. In pursuing these goals, progressives substantially altered the composition of the electorate and strengthened government regulation of voting. The results were contradictory. On the one hand, progressives enlarged the electorate by extending the right to vote to women; on the other hand, they either initiated or tolerated laws that barred large numbers of minority and poor voters from the polls.

The Australian Ballot

Government regulation of voting had begun in the 1890s, when virtually every state adopted the **Australian,** or secret, **ballot.** This reform required voters to vote in private rather than in public. It also required the government, rather than political parties, to print the ballots and supervise the voting. Before this time, each political party had printed its own ballot with only its candidates listed. At election time, each party mobilized its loyal supporters. Party workers offered liquor, free meals, and other bribes to entice voters to the polls and to "persuade" them to cast the party ballot. Because the ballots were cast in public, few voters who had accepted gifts of liquor and food dared to cross watchful party officials. Critics argued that the system corrupted the electoral process. They also pointed out that it made "ticketsplitting"—dividing one's vote between candidates of two or more parties—virtually impossible.

The Australian ballot solved these problems. Although it predated progressivism, it embodied the progressives' determination to use government power to encourage citizens to cast their votes responsibly and wisely.

Personal Registration Laws

That same determination was apparent in the progressives' support for the personal registration laws that virtually every state passed between 1890 and 1920. These laws allowed prospective voters to register to vote only if they appeared at a designated government office with proper identification. Frequently, these laws also mandated a certain period of residence in the state before registration and a certain interval between registration and actual voting.

Personal registration laws were meant to disenfranchise citizens who showed no interest in voting until election day, when a party worker arrived with a few dollars and offered a free ride to the polls. However, they also excluded many hardworking, responsible, poor people who wanted to vote but had failed to register, either because their work schedules made it impossible or because they were intimidated by the complex regulations. The laws were particularly frustrating for immigrants with limited knowledge of American government and of the English language.

Disenfranchisement

Progressives also promoted election laws expressly designed to keep noncitizen immigrants from voting. In the 1880s, 18 states had passed laws allowing immigrants to vote without first becoming citizens. Progressives reversed this trend. At the same time, the newly formed Bureau of Immigration and Naturalization (1906) made it more difficult to become a citizen. Applicants for citizenship now had to appear before a judge, who interrogated them, in the English language, on American history and civics. In addition, immigrants were required to provide two witnesses to vouch for their "moral character" and their "attachment to the principles of the Constitution." Finally, immigrants had to swear (and, if necessary, prove) that they were not anarchists or polygamists and that they had resided continuously in the United States for five years.

Most progressives defended the new rigor of the process. U.S. citizenship, they believed, carried responsibilities; it was not to be bestowed lightly. This position was understandable, given the electoral abuses progressives had exposed. Nevertheless, the reforms also denied the vote to a large proportion of the population. In cities and towns where immigrants dominated the workforce, the numbers of registered voters fell steeply. Nowhere was exclusion more startling than in the South, where between 1890 and 1904, every ex-Confederate state passed laws designed to strip blacks of their right to vote. Because laws explicitly barring blacks from voting would have violated the 15th Amendment, this exclusion had to be accomplished indirectly—through literacy tests, property qualifications, and poll taxes mandated by the legislatures of the ex-Confederate states. Any citizen who failed a reading test, or who could not sign his name, or who did not own a minimum amount of property, or who could not pay a poll tax, lost his right to vote. The citizens who failed these tests most frequently were blacks—who formed the poorest and least educated segment of the southern population—but a large portion of the region's poor whites also failed the tests. The effects of **disenfranchisement** were stark. In 1900, only 1,300 blacks voted in Mississippi elections, down from 130,000 in the 1870s. Virginia's voter turnout dropped from 60 percent of adult men (white and black) in 1900 to 28 percent in 1904.

Many progressives in the North, such as Governor Robert La Follette of Wisconsin, criticized southern disenfranchisement. Some, including Jane Addams and John Dewey, joined in 1910 with W. E. B. Du Bois and other black reformers to found the National Association for the Advancement of Colored People (NAACP), an interracial political organization that made black equality its primary goal. In the South, however, white progressives rarely challenged disenfranchisement, and most had little difficulty

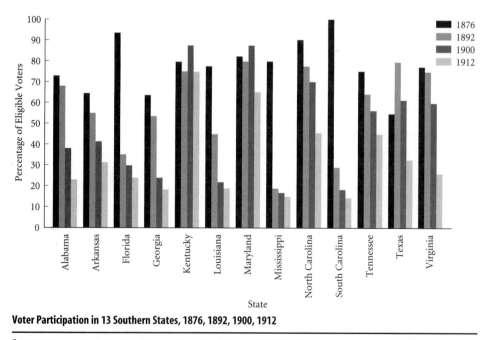

Voter Participation in 13 Southern States, 1876, 1892, 1900, 1912

Source: Data from *Historical Statistics of the United States, Colonial Times to 1970* (White Plains, N.Y.: Kraus International, 1989).

justifying it with progressive ideology. Because progressives everywhere considered the right to vote a precious gift granted only to those who could handle its responsibilities, they equally believed that it must be withheld from people who were deemed racially or culturally unfit. Progressives in the North excluded many immigrants on just those grounds. Progressives in the South saw the disenfranchisement of African Americans in the same light.

Disillusionment with the Electorate

In the process of identifying those groups "unfit" to hold the franchise, some progressives soured on the electoral process altogether. The more they looked for rational and virtuous voters, the fewer they found. In *Drift and Mastery* (1914), Walter Lippmann argued that ordinary people had been overwhelmed by industrial and social changes. Because these changes seemed beyond their comprehension or control, they "drifted," unable to "master" the circumstances of modern life or take charge of their own destiny. Lippmann did not suggest that such ordinary people should be barred from voting, but he did argue that more political responsibility should rest with appointed officials who possessed the training and knowledge necessary to make government effective and just. The growing disillusionment with the electorate, in combination with intensifying restrictions on the franchise, created an environment in which fewer and fewer Americans actually went to the polls. Voting participation rates fell from 79 percent in 1896 to only 49 percent in 1920.

Woman Suffrage

The major exception to this trend was the enfranchisement of women. This momentous reform was adopted by several states during the 1890s and the first two decades of the 20th century and became federal law with the ratification of the 19th Amendment to the Constitution in 1920.

Launched in 1848 at the famous Seneca Falls convention (see chapter 12), the women's rights movement floundered in the 1870s and 1880s. In 1890, suffragists came together in a new organization, the **National American Woman Suffrage Association** (NAWSA), led by Elizabeth Cady Stanton and Susan B. Anthony. Thousands of young, college-educated women campaigned door-to-door, held impromptu rallies, and pressured state legislators.

Wyoming, which attained statehood in 1890, became the first state to grant women the right to vote, followed in 1893 by Colorado and in 1896 by Idaho and Utah. The main reason for success in these sparsely populated western states was not egalitarianism but rather the conviction that women's supposedly gentler and more nurturing nature would tame and civilize the men who had populated the frontier.

This notion reflected a subtle but important change in the suffrage movement. Earlier generations had insisted that women were fundamentally equal to men, but the new suffragists argued that women were different from men. Women, they stressed, possessed a moral sense and a nurturing quality that men lacked. Consequently, they understood the civic obligations implied by the franchise and could be trusted to vote virtuously. Their votes would hasten to completion the progressive task of cleansing the political process of corruption. Their experience as mothers and household managers, moreover, would enable them to guide local and state governments in efforts to improve education, sanitation, family wholesomeness, and the condition of women and children in the workforce. In other words, the enfranchisement of women would enhance the quality of both public and private life without insisting they were the equals of men in all respects.

Suffragists were slow to ally themselves with blacks, Asians, and other disenfranchised groups. In fact, many suffragists, especially those in the South and West, opposed the franchise for Americans of color. They, like their male counterparts, believed that members of these groups lacked moral strength and thus did not deserve the right to vote. Unlike the suffrage pioneers of the 1840s and 1850s, many progressive-era suffragists were little troubled by racial discrimination and injustice. **(See Map 21.1, Woman Suffrage Before 1920, in the color insert following page 816.)**

Washington, California, Kansas, Oregon, and Arizona followed the lead of the other western states by enfranchising women in the years from 1910 to 1912. After a series of setbacks in eastern and midwestern states, the movement regained momentum under the leadership of the strategically astute Carrie Chapman Catt, who became president of NAWSA in 1915 and successfully coordinated myriad grassroots campaigns. Equally important was Alice Paul, a radical who founded the Congressional Union in 1913 and later renamed it the National Woman's Party. Paul and her supporters focused their attention on the White House, picketing President Wilson's home 24 hours a day, brandishing large posters that chastised him for abandoning his democratic principles, and daring the police to arrest them. Several suffrage demonstrators were jailed, where they continued their protests by going on hunger strikes (refusing to eat). Aided by a heightened enthusiasm for democracy generated by America's participation in the First World War (see chapter 23), which generated a more positive popular response to Paul's tactics than might otherwise have been the case, the suffragists achieved their goal of universal woman suffrage in 1920.

Predictions that suffrage for women would radically alter politics turned out to be false. The political system was neither cleansed of corruption, nor did the government rush headlong to address the private needs of women and their families. Although the numbers of voters increased after 1920, voter participation rates continued to decline. Still, the extension of the vote to women, 144 years after the founding of the nation, was a major political achievement.

Economic and Social Reform in the States

In some states, progressive reform extended well beyond political parties and the electorate. Progressives also wanted to limit corporate power, strengthen organized labor, and offer social welfare protection to the weak. State governments were pressured into passing such legislation by progressive alliances of middle-class and working-class reformers and by dynamic state governors.

Robert La Follette and Wisconsin Progressivism

Nowhere did the progressives' campaign for social reform flourish as it did in Wisconsin. The movement arose first in the 1890s, in hundreds of Wisconsin cities and towns, as citizens began to mobilize against the state's corrupt Republican Party and the special privileges the party had granted to private utilities and railroads. These reform-minded citizens came from varied backgrounds. They were middle class and working class, urban and rural, male and female, intellectual and evangelical, Scandinavian Protestant and German Catholic. Wisconsin progressivism had already gained considerable momentum by 1897, when Robert La Follette assumed its leadership.

La Follette was born into a prosperous farming family in 1855. He entered politics as a Republican in the 1880s and embraced reform in the late 1890s. Elected governor in 1900, he secured for Wisconsin both a direct primary and a tax law that stripped the railroad corporations of tax exemptions they had long enjoyed. In 1905, he pushed through a civil service law mandating that every state employee meet a certain level of competence.

Wisconsin Historical Society

Robert La Follette, Wisconsin Progressive This photograph of La Follette campaigning in Wisconsin in 1897 captures the intensity and combativeness that "Fighting Bob" brought to progressivism.

A tireless campaigner and a spellbinding speaker, "Fighting Bob" won election to the U.S. Senate in 1906. Meanwhile, Wisconsin's advancing labor and socialist movements impelled progressive reformers to focus their legislative efforts on issues of corporate greed and social welfare. By 1910, reformers had passed state laws that regulated railroad and utility rates, instituted the nation's first state income tax, and provided workers with compensation for injuries, limitations on work hours, restrictions on child labor, and minimum wages for women.

Many of these laws were written by social scientists at the University of Wisconsin, with whom reformers had close ties. In the first decade of the 20th century, John R. Commons, University of Wisconsin economist, drafted Wisconsin's civil service and public utilities laws. In 1911, Commons designed and won legislative approval for the Wisconsin Industrial Commission, which brought together employers, trade unionists, and professionals and gave them broad powers to investigate and regulate relations between industry and labor throughout the state. Never before had a state government so plainly committed itself to the cause of industrial justice. For the first time, the rights of labor would be treated with the same respect as the rights of industry. Equally important was the responsibility the commission delegated to nonelected professionals: social scientists, lawyers, engineers, and others. These professionals, Wisconsin reformers believed, would succeed where political parties had failed—namely, in providing the public with expert and honest government.

The "Wisconsin idea" found quick adoption in Ohio, Indiana, New York, and Colorado; and in 1913, the federal government established its own Industrial Relations Commission and hired Commons to direct its investigative staff. In other areas, too, reformers began urging state and federal governments to shift the policy-making initiative away from political parties and toward administrative agencies staffed by professionals.

Progressive Reform in New York

New York was second only to Wisconsin in the vigor and breadth of its progressive movement. As in Wisconsin, New York progressives focused first on fighting political corruption. Revelations of close ties between leading Republican politicians and life insurance companies vaulted reform lawyer Charles Evans Hughes into the governor's mansion in 1907. Hughes immediately established several public service commissions to regulate railroads and utility companies. Also, as in Wisconsin, the labor movement exercised its influence. New York City garment workers struck and forced state legislators to regulate working conditions. With the establishment of the Factory Investigating Committee, New York, like Wisconsin, became a pioneer in labor and social welfare policy.

New York state legislators also faced pressure from middle-class reformers—settlement house workers such as Lillian Wald of the Henry Street Settlement and lawyers such as Louis Brandeis—who had become convinced of the need for new laws to protect the disadvantaged. This combined pressure from working-class and middle-class constituencies persuaded some state Democrats, including Assemblyman Alfred E. Smith and Senator Robert F. Wagner, to convert from machine to reform politics. Their appearance in the progressive ranks represented the arrival of a new reform sensibility. Wagner and Smith were both ethnic Catholics (Wagner was born in Germany, and Smith was the grandchild of Irish immigrants). They opposed prohibition, city commissions, voter registration laws, and other reforms whose intent seemed anti-immigrant or anti-Catholic. Meanwhile, they supported reforms meant to improve the working and living conditions of New York's urban poor. They agitated for a minimum wage, factory safety, workmen's compensation, the right of workers to join unions, and the regulation of excessively powerful corporations. Their participation in progressivism accelerated the movement's shift, first in New York and then elsewhere, away from a preoccupation with political parties and electorates and toward questions of economic justice and social welfare.

A Renewed Campaign for Civil Rights

Focus Question

How did W. E. B. Du Bois's approach to African American reform differ from that of Booker T. Washington?

At the same time that politicians such as Smith and Wagner introduced an ethnic sensibility into progressivism, a new generation of African American activists began insisting that the issue of racial equality also be placed on the reform agenda.

The Failure of Accommodationism

Booker T. Washington's message—that blacks should accept segregation and disenfranchisement as unavoidable and focus their energies instead on self-help and self-improvement— faced increasing criticism from black activists such as **W. E. B. Du Bois**, Ida B. Wells, Monroe Trotter, and others. Washington's accommodationist leadership (see chapter 18), in their eyes, brought southern blacks no reprieve from racism. More than 100 blacks had been lynched in 1900 alone; between 1901 and 1914, at least 1,000 others would be hanged.

Increasingly, unsubstantiated rumors of black assaults on whites became occasions for white mobs to rampage through black neighborhoods and indiscriminately destroy life and property. In 1908, a mob in Springfield, Illinois, attacked black businesses and individuals; a force of 5,000 state militia was required to restore order. The troops were too late, however, to stop the lynching of two innocent black men, one a successful barber and the other an 84-year-old man who had been married to a white woman for more than 30 years. There was a sad irony in the deaths of these African Americans. Murdered in Abraham Lincoln's hometown and within walking distance of his grave, they died just as black and white Americans everywhere were preparing to celebrate the centennial of the Great Emancipator's birth.

Booker T. Washington had long believed that blacks who educated themselves or who succeeded in business would be accepted as equals by whites. As Du Bois and other black militants observed, however, white rioters made no distinction between rich blacks and

Antiblack Violence   In 1913, a white mob destroyed a large part of the black section of Omaha, Nebraska. Race riots of this scale and devastation in early 20th-century America convinced many blacks that Booker T. Washington's message of accommodation was not working

poor, or between solid citizens and petty criminals. All that had seemed to matter was the color of one's skin. Similarly, many black militants knew from personal experience that individual accomplishment was not enough to overcome racial prejudice. Du Bois was a brilliant scholar who became, in 1899, the first African American to receive a doctorate from Harvard University. Had he been white, Du Bois would have been asked to teach at Harvard or another elite academic institution, but no prestigious white university, in the South or North, made him an offer.

From the Niagara Movement to the NAACP

Seeing no future in accommodation, Du Bois and other young black activists came together at Niagara Falls in 1905 to fashion a new political agenda. They demanded that African Americans regain the right to vote in states that had taken it away, that segregation be abolished, and that the many discriminatory barriers to black advancement be removed. They declared their commitment to freedom of speech, the brotherhood of all men, and respect for the working man. Although their numbers were small, the members of the so-called Niagara movement were inspired by the example of the antebellum

abolitionists. Meeting in Boston, Oberlin, and Harpers Ferry—all places of special significance to the abolitionist cause—they hoped to rekindle the militant, uncompromising
spirit of that earlier crusade (see chapters 12 and 14).

The 1908 Springfield riot had shaken many whites. Some, especially those already working for social and economic reform, now joined in common cause with the Niagara movement. Together, black and white activists planned a conference for Lincoln's birthday in
1909 to revive, in the words of author William English Walling, "the spirit of the abolitionists"
and to "treat the Negro on a plane of absolute political and social equality." Oswald Garrison
Villard, the grandson of William Lloyd Garrison, called on "all believers in democracy to join
in a National conference for the discussion of present evils, the voicing of protests, and the
renewal of the struggle for civil and political liberty." The conference brought together distinguished progressives, white and black, including Mary White Ovington, Jane Addams,
John Dewey, William Dean Howells, Ida B. Wells, and Du Bois. They drew up plans to establish an organization dedicated to fighting racial discrimination and prejudice. In May 1910,
the **National Association for the Advancement of Colored People** (NAACP) was officially
launched, with Moorfield Storey of Boston as president, Walling as chairman of the executive committee, and Du Bois as the director of publicity and research.

The formation of the NAACP marked the beginning of the modern civil-rights movement. The organization launched a magazine, *The Crisis,* edited by Du Bois, to publicize
and protest the lynchings, riots, and other abuses directed against black citizens. Equally
important was the Legal Redress Committee, which initiated lawsuits against city and state
governments for violating the constitutional rights of African Americans. The committee
scored its first major success in 1915, when the U.S. Supreme Court ruled that the so-
called grandfather clauses of the Oklahoma and Maryland constitutions violated the 15th
Amendment. (These clauses allowed poor, uneducated whites—but not poor, uneducated
blacks—to vote, even if they failed to pay their state's poll tax or to pass its literacy test,
by exempting the descendants of men who had voted before 1867.) NAACP lawyers won
again in 1917 when the Supreme Court declared unconstitutional a Louisville, Kentucky,
law that required all blacks to reside in predetermined parts of the city.

By 1914, the NAACP had enrolled thousands of members in scores of branches
throughout the United States. The organization's success generated other civil-rights
groups. The National Urban League, founded in 1911, worked to improve the economic
and social conditions of blacks in cities. It pressured employers to hire blacks, distributed
lists of available jobs and housing in African American communities, and developed social
programs to ease the adjustment of rural black migrants to city life.

Progress toward racial equality was sluggish. Attacking segregation and discrimination
through lawsuits was, by its nature, a slow strategy that would take decades to complete.
The growing membership of the NAACP, although impressive, was not large enough to
qualify it as a mass movement, and its interracial character made the organization seem dangerously radical to millions of whites. White NAACP leaders responded to this hostility by
limiting the number and power of African Americans who worked for the organization.

This policy, in turn, outraged black militants who argued that no civil-rights organization should be in the business of appeasing white racists.

Despite its limitations, the NAACP made significant strides. It gave Du Bois the security and visibility he needed to carry on his fight against Booker T. Washington's accommodationist philosophy. Even before his death in 1915, Washington's influence in black and white communities had receded. The NAACP, more than any other organization, helped resurrect the issue of racial equality at a time when many white Americans had accepted as normal the practices of racial segregation and discrimination.

National Reform

Focus Question
What were the key similarities and differences in the progressive politics of Theodore Roosevelt and Woodrow Wilson?

The more progressives focused on economic and social matters, the more they sought to increase their influence in national politics. Certain problems demanded national solutions. No patchwork of state regulations, for example, could adequately curtail the power of the trusts, protect workers, or monitor the quality of consumer goods. Moreover, state and federal courts often were hostile toward progressive goals: They repeatedly struck down as unconstitutional reform laws regulating working hours or setting minimum wages, on the grounds that they impinged on the freedom of contract and trade. A national progressive movement could force passage of laws that were less vulnerable to judicial veto or elect a president who could overhaul the federal judiciary with progressive-minded judges.

National leadership would not emerge from Congress. The Democratic Party had been scarred by the Populist challenge of the 1890s. Divided between the radical Bryanites and the conservative followers of Grover Cleveland, and consequently unable to speak with one voice on questions of social and economic policy, after 1896 the Democrats seemed incapable of winning a national election. The Republican Party was more unified and popular, but it was controlled by a conservative Old Guard. Led by Senator Nelson Aldrich of Rhode Island and House Speaker Joseph G. Cannon of Illinois, the Republican Old Guard was pro-business and devoted to a 19th-century style of backroom patronage. When Robert La Follette arrived in the Senate from Wisconsin in 1907, the Old Guard ostracized him as a dangerous radical.

National progressive leadership came from the executive rather than the legislative branch, and from two presidents in particular, Republican Theodore Roosevelt and Democrat Woodrow Wilson. These two presidents sponsored reforms that profoundly affected the lives of Americans and altered the nature of the American presidency.

The Roosevelt Presidency

When the Republican bosses chose Theodore Roosevelt as William McKinley's running mate in 1900, their purpose was more to remove this headstrong, unpredictable character from New York state politics than to groom him for national leadership. As governor of New York, Roosevelt had been a moderate reformer, but even his modest efforts to rid the state's Republican Party of corruption and to institute civil service reform were too much for the state party machine, led by Thomas C. Platt. Consigning Roosevelt to the vice presidency seemed a safe solution. McKinley was a young, vigorous politician, fully in control of his party and his presidency. Less than a year into his second term, in September 1901, McKinley was shot by an anarchist assassin. The president clung to life for nine days, and then died. Upon succeeding McKinley, Theodore Roosevelt, age 42, became the youngest chief executive in the nation's history.

Born to an aristocratic New York City family, Roosevelt nevertheless developed an uncommon affection for "the people." Asthmatic, sickly, and nearsighted as a boy, he remade himself into a vigorous adult. With an insatiable appetite for high-risk adventure—everything from "dude ranching" in the Dakota Territory, to big-game hunting in Africa, to wartime combat—he was also a voracious reader and an accomplished writer. Aggressive and swaggering in his public rhetoric, he was in private a skilled, patient negotiator. A believer in the superiority of the English-speaking peoples, he nevertheless appointed members of "inferior" races to important posts in his administration. Rarely has a president's personality so enthralled the American public. He is the only 20th-century president immortalized on Mount Rushmore.

Regulating the Trusts

Roosevelt quickly revealed his flair for the dramatic. In 1902, he ordered the Justice Department to prosecute the Northern Securities Company, a $400 million monopoly that controlled all railroad lines and traffic in the Northwest from Chicago to Washington state. Never before had an American president sought to use the Sherman Antitrust Act to break up a business monopoly. The news shocked J. P. Morgan, the banker who had brokered the deal that had created Northern Securities. Morgan rushed to the White House, where he is said to have told Roosevelt, "If we have done anything wrong, send your man to my man and they can fix it up." Roosevelt would have none of this "fixing." In 1903, a federal court ordered Northern Securities dissolved, and the U.S. Supreme Court upheld the decision the next year. Roosevelt was hailed as the nation's "trust-buster."

Roosevelt, however, did not believe in breaking up all, or even most, large corporations. Industrial concentration, he believed, brought the United States wealth, productivity, and a rising standard of living. Rather than bust them up, Roosevelt argued, government should regulate the industrial giants and punish those that used their power improperly. This new role would require the federal government to expand its powers. A newly fortified government—the centerpiece of a political program that Roosevelt would later call the **New Nationalism**—was to be led by a forceful president, who was willing to use all of the powers at his disposal to achieve prosperity and justice.

Toward a "Square Deal"

Roosevelt displayed his willingness to use government power to protect the economically weak in a 1902 coal miners' strike. Miners in the anthracite fields of eastern Pennsylvania wanted recognition for their union, the United Mine Workers (UMW). They also wanted a 10 percent to 20 percent increase in wages and an eight-hour day. When their employers, led by George F. Baer of the Reading Railroad, refused to negotiate, they went on strike. In October, the fifth month of the strike, Roosevelt summoned the mine owners and John Mitchell, the UMW president, to the White House. Baer expected Roosevelt to threaten the striking workers with arrest by federal troops if they failed to return to work. Instead, Roosevelt supported Mitchell's request for arbitration and warned the mine owners that if they refused to go along, 10,000 federal troops would seize their property. Stunned, the mine owners agreed to submit the dispute to arbitrators, who awarded the unionists a 10 percent wage increase and a nine-hour day.

The mere fact that the federal government had ordered employers to compromise with their workers carried great symbolic weight. Roosevelt enjoyed a surge of support from Americans convinced that he shared their dislike for ill-gotten wealth and privilege. He also raised the hopes of African Americans when, only a month into his presidency, he dined with Booker T. Washington at the White House and then shrugged off the protests of white southerners, who accused him of undermining segregation.

In his 1904 election campaign, Roosevelt promised that, if reelected, he would offer every American a "square deal." The slogan resonated with voters and helped carry Roosevelt to a victory (57 percent of the popular vote) over the conservative Democrat Alton B. Parker. To the surprise of many observers, Roosevelt had aligned the Republican Party with the cause of reform.

Expanding Government Power: The Economy

Emboldened by his victory, the president intensified his efforts to extend government regulation of economic affairs. His most important proposal was to give the government power to set railroad shipping rates and thereby to eliminate the industry's discriminatory marketing practices. The government, in theory, already possessed this power through the Interstate Commerce Commission (ICC), a regulatory body established by Congress in 1887, but the courts had so weakened the ICC's oversight and regulatory functions as to render it virtually powerless. Roosevelt achieved his goal in 1906, when Congress passed the Hepburn Act, which significantly increased the ICC's powers of rate review and enforcement. Roosevelt supported the Pure Food and Drug Act, passed by Congress that same year, which protected the public from fraudulently marketed and dangerous foods and medications. He also campaigned for the Meat Inspection Act (1906), which committed the government to monitoring the quality and safety of meat being sold to American consumers.

Expanding Government Power: The Environment

Roosevelt also did more than any previous president to extend federal control over the nation's physical environment. Roosevelt was not a "preservationist" in the manner of John Muir, founder of the Sierra Club, who insisted that the beauty of the land and the well-being of its wildlife should be protected from all human interference. Instead, Roosevelt viewed the wilderness as a place to live strenuously, to test oneself against the rough outdoors, and to match wits against strong and clever game. Roosevelt further believed that in the West— that land of ancient forests, lofty mountain peaks, and magnificent canyons—Americans could learn something important about their nation's roots and destiny. To preserve this West, Roosevelt oversaw the creation of 5 new national parks, 16 national monuments, and 53 wildlife reserves. The work of his administration led directly to the formation of the National Park Service in 1916.

Roosevelt also emerged a strong supporter of the **"conservationist"** movement. Conservationists cared little for national parks or grand canyons. They wanted to manage the environment, so as to ensure that the nation's resources were put to the most efficient economic use. Roosevelt shared the conservationists' belief that the plundering of western timberlands, grazing areas, water resources, and minerals had reached crisis proportions. Only broad regulatory controls would restore the West's economic potential.

To that end, Roosevelt appointed a Public Lands Commission in 1903 to survey public lands, inventory them, and establish permit systems to regulate the kinds and numbers of users. Soon after, the Departments of Interior and Agriculture placed certain western lands rich in natural resources and waterpower off-limits to agricultural users. Government officials also limited waterpower development by requiring companies to acquire permits and pay fees for the right to generate electricity on public land. When political favoritism and corruption within the Departments of the Interior and Agriculture threatened these efforts at regulation, Roosevelt authorized the hiring of university-trained experts to replace state and local politicians. Scientific expertise, rather than political connections, would now determine the distribution and use of western territory.

Gifford Pinchot, a specialist in forestry management and Roosevelt's close friend, led the drive for scientific management of natural resources. In 1905, he persuaded Roosevelt to relocate jurisdiction for the national forests from the Department of the Interior to the Department of Agriculture, which, Pinchot argued, was the most appropriate department to oversee the efficient "harvest" of the nation's forest crop. The newly created National Forest Service, under Pinchot's control, quickly instituted a system of competitive bidding for the right to harvest timber on national forest lands. Pinchot and his expanding staff of college-educated foresters also implemented a new policy that exacted user fees from livestock ranchers who had previously used national forest grazing lands for free. Armed with new legislation and authority, Pinchot and fellow conservationists in the Roosevelt administration declared vast stretches of federal land in the West off-limits to mining and dam construction.

The Republican Old Guard disliked these initiatives. When Roosevelt recommended prosecution of cattlemen and lumbermen who were illegally using federal land for private gain, congressional conservatives struck back with legislation (in 1907) that curtailed the president's power to create new government land reserves. Roosevelt responded by seizing another 17 million acres for national forest reserves before the new law went into effect. To his conservative opponents, excluding commercial activity from public land—a program they regarded as socialistic—was bad enough, but flouting the will of Congress with a 17-million-acre land grab violated constitutional principles governing the separation of powers. Yet, to millions of American voters, Roosevelt's willingness to defy western cattle barons, mining tycoons, and other "malefactors of great wealth" increased his popularity.

Progressivism: A Movement for the People?

Historians have long debated how much Roosevelt's economic and environmental reforms altered the balance of power between the "interests" and the people. Some have demonstrated that many corporations were eager for federal government regulation—that railroad corporations wanted relief from the rate wars that were driving them into bankruptcy, for example, and that the larger meatpackers believed that the costs of government food inspections would drive smaller meatpackers out of business. So, too, historians have shown that agribusinesses, timber companies, and mining corporations in the West believed that government regulation would aid them and hurt smaller competitors. According to this view, government regulation benefited the corporations more than it benefited workers, consumers, and small businessmen.

This view has some validity. These early reforms often curtailed corporate power only to a limited extent. Corporations fought with some success to turn the final versions of the reform laws to their advantage. But in 1907, the progressive program was still evolving. Popular anger over corporate power and political corruption remained a driving force of progressivism. The presence in the Senate of La Follette, Albert Beveridge of Indiana, and other anticorporate Republicans gave that anger an influential national voice. Whether the corporations or the people would benefit most from progressive reforms had yet to be determined.

The Republicans: A Divided Party

The financial panic of 1907 further strained relations between Roosevelt reformers and Old Guard conservatives in the Republican Party. When several New York banks failed in a speculative effort to corner the copper market, they triggered a run on banks, a short but severe dip in industrial production, and widespread layoffs. Everywhere, people worried that a major depression, like that of the 1890s, was in the offing. Only the timely decision of J. P. Morgan and his fellow bankers to pour private cash into the collapsing banks saved the nation from an economic crisis. Prosperity quickly returned, but the panic jitters lingered. Conservatives blamed Roosevelt's "radical" economic policies for the fiasco. To Roosevelt and his fellow progressives, however, the panic merely pointed out how little impact their reforms had actually made on the reign of "speculation, corruption, and fraud."

Roosevelt, as a result, began calling for an overhaul of the banking system and regulation of the stock market. The Republican Old Guard, meanwhile, was more determined than ever to run the "radical" Roosevelt out of the White House. Sensing that he might fail to win his party's nomination, and mindful of a rash promise he had made in 1904 not to run again in 1908, Roosevelt decided not to seek reelection. It was a decision he would soon regret. Barely 50 years old, he was too young and energetic to end his political career, and much of his reform program had yet to win Congressional approval.

The Taft Presidency

Roosevelt thought he had found in **William Howard Taft,** his secretary of war, an ideal successor. Taft had worked closely with Roosevelt on foreign and domestic policies. He had supported Roosevelt's progressive reforms and offered him shrewd advice. Roosevelt believed Taft possessed both the ideas and the skills to complete the reform Republican program.

To reach that conclusion, however, Roosevelt had to ignore some obvious differences between Taft and himself. Taft neither liked nor was particularly adept at politics. With the exception of a judgeship in an Ohio superior court, he had never held elective office. He was by nature a cautious and conservative man. As Roosevelt's handpicked successor, Taft easily won the election of 1908, defeating Democrat William Jennings Bryan with 52 percent of the vote. His conservatism soon revealed itself in his choice of corporation lawyers, rather than reformers, for cabinet positions.

Battling Congress

Taft's troubles began when he appeared to side against progressives in an acrimonious congressional battle over tariff legislation. Progressives had long desired tariff reduction, believing that competition from foreign manufacturers would benefit American consumers and check the economic power of American manufacturers. Taft had raised expectations for tariff reduction when he called Congress into special session to consider a reform bill that called for a modest reduction of tariffs and an inheritance tax. The bill passed the House but was gutted in the Senate. When congressional progressives pleaded with Taft to use his power to whip conservative senators into line, he pressured the Old Guard into including a 2 percent corporate income tax in their version of the bill, but he did not insist on tariff reductions. As a result, the Payne-Aldrich Tariff he signed into law on August 5, 1909, did nothing to encourage imports. Progressive Republicans, bitterly disappointed, held Taft responsible.

They were further angered when Taft withdrew his support of their efforts to strip Speaker Joe Cannon of his legislative powers. By 1910, Republican insurgents had entered into an alliance with reform-minded congressional Democrats. Then a bruising fight over Taft's conservation policies brought relations between Taft and the insurgent Republicans to the breaking point.

The Ballinger-Pinchot Controversy

Richard A. Ballinger, secretary of the interior, had aroused progressives' suspicions by reopening for private commercial use 1 million acres of land that the Roosevelt administration had previously brought under federal protection. Gifford Pinchot, still head of the National Forest Service, obtained information implicating Ballinger in the sale of Alaskan coal deposits to a private syndicate. Pinchot showed the information, including an allegation that Ballinger had personally profited from the sale, to Taft. Taft defended Ballinger, Pinchot went public with his charges, and a contentious congressional investigation ensued. Whatever hope Taft may have had of escaping political damage disappeared when Roosevelt, returning from an African hunting trip by way of Europe in spring 1910, staged a publicized rendezvous with Pinchot in England. In so doing, Roosevelt signaled his continuing support for his old friend Pinchot and his displeasure with Taft.

Roosevelt's Return

When Roosevelt arrived in the United States later that summer, he quickly returned to politics. In September, Roosevelt embarked on a speaking tour, the high point of which was his elaboration at Osawatomie, Kansas, of his New Nationalism, an ambitious reform program that called for the federal government to stabilize the economy, protect the weak, and restore social harmony.

The 1910 congressional elections confirmed the popularity of Roosevelt's positions. Insurgent Republicans trounced conservative Republicans in primary after primary, and the Democrats' embrace of reform brought them a majority in the House of Representatives for

Brown Brothers

Theodore Roosevelt Launches His New Nationalism Campaign, 1910   This photograph of Roosevelt at Osawatomie, Kansas, captures some of the strength and exuberance of Roosevelt's public style. Roosevelt's appearance at Osawatomie marked his formal return to politics. For the occasion, he unveiled his New Nationalism, a far-reaching program of reform that called on the government to control the powerful corporations in the interests of the commonweal.

the first time since 1894. When Robert La Follette, who was challenging Taft for the Republican presidential nomination, seemed to suffer a nervous breakdown in February 1912, Roosevelt announced his own candidacy. In the 13 states sponsoring preferential primaries, Roosevelt won nearly 75 percent of the delegates, but the party's national leadership remained in the hands of the Old Guard, and they were determined to deny Roosevelt the Republican nomination. At the Republican convention in Chicago, Taft won renomination on the first ballot.

The Bull Moose Campaign

Roosevelt had expected this outcome. The night before the convention opened, he had told an assembly of 5,000 supporters that the party leaders would not succeed in derailing their movement. "We stand at Armageddon," he declared, and "we battle for the Lord." The next day, Roosevelt and his supporters withdrew from the convention and from the Republican Party. In August, the reformers reassembled as the new **Progressive Party**, nominated Roosevelt for president and California governor Hiram W. Johnson for vice president, and hammered out the reform platform they had long envisioned: sweeping regulation of the corporations, extensive protections for workers, a sharply graduated income tax, and woman suffrage. "I am as strong as a bull moose," Roosevelt roared as he readied for combat; his proud followers took to calling themselves **"Bull Moosers."**

Some of them, however, probably including Roosevelt, knew that their mission was futile. They had failed to enroll many Republican insurgents who had supported Roosevelt in the primaries but who now refused to abandon the GOP. Consequently, the Republican vote would be split between Roosevelt and Taft, making them both vulnerable to the Democrats' candidate, Woodrow Wilson.

The Rise of Woodrow Wilson

Few would have predicted in 1908 that the distinguished president of Princeton University, Woodrow Wilson, would be the 1912 Democratic nominee for president of the United States. Before 1910, Wilson had never run for elective office, nor had he ever held an appointed post in a local, state, or federal administration. The son of a Presbyterian minister from Virginia, Wilson had practiced law for a short time after graduating from Princeton (then still the College of New Jersey) in 1879 before settling on an academic career. Earning his doctorate in political science from Johns Hopkins in 1886, he taught history and political science at Bryn Mawr and Wesleyan (Connecticut) before returning to Princeton in 1890. He became president of Princeton in 1902, a post he held until he successfully ran for the governorship of New Jersey in 1910.

Identifying himself with the anti-Bryan wing of the Democratic Party, Wilson attracted the attention of wealthy conservatives, who saw him as a potential presidential candidate. They convinced the bosses of the New Jersey Democratic machine to nominate Wilson for governor in 1910. Wilson accepted the nomination and won the governorship handily. He then shocked his conservative backers by declaring his independence from the state's

Democratic machine and moving New Jersey into the forefront of reform. Wilson's Presbyterian upbringing had instilled in him a strong sense that society should be governed by God's moral law. As a young man in the 1880s, he had come to believe that the social consequences of unregulated industrialization were repugnant to Christian ethical principles. Although these beliefs had receded from view somewhat during his tenure as Princeton University president, they had not disappeared. Their presence in his consciousness helps to explain his emergence in 1911 and 1912 as one of the nation's leading progressives.

The Election of 1912

At the Democratic convention of 1912, Wilson was something of a dark horse, running a distant second to House Speaker Champ Clark of Missouri. When the New York delegation gave Clark a simple majority of delegates, virtually everyone assumed that Clark would soon command the two-thirds majority needed to win the nomination. But Wilson's managers held onto Wilson's delegates and began chipping away at Clark's lead. On the fourth day, on the 46th ballot, Wilson won the nomination. The exhausted Democrats closed ranks behind their candidate.

Given the split in Republican ranks, Democrats had their best chance in 20 years of regaining the White House. A Wilson victory, moreover, would give the country its first southern-born president in almost 50 years. Finally, whatever its outcome, the election promised to deliver a hefty vote for reform. Both Roosevelt and Wilson were running on reform platforms, and the Socialist Party candidate, Eugene V. Debs, was attracting larger crowds and generating greater enthusiasm than had been expected. Taft was so certain of defeat that he barely campaigned.

Debate among the candidates focused on the trusts. All three reform candidates—Roosevelt, Wilson, and Debs—agreed that corporations had acquired too much economic power. Debs argued that the only way to ensure popular control of that power was for the federal government to assume ownership of the trusts. Roosevelt called for the establishment of a powerful government that

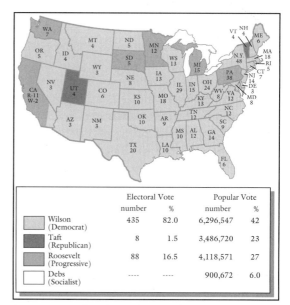

	Electoral Vote		Popular Vote	
	number	%	number	%
Wilson (Democrat)	435	82.0	6,296,547	42
Taft (Republican)	8	1.5	3,486,720	23
Roosevelt (Progressive)	88	16.5	4,118,571	27
Debs (Socialist)	----	----	900,672	6.0

Map 21.2 Presidential Election, 1912 Taft and Roosevelt split the Republican vote, allowing Wilson to win with a plurality of the popular vote (42 percent) and a big majority (82 percent) of the electoral vote.

would regulate and, if necessary, curb the power of the trusts. This was the essence of his New Nationalism, the program he had been advocating since 1910.

Rather than regulate the trusts, Wilson declared his intention to break them up. He wanted to reverse the tendency toward economic concentration and thus restore opportunity to the people. This philosophy, which Wilson labeled the **New Freedom,** called for a temporary concentration of governmental power in order to dismantle the trusts. But once that was accomplished, Wilson promised, the government would relinquish its power.

Wilson won the November election with 42 percent of the popular vote to Roosevelt's 27 percent and Taft's 23 percent; Debs made a strong showing with 6 percent, the largest in his party's history. The three candidates who had pledged themselves to reform programs—Wilson, Roosevelt, and Debs—together won a remarkable 75 percent of the vote.

The Wilson Presidency

Wilson quickly assembled a cabinet of talented men who could be counted on for wise counsel, loyalty, and influence over vital Democratic constituencies. He cultivated a public image of himself as a president firmly in charge of his party and as a faithful tribune of the people.

Tariff Reform and a Progressive Income Tax

Like his predecessor, Wilson first turned his attention to tariff reform. The House passed a tariff-reduction bill within a month, and Wilson used his leadership skills to push the bill through a reluctant Senate. The resulting Underwood-Simmons Tariff of 1913 reduced tariff barriers from approximately 40 percent to 25 percent. To make up for revenue lost to tariff reductions, Congress then passed an income tax law. The 16th Amendment to the Constitution, ratified by the states in 1913, had already given the government the right to impose an income tax. The law passed by Congress made good on the progressive pledge to reduce the power and privileges of wealthy Americans by requiring them to pay taxes on a greater *percentage* of their income than the poor.

The Federal Reserve Act

Wilson then asked Congress to overhaul the nation's financial system. Virtually everyone in both parties agreed on the need for greater regulation of banks and currency, but they differed sharply over how to proceed. The banking interests and their congressional supporters wanted the government to give the authority to regulate credit and currency flows either to a single bank or to several regional banks. Progressives opposed the vesting of so much financial power in private hands and insisted that any reformed financial system must be publicly controlled. Wilson worked out a compromise plan that included both private and public controls, and he marshaled the votes to push it through both the House and the Senate. By the end of 1913, Wilson had signed the **Federal Reserve Act,** the most important law passed in his first administration.

The Federal Reserve Act established 12 regional banks, each controlled by the private banks in its region. Every private bank in the country was required to deposit an average of 6 percent of its assets in its regional Federal Reserve bank. The reserve would be used to make loans to member banks and to issue paper currency (Federal Reserve notes) to facilitate financial transactions. The regional banks were also instructed to use their funds to shore up member banks in distress and to respond to sudden changes in credit demands by easing or tightening the flow of credit. A Federal Reserve Board appointed by the president and responsible to the public rather than to private bankers would set policy and oversee activities within the 12 reserve banks.

The Federal Reserve system strengthened the nation's financial structure and was in most respects an impressive political achievement for Wilson. In its final form, however, it revealed that Wilson was retreating from his New Freedom pledge. The Federal Reserve Board was a less powerful and less centralized federal authority than a national bank would have been, but it nevertheless represented a substantial increase in government control of banking. Moreover, the bill authorizing the system made no attempt to break up private financial institutions that had grown too powerful or to prohibit the interlocking directorates that large banks used to augment their power. Because it sought to work with large banks rather than to break them up, the Federal Reserve system seemed more consonant with the principles of Roosevelt's New Nationalism than with those of Wilson's New Freedom.

From the New Freedom to the New Nationalism

Wilson's failure to mount a vigorous antitrust campaign confirmed his drift toward the New Nationalism. For example, in 1914, Wilson supported the Federal Trade Commission Act, which created a government agency by that name to regulate business practices. The Federal Trade Commission (FTC) had wide powers to collect information on corporate pricing policies and on cooperation and competition among businesses. The FTC might have attacked trusts for "unfair trade practices," but the Senate stripped the FTC Act's companion legislation, the Clayton Antitrust Act, of virtually all provisions that would have allowed the government to prosecute the trusts. Wilson supported this weakening of the Clayton Act, having decided that the breakup of large-scale industry was no longer practical or preferable. The FTC, in Wilson's eyes, would help businesses, large and small, to regulate themselves in ways that contributed to national well-being. In accepting giant industry as an inescapable feature of modern life and in seeking to regulate industrial behavior by means of government agencies such as the FTC, Wilson had become, in effect, a New Nationalist.

At first, Wilson's drift to New Nationalist policies led him to support business interests. His nominations to the Federal Reserve Board, for example, were generally men who had worked for Wall Street firms and large industrial corporations. At the same time, he usually refused to use government powers to aid organized groups of workers and farmers. Court rulings had made worker and farmer organizations vulnerable to prosecution under the terms of the Sherman Antitrust Act of 1890. AFL president Samuel Gompers and other labor leaders tried but failed to convince Wilson to insert into the Clayton Antitrust Act a clause that would unambiguously grant labor and farmer organizations immunity from further antitrust prosecutions.

Nor did Wilson, at this time, view with any greater sympathy the campaign for African American political equality. He supported efforts by white southerners in his cabinet, such as Postmaster General Albert Burleson and Treasury Secretary William McAdoo, to segregate their government departments, and he largely ignored pleas from the NAACP to involve the federal government in a campaign against lynching.

In late 1915, however, Wilson moved to the left, in part because he feared losing his reelection in 1916. The Bull Moosers of 1912 were retreating back to the Republican Party. Wilson remembered how much his 1912 victory, based on only 42 percent of the popular vote, had depended on the Republican split. To halt the progressives' rapprochement with the GOP, he made a bid for their support. In January 1916, he nominated Louis Brandeis to the Supreme Court. Not only was Brandeis one of the country's most respected progressives, but he was also the first Jew nominated to serve on the country's highest court. Congressional conservatives did everything they could to block the confirmation of a man they regarded as dangerously radical, but Wilson, as usual, was better organized, and by June his forces in the Senate had emerged victorious.

Wilson followed up this victory by pushing through Congress the first federal workmen's compensation law (the Kern-McGillicuddy Act, which covered federal employees), the first federal law outlawing child labor (the Keating-Owen Act), and the first federal law guaranteeing workers an eight-hour day (the Adamson Act, which covered the nation's 400,000 railway workers). The number of Americans affected by these acts was rather small. Nevertheless, Wilson had reoriented the Democratic Party to a New Nationalism that cared as much about the interests of the powerless as the interests of the powerful.

Trade unionists flocked to Wilson, as did most of the prominent progressives who had followed the Bull Moose in 1912. Meanwhile, Wilson had appealed to the supporters of William Jennings Bryan by supporting legislation that made federal credit available to farmers in need. He had put together a reform coalition capable of winning a majority at the polls. In the process, he had transformed the Democratic Party. From 1916 on, the Democrats, rather than the Republicans, became the chief guardians of the American reform tradition.

That Wilson did so is a sign of the strength of the reform and radical forces in American society. By 1916, the ranks of middle-class progressives had grown broad and deep. Working-class protest had also accelerated in scope and intensity. In Lawrence, Massachusetts, in 1912, and in Paterson, New Jersey, in 1913, for example, the IWW organized strikes of textile workers that drew national attention, as did the 1914 strike by Colorado mine workers that ended with the infamous Ludlow massacre (see chapter 20). These protests reflected the mobilization of those working-class constituencies—immigrants, women, the unskilled—long considered inconsequential both by mainstream labor leaders and party politicians. Assisted by radicals, these groups had begun to fashion a more inclusive and politically ambitious labor movement. Wilson and other Democrats understood the potential strength of this new labor movement, and the president's pro-labor legislative agenda in 1916 can be understood, in part, as an effort to channel labor's new constituents into the Democratic Party. It was a successful strategy that contributed to Wilson's reelection in 1916.

Conclusion

By 1916, the progressives had accomplished a great deal. They demonstrated that traditional American concerns with democracy and liberty could be adapted to an industrial age. They exposed and curbed some of the worst abuses of the American political system. They enfranchised women and took steps to protect the environment. They broke the hold of laissez-faire economic policies on national politics and replaced it with the idea of a strong federal government committed to economic regulation and social justice. They transformed the presidency into a post of legislative and popular leadership. They enlarged the executive branch by establishing new commissions and agencies charged with administering government policies.

The progressives, in short, had presided over the emergence of a new national government, one in which power increasingly flowed away from municipalities and states and toward Washington. This reorientation followed a compelling logic: A national government stood a better chance of solving the problems of growing economic inequality, mismanagement of natural resources, and consumer fraud than did local and state governments. This emphasis on involving the federal government in economic and social affairs became progressivism's most enduring legacy. It made the movement a forerunner of the liberalism and "New Deal" that emerged under Franklin Roosevelt's leadership in the 1930s (see chapter 25).

The promise of effective federal government intervention, however, also brought a new danger: the possibility that government administrators might use their power to fashion themselves into a new bureaucratic elite impervious to popular control. Some progressives, such as Walter Lippmann, were already arguing that their knowledge, objectivity, and dedication equipped them to make critical decisions on behalf of the people without consulting them. Other progressives in government claimed to be responsive to the people while they cultivated close ties with corporations that they were expected to regulate on the people's behalf. In some instances, in other words, progressive reformers were doing as much to advance their own bureaucratic interests or those of their corporate allies as they were helping to improve the welfare of ordinary Americans.

These elitist tendencies did not go unchallenged. The democratic movements of the progressive era—those involving workers, women, minorities, consumers, and environmentalists—were determined to hold both elected and appointed government officials accountable to the popular will. Their success in moving Wilson to the left in 1916 demonstrated that the forces of democracy could win. But the struggle between the contrasting progressive impulses toward democracy and elitism would go on, manifesting itself not simply in domestic politics but also in foreign affairs, where the United States was seeking to balance its interest in spreading liberty with the protection of its international economic interests.

SUGGESTED READINGS

No topic in 20th-century American history has generated as large and rapidly changing a scholarship as has progressivism. Today, few scholars treat this political movement in the terms set forth by the progressives themselves: as a movement of "the people" against the "special interests." In

The Age of Reform: From Bryan to FDR (1955), **Richard Hofstadter** argues that progressivism was the expression of a declining Protestant middle class at odds with the new industrial order. In *The Search for Order, 1877–1920* (1967), **Robert Wiebe** finds the movement's core in a rising middle class, closely allied to the corporations and bureaucratic imperatives that were defining this new order. **Gabriel Kolko**, *The Triumph of Conservatism: A Reinterpretation of American History* (1963), and **James Weinstein**, *The Corporate Ideal in the Liberal State, 1900–1918* (1969), both argue that progressivism was the work of businessmen, who were eager to ensure corporate stability and profitability in a dangerously unstable capitalist economy.

Without denying the importance of this corporate search for order, **Nell Irvin Painter**, *Standing at Armageddon: The United States, 1877–1919* (1987), and **Alan Dawley**, *Struggles for Justice: Social Responsibility and the Liberal State* (1991), insist on the role of the working class, men and women, whites and blacks, in shaping the progressive agenda. **James T. Kloppenberg**, *Uncertain Victory: Social Democracy and Progressivism in European and American Thought, 1870–1920* (1986), and **Thomas J. Knock**, *To End All Wars: Woodrow Wilson and the Quest for a New World Order* (1992), emphasize the influence of socialism on progressive thought, while **Martin J. Sklar**, *The Corporate Reconstruction of American Capitalism, 1900–1916: The Market, the Law and Politics* (1988), stresses the role of progressivism in "containing" or taming socialism.

Daniel T. Rodgers reconstructs the international networks of reform that nourished progressivism in *Atlantic Crossings: Social Politics in a Progressive Age* (1998). **Nick Salvatore** superbly captures the charisma and enigma of Debs in his *Eugene V. Debs: Citizen and Socialist* (1982). **Paul Boyer**, *Urban Masses and Moral Order in America, 1820–1920* (1978), treats progressivism as a cultural movement to enforce middle-class norms on unruly urban and immigrant populations. **Theda Skocpol**, *Protecting Soldiers and Mothers: The Political Origins of Social Policy in the United States* (1992), and **Robyn Muncy**, *Creating a Female Dominion in American Reform, 1890–1935* (1991), reconstruct the central role of middle-class Protestant women in shaping progressive social policy, while **Robert M. Crunden**, *Ministers of Reform: The Progressives' Achievement in American Civilization, 1889–1920* (1982), stresses the religious roots of progressive reform. **Michael Kazin**, *A Godly Hero: the Life of William Jennings Bryan* (2006), is indispensable not just on Bryan but also on the religious dimensions of progressivism, while **Alexander Keyssar**, *The Right to Vote: The Contested History of Democracy in the United States* (2000) is an essential guide to political reform during this period. An impressive recent attempt to synthesize the literature on progressivism is **Michael McGerr**, *A Fierce Discontent: The Rise and Fall of the Progressive Movement in America, 1870–1920* (2003).

Visit the Liberty Equality Power Companion Web site for resources specific to this textbook: http://www.thomsonedu.com/history/murrin

Also find self-tests and additional resources at ThomsonNOW. ThomsonNOW is an integrated online suite of services and resources with proven ease of use and efficient paths to success, delivering the results you want-NOW!

www.thomsonedu.com/login/

22

Becoming a World Power, 1898–1917

For much of the 19th century, most Americans were preoccupied by continental expansion. They treasured their distance from European societies, monarchs, and wars. Elections rarely turned on international events, and presidents rarely made their reputations as statesmen in the world arena. The diplomatic corps, like most agencies of the federal government, was small and inexperienced. The government projected its limited military power westward and possessed virtually no capacity or desire for involvement overseas.

The nation's rapid industrial growth in the late 19th century forced a turn away from such continentalism. Technological advances, especially the laying of transoceanic cables and the introduction of steamship travel, diminished America's physical isolation. The babel of languages one could hear in American cities testified to how much the Old World had penetrated the New. Then, too, Americans watched anxiously as England, Germany, Russia, Japan, and other industrial powers intensified their competition for overseas markets and colonies, and some believed America too needed to enter this contest. The voices making this argument grew more insistent and persuasive as the economic depression of the 1890s stripped the United States of its prosperity and pride.

A war with Spain in 1898 gave the United States an opportunity to upgrade its military and acquire colonies and influence in the Western Hemisphere and Asia. Under Presidents William McKinley and Theodore Roosevelt, the United States pursued these initiatives and established a small but strategically important empire. Not all Americans supported this imperial project, and many protested the subjugation of the peoples of Cuba, Puerto Rico, and the Philippines that imperial expansion seemed to entail. In the eyes of anti-imperialists, the United States seemed to be becoming the kind of nation that many Americans had long despised—one that valued power more than liberty.

Roosevelt brushed aside these objections and set about creating an international system in which a handful of industrial nations pursued their global economic interests, dominated world trade, and kept the world at peace. Woodrow Wilson, however, was more troubled by America's imperial turn. His doubts became apparent in his efforts to devise a policy toward postrevolutionary Mexico that restrained American might and respected Mexican desires for liberty. It was a worthy ambition but one that proved exceedingly difficult to achieve.

CHRONOLOGY

1893	Frederick Jackson Turner publishes an essay announcing the end of the frontier
1898	Spanish-American War (April 14–August 12) • Treaty of Paris signed (December 10), giving U.S. control of Philippines, Guam, and Puerto Rico • U.S. annexes Hawaii
1899–1902	American-Filipino War
1899–1900	U.S. pursues Open Door policy toward China
1900	U.S. annexes Puerto Rico • U.S. and other imperial powers put down Chinese Boxer Rebellion
1901	U.S. forces Cuba to adopt constitution favorable to U.S. interests
1903	Hay–Bunau-Varilla Treaty signed, giving U.S. control of Panama Canal Zone
1904	"Roosevelt corollary" to Monroe Doctrine proclaimed
1905	Roosevelt negotiates end to Russo-Japanese War
1906–17	U.S. intervenes in Cuba, Nicaragua, Haiti, Dominican Republic, and Mexico
1907	Roosevelt and Japanese government reach a "gentlemen's agreement" restricting Japanese immigration to U.S. and ending the segregation of Japanese schoolchildren in California
1907–09	Great White Fleet circles the world
1909–13	William Howard Taft conducts "dollar diplomacy"
1910	Mexican Revolution
1914	Panama Canal opens
1914–17	Wilson struggles to develop a policy toward Mexico
1917	U.S. purchases Virgin Islands from Denmark

The United States Looks Abroad

By the late 19th century, sizable numbers of Americans had become interested in extending their country's influence abroad. The most important groups were Protestant missionaries, businessmen, and imperialists.

Protestant Missionaries

Protestant missionaries were among the most active promoters of American interests abroad. Overseas missionary activity grew quickly between 1870 and 1900, most of it directed toward China. Between 1880 and 1900, the number of women's missionary societies doubled, from 20 to 40; by 1915, these societies enrolled 3 million women. Convinced of the superiority of the Anglo-Saxon race, Protestant missionaries considered it their Christian duty to teach the Gospel to the "ignorant" Asian masses and save their souls. Missionaries also believed that their efforts would free those masses from their racial destiny, enabling them to become "civilized." In this "civilizing" effort, missionaries resembled progressive reformers who sought to uplift America's immigrant masses at home.

Businessmen

For different reasons, industrialists, traders, and investors also began to look overseas, sensing that they could make fortunes in foreign lands. Exports of American manufactured goods rose substantially after 1880. By 1914, American foreign investment already equaled a sizable 7 percent of the nation's gross national product. Companies such as Eastman Kodak (film and cameras), Singer Sewing Machine Company, Standard Oil, American Tobacco, and International Harvester had become multinational corporations with overseas branch offices.

Some industrialists became entranced by the prospect of clothing, feeding, housing, and transporting the 400 million people of China. James B. Duke, who headed American Tobacco, was selling 1 billion cigarettes per year in East Asian markets. Looking for ways to fill empty boxcars heading west from Minnesota to Tacoma, Washington, the railroad tycoon James J. Hill imagined stuffing them with wheat and steel destined for China and Japan. He actually published and distributed wheat cookbooks throughout East Asia to convince Asians to shift from a rice-based to a bread-based diet (so that there would be a market there for U.S. flour exports). Although export trade with East Asia during this period never fulfilled the expectations of Hill and other industrialists, their talk about the "wealth of the Orient" impressed on politicians its importance to American economic health.

Events of the 1890s only intensified the appeal of foreign markets. First, the 1890 U.S. census announced that the frontier had disappeared and that America had completed the task of westward expansion. Then, in 1893, a young historian named Frederick Jackson Turner published an essay, "The Significance of the Frontier in American History," that articulated what many Americans feared: that the frontier had been essential to the growth of the economy and to the cultivation of democracy.

Living in the wilderness, Turner argued, had transformed the Europeans who settled the New World into Americans. They shed their European clothing styles, social customs, and political beliefs, and acquired distinctively American characteristics—rugged individualism, egalitarianism, and a democratic faith. How, Turner wondered, could the nation continue to prosper now that the frontier had gone?

In recent years, historians of the American West have criticized **Turner's "frontier thesis."** They have argued that the very idea of the frontier as uninhabited wilderness overlooked the tens of thousands of Indians who occupied the region and that much else of what Americans believed about the West was based more on myth than on reality. They have also pointed out that it makes little sense to view the 1890s as a decade in which opportunities for economic gain disappeared in the West.

Even though these points are valid, they would have meant little to Americans living in Turner's time. For them, as for Turner, concern about the disappearing frontier expressed a fear that the increasingly urbanized and industrialized nation had lost its way. Turner's essay appeared just as the country was entering the deepest, longest, and most conflict-ridden depression in its history (see chapter 19). What could the republic do to regain its economic prosperity and political stability? Where would it find its new frontiers? One answer to these questions focused on the pursuit of overseas expansion. As Senator Albert J. Beveridge of Indiana declared in 1899: "We are raising more than we can consume. . . . We are making more than we can use. Therefore, we must find new markets for our produce, new occupation for our capital, new work for our labor."

Imperialists

Eager to assist in the drive for overseas expansion was a group of politicians, intellectuals, and military strategists who viewed such expansion as a key ingredient in the pursuit of world power. They wanted the United States to take its place alongside Britain, France, Germany, and Russia as a great imperial nation. They believed that the United States should build a strong navy, solidify a sphere of influence in the Caribbean, and extend markets into Asia. Their desire to control ports and territories beyond the continental borders of their own country made them **imperialists.** Many of them were also Social Darwinists (see chapter 19) who believed that America's destiny required that it prove itself the military equal of the strongest European nations and the master of the "lesser" peoples of the world.

One of the best-known imperialists of the period was Admiral **Alfred Thayer Mahan.** In an influential book, *The Influence of Sea Power upon History, 1660–1783* (1890), Mahan argued that past empires, beginning with Rome, had relied on their capacity to control the seas. Mahan called for the construction of a U.S. navy with enough ships and firepower to make its presence felt everywhere in the world. To be effective, that global fleet would require a canal across Central America through which U.S. warships could pass swiftly from the Atlantic to the Pacific oceans. It would also require a string of far-flung service bases from the Caribbean to the southwestern Pacific. Mahan recommended that the U.S. government take possession of Hawaii and other strategically located Pacific islands with superior harbor facilities.

Presidents William McKinley and Theodore Roosevelt would eventually make almost the whole of Mahan's vision a reality, but in the early 1890s, Mahan doubted that Americans would accept the responsibility and costs of empire. Although the imperialists counted in their ranks such prominent figures as Theodore Roosevelt and Senator Henry Cabot Lodge of Massachusetts, many Americans still insisted that the United States should not aspire to world power by acquiring overseas bases and colonizing foreign peoples.

Mahan underestimated, however, the government's alarm over the scramble of Europeans to extend their imperial control. Every U.S. administration from the 1880s on committed itself to a "big navy" policy. By 1898, the U.S. Navy ranked fifth in the world, and by 1900, it ranked third. Already in 1878, the United States had secured rights to Pago Pago, a superb deep-water harbor in Samoa (a collection of islands in the southwest Pacific inhabited by Polynesians), and in 1885, it had leased Pearl Harbor from the Hawaiians. Both harbors were expected to serve as fueling stations for the growing U.S. fleet.

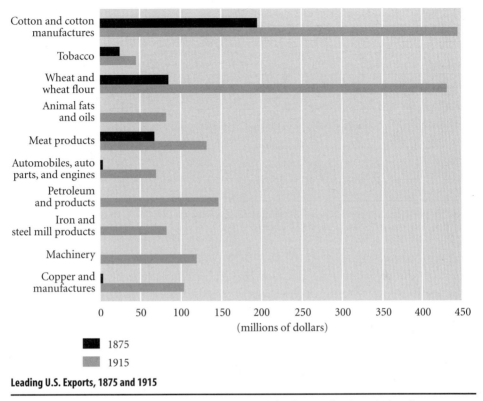

Leading U.S. Exports, 1875 and 1915

Source: Data from *Historical Statistics of the United States, Colonial Times to 1970* (White Plains, N.Y.: Kraus International, 1989).

These attempts to project U.S. power overseas had already deepened the government's involvement in the affairs of distant lands. In 1889, the United States established a protectorate over part of Samoa, a move meant to forestall German and British efforts to weaken American influence on the islands. In the early 1890s, President Grover Cleveland's administration was increasingly drawn into Hawaiian affairs, as tensions between American sugar plantation owners and native Hawaiians upset the islands' economic and political stability. In 1891, U.S. plantation owners succeeded in deposing the Hawaiian king and putting into power Queen Liliuokalani. But when Liliuokalani strove to establish her independence from American interests, the planters, assisted by U.S. sailors, overthrew her regime, too. Cleveland declared Hawaii a protectorate in 1893, but he resisted the imperialists in Congress who wanted to annex the islands.

Still, imperialist sentiment in Congress and across the nation continued to gain strength, fueled by "jingoism." Jingoists were nationalists who thought that a swaggering foreign policy and a willingness to go to war would enhance their nation's glory. They were constantly on the alert for insults to their country's honor and swift to call for military

The U.S. Navy, 1890–1914: Expenditures and Battleship Size

Fiscal year	Total Federal Expenditures	Naval Expenditures	Naval Expenditures as Percentage of Total Federal Expenditures	Size of Battleships (average tons displaced)
1890	$318,040,711	$ 22,006,206	6.9%	11,000
1900	520,860,847	55,953,078	10.7	12,000
1901	524,616,925	60,506,978	11.5	16,000
1905	657,278,914	117,550,308	20.7	16,000
1909	693,743,885	115,546,011	16.7	27,000 (1910)
1914	735,081,431	139,682,186	19.0	32,000

Sources: (for expenditures) E. B. Potter, *Sea Power: A Naval History* (Annapolis: Naval Institute Press, 1982), p. 187; (for size of ships) Harold Sprout, *Toward a New Order of Sea Power* (New York: Greenwood Press, 1976), p. 52.

retaliation. This predatory brand of nationalism emerged in each of the world's big powers in the late 19th century. In the United States, it manifested itself in terms of an eagerness for war. The anti-imperialist editor of the *Nation*, E. L. Godkin, exclaimed in 1894: "The number of men and officials of this country who are now mad to fight somebody is appalling." Recent feminist scholarship has emphasized the degree to which men of the 1890s saw war as an opportunity to revive frontier-like notions of masculinity—of men as warriors and conquerors—that were proving difficult to sustain in industrializing and bureaucratizing America. Spain's behavior in Cuba in the 1890s gave those men the war they sought.

The Spanish-American War

Focus Question
In going to war against Spain in 1898, was the United States impelled more by imperialist or anti-imperialist motives?

By the 1890s, the islands of Cuba and Puerto Rico were virtually all that remained of the vast Spanish empire in the Americas. Relations between the Cubans and their Spanish rulers had long been deteriorating. The Spanish had taken 10 years to subdue a revolt begun in 1868. In 1895, the Cubans staged another revolt, sparked by their continuing resentment of Spanish control and by a depressed economy caused in part by an 1894 U.S. tariff law that made Cuban sugar too expensive for the U.S. market. The fighting was brutal. Cuban forces destroyed large areas of the island to make it uninhabitable by the Spanish. The Spanish army, led by General Valeriano Weyler, responded in kind, forcing large numbers of Cubans into concentration camps. Denied adequate food, shelter, and sanitation, an estimated 200,000 Cubans—one-eighth of the island's population—died of starvation and disease.

Uncle Sam Gives Spain More Than It Can Handle   By going to war in 1898, this poster suggests, the United States had toppled "brutal Spain" and the remnants of its empire.

Such tactics, especially those ascribed to "Butcher" Weyler (as he was known in much of the U.S. press), inflamed American opinion. Many Americans sympathized with the Cubans, who seemed to be fighting the kind of anticolonial war Americans had waged more than 100 years earlier. Americans stayed well informed about the atrocities by reading the *New York Journal,* owned by William Randolph Hearst, and the *New York World,* owned by Joseph Pulitzer. Hearst and Pulitzer were transforming newspaper publishing in much the same way Sam McClure and others had revolutionized the magazine business (see chapter 21). To boost circulation, they sought out sensational and shocking stories and described them in lurid detail. They were accused of engaging in **"yellow journalism"**—embellishing stories with titillating details when the true reports did not seem dramatic enough.

The sensationalism of the yellow press and its frequently jingoistic accounts failed to bring about American intervention in Cuba, however. In the final days of his administration, President Cleveland resisted mounting pressure to intervene. William McKinley, who succeeded him in 1897, denounced the Spanish even more harshly, with the aim of forcing Spain into concessions that would satisfy the Cuban rebels and end the conflict. Initially, this strategy seemed to be working: Spain relieved "Butcher" Weyler of his command, began releasing incarcerated Cubans from concentration camps, and granted Cuba limited autonomy. Still, Spaniards living on the island refused to be ruled by a Cuban government, and the Cuban rebels continued to demand full independence. Late in 1897, when riots broke out in Havana, McKinley ordered the battleship *Maine* into Havana harbor to protect U.S. citizens and their property. Two unexpected events then set off a war.

The first was the February 9, 1898, publication in Hearst's *New York Journal* of a letter stolen from Depuy de Lôme, the Spanish minister to Washington, in which he described McKinley as "a cheap politician" and a "bidder for the admiration of the crowd." The de Lôme letter also implied that the Spanish cared little about resolving the Cuban crisis through negotiation and reform. The news embarrassed Spanish officials and outraged U.S. public opinion. Then, only six days later, the *Maine* exploded in Havana harbor, killing 260 American sailors. Although subsequent investigations revealed that the most probable cause of the explosion was a malfunctioning boiler, Americans were certain that it had been the work of Spanish agents. "Remember the Maine!" screamed the headlines in the yellow press. On March 8, Congress responded to the clamor for war by authorizing $50 million to mobilize U.S. forces. In the meantime, McKinley notified Spain of his conditions for avoiding war: Spain would pay an indemnity for the *Maine,* abandon its concentration camps, end the fighting with the rebels, and commit itself to Cuban independence. On April 9, Spain accepted all the demands but the last. Nevertheless, on April 11, McKinley asked Congress for authority to go to war. Three days later, Congress approved a war resolution, which included a declaration (spelled out in the Teller Amendment) that the United States would not use the war as an opportunity to acquire territory in Cuba. On April 24, Spain responded with a formal declaration of war against the United States.

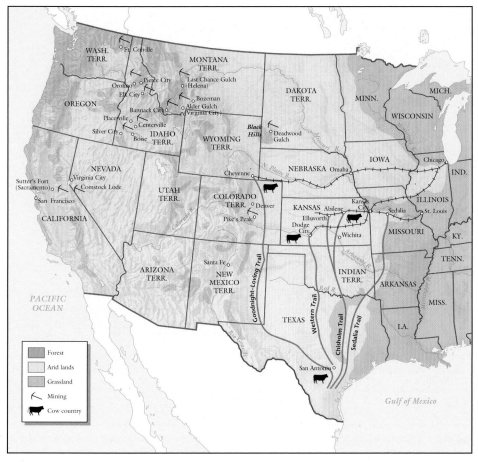

Map 18.1 Mining and Cattle Frontiers, 1870s Most of the mines shown on this map produced gold and silver. The next generation would begin to exploit the copper to be found in Montana and Arizona, and later generations would extract oil from Texas and Oklahoma and coal and oil from Wyoming.

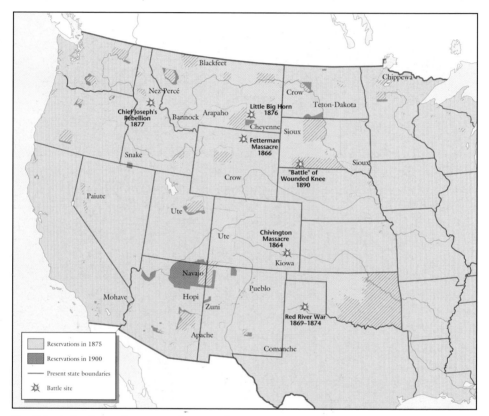

Map 18.2   Indian Reservations, 1875 and 1900   Before the Civil War, Indians had hunted and trapped over most of this vast region. The shrinking areas on which they were confined by the reservation policy vividly illustrates that for the first Americans, the story was not "the expansion of America" but "the contraction of America."

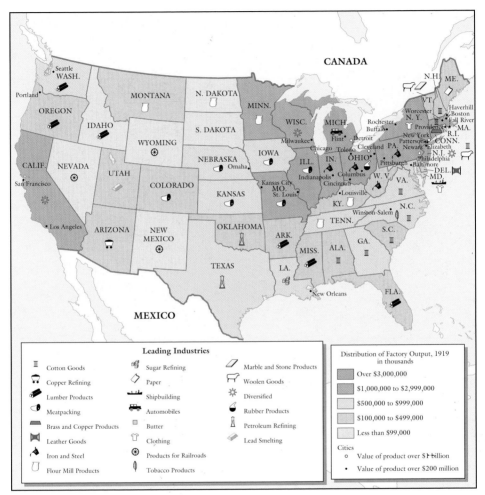

Leading Industries

Cotton Goods	
Copper Refining	
Lumber Products	
Meatpacking	
Brass and Copper Products	
Leather Goods	
Iron and Steel	
Flour Mill Products	

Sugar Refining	
Paper	
Shipbuilding	
Automobiles	
Butter	
Clothing	
Products for Railroads	
Tobacco Products	

Marble and Stone Products	
Woolen Goods	
Diversified	
Rubber Products	
Petroleum Refining	
Lead Smelting	

**Distribution of Factory Output, 1919
in thousands**

- Over $3,000,000
- $1,000,000 to $2,999,000
- $500,000 to $999,000
- $100,000 to $499,000
- Less than $99,000

Cities
- Value of product over $1 billion
- Value of product over $200 million

Map 20.1 Industrial America, 1900–1920   This map shows that the Northeast, Midwest, and California dominated factory production in the United States from 1900 to 1920. It also reveals the state-by-state distribution of various industries—clothing in New York, automobiles in Michigan, petroleum refining in Texas and Oklahoma, and lumber in Oregon, Washington, and Idaho. View an animated version of this map or related maps at http://www.thomsonedu.com/history/murrin.

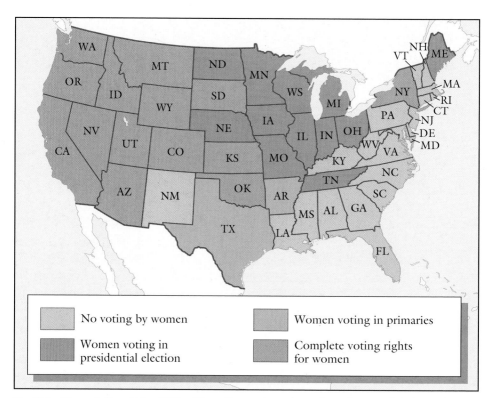

Map 21.1 Woman Suffrage Before 1920 This map illustrates how woman suffrage prior to 1920 had advanced furthest in the West.

"A Splendid Little War"

Secretary of State John Hay called the fight with Spain "a splendid little war." Begun in April, it ended in August. More than 1 million men volunteered to fight, and fewer than 500 were killed or wounded in combat. The American victory over Spain was complete, not just in Cuba but in the neighboring island of Puerto Rico and in the Philippines, Spain's strategic possession in the Pacific.

Actually, the war was more complicated than it seemed. The main reason for the easy victory was U.S. naval superiority. In the war's first major battle, a naval engagement in Manila harbor in the Philippines on May 1, a U.S. fleet commanded by Commodore George Dewey destroyed an entire Spanish fleet and lost only one sailor (to heat stroke). On land, the story was different. On the eve of war, the U.S. Army consisted of only 26,000 troops. These soldiers were skilled at skirmishing with Indians but ill-prepared and ill-equipped for all-out war. A force of 80,000 Spanish regulars awaited them in Cuba, with another 50,000 in reserve in Spain. Congress immediately increased the army to 62,000 and called for an additional 125,000 volunteers. The response to this call was astounding, but outfitting, training, and transporting the new recruits overwhelmed the army's capacities. Its standard-issue, blue flannel uniforms proved too heavy for fighting in tropical Cuba. Rations were so poor that soldiers referred to one common item as "embalmed beef." Most of the volunteers had to make do with ancient Civil War rifles that still used black, rather than smokeless, powder. The initial invasion force of 16,000 men took more than five days to sail the short distance from Tampa, Florida, to Daiquiri, Cuba. Moreover, the army was unprepared for the effects of malaria and other tropical diseases.

That the Cuban revolutionaries were predominantly black also came as a shock to the U.S. forces. In their attempts to arouse support for the Cuban cause, U.S. newspapers had portrayed Cuban rebels as fundamentally similar to white Americans. They were described as intelligent, civilized, and democratic, possessing an "Anglo-Saxon tenacity of purpose." And, they were "fully nine-tenths" white, according to one report. The Spanish oppressors, by contrast, were depicted as dark-complexioned— "dark cruel eyes, dark swaggering men" wrote author Sherwood Anderson—and as possessing the characteristics of their "dark race": barbarism, cruelty, and indolence. The U.S. troops' first encounters with Cuban and Spanish forces challenged these stereotypes. Their Cuban allies appeared poorly outfitted, rough in their manners, and primarily black-skinned. The Spanish soldiers appeared well disciplined, tough in battle, and light complexioned.

The Cuban rebels were actually skilled guerrilla fighters, but racial prejudice prevented most U.S. soldiers and reporters from crediting their military expertise. Instead, they judged the Cubans harshly—as primitive, savage, and incapable of self-control or self-government. White U.S. troops preferred not to fight alongside the Cubans; increasingly, they refused to coordinate strategy with them.

At first, the U.S. Army's logistical unpreparedness and its racial misconceptions did little to diminish the soldiers' hunger for a good fight. No one was more eager for battle than Theodore Roosevelt, who, along with Colonel Leonard Wood, led a volunteer cavalry unit

Map 22.1   Spanish-American War in Cuba, 1898   This map shows the following: the routes taken by U.S. ships transporting troops from Florida to Cuba; the concentration of troop landings and battles around Santiago, Cuba; and a U.S. naval blockade, stretching hundreds of miles from Puerto Rico to Cuba, that attempted to keep the Spanish troops in Cuba and Puerto Rico from being reinforced.
View an animated version of this map or related maps at http://www.thomsonedu.com/history/murrin.

composed of Ivy League gentlemen, western cowboys, sheriffs, prospectors, Indians, and small numbers of Hispanics and ethnic European Americans. Roosevelt's **Rough Riders,** as the unit came to be known, landed with the invasion force and played an active role in the three battles fought in the hills surrounding Santiago. Their most famous action, the one on which Roosevelt would build his lifelong reputation as a military hero, was a furious charge up Kettle Hill into the teeth of Spanish defenses. Roosevelt's bravery was stunning, although his judgment was faulty. Nearly 100 men were killed or wounded in the charge. Reports of Roosevelt's bravery overshadowed the equally brave performance of other troops, notably the **9th and 10th Negro Cavalries,** which played a pivotal role in clearing away Spanish fortifications on Kettle Hill and allowing Roosevelt's Rough Riders to make their charge. One Rough Rider commented: "If it had not been for the Negro cavalry, the Rough Riders would have been exterminated." Another added: "I am a Southerner by birth, and I never thought much of the colored man. But . . . I never saw such fighting as those Tenth Cavalry men did. They didn't seem to know what fear was, and their battle hymn was 'There'll be a hot time in the old town tonight.'" The 24th and 25th Negro Infantry Regiments performed equally vital tasks in the U.S. Army's conquest of the adjacent San Juan Hill.

Theodore Roosevelt saw the Rough Rider regiment that he commanded in the Spanish-American War as a melting pot of different groups of white Americans. Combat, he further believed, would forge these many groups into one, as war had always done in the American past. African Americans were the group most conspicuously absent from the Rough Rider mix. Yet the fury of the fighting on Kettle Hill and San Juan Hill so scrambled the white and black regiments that by the time the troops reached the San Juan summit, they were racially intermixed. Combat had brought blacks into the great American melting pot, a phenomenon that Roosevelt celebrated at the time. The black troops, he declared, were "an excellent breed of Yankee," and no "Rough Rider will ever forget," he added, "the tie that binds us to the Ninth and Tenth Cavalry."

But Roosevelt did not truly believe that blacks were the equals of whites or that they could be absorbed into the American nation. So, a few months after returning home, he began downplaying the role of black troops and questioned their ability to fight. The heroic role of black soldiers disappeared not only from Roosevelt's own memory but also from accounts and illustrations of the great charge. The attack on black fighting abilities would become so widespread that by the start of the First World War, the U.S. military had largely excluded black troops from combat roles. Thus, an episode that had demonstrated the possibility of interracial cooperation in America ended in the hardening of racial boundaries.

The taking of Kettle Hill, San Juan Hill, and other high ground surrounding Santiago gave the U.S. forces a substantial advantage over the Spanish defenders in Santiago. Nevertheless, logistical and medical problems nearly did them in. The troops were short of food, ammunition, and medical facilities. Their ranks were devastated by malaria, typhoid, and dysentery, and more than 5,000 soldiers died from disease. Even the normally ebullient Roosevelt was close to despair: "We are within measurable distance of a terrible military disaster," he wrote his friend Henry Cabot Lodge on July 3.

Fortunately, the Spanish had lost the will to fight. On the very day Roosevelt wrote to Lodge, Spain's Atlantic fleet tried to retreat from Santiago harbor and was promptly destroyed by a U.S. fleet. The Spanish army in Santiago surrendered on July 16; on July 18, the Spanish government asked for peace. While negotiations for an armistice proceeded, U.S. forces overran the neighboring island of Puerto Rico. On August 12, the U.S. and Spanish governments agreed to an armistice, but before the news could reach the Philippines, the United States had captured Manila and had taken prisoner 13,000 Spanish soldiers.

The armistice required Spain to relinquish its claim to Cuba, cede Puerto Rico and the Pacific island of Guam to the United States, and tolerate the American occupation of Manila until a peace conference could be convened in Paris on October 1, 1898. At that conference, American diplomats startled their Spanish counterparts by demanding that Spain also cede the Philippines to the United States. After two months of stalling, the Spanish government agreed to relinquish their coveted Pacific colony for $20 million. The transaction was sealed by the Treaty of Paris on December 10, 1898.

Rough Riders and 10th Cavalry   Roosevelt poses with his Rough Riders (above) while members of the 10th Cavalry appear below. Both groups played pivotal roles in the battles of San Juan and Kettle Hills, but America would celebrate only the Rough Riders, not the black cavalrymen.

The United States Becomes a World Power

Focus Question
What different mechanisms of control did the United States use to achieve its aims in Hawaii, Cuba, the Philippines, Puerto Rico, and China?

America's initial war aim had been to oust the Spanish from Cuba—an aim that both imperialists and anti-imperialists supported, but for different reasons. Imperialists hoped to incorporate Cuba into a new American empire; anti-imperialists hoped to see the Cubans gain their independence. But only the imperialists condoned the U.S. acquisition of Puerto Rico, Guam, and particularly the Philippines, which they viewed as integral to the extension of U.S. interests into Asia. Soon after the war began, President McKinley had cast his lot with the imperialists. First, he annexed Hawaii, giving the United States permanent control of Pearl Harbor. Next, he set his sights on setting up a U.S. naval base at Manila. Never before had the United States sought such a large military presence outside the Western Hemisphere.

In a departure of equal importance, McKinley announced his intent to administer much of this newly acquired territory as U.S. colonies. Virtually all territory the United States had obtained in the 19th century had been part of the North American continent. These lands had been settled by Americans, who had eventually petitioned for statehood. By 1900, most of these territories had been admitted to the Union with the same rights as existing states; others, such as New Mexico, Arizona, and Oklahoma, would soon acquire statehood status. In the case of the new overseas territories, however, only Hawaii would be allowed to follow this traditional path toward statehood. There, the powerful U.S. sugar plantation owners prevailed on Congress to pass an act in 1900 extending U.S. citizenship to all Hawaiian citizens and putting Hawaii on the road to statehood. No such influential group of Americans resided in the Philippines. The country was made a U.S. colony and placed under a U.S. administration that took its orders from Washington rather than from the Filipino people. Such colonization was necessary, in the eyes of American imperialists, to prevent other powers, such as Japan and Germany, from gaining a foothold somewhere in the 400-island archipelago and launching attacks on the U.S. naval base in Manila.

The McKinley administration might have taken a different course. The United States might have negotiated an arrangement with **Emilio Aguinaldo,** the leader of an anticolonial movement in the Philippines, that would have given the Philippines independence in exchange for a U.S. naval base at Manila. An American fleet stationed there would have been able to protect both American interests and the fledgling Philippine nation from predatory assaults by Japan, Germany, or Britain. Alternatively, the United States might have annexed the Philippines outright and offered Filipinos U.S. citizenship as the first step toward statehood. McKinley and his supporters, however, believed that the "inferior" Filipino people lacked the capacity for self-government. The United States would undertake a solemn mission to "civilize" the Filipinos and thereby prepare them for independence,

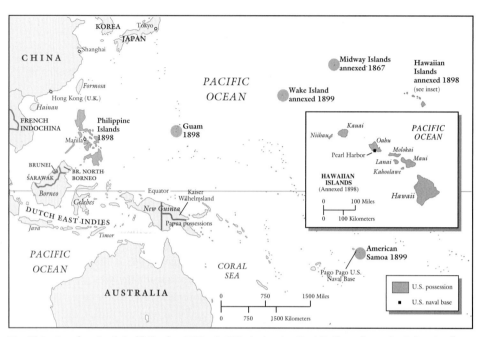

Map 22.2   American South Pacific Empire, 1900   By 1900, the American South Pacific empire consisted of a series of strategically located islands with superior harbor facilities, stretching from the Hawaiian Islands and Samoa in the middle of the Pacific to the Philippines on the ocean's western edge.

but until that mission was complete, the Philippines would submit to rule by presidentially appointed U.S. governors.

The Debate over the Treaty of Paris

The proposed acquisition of the Philippines aroused opposition both in the United States and in the Philippines. The Anti-Imperialist League, strong in the Northeast, enlisted the support of several elder statesmen in McKinley's own party, as well as the former Democratic President Grover Cleveland, the industrialist Andrew Carnegie, and the labor leader Samuel Gompers. William Jennings Bryan, meanwhile, marshaled a vigorous anti-imperialist protest among Democrats in the South and West, while Mark Twain, William James, William Dean Howells, and other men of letters lent the cause their prestige. Some anti-imperialists believed that subjugating the Filipinos would violate the nation's most precious principle: the right of all people to independence and self-government. Moreover, they feared that the military and diplomatic establishment needed to administer the colony would threaten political liberties at home.

Other anti-imperialists were motivated more by self-interest than by democratic ideals. U.S. sugar producers, for example, feared competition from Filipino producers. Trade unionists worried that poor Filipino workers would flood the U.S. labor market and depress wage rates. Some businessmen warned that the costs of maintaining an imperial outpost would exceed any economic benefits that the colony might produce. Many Democrats, meanwhile, simply wanted to gain partisan advantage by opposing the Republican administration's foreign policy. Still other anti-imperialists feared the contaminating effects of contact with "inferior" Asian races.

The contrasting motivations of the anti-imperialists weakened their opposition. Even so, they almost dealt McKinley and his fellow imperialists a defeat in the U.S. Senate. On February 6, 1899, the Senate voted 57 to 27 in favor of the Treaty of Paris, only one vote beyond the minimum two-thirds majority required for ratification. Two last-minute developments may have brought victory. First, William Jennings Bryan, in the days before the vote, abandoned his opposition and announced his support for the treaty. (He would later explain that he had decided for ratification in order to end the war with Spain, intending to continue his work for Filipino independence through diplomatic means.) Second, on the eve of the vote, Filipinos rose in revolt against the U.S. army of occupation. With another war looming and the lives of American soldiers imperiled, a few senators who had been reluctant to vote for the treaty may have felt obligated to support the president.

The American-Filipino War

The acquisition of the Philippines immediately embroiled the United States in a long, brutal war to subdue the Filipino rebels. In four years of fighting, more than 120,000 American soldiers served in the Philippines and more than 4,200 of them died. The war cost $160 million, or eight times what the United States had paid Spain to acquire the archipelago. The war brought Americans face-to-face with an unpleasant truth: that American actions in the Philippines were virtually indistinguishable from Spain's actions in Cuba. Like Spain, the United States refused to acknowledge a people's aspiration for self-rule. Like "Butcher" Weyler, American generals permitted their soldiers to use savage tactics. Whole communities suspected of harboring guerrillas were driven into concentration camps, and their houses, farms, and livestock were destroyed. American soldiers killed so many Filipino rebels (whom they called "goo-goos") that the ratio of Filipino dead to wounded reached 15 to 1, a statistic that made the American Civil War, in which one soldier had died for every five wounded, seem relatively humane. One New York infantryman wrote home that his unit had killed 1,000 Filipinos—men, women, and children—in retaliation for the murder of a single American soldier: "I am in my glory when I can sight my gun on some dark skin and pull the trigger," he exclaimed. A total of 15,000 Filipino soldiers died in the fighting. Estimates of total Filipino deaths from gunfire, starvation, and disease range from 50,000 to 200,000.

The United States finally gained the upper hand in the war after General Arthur MacArthur (father of Douglas) was appointed commander of the islands in 1900. MacArthur did not lessen the war's ferocity, but he understood that it could not be won by guns alone. He offered amnesty to Filipino guerrillas who agreed to surrender, and he cultivated close relations with the islands' economic elites. McKinley supported this effort to build a Filipino constituency sympathetic to the U.S. presence. To that end, he sent

William Howard Taft to the islands in 1900 to establish a civilian government. In 1901, Taft became the colony's first "governor-general" and declared that he intended to prepare the Filipinos for independence. He transferred many governmental functions to Filipino control and launched a program of public works (roads, bridges, schools) that would give the Philippines the infrastructure necessary for economic development and political independence. By 1902, this dual strategy of ruthless war against those who had taken up arms and concessions to those who were willing to live under benevolent American rule had crushed the revolt. Though sporadic fighting continued until 1913, Americans had secured control of the Philippines. The explicit commitment of the United States to Philippine independence (a promise that was deferred until 1946), together with an extensive program of internal improvements, eased the nation's conscience.

Controlling Cuba and Puerto Rico

Helping the Cubans achieve independence had been a major rationalization for the war against Spain. Even so, in 1900, when General Leonard Wood, now commander of U.S. forces in Cuba, authorized a constitutional convention to write the laws for a Cuban republic, the McKinley administration made clear it would not easily relinquish control of the island. At McKinley's urging, the U.S. Congress attached to a 1901 army appropriations bill the **Platt Amendment** (Orville Platt was the Republican senator from Connecticut), delineating three conditions for Cuban independence: (1) Cuba would not be permitted to make treaties with foreign powers; (2) the United States would have broad authority to intervene in Cuban political and economic affairs; and (3) Cuba would sell or lease land to the United States for naval stations. The delegates to Cuba's constitutional convention were so outraged by these conditions that they refused even to vote on them. But the dependence of Cuba's vital sugar industry on the U.S. market and the continuing presence of a U.S. army on Cuban soil rendered resistance futile. In 1901, by a vote of 15 to 11, the delegates reluctantly wrote the Platt conditions into their constitution. "There is, of course, little or no independence left Cuba under the Platt Amendment," Wood candidly admitted to his friend Theodore Roosevelt, who had recently succeeded the assassinated McKinley as president.

Cuba's status, in truth, differed little from that of the Philippines. Both were colonies of the United States. In the case of Cuba, economic dependence closely followed political subjugation. Between 1898 and 1914, U.S. trade with Cuba increased more than tenfold (from $27 million to $300 million), while investments more than quadrupled (from $50 million to $220 million). In 1903, the United States compelled Cuba to lease it 45 square miles of land and water on the island nation's southeast coast. There the United States built the U.S. Naval Station at Guantanamo Bay, a facility that it maintains to this day. The United States also intervened in Cuban political affairs five times between 1906 and 1921 to protect its economic interests and those of the indigenous ruling class with whom it had become closely allied. The economic, political, and military control that the United States imposed on Cuba would fuel anti-American sentiment there for years to come.

Puerto Rico received somewhat different treatment. The United States did not think independence appropriate, even though under Spanish rule the island had enjoyed a large measure of political autonomy and a parliamentary form of government. Nor did the United States follow its Cuban strategy by granting Puerto Rico nominal independence under informal economic and political controls. Instead, it annexed the island outright with the Foraker Act (1900). Unlike every previous annexation authorized by Congress since 1788, this act contained no provision for making the inhabitants of Puerto Rico citizens of the United States. Instead, Puerto Rico was designated an "unincorporated" territory, which meant that Congress would dictate the island's government and specify the rights of its inhabitants. Puerto Ricans were allowed no role in designing their government, nor was their consent to its establishment sought. With the Foraker Act, Congress had, in effect, invented a new, imperial mechanism for ensuring sovereignty over lands deemed vital to U.S. economic and military security. The U.S. Supreme Court upheld the constitutionality of this mechanism in a series of historic decisions, known as the Insular Cases, in the years from 1901 to 1904.

In some respects, Puerto Rico fared better than "independent" Cuba. Puerto Ricans were granted U.S. citizenship in 1917 and won the right to elect their own governor in 1947. Still, Puerto Ricans enjoyed fewer political rights than Americans in the 48 states. Moreover, throughout the 20th century, they endured a poverty rate far exceeding that of

"A Philippine Album: American Era Photographs" by Jonathan Best. (Bookmark, Manila 1998)

The "Water Cure" in the Philippines   This extraordinary photograph shows U.S. soldiers forcing water into the mouth of a Filipino guerrilla to the point where it would overflow his esophagus and pour into his breathing channels, creating the sensation of drowning. It reveals U.S. forces using brutal tactics to break down the resistance of their Filipino opponents.

the mainland. As late as 1948, for example, three-fourths of Puerto Rican households subsisted on $1,000 or less annually, a figure below the U.S. poverty line. In its skewed distribution of wealth and its lack of industrial development, Puerto Rico resembled the poorly developed nations of Central and South America more than it did the affluent country that took over its government in 1900.

The subjugation of Cuba and the annexation of Puerto Rico troubled Americans far less than the U.S. takeover in the Philippines. Since the first articulation of the Monroe Doctrine in 1823, the United States had, in effect, claimed the Western Hemisphere as its sphere of influence. Within that sphere, many Americans believed, the United States possessed the right to act unilaterally to protect its interests. Before 1900, most of its actions (with the exception of the Mexican War) had been designed to limit the influence of European powers—Britain, France, Russia, and Spain—on the countries of the hemisphere. After 1900, however, the United States assumed a more aggressive role, seizing land, overturning governments it did not like, and forcing its economic and political policies on weaker neighbors in order to turn the Caribbean Sea into what policy makers called (with the example of ancient Rome in mind) an American Mediterranean.

China and the "Open Door"

Except for the Philippines and Guam, the United States made no effort to take control of Asian lands. Such a policy might well have triggered war with other world powers that were already well established in the area. Nor were Americans prepared to tolerate the financial and political costs Asian conquest would have entailed. The United States opted for a diplomatic rather than a military strategy to achieve its foreign policy objectives. For China, in 1899 and 1900, it proposed the policy of the "open door."

The United States was concerned that the actions of the other world powers in China would block its own efforts to open up China's markets to American goods. Britain, Germany, Japan, Russia, and France each coveted their own chunk of China, where they could monopolize trade, exploit cheap labor, and establish military bases. By the 1890s, each of these powers was building a sphere of influence, either by wringing economic and territorial concessions from the weak Chinese government or by seizing outright the land and trading privileges they desired.

To prevent China's breakup and to preserve U.S. economic access to the whole of China, McKinley's secretary of state, John Hay, sent **"open door" notes** to the major world powers. The notes asked each power to open its Chinese sphere of influence to the merchants of other nations and to grant them reasonable harbor fees and railroad rates. Hay also asked each power to respect China's sovereignty by enforcing Chinese tariff duties in the territory it controlled.

None of the world powers embraced either of Hay's requests, although Britain and Japan gave provisional assent. France, Germany, Russia, and Italy responded evasively, indicating their support for the Open Door policy in theory but insisting that they could not implement it until all of the other powers had done so. Hay put the best face on their

Challenges to America's Open Door China Policy   Although imperial powers had defeated the Chinese Boxers, here depicted as a slain Chinese dragon, this cartoon suggests that they would soon be fighting each other for the spoils of victory. Appearing in the British magazine, *Puck*, the cartoon presents Russia (the bear) and Britain (the lion) as the two principal antagonists, with menacing France (the fox) and Japan (mountain cat) snarling in the foreground, and various birds of prey (the United States, Germany, Austria, and Italy) hovering over the kill.

responses by declaring that all of the powers had agreed to observe his Open Door principles and that he regarded their assent as "final and definitive." Americans took Hay's bluff as evidence that the United States had triumphed diplomatically over its rivals. The rivals may have been impressed by Hay's diplomacy, but whether they intended to uphold the United States' Open Door policy was not at all clear.

The first challenge to Hay's policy came from the Chinese. In May 1900, a Chinese organization, colloquially known as the **"Boxers,"** sparked an uprising to rid China of all "foreign devils" and foreign influences. Hundreds of Europeans were killed, as were many Chinese men and women who had converted to Christianity. When the Boxers laid siege to the foreign legations in Beijing and cut off communication between that city and the outside world, the imperial powers raised an expeditionary force to rescue the diplomats and punish the Chinese rebels. The force, which included 5,000 U.S. soldiers, rushed over from the Philippines, broke the Beijing siege in August, and ended the Boxer Rebellion soon thereafter.

Hay feared that other major powers would use the rebellion as a reason to demand greater control over Chinese territory. He sent out a second round of Open Door notes, now asking each power to respect China's political independence and territorial integrity, in addition to guaranteeing unrestricted access to its markets. Impressed by America's show of military strength and worried that the Chinese rebels might strike again, the imperialist rivals responded more favorably to this second round of notes. Britain, France, and Germany endorsed Hay's policy outright. With that support, Hay was able to check Russian and Japanese designs on Chinese territory. Significantly, when the powers decided that the Chinese government should pay them reparations for their property and personnel losses during the Boxer Rebellion, Hay convinced them to accept payment in cash rather than in territory. By keeping China intact and open to free trade, the United States had achieved a major foreign policy victory. Americans began to see themselves as China's savior as well.

Theodore Roosevelt, Geopolitician

Focus Question
What were the similarities and differences in the foreign policies of Theodore Roosevelt, William Howard Taft, and Woodrow Wilson?

Roosevelt had been a driving force in the transformation of U.S. foreign policy during the McKinley Administration. As assistant secretary of the navy, as a military hero, as a speaker and writer, and then as vice president, Roosevelt worked tirelessly to remake the country into one of the world's great powers. He believed that the Americans were a racially superior people destined for supremacy in economic and political affairs. He did not assume, however, that international supremacy would automatically accrue to the United States. A nation, like an individual, had to strive for greatness and cultivate physical and mental fitness; it had to build a military force that could convincingly project power overseas; and it had to be prepared to fight. All great nations, Roosevelt declared, ultimately depended on the skill and dedication of their warriors.

Roosevelt's appetite for a good fight caused many people to rue the ascension of this "cowboy" to the White House after McKinley's assassination in 1901. But behind his blustery exterior lay a shrewd analyst of international relations. As much as he craved power for himself and the nation, he understood that the United States could not rule every portion of the globe through military or economic means. Consequently, he sought a balance of power among the industrial nations through negotiation rather than war. Such a balance would enable each imperial power to safeguard its key interests and contribute to world peace and progress. (**See Map 22.3, Colonial Possessions, 1900, in the color insert following page 912.**)

Absent from Roosevelt's geopolitical thinking was concern for the interests of less powerful nations. Roosevelt had little patience with the claims to sovereignty of small countries or the human rights of weak peoples. In his eyes, the peoples of Latin America, Asia (with the exception of Japan), and Africa were racially inferior and thus incapable of self-government or industrial progress. They were better suited to subservience and subsistence than to independence and affluence.

The Roosevelt Corollary

Ensuring U.S. dominance in the Western Hemisphere ranked high on Roosevelt's list of foreign policy objectives. In 1904, he issued a "corollary" to the Monroe Doctrine, which had asserted the right of the United States to keep European powers from meddling in hemispheric affairs. In his corollary, Roosevelt declared that the United States possessed a further right: the right to intervene in the domestic affairs of nations in the Western Hemisphere to quell disorder and forestall European intervention. The **Roosevelt corollary** formalized a policy that the United States had already deployed against Cuba and Puerto Rico in 1900 and 1901. Subsequent events in Venezuela and the Dominican Republic had further convinced Roosevelt of the need to expand the scope of U.S. intervention in hemispheric affairs.

Both Venezuela and the Dominican Republic were controlled by dictators who had defaulted on debts owed to European banks. Their delinquency prompted a German-led European naval blockade and bombardment of Venezuela in 1902 and a threatened invasion of the Dominican Republic by Italy and France in 1903. The United States forced the German navy to retreat from the Venezuelan coast in 1903. In the Dominican Republic, after a revolution had chased the dictator from power, the United States assumed control of the nation's customs collections in 1905 and refinanced the Dominican national debt through U.S. bankers.

The willingness of European bankers to loan money to Latin America's corrupt regimes had created the possibility that the countries ruled by these regimes would suffer bankruptcy, social turmoil, and foreign intervention. The United States, under Roosevelt, did not hesitate to intervene to make sure that loans were repaid and social stability was restored. But rarely in Roosevelt's tenure did the United States show a willingness to help the people who had suffered under these regimes establish democratic institutions or achieve social justice. When Cubans seeking true national independence rebelled against their puppet government in 1906, the United States sent in the Marines to silence them. **(See Map 22.4, United States Presence in Latin America, 1895–1934, in the color insert following page 912.)**

The Panama Canal

Roosevelt's varied interests in Latin America embraced the building of a canal across Central America. The president had long believed, along with Admiral Mahan, that the nation needed a way of moving its ships swiftly from the Pacific Ocean to the Atlantic Ocean, and back again. Central America's narrow width, especially in its southern half, made it the logical place to build a canal. In fact, a French company had obtained land rights and had begun construction of a canal across the Colombian province of Panama in the 1880s. But even though a "mere" 40 miles of land separated the two oceans, the French were stymied by technological difficulties and by the financial costs of literally moving mountains. Moreover, French doctors found they were unable to check the spread of malaria and yellow fever among their workers. By the time Roosevelt entered the White House in 1901, the French Panama Company had gone bankrupt.

Roosevelt was not deterred by the French failure. He first presided over the signing of the Hay-Pauncefote Treaty with Great Britain in 1901, releasing the United States from an

1850 agreement that prohibited either country from building a Central American canal without the other's participation. He then instructed his advisers to develop plans for a canal across Nicaragua. The Panamanian route chosen by the French was shorter than the proposed Nicaraguan route, and the canal begun by the French was 40 percent complete, but the French company wanted $109 million for it, more than the United States was willing to pay. In 1902, however, the company reduced the price to $40 million, a sum that Congress deemed appropriate. Secretary of State Hay quickly negotiated an agreement with Tomas Herran, the Colombian chargé d'affaires in Washington. The agreement, formalized in the Hay-Herran Treaty, accorded the United States a six-mile-wide strip across **Panama** on which to build the **canal.** Colombia was to receive a onetime $10 million payment and annual rent of $250,000.

The Colombian legislature, however, rejected the proposed payment as insufficient and sent a new ambassador to the United States with instructions to ask for a onetime payment of $20 million and a share of the $40 million being paid to the French company. Actually, the Colombians (not unreasonably) were hoping to stall negotiations until 1904, when they would regain the rights to the canal zone and consequently to the $40 million sale price promised to the French company.

As negotiations failed to deliver the result he desired, Roosevelt encouraged the Panamanians to revolt against Colombian rule. Panamanians had staged several rebellions in the previous 25 years, all of which had failed, but the 1903 rebellion succeeded, mainly because a U.S. naval force prevented the Colombian government from landing troops in its Panama province. Meanwhile, the U.S.S. *Nashville* put U.S. troops ashore to help the new nation secure its independence. The United States formally recognized Panama as a sovereign state only two days after the rebellion against Colombia began.

Philippe Bunau-Varilla, a director of the French company from which the United States had bought the rights to the canal, declared himself Panama's diplomatic representative, even though he was a French citizen operating out of a Wall Street law firm and hadn't set foot in Panama in 15 years. Before the true Panamanian delegation (appointed by the new Panamanian government) even reached the United States for negotiations over the canal, Bunau-Varilla had gone to Washington, where he and Secretary of State Hay signed the Hay–Bunau-Varilla Treaty (1903). The treaty granted the United States a 10-mile-wide canal zone in Panama in return for the package Colombia had rejected—$10 million down and $250,000 annually. Thus the United States secured its canal, not by dealing with the newly installed Panamanian government, but with Bunau-Varilla's French company. When the Panamanian delegation arrived in Washington and read the treaty, one of them became so enraged that he knocked Bunau-Varilla cold. Under the circumstances, however, the Panamanian delegation's hands were tied. If it objected to the counterfeit treaty, the United States might withdraw its troops from Panama, leaving the new country at the mercy of Colombia. The instrument through which the United States secured the Canal Zone is known in Panamanian history as "the treaty which no Panamanian signed," and it bedeviled relations between the two countries for much of the 20th century.

Roosevelt's severing of Panama from Colombia prompted angry protests in Congress. The Hearst newspapers decried the Panama foray as "nefarious" and "a quite unexampled instance of foul play in American politics." Roosevelt was not perturbed. Elihu Root (secretary of state in Roosevelt's second administration), after hearing Roosevelt defend his action before a meeting of his cabinet, jokingly told the president, "You have shown that you were accused of seduction and you have conclusively proved that you were guilty of rape." Roosevelt later gloated, "I took the Canal Zone and let Congress debate!"

Roosevelt turned the building of the canal into a test of American ingenuity and willpower. Engineers overcame every obstacle; doctors developed drugs to combat malaria and yellow fever; armies of construction workers "made the dirt fly." The canal remains a testament to the labor of some 30,000 workers, imported mainly from the West Indies, who, over a 10-year period, labored 10 hours a day, 6 days a week, for 10 cents an hour. Roosevelt visited the canal site in 1906, the first American president to travel overseas while in office. When the canal was triumphantly opened to shipping in 1914, the British ambassador James Bryce described it as "the greatest liberty Man has ever taken with Nature." The canal shortened the voyage from San Francisco to New York by more than 8,000 miles and significantly enhanced the international prestige of the United States. The

Map 22.5 Panama Canal Zone, 1914   This map shows the route of the completed canal through Panama and the 10-mile-wide zone surrounding it that the United States controlled. The inset map locates the Canal Zone in the context of Central and South America.

strategic importance of the canal, in turn, made the United States even more determined to preserve political order in Central America and the Caribbean.

In 1921, the United States paid the Colombian government $25 million as compensation for its loss of Panama. Panama waited more than 70 years, however, to regain control of the 10-mile-wide strip of land that Bunau-Varilla, in connivance with the U.S. government, had bargained away in 1903. President Jimmy Carter signed a treaty in 1977 providing for the reintegration of the Canal Zone into Panama, and the canal was transferred to Panama in 2000.

Keeping the Peace in East Asia

In East Asia, Roosevelt strove to preserve the Open Door policy in China and the balance of power throughout the region. The chief threats came from Russia and Japan, both of whom wanted to seize large chunks of China. At first, Russian expansion into Manchuria and Korea prompted Roosevelt to support Japan's 1904 attack on the Russian Pacific fleet anchored at Port Arthur, China. Once the ruinous effects of the war on Russia became clear, however, Roosevelt entered into secret negotiations to arrange a peace. He invited representatives of Japan and Russia to Portsmouth, New Hampshire, and prevailed on them to negotiate a compromise. The settlement favored Japan by perpetuating its control over most of the territories it had won during the brief **Russo-Japanese War.** Its chief prize was Korea, which became a protectorate of Japan, but Japan also acquired the southern part of Sakhalin Island, Port Arthur, and the South Manchurian Railroad. Russia avoided paying Japan a huge indemnity and it retained Siberia, thus preserving its role as an East Asian power. Finally, Roosevelt protected China's territorial integrity by inducing the armies of both Russia and Japan to leave Manchuria. Roosevelt's success in ending the Russo-Japanese War won him the Nobel Prize for Peace in 1906; he was the first American to earn that award.

Although Roosevelt succeeded in negotiating a peace between these two world powers, he subsequently ignored, and sometimes encouraged, challenges to the sovereignty of weaker Asian nations. In a secret agreement with Japan (the Taft-Katsura Agreement of 1905), for example, the United States agreed that Japan could dominate Korea in return for a Japanese promise not to attack the Philippines. And in the Root-Takahira Agreement of 1908, the United States tacitly reversed its earlier stand on the inviolability of Chinese borders by recognizing Japanese expansion into southern Manchuria.

In Roosevelt's eyes, the overriding need to maintain peace with Japan justified ignoring the claims of Korea and, increasingly, of China. Roosevelt admired Japan's industrial and military might and regarded Japanese expansion into East Asia as a natural expression of its imperial ambition. The task of American diplomacy, he believed, was first to allow the Japanese to build a secure sphere of influence in East Asia (much as the United States had done in Central America and the Caribbean), and second to encourage them to join the United States in pursuing peace rather than war. This was a delicate diplomatic task that required both sensitivity and strength, especially when anti-Japanese agitation broke out in California in 1906.

North Wind Picture Archive

Anti-Asian Hysteria in San Francisco   In 1906, in the midst of a wave of anti-Asian prejudice in California, the San Francisco school board ordered the segregation of all Asian schoolchildren. Here, a nine-year-old Japanese student submits an application for admission to a public primary school and is refused by the principal, Miss M. E. Dean.

White Californians had long feared the presence of East Asian immigrants (see chapter 20). They had pressured Congress into passing the Chinese Exclusion Act of 1882, which ended most Chinese immigration to the United States. They next turned their racism on Japanese immigrants, whose numbers in California had reached 24,000. In 1906, the San Francisco school board ordered the segregation of Asian schoolchildren, so that they would not "contaminate" white children. In 1907, the California legislature debated a law to end Japanese immigration to the state. Anti-Asian riots erupted in San Francisco and Los Angeles, encouraged in part by hysterical stories in the press about the "Yellow Peril."

Outraged militarists in Japan began talking of a possible war with the United States. Roosevelt assured the Japanese government that he too was appalled by the Californians' behavior. In 1907, he reached a **"gentlemen's agreement"** with the Japanese, by which the Tokyo government promised to halt the immigration of Japanese adult male laborers to the United States in return for Roosevelt's pledge to end anti-Japanese discrimination in California. Roosevelt did his part by persuading the San Francisco school board to rescind its segregation ordinance.

At the same time, Roosevelt worried that the Tokyo government would interpret his sensitivity to Japanese honor as weakness. So he ordered the main part of the U.S. fleet, consisting of 16 battleships, to embark on a 45,000-mile world tour, including a splashy stop in Tokyo Bay. Many Americans deplored the cost of the tour and feared that the appearance of the U.S. Navy in a Japanese port would provoke military retaliation. Roosevelt brushed his critics aside, and, true to his prediction, the Japanese were impressed by the **Great White Fleet's** show of strength. Their response seemed to lend validity to the African proverb Roosevelt often invoked: "Speak softly and carry a big stick."

In fact, Roosevelt's handling of Japan was arguably the most impressive aspect of his foreign policy. Unlike many other Americans, he refused to let racist attitudes cloud his thinking. He knew when to make concessions and when to stand firm. His policies lessened the prospect of a war with Japan while preserving a strong U.S. presence in East Asia.

William Howard Taft, Dollar Diplomat

William Howard Taft brought impressive foreign policy credentials to the job of president. He had gained valuable experience in colonial administration as the first governor-general of the Philippines. As Roosevelt's secretary of war and chief negotiator for the Taft-Katsura agreement of 1905, he had learned a great deal about conducting diplomacy with imperialist rivals. Yet Taft lacked Roosevelt's grasp of balance-of-power politics and capacity for leadership in foreign affairs. Furthermore, Taft's secretary of state, Philander C. Knox, a corporation lawyer from Pittsburgh, lacked diplomatic expertise. Knox's conduct of foreign policy seemed directed almost entirely toward expanding opportunities for corporate investment overseas, a disposition that prompted critics to deride his policies as **"dollar diplomacy."**

Taft and Knox believed that U.S. investments would effectively substitute "dollars for bullets," and thus offer a more peaceful and less coercive way of maintaining stability and order. Taking a swipe at Roosevelt's "big stick" policy, Taft announced that "modern diplomacy is commercial."

The inability of Taft and Knox to grasp the complexities of power politics, however, led to a diplomatic reversal in East Asia. Prodded by banker associates, Knox sought to expand American economic activities in China—even in Manchuria, where they encroached on the Japanese sphere of influence. In 1911, Knox proposed that a syndicate of European and American bankers buy the Japanese-controlled South Manchurian Railroad to open up North China to international trade. Japan reacted by signing a friendship treaty with Russia, its former enemy, which signaled their joint determination to exclude American, British, and French goods from Manchurian markets. Knox's plan to purchase the railroad collapsed, and the United States' Open Door policy suffered a serious blow. Knox's further efforts to increase American trade with Central and South China triggered further hostile responses from the Japanese and the Russians and contributed to the collapse of the Chinese government and the onset of the Chinese Revolution in 1911.

Dollar diplomacy worked better in the Caribbean, where no major power contested U.S. policy. Knox encouraged U.S. investment. Companies such as United Fruit of Boston, which established extensive banana plantations in Costa Rica and Honduras, grew powerful enough to influence both the economies and the governments of Central

American countries. When political turmoil threatened their investments, the United States simply sent in its troops. Thus, when Nicaraguan dictator José Santos Zelaya reportedly began negotiating with a European country to build a second trans-Isthmian canal in 1910, a force of U.S. Marines toppled his regime. Marines landed again in 1912 when Zelaya's successor, Adolfo Diaz, angered Nicaraguans with his pro-American policies. This time the Marines were instructed to keep the Diaz regime in power. Except for a brief period in 1925, U.S. troops would remain in Nicaragua continuously from 1912 until 1933. Under Taft, the United States continued to do whatever American policy makers deemed necessary to bolster friendly governments and maintain order in Latin America.

Woodrow Wilson, Struggling Idealist

Woodrow Wilson's foreign policy in the Caribbean initially appeared no different from that of his Republican predecessors. In 1915, the United States sent troops to Haiti to put down a revolution; they remained as an army of occupation for 21 years. In 1916, when the people of the Dominican Republic (who shared the island of Hispaniola with the Haitians) refused to accept a treaty making them more or less a protectorate of the United States, Wilson forced them to accept the rule of a U.S. military government. When German influence in the Danish West Indies began to expand, Wilson purchased the islands from Denmark, renamed them the Virgin Islands, and added them to the U.S. Caribbean empire. By the time Wilson left office in 1921, he had intervened militarily in the Caribbean more often than any American president before him.

Wilson's relationship with Mexico in the wake of its revolution, however, reveals that he was troubled by a foreign policy that ignored a less powerful nation's right to determine its own future. He deemed the Mexicans capable of making democracy work and, in general, showed a concern for morality and justice in foreign affairs—matters to which Roosevelt and Taft had paid scant attention. Wilson wanted U.S. foreign policy to advance democratic ideals and institutions in Mexico.

Wilson's Mexican dealings were motivated by more than his fondness for democracy. He also feared that political unrest in Mexico could lead to violence, social disorder, and a revolutionary government hostile to U.S. economic interests. With a U.S.-style democratic government in Mexico, Wilson believed, property rights would be respected and U.S. investments would remain secure. Wilson's desire both to encourage democracy and to limit the extent of social change made it difficult to devise a consistent foreign policy toward Mexico.

The Mexican Revolution broke out in 1910 when dictator Porfirio Diaz, who had ruled for 34 years, was overthrown by democratic forces led by Francisco Madero. Madero's talk of democratic reform frightened many foreign investors, especially those in the United States and Great Britain, who owned more than half of all Mexican real estate, 90 percent of its oil reserves, and practically all of its railroads. Thus, when Madero was overthrown early in 1913 by Victoriano Huerta, a conservative general who promised to protect foreign investments, the dollar diplomatists in the Taft administration and in Great Britain breathed a sigh of relief. Henry Lane Wilson, the U.S. ambassador to Mexico, had helped engineer Huerta's coup. Before close relations between the United States and Huerta could be worked out, however, Huerta's men murdered Madero.

Woodrow Wilson, who became president shortly after Madero's assassination in 1913, might have overlooked it (as did the European powers) and entered into close ties with Huerta on condition that he protect U.S. property. Instead, Wilson refused to recognize Huerta's "government of butchers" and demanded that Mexico hold democratic elections. Wilson favored Venustiano Carranza and **Francisco ("Pancho") Villa,** two enemies of Huerta who commanded rebel armies and who claimed to be democrats. In April 1914, Wilson used the arrest of several U.S. sailors by Huerta's troops as a reason to send a fleet into Mexican waters. He ordered the U.S. Marines to occupy the Mexican port city of Veracruz and to prevent a German ship there from unloading munitions meant for Huerta's army. In the resulting battle between U.S. and Mexican forces, 19 Americans and 126 Mexicans were killed. The battle brought the two countries dangerously close to war. Eventually, however, American control over Veracruz weakened and embarrassed Huerta's regime to the point where Carranza was able to take power.

Carranza did not behave as Wilson had expected. Rejecting Wilson's efforts to shape a new Mexican government, he announced a bold land reform program. That program called for the distribution of some of Mexico's agricultural land to impoverished peasants and the transfer of developmental rights on oil lands from foreign corporations to the Mexican government. If the program went into effect, U.S. petroleum companies would lose control of their Mexican properties, a loss that Wilson deemed unacceptable. Wilson now threw his support to Pancho Villa, who seemed more willing than Carranza to protect U.S. oil interests. When Carranza's forces defeated Villa's forces in 1915, Wilson reluctantly withdrew his support of Villa and prepared to recognize the Carranza government.

Furious that Wilson had abandoned him, Villa and his soldiers pulled 18 U.S. citizens from a train in northern Mexico and murdered them, along with another 17 in an attack on Columbus, New Mexico. Determined to punish Villa, Wilson received permission from Carranza to send a U.S. expeditionary force under General John J. Pershing into Mexico to hunt down Villa's "bandits." Pershing's troops pursued Villa's forces 300 miles into Mexico but failed to catch them. The U.S. troops did, however, clash twice with Mexican troops under Carranza's command, once again bringing the countries to the brink of war. The United States, about to enter the First World War, could not afford a fight with Mexico; in 1917, Wilson quietly ordered Pershing's troops home and grudgingly recognized the Carranza government.

Wilson's policies toward Mexico in 1913–17 seemed to have produced few concrete results, except to reinforce an already deep antagonism among Mexicans toward the United States. His repeated changes in strategy, moreover, seemed to indicate a lack of skill and decisiveness in foreign affairs. Actually, however, Wilson recognized something that Roosevelt and Taft had not: that more and more peoples of the world were determined to control their own destinies. The United States, under Wilson, was looking for a way to support these peoples' democratic aspirations while also safeguarding its own economic interests. The First World War would make this quest for a balance between democratic principles and national self-interest all the more urgent.

Conclusion

We can assess the dramatic turn in U.S. foreign policy after 1898 either in relation to the foreign policies of rival world powers or against America's own democratic ideals. By the first standard, U.S. foreign policy looks impressive. The United States achieved its major objectives in world affairs: It tightened its control over the Western Hemisphere and projected its military and economic power into Asia. It did so while sacrificing relatively few American lives and while constraining the jingoistic appetite for truly extensive military adventure and conquest. The United States added only 125,000 square miles to its empire in the years from 1870 to 1900, while Great Britain, France, and Germany enlarged their empires by 4.7, 3.5, and 1.0 million square miles, respectively. Relatively few foreigners were subjected to U.S. colonial rule. By contrast, in 1900, the British Empire extended more than 12 million square miles and embraced one-fourth of the world's population. At times, American rule could be brutal, as it was to Filipino soldiers and civilians alike, but on the whole it was no more severe than British or French rule and significantly less severe than that of German, Belgian, or Japanese imperialists. McKinley, Roosevelt, Taft, and Wilson all placed limits on American expansion and avoided, until 1917, extensive foreign entanglements and wars.

If measured against the standard of America's own democratic ideals, however, U.S. foreign policy after 1898 must be judged more harshly. It demeaned the peoples of the Philippines, Puerto Rico, Guam, Cuba, and Colombia as inferior and primitive and denied them the right to govern themselves. In choosing to behave like the imperialist powers of Europe, the United States abandoned its longstanding claim to being a different kind of nation—one that valued liberty more than power.

Many Americans of the time judged their nation by both standards and thus faced a dilemma that would extend throughout the 20th century. On the one hand, they believed with Roosevelt that the size, economic strength, and honor of the United States required it to accept the role of world power and policeman. On the other hand, they continued to believe with Wilson that they had a mission to spread the democratic values of 1776 to the farthest reaches of the earth. The Mexico example demonstrates how hard it was for the United States to reconcile these two very different approaches to world affairs.

SUGGESTED READINGS

General works on America's imperialist turn in the 1890s and early years of the 20th century include **John Dobson,** *America's Ascent: The United States Becomes a Great Power, 1880–1914* (1978); **Walter LaFeber,** *The Cambridge History of Foreign Relations: The Search for Opportunity, 1865–1913* (1993); and **Emily Rosenberg,** *Spreading the American Dream: American Economic* *and Cultural Expansion, 1890–1945* (1982). **David F. Trask,** *The War with Spain in 1898* (1981) is a comprehensive study of the Spanish-American War, but it should be supplemented with **Philip S. Foner,** *The Spanish-Cuban-American War and the Birth of American Imperialism,* 2 vols. (1972). **Gerald F. Linderman,** *The Mirror of War: American Society and the Spanish-American War* (1974) brilliantly recaptures the shock that overtook Americans who discovered that their Cuban allies were black and the Spanish enemies were white. The role of gender in the Spanish-American War is explored in **Kristin L. Hoganson,** *Fighting for American Manhood: How Gender Politics Provoked the Spanish-American and Philippine-American Wars* (1998).

Stuart Creighton Miller, *"Benevolent Assimilation": The American Conquest of the Philippines, 1899–1903* (1982) examines the Filipino-American war, while **Paul A. Kramer,** *The Blood of Government: Race, Empire, the United States, and the Philippines* (2006) analyzes the effects of U.S. colonialism on the Philippines and America. **Louis A. Perez,** *Cuba under the Platt Amendment, 1902–1934* (1986), explores the extension of U.S. control over Cuba, while **Marilyn B. Young,** *The Rhetoric of Empire: American China Policy, 1895–1901* (1968) examines the unfolding Open Door policy. The acquisition of Guam and Samoa is the subject of **Paul M. Kennedy,** *The Samoan Tangle* (1974), and the history of Puerto Rico following its annexation by the United States is explored in **Raymond Carr,** *Puerto Rico: A Colonial Experiment* (1984). The anti-imperialist movement is analyzed in **E. Berkeley Tompkins,** *Anti-Imperialism in the United States, 1890–1920: The Great Debate* (1970).

Howard K. Beale, *Theodore Roosevelt and the Rise of America to World Power* (1956), is still a crucial work on Roosevelt's foreign policy, but it should be supplemented with **Richard H. Collin,** *Theodore Roosevelt's Caribbean: The Panama Canal, the Monroe Doctrine and the Latin American Context* (1990). Consult **Emily Rosenberg,** *Financial Missionaries to the World: The Politics and Culture of Dollar Diplomacy, 1900–1930* (1999), on the "dollar diplomacy" that emerged during the Taft Administration. On Wilson's foreign policy, see **Thomas J. Knock,** *To End All Wars: Woodrow Wilson and the Quest for a New World Order* (1992); **Lloyd C. Gardner,** *Safe for Democracy: The Anglo-American Response to Revolution, 1913–1923* (1984); **John S. D. Eisenhower,** *Intervention: The United States and the Mexican Revolution, 1913–1917* (1993); and **Mary A. Renda,** *Taking Haiti: Military Occupation and the Culture of U.S. Imperialism, 1915–1940* (2001).

Visit the Liberty Equality Power Companion Web site for resources specific to this textbook: http://www.thomsonedu.com/history/murrin

Also find self-tests and additional resources at ThomsonNOW. ThomsonNOW is an integrated online suite of services and resources with proven ease of use and efficient paths to success, delivering the results you want-NOW!

www.thomsonedu.com/login/

War and Society, 1914–1920

The First World War broke out in Europe in August 1914. The **Triple Alliance** of Germany, Austria-Hungary, and the Ottoman Empire squared off against the **Triple Entente** of Great Britain, France, and Russia. The United States entered the war on the side of the Entente (the Allies, or Allied Powers, as they came to be called) in 1917. Over the next year and a half, the United States converted its large, sprawling economy into a disciplined war production machine, raised a 5-million-man army, and provided both the war matériel and troops that helped propel the Allies to victory. The United States emerged from the war as the world's mightiest country. In these and other respects, the war was a great triumph.

But the war also convulsed American society more deeply than any event since the Civil War. This was the first **"total" war**, meaning that combatants devoted virtually all of their resources to the fight. Thus the U.S. government had no choice but to pursue a degree of industrial control and social regimentation that was unprecedented in American history. Needless to say, this degree of government control was a controversial measure in a society that had long distrusted state power. Moreover, significant numbers of Americans from a variety of constituencies opposed the war. To overcome this opposition, Wilson couched American war aims in disinterested and idealistic terms: The United States, he claimed, wanted a "peace without victory," a "war for democracy," and liberty for the world's oppressed peoples. Because these words drew deeply on American political traditions, Wilson believed that Americans would find them inspiring, put aside their suspicions, and support him.

Although many people in the United States and abroad responded enthusiastically to Wilson's ideals, Wilson needed England and France's support to deliver peace without victory, and this support never came. At home, disadvantaged groups stirred up trouble by declaring that American society had failed to live up to its democratic and egalitarian ideals. Wilson supported repressive policies to silence these rebels and to enforce unity and conformity on the American people. In the process, he tarnished the ideals for which America had been fighting. Only a year after the war ended, Wilson's hopes for peace without victory abroad had been destroyed, and America was being torn apart by violent labor disputes and race riots at home.

CHRONOLOGY

1914	First World War breaks out (July–August)
1915	German submarine sinks the *Lusitania* (May 7)
1916	Woodrow Wilson unveils peace initiative • Wilson reelected as "peace president"
1917	Germany resumes unrestricted submarine warfare (February) • Tsar Nicholas II overthrown in Russia (March) • U.S. enters the war (April 6) • Committee on Public Information established • Congress passes Selective Service Act, Espionage Act, Immigration Restriction Act • War Industries Board established • Lenin's Bolsheviks come to power in Russia (November)
1918	Lenin signs treaty with Germany, pulls Russia out of war (March) • Germany launches offensive on western front (March–April) • Congress passes Sabotage Act and Sedition Act • French, British, and U.S. troops repel Germans, advance toward Germany (April–October) • Eugene V. Debs jailed for making antiwar speech • Germany signs armistice (November 11)
1919	Treaty of Versailles signed (June 28) • Chicago race riot (July) • Wilson suffers stroke (October 2) • Police strike in Boston • 18th Amendment (Prohibition) ratified
1919–20	Steelworkers strike in Midwest • Red Scare prompts "Palmer raids" • Senate refuses to ratify Treaty of Versailles • Universal Negro Improvement Association grows under Marcus Garvey's leadership
1920	Anarchists Sacco and Vanzetti convicted of murder
1923	Marcus Garvey convicted of mail fraud
1924	Woodrow Wilson dies
1927	Sacco and Vanzetti executed

Europe's Descent into War

Europe began its descent into war on June 28, 1914, in Sarajevo, Bosnia, when a Bosnian nationalist assassinated Archduke Franz Ferdinand, heir to the Austro-Hungarian throne. This act was meant to protest the Austro-Hungarian imperial presence in the Balkans and to encourage the Bosnians, Croatians, and other Balkan peoples to join the Serbs in establishing independent nations. Austria-Hungary responded to this provocation on July 28 by declaring war on Serbia, holding it responsible for the archduke's murder.

The conflict might have remained local if an intricate series of treaties had not divided Europe into two hostile camps. Germany, Austria-Hungary, and Italy, the so-called Triple Alliance, had promised to come to each other's aid if attacked. Italy would soon opt out of this alliance, to be replaced by the Ottoman Empire. Arrayed against the nations of the Triple Alliance were Britain, France, and Russia in the Triple Entente. Russia was obligated by another treaty to defend Serbia against Austria-Hungary, and consequently on July 30, it mobilized its armed forces to go to Serbia's aid. That brought

Germany into the conflict to protect Austria-Hungary from Russian attack. On August 3, German troops struck not at Russia but at France, Russia's western ally. To reach France, German troops had marched through neutral Belgium. On August 4, Britain reacted by declaring war on Germany. Within the space of only a few weeks, Europe was engulfed in war.

Complicated alliances and defense treaties of the European nations undoubtedly hastened the rush toward war. But equally important was the competition among the European powers to build the strongest economies, the largest armies and navies, and the grandest colonial empires. Britain and Germany, in particular, were engaged in a bitter struggle for European and world supremacy. Few Europeans had any idea that these military buildups might lead to a terrible war that would kill nearly an entire generation of young men and expose the barbarity lurking in their civilization. Historians now believe that several advisers close to the German emperor, Kaiser Wilhelm II, were actually eager to engage Russia and France in a fight for supremacy on the European continent. They expected that a European war would be swift and decisive—in Germany's favor. England and France also believed in their own superiority. Millions of young men, rich and poor, rushed to join the armies on both sides and share in the expected glory.

Victory was not swift. The two camps were evenly matched. Moreover, the first wartime use of machine guns and barbed wire made defense against attack easier than staging an offensive. (Both tanks and airplanes had been invented by this time, but military strategists on both sides were slow to put them to offensive use.) On the western front, after the initial German attack narrowly failed to take Paris in 1914, the two opposing armies confronted each other along a battle line stretching from Belgium in the north to the Swiss border in the south. Troops dug trenches to protect themselves from artillery bombardment and poison gas attacks. Commanders on both sides mounted suicidal ground assaults on the enemy by sending tens of thousands of infantry, armed only with rifles, bayonets, and grenades, out of the trenches and directly into enemy fire. Barbed wire further retarded forward progress, enabling enemy artillery and machine guns to cut down appalling numbers of men. In 1916, during one 10-month German offensive at Verdun (France), 600,000 German troops died; 20,000 British troops were killed during only the first day of an Entente assault on the Somme River (also in France). Many of those who were not killed in combat succumbed to disease that spread rapidly in the cold, wet, and rat-infested trenches. In Eastern Europe, the armies of Germany and Austria-Hungary squared off against those of Russia and Serbia. Although that front did not employ trench warfare, the combat was no less lethal. By the time the First World War ended, an estimated 8.5 million soldiers had died and more than twice that number had been wounded. Total casualties, both military and civilian, had reached 37 million. Europe had lost a generation of young men, as well as its confidence, stability, and global supremacy.

Map 23.1 Europe Goes to War In the First World War, Great Britain, France, and Russia squared off against Germany, Austria-Hungary, and the Ottoman Empire. Most of the fighting occurred in Europe along the western front in France (solid line) or the eastern front in Russia (dashed line). This map also shows Britain's blockade of German ports. British armies based in Egypt (then a British colony) clashed with Ottoman armies in Arabia and other parts of the Ottoman Empire. View an animated version of this map or related maps at http://www.thomsonedu.com/history/murrin.

American Neutrality

Focus Question
Why did the U.S. policy of neutrality fail, and why did the United States get drawn into war?

Soon after the fighting began, Woodrow Wilson told Americans that this was a European war; neither side was threatening a vital American interest. The United States would therefore proclaim its **neutrality** and maintain normal relations with both sides while seeking to secure peace. Normal relations meant that the United States would continue trading with both camps. Wilson's neutrality policy met with lively opposition, especially from Theodore Roosevelt, who was convinced that the United States should join the Entente to check German power and expansionism. Most Americans, however, applauded Wilson's determination to keep the country out of war.

Neutrality was easier to proclaim than to achieve, however. Many Americans, especially those with economic and political power, identified culturally more with Britain than with Germany. They shared with the English a language, a common ancestry, and a commitment to liberty. Wilson revered the British parliamentary system of government. His closest foreign policy adviser, Colonel Edward M. House, was pro-British, as was Robert Lansing, a trusted counselor in the State Department. William Jennings Bryan, Wilson's secretary of state, objected to this pro-British tilt, but he was a lone voice in Wilson's Cabinet. Germany had no such attraction for U.S. policy makers. On the contrary, Germany's acceptance of monarchical rule, the prominence of militarists in German politics, and its lack of democratic traditions inclined U.S. officials to judge Germany harshly.

The United States had strong economic ties to Great Britain as well. In 1914, the United States exported more than $800 million in goods to Britain and its allies, compared with $170 million to Germany and Austria-Hungary (which came to be known as the Central Powers). As soon as the war began, the British and then the French turned to the United States for food, clothing, munitions, and other war supplies. The U.S. economy, which had been languishing in 1914, enjoyed a boom as a result. Bankers began to issue loans to the Allied Powers, further knitting together the American and British economies and giving American investors a direct stake in an Allied victory. Moreover, the British navy had blockaded German ports, which damaged the United States' already limited trade with Germany. By 1916, U.S. exports to the Central Powers had plummeted to barely $1 million, a fall of more than 99 percent in two years.

The British blockade of German ports clearly violated American neutrality. The Wilson administration protested the British navy's search and occasional seizure of American merchant ships, but it never retaliated by suspending loans or exports to Great Britain. To do so would have plunged the U.S. economy into a recession. In failing to protect its right to trade with Germany, however, the United States compromised its neutrality and allowed itself to be drawn into war.

Submarine Warfare

To combat British control of the seas and to check the flow of U.S. goods to the Allies, Germany unveiled a terrifying new weapon, the *Unterseeboot,* or U-boat, the first militarily effective submarine. Early in 1915, Germany announced its intent to use its U-boats to sink on sight enemy ships en route to the British Isles. On May 7, 1915, without warning, a German U-boat torpedoed the British passenger liner **Lusitania,** en route from New York to London. The ship sank in 22 minutes, killing 1,198 men, women, and children, 128 of them U.S. citizens. Americans were shocked by the sinking. Innocent civilians who had been given no warning of attack and no chance to surrender had been murdered in cold blood. The attack appeared to confirm what anti-German agitators were saying: that the Germans were by nature barbaric and uncivilized. The circumstances surrounding the sinking of the *Lusitania,* however, were more complicated than most Americans realized.

Before its sailing, the Germans had alleged that the *Lusitania* was secretly carrying a large store of munitions to Great Britain (a charge later proved true), and that it therefore was subject to U-boat attack. Germany had warned American passengers not to travel on British passenger ships that carried munitions. Moreover, Germany claimed, with some justification, that the purpose of the U-boat attacks—the disruption of Allied supply lines—was no different from Britain's purpose in blockading German ports. Because its surface ships were outnumbered by the British navy, Germany claimed it had no alternative but to choose the underwater strategy. If a submarine attack seemed more reprehensible than a conventional sea battle, the Germans argued, it was no more so than the British attempt to starve the German people into submission with a blockade.

American political leaders might have used the *Lusitania* incident to denounce both Germany's U-boat strategy and Britain's blockade as actions that violated the rights of citizens of neutral nations. Only Secretary of State Bryan had the courage to say so, however, and his stand proved so unpopular in Washington that he resigned from office; Wilson chose the pro-British Lansing to take his place. Wilson denounced the sinking of the *Lusitania* and demanded that Germany pledge never to launch another attack on the citizens of neutral nations, even when they were traveling in British or French ships. Germany acquiesced to Wilson's demand.

The resulting lull in submarine warfare was short-lived, however. In early 1916, the Allies began to arm their merchant vessels with guns and depth charges capable of destroying German U-boats. Considering this a provocation, Germany renewed its campaign of surprise submarine attacks. In March 1916, a German submarine torpedoed the French passenger liner *Sussex,* causing a heavy loss of life and injuring several Americans. Again Wilson demanded that Germany spare civilians from attack. In the so-called *Sussex* pledge, Germany once again relented but warned that it might resume unrestricted submarine warfare if the United States did not prevail on Great Britain to permit neutral ships to pass through the naval blockade.

The German submarine attacks strengthened the hand of Theodore Roosevelt and others who had been arguing that war with Germany was inevitable and that the United States must prepare to fight. By 1916, Wilson could no longer ignore these critics. Between January and September of that year, he sought and won congressional approval for bills to increase the size of the army and navy, tighten federal control over National Guard forces, and authorize the building of a merchant fleet. Although Wilson had conceded ground to the pro-war agitators, he did not share their belief that war with Germany was either inevitable or desirable. To the contrary, he accelerated his diplomatic initiatives to secure peace, and he dispatched Colonel House to London in January 1916 to draw up a peace plan with the British foreign secretary, Lord Grey. This initiative resulted in the House-Grey memorandum of February 22, 1916, in which Britain agreed to ask the United States to negotiate a settlement between the Allies and the Central Powers. The British believed that the terms of such a peace settlement would favor the Allies. They were furious when Wilson revealed that he wanted an impartial, honestly negotiated peace in which the claims of the Allies and Central Powers would be treated with equal respect and consideration. Britain now rejected U.S. peace overtures, and relations between the two countries grew unexpectedly tense.

The Peace Movement

Underlying Wilson's 1916 peace initiative was a vision of a new world order in which relations between nations would be governed by negotiation rather than war and in which justice would replace power as the fundamental principle of diplomacy. In a major foreign policy address on May 27, 1916, Wilson formally declared his support for what he would later call the League of Nations, an international parliament dedicated to the pursuit of peace, security, and justice for all the world's peoples.

Many Americans supported Wilson's efforts to commit national prestige to the cause of international peace rather than conquest and to keep the United States out of war. Carrie Chapman Catt, president of the National American Woman Suffrage Association, and Jane Addams, founder of the Women's Peace Party, actively opposed the war. In 1915, an international women's peace conference at The Hague (in the Netherlands) had drawn many participants from the United States. A substantial pacifist group emerged among the nation's Protestant clergy. Midwestern progressives such as Robert La Follette, William Jennings Bryan, and George Norris urged that the United States steer clear of this European conflict, as did leading socialists such as Eugene V. Debs. In April 1916, many of the country's most prominent progressives and socialists joined hands in the American Union Against Militarism and pressured Wilson to continue pursuing the path of peace.

Wilson's peace campaign also attracted support from the country's sizable Irish and German ethnic populations, who wanted to block a formal military alliance with Great Britain. That many German ethnics, who continued to feel affection for their native land and culture, would oppose U.S. entry into the war is hardly surprising. And the Irish viewed England as an arrogant imperial power that kept Ireland subjugated. That view was confirmed when England crushed the Easter Rebellion that Irish nationalists had launched on Easter Monday 1916 to win their country's independence. The Irish in America, like those in Ireland, wanted to see Britain's strength sapped (and Ireland's prospects for freedom enhanced) by a long war.

Wilson's Vision: "Peace without Victory"

The 1916 presidential election revealed the breadth of peace sentiment. At the Democratic convention, Governor Martin Glynn of New York, the Irish American speaker who renominated Wilson for a second term, praised the president for keeping the United States out

UNITED WE STAND - DIVIDED WE FALL

UNITED
MINE WORKERS
JOURNAL

AFTER TWO YEARS—WHO WANTS ME?

INDIANAPOLIS, IND., AUGUST 3, 1916

Wisconsin Historical Society

The Horror of War   This cover of the *United Mine Workers Journal* (1916) presents the Great War in the bleakest possible terms: as giving the Grim Reaper license to claim the bodies and souls of Europe's young men. Progressive labor unions were part of the broad coalition in the United States opposed to America's entry into war.

of war. His portrayal of Wilson as the "peace president" electrified the convention and made "He kept us out of war" a campaign slogan. The slogan proved particularly effective against Wilson's Republican opponent, Charles Evans Hughes, whose close ties to Theodore Roosevelt seemed to place him in the pro-war camp. Combining the promise of peace with a pledge to push ahead with progressive reform, Wilson won a narrow victory.

Emboldened by his electoral triumph, Wilson intensified his quest for peace. On December 16, 1916, he sent a peace note to the belligerent governments, entreating them to consider ending the conflict and, to that end, to state their terms for peace. Although Germany refused to specify its terms and Britain and France announced a set of conditions too extreme for Germany ever to accept, Wilson pressed ahead, initiating secret peace negotiations with both sides. To prepare the American people for what he hoped would be a new era of international relations, Wilson appeared before the Senate on January 22, 1917, to outline his plans for peace. In his speech, he reaffirmed his commitment to the League of Nations, but for such a league to succeed, Wilson argued, it would have to be handed a sturdy peace settlement. This entailed a **"peace without victory."** Only a peace settlement that refused to crown a victor or humiliate a loser would ensure the equality of the combatants, and "only a peace between equals can last."

Wilson listed the crucial principles of a lasting peace: freedom of the seas; disarmament; and the right of every people to self-determination, democratic self-government, and security against aggression. He was proposing a revolutionary change in world order, one that would allow all of the world's peoples, regardless of their size or strength, to achieve political independence and to participate as equals in world affairs. These views, rarely expressed by the leader of a world power, stirred the despairing masses of Europe and elsewhere caught in deadly conflict.

German Escalation

Wilson's oratory came too late to serve the cause of peace. Sensing the imminent collapse of Russian forces on the eastern front, Germany had decided, in early 1917, to throw its full military might at France and Britain. On land it planned to launch a massive assault on the trenches, and at sea it prepared to unleash its submarines to attack all vessels heading for British ports. Germany knew that this last action would compel the United States to enter the war, but it was gambling on being able to strangle the British economy and leave France isolated before significant numbers of American troops could reach European shores.

On February 1, the United States broke off diplomatic relations with Germany. Wilson continued to hope for a negotiated settlement, however, until February 25, when the British intercepted and passed on to the president a telegram from Germany's foreign secretary, Arthur Zimmermann, to the German minister in Mexico. The infamous **"Zimmermann telegram"** instructed the minister to ask the Mexican government to attack the United States in the event of war between Germany and the United States. In return, Germany would pay the Mexicans a large fee and regain for them the "lost provinces" of Texas, New Mexico, and Arizona. Wilson, Congress, and the American public were outraged by the story.

In March, news arrived that Tsar Nicholas II's autocratic regime in Russia had collapsed and had been replaced by a liberal-democratic government under the leadership of Alexander Kerensky. As long as the tsar ruled Russia and stood to benefit from the Central Powers' defeat, Wilson could not honestly claim that America's going to war against Germany would bring democracy to Europe. The fall of the tsar and the need of Russia's fledgling democratic government for support gave Wilson the rationale he needed to justify American intervention.

Appearing before a joint session of Congress on April 2, Wilson declared that the United States must enter the war because "the world must be made safe for democracy." He continued:

> We shall fight for the things which we have always carried nearest our hearts—for democracy, for the right of those who submit to authority to have a voice in their own Governments, for the rights and liberties of small nations, for a universal dominion of right by such a concert of free peoples as shall bring peace and safety to all nations and make the world itself at last free. To such a task we dedicate our lives and our fortunes.

Inspired by his words, Congress broke into thunderous applause. On April 6, Congress voted to declare war by a vote of 373 to 50 in the House and 82 to 6 in the Senate.

The United States thus embarked on a grand experiment to reshape the world. Wilson had given millions of people around the world reason to hope, both that the terrible war would end soon and that their strivings for freedom and social justice would be realized. Although he was taking America to war on the side of the Allies, he stressed that America would fight as an "associated power," a phrase meant to underscore America's determination to keep its war aims separate from and more idealistic than those of the Allies.

Still, Wilson understood all too well the risks of his undertaking. A few days before his speech to Congress, he had confided to a journalist his worry that the American people, once at war, will "forget there ever was such a thing as tolerance. To fight you must be brutal and ruthless, and the spirit of ruthless brutality will enter into the very fibre of our national life, infecting Congress, the courts, the policeman on the beat, the man in the street."

American Intervention

The entry of the United States into the war gave the Allies the muscle they needed to defeat the Central Powers, but it almost came too late. Germany's resumption of unrestricted submarine warfare took a frightful toll on Allied shipping. From February through July 1917, German subs sank almost 4 million tons of shipping, more than one-third of Britain's entire merchant fleet. One of every four large freighters departing Britain in those months never returned; at one point, the British Isles were down to a mere four weeks of provisions. American intervention ended Britain's vulnerability in dramatic fashion. U.S. and British naval commanders now grouped merchant ships into convoys and provided them with warship escorts through the most dangerous stretches of the North Atlantic. Destroyers armed with depth charges were particularly effective as escorts. Their shallow draft made them invulnerable to torpedoes, and their great acceleration and speed allowed them to pursue slow-moving U-boats. The U.S. and British navies had begun to use sound waves (later called "sonar") to pinpoint the location of underwater craft, and this new technology increased the effectiveness of destroyer attacks. By the end of 1917, the tonnage of Allied shipping lost each month to U-boat attacks had declined by two-thirds, from almost 1 million tons in April to 350,000 tons in December. The increased flow of supplies stiffened the resolve of the exhausted British and French troops.

The French and British armies had bled themselves white by taking the offensive in 1916 and 1917 and had scarcely budged the trench lines. The Germans had been content in those years simply to hold their trench position in the West because they were engaged in a huge offensive against the Russians in the East. The Germans intended first to defeat Russia and then to shift their eastern armies to the West for a final assault on the weakened British and French lines. Their opportunity came in the winter and spring of 1918.

A second Russian revolution in November 1917 had overthrown Kerensky's liberal-democratic government and had brought to power a revolutionary socialist government under Vladimir Lenin and his Bolshevik Party. Lenin pulled Russia out of the war on the grounds that the war did not serve the best interests of the working classes, that it was a conflict between rival capitalist elites interested only in wealth and power (and indifferent to the slaughter of soldiers in the trenches). In March 1918, Lenin signed a treaty at Brest-Litovsk that added to Germany's territory and resources and enabled Germany to shift its eastern forces to the western front.

Russia's exit from the war hurt the Allies. Not only did it expose French and British troops to a much larger German force, but it also challenged the Allied claim that they were fighting a just war against German aggression. Lenin had published the texts of secret Allied treaties showing that Britain and France, like Germany, had plotted to enlarge their nations and empires through war. The revelation that the Allies were fighting for land and riches rather than democratic principles outraged large numbers of people in France and Great Britain, demoralized Allied troops, and threw the French and British governments into disarray.

The treaties also embarrassed Wilson, who had brought America into the war to fight for democracy, not territory. Wilson quickly moved to restore the Allies' credibility by unveiling, in January 1918, a concrete program for peace. His **Fourteen Points** reaffirmed America's commitment to an international system governed by laws rather than by might and renounced territorial aggrandizement as a legitimate war aim. This document provided the ideological cement that held the Allies together at a critical moment. (The Fourteen Points are discussed more fully in the section "The Failure of the International Peace.")

In March and April 1918, Germany launched its huge offensive against British and French positions, sending Allied troops reeling. A ferocious assault against French lines on May 27 met with little resistance; German troops advanced 10 miles a day—a faster pace than any on the western front since the earliest days of the war—until they reached the Marne River, within striking distance of Paris. The French government prepared to evacuate the city. At this perilous moment, a large American army—fresh, well-equipped, and oblivious to the horrors of trench warfare—arrived to reinforce what remained of the French lines.

In fact, these American troops, part of the American Expeditionary Force (AEF) commanded by General **John J. Pershing**, had begun landing in France almost a year earlier. During the intervening months, the United States had had to create a modern army from scratch, because its existing force was so small, ranking only 17th in the world. Men had to be drafted, trained, and supplied with food and equipment; ships for transporting them to Europe had to be found or built. In France, Pershing put his troops through additional training before committing them to battle. He was determined that the American soldiers—or "doughboys," as they were called—should acquit themselves well on the battlefield. The army he ordered into battle to counter the German spring offensive of 1918 fought well. Many American soldiers fell, but the German offensive ground to a halt. Paris was saved, and Germany's best chance for victory slipped from its grasp.

Buttressed by this show of AEF strength, the Allied troops staged a major offensive of their own in late September. Millions of Allied troops (including more than a million from the AEF) advanced across the 200-mile-wide Argonne forest in France, cutting German supply lines. By late October, they had reached the German border. Faced with an invasion of their homeland and with rapidly mounting popular dissatisfaction with the war, German leaders asked for an armistice, to be followed by peace negotiations based on Wilson's Fourteen Points. Having forced the Germans to agree to numerous concessions, the Allies ended the war on November 11, 1918. The carnage was finally over.

Mobilizing for "Total" War

Focus Question
What problems did the United States encounter in mobilizing for total war, and how successfully were those problems overcome?

Compared to Europe, the United States suffered little from the war. The deaths of 112,000 American soldiers paled in comparison to European losses: 900,000 by Great Britain, 1.2 million by Austria-Hungary, 1.4 million by France, 1.7 million by Russia, and 2 million by Germany. The U.S. civilian population was spared most of the war's ravages—the destruction of homes and industries, the shortages of food and medicine, the spread of disease—that afflicted millions of Europeans. Only with the flu epidemic that swept across the Atlantic from Europe in 1919 to claim approximately 500,000 lives did Americans briefly experience wholesale suffering and death.

Still, the war had a profound effect on American society. Every military engagement the United States had fought since the Civil War—the Indian wars, the Spanish-American War, the American-Filipino War, the Boxer Rebellion, the Latin American interventions—had been limited in scope. Even the troop mobilizations that seemed large at the time—the more than 100,000 needed to fight the Spanish and then the Filipinos—failed to tax severely American resources.

The First World War was different. It was a "total" war to which every combatant had committed virtually all of its resources. The scale of the effort in the United States became apparent early in 1917 when Wilson asked Congress for a conscription law that would permit the federal government to raise a multimillion-man army. The United States would also have to devote much of its agricultural, transportation, industrial, and population resources to the war effort if it wished to end the European stalemate. Who would organize this massive effort? Who would pay for it? Would Americans accept the sacrifice and regimentation it would demand? These were vexing questions for a nation long committed to individual liberty, small government, and a weak military.

Organizing Industry

At first, Wilson pursued a decentralized approach to mobilization, delegating tasks to local defense councils throughout the country. When that effort failed, however, Wilson created several centralized federal agencies, each charged with supervising nationwide activity in its assigned economic sector.

The success of these agencies varied. The Food Administration, headed by mining engineer and executive Herbert Hoover, substantially increased production of basic foodstuffs and put in place an efficient distribution system that delivered food to millions of troops and European civilians. Treasury Secretary William McAdoo, as head of the U.S. Railroad Administration, also performed well in shifting the rail system from private to public control, coordinating dense train traffic, and making capital improvements that allowed goods to move rapidly to eastern ports, where they were loaded onto ships and sent to Europe. At the other extreme, the Aircraft Production Board and Emergency Fleet Corporation did a poor job of supplying the Allies with combat aircraft and merchant vessels. On balance, the U.S. economy performed wonders in supplying troops with uniforms, food, rifles, munitions, and other basic items; it failed badly, however, in producing more sophisticated weapons and machines such as artillery, aircraft, and ships.

At the time, many believed that the new government war agencies possessed awesome power over the nation's economy and thus represented a near revolution in government. Most such agencies, however, were more powerful on paper than in fact. Consider, for example, the **War Industries Board** (WIB), an administrative body established by Wilson in July 1917 to harness manufacturing might to military needs. The WIB floundered for its first nine months, lacking the statutory authority to force manufacturers and the military to adopt its plans. Only the appointment of Wall Street investment banker Bernard

Baruch as WIB chairman in March 1918 turned the agency around. Rather than attempting to force manufacturers to do the government's bidding, Baruch permitted industrialists to charge high prices for their products. He won exemptions from antitrust laws for corporations that complied with his requests. In general, he made war production too lucrative an activity to resist; however, he did not hesitate to unleash his wrath on corporations that resisted WIB enticements.

Baruch's forceful leadership worked reasonably well throughout his nine months in office. War production increased, and manufacturers discovered the financial benefits of cooperation between the public and private sectors. But Baruch's approach created problems, too. His favoritism toward large corporations hurt smaller competitors. Moreover, the cozy relationship between government and corporation that he encouraged violated the progressive pledge to protect the people against the "interests." Achieving cooperation by boosting corporate profits, finally, was a costly way for the government to do business. The costs of the war soared to $33 billion, a figure more than three times expectations.

Securing Workers, Keeping Labor Peace

The government worried as much about labor's cooperation as about industry's compliance, for the best-laid production plans could be disrupted by a labor shortage or an extended strike. War increased the demand for industrial labor while cutting the supply. European immigrants had long been the most important source of new labor for American industry, and during the war they stopped coming. Meanwhile, millions of workers already in America were conscripted into the military and thus lost to industry.

Manufacturers responded to the labor shortage by recruiting new sources of labor from the rural South; a half million African Americans migrated to northern cities between 1916 and 1920. Another half million white southerners followed the same path during that period. Hundreds of thousands of Mexicans fled their revolution-ridden homeland for jobs in the Southwest and Midwest. Approximately 40,000 northern women found work as streetcar conductors, railroad workers, metalworkers, munitions makers, and in other jobs customarily reserved for men. The number of female clerical workers doubled between 1910 and 1920, with many of these women finding work in the government war bureaucracies. Altogether, a million women toiled in war-related industries.

These workers alleviated but did not eliminate the nation's labor shortage. Unemployment, which had hovered around 8.5 percent in 1915, plunged to 1.2 percent in 1918. Workers were quick to recognize the benefits of the tight labor market. They quit jobs they did not like and took part in strikes and other collective actions in unprecedented numbers. From 1916 to 1920, more than 1 million workers went on strike every year. Union membership almost doubled, from 2.6 million in 1915 to 5.1 million in 1920. Workers commonly sought higher wages and shorter hours through strikes and unionization. Wages rose an average of 137 percent from 1915 to 1920, although inflation largely negated these gains. The average workweek declined in that same period from 55 to 51 hours. Workers also struck in response to managerial attempts to speed up production and tighten discipline. As time passed, increasing numbers of workers began to wonder why the war for democracy in Europe had no counterpart in their factories at home. "Industrial democracy" became the battle cry of an awakened labor movement.

Wilson's willingness to include labor in his 1916 progressive coalition reflected his awareness of labor's potential power (see chapter 21). In 1918, he bestowed prestige on the newly formed **National War Labor Board** (NWLB) by appointing former president William Howard Taft to be co-chair alongside Samuel Gompers, president of the American Federation of Labor. The NWLB brought together representatives of labor, industry, and the public to resolve labor disputes.

Raising an Army

To raise an army, the Wilson administration committed itself to conscription—the drafting of most men of a certain age, irrespective of their family's wealth, ethnic background, or social standing. The Selective Service Act of May 1917 empowered the administration to do just that. By war's end, local Selective Service boards had registered 24 million young men age 18 and older and had drafted nearly 3 million of them into the military; another 2 million volunteered for service.

Relatively few men resisted the draft, even among recently arrived immigrants. Foreign-born men constituted 18 percent of the armed forces—a percentage greater than their share of the total population. Almost 400,000 African Americans served, representing

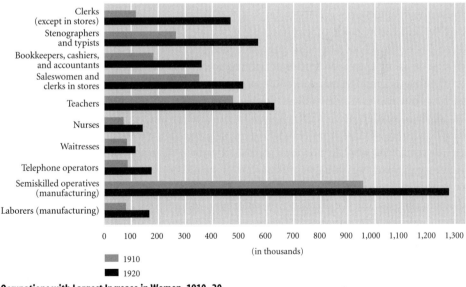

Occupations with Largest Increase in Women, 1910–20

Source: Joseph A. Hill, *Women in Gainful Occupations, 1870–1920*, U.S. Bureau of the Census, Monograph no. 9 (Washington, DC: Government Printing Office, 1929), p. 33.

National Archives

Women Doing "Men's Work" Labor shortages during the war allowed thousands of women to take industrial jobs customarily reserved for men. Here women operate pneumatic hammers at the Midvale Steel and Ordnance Company, Nicetown, Pennsylvania, 1918.

approximately 10 percent of armed forces, the same as the percentage of African Americans in the total population.

The U.S. Army, under the command of Chief of Staff Peyton March and General John J. Pershing, faced the difficult task of fashioning these ethnically and racially diverse millions into a professional fighting force. Teaching raw recruits to fight was hard enough, Pershing and March observed; the generals refused the task of teaching them to put aside their prejudices. Rather than integrate the armed forces, they segregated black soldiers from white. Virtually all African Americans were assigned to all-black units and barred from combat. Being stripped of a combat role was particularly galling to blacks, who, in previous wars, had proven themselves to be among the best American fighters. Pershing was fully aware of the African American contribution. He had commanded African American troops in the 10th Cavalry, the all-black regiment that had distinguished itself in the Spanish-American War (chapter 22). Pershing's military reputation had depended so heavily on the black troops who fought for him that he had acquired the nickname Black Jack.

For a time, the military justified its intensified discrimination against blacks by referring to the results of rudimentary IQ (intelligence quotient) tests administered by psychologists to 2 million AEF soldiers. These tests allegedly "proved" that native-born Americans and immigrants from the British Isles, Germany, and Scandinavia were well endowed with intelligence, whereas African Americans and immigrants from Southern and Eastern

Europe were poorly endowed. The tests were scientifically so ill-conceived, however, that their findings revealed nothing about the true distribution of intelligence in the soldier population. Their most sensational revelation was that more than half of the soldiers in the AEF—white and black—were "morons," men who had failed to reach the mental age of 13. After trying to absorb the apparent news that most U.S. soldiers were feeble-minded, the military sensibly rejected the pseudo-science on which these intelligence findings were based. In 1919, it discontinued the IQ testing program.

Given the racial and ethnic differences among American troops and the short time Pershing and his staff had to train recruits, the AEF's performance was impressive. The United States increased the army from a mere 100,000 to 5 million in little more than a year. The Germans sank no troop ships, nor were any soldiers killed during the dangerous Atlantic crossing. In combat, U.S. troops became known for their sharpshooting skills. The most decorated soldier in the AEF was Sergeant Alvin C. York of Tennessee, who captured 35 machine guns, took 132 prisoners, and killed 17 German soldiers with 17 bullets. York had learned his marksmanship hunting wild turkeys in the Tennessee hills. "Of course, it weren't no trouble no how for me to hit them big [German] army targets," he later commented. "They were so much bigger than turkeys' heads." One of the most decorated AEF units was **New York's 369th Regiment,** a black unit recruited in Harlem. Bowing to pressure from civil

National Archives

The 369th Returns to New York Denied the opportunity to fight in the U.S. Army, this unit fought for the French. For the length and distinction of its service in the front lines, this entire unit was awarded the *Croix de Guerre* (War Cross) by the French government.

rights groups to allow some black troops to fight, Pershing had offered the 369th to the French army. The 369th entered the French front line, served in the forward Allied trenches for 191 days (longer than any other U.S. regiment), and scored several major successes. In gratitude for its service, the French government decorated the entire unit with one of its highest honors—the *Croix de Guerre* (War Cross).

Paying the Bills

The government incurred huge debts buying food, uniforms, munitions, weapons, vehicles, and sundry other items for the U.S. military. To help pay its bills, it sharply increased tax rates. The new taxes hit the wealthiest Americans the hardest: The richest were slapped with a 67 percent income tax and a 25 percent inheritance tax. Corporations were ordered to pay an "excess profits" tax. Proposed by the Wilson administration and backed by Robert La Follette and other congressional progressives who feared that the "interests" would use the war to enrich themselves, these taxes were meant to ensure that all Americans would sacrifice something for the war.

Tax revenues, however, provided only about one-third of the $33 billion that the government ultimately spent on the war. The rest came from the sale of **Liberty Bonds.** These 30-year government bonds offered individual purchasers a return of 3.5 percent in annual interest. The government offered five bond issues between 1917 and 1920, and all quickly sold out, thanks, in no small measure, to a high-powered sales pitch, orchestrated by Treasury Secretary William G. McAdoo, that equated bond purchases with patriotic duty. McAdoo's agents blanketed the country with posters, sent bond "salesmen" into virtually every American community, enlisted Boy Scouts to go door-to-door, and staged rallies at which movie stars such as Mary Pickford, Douglas Fairbanks, and Charlie Chaplin stumped for the war.

Arousing Patriotic Ardor

The Treasury's bond campaign was only one aspect of an extraordinary government effort to arouse public support for the war. In 1917, Wilson set up a new agency, the **Committee on Public Information** (CPI), to popularize the war. Under the chairmanship of George Creel, a midwestern progressive and a muckraker, the CPI distributed 75 million copies of pamphlets explaining U.S. war aims in several languages. It trained a force of 75,000 "Four-Minute Men" to deliver succinct, uplifting war speeches to numerous groups in their home cities and towns. It papered the walls of virtually every public institution (and many private ones) with posters, placed advertisements in mass-circulation magazines, sponsored exhibitions, and peppered newspaper editors with thousands of press releases on the progress of the war.

Faithful to his muckraking past (see chapter 21), Creel wanted to give the people the facts of the war, believing that well-informed citizens would see the wisdom of Wilson's policies. He also saw his work as an opportunity to achieve the progressive goal of uniting all Americans into a single moral community. Americans everywhere learned that the United States had entered the war "to make the world safe for democracy," to help the world's weaker peoples achieve self-determination, and to bring a measure of justice into the conduct of international affairs. Americans were asked to affirm those ideals by doing everything they could to support the war.

This uplifting message affected the American people, although not necessarily in ways anticipated by CPI propagandists. It imparted to many a deep love of country and a sense of participation in a grand democratic experiment. Among others, particularly those experiencing poverty and discrimination, it sparked a new spirit of protest. Workers, women, European ethnics, and African Americans began demanding that America live up to its democratic ideals at home as well as abroad. Workers rallied to the cry of "industrial democracy." Women seized on the democratic fervor to bring their fight for suffrage to a successful conclusion (see chapter 21). African Americans began to dream that the war might deliver them from second-class citizenship. European ethnics believed that Wilson's support of their countrymen's rights abroad would improve their own chances for success in the United States.

Although the CPI had helped to unleash it, this new democratic enthusiasm troubled Creel and others in the Wilson administration. The United States, after all, was still deeply divided along class, ethnic, and racial lines. Workers and industrialists regarded each other with suspicion. Cultural differences compounded this class division, for the working class was overwhelmingly ethnic in composition, and the industrial and political elites consisted mainly of the native-born whose families had been Americans for generations. Progressives had fought hard to overcome these divisions. They had tamed the power of capitalists, improved the condition of workers, encouraged the Americanization of immigrants, and articulated a new, more inclusive idea of who could belong to the American nation.

But their work was far from complete when the war broke out, and the war opened up new social and cultural divisions. German immigrants still formed the largest foreign-born population group at 2.3 million. Another 2.3 million immigrants came from some part of the Austro-Hungarian Empire, and more than 1 million Americans—native-born and immigrants—supported the Socialist Party and the Industrial Workers of the World, both of which had opposed the war. The decision to authorize the CPI's massive unity campaign indicates that the progressives understood how widespread the discord was. Still, they had not anticipated that the promotion of democratic ideals at home would exacerbate, rather than lessen, the nation's social and cultural divisions.

Wartime Repression

By early 1918, the CPI's campaign had developed a darker, more coercive side. Inflammatory advertisements called on patriots to report on neighbors, coworkers, and ethnics whom they suspected of subverting the war effort. Propagandists called on all immigrants, especially those from Central, Southern, and Eastern Europe, to pledge themselves to "100 percent Americanism" and to repudiate all ties to their homeland, native language, and ethnic customs. The CPI aroused hostility toward Germans by spreading lurid tales of German atrocities and encouraging the public to see movies such as *The Prussian Cur* and

Renamed German American Words

Original German Name	Renamed "Patriotic" Name
hamburger	salisbury steak, liberty steak, liberty sandwich
sauerkraut	liberty cabbage
Hamburg Avenue, Brooklyn, New York	Wilson Avenue, Brooklyn, New York
Germantown, Nebraska	Garland, Nebraska
East Germantown, Indiana	Pershing, Indiana
Berlin, Iowa	Lincoln, Iowa
pinochle	liberty
German shepherd	Alsatian shepherd
Deutsches Hans of Indianapolis	Athenaeum of Indiana
Germania Maennerchor of Chicago	Lincoln Club
Kaiser Street	Maine Way

Sources: From La Vern J. Rippley, *The German Americans* (Boston: Twayne Publishers, 1976), p. 186; and Robert H. Ferrell, *Woodrow Wilson and World War I, 1917–1921* (New York: Harper and Row, 1985), pp. 205–206.

The Beast of Berlin. The Justice Department arrested thousands of German and Austrian immigrants whom it suspected of subversive activities. Congress passed the Trading with the Enemy Act, which required foreign-language publications to submit all war-related stories to post office censors for approval.

German Americans became the objects of popular hatred. American patriots sought to expunge every trace of German influence from American culture. In Boston, performances of Beethoven's symphonies were banned, and the German-born conductor of the Boston Symphony Orchestra was forced to resign. Although Americans would not give up the German foods they had grown to love, they would no longer call them by their German names. Sauerkraut was rechristened "liberty cabbage," and hamburgers became "liberty sandwiches." Libraries removed works of German literature from their shelves, and Theodore Roosevelt and others urged school districts to prohibit the teaching of the German language. Patriotic school boards in Lima, Ohio, and elsewhere burned the German books in their districts.

German Americans risked being fired from work, losing their businesses, and being assaulted on the street. A St. Louis mob lynched an innocent German immigrant whom they suspected of subversion. After only 25 minutes of deliberation, a St. Louis jury acquitted the mob leaders, who had brazenly defended their crime as an act of patriotism. German Americans began hiding their ethnic identity, changing their names, speaking German only in the privacy of their homes, and celebrating their holidays only with trusted friends. This experience devastated the once-proud German American community; many would never recover from the shame and vulnerability they experienced in those years.

The anti-German campaign escalated into a general anti-immigrant crusade. Congress passed the **Immigration Restriction Act of 1917,** over Wilson's veto, which declared that all adult immigrants who failed a reading test would be denied admission to the United States. The act also banned the immigration of laborers from India, Indochina, Afghanistan, Arabia, the East Indies, and several other countries within an Asiatic Barred Zone. This legislation marked the beginning of a movement in Congress that, four years later, would close the immigration door to virtually all transoceanic peoples.

Congress also passed the 18th Amendment to the Constitution, which prohibited the manufacture and distribution of alcoholic beverages (see chapter 21). The crusade for prohibition was not new, but anti-immigrant feelings generated by the war gave it added impetus. Prohibitionists pictured the nation's urban ethnic ghettos as scenes of drunkenness, immorality, and disloyalty.

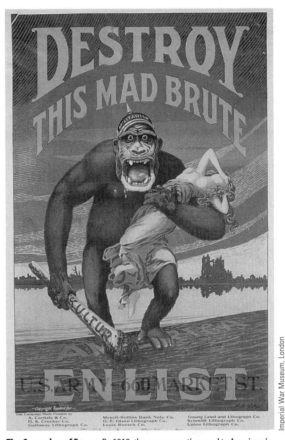

The Campaign of Fear By 1918, the government's appeal to Americans' best aspirations—to spread liberty and democracy—had been replaced by a determination to arouse fear of subversion and conquest. Here the German enemy is depicted as a terrifying brute who violates Lady Liberty and uses his *kultur* club to destroy civilization.

They also accused German American brewers of operating a "liquor trust" to sap people's will to fight. The states quickly ratified the 18th Amendment, and in 1919, Prohibition became the law of the land.

More and more, the Wilson administration relied on repression to achieve domestic unity. In the **Espionage, Sabotage, and Sedition Acts** passed in 1917 and 1918, Congress gave the administration sweeping powers to silence and imprison dissenters. These acts went far beyond outlawing behavior that no nation at war could be expected to tolerate, such as spying for the enemy, sabotaging war production, and calling for the enemy's victory. Now citizens could be prosecuted for writing or uttering any statement that could be construed as profaning the flag, the Constitution, or the military. These acts constituted the most drastic restrictions of free speech at the national level since the Alien and Sedition Acts of 1798 (see chapter 8).

Government repression fell most heavily on the IWW and the Socialist Party. Both groups had opposed intervention before 1917. Although they subsequently muted their opposition, they continued to insist that the true enemies of American workers were to be found in the ranks of American employers, not in Germany or Austria-Hungary. The government responded by banning many socialist materials from the mails and by disrupting socialist and IWW meetings. By spring 1918, government agents had raided countless IWW offices and had arrested 2,000 IWW members, including its entire executive board. Many of those arrested would be sentenced to long jail terms. William Haywood, the IWW president, fled to Europe and then to the Soviet Union rather than go to jail. Eugene V. Debs, the head of the Socialist Party, received a 10-year jail term for making an antiwar speech in Canton, Ohio, in summer 1918.

This federal repression, carried out in an atmosphere of supercharged patriotism, encouraged local governments and private citizens to initiate their own antiradical crusades. In the mining town of Bisbee, Arizona, a sheriff with an eager force of 2,000 deputized citizens kidnapped 1,200 IWW members, herded them into cattle cars, and dumped them onto the New Mexico desert with little food or water. Vigilantes in Butte, Montana, chained an IWW organizer to a car and let his body scrape the pavement as they drove the vehicle through city streets. Next, they strung him up to a railroad trestle, castrated him, and left him to die. The 250,000 members of the American Protective League, most of them businessmen and professionals, routinely spied on fellow workers and neighbors. They opened mail and tapped phones and otherwise harassed those suspected of disloyalty. Attorney General Thomas Gregory publicly endorsed the group and sought federal funds to support its "police" work.

The spirit of coercion even infected institutions that had long prided themselves on tolerance. In July 1917, Columbia University fired two professors for speaking out against U.S. intervention in the war. The National Americanization Committee, which before 1917 had pioneered a humane approach to the problem of integrating immigrants into American life, now supported surveillance, internment, and deportation of aliens suspected of anti-American sentiments.

Wilson bore responsibility for this climate of repression. He did attempt to block certain pieces of repressive legislation; for example, he vetoed both the Immigration Restriction Act and the Volstead Act (the act passed to enforce Prohibition), only to be overridden by Congress. But Wilson did little to halt Attorney General Gregory's prosecution of radicals or Postmaster General Burleson's campaign to exclude Socialist Party publications from the mail. He ignored pleas from progressives that he intervene in the Debs case to prevent the ailing 62-year-old from going to jail. His acquiescence in these matters cost him dearly among progressives and socialists. Wilson believed, however, that once the Allies, with U.S. support, won the war and arranged a just peace in accordance with the Fourteen Points, his administration's wartime actions would be forgiven and the progressive coalition would be restored.

The Failure of the International Peace

Focus Question
What were Woodrow Wilson's peace proposals, and how did they fare?

In the month following Germany's surrender on November 11, 1918, Wilson was confident about the prospects of achieving a just peace. Both Germany and the Allies had publicly accepted the Fourteen Points as the basis for negotiations. Wilson's international prestige was enormous. People throughout the world were inspired by his dream of a democratic, just, and harmonious world order free of poverty, ignorance, and war. Poles, Lithuanians, and other Eastern Europeans whose pursuit of nationhood had been frustrated for 100 years or more now believed that independence might be within their reach. Zionist Jews in Europe and the United States dared to dream of a Jewish homeland within their lifetimes. Countless African and Asian peoples imagined achieving their freedom from colonial domination.

To capitalize on his fame and to maximize the chances for a peace settlement based on his Fourteen Points, Wilson broke with diplomatic precedent and decided to head the American delegation to the Paris Peace Conference in January 1919. Enormous crowds of enthusiastic Europeans turned out to hail Wilson's arrival on the Continent in December. Some 2 million French citizens—the largest throng ever assembled on French soil—lined the parade route in Paris to catch a glimpse of "Wilson, *le juste* [the just]." In Rome, Milan, and La Scala, Italians acclaimed him "The Savior of Humanity" and "The Moses from Across the Atlantic."

In the Fourteen Points, Wilson had translated his principles for a new world order into specific proposals for international peace and justice. The first group of points called for all nations to abide by a code of conduct that embraced free trade, freedom of the seas, open diplomacy, disarmament, and the resolution of disputes through mediation. A second group, based on the principle of self-determination, proposed redrawing the map of Europe to give the subjugated peoples of the Austro-Hungarian, Ottoman, and Russian empires national sovereignty. The last point called for establishing the League of Nations, an assembly in which all nations would be represented and in which all international disputes would be given a fair hearing and an opportunity for peaceful solutions.

The Paris Peace Conference and the Treaty of Versailles

Although representatives of 27 nations began meeting in Paris on January 12, 1919, to discuss Wilson's Fourteen Points, negotiations were controlled by the "Big Four": Wilson, Prime Minister David Lloyd George of Great Britain, Premier Georges Clemenceau of France, and Prime Minister Vittorio Orlando of Italy. When Orlando quit the conference after a dispute with Wilson, the Big Four became the Big Three. Wilson quickly learned that his negotiating partners' support for the Fourteen Points was much weaker than he had believed. The cagey Clemenceau mused: "God gave us the Ten Commandments, and we broke them. Wilson gives us Fourteen Points. We shall see." Clemenceau and Lloyd George refused to include most of Wilson's points in the peace treaty. The points having to do with freedom of the seas and free trade were omitted, as were the proposals for open diplomacy and Allied disarmament. Wilson won partial endorsement of the principle of self-determination: Belgian sovereignty was restored, Poland's status as a nation was affirmed, and the new nations of Czechoslovakia, Yugoslavia, Finland, Lithuania, Latvia, and Estonia were created. In addition, some lands of the former Ottoman Empire—Armenia, Palestine, Mesopotamia, and Syria—were to be placed under League of Nations' trustee-ships with the understanding that they would someday gain their independence. Wilson failed in his efforts to block a British plan to transfer former German colonies in Asia to Japanese control, an Italian plan to annex territory inhabited by 200,000 Austrians, and a French plan to take from Germany its valuable Saar coal mines. (**See Map 23.2, Europe and the Near East After the First World War, in the color insert following page 912.**)

Nor could Wilson blunt the drive to punish Germany for its wartime aggression. In addi-tion to awarding the Saar basin to France, the Allies gave portions of northern Germany to Denmark and portions of eastern Germany to Poland and Czechoslovakia. Germany was stripped of virtually its entire navy and air force, and forbidden to place soldiers or forti-fications in western Germany along the Rhine. It was allowed to keep an army of only 100,000 men. In addition, Germany was forced to admit its responsibility for the war. In accepting this "war guilt," Germany was, in effect, agreeing to compensate the victors in cash (reparations) for the pain and suffering it had inflicted on them.

Lloyd George and Clemenceau brushed off the protests of those who viewed this desire to prostrate Germany as a cruel and vengeful act. That the German people, after their nation's 1918 defeat, had overthrown the monarch (Kaiser Wilhelm II) who had taken them to war, and had reconstituted their nation as a democratic republic—the first in their country's history—won them no leniency. On June 28, 1919, Great Britain, France, the United States, Germany, and other European nations signed the Treaty of Versailles. In 1921, an Allied commission notified the Germans that they were to pay the victors $33 billion, a sum well beyond the resources of a defeated and economically ruined Germany.

The League of Nations

The Allies' single-minded pursuit of self-interest disillusioned many liberals and socialists in the United States, but Wilson seemed undismayed. He had won approval of the most important of his Fourteen Points—that which called for the creation of the League of Nations. The League, whose structure and responsibilities were set forth in the Covenant attached to the peace treaty, would usher in Wilson's new world order. Drawing its mem-bership from the signatories to the Treaty of Versailles (except, for the time being, Germany), the League would function as an international parliament and judiciary, establishing rules of international behavior and resolving disputes between nations through rational and

Wilson in Paris, 1919   This photograph shows President Wilson (on right), recently arrived in Paris to negotiate the Treaty of Versailles, striding confidently and comfortably alongside his two allies, British Prime Minister Lloyd George (on left) and French Premier Clemenceau (in center). In the negotiations themselves, Lloyd George and Clemenceau would prove to be as much adversaries as allies to Wilson.

peaceful means. A nine-member executive council—the United States, Britain, France, Italy, and Japan would have permanent seats on the council, while the other four seats would rotate among the smaller powers—was charged with administering decisions.

Wilson believed that the League would redeem the failures of the Paris Peace Conference. Under its auspices, free trade and freedom of the seas would be achieved, reparations against Germany would be reduced or eliminated, disarmament of the Allies would proceed, and the principle of self-determination would be extended to peoples outside Europe. Moreover, the **Covenant (Article X)** would endow the League with the power to punish aggressor nations through economic isolation and military retaliation.

Wilson versus Lodge: The Fight over Ratification

The League's success, however, depended on Wilson's ability to convince the U.S. Senate to ratify the Treaty of Versailles. Wilson knew that this would not be easy. The Republicans had gained a majority in the Senate in 1918, and two groups within their ranks were determined to frustrate Wilson's ambitions. One group was a caucus of 14 midwesterners and westerners known as the **"irreconcilables."** Most of them were conservative isolationists who wanted the United States to preserve its separation from Europe, but a few were prominent progressives—Robert La Follette, William Borah, and Hiram Johnson— who had voted against the declaration of war in 1917. The self-interest displayed by England and France at the peace conference convinced this group that the Europeans were incapable of decent behavior in international matters.

Senator **Henry Cabot Lodge** of Massachusetts led the second opposition group. Its members rejected Wilson's belief that every group of people on earth had a right to form their own nation; that every state, regardless of its size, its economic condition, and the vigor and intelligence of its people, should have a voice in world affairs; and that disputes between nations could be settled in open, democratic forums. They subscribed instead to Theodore Roosevelt's vision of a world controlled by a few great nations, each militarily strong, secure in its own sphere of influence, and determined to avoid war through a carefully negotiated balance of power. These Republicans preferred to let Europe return to the power politics that had prevailed before the war rather than experiment with a new world order that might constrain and compromise U.S. power and autonomy.

This Republican critique was a cogent one that merited extended discussion. Particularly important were questions that Republicans raised about Article X, which gave the League the right to undertake military actions against aggressor nations. Did Americans want to authorize an international organization to decide when the United States would go to war? Was this not a violation of the Constitution, which vested war-making power solely in the Congress? Even if the constitutional problem could be solved, how could the United States ensure that it would not be forced into a military action that might damage its national interest?

It soon became clear, however, that several Republicans, including Lodge, were as interested in humiliating Wilson as in developing an alternative approach to foreign policy. They accused Wilson of promoting socialism through his wartime expansion of government power. They were angry that he had failed to include any distinguished Republicans, such as Lodge, Elihu Root, or William Howard Taft, in the Paris peace delegation. And they were still bitter about the 1918 congressional elections, when Wilson had argued that a Republican victory would embarrass the nation abroad. Although Wilson's electioneering had failed to sway the voters (the Republicans won a majority in both Houses), his suggestion that a Republican victory would injure national honor had infuriated Theodore Roosevelt and his supporters. Roosevelt died in 1919, but his close friend Lodge kept his rage alive: "I never thought I could hate a man as much as I hate Wilson," Lodge conceded in a moment of candor.

As chairman of the Senate Foreign Relations Committee, charged with considering the treaty before reporting it to the Senate floor, Lodge did everything possible to obstruct ratification. He packed the committee with senators who were likely to oppose the treaty. He delayed action by reading every one of the treaty's 300 pages aloud and by subjecting it to endless criticism in six long weeks of public hearings. When his committee finally reported the treaty to the full Senate, it came encumbered with nearly 50 amendments whose adoption Lodge made a precondition of his support. Some of the amendments expressed reasonable concerns—namely, that participation in the League not diminish the role of Congress in determining foreign policy, compromise American sovereignty, or involve the United States in an unjust or ill-advised war—but many were meant only to complicate the task of ratification.

Despite Lodge's obstructionism, the treaty's chances for ratification by the required two-thirds majority of the Senate remained good. Many Republicans were prepared to vote for ratification if Wilson indicated his willingness to accept some of the proposed amendments. Wilson could have salvaged the treaty and, along with it, U.S. participation in the League of Nations, but he refused to compromise with the Republicans and announced that he would carry his case directly to the American people instead. In September 1919, Wilson undertook a whirlwind cross-country tour that covered more than 8,000 miles with 37 stops. He addressed as many crowds as he could reach, sometimes speaking for an hour at a time, four times a day.

On September 25, after giving a speech at Pueblo, Colorado, Wilson suffered excruciating headaches throughout the night. His physician ordered him back to Washington, where on October 2 he suffered a near-fatal stroke. Wilson hovered near death for two weeks and remained seriously disabled for another six. His condition improved somewhat in November, but his left side remained paralyzed, his speech was slurred, his energy level low, and his emotions unstable. Wilson's wife, Edith Bolling Wilson, and his doctor isolated him from Congress and the press, withholding news they thought might upset him and preventing the public from learning how much his body and mind had deteriorated.

Many historians believe that the stroke impaired Wilson's political judgment. He refused to consider any of the Republican amendments to the treaty, even after it had become clear that compromise offered the only chance of winning U.S. participation in the League of Nations. When Lodge presented an amended treaty for a ratification vote on November 19, Wilson ordered Senate Democrats to vote against it; 42 (of 47) Democratic senators complied, and with the aid of 13 Republican irreconcilables, the Lodge version was defeated. Only moments later, the unamended version of the treaty—Wilson's version—received only 38 votes.

The Treaty's Final Defeat

As the magnitude of the calamity became apparent, supporters of the League in Congress, the nation, and the world urged the Senate and the president to reconsider. Wilson would not budge. A bipartisan group of senators desperately tried to work out a compromise without consulting him. When that effort failed, the Senate put to a vote, one more time, the Lodge version of the treaty. Because 23 Democrats, most of them southerners, still refused to break with Wilson, this last-ditch effort at ratification failed on March 8, 1920, by a margin of seven votes. Wilson's dream of a new world order died that day. The crumpled figure in the White House seemed to bear little resemblance to the hero who, barely 15 months before, had been greeted in Europe as the world's savior. Wilson filled out his remaining 12 months in office as an invalid, presiding over the interment of progressivism. He died in 1924.

The judgment of history lies heavily on these events, for many believe that the flawed treaty and the failure of the League contributed to Adolf Hitler's rise in Germany and the outbreak of a second world war more devastating than the first. It is necessary to ask, then,

Woodrow Wilson's Fourteen Points, 1918: Record of Implementation

1. Open covenants of peace openly arrived at	Not fulfilled
2. Absolute freedom of navigation upon the seas in peace and war	Not fulfilled
3. Removal of all economic barriers to the equality of trade among nations	Not fulfilled
4. Reduction of armaments to the level needed only for domestic safety	Not fulfilled
5. Impartial adjustments of colonial claims	Not fulfilled
6. Evacuation of all Russian territory; Russia to be welcomed into the society of free nations	Not fulfilled
7. Evacuation and restoration of Belgium	Fulfilled
8. Evacuation and restoration of all French lands; return of Alsace-Lorraine to France	Fulfilled
9. Readjustment of Italy's frontiers along lines of Italian nationality	Compromised
10. Self-determination for the former subjects of the Austro-Hungarian Empire	Compromised
11. Evacuation of Romania, Serbia, and Montenegro; free access to the sea for Serbia	Compromised
12. Self-determination for the former subjects of the Ottoman Empire; secure sovereignty for Turkish portion	Compromised
13. Establishment of an independent Poland with free and secure access to the sea	Fulfilled
14. Establishment of a League of Nations affording mutual guarantees of independence and territorial integrity	Compromised

Sources: From G. M. Gathorne-Hardy, *The Fourteen Points and the Treaty of Versailles,* Oxford Pamphlets on World Affairs, no. 6 (1939), pp. 8–34; and Thomas G. Paterson et al., *American Foreign Policy: A History,* 2nd ed. (Lexington, MA: Heath, 1983), vol. 2, pp. 282–93.

whether American participation in the League would have significantly altered the course of world history.

The mere fact of U.S. membership in the League would not have magically solved Europe's postwar problems. The U.S. government was inexperienced in diplomacy and prone to mistakes. Its freedom to negotiate solutions to international disputes would have been limited by the large number of American voters who remained strongly opposed to U.S. entanglement in European affairs. Even if such opposition could have been overcome, the United States would still have confronted European countries determined to go their own way.

Nevertheless, one thing is clear: No stable international order could have arisen after the First World War without the full involvement of the United States. The League of Nations required American authority and prestige in order to operate effectively as an international parliament. We cannot know whether the League, with American involvement, would have offered the Germans a less humiliating peace, allowing them to rehabilitate their economy and salvage their national pride; nor whether an American-led League would have stopped Hitler's expansionism before it escalated into full-scale war in 1939. Still, it seems fair to suggest that American participation would have strengthened the League and improved its ability to bring a lasting peace to Europe.

The Postwar Period: A Society in Convulsion

Focus Question
What issues convulsed American society in the immediate aftermath of war, and how were they resolved?

The end of the war brought no respite from the forces convulsing American society. Workers were determined to regain the purchasing power they had lost to inflation. Employers were determined to halt or reverse the wartime gains labor had made. Radicals saw in this conflict between capital and labor the possibility of a socialist revolution. Conservatives were certain that the revolution had already begun. Returning white servicemen were nervous about regaining their civilian jobs and looked with hostility on the black, Hispanic, and female workers who had been recruited to take their places. Black veterans were in no mood to return to segregation and subordination. The federal government, meanwhile, uneasy over the centralization of power during the war, quickly dismantled such agencies as the War Industries Board and the National War Labor Board. By so doing, it deprived itself of mechanisms that might have enabled it to intervene in social conflicts and keep them from erupting into rage and violence.

Labor-Capital Conflict

Nowhere was the escalation of conflict more evident than in the workplace. In 1919, 4 million workers—one-fifth of the nation's manufacturing workforce—went on strike. In January 1919, a general strike paralyzed the city of Seattle when 60,000 workers walked off their jobs. By August, walkouts had been staged by 400,000 eastern and midwestern coal miners, 120,000 New England textile workers, and 50,000 New York City garment workers. Then came two strikes that turned public opinion sharply against labor. In September, Boston policemen walked off their jobs after the police commissioner refused to negotiate with their newly formed union. Rioting and looting soon broke out. Massachusetts Governor Calvin Coolidge, outraged by the policemen's betrayal of their sworn public duty, refused to negotiate with them, called out the National Guard to restore order, and fired the entire police force. His tough stand would bring him national fame and the Republican vice presidential nomination in 1920.

Hard on the heels of the policemen's strike came a strike by more than 300,000 steelworkers in the Midwest. No union had established a footing in the steel industry since the 1890s, when Andrew Carnegie had ousted the ironworkers' union from his Homestead, Pennsylvania, mills. Most steelworkers labored long hours (the 12-hour shift was still standard) for low wages in dangerous workplaces. The organizers of the **1919 steel strike** had somehow managed to persuade steelworkers with varied skill levels and ethnic backgrounds to put aside their differences and demand an eight-hour day and union recognition. When the employers rejected those demands, the workers walked off their jobs. The employers responded by procuring armed guards to beat up the strikers and by hiring nonunion labor to keep the plants running. In many areas, local and state police prohibited union meetings, ran strikers out of town, and opened fire on those who disobeyed orders. In Gary, Indiana, a confrontation between unionists and armed guards left 18 strikers dead. To arouse public support for their antiunion campaign, industry leaders portrayed the strike leaders as dangerous and violent radicals bent on the destruction of political liberty and economic freedom. They succeeded in arousing public opinion against the steelworkers, and the strike collapsed in January 1920.

Radicals and the Red Scare

The steel companies succeeded in putting down the strike by fanning the public's fear that revolutionary sentiment was spreading among workers. Radical sentiment was indeed on the rise. Mine workers and railroad workers had begun calling for the permanent nationalization of coal mines and railroads. Longshoremen in San Francisco and Seattle refused to load ships carrying supplies to the White Russians who had taken up arms against Lenin's Bolshevik government. Socialist trade unionists mounted the most serious challenge to Gompers's control of the AFL in 25 years. In 1920, nearly a million Americans voted for the Socialist presidential candidate Debs, who ran his campaign from the Atlanta Federal Penitentiary. Small groups of anarchists contemplated, and occasionally carried out, bomb attacks on businessmen and public officials.

This radical surge did not mean, however, that leftists had fashioned themselves into a single movement or political party. On the contrary, the Russian Revolution had split the American Socialist Party. One faction, which would keep the name Socialist and would continue under Debs's leadership, insisted that radicals follow a democratic path to socialism.

The other group, which would take the name Communist, wanted to establish a Lenin-style "dictatorship of the proletariat." Small groups of anarchists, some of whom advocated campaigns of terror to speed the revolution, represented yet a third radical tendency.

Few Americans noticed the disarray in the radical camp. Most assumed that radicalism was a single, coordinated movement bent on establishing a communist government on American soil. They saw the nation's immigrant communities as breeding grounds for Bolshevism. Beginning in 1919, this perceived **"red scare"** prompted government officials and private citizens to embark on yet another campaign of repression.

The postwar repression of radicalism closely resembled the wartime repression of dissent. Thirty states passed sedition laws to punish those who advocated revolution. Numerous public and private groups intensified Americanization campaigns designed to strip foreigners of their subversive ways and remake them into loyal citizens. Universities fired radical professors, and vigilante groups wrecked the offices of socialists and assaulted IWW agitators. A newly formed veterans' organization, the American Legion, took on the American Protective League's role of identifying seditious individuals and organizations and ensuring the public's devotion to "100 percent Americanism."

The Red Scare reached its climax on New Year's Day 1920, when federal agents broke into the homes and meeting places of thousands of suspected revolutionaries in 33 cities. Directed by Attorney General A. Mitchell Palmer, these widely publicized "Palmer raids" were meant to expose the extent of revolutionary activity. Palmer's agents uncovered three pistols, no rifles, and no explosives. Nevertheless, they arrested more than 4,000 people and kept many of them in jail for weeks without formally charging them with a crime. Finally, those who were not citizens (approximately 600) were deported and the rest were released.

Palmer's failure to expose a revolutionary plot blunted support for him in official circles, but, undeterred, Palmer now alleged that revolutionaries were planning a series of assaults on government officials and government buildings for May 1, 1920. When nothing happened on that date, his credibility suffered another blow.

As Palmer's exaggerations of the Red threat became known, many Americans began to reconsider their near-hysterical fear of dissent and subversion. Even so, the political atmosphere remained hostile to radicals, as the **Sacco and Vanzetti case** revealed. In May 1920, two Italian-born anarchists, Nicola Sacco and Bartolomeo Vanzetti, were arrested in Brockton, Massachusetts, and charged with armed robbery and murder. Both men proclaimed their innocence and insisted that they were being punished for their political beliefs. Their foreign accents and their defiant espousal of anarchist doctrines in the courtroom inclined many Americans, including the judge who presided at their trial, to view them harshly. Despite the weak case against them, they were convicted of first-degree murder and sentenced to death. Their lawyers attempted numerous appeals, all of which failed. Anger over the verdicts began to build among Italian Americans, radicals, and liberal intellectuals. Protests compelled the governor of Massachusetts to appoint a commission to review the case, but no new trial was ordered. On August 23, 1927, Sacco and Vanzetti were executed, still insisting they were innocent.

Reds (1981)

Directed by Warren Beatty. Starring Warren Beatty (John Reed), Diane Keaton (Louise Bryant), Edward Herrmann (Max Eastman), Jerzy Kosinski (Grigory Zinoviev), Jack Nicholson (Eugene O'Neill), and Maureen Stapleton (Emma Goldman).

In this epic film, Warren Beatty, producer, director, and screenplay cowriter, attempts to integrate the history of the American Left in the early 20th century with a love story about two radicals of that era, John "Jack" Reed and Louise Bryant. Reed was a well-known radical journalist whose dispatches from Russia during its 1917 revolution were published as a book, *Ten Days That Shook the World*, that brought him fame and notoriety. Bryant never developed the public reputation that Reed enjoyed, but she was an integral member of the radical circles that gathered in apartments and cafés in New York's Bohemian Greenwich Village before and during the First World War.

At times, the love principals in this movie seem to resemble Warren Beatty and Diane Keaton more than they do the historical figures they are meant to represent. In general, however, the movie keeps love and politics in balance and thus successfully conveys an important and historically accurate message about the American Left, especially before the First World War: namely, that its participants wanted to revolutionize the personal as well as the political. Thus equality between men and women, women's right to enjoy the same sexual freedom as men, and marriage's impact on personal growth and adventure were issues debated with the same fervor as building a radical political party and accelerating the transition to socialism. (See the section entitled, The New Sexuality and the Rise of Feminism," in chapter 20.)

Reds is also an exceptionally serious film about political parties and ideologies. The film follows the arc of John Reed's and Louise Bryant's lives from their prewar days as discontented members of the Portland, Oregon, social elite, through their flight to the freedom and radicalism of Greenwich Village, to the hardening of their radicalism as a result of repression during the First World War at home and the Bolshevik triumph in November 1917. In this movie, Beatty has recreated detailed and complex stories about internal fights within the Left both in the United States and Russia, through which he seeks to show how hopes for social transformation went awry. To give this film added historical weight, Beatty introduces "witnesses," individuals who actually knew the real Reed and Bryant and who appear on screen periodically to share their memories, both serious and whimsical, about the storied couple and the times in which they lived.

© Paramount Pictures/Courtesy: Everett Collection.

Diane Keaton as Louise Bryant and Warren Beatty as John Reed, together in Russia in the midst of that country's socialist revolution.

Racial Conflict and the Rise of Black Nationalism

The more than 400,000 blacks who served in the armed forces believed that a victory for democracy abroad would help them achieve democracy for their people at home. At first, despite the discrimination they encountered in the military, they maintained their conviction that they would be treated as full-fledged citizens upon their return. Many began to talk about the birth of a New Negro—independent and proud. Thousands joined the National Association for the Advancement of Colored People (NAACP), an organization at the forefront of the fight for racial equality. By 1918, 100,000 African Americans subscribed to the NAACP's magazine, *The Crisis,* whose editor, W. E. B. Du Bois, had urged them to support the war.

This wartime optimism made the postwar discrimination and hatred African Americans encountered difficult to endure. Many black workers who had found jobs in the North were fired to make way for returning white veterans. Returning black servicemen, meanwhile, had to scrounge for poorly paid jobs as unskilled laborers. In the South, lynch mobs targeted black veterans who refused to tolerate the usual insults and indignities; 10 of the 70 blacks lynched in the South in 1919 were veterans.

The worst anti-black violence that year occurred in the North, however. Crowded conditions during the war had forced black and white ethnic city dwellers into uncomfortably close proximity. Many white ethnics regarded blacks with a mixture of fear and prejudice. They resented having to share neighborhoods, trolleys, parks, streets, and workplaces with blacks. Many also wanted African Americans barred from unions, seeing them as threats to their job security.

Racial tensions escalated into race riots. The deadliest explosion occurred in Chicago in July 1919, when a black teenager who had been swimming in Lake Michigan was killed by whites after coming too close to a whites-only beach. Rioting soon broke out, with white mobs invading black neighborhoods, torching homes and stores, and attacking innocent residents. Led by war veterans, some of whom were armed, blacks fought back, turning the border areas between white and black neighborhoods into battle zones. Fighting raged for five days, leaving 38 dead (23 black, 15 white) and more than 500 injured. Race rioting in other cities pushed the death toll to 120 before summer's end.

The riots made it clear to blacks that the North was not the Promised Land. Confined to unskilled jobs and to segregated neighborhoods with substandard housing and exorbitant rents, black migrants in Chicago, New York, and other northern cities suffered economic hardship throughout the 1920s. The NAACP carried on its campaign for civil rights and racial equality, but many blacks no longer shared its belief that they would one day be accepted as first-class citizens. They turned instead to a leader from Jamaica, **Marcus Garvey,** who gave voice to their bitterness: "The first dying that is to be done by the black man in the future," Garvey declared in 1918, "will be done to make himself free. And then when we are finished, if we have any charity to bestow, we may die for the white man. But as for me, I think I have stopped dying for him."

Garvey called on blacks to give up their hopes for integration and to set about forging a separate black nation. He reminded blacks that they possessed a rich culture stretching

Library of Congress, Prints and Photographs Division

Marcus Garvey, Black Nationalist This portrait was taken in 1924, after Garvey's conviction on mail fraud charges.

back over the centuries that would enable them to achieve greatness as a nation. Garvey's ambition was to build a black nation in Africa that would bring together all of the world's people of African descent. In the short term, he wanted to help American and Caribbean blacks to achieve economic and cultural independence.

Garvey's call for black separatism and self-sufficiency—or black nationalism, as it came to be known—elicited a favorable response among African Americans. In the early 1920s, the Universal Negro Improvement Association (UNIA), which Garvey had founded, enrolled millions of members in 700 branches in 38 states. His newspaper, the *Negro World,* reached a circulation of 200,000. The New York chapter of UNIA undertook an economic development program that included the establishment of grocery stores, restaurants, and factories. Garvey's most visible economic venture was the Black Star Line, a shipping company with three ships flying the UNIA flag from their masts.

This black nationalist movement did not endure for long. Garvey entered into bitter disputes with other black leaders, including W. E. B. Du Bois, who regarded him as a flamboyant, self-serving demagogue. Garvey sometimes showed poor judgment, as when he expressed support for the Ku Klux Klan on the grounds that it shared his pessimism about the possibility of racial integration. Inexperienced in economic matters, Garvey squandered

UNIA money on abortive business ventures. The U.S. government regarded his rhetoric as inflammatory and sought to silence him. In 1923, he was convicted of mail fraud involving the sale of Black Star stocks and was sentenced to five years in jail. In 1927, he was deported to Jamaica, and the UNIA folded. Nevertheless, Garvey's philosophy of black nationalism endured.

Conclusion

The resurgence of racism in 1919 and the consequent turn to black nationalism among African Americans were signs that the high hopes of the war years had been dashed. Industrial workers, immigrants, and radicals also found their pursuit of liberty and equality interrupted by the fear, intolerance, and repression unleashed by the war. They came to understand as well that Wilson's commitment to these ideals counted for less than did his administration's and Congress's determination to discipline a people whom they regarded as dangerously heterogeneous and unstable. Of the reform groups, only woman suffragists made enduring gains—especially the right to vote—but, for the feminists in their ranks, these steps forward failed to compensate for the collapse of the progressive movement and, with it, their program of achieving equal rights for women across the board.

A similar disappointment engulfed those who had embraced and fought for Wilson's dream of creating a new and democratic world order. The world in 1919 appeared as volatile as it had been in 1914. More and more Americans—perhaps even a majority— were coming to believe that U.S. intervention had been a mistake.

In other ways, the United States benefited a great deal from the war. By 1919, the American economy was by far the world's strongest. Many of the nation's leading corporations had improved productivity and management during the war. U.S. banks were poised to supplant those of London as the most influential in international finance. The nation's economic strength triggered an extraordinary burst of growth in the 1920s, and millions of Americans rushed to take advantage of the prosperity that this "people's capitalism" had put within their grasp. But even affluence failed to dissolve the class, ethnic, and racial tensions that the war had exposed. And the failure of the peace process added to Europe's problems, delayed the emergence of the United States as a leader in world affairs, and created the preconditions for another world war.

SUGGESTED READINGS

On America's neutrality and road to war, consult **Arthur S. Link, *Woodrow Wilson: Revolution, War and Peace*** (1979), and **John Milton Cooper Jr., *The Vanity of Power: American Isolationism and the First World War, 1914–1917*** (1969). **Roland C. Marchand, *The American Peace Movement and Social Reform, 1898–1918*** (1972), reconstructs the large and influential antiwar movement, while **John W. Chambers, *To Raise an Army: The Draft Comes to Modern America*** (1987), analyzes American efforts to prepare for war by raising a multimillion-man fighting machine. **David Kennedy, *Over Here: The First World War and American Society*** (1980), is a superb account of the effects of war on American society. For details on industrial mobilization, consult **Robert D. Cuff,** *The War Industries Board: Business-Government Relations during World War I* (1973). **David Montgomery,** *The Fall of the House of Labor: The Workplace, the State, and American Labor Activism, 1865–1925* (1987), expertly reconstructs the escalation of labor-management tensions during the war, but it should be read alongside **Joseph A. McCartin,** *Labor's Great War: The Struggle for Industrial Democracy and the Origins of Modern Labor Relations, 1912–1921* (1997).

For a pioneering effort to situate U.S. domestic politics during the war in an international context, see **Alan Dawley,** *Changing the World: American Progressives in War and Revolution* (2003). On the migration of African Americans to northern industrial centers and the movement of women into war production, see **Joe William Trotter Jr., ed.,** *The Great Migration in Historical Perspective: New Dimensions of Race, Class, and Gender* (1991), and **Maurine W. Greenwald,** *Women, War and Work* (1980). **Stephen Vaughn,** *Holding Fast the Inner Lines: Democracy, Nationalism, and the Committee on Public Information* (1980), is an important account of the CPI, the government's central propaganda agency. **Harry N. Scheiber,** *The Wilson Administration and Civil Liberties, 1917–1921* (1960) and **Geoffrey R. Stone,** *Perilous Times: Free Speech in War Time from the Sedition Act of 1798 to the War on Terrorism* (2004), analyze the repression of dissent.

On Wilson, Versailles, and the League of Nations, consult **Thomas J. Knock,** *To End All Wars: Woodrow Wilson and the Quest for a New World Order* (1992); **Arno Mayer,** *The Politics and Diplomacy of Peacemaking: Containment and Counterrevolution at Versailles, 1918–1919* (1967); **Lloyd C. Gardner,** *Safe for Democracy: The Anglo-American Response to Revolution, 1913–1923* (1984); **John Milton Cooper, Jr.,** *Breaking the Heart of the World: Woodrow Wilson and the Fight for the League of Nations* (2001); and **Katherine A. S. Siegel,** *Loans and Legitimacy: The Evolution of Soviet-American Relations, 1919–1933* (1996). On Republican opposition to the League of Nations, see **William C. Widenor,** *Henry Cabot Lodge and the Search for an American Foreign Policy* (1980).

Nell Irvin Painter, *Standing at Armageddon: The United States, 1877–1919* (1987), offers a good overview of the class and racial divisions that convulsed American society in 1919. On the Red Scare, consult **Robert K. Murray,** *Red Scare: A Study in National Hysteria* (1955). **William Tuttle, Jr.,** *Race Riot: Chicago in the Red Summer of 1919* (1970), examines race conflict after the First World War, while **Judith Stein,** *The World of Marcus Garvey: Race and Class in Modern Society* (1986), explores the emergence of Marcus Garvey and the Universal Negro Improvement Association.

Visit the Liberty Equality Power Companion Web site for resources specific to this textbook: http://www.thomsonedu.com/history/murrin

Also find self-tests and additional resources at ThomsonNOW. ThomsonNOW is an integrated online suite of services and resources with proven ease of use and efficient paths to success, delivering the results you want—NOW!

www.thomsonedu.com/login/

24

The 1920s

In 1920, Americans elected as president, Warren G. Harding, a man who could not have been more different from his predecessor Woodrow Wilson. A Republican, Harding presented himself as a common man with common desires. In his 1920 campaign, he called for a "return to normalcy." Although he died in office in 1923, his carefree spirit is thought to characterize the 1920s.

To many Americans, the decade was one of fun rather than reform, of good times rather than high ideals. It was, in the words of novelist F. Scott Fitzgerald, the "Jazz Age," a time when the search for personal gratification seemed to replace the quest for public welfare.

Despite Harding's call for a return to a familiar past, America seemed to be rushing headlong into the future. The word *modern* began appearing everywhere: modern times, modern women, modern technology, the modern home, modern marriage. Although the word was rarely defined, it connoted certain beliefs: that science was a better guide to life than religion; that people should be free to choose their own lifestyles; that sex should be a source of pleasure for women as well as men; that women and minorities should be equal to white men and enjoy the same rights.

Many other Americans, however, reaffirmed their belief that God's word transcended science; that people should obey the moral code set forth in the Bible; that women were not equal to men; and that blacks, Mexicans, and Eastern European immigrants were inferior to Anglo-Saxon whites. They made their voices heard in a resurgent **Ku Klux Klan** and the fundamentalist movement, and on issues such as evolution and immigration. In seeking to restore an older America, some in their ranks were prepared to deny individual Americans the liberty to choose their own ways of living and to insist that all people were not fundamentally equal.

Modernists and traditionalists confronted each other in party politics, in legislatures, in courtrooms, and in the press. Their battles belie the vision of the 1920s merely as a time for the pursuit of leisure.

Prosperity

Focus Question
What were the achievements and limitations of "people's capitalism" in the 1920s?

CHRONOLOGY

1920	Prohibition goes into effect • Warren G. Harding defeats James M. Cox for presidency • Census reveals that a majority of Americans live in urban areas • 8 million cars on road
1921	Sheppard-Towner Act passed
1922	United States, Britain, Japan, France, and Italy sign Five-Power Treaty, agreeing to reduce size of their navies
1923	Teapot Dome scandal lands Secretary of the Interior Albert Fall in jail • Harding dies in office; Calvin Coolidge becomes president
1924	Dawes Plan to restructure Germany's war debt put in effect • Coolidge defeats John W. Davis for presidency • Ku Klux Klan membership approaches 4 million • Johnson-Reed Act cuts immigration by 80 percent and discriminates against East and South Asians and Southern and Eastern Europeans
1925	Scopes trial upholds right of Tennessee to bar teaching of evolution in public schools • *Survey Graphic* publishes a special issue announcing the Harlem Renaissance • F. Scott Fitzgerald publishes *The Great Gatsby* • U.S. withdraws Marines from Nicaragua
1926	Revenue Act cuts income and estate taxes • U.S. sends Marines back to Nicaragua to end civil war and protect U.S. property
1927	Coolidge vetoes McNary-Haugen bill, legislation meant to relieve agricultural distress • Babe Ruth hits 60 home runs • Charles Lindbergh flies across the Atlantic
1928	15 nations sign Kellogg-Briand pact, pledging to avoid war • Coolidge vetoes McNary-Haugen bill again • Herbert Hoover defeats Alfred E. Smith for presidency
1929	Union membership drops to 3 million • 27 million cars on roads • William Faulkner publishes *The Sound and the Fury* • Josh Gibson joins the National Negro League
1930	Los Angeles's Mexican population reaches 100,000

On balance, the First World War had been good for the American economy. American industries had emerged intact, even strengthened, from the war. The war needs of the Allies had created an insatiable demand for American goods and capital. Manufacturers and bankers had exported so many goods and extended so many loans to the Allies that by war's end, the United States was the world's leading creditor nation. New York City challenged London as the hub of world finance. At home, the government had helped large corporations and banks to consolidate their power. Corporate America had responded by raising productivity and efficiency to new heights through advances in technology and management.

Postwar economic turmoil and depression hampered these advances for a time. From 1919 to 1921, the country struggled to redirect industry from wartime to civilian production, a process slowed by the government's hasty withdrawal from its wartime role as economic regulator and stabilizer. Workers went on strike to protest wage reductions or increases in the workweek. Farmers were hit by a depression as the overseas demand for American foodstuffs fell from its 1918–19 peak. Disgruntled workers and farmers even joined forces to form statewide farmer-labor parties, which for a time threatened to disrupt the country's two-party system in the upper Midwest. In 1924, the two groups formed a national Farmer-Labor Party. Robert La Follette, their presidential candidate, received an impressive 16 percent of the vote that year, but then the third-party movement fell apart.

Its collapse reflected a rising public awareness of how vigorous and productive the economy had become. Beginning in 1922, the nation embarked on a period of remarkable growth. From 1922 to 1929, the gross national product grew at an annual rate of 5.5 percent, rising from $149 billion to $227 billion. The unemployment rate never exceeded 5 percent, and real wages rose about 15 percent.

A Consumer Society

The variety of products being produced matched the rate of economic growth. In the 19th century, economic growth had rested primarily on the production of capital goods, such as factory machinery and railroad tracks. In the 1920s, however, growth rested more on consumer goods. Some products, such as cars and telephones, had been available since the early 1900s, but in the 1920s their sales reached new levels. In 1920, just 12 years after Ford introduced the Model T, 8 million cars were on the road. By 1929, there were 27 million— one for every five Americans. Other consumer goods became available for the first time: tractors, washing machines, refrigerators, electric irons, radios, and vacuum cleaners. The term **"consumer durable"** was coined to describe such goods, which, unlike food, clothing, and other perishables, were meant to last. Even perishables took on new allure. Scientists had discovered the importance of vitamins in the diet and began urging Americans to consume more fresh fruits and vegetables. The agricultural economy of southern California grew rapidly as urban demand for the region's fresh fruits and vegetables skyrocketed. Improvements in refrigeration and in packaging, meanwhile, allowed fresh produce to travel long distances and extended its shelf life in grocery stores. And more stores were being operated by large grocery chains that could afford the latest refrigeration and packaging technology.

The public responded to these innovations with excitement. American industry had made fresh food and stylish clothes available to the masses. Refrigerators, vacuum cleaners, and washing machines would spare women the drudgery of housework. Radios would expand the public's cultural horizons. Cars, asphalt roads, service stations, hot dog stands, "tourist cabins" (the forerunners of motels), and traffic lights seemed to herald a wholly new automobile civilization. By the middle of the decade, the country possessed a network of paved roads. City dwellers now had easy access to rural areas and made a ritual of day-long excursions. Camping trips and long-distance vacations became routine. Farmers and their families could now hop into their cars and head for the nearest town with its stores, movies, amusement parks, and sporting events. Suburbs proliferated, billed as the perfect mix of urban and rural life. Young men and women everywhere discovered that cars were a place where they could "make out," and even make love, without fear of reproach by prudish parents or prying neighbors.

In the 1920s, some Americans also discovered the benefits of owning stocks. The number of stockholders in AT&T, the nation's largest corporation, rose from 140,000 to 568,000. U.S. Steel stockholder numbers increased from 96,000 to 146,000. By 1929, as many as 7 million Americans owned stock, most of them people of middle-class or upper-class means. This spread of stock ownership reflected the need for working capital among the nation's corporations. Because privately held wealth could not satisfy that need, corporations sought to sell their stocks and bonds to the general public. The New York Stock Exchange, first organized in 1792, assisted in processing complicated transactions.

A People's Capitalism

Capitalists boasted that they had created a **"people's capitalism"** in which virtually all Americans could participate. Now, everyone could own a piece of corporate America. Now, everyone could have a share of luxuries and amenities. Poverty, capitalists claimed, was banished, and the gap between rich and poor all but closed. If every American could own a car and house, buy quality clothes, own stock, take vacations, and go to the movies, then economic inequality would cease to matter as a political issue.

Actually, although wages were rising, millions of Americans still earned too little to partake fully of the marketplace. The percentage of Americans owning stocks remained small. Social scientists Robert and Helen Lynd discovered, in their celebrated 1929 study of Muncie, Indiana, that working-class families who bought a car often lacked money for other goods. One housewife admitted, "We don't have no fancy clothes when we have the car to pay for. . . . The car is the only pleasure we have." Another declared, "I'll go without food before I'll see us give up the car." Many industrialists resisted pressure to increase wages, and workers lacked the organizational strength to force them to pay more.

One solution came with the introduction of consumer credit. Car dealers, home appliance salesmen, and other merchants began to offer installment plans that enabled consumers to purchase a product by making a down payment and promising to pay the rest in installments. By 1930, 15 percent of all purchases—including 60 percent of all cars and 75 percent of all radios—were made on the installment plan.

Even so, many poor Americans benefited little from the consumer revolution. Middle-class Americans acquired a disproportionate share of consumer durables. They also could afford to purchase far more fresh fruits and vegetables and stocks than most working-class Americans.

The Rise of Advertising and Mass Marketing

But even middle-class consumers had to be wooed. How could they be persuaded to buy another car only a few years after they had bought their first one? General Motors had the answer. In 1926, it introduced the concept of the annual model change. GM cars took on a different look every year as GM engineers changed headlights and chassis colors, stream-lined bodies, and added new features. The strategy worked. GM leaped past Ford and became the world's largest car manufacturer.

Henry Ford reluctantly introduced his Model A in 1927 to provide customers with a colorful alternative to the drab Model T. Having spent his lifetime selling a product renowned for its utility and reliability, Ford rejected the idea that sales could be increased by appealing to the intangible hopes and fears of consumers. He was wrong. The desire to be beautiful, handsome, or sexually attractive; to exercise power and control; to demon-strate competence and success; to escape anonymity, loneliness, and boredom; to experi-ence pleasure—all such desires, once activated, could motivate a consumer to buy a new car even when the old one was still serviceable, or to spend money on goods that might have once seemed frivolous.

Arousing such desires required more than bright colors, sleek lines, and attractive pack-aging. It called for advertising campaigns intended to make a product seem to be the answer to the consumer's desires. To create those campaigns, corporations turned to a new kind of company: professional advertising firms. The new advertising entrepreneurs, people such as Edward Bernays, Doris Fleischmann, and Bruce Barton, tended to be well-educated, sen-sitive to public taste, and knowledgeable about human psychology. In their campaigns, these advertisers played on the emotions and vulnerabilities of their target audiences. One cosmetics ad decreed: "Unless you are one woman in a thousand, you must use powder and rouge. Modern living has robbed women of much of their natural color." A perfume manufacturer's ad pronounced: "The first duty of woman is to attract. . . . It does not mat-ter how clever or independent you may be, if you fail to influence the men you meet, con-sciously or unconsciously, you are not fulfilling your fundamental duty as a woman." A mouthwash ad warned about one unsuspecting gentleman's bad breath—"the truth that his friends had been too delicate to mention," while a tobacco ad matter-of-factly declared: "Men at the top are apt to be pipe-smokers. . . . It's no coincidence—pipe-smoking is a calm and deliberate habit—restful, stimulating. His pipe helps a man think straight. A pipe is back of most big ideas."

Advertising professionals believed they were helping people to manage their lives in ways that would increase their satisfaction and pleasure. American consumers responded enthusiastically. Their interest in fashion, their eagerness to fill their homes with the lat-est products, their alacrity to take up the craze of the moment (the mah-jongg card game, crossword puzzles, miniature golf)—all evidenced Americans' preoccupation with self-improvement and personal pleasure. The most enthusiastic of all were middle-class Americans, who could afford to buy what the advertisers were selling. Many of them were newcomers to middle-class ranks, searching for ways to affirm—or even create—their new identity. The aforementioned ad for pipe tobacco, for example, was targeted at the new middle-class man, imagined by advertisers to be someone holding a salaried position in a corporate office or bank, or working as a commission salesman, or owning a small business.

Selling Beauty and Health   This advertisement hints at the negative health effects of smoking, but touts "Luckies" as a healthful cigarette more appropriate for the delicate bodies of beautiful women.

As male wage earners moved into the new middle class, their wives were freed from the necessity of working outside the home. Advertisers appealed to the new middle-class woman, too, as she refocused her attention toward dressing in the latest fashion, managing the household, and raising children. Vacuum cleaners and other consumer durables would make her more efficient, and books on child-rearing, many imbued with a popularized Freudianism, would enable her to mold her children for future success in work and marriage. Cosmetics would aid women in their "first duty"—to be beautiful and sexual for their husbands and boyfriends.

Changing Attitudes toward Marriage and Sexuality

That husbands and wives were encouraged to pursue sexual satisfaction together was one sign of how prescriptions for married life had changed since the 19th century, when women were thought to lack sexual passion and men were tacitly expected to satisfy their drives through extramarital liaisons. Modern husbands and wives were expected to share other leisure activities as well—dining out, playing cards with friends, going to the movies, attending concerts, and discussing the latest selection from the newly formed Book-of-the-Month Club. Husbands and wives now aspired to a new ideal—to be best friends, full partners in the pursuit of happiness.

The public pursuit of pleasure was also noticeable among young and single middle-class women. The so-called **flappers** of the 1920s set out to break the informal rules governing young women's lives: they donned short dresses, rolled their stockings down, wore red lipstick, and smoked in public. They took their inspiration from depictions of saucy, working-class women of the previous decade that moviemakers had popularized and refined. Flappers were signaling their desire for independence and equality, but they had little thought of achieving those goals through politics, as had their middle-class predecessors in the woman suffrage movement. Rather, they aimed to create a new female personality endowed with self-reliance, outspokenness, and a new appreciation for the pleasures of life.

An Age of Celebrity

Focus Question

What was the age of celebrity and what caused it to arise?

The pursuit of pleasure became both an individual and a group endeavor. Mass marketers began to understand that big sums of money could be made by staging mega-events, mostly connected to sports, that tens of thousands would attend and that radio announcers would broadcast to a virtual audience of millions. Newspapers and word-of-mouth would ensure that enthusiasts would discuss these events for days, even weeks and months. Baseball and boxing became the two sports where mass marketing had advanced the furthest. When Yankee Stadium opened in 1923, it set a new standard for the scale and magnificence of sports amphitheaters. Boxing matches began drawing audiences that would have been unimaginable 20 years earlier. To succeed on this scale, these sports required not just stirring athletic competitions but also individual athletes who seemed larger than life and whose exploits and character could be endlessly promoted.

No sports figure achieved greater fame than did George Herman "Babe" Ruth, who overcame the hardships of a poor and orphaned youth in Baltimore to become the slugging star, the "Sultan of Swat," of the New York Yankees. In the 1920s, Ruth hit more home runs than baseball experts had thought humanly possible, culminating in 1927, when he hit a magical 60, a record that would last for 34 years and that would be surpassed only three times in the 20th century. A close second in popularity to Ruth was heavyweight prizefighter Jack Dempsey, whose combination of ruthlessness and efficiency in the ring with gentleness outside it enthralled millions.

Americans also drew their celebrities from the movies, where stars such as comedian Charles Chaplin and the exotically handsome Rudolph Valentino stirred laughter and sexual longings, respectively, in audiences. These and other figures became so familiar on the silver screen that they created an insatiable appetite among movie fans for news about their private lives as well, an interest that the movie industry was only too eager to exploit.

The popular figures of the 1920s did not earn their status through their accomplishments in politics or war, but through their prowess at a game or their skill at acting in front of a camera. Historians have tended to criticize such celebrity worship, especially when the lionized individual seemed to possess no quality greater than the ability to hit a ball 400 feet or to smash an opponent's face. But such scholarly criticism perhaps has been too quick to overlook the human longing to experience the intensity of emotions associated with competition and triumph or to draw close to someone who demonstrates that the impossible— whether in the form of a physical feat, or a love relationship, or an escape from a confining life—could be accomplished.

Some of these sentiments can be discerned in the adulation bestowed on **Charles A. Lindbergh,** the young pilot who, in 1927, became the first individual to cross the Atlantic in a solo flight. Piloting his single-engine white monoplane, *The Spirit of St. Louis,* Lindbergh flew nonstop (and without sleep) for 34 hours from the time he took off from Long Island until he landed at Le Bourget Airport in Paris. Thousands of Parisians were waiting for him at the airfield and began charging his plane as soon as it landed. When he returned to New York, an estimated 4 million fans lined the parade route. This shy young man from Minnesota instantly became the most famous and adored man in America, mobbed by crowds everywhere he went. None of this fame could have happened without the new machinery of celebrity culture—aggressive journalists and radio commentators, promoters, and others who understood how fame could yield a profit. It mattered, too, that Lindbergh performed his feat in an airplane, one of the era's newest and most exciting innovations. But Lindbergh's celebrity involved more than hype and technology: He accomplished what others said could not be done, and he did it on his own in a time when corporations and other private institutions of power seemed to be shrinking the realm for individual initiative. Some of Lindbergh's popularity no doubt rested on his ability to demonstrate that an individual of conviction and skill could still make a difference in an increasingly industrialized and bureaucratized world.

Celebrating Business Civilization

Industrialists, advertisers, and merchandisers in the 1920s began to claim that their accomplishments lay at the heart of American civilization. Business, they argued, made America great, and businessmen provided the nation with its wisest, most vigorous leadership. In

1924, President Calvin Coolidge declared that "the business of America is business." Even religion became a business. Bruce Barton, in his best seller *The Man Nobody Knows* (1925), depicted Jesus as a business executive "who picked up twelve men from the bottom ranks of business and forged them into an organization that conquered the world." Elsewhere, Barton hailed Jesus as an early "national advertiser," and proclaimed that Peter and Paul were really not so different from Americans who sold vacuum cleaners.

Some corporate leaders adopted benevolent attitudes toward their employees. They set up workplace cafeterias, hired doctors and nurses to staff on-site medical clinics, and engaged psychologists to counsel troubled workers. They built ball fields and encouraged employees to join industry-sponsored leagues. They published employee newsletters and gave awards to employees who did their jobs well and with good spirit. Some employers set up profit-sharing plans and offered stock options to reward employees for their efforts, and some even gave employees a voice in determining working conditions.

The real purpose of these measures—collectively known as welfare capitalism—was to encourage employees to be loyal to their firm and to convince them (contrary to what labor union critics had been arguing) that industry did have the best interests of its employees at heart. Management had an understandable fear of union power, arising from the paralyzing strikes of 1919. As the decade proceeded and as prosperity rolled on, welfare capitalism reflected the confidence that capitalism had become more responsive to employee concerns and thus more humane.

Industrial Workers

Many industrial workers benefited from the nation's prosperity. Most of them enjoyed rising wages and a reasonably steady income. Skilled craftsmen in the older industries of construction, railroad transportation, and printing fared especially well. Their real wages rose by 30 percent to 50 percent over the decade. The several million workers employed in the large mass-production industries (such as automobile and electrical equipment manufacture) also did well. Their wages were relatively high, and some of them enjoyed good benefits—paid sick leave, paid vacations, life insurance, stock options, and retirement pensions. Although all workers in companies with these programs were eligible for such benefits, skilled workers were in the best position to claim them.

Semiskilled and unskilled industrial workers had to contend with a labor surplus throughout the decade. As employers replaced workers with machines, the aggregate demand for industrial labor increased at a lower rate than it had in the preceding 20 years. Despite a weakening demand for labor, rural whites, rural blacks, and Mexicans continued their migration to the cities, stiffening the competition for factory jobs. Employers could hire and fire as they saw fit and could therefore keep wage increases lagging behind increases in productivity.

This softening demand for labor helps explain why many working-class families benefited little from the decade's prosperity or from its consumer revolution. An estimated 40 percent of workers remained mired in poverty, unable to afford a healthy diet or adequate housing, much less any of the more costly consumer goods. In 1930, for instance, only 25 percent to 40 percent of American households owned a washing machine, a vacuum cleaner, and a radio, and only 50 percent had a car.

The million or more workers who labored in the nation's two largest industries, coal and textiles, suffered the most during the 1920s. Throughout the decade, both industries experienced severe overcapacity. By 1926, only half of the coal mined each year was being sold. Many New England textile cities experienced levels of unemployment that sometimes approached 50 percent. One reason was that many textile industrialists had shifted their operations to the South, where taxes and wages were lower. But the southern textile industry also suffered from excess capacity, exerting a downward pressure on prices and wages there as well. Plant managers pressured their workers to speed up production. Workers loathed the frequent "speed-ups" of machines and the "stretch-outs" in the number of spinning or weaving machines each worker was expected to tend. By the late 1920s, labor strife and calls for unionization were rising among disgruntled workers in both the South and the North.

Unionization of textiles and coal, and of more prosperous industries as well, would have brought workers a larger share of the decade's prosperity. Some labor leaders, such as Sidney Hillman of the Amalgamated Clothing Workers, argued that unionization would actually increase corporate profits by compelling employers to observe uniform wage and hour schedules that would restrain ruinous competition. Hillman pointed out—as Henry Ford had in the preceding decade—that rising wages would enable workers to purchase

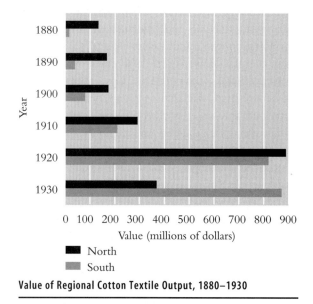

Value of Regional Cotton Textile Output, 1880–1930

Source: Data from Nancy F. Kane, *Textiles in Transition: Technology, Wages, and Industry Relocation in the U.S. Textile Industry, 1880–1939* (New York: Greenwood Press, 1988), p. 29.

more consumer goods and thus increase corporate sales and revenues, but Hillman's views were ignored outside the garment industry.

Elsewhere, unions lost ground as business and government, backed by middle-class opinion, remained hostile to labor organization. Employers attacked unions as un-American. A conservative Supreme Court whittled away at labor's legal protections. In 1921, it ruled that lower courts could issue injunctions against union members, prohibiting them from striking or picketing an employer. State courts also enforced what union members called **"yellow dog" contracts,** written pledges by which employees promised not to join a union while they were employed. Any employee who violated that pledge was subject to immediate dismissal.

These measures crippled efforts to organize trade unions. Membership fell from a high of 5 million in 1920 to less than 3 million in 1929, a mere 10 percent of the nation's industrial workforce. Other forces contributed to the decline, too. Many workers, especially those benefiting from welfare capitalist programs, decided they no longer needed trade unions. And the labor movement hurt itself by moving too slowly to open its ranks to semiskilled and unskilled factory workers.

Women and Work

Women workers experienced the same hardships as men in the industrial workforce and fewer of the benefits. They were largely excluded from the ranks of the skilled craftsmen and thus missed out on the substantial wage increases that the men in those positions enjoyed. Women also had trouble finding work in the automobile industry, the highest paying of the mass-production industries. They had better access to the electrical equipment and meat-packing industries, although they were often segregated in departments given over to "women's work." Where women were allowed to compete for the same jobs as men, they usually earned less. Thus, a female trimmer in a meat-packing plant typically made 37 cents per hour, only two-thirds of what a male trimmer earned. The textile industry had long been a major source of employment for women, but, in the 1920s, women and men alike in this ailing manufacturing sector suffered high rates of unemployment and declining wages.

White-collar work established itself, in the 1920s, as a magnet for women. This sector grew rapidly in a decade in which corporations expanded and refined their managerial and accounting practices. Discrimination prevented women from becoming managers, accountants, or supervisors, but they did dominate the lower-level ranks of secretaries, typists, filing clerks, bank tellers, and department store clerks. By the 1930s, 2 million women, or 20 percent of the female workforce, labored in these and related occupations. Initially, these positions had a glamour that factory work lacked. Work environments were cleaner and brighter, and women had the opportunity—indeed were expected—to dress well and fashionably. But wages were low and managerial authority was absolute. Unions had virtually no presence in white-collar places of employment, and workers had difficulty finding alternative ways of protesting unfair managers or difficult working conditiosns.

© Hulton-Deutsch Collection/CORBIS

Amelia Earhart, Aviation Pioneer   Earhart strikes a flapper pose in front of the biplane that she was preparing to fly across the Atlantic.

Women with ambitious work aspirations most often pursued the "female" professions, such as teaching, nursing, social work, and librarianship. Opportunities in several of these fields, especially teaching and social work, were growing, and women responded by enrolling in college in large numbers. The number of female college students increased by 50 percent during the 1920s. Some of these college graduates used their new skills in new fields, such as writing for women's magazines. A few, drawing strength from their feminist forebears during the progressive era, managed to crack such male bastions of work as mainstream journalism and university research and teaching. In every field of endeavor, even such new and exotic ones as airplane flying, at least one woman arose to demonstrate that her sex had the necessary talent and drive to match or exceed what men had done.

Thus in 1932, Amelia Earhart became the first woman to fly the Atlantic solo, matching Lindbergh's feat and inspiring women everywhere. Even so, Earhart's feat failed to improve substantially opportunities for women who wanted to work as pilots in the airline industry. In this industry, as in most lines of work, gender prejudices remained too entrenched, and the women who had broken the gender line remained, by and large, solitary figures.

The Women's Movement Adrift

Many supporters of the 19th Amendment to the Constitution, which, in 1920, gave women the right to vote, expected it to transform American politics. Women voters would reverse the decline in voter participation, cleanse politics of corruption, and launch a variety of reform initiatives that would improve the quality of life for women and men alike. This female-inspired transformation, however, failed to materialize. Voter participation rates did not increase, nor did American politics become imbued with female-inspired virtue and honesty. The women's movement, instead, seemed to succumb to the same exhaustion and frustration as had the more general progressive movement from which it had emerged 20 years earlier. Younger women searching for independence and equality (such as the flappers discussed earlier in this chapter) often turned away from reform altogether, preferring a lifestyle that emphasized private achievement and personal freedom to a political career devoted to improving the collective status of America's women. Those who continued to agitate for reform found progress more difficult to achieve once the conservative Republican administrations of Harding and Coolidge took office.

Despite the difficult political environment in which they had to work, some female reformers made significant strides in the 1920s. In 1921, one group succeeded in getting Congress to pass the **Sheppard-Towner Act,** a major social welfare program that provided federal funds for prenatal and child health care centers throughout the United States. It remained in effect until 1929. In 1923, Alice Paul, still head of the National Woman's Party (NWP, see chapter 20), and her allies prevailed on Congress to consider an Equal Rights Amendment (ERA) to the Constitution, phrased as follows: "Men and women shall have equal rights throughout the United States and every place subject to its jurisdiction." And the National American Woman Suffrage Association, the major force behind the struggle for suffrage, transformed itself in 1920 into the **League of Women Voters** (LWV). During the next decade, the LWV launched numerous initiatives to encourage women to run for elective office, to educate voters about the issues before them, and to improve the condition of those Americans—the poor, female and child laborers, the mentally ill—who needed assistance.

Sometimes the women's movement was stymied not just by external opposition but also by internal division— as it was over the ERA. The NWP and other supporters of the ERA insisted that there could be no compromise with the proposition that women were the equals of men in every respect. But, the LWV countered, child-rearing and mothering duties did render women different from men in key respects and thus, in some instances, in need of special treatment by Congress and other lawmaking bodies.

The question of female difference crystallized around the issue of protective labor legislation for women. Over the years, a series of state and federal laws had given women protections at the workplace—limitations on the hours of labor, prohibitions on overnight work, and other such measures—that men did not have. Many women reformers supported these measures, believing they were vital to protecting the masses of women workers from the worst forms of exploitation and thus enabling them to have enough time and energy to perform their vital roles as mothers and wives. Fearing that a successful ERA would render this protective legislation unconstitutional, the LWV and its allies opposed the ERA. Alice Paul and her allies countered by arguing that female protective laws did not really benefit women. Instead, employers used these laws as an excuse to segregate women in stereotyped jobs that were mostly low status and low paying and thus to deny women the opportunities for advancement and fulfillment open to men.

This issue of whether women should be treated like men in all respects or offered some protections that no men enjoyed was a genuinely complicated one, and women activists would continue to argue about it with each other for decades. In the 1920s, however, their inability to speak with a single voice on this matter weakened their cause in the eyes of their adversaries.

The Politics of Business

Focus Question
What were the similarities and differences in the politics of Harding, Coolidge, and Hoover?

Republican presidents governed the country from 1921 to 1933. In the beginning, this transition engulfed national politics in scandal, as Warren Harding, the first of the decade's three Republican presidents, allowed high-ranking members of his administration to indulge in spectacular forms of corruption. But his successor, Calvin Coolidge, restored virtue and honor to the presidency while carrying out his 1924 campaign pledge to overturn the legacy of progressivism and reduce the role of the government in economic affairs. The most significant challenge to Coolidge's small government program came from his own secretary of commerce and then his successor as president, Herbert Hoover, who sought to sustain the spirit of activist government that Theodore Roosevelt had introduced to Republican politics, albeit in somewhat altered form.

Harding and the Politics of Personal Gain

Warren Gamaliel Harding defeated Democrat James M. Cox for the presidency in 1920. From modest origins as a newspaper editor in the small town of Marion, Ohio, Harding had risen to the U.S. Senate chiefly because the powerful Ohio Republican machine knew it could count on him to do its bidding. He gained the presidency for the same reason. The Republican Party bosses believed that almost anyone they nominated in 1920 could defeat the Democratic opponent. They chose Harding because they could control him. Harding's good looks and geniality made him a favorite with voters, and he swept into office with 61 percent of the popular vote, the greatest landslide since 1820.

To his credit, Harding released the aging Socialist Party leader Eugene V. Debs from jail and took other measures to cool the passions unleashed by the Red Scare. He also included

Warren G. Harding with Friends and Attendants   This photograph was shot in St. Augustine, Florida. Harding is third from the right. Attorney General Harry M. Daugherty, boss of the Ohio Republican machine, stands to the left of the President, dressed in black and supporting himself with a cane.

talented men in his cabinet. His choices of Herbert Hoover as secretary of commerce, Charles Evans Hughes as secretary of state, and Andrew Mellon as secretary of the treasury were particularly impressive appointments. Still, Harding lacked the will to alter his ingrained political habits. He had built his political career on a willingness to please the lobbyists who came to his Senate office asking for favors and deals. He had long followed Ohio boss Harry M. Daugherty's advice and would continue to do so with Daugherty as his attorney general. Harding apparently did not consider men such as Daugherty self-serving or corrupt. They were his friends; they had been with him since the beginning of his political career. He made sure the "boys" had jobs in his administration, and he continued to socialize with them. Many a night he could be found drinking (despite **Prohibition**), gambling, and womanizing with the "Ohio Gang" at its K Street hangout. Sometimes the gang even convened in the White House. Alice Roosevelt Longworth, Theodore Roosevelt's daughter, once came into the White House study and found the air "heavy with tobacco smoke," its tables cluttered with "bottles containing every imaginable brand of whiskey, . . . [and] cards and poker chips at hand."

The K Street house was more than a place to carouse. It was a place of business where the Ohio Gang became rich selling government appointments, judicial pardons, and police protection to bootleggers. By 1923, the corruption could no longer be concealed. Journalists and senators began to focus public attention on the actions of Secretary of the Interior Albert Fall, who had persuaded Harding to transfer control of large government oil reserves at **Teapot Dome,** Wyoming, and Elk Hills, California, from the navy to the Department of the Interior. Fall had immediately leased the deposits to two oil tycoons, Harry F. Sinclair and Edward L. Doheny, who pumped oil from the wells in exchange for providing the navy with a system of fuel tank reserves. Fall had issued the leases secretly, without allowing other oil corporations to compete for them, and he had accepted almost $400,000 from Sinclair and Doheny.

Fall would pay for this shady deal with a year in jail. He was not the only Harding appointee to do so. Charles R. Forbes, head of the Veterans' Bureau, would go to Leavenworth Prison for swindling the government out of $200 million in hospital supplies. The exposure of Forbes's theft prompted his lawyer, Charles Cramer, to commit suicide; Jesse Smith, Attorney General Daugherty's close friend and housemate, also killed himself, apparently to avoid being indicted and brought to trial. Daugherty managed to escape conviction and incarceration for bribery by burning incriminating documents held by his brother's Ohio bank. Still, Daugherty left government service in disgrace.

Harding initially kept himself blind to this widespread use of public office for private gain but grew depressed when he finally realized what had been going on. In summer 1923, in poor spirits, he left Washington for a West Coast tour. He fell ill in Seattle and died from a heart attack in San Francisco. The train returning his body to Washington attracted crowds of grief-stricken mourners who little suspected the web of corruption and bribery in which Harding had been caught. Even as the revelations poured forth in 1924 and 1925, few Americans seemed bothered. Some of this insouciance reflected the carefree atmosphere of the 1920s, but much of it had to do with the character of the man who succeeded Harding.

Coolidge and Laissez-Faire Politics

Calvin Coolidge rarely smiled. At the many dinners he attended as vice president, he said hardly a word. Silence was his public creed, much to the chagrin of Washington's socialites. He was never enticed into carousing with the "boys," nor did he ever stand by as liquor was being served. He believed that the best government was the government that governed least, and that the welfare of the country hinged not on politicians but on the people—their willingness to work hard, to be honest, and to live within their means.

Born in Vermont and raised in Massachusetts, Calvin Coolidge gained national visibility in September 1919, when as governor of Massachusetts he took a firm stand against Boston's striking policemen (see chapter 23). His reputation as a man who battled labor radicals earned him a place on the 1920 national Republican ticket. His image as an ordinary man helped convince voters in 1920 that the Republican Party would return the country to its commonsensical ways after eight years of reckless reforms. Coolidge won his party's presidential nomination handily in 1924 and easily defeated his Democratic opponent, John W. Davis. Coolidge's popularity remained strong throughout his first full term, and he probably would have been re-nominated and reelected in 1928, but he chose not to run.

Coolidge took greatest pride in those measures that reduced the government's control over the economy. The Revenue Act of 1926 slashed the high income and estate taxes that progressives had pushed through Congress during the First World War. Coolidge curtailed the power of the Federal Trade Commission to regulate business affairs and endorsed Supreme Court decisions invalidating progressive era laws that had strengthened organized labor and protected children and women from employer exploitation.

Hoover and the Politics of Associationalism

Republicans in the 1920s did more than simply remove government restraints and regulations from the economy. Some, led by Secretary of Commerce Herbert Hoover, conceived of government as a dynamic, even progressive, economic force. Hoover did not want government to control industry, but he did want government to persuade private corporations to abandon their wasteful, selfish ways and turn to cooperation and public service. Hoover envisioned an economy built on the principle of association. Industrialists, wholesalers, retailers, operators of railroad and shipping lines, small businessmen, farmers, workers, doctors—each of these groups would form a trade association whose members would share economic information, discuss problems of production and distribution, and seek ways of achieving greater efficiency and profit. Hoover believed that the very act of associating in this way—an approach that historian Ellis Hawley has called **"associationalism"**—would convince participants of the superiority of cooperation over competition, of negotiation over conflict, of public service over selfishness.

A graduate of Stanford University, Hoover had worked first as a mining engineer and then as an executive in multinational mining corporations. During the war, he had directed the government's Food Administration (see chapter 23). From that experience, he had come to appreciate the role that government could play in coordinating the activities of thousands of producers and distributors scattered across the country.

Hoover's ambition as secretary of commerce was to make the department the grand orchestrator of economic cooperation. During his eight years in that post (1921–29), he organized more than 250 conferences and repeatedly brought together government officials, representatives of business, policy makers, and others who had a stake in strengthening the economy.

Hoover achieved some notable successes. He persuaded farmers to join together in marketing cooperatives, steel executives to abandon the 12-hour day for their employees, and some groups of bankers in the South to organize their institutions into regional associations with adequate resources and expertise. Hoover's dynamic conception of government did not endear him to Coolidge, who declared in 1927: "That man has offered me unsolicited advice for six years, all of it bad."

The Politics of Business Abroad

Republican domestic policy disagreements over whether to pursue laissez-faire or associationalism spilled over into foreign policy as well. As secretary of commerce, Hoover intended to apply associationalism to international relations. He wanted the world's leading nations to meet regularly in conferences, to limit military buildups, and to foster an international environment in which capitalism could flourish. Aware that the United States must help create such an environment, Hoover hoped to persuade American bankers to adopt investment and loan policies that would aid European recovery. If they refused to do so, he was prepared to urge the government to take an activist, supervisory role in foreign investment.

In 1921 and 1922, Hoover helped design the Washington Conference on the Limitation of Armaments. Although he did not serve as a negotiator at the conference—Secretary of State Charles Evans Hughes reserved that role for himself and his subordinates—Hoover did supply Hughes's team with a wealth of economic information, and he helped Hughes to use that information to design forceful, detailed proposals for disarmament. Those proposals gave U.S. negotiators a decided advantage over their European and Asian counterparts and helped them win a stunning accord, the **Five-Power Treaty,** by which the United States, Britain, Japan, France, and Italy agreed to scrap more than 2 million tons of warships. Hughes also obtained pledges from all of the signatories that they would respect the "Open Door" in China, long a U.S. foreign policy objective (see chapter 22).

These triumphs redounded to Hughes's credit but not to Hoover's, and Hughes used it to consolidate his control over foreign policy. He rebuffed Hoover's efforts to put international economic affairs under the direction of the Commerce Department and rejected Hoover's suggestion to intervene in the international activities of U.S. banks.

Hughes was not entirely laissez faire in approach, as he demonstrated in his 1923 reaction to a crisis in Franco-German relations. The victorious Allies had imposed on Germany an obligation to pay $33 billion in war reparations (see chapter 23). In 1923, when the impoverished German government suspended its payments, France sent troops to occupy the Ruhr valley, whose industry was vital to the German economy. German workers retaliated by going on strike, and the crisis threatened to undermine Europe's precarious economic recovery. Hughes did not stand on the sidelines. He intensified American financial pressure on the French and compelled them to attend a U.S.-sponsored conference in 1924 to restructure Germany's debt obligation.

The conference produced the **Dawes Plan** (after the Chicago banker and chief negotiator, Charles G. Dawes), which reduced German reparations from $542 million to $250 million annually and called on U.S. and foreign banks to stimulate the German economy with a quick infusion of $200 million in loans. Within a matter of days, banker J. P. Morgan, Jr., raised more than $1 billion from American investors. Money poured into German financial markets, and the German economy appeared to stabilize.

The Dawes Plan won applause on both sides of the Atlantic, but soon the U.S. money flooding into Germany created its own problems. American investors were so eager to lend to Germany that their investments became speculative and unsound. At this point, a stronger U.S. government effort to direct loans to sound investments, a strategy that Hoover supported, might have helped. But neither Hughes nor his successor as secretary of state, Frank Kellogg, was interested in such initiatives, and neither was Secretary of the Treasury Mellon. The laissez-faire approach had reasserted itself, and Hoover's plan to involve the U.S. government directly in international economic matters had been rebuffed.

The Republicans' continued pursuit of disarmament and world peace seemed to diverge from their general reluctance to involve the U.S. government in foreign affairs. To follow up the success of the 1922 Five-Power treaty, Secretary of State Kellogg drew up a treaty with Aristide Briand, the French foreign minister, outlawing war as a tool of national policy. In 1928, representatives of the United States, France, and 13 other nations met in Paris to sign the Kellogg-Briand pact, an agreement that soon attracted the support of 48 other nations. Coolidge viewed Kellogg-Briand, however, not as a way of extending U.S. government power abroad but as a way of reducing further the size of the U.S. government at home. With the threat of war removed, the United States could scale back its military forces and eliminate much of the bureaucracy needed to support a large standing army and navy. Unfortunately, the pact contained no enforcement mechanism, thus rendering itself ineffective as a foreign policy tool.

The Republican administrations flexed U.S. power more effectively in Latin American affairs. U.S. investments in the region more than doubled from 1917 to 1929, and the U.S. government continued its policy of intervening in the internal affairs of Latin America to protect U.S. interests. Republican administrations did attempt initially to curtail American military involvement in the Caribbean. The Coolidge administration pulled American troops out of the Dominican Republic in 1924 and Nicaragua in 1925. In the case of Nicaragua, however, U.S. Marines returned in 1926 to end a war between liberal and conservative Nicaraguans and to protect American property; this time they stayed until 1934. U.S. troops, meanwhile, occupied Haiti continuously between 1919 and 1934, keeping in power governments friendly to U.S. interests. Opposition to such heavy-handed tactics continued to build in the United States, but it would not yield a significant change in U.S. policy until the 1930s (see chapter 25).

Farmers, Small-Town Protestants, and Moral Traditionalists

Focus Question
What did farmers and conservative Protestants fear in the 1920s, and what policies did they support?

Although many Americans benefited from the prosperity of the 1920s, others did not. Overproduction was impoverishing substantial numbers of farmers. Beyond these economic hardships, many moral-traditionalist white Protestants, especially those in rural areas and small towns, believed that the country was being overrun by racially inferior and morally suspect foreigners.

Agricultural Depression

The 1920s brought hard times to the nation's farmers after the boom period of the war years. During the war, domestic demand for farm products had risen steadily and foreign demand had exploded as the war disrupted agricultural production in France, Ukraine,

Price of Major Crops, 1914–1929

Source: Data from *Historical Statistics of the United States, Colonial Times to 1970* (White Plains, N.Y.: Kraus International, 1989), pp. 511–12.

and other European food-producing regions. Soon after the war, however, Europe's farmers quickly resumed their customary levels of production. Foreign demand for American foodstuffs fell precipitously, leaving U.S. farmers with an oversupply and depressed prices.

A rise in agricultural productivity made possible by the tractor also worsened the plight of many farmers. The number of tractors in use almost quadrupled in the 1920s, and 35 million new acres came under cultivation. Produce flooded the market. Prices fell even further, as did farm incomes. By 1929, the annual per capita income of rural Americans was only $223, one-quarter that of the non-farm population. Hundreds of thousands had to sell their farms and either scrape together a living as tenants or abandon farming altogether. Many chose to abandon farm life, packed their belongings into jalopies or loaded them onto trains, and headed for the city.

Those who stayed on the land grew increasingly assertive in their demands. Early in the decade, radical farmers working through such organizations as the Nonpartisan League of North Dakota and farmer-labor parties in Minnesota, Wisconsin, and other midwestern states led the movement. By the second half of the decade, however, leadership had passed from farming radicals to farming moderates, and from small farmers in danger of dispossession to larger farmers and agribusinesses seeking to extend their holdings. By lobbying through such organizations as the Farm Bureau Federation, the more powerful agricultural interests pressured Congress to set up economic controls that would protect them from failure. Their proposals, embodied in the McNary-Haugen Bill, called on the government to erect high tariffs on foreign produce and to purchase surplus U.S. crops. The government would then sell the surplus crops on the world market for whatever prices they fetched. Any money lost in international sales would be absorbed by the government rather than by the farmers. The McNary-Haugen Bill passed Congress in 1927 and in 1928, only to be vetoed by President Coolidge both times.

Cultural Dislocation

Added to the economic plight of the farmers was a sense of cultural dislocation among the majority who were white, Protestant, and of northwest European descent. These farmers had long perceived themselves as the backbone of the nation—hardworking, honest, God-fearing yeomen, guardians of independence and liberty.

The 1920 census challenged the validity of that view. For the first time, a slight majority of Americans now lived in urban areas. That finding in itself signified little because the census classified as "urban" those towns with a population as small as 2,500. But the census figures did reinforce the widespread perception that both the economic and cultural vitality of the nation had shifted from the countryside to the metropolis. Industry, the chief engine of prosperity, was an urban phenomenon. Commercialized leisure—the world of amusement parks, department stores, professional sports, movies, cabarets, and theaters—was to be enjoyed in cities; so too were flashy fashions and open sexuality. Catholics, Jews, and African Americans, who together outnumbered white Protestants in many cities, seemed to be the principal creators of this new world. They were also thought to be the

Brown Brothers

Consumer Culture Penetrates the Countryside   By the 1920s, cars, Coca-Cola, radios, and other commodities had found their way to the country's smallest towns. Here a farmer tunes his radio as he milks his cow.

purveyors of Bolshevism and other modes of radicalism. Cities, finally, were the home of secular intellectuals who had scrapped their belief in Scripture and in God and had embraced science as their new, unimpeachable authority.

Throughout the progressive era, rural white Americans had believed that the cities could be redeemed, that city dwellers could be reformed, that the Protestant values of rural America would triumph. War had crushed that confidence and had replaced it with the fear that urban culture and urban people would undermine all that "true" Americans held dear.

These fears grew even more intense with the changes brought by prosperity. Urban-industrial America increased in power and affluence and spread its consumer culture and its commodities to the countryside as never before. Even small towns now sported movie theaters and automobile dealerships. Radio waves carried news of city life into isolated farmhouses. The growth in the circulation of national magazines also broke down the wall separating country from city. Mail-order catalogs—Sears, Roebuck, and Company and others—invited farmers to fantasize that they too could fill their homes with refrigerators, RCA Victrolas, and Hoover vacuum cleaners. **(See Map 24.1, Urbanization, 1920, in the color insert following page 912.)**

Rural white Americans showed ambivalence toward this cultural invasion. On the one hand, most country dwellers were eager to participate in the consumer marketplace. On the other hand, many worried that doing so would expose the countryside to atheism, immorality, and radicalism. They expressed their determination to protect their imperiled way of life in their support for Prohibition, the Ku Klux Klan, immigration restriction, and religious fundamentalism.

Prohibition

The 18th Amendment to the Constitution, which prohibited the manufacture and sale of alcohol, went into effect in January 1920. Initially it drew support from a large and varied constituency that included farmers, middle-class city dwellers, feminists, and progressive reformers who loathed the powerful "liquor trust" and who saw firsthand the deleterious effects of drink on the urban poor. It soon became apparent, however, that Prohibition was doing as much to encourage law-breaking as abstinence. With only 1,500 federal agents to enforce the law, the government could not possibly police the drinking habits of 110 million people. With little fear of punishment, those who wanted to drink did so, either brewing liquor at home or buying it from speakeasies and bootleggers.

Because the law prevented legitimate businesses from manufacturing liquor, organized crime added alcohol to its portfolio. Mobsters procured much of their liquor from Canadian manufacturers, smuggled it across the border, protected it in warehouses, and distributed it to speakeasies. Al Capone's Chicago-based mob alone employed 1,000 men to protect its liquor trafficking, which was so lucrative that Capone became the richest (and most feared) gangster in America. Blood flowed in the streets of Chicago and other northern cities as rival mobs fought one another to enlarge their share of the market.

These unexpected consequences caused many early advocates of Prohibition, especially in the cities, to withdraw their support. Not so for Prohibition's rural, white Protestant supporters, however. The violence spawned by liquor trafficking confirmed their view of alcohol as evil. The high-profile participation of Italian, Irish, and Jewish gangsters in the bootleg trade reinforced their belief that Catholics and Jews were threats to law and morality. Many rural white Protestants became more, not less, determined to rid the country of liquor once and for all; some among them resolved to rid the country of Jews and Catholics as well.

The Ku Klux Klan

The original Ku Klux Klan, formed in the South in the late 1860s, had died out with the defeat of Reconstruction and the reestablishment of white supremacy (see chapter 17). The new Klan was created in 1915 by William Simmons, a white southerner who had been inspired by D. W. Griffith's racist film, *Birth of a Nation,* in which the early Klan was depicted as having saved the nation from predatory blacks. By the 1920s, control of the Klan had passed from Simmons to a Texas dentist, Hiram Evans, and its ideological focus had expanded from a loathing of blacks to a hatred of Jews and Catholics as well. Evans's Klan propagated a nativist message that the country should contain—or better yet, eliminate—the influence of Jews and Catholics and restore "Anglo-Saxon" racial purity, Protestant supremacy, and traditional morality to national life. This message swelled Klan ranks and expanded its visibility and influence in the North and South alike.

By 1924, as many as 4 million Americans are thought to have belonged to the Klan, including the half-million members of its female auxiliary, Women of the Ku Klux Klan. Not only was the Klan strong in states of the Old Confederacy such as Louisiana and Texas and in border states such as Oklahoma and Kansas, but it thrived, too, in such northern states as Indiana, Pennsylvania, Washington, and Oregon. It even drew significant membership from the cities of those states. Indiana, for example, was home to 500,000 Klansmen and women, many of them in the Indianapolis area. In 1924, Indiana voters elected a Klansman to the governorship and sent several other Klan members to the statehouse.

In some respects, the Klan resembled other fraternal organizations. It offered its members friendship networks, social services, and conviviality. Its rituals, regalia, and mock-medieval language (the Imperial Wizard, Exalted Cyclops, Grand Dragons, and such) gave initiates a sense of superiority, valor, and mystery similar to what other fraternal societies, from the Masons to the Knights of Columbus, imparted to their members.

But the Klan also thrived on hate. It spread lurid tales of financial extortion by Jewish bankers and sexual exploitation by Catholic priests. The accusations were sometimes general, as in the claim that an international conspiracy of Jewish bankers had caused the agricultural depression, or allegations that the pope had sent agents to the United States with instructions to destroy liberty and democracy. More common, and more incendiary, however, were the seemingly plausible, yet totally manufactured, tales of Jewish or Catholic depravity. Stories circulated of Jewish businessmen who had opened amusement parks and dance halls to which they lured innocent adolescents, tempting them with sexual transgression and profiting handsomely from their moral debasement. Likewise, Catholic priests and nuns were said to prey on Protestant girls and boys who had been forced into convents and Catholic orphanages. These outrageous stories sometimes provoked attacks on individual Jews and Catholics. More commonly, they prompted campaigns to boycott Jewish businesses and Catholic institutions, and to ruin reputations.

The emphasis on sexual exploitation in these stories reveals the anxiety Klan members felt about society's growing acceptance of sexual openness and sexual gratification. Many Klan supporters lived in towns suffused with these modern attitudes. That such attitudes might reflect the yearnings of Protestant children rather than the manipulation of deceitful Jews and Catholics was a truth some Protestant parents found difficult to accept.

Immigration Restriction

Although most white Protestants never joined the Klan, many of them did respond to the Klan's nativist argument that the country and its values would best be served by limiting the entry of outsiders. That was the purpose of the Johnson-Reed **Immigration Restriction Act of 1924.**

By the early 1920s, most Americans believed that the country could no longer accommodate the million immigrants who had been arriving each year before the war and the more than 800,000 who arrived in 1921. Industrialists no longer needed unskilled European laborers to operate their factories, their places having been taken either by machines or by

African American and Mexican workers. Most labor movement leaders were convinced that the influx of workers unfamiliar with English and with trade unions had weakened labor solidarity. Progressive reformers no longer believed that immigrants could be easily Americanized or that harmony between the native-born and the foreign-born could be readily achieved. Congress responded to constituents' concerns by passing an immigration restriction act in 1921. In 1924, the more comprehensive Johnson-Reed Act imposed a yearly quota of 165,000 immigrants from countries outside the Western Hemisphere, effectively reducing total immigration to only 20 percent of the prewar annual average.

The sponsors of the 1924 act believed that certain groups—British, Germans, and Scandinavians, in particular—were racially superior and that, consequently, these groups should be allowed to enter the United States in greater numbers; however, because the Constitution prohibited the enactment of explicitly racist laws, Congress had to achieve this racist aim through subterfuge. Lawmakers established a formula to determine the annual immigrant quota for each foreign country, which was to be computed at 2 percent of the total number of immigrants from that country already resident in the United States in the year 1890. In 1890, immigrant ranks had been dominated by the British, Germans, and Scandinavians, so the new quotas would thus allow for a relatively larger cohort of immigrants from those countries. Immigrant groups that were poorly represented in the 1890 population—Italians, Greeks, Poles, Slavs, and Eastern European Jews—were effectively locked out.

The Johnson-Reed Act also reaffirmed the long-standing policy of excluding Chinese immigrants, and it added Japanese and other groups of East and South Asians to the list of groups that were altogether barred from entry. The act did not officially limit immigration from nations in the Western Hemisphere, chiefly because agribusiness interests in Texas and California had convinced Congress that cheap Mexican labor was indispensable to their industry's prosperity. Still, the establishment of a Border Patrol along the U.S.–Mexican border and the imposition of a $10 head tax on all prospective Mexican immigrants made entry into the United States more difficult than it had been.

The Johnson-Reed Act accomplished Congress's underlying goal. Annual immigration from transoceanic nations fell by 80 percent. The large number of available slots for English and German immigrants regularly went unfilled, while the smaller number of available slots for Italians, Poles, Russian Jews, and others prevented hundreds of thousands of them from entering the country. A "national origins" system put in place in 1927 further reduced the total annual quota to 150,000 and reserved more than 120,000 of these slots for immigrants from northwestern Europe. Except for minor modifications in 1952, the Johnson-Reed Act would govern U.S. immigration policy until 1965.

Remarkably few Americans, outside of the ethnic groups being discriminated against, objected to these laws at the time they were passed—an indication of how broadly acceptable racism and nativism had become. In fact, racism and religious bigotry enjoyed a resurgence during the Jazz Age. The pseudoscience of eugenics, based on the idea that nations could improve the racial quality of their population by expanding its stronger racial strains

Annual Immigrant Quotas under the Johnson-Reed Act, 1925–1927

Northwest Europe and Scandinavia		Eastern and Southern Europe		Other Countries	
Country	Quota	Country	Quota	Country	Quota
Germany	51,227	Poland	5,982	Africa (other than Egypt)	1,100
Great Britain and Northern Ireland	34,007	Italy	3,845	Armenia	124
		Czechoslovakia	3,073		
Irish Free State (Ireland)	28,567	Russia	2,248	Australia	121
		Yugoslavia	671	Palestine	100
Sweden	9,561	Romania	603	Syria	100
Norway	6,453	Portugal	503	Turkey	100
France	3,954	Hungary	473	New Zealand and Pacific Islands	100
Denmark	2,789	Lithuania	344		
Switzerland	2,081	Latvia	142	All others	1,900
Netherlands	1,648	Spain	131		
Austria	785	Estonia	124		
Belgium	512	Albania	100		
Finland	471	Bulgaria	100		
Free City of Danzig	228	Greece	100		
Iceland	100				
Luxembourg	100				
Total (number)	142,483	Total (number)	18,439	Total (number)	3,745
Total (%)	86.5%	Total (%)	11.2%	Total (%)	2.3%

Note: Total annual immigrant quota was 164,667.
Source: From *Statistical Abstract of the United States* (Washington, D.C.: Government Printing Office, 1929), p. 100.

and shrinking its weaker ones, found supporters not only in Congress but among the ranks of prestigious scientists as well. Universities such as Harvard and Columbia set quotas similar to those of the Johnson-Reed Act to reduce the proportion of Jews among their undergraduates.

Fundamentalism versus Liberal Protestantism

Of all the movements protesting against the modern elements of urban life in the 1920s, Protestant fundamentalism was perhaps the most enduring. **Fundamentalists** regarded the Bible as God's word and thus the source of all "fundamental" truth. They believed that every event depicted in the Bible, from the creation of the world in six days to the resurrection of

Christ, happened exactly as the Bible described it. For fundamentalists, God was a deity who intervened directly in the lives of individuals and communities and who made known both his pleasure and his wrath to those who acknowledged his divinity. Sin had to be actively purged, and salvation actively sought.

The rise of the fundamentalist movement from the 1870s through the 1920s roughly paralleled the rise of urban-industrial society. Fundamentalists recoiled from the "evils" of the city—from what they perceived as its poverty, its moral degeneracy, its irreligion, and its crass materialism. Fundamentalism took shape in reaction against two additional aspects of urban society: the growth of liberal Protestantism and the revelations of science.

Liberal Protestants believed that religion had to be adapted to the skeptical and scientific temper of the modern age. No biblical story in which a sea opens up, the sun stands still, or a woman springs forth from a man's rib could possibly be true. The Bible was to be mined for its ethical values rather than for its literal truth. Liberal Protestants removed God from his active role in history and refashioned him into a distant and benign deity who watched over the world but did not intervene to punish or to redeem. They turned religion away from the quest for salvation and toward the pursuit of good deeds, social conscience, and love for one's neighbor. Although those with a liberal bent constituted only a minority of Protestants, they were articulate, visible, and influential in social reform movements. Fundamentalism arose in part to counter the "heretical" claims of the liberal Protestants.

Liberal Protestants and fundamentalists both understood that science was the source of most challenges to Christianity. Scientists believed that rational inquiry was a better guide to the past and to the future than prayer and revelation. Scientists even challenged the ideas that God had created the world and had fashioned humankind in his own image. These were assertions that many religious peoples, particularly fundamentalists, simply could not accept. Conflict was inevitable. It came in 1925, in Dayton, Tennessee.

The Scopes Trial

No aspect of science aroused more anger among fundamentalists than Charles Darwin's theory of evolution. There was no greater blasphemy than to suggest that man emerged from lower forms of life instead of being created by God. In Tennessee in 1925, fundamentalists succeeded in passing a law that forbade teaching "any theory that denies the story of the divine creation of man as taught in the Bible."

For Americans who accepted the authority of science, denying the truth of evolution was as ludicrous as insisting that the sun revolved around the earth. They ridiculed the fundamentalists, but they worried that the passage of the Tennessee law might signal the onset of a campaign to undermine First Amendment guarantees of free speech. The American Civil Liberties Union (ACLU), founded by liberals during the Red Scare of 1919 and 1920, began searching for a teacher who would be willing to challenge the constitutionality of the Tennessee law. They found their man in John T. Scopes, a 24-year-old biology teacher in Dayton, Tennessee. After confessing that he had taught evolution to his students, Scopes was

INHERIT THE WIND (1960)

Directed by Stanley Kramer.
Starring Fredric March (Matthew Harrison Brady), Spencer Tracy (Henry Drummond), Gene Kelly
(E. K. Hornbeck), Dick York (Bertram T. Cates), Claude Akins (Rev. Jeremiah Brown), and Donna Anderson
(Rachel Brown).

Inherit the Wind is a fictionalized drama about the 1925 Scopes Trial in Dayton, Tennessee (see p. 891 for a discussion of the actual trial). It begins with the arrest of Bertram T. Cates (the name given by the moviemakers to the John T. Scopes character) and ends with Cates's conviction on the charge of breaking a state law prohibiting the teaching of evolution in Tennessee schools. The climactic moment in the movie, as in the real Scopes story, is the courtroom clash between Matthew Harrison Brady (a thinly fictionalized version of William Jennings Bryan) and Henry Drummond (the Clarence Darrow character) over the Bible, truth, and scientific inquiry. That the two actors who played Brady and Drummond, Fredric March and Spencer Tracy, were as prominent in American cinema as Bryan and Darrow had been in American politics enhanced the movie's appeal. A popular film, *Inherit the Wind* shaped how a generation that came of age in the 1960s interpreted the meaning of the Scopes trial. The film's broad influence makes it a particularly important and interesting historical document to explore.

The director of *Inherit the Wind*, Stanley Kramer, liked to engage important political issues in his movies: *Home of the Brave* (1949) explored racism in the U.S. army; *On the Beach* (1959) examined the social consequences of nuclear war; and *Judgment at Nuremberg* (1961) investigated the nature of Nazi criminality. Some movie critics have expressed frustration with these "message movies," charging that Kramer often sacrificed historical and personal nuance in order to drive his political point home. He does this in *Inherit the Wind* by portraying the Scopes camp in the most positive possible light. To help us identify with E. K. Hornbeck (meant to represent the irascible Baltimore-based journalist, H. L. Mencken, for example, he casts the amiable Gene Kelly in the role. Kramer celebrates Drummond (representing Darrow) not just for his commitment to defending science and reason but for having more integrity than anyone else in the courtroom. Kramer does try to endow Brady with some positive qualities and to honor him for his past achievements in politics. Ultimately, however, Kramer cannot resist depicting Brady as pompous, calculating, and, by the trial's end, dangerously out of control.

This caricature of Brady/Bryan reveals the roots of *Inherit the Wind* in a 1955 play by the same name. The creators of that play were not especially concerned about making their Brady character resemble Bryan. Instead, they wanted Brady to represent an entirely different figure in American politics, Senator Joseph McCarthy, who led a campaign in the 1950s to oust communists and their supporters from their jobs in the U.S. government. McCarthy's anticommunist operation was terrifying not just to the radicals he sought to expose but also to liberals and others who believed that McCarthy's unscrupulous methods were threatening the core political values of the American republic (see chapter 27). In identifying Brady with McCarthy, the playwrights sought to discredit both men.

The play and movie also criticize McCarthyism by introducing to the 1920s evolution battle an entirely fictitious fire and brimstone preacher, Reverend Jeremiah Brown, who, in the manner of a 1950s McCarthyite anticommunist, viciously and publicly condemns those, including his own daughter, Rachel, who dare to challenge the authority of those in power. Both Brown and Brady are portrayed in the play and movie as successful manipulators of public opinion, much as McCarthy was thought to have distorted the minds of Americans everywhere with his messages of fear and hate.

Spencer Tracy playing Henry Drummond (the fictional Clarence Darrow) on left and Fredric March playing Matthew Harrison Brady (the fictional William Jennings Bryant) on right.

That Kramer allowed his movie about a trial in the 1920s to be influenced by events that he lived through in the 1950s is itself an interesting subject to discuss. It causes us to ask how much historians' views of the past are themselves shaped by the times in which these historians lived. But however much we come to see *Inherit the Wind* as a commentary on politics in 1950s America, we still need to acknowledge the power of the final courtroom scene in the movie, in which Drummond and Brady battle each other about the meaning of science and religion. Their confrontation allows us to glimpse what was at stake in 1925 when a trial in the small town of Dayton, Tennessee, transfixed the nation.

arrested. The case quickly attracted national attention. William Jennings Bryan, the former Populist, progressive, and secretary of state, announced that he would help prosecute Scopes, and the famous liberal trial lawyer Clarence Darrow rushed to Dayton to lead Scopes's defense. That Bryan and Darrow had once been allies in the progressive movement only heightened the drama. A small army of journalists descended on Dayton, led by H. L. Mencken, a Baltimore-based journalist famous for his savage critiques of the alleged stupidity and prudishness of small-town Americans.

The trial dragged on, and most of the observers expected Scopes to be convicted. He was, but the hearing took an unexpected turn when Darrow persuaded the judge to let Bryan testify as an "expert on the Bible." Darrow knew that Bryan's testimony would have no bearing on the question of Scopes's innocence or guilt. The jury was not even allowed to hear it. His aim was to expose Bryan as a fool for believing that the Bible was a source of literal truth and thus to embarrass the fundamentalists. In a riveting confrontation, Darrow made Bryan's defense of the Bible look problematic and led Bryan to admit that the "truth" of the Bible was not always easy to determine. But Darrow could not shake Bryan's belief that the Bible was God's word and thus the source of all truth.

In his account of the trial, Mencken portrayed Bryan as a pathetic figure devastated by his humiliating experience on the witness stand, a view popularized in the 1960 movie *Inherit the Wind.* When Bryan died only a week after the trial ended, Mencken claimed that the trial had broken Bryan's heart. Bryan deserved a better epitaph than the one Mencken had given him. Diabetes caused his death, not a broken heart. Nor was Bryan the innocent fool that Mencken made him out to be. He remembered when social conservatives had used Darwin's phrase "survival of the fittest" to prove that the wealthy and politically powerful were racially superior to the poor and powerless. His rejection of Darwinism evidenced his democratic faith that all human beings were creatures of God and thus capable of striving for perfection and equality.

The public ridicule attendant on the Scopes trial took its toll on fundamentalists. Many of them retreated from politics and refocused their attention on purging sin from their own hearts rather than from the hearts of others. In the end, the fundamentalists prevailed on three more states to prohibit the teaching of evolution, but the controversy had even more far-reaching effects. Worried about losing sales, publishers quietly removed references to Darwin from their science textbooks, a policy that would remain in force until the 1960s. In this respect, the fundamentalists had scored a significant victory.

Ethnic and Racial Communities

Focus Question
How were the experiences of ethnic and racial groups in 1920s America similar and how were they different?

The 1920s were a decade of change for ethnic and racial minorities. Government policy simultaneously discouraged the continued immigration of "new immigrants" from Southern and Eastern Europe and encouraged the migration of African Americans from the South to the North and of Mexicans across the Rio Grande and into the American Southwest. Some minorities benefited from the prosperity of the decade; others created and sustained vibrant subcultures. All, however, experienced a surge in religious and racial discrimination that made them uneasy in Jazz Age America.

European American Ethnics

European American ethnics—and especially the Southern and Eastern European majority among them—were concentrated in the cities of the Northeast and Midwest. Many were semiskilled and unskilled industrial laborers who suffered economic insecurity. In addition, they faced cultural discrimination. Catholics and Jews were targets of the Klan and its politics of hate. Catholics generally opposed Prohibition, viewing it as a crude attempt by Protestants to control their behavior. Southern and Eastern Europeans, particularly Jews and Italians, resented immigration restriction and the implication that they were inferior to Anglo-Saxon whites. Many Italians were outraged by the execution of Nicola Sacco and Bartolomeo Vanzetti in 1927 (chapter 23). If the two men had been native-born white Protestants, Italians argued, their lives would have been spared.

Southern and Eastern Europeans everywhere endured intensive Americanization campaigns. State after state passed laws requiring public schools to instruct children in the essentials of citizenship. Several states, including Rhode Island, extended these laws to private schools as well, convinced that the children of immigrants who were attending Catholic parochial schools were spending too much time learning about their native religion, language, and country. An Oregon law tried to eliminate Catholic schools altogether by ordering all children aged 8 to 16 to enroll in public schools. But attending a public school was no guarantee of acceptance, either—a lesson learned by Jewish children who had excelled in their studies only to be barred from Harvard, Columbia, and other elite universities.

Southern and Eastern Europeans responded to these insults and attacks by strengthening the very institutions and customs Americanizers sought to undermine. Ethnic associations flourished in the 1920s—Catholic churches and Jewish synagogues, fraternal and mutual benefit societies, banks and charitable organizations, athletic leagues and youth groups. Children learned their native languages and customs at home and at church if not at school, and they joined with their parents to celebrate their ethnic heritage. Among Italians and French Canadians, saints' days were occasions for parades, speeches, band concerts, games, and feasts, all serving to solidify ethnic bonds and affirm ethnic identity.

Many of these immigrants and their children, however, also embraced the new consumer culture. They flocked to movies and amusement parks, to baseball games and boxing matches. Children usually entered more enthusiastically into the world of American mass culture than did their immigrant parents, a behavior that often set off family conflicts.

Democratic Presidential Voting in Chicago by Ethnic Groups, 1924 and 1928

	Percent Democratic	
	1924	1928
Czechoslovaks	40%	73%
Poles	35	71
Lithuanians	48	77
Yugoslavs	20	54
Italians	31	63
Germans	14	58
Jews	19	60

Source: From John M. Allswang, *A House for All Peoples: Ethnic Politics in Chicago, 1890–1936* (Lexington: University Press of Kentucky), p. 42.

The famed New York Yankee, Lou Gehrig, had to fight to convince his German-born mother that playing baseball was honorable work. But many ethnics found it possible to reconcile their own culture with American culture. Youngsters who went to the movies did so with friends from within their community. Ethnics also played baseball in leagues organized around churches or ethnic associations. In these early days of radio, ethnics living in large cities could always find programs in their native language and music from their native lands.

European American ethnics also resolved to develop sufficient political muscle to defeat the forces of nativism and to turn government policy in a more favorable direction. One sign of this determination was a sharp rise in the number of immigrants who became U.S. citizens. The percentage of immigrant Poles, Slavs, Italians, Lithuanians, and Hungarians who became naturalized citizens nearly doubled during the decade; the percentage of naturalized Greeks almost tripled. Armed with the vote, ethnics turned out on election day to defeat unsympathetic city councilmen, mayors, state representatives, and even an occasional governor. Their growing national strength first became apparent at the Democratic national convention of 1924, when urban-ethnic delegates almost won approval of planks calling for the repeal of Prohibition and condemnation of the Klan. After denying the presidential nomination to William G. McAdoo—Woodrow Wilson's treasury secretary, son-in-law, and heir apparent—they nearly secured it for their candidate, **Alfred E. Smith**, the Irish American governor of New York. McAdoo represented the rural and southern constituencies of the Democratic Party. His forces ended up battling Smith's urban-ethnic forces for 103 ballots, until both men gave up and supporters from each camp switched their votes to a compromise candidate, the corporate lawyer John W. Davis.

The nomination fight damaged the Democratic Party in the short term, and popular Calvin Coolidge easily defeated the little-known Davis. This split between the party's rural

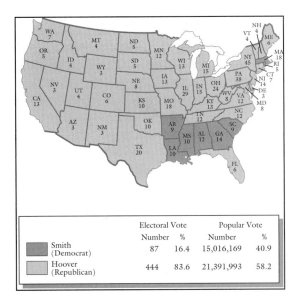

Map 24.2   Presidential Election, 1928   This map shows Hoover's landslide victory in 1928, as he carried all but eight states and won almost 84 percent of the electoral vote.

Protestant and urban-ethnic constituencies would keep the Democrats from the White House for nearly a decade, but the convention upheaval of 1924 also marked an important milestone in the bid by European American ethnics for political power. They would achieve a second milestone at the Democratic national convention of 1928 when, after another bitter nomination struggle, they secured the presidential nomination for Al Smith. Never before had a major political party nominated a Catholic for president. Herbert Hoover crushed Smith in the general election, as nativists stirred up anti-Catholic prejudice yet again and as large numbers of southern Democrats either stayed home or voted Republican. Even so, the campaign offered encouraging signs, none more so than Smith's beating Hoover in the nation's 12 largest cities. European American ethnics would yet have their day.

African Americans

Despite the urban race riots of 1919 (see chapter 23), African Americans continued to leave their rural homes for the industrial centers of the South and the North. In the 1920s alone, nearly a million blacks traveled North. In New York City and Chicago, their numbers grew so large—300,000 in New York and 234,000 in Chicago—that they formed cities unto themselves. When word of New York City's urban black enclave reached the Caribbean, thousands of West Indian blacks set off for Harlem. Within these black metropolises emerged complex societies consisting of workers, businessmen, professionals,

Death Rates from Selected Causes for New York City Residents, 1925

Cause of Death	Total Population	African American Population
General death rate (per 1,000 population)	11.4	16.5
Pneumonia	132.8	282.4
Pulmonary tuberculosis	75.5	258.4
Infant mortality (per 1,000 live births)	64.6	118.4
Maternal mortality (per 1,000 total births)	5.3	10.2
Stillbirths (per 1,000 births)	47.6	82.7
Homicide	5.3	19.5
Suicide	14.8	9.7

Note: Rate is per 100,000 population, unless noted.
Source: Cheryl Lynn Greenberg, *"Or Does It Explode?" Black Harlem in the Great Depression* (New York: Oxford University Press, 1991), p. 32.

intellectuals, artists, and entertainers. Social differentiation intensified as various groups—long-resident northerners and newly arrived southerners, religious conservatives and cultural radicals, African Americans and African Caribbeans—found reason to disapprove of one another's ways. Still, the diversity and complexity of urban black America were thrilling, nowhere more so than in Harlem, the "Negro capital." Black writer James Weldon Johnson described Harlem in the 1920s:

> Throughout colored America Harlem is the recognized Negro capital. Indeed, it is Mecca for the sightseer, the pleasure-seeker, the curious, the adventurous, the enterprising, the ambitious, and the talented of the entire Negro world. . . . Not merely a colony or a community or a settlement—not at all a "quarter" or a slum or a fringe—[Harlem is] . . . a black city, located in the heart of white Manhattan, and containing more Negroes to the square mile than any other spot on earth. It strikes the uninformed observer as a phenomenon, a miracle straight out of the skies.

Not even the glamour of Harlem could erase the reality of racial discrimination, however. Most African Americans could find work only in New York City's least-desired and lowest-paying jobs. Because they could rent apartments only in areas that real estate agents and banks had designated as "colored," African Americans suffered the highest rate of residential segregation of any minority group. Although Harlem had its fashionable districts where affluent blacks lived, much of the area's housing stock was poor and rents were high. Harlem became a black ghetto, an area set apart from the rest of the city by the skin color of its inhabitants, by its higher population density and poverty rate, by its higher incidence of infectious diseases, and by the lower life expectancy of its people.

Blacks did enjoy some important economic breakthroughs in the 1920s. Henry Ford, for example, hired large numbers of African Americans to work in his Detroit auto factories. Even here, however, a racist logic was operating, for Ford believed that black and white workers, divided along racial lines, would not challenge his authority. Until the 1940s, in fact, unions made less headway at Ford plants than at the plants of other major automobile manufacturers.

Racial divisions carried over from work to play. African Americans loved baseball as much as white Americans did, and Babe Ruth enjoyed a large black following, but black baseball players were barred from playing in the lily-white major leagues. In response, they formed their own Negro Leagues in the United States and also played professional ball in Mexico and the Caribbean, where they earned extra income and escaped some of the prejudice that met them everywhere in the United States. Cuba, Puerto Rico, Mexico, and other countries in which African Americans played did not organize baseball along racial lines.

The greatest black baseball player was probably Josh Gibson, who joined the Homestead Grays of the National Negro League in 1929 at the age of 18. In his 17-year career, he compiled statistics that surpassed those of any professional ballplayer of his era, white or black, including those of the legendary Babe Ruth. Gibson slugged 962 career home runs, hit 84 home runs in a single season, and compiled a .373 lifetime batting average. Because he died in 1947, at the age of 35, just months before the integration of major league baseball, Gibson never got the opportunity to test his skills against the best white ballplayers, and they never got a chance to play against him.

African Americans grew pessimistic about achieving racial equality. After Marcus Garvey's black nationalist movement collapsed in the mid-1920s (see chapter 23), no comparable organization arose to take its place. The NAACP continued to fight racial discrimination, and the Urban League carried on quiet negotiations with industrial elites to secure jobs for African Americans. Black socialists led by A. Philip Randolph built a strong all-black union, the Brotherhood of Sleeping Car Porters, but the victories were small and white allies were scarce. The political initiatives emerging among European American ethnics had few counterparts in the African American community.

In terms of black culture, however, the 1920s were vigorous and productive. Black musicians coming north to Chicago and New York brought with them their distinctive musical styles, most notably the blues and ragtime. Influenced by the harmonies and techniques of European classical music, which black musicians learned from their European American ethnic counterparts, these southern styles metamorphosed into jazz. Urban audiences, first black and then white, found this new music alluring. They responded to its melodies, its sensuality, its creativity, its savvy. In Chicago, Detroit, New York, New Orleans, and elsewhere, jazz musicians came together in cramped apartments, cabarets, and nightclubs to jam, compete, and entertain. Willie Smith, Charles P. Johnson, Count Basie, Fats Waller, Duke Ellington, and Louis Armstrong were among the most famous musicians of the day. By the late 1920s, they were being hailed in Europe as well.

Jazz seemed to express something quintessentially modern. Jazz musicians broke free of convention, improvised, and produced new sounds that created new sensations. Both blacks and whites found in jazz an escape from the routine, the predictability, and the conventions of their everyday lives.

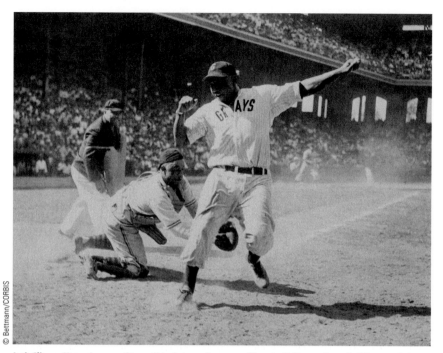

© Bettmann/CORBIS

Josh Gibson, Negro Leagues Star   This photograph captures Gibson in 1944, near the end of his career, being tagged out at home plate by Ted Radcliffe in the 10th annual East-West All Star Game at Comiskey Park, Chicago.

The Harlem Renaissance

Paralleling the emergence of jazz was a black literary and artistic awakening known as the **Harlem Renaissance.** Black novelists, poets, painters, sculptors, and playwrights set about creating works rooted in their own culture instead of imitating the styles of white Europeans and Americans. The movement had begun during the war, when blacks sensed that they might at last be advancing to full equality. It was symbolized by the image of the "New Negro," a black man or woman who would no longer be deferential to whites but who would display his or her independence through talent and determination. The "New Negro" would be assertive in every field—at work, in politics, in the military, and in arts and letters. As racial discrimination intensified after the war, cultural activities took on special significance. The world of culture was one place where blacks could express their racial pride and demonstrate their talent.

Langston Hughes, a young black poet, said of the Harlem Renaissance: "We younger Negro artists who create now intend to express our individual dark-skinned selves without fear or shame. If white people are pleased, we are glad. If they are not, it doesn't matter. We know we are beautiful. And ugly, too." Writers Claude McKay, Jean Toomer, and Zora Neale Hurston; poet Countee Cullen; and painter Aaron Douglas were other prominent Renaissance participants. In 1925, *Survey Graphic,* a white liberal magazine, devoted an entire issue to "Harlem—the Mecca of the New Negro." Alain Locke, an art and literary critic and professor of philosophy at Howard University in Washington, D.C., edited both the issue and the book *The New Negro*, published later that year. Locke became the movement's leading visionary and philosopher.

But even these cultural advances failed to escape white prejudice. The most popular jazz nightclubs in Harlem, most of which were owned and operated by whites, often refused to admit black customers. The only African Americans permitted inside were the jazz musicians, singers and dancers, prostitutes, and kitchen help. Moreover, the musicians often had to perform what the white patrons wanted to hear. Duke Ellington, for example, was called on to play "jungle music," which for whites revealed the "true" African soul—sensual, innocent, primitive. Such pressures curtailed the artistic freedom of black musicians and reinforced racist stereotypes of African Americans as inferior people who were closer to nature than the "more civilized" white audiences who came to hear their music.

Black artists and writers experienced similar pressures. Many of them depended for their sustenance on the support of wealthy white patrons. Those patrons were generous, but they wanted a return on their investment. Charlotte Mason, the New York City matron who supported Hughes and Hurston, for example, expected them to entertain her friends by demonstrating "authentic Negritude" in their work. Hurston accepted this role, but for Hughes it became intolerable. Both Hughes and Hurston paid a price for their patron's support, including the collapse of their once-close friendship with each other.

Mexican Americans

After the Johnson-Reed Act of 1924, Mexicans became the country's chief source of immigrant labor. A total of 500,000 Mexicans came to the United States in the 1920s. Some headed for the steel, auto, and meatpacking plants of the Midwest, but most settled in the Southwest, where they worked on the railroads and in construction, agriculture, and manufacturing. In Texas, three of every four construction workers and eight of every ten migrant farm workers were Mexicans. An official of the San Antonio Chamber of Commerce declared: "Mexican farm labor is rapidly proving the making of this State." In California, Mexican immigrants made up 75 percent of the state's agricultural workforce.

Mexican farm laborers in Texas worked long hours for little money. As a rule, they earned 50 cents to a dollar less per day than Anglo workers. They were usually barred from becoming machine operators or assuming other skilled positions. Forced to follow the crops, they had little opportunity to develop settled homes and communities. Mexican farm workers depended for shelter on whatever facilities farm owners offered. Because farm owners rarely required the services of Mexican workers for more than several days or weeks, few were willing to spend the money required to provide decent homes and schools. Houses typically lacked even wooden floors or indoor plumbing. Mexican laborers found it difficult to protest these conditions because their knowledge of English was limited. Few owned cars or trucks that would have allowed them to escape a bad employer

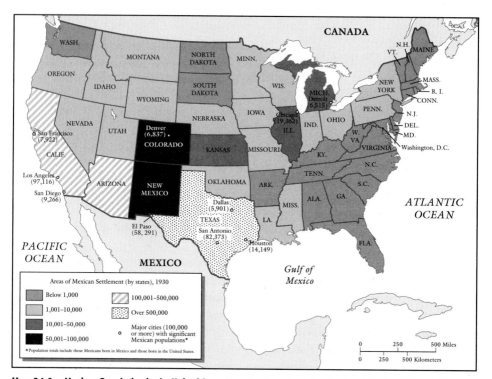

Map 24.3   Mexican Population in the United States, 1930   By 1930, Mexican immigrants had established their pattern of settling primarily in the U.S. Southwest. Texas had the largest concentration of Mexican immigrants, followed by California and Arizona, and then by New Mexico and Colorado. Though Texas had a larger overall population, Los Angeles had surpassed San Antonio as the city with the largest single Mexican community in the United States.

and search for a good one. Many were in debt to employers who had advanced them money and who threatened them with jail if they failed to fulfill the terms of their contract. Others feared deportation; they lacked visas, having slipped into the United States illegally rather than pay the immigrant tax or endure harassment from the Border Patrol.

Increasing numbers of Mexican immigrants, however, found their way to California, where, on the whole, wages exceeded those in Texas. Some escaped agricultural labor altogether for construction and manufacturing jobs. Many Mexican men in Los Angeles, for example, worked in the city's large railroad yards, at the city's numerous construction sites, and as unskilled workers in local factories. Mexican women labored in the city's garment shops, fish canneries, and food processing plants. By 1930, Los Angeles had become the largest area of settlement for Mexicans in the United States.

The Los Angeles Mexican American community increased in complexity as it grew in size. By the mid-1920s, it included a growing professional class, a proud group of **californios** (Spanish-speakers who had been resident in California for generations), many musicians and entertainers, a small but energetic band of entrepreneurs and businessmen,

Map 22.3 Colonial Possessions, 1900 In 1900, the British Empire was the largest in the world, followed by the French and Russian Empires. The U.S. Empire, if measured by the square miles of land held as colonial possessions, was small by comparison.

Map 22.4 **United States Presence in Latin America, 1895–1934** The United States possessed few colonies in Latin America but intervened (often repeatedly) in Mexico, Cuba, Nicaragua, Panama, Haiti, the Dominican Republic, and Venezuela to secure its economic and political interests.

Map 23.2   Europe and the Near East After the First World War   The First World War and the Treaty of Versailles changed the geography of Europe and the Near East. Nine nations in Europe, stretching from Yugoslavia in the south to Finland in the north, were created (or reformed) out of the defeated Austro-Hungarian and Ottoman Empires. In the Near East, meanwhile, Syria, Lebanon, Palestine, Transjordan, and Iraq were carved out of the Ottoman Empire, placed under British or French control, and promised eventual independence.

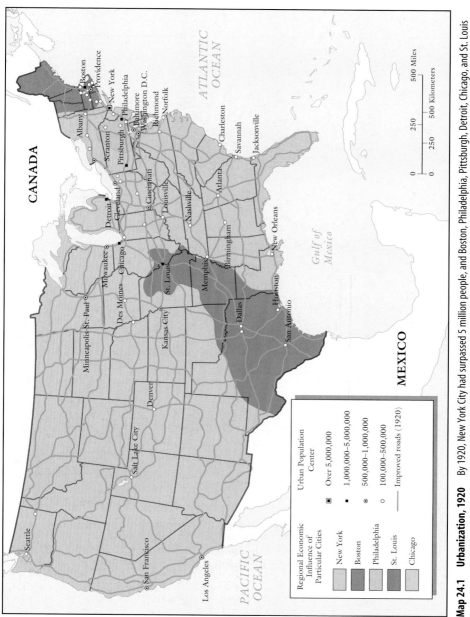

Map 24.1 Urbanization, 1920 By 1920, New York City had surpassed 5 million people, and Boston, Philadelphia, Pittsburgh, Detroit, Chicago, and St. Louis had surpassed 1 million. Another 10 cities, from Los Angeles, California, to Buffalo, New York, had surpassed 500,000. This map, through its color coding, also shows the regions in which the country's five largest cities exercised economic influence.

conservative clerics and intellectuals who had fled or been expelled from revolutionary Mexico, and Mexican government officials who had been sent to counter the influence of the conservative exiles and to strengthen the ties of the immigrants to their homeland. This diverse mix created much internal conflict, but it also generated considerable cultural vitality. Los Angeles became the same kind of magnet for Mexican Americans that Harlem had become for African Americans.

Mexican musicians flocked to Los Angeles, as did Mexican playwrights. The city supported a vigorous Spanish-language theater. Mexican musicians performed on street corners, at ethnic festivals and weddings, at cabarets, and on the radio. Especially popular were folk ballads, called *corridos,* that spoke to the experiences of Mexican immigrants. Although different in form and melody from the African American blues, *corridos* resembled the blues in their emphasis on the suffering, hope, and frustrations of ordinary people.

This flowering of Mexican American culture in Los Angeles could not erase the low wages, high rates of infant mortality, racial discrimination, and other hardships Mexicans faced; nor did it encourage Mexicans, in Los Angeles or elsewhere, to mobilize themselves

Security Pacific Collection/Los Angeles Public Library

Mexican American Women Workers, 1920s   These women were employed at a tortilla factory in Los Angeles.

as a political force. Unlike European immigrants, Mexican immigrants showed little interest in becoming American citizens and acquiring the vote. Yet the cultural vibrancy of the Mexican immigrant community did sustain many individuals who were struggling to survive in a strange, and often hostile, environment.

The "Lost Generation" and Disillusioned Intellectuals

Focus Question
To whom did the phrase "Lost Generation" refer and what caused these individuals to become disillusioned?

Many native-born white artists and intellectuals also felt uneasy in America in the 1920s. Their unease arose not from poverty or discrimination but from alienation. They despaired of American culture and regarded the average American as anti-intellectual, small-minded, materialistic, and puritanical. The novelist Sinclair Lewis, for example, ridiculed small-town Americans in *Main Street* (1920), "sophisticated" city dwellers in *Babbitt* (1922), physicians in *Arrowsmith* (1925), and evangelicals in *Elmer Gantry* (1927).

Before the First World War, intellectuals and artists had been deeply engaged with "the people." Although they were critical of many aspects of American society, they believed they could help bring about a new politics and improve social conditions. Some of them joined the war effort on the side of the Allies before the United States had officially intervened. Ernest Hemingway, John Dos Passos, and e. e. cummings, among others, sailed to Europe and volunteered their services, usually as ambulance drivers carrying wounded Allied soldiers from the front.

America's intellectuals were shaken by the war's effect on American society. The wartime push for consensus created intolerance of radicals, immigrants, and blacks. Intellectuals had been further dismayed by Prohibition, the rebirth of the Ku Klux Klan, the rise of fundamentalism, and the execution of Sacco and Vanzetti. Not only had many Americans embraced conformity for themselves, but they seemed determined to force conformity on others. The young critic Harold Stearns wrote in 1921 that "the most moving and pathetic fact in the social life of America today is emotional and aesthetic starvation." Before these words were published, Stearns had sailed for France. So many alienated young men like Stearns showed up in Paris that Gertrude Stein, an American writer whose Paris apartment became a gathering place for them, took to calling them the **"Lost Generation."**

Their indictment of America was often too harsh. Most of these writers possessed little knowledge of how most Americans lived. Few expressed sympathy for the plight of farmers or the working-class poor. Few knew much about the rich cultural heritage of immigrant communities. Still, they managed to convert their disillusionment into a rich literary sensibility. The finest works of the decade focused on the psychological toll of living in what the poet T. S. Eliot referred to as *The Waste Land* (1922).

F. Scott Fitzgerald's novel *The Great Gatsby* (1925) told of a man destroyed by his desire to be accepted into a world of wealth, fancy cars, and fast women. In the novel *A Farewell to Arms* (1929), Ernest Hemingway wrote of an American soldier overwhelmed by the senselessness and brutality of war who deserts the army for the company of a woman he loves. Playwright Eugene O'Neill created characters haunted by despair, loneliness, and unfulfilled longing. Writers created innovations in style as well as in content. Sherwood Anderson, in his novel *Winesburg, Ohio* (1919), blended fiction and autobiography. John Dos Passos, in *Manhattan Transfer* (1925), mixed journalism with more traditional literary methods. Hemingway wrote in an understated, laconic prose that somehow drew attention to his characters' rage and vulnerability.

White Southern writers found a tragic sensibility surviving from the South's defeat in the Civil War that spoke to their own loss of hope. One group of such writers, calling themselves the Agrarians, argued that the enduring agricultural character of their region offered a more hopeful path to the future than did the mass-production and mass-consumption regime that had overtaken the North. In 1929, William Faulkner published *The Sound and the Fury,* the first in a series of novels set in northern Mississippi's fictional Yoknapatawpha County. Faulkner explored the violence and terror that marked relationships among family members and townspeople, while maintaining compassion and understanding. Faulkner, Lewis, Hemingway, O'Neill, and Eliot would each receive the Nobel Prize for Literature.

Democracy on the Defensive

Disdain for the masses led many intellectuals to question democracy. If ordinary people were as stupid, prejudiced, and easily manipulated as they seemed, how could they be entrusted with the fate of the nation? Although few intellectuals were as frank as Mencken, who dismissed democracy as "the worship of jackals by jackasses," their distrust of democracy ran deep. Walter Lippmann, a former radical and progressive, declared that modern society had rendered democracy obsolete. In his view, average citizens, buffeted by propaganda emanating from powerful opinion makers, could no longer make the kind of informed, rational judgments needed to make democracy work. They were vulnerable to demagogues who played on their emotions and fears. Lippmann's solution, and that of many other political commentators, was to shift government power from the people to educated elites. Those elites, who would be appointed rather than elected, would conduct foreign and domestic policy in an informed, intelligent way. Only then, in Lippmann's view, could government be effective and just.

Mencken and Lippmann enjoyed especially strong influence and prestige among university students, whose ranks and political significance were growing. But their antidemocratic views did not go uncontested. The philosopher **John Dewey,** who taught at Columbia University but whose reputation and influence extended well beyond academia, was the most articulate spokesman for the "pro-democracy" position. He acknowledged that the concentration of power in giant organizations had eroded the authority of Congress, the presidency, and other democratic institutions, but democracy, he insisted, was not doomed. The people could reclaim their freedom by making big business subject to government control. Government could use its power to democratize corporations and to regulate the communications industry to ensure that every citizen had access to the facts needed to make reasonable, informed political decisions.

Dewey's views attracted the support of a wide range of liberal intellectuals and reformers, including Robert and Helen Lynd; Rexford Tugwell, professor of economics at Columbia; and Felix Frankfurter, a rising star at Harvard's law school. Some of these activists had ties to labor leaders and to New York Governor Franklin D. Roosevelt. They formed the vanguard of a new liberal movement committed to taking up the work the progressives had left unfinished.

But these reformers were utterly without power, except in a few states. The Republican Party had driven reformers from its ranks. The Democratic Party was a fallen giant, crippled by a split between its principal constituencies—rural Protestants and urban ethnics—over Prohibition, immigration restriction, and the Ku Klux Klan. The labor movement was moribund. The Socialist Party had never recovered from the trauma of war and Bolshevism. La Follette's Farmer-Labor Party had stalled after a promising debut. John Dewey and his friends tried to launch yet another third party, but they failed to raise money or arouse mass support.

Reformers took little comfort in the presidential election of 1928. Hoover's smashing victory suggested that the trends of the 1920s—the dominance of the Republicans, the centrality of Prohibition to political debate, the paralysis of the Democrats, the growing economic might of capitalism, and the pervasive influence of the consumer culture—would continue unabated.

Conclusion

Signs abounded in the 1920s that Americans were creating a new and bountiful society. The increased accessibility of cars, radios, vacuum cleaners, and other consumer durables; rising real wages, low unemployment, and installment buying; the widening circle of stock owners; the spread of welfare capitalism—all these pointed to an economy that had become more prosperous, more consumer-oriented, even somewhat more egalitarian. Moves to greater equality within marriage and to enhanced liberty for single women suggested that economic change was propelling social change as well.

Even so, many working-class and rural Americans benefited little from the decade's prosperity. Moreover, the decade's social changes aroused resistance, especially from white farmers and small-town Americans, who feared that the rapid growth of cities and the large urban settlements of European and Mexican Catholics, Jews, and African Americans were rendering their white Protestant America unrecognizable.

In the Democratic Party, farmers, small-town Americans, and moral traditionalists fought bitterly against the growing power of urban, ethnic constituencies. Elsewhere, the traditionalists battled hard to protect religion's authority against the inroads of science and to purge the nation of "inferior" population streams. In the process they arrayed themselves against American traditions of liberty and equality, even as they posed as the defenders of the best that America had to offer.

Their resistance to change caused many of the nation's most talented artists and writers to turn away from their fellow Americans in disgust. Meanwhile, although ethnic and racial minorities experienced high levels of discrimination, they nevertheless found enough freedom to create vibrant ethnic and racial communities and to launch projects—as in the case of African Americans in Harlem and Mexican Americans in Los Angeles—of cultural renaissance.

The Republican Party, having largely shed its reputation for reform, took credit for engineering the new economy of consumer plenty. It looked forward to years of political dominance. A steep and unexpected economic depression, however, would soon dash that expectation, revive the Democratic Party, and destroy Republican political power for a generation.

SUGGESTED READINGS

William Leuchtenberg, *The Perils of Prosperity, 1914–1932* (1958), and Ellis Hawley, *The Great War and the Search for a Modern Order: A History of the American People and Their Institutions, 1917–1933* (1979), offer useful overviews of the 1920s. Important works on the consumer revolution include Warren I. Susman, *Culture as History: The Transformation of American Society in the Twentieth Century* (1984); Roland Marchand, *Advertising the American Dream: Making Way for Modernity, 1920–1940* (1985); and Kathy Lee Peiss, *Hope in a Jar: The Making of America's Beauty Culture* (1998). John D. Hicks, *Republican Ascendancy, 1921–1933* (1960) still serves as a good introduction to national politics, but consult, too, Thomas B. Silver, *Coolidge and the Historians* (1982); Ellis Hawley, ed., *Herbert Hoover as Secretary of Commerce: Studies in New Era Thought and Practice* (1974); and John W. Dean, *Warren G. Harding* (2004). For a penetrating look at U.S. imperialism in the Caribbean in the 1920s, see Mary A. Renda, *Taking Haiti: Military Occupation and the Culture of U.S. Imperialism* (2001).

On agricultural distress and protest, see Theodore Saloutos and John D. Hicks, *Twentieth Century Populism: Agricultural Discontent in the Middle West, 1900–1939* (1951). For an examination of the economic and social effects of Prohibition, see Norman Clark, *Deliver Us From Evil: An Interpretation of American Prohibition* (1976). The best treatment of the Scopes trial can be found in Michael Kazin, *A Godly Hero: The Life of William Jennings Bryan* (2006). On the 1920s resurgence of the Ku Klux Klan, consult Nancy MacLean, *Behind the Mask of Chivalry: The Making of the Second Ku Klux Klan* (1994). Frederic Morton Szasz, *The Divided Mind of Protestant America, 1880–1930* (1982), expertly analyzes the split in Protestant ranks between liberals and fundamentalists. John Higham, *Strangers in the Land: Patterns of American Nativism, 1865–1925* (1955), remains an excellent work on the spirit of intolerance that gripped America in the 1920s. On hostility toward immigrants and ethnics, see, also, Mae Ngai, *Impossible Subjects: Illegal Aliens and the Making of Modern America* (2004) and Jerome Karabel, *The Chosen: The Hidden History of Admission and Exclusion at Harvard, Yale, and Princeton* (2005). Irving Bernstein, *The Lean Years: A History of the American Worker, 1920–1933* (1960), remains the most thorough examination of 1920s workers.

On ethnic communities, Americanization, and political mobilization in the 1920s, see **Gary Gerstle**, *Working-Class Americanism: The Politics of Labor in a Textile City, 1914–1960* (1989); George J. Sánchez, *Becoming Mexican American: Ethnicity, Culture and Identity in Chicano Los Angeles, 1900–1945* (1993); and **Kristi Andersen**, *The Creation of a Democratic Majority, 1928–1936* (1979). On the Harlem Renaissance, see **Nathan Huggins**, *Harlem Renaissance* (1971). Malcolm Cowley, *Exiles Return* (1934), is a marvelous account of the writers and artists who comprised the "Lost Generation." For a provocative interpretation of the intertwined character of white and black literary cultures in 1920s New York, see **Ann Douglas**, *Terrible Honesty: Mongrel Manhattan in the 1920s* (1995).

Visit the Liberty Equality Power Companion Web site for resources specific to this textbook: http://www.thomsonedu.com/history/murrin

Also find self-tests and additional resources at ThomsonNOW. ThomsonNOW is an integrated online suite of services and resources with proven ease of use and efficient paths to success, delivering the results you want—NOW!

www.thomsonedu.com/login/

The Great Depression and the New Deal, 1929–1939

The **Great Depression** began on October 29, 1929 (Black Tuesday) with a spectacular stock market crash. On that one day, stock values plummeted $14 billion. By the end of that year, stock prices had fallen 50 percent from their September highs. By 1932, the worst year of the depression, they had fallen another 30 percent. In three years, $74 billion of wealth had simply vanished. Meanwhile, the unemployment rate had soared to 25 percent.

Many Americans who lived through the Great Depression could never forget the scenes of misery they saw everywhere. In cities, the poor meekly awaited their turn for a piece of stale bread and thin gruel at ill-funded soup kitchens. Scavengers poked through garbage cans for food, scoured railroad tracks for coal that had fallen from trains, and sometimes ripped up railroad ties for fuel. Hundreds of thousands of Americans built makeshift shelters out of cardboard, scrap metal, and whatever else they could find in the city dump. They called their towns "Hoovervilles," after the president whom they despised for his apparent refusal to help them.

The Great Depression brought cultural crisis as well as economic crisis. In the 1920s, American business leaders had successfully redefined the national culture in business terms, as Americans' values became synonymous with the values of business: economic growth, freedom of enterprise, and acquisitiveness. But the swagger and bluster of American businessmen during the 1920s made them vulnerable to attack in the 1930s, as jobs, incomes, and growth all disappeared. With the prestige of business and business values in decline, how could Americans regain their hope and recover their confidence in the future? The first years of the 1930s held no convincing answers.

The gloom broke in early 1933 when Franklin Delano Roosevelt became president and unleashed the power of government to regulate capitalist enterprises, to restore the economy to health, and to guarantee the social welfare of Americans who were unable to help themselves. Roosevelt called his pro-government program a "new deal for the American people," and it would dominate national politics for the next 40 years. Hailed as a hero, Roosevelt became (and remains) the only president to serve more than two terms. In the short term, the New Deal failed to restore prosperity to America, but the "liberalism" it championed found acceptance among millions, who agreed with Roosevelt that only a large and powerful government could guarantee Americans their liberty.

CHRONOLOGY

1929	Herbert Hoover assumes the presidency • Stock market crashes on "Black Tuesday"
1930	Tariff Act (Hawley-Smoot) raises tariffs
1931	More than 2,000 U.S. banks fail
1932	Unemployment rate reaches 25 percent • Reconstruction Finance Corporation established • Bonus Army marches on Washington • Roosevelt defeats Hoover for presidency
1933	Roosevelt assumes presidency • Hundred Days legislation defines First New Deal (March–June) • Roosevelt administration recognizes the Soviet Union • Good Neighbor Policy toward Latin America launched
1934	Father Charles Coughlin and Huey Long challenge conservatism of First New Deal • 2,000 strikes staged across country • Democrats overwhelm Republicans in off-year election • Radical political movements emerge in Wisconsin, Minnesota, Washington, and California • Indian Reorganization Act restores tribal land, provides funds, and grants limited right of self-government to American Indians • Reciprocal Trade Agreement lowers tariffs
1935	Committee for Industrial Organization (CIO) formed • Supreme Court declares NRA unconstitutional • Roosevelt unveils his Second New Deal • Congress passes Social Security Act • National Labor Relations Act (Wagner Act) guarantees workers' right to join unions • Holding Company Act breaks up utilities' near-monopoly • Congress passes Wealth Tax Act • Emergency Relief Administration Act passed; funds Works Progress Administration and other projects • Rural Electrification Administration established • Number of Mexican immigrants returning to Mexico reaches 500,000
1936	Roosevelt defeats Alf Landon for second term • Supreme Court declares AAA unconstitutional • Congress passes Soil Conservation and Domestic Allotment Act to replace AAA • Farm Security Administration established
1937	United Auto Workers defeat General Motors in sit-down strike • Roosevelt attempts to "pack" the Supreme Court • Supreme Court upholds constitutionality of Social Security and National Labor Relations acts • Severe recession hits
1938	Conservative opposition to New Deal does well in off-year election • *Superman* comic debuts
1939	75,000 gather to hear Marian Anderson sing at Lincoln Memorial.

Causes of the Great Depression

Focus Question

What caused the crash of 1929, and why did the ensuing Depression last so long?

America had experienced other depressions, or "panics," and no one would have been surprised if the boom of the 1920s had been followed by a one- or two-year economic downturn. No one was prepared, however, for the economic catastrophe of the 1930s.

Stock Market Speculation

In 1928 and 1929, the New York Stock Exchange had undergone a remarkable run-up in prices. In less than two years, the Dow Jones Industrial Average had doubled. Money had poured into the market, but many investors were buying on 10 percent "margin," putting up only 10 percent of the price of a stock and borrowing the rest from brokers or banks. Few thought they would ever have to repay these loans with money out of their own pockets. Instead, investors expected to resell their shares within a few months at dramatically higher prices, pay back their loans from the proceeds, and still clear a handsome profit. And, for a while, that is exactly what they did. In 1928 alone, for example, RCA stock value increased 400 percent.

The possibility of making a fortune by investing a mere a few thousand dollars only intensified investors' greed. As speculation became rampant, money flowed indiscriminately into all kinds of risky enterprises. The stock market spiraled upward, out of control. When, in October 1929, confidence in future earnings finally faltered, creditors began demanding that investors who had bought stocks on margin repay their loans. The market crashed from its dizzying heights.

Still, the crash, by itself, fails to explain why the Great Depression lasted as long as it did. Poor decision making by the Federal Reserve Board, an ill-advised tariff that took effect soon after the depression hit, and a lopsided concentration of wealth in the hands of the rich deepened the economic collapse and made recovery more difficult.

Mistakes by the Federal Reserve Board

In 1930 and 1931, the Federal Reserve curtailed the amount of money in circulation and raised interest rates, thereby making credit more difficult for the public to secure. Although employing a tight money policy during the boom years of 1928 or 1929 might have restrained the stock market and strengthened the economy, it was disastrous once the market had crashed. What the economy needed in 1930 and 1931 was an expanded money supply, lower interest rates, and easier credit. Such a course would have made it easier for debtors to pay their creditors. Instead, by choosing the opposite course, the Federal Reserve plunged an economy starved for credit deeper into depression. Higher interest rates also triggered an international crisis, as the banks of Germany and Austria, heavily dependent on U.S. loans, went bankrupt. The German-Austrian collapse, in turn, spread financial panic through Europe and ruined U.S. manufacturers and banks specializing in European trade and investment.

An Ill-Advised Tariff

The Tariff Act of 1930, also known as the Hawley-Smoot Tariff Act, accelerated economic decline abroad and at home. Throughout the 1920s, agricultural interests had sought higher tariffs to protect American farmers against foreign competition. But Hawley-Smoot not only raised tariffs on 75 agricultural goods from 32 percent to 40 percent (the highest

© Bettmann/CORBIS

Unemployed Men in New York City, 1931   The thousands of men waiting to register at the Emergency Unemployment Relief office became so frustrated that they rioted. Police reserves arrived to restore order.

rate in American history), it also raised tariffs by a similar percentage on 925 manufactured products. Industrialists had convinced their supporters in the Republican-controlled Congress that such protection would give American industry much-needed assistance. The legislation was a disaster. Angry foreign governments retaliated by raising their own tariff rates to keep out American goods. International trade, already weakened by the tight credit policies of the Federal Reserve, took another blow at the very moment when it desperately needed a boost.

A Maldistribution of Wealth

A maldistribution in the nation's wealth that had developed in the 1920s also stymied economic recovery. Although average income rose in the 1920s, the incomes of the wealthiest families rose higher than the rest. Between 1918 and 1929, the share of the national income that went to the wealthiest 20 percent of the population rose by more than 10 percent, while the share that went to the poorest 60 percent fell by almost 13 percent. The Coolidge administration contributed to this maldistribution by lowering taxes on the wealthy, thereby increasing the proportion of the national wealth concentrated in their hands. The deepening inequality of income distribution slowed consumption and held back the growth of consumer-oriented industries (cars, household appliances, processed and packaged foods, recreation), the most dynamic elements of the U.S. economy. Even when the rich spent their money lavishly—building huge mansions, buying expensive cars, vacationing on the French Riviera—they still spent a smaller proportion of their total incomes on consumption than wage earners did. The average 1920s wage earner, for example, might spend one-quarter to one-half of his annual earnings to buy a car.

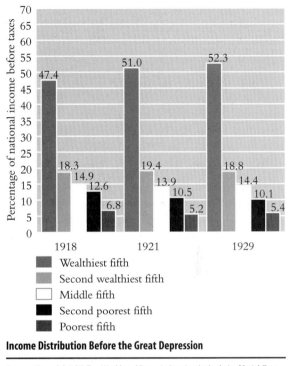

Income Distribution Before the Great Depression

Source: From Gabriel Kolko, *Wealth and Power in America: An Analysis of Social Class and Income Distribution* (New York: Praeger, 1962), p. 14.

Putting more of the total increase in national income into the pockets of average Americans during the 1920s would have steadied the demand for consumer goods and kept the newer consumer industries correspondingly stronger. Such an economy might have recovered relatively quickly from the stock market crash of 1929. Instead, recovery from the Great Depression lagged until 1941, more than a decade later.

Hoover: The Fall of a Self-Made Man

In 1928, Herbert Hoover seemed to embody the American dream. From modest beginnings, Hoover had parlayed his intelligence and drive into gaining admission to Stanford University, becoming a mining engineer, and then rising rapidly to top management positions in the corporate world. A talented and tireless administrator, Hoover won an international reputation in the First World War for his success, as head of the U.S. Food Administration, in feeding millions of European soldiers and civilians. Then, in the 1920s, he became an active and influential secretary of commerce (see chapters 23 and 24). As the decade wound down, no American seemed better qualified to become president of the United States, an office that Hoover assumed in March 1929. Hoover was certain he could make prosperity a permanent feature of American life. "We in America today are nearer to the final triumph over poverty than ever before in the history of any land," he declared in August 1928. A little more than a year later, the Great Depression struck.

Hoover's Program

To cope with the crisis, Hoover first turned to the associational principles he had followed as secretary of commerce (see chapter 24). He encouraged organizations of farmers, industrialists, and bankers to share information, bolster one another's spirits, and devise policies to aid economic recovery. He urged farmers to restrict output, industrialists to hold wages at pre-depression levels, and bankers to help each other remain solvent. The federal government would provide them with information, strategies of mutual aid, occasional loans, and morale-boosting speeches.

Hoover turned to other aggressive policies once he realized that associationalism was failing. To ease the European crisis, Hoover secured a one-year moratorium on loan payments that European governments owed American banks. He steered through Congress the Glass-Steagall Act of 1932, which was intended to help American banks meet the demands of European depositors who wished to convert their dollars to gold. And to ease the crisis at home, he began to expand the government's economic role. The Reconstruction Finance Corporation (RFC), created in 1932, made $2 billion available in loans to ailing banks and to corporations willing to build low-cost housing, bridges, and other public works. The RFC was the biggest federal peacetime intervention in the economy up to that point in American history. The Home Loan Bank Board, set up that same year, offered funds to savings and loans, mortgage companies, and other financial institutions that lent money for home construction and mortgages.

Despite this new government activism, Hoover was uncomfortable with the idea that the government should be responsible for restoring the nation's economic welfare. When RFC expenditures, in 1932, created the largest peacetime deficit in U.S. history, Hoover tried to balance the federal budget. He supported the Revenue Act of 1932, which aimed to erase the deficit by raising taxes. He also insisted that the RFC issue loans only to relatively healthy institutions that were capable of repaying them and that it favor public works, such as toll bridges, that were likely to become self-financing. As a result of these constraints, the RFC spent considerably less than Congress had authorized. Hoover was especially reluctant to engage the government in providing relief to unemployed and homeless Americans. To give money to the poor, he insisted, would destroy their desire to work, undermine their sense of self-worth, and erode their capacity for citizenship.

Hoover saw no similar peril in extending government assistance to ailing banks and businesses. Critics pointed to the seeming hypocrisy of Hoover's policies. For example, in 1930, Hoover refused a request of $25 million to help feed Arkansas farmers and their families but approved $45 million to feed the same farmers' livestock. In 1932, shortly after rejecting an urgent request from the city of Chicago for aid to help pay its teachers and municipal workers, Hoover approved a $90 million loan to rescue that city's Central Republic Bank.

The Bonus Army

In spring 1932, a group of army veterans mounted a particularly emotional challenge to Hoover's policies. In 1924, Congress had authorized a $1,000 bonus for First World War veterans in the form of compensation certificates that would mature in 1945. Now the veterans were demanding that the government pay the bonus immediately. A group of Portland, Oregon, veterans, calling themselves the Bonus Expeditionary Force, hopped onto empty boxcars of freight trains heading east, determined to stage a march on Washington. As the impoverished "army" moved eastward, its ranks multiplied, so that by the time it reached Washington its numbers had swelled to 20,000, including wives and children. The so-called **Bonus Army** set up camp in the Anacostia Flats, southeast of the Capitol, and petitioned Congress for early payment of the promised bonus. The House of Representatives agreed, but the Senate turned them down. Hoover refused to meet with the veterans. In July, federal troops led by Army Chief of Staff Douglas MacArthur and 3rd Cavalry Commander George Patton entered the veterans' Anacostia encampment, set the tents and shacks ablaze, and dispersed the protestors. In the process, more than 100 veterans were wounded and one infant died.

News that veterans and their families had been attacked in the nation's capital served only to harden anti-Hoover opinion. In the 1932 elections, the discredited Republicans were voted out of office after having dominated national politics (excepting Woodrow Wilson's two terms) for 36 years. Hoover received only 39.6 percent of the popular vote

The Bonus Army's Encampment Set Ablaze   U.S. troops under the command of General Douglas MacArthur torched the tents and shacks that housed thousands of First World War veterans who had come to Washington to demand financial assistance from the government.

© Bettmann/CORBIS

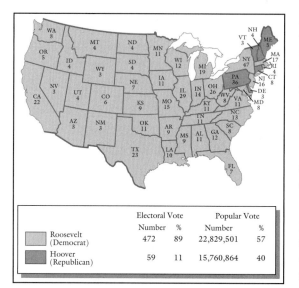

Map 25.1 Presidential Election, 1932 The trauma of the Great Depression can be gauged by the shifting fortunes of President Herbert Hoover. In 1928, he had won 444 electoral votes and carried all but eight states (see Map 24.2, p. 897). In 1932, by contrast, he won only 59 electoral votes and carried only seven states. His Democratic opponent, Franklin D. Roosevelt, was the big winner.

and just 59 (of 531) electoral votes. Hoover left the presidency in 1933 a bewildered man, reviled by Americans for his seeming indifference to suffering and his ineptitude in dealing with the economy's collapse.

A Culture in Crisis

The economic crisis of the early 1930s expressed itself not just in politics but also in culture, especially in the literature and cinema of the time. Many writers who, in the 1920s, had castigated ordinary Americas for their small-mindedness and crass materialism now felt compelled to travel among them, learn about their condition, and seek signs of social renewal. But writers found mostly economic misery and a deep spiritual depression. Edmund Wilson, a literary critic, traveled the country in 1930 and 1931 and wrote numerous essays about how Americans had lost their way and knew not where to turn. When he reached San Diego, he got hold of the city's coroner reports on the numerous individuals who, in desperation, had taken their own lives. Wilson had believed that San Diego, that lovely outpost of the American frontier sitting astride the great and beckoning Pacific, would be a place where the American dream still thrived. But here, too, Wilson claimed, failure and death suffused life and snuffed out hope. He reported on the city's suicides in this fashion:

> They drive their cars into dark alleys, get into the back seat and shoot themselves; they hang themselves in hotel bedrooms, take overdoses of suphonal or barbital; they slip off to the municipal golf-links and there stab themselves with carving-knives; or they throw themselves into the bay, blue and placid, where gray battleships and cruisers guard the limits of their broad-belting nation.

A sense of aimlessness and hopelessness characterized one of the major literary works of the early 1930s, the Studs Lonigan trilogy (1932–35) written by the Chicago-born writer James T. Farrell. In another decade, one easily imagines that Farrell might have cast his scrappy Irish-American protagonist, Studs, as an American hero whose pluck and guile enable him to achieve wealth, success, and influence. But Studs lacks the necessary focus and is too easily overcome by the harshness of his environment. He dies poor and alone, not even having reached the age of 30. The popular writer Nathaniel West, meanwhile, was publishing *Miss Lonelyhearts* (1933) and *A Cool Million* (1934), novels similarly organized around central characters succumbing to failure, drift, and even insanity.

One can detect parallel themes of despair in the period's cinema, especially in such movies as *Fugitive from a Chain Gang* (1932), in which an industrious and honorable man, James Allen, returns from Europe a war hero, only to sink into vagabondage. Caught by the police when he becomes an innocent accessory to a crime, Allen is sentenced to 10 years on a Georgia chain gang. Unable to tolerate the hardship and injustice of his punishment, Allen escapes from jail and uses his intelligence and character to start a new life for himself under an alias. He finds himself a woman and satisfying work as an engineer, but must abandon both once his true identity is revealed. His desire to stay out of prison condemns him to being a man always on the run, unable to prove his innocence or to earn a decent living or build enduring relationships. It is a powerful and bleak film that was, nevertheless, popular with moviegoers and given an Academy Award for Best Picture.

Less grim but still sobering were the gangster movies of the early 1930s, especially *Little Caesar* (1930) and *The Public Enemy* (1931), which told stories of hard-nosed, crooked, and violent men who made themselves into figures of wealth and influence by living outside the law and bending the social environment in which they lived to their will. These gangsters usually had to pay for their sins by dying or going to jail, but, before that happened, they were often portrayed sympathetically, as individuals who, against all odds, found a way to succeed. Moviegoers liked the intensity, suspense, and violence of gangster–police confrontations offered in these films but they were drawn, too, to the gangsters, modern-day outlaws who demonstrated how tough it was to succeed in America and how necessary it might be to break the rules.

The lawlessness that was so integral to the gangster movies also surfaced in the wild comedy of Groucho, Chico, Harpo, and Zeppo Marx, entertainers who, in the 1920s and 1930s, made the transition from vaudeville stage to silver screen. In their films, the Marx Brothers ridiculed figures of authority, broke every rule of etiquette, smacked around their antagonists (and each other), and deliberately and delightfully mangled the English language. Anarchy ruled their world. Many of the moviegoers who went to see the Marx Brothers on the big screen simply wanted to enjoy 90 minutes of side-splitting laughter, if only to escape the harshness of their daily lives.

But some of the Marx Brothers movies carried a more serious political message, perhaps none more so than *Duck Soup* (1933), a withering political satire set in the fictional nation of Fredonia. Fredonia's dictatorial leaders are pompous and small-minded, its legal system is a fraud, and its citizens are clueless and easily misled; by the movie's end, the latter are called to arms through spectacularly ludicrous song and dance scenes, and then led off to fight a meaningless but deadly war. In one of the film's most famous and controversial lines, Rufus T. Firefly, leader of Fredonia (played by Groucho Marx), declares to his troops: "And remember while you're out there risking life and limb through shot and shell, we'll be in here thinking what a sucker you are."

Duck Soup contains some of the funniest scenes the Marx Brothers ever filmed, but it also delivers the dispiriting message that people could not hope to better themselves through politics, which had been emptied of meaning and honesty. This cinematic sentiment paralleled the conviction held by many Americans in 1932 and early 1933 that their own politicians, especially Hoover and the Republicans, had failed them in a time of need. In such ways did the political pessimism of the early 1930s seep into the era's culture.

The Democratic Roosevelt

Between 1933 and 1935, the mood of the country shifted sharply, and politics would, once again, generate hope rather than despair. This change was largely attributable to the personality and policies of Hoover's successor, **Franklin D. Roosevelt,** and to the social movements that emerged during his presidency.

An Early Life of Privilege

Roosevelt was born in 1882 into a patrician family descended, on his father's side, from Dutch gentry who in the 17th century had built large estates on the fertile land along the Hudson River. By the 1880s, the Hyde Park manor where Roosevelt grew up had been in the family for more than 200 years. His mother's family—the Delanos—traced its ancestry back to the *Mayflower*. Roosevelt's education at Groton, Harvard College, and Columbia Law School was typical of the path followed by the sons of America's elite.

The Roosevelt family was wealthy, although not spectacularly so by the standards of the late 19th century. His parents' net worth of more than $1 million was relatively small in comparison to the fortunes being amassed by industrialists and railroad tycoons, many of whom commanded fortunes of $50 million to $100 million or more. This widening gap in wealth concerned families like the Roosevelts, who worried that the new industrial elite would dislodge them from their social position. Moreover, they took offense at the newcomers' allegedly vulgar displays of wealth, lack of taste and etiquette, indifference to the natural environment, and hostility toward those less fortunate than themselves. Theodore Roosevelt, an older cousin of Franklin Roosevelt, had called on the men of his gentry class to set a better example by devoting themselves to public service and the public good.

Though young Franklin wanted to follow in his famous cousin's footsteps, it took a long time for him to show Teddy's seriousness of purpose. He distinguished himself neither at school nor at law. Prior to the 1920s, he could point to few significant political achievements, and he owed much of his political ascent in the Democratic Party to his famous name. He was charming, gregarious, and fun-loving, always eager to sail, party, and enjoy the company of women other than his wife, Eleanor. Then, in 1921, at the age of 39, Roosevelt was both stricken and transformed by a devastating illness, polio, which paralyzed him from the waist down for the rest of his life.

During the two years that Roosevelt spent bedridden, he seemed to acquire a new determination and focus. He developed a compassion for those suffering misfortune that would later enable him to reach out to the millions caught in the Great Depression. Roosevelt's physical debilitation also transformed his relationship with Eleanor, with whom he had shared a testy and increasingly loveless marriage. Eleanor's dedication to nursing Franklin back to health forged a new bond between them. More conscious of his dependence on others, he now welcomed her as a partner in his career. Eleanor soon displayed a talent for political organization and public speaking that surprised those who knew her only as a shy, awkward woman. She was an indispensable player in the revival of Franklin's political fortunes, which began in 1928 with his election to the governorship of New York state. Eleanor would also become an active, eloquent First Lady, her husband's trusted ally, and an architect of American liberalism.

Roosevelt Liberalism

As governor of New York for four years (1929–33), Roosevelt had initiated various reform programs, and his success made him the front-runner for the 1932 Democratic presidential nomination. Even so, he had little assurance that he would be the party's choice. Since 1924, the Democrats had been divided between southern and midwestern agrarians on the one hand and northeastern ethnics on the other. The agrarians favored government regulation—both of the nation's economy and of the private affairs of its citizens. Their support of government intervention in the pursuit of social justice marked them as economic progressives, while their advocacy of Prohibition revealed a cultural conservatism as well as a nativistic strain. By contrast, urban ethnics opposed Prohibition and other forms of government interference in the private lives of its citizens. Urban ethnics were divided over whether the government should regulate the economy, with former New York governor Al Smith increasingly committed to a laissez-faire policy, and Senator Robert Wagner of New York and others supporting more federal control.

Roosevelt understood the need to carve out a middle ground. As governor of New York, and then as a presidential candidate in 1932, he surrounded himself with men and women who embraced the new reform movement called liberalism. **Frances Perkins**, Harry Hopkins, Raymond Moley, Rexford Tugwell, Adolph Berle, Samuel Rosenman—all were interventionist in economic matters and libertarian on questions of personal behavior. They shared with the agrarians and Wagner's supporters a desire to regulate capitalism, but they agreed with Al Smith that the government had no business telling people how to live their lives. Although it seemed unlikely at first, Roosevelt did manage to unite the party behind him at the 1932 Democratic Party convention. In his convention acceptance speech, he declared: "Ours must be the party of liberal thought, of planned action, of enlightened international outlook, and of the greatest good for the greatest number of citizens." He promised "a new deal for the American people."

The First New Deal, 1933–1935

Focus Question
What do you consider to be the three or four most important pieces of legislation in the First New Deal? Why?

© The Granger Collection, New York

From Herbert Hoover to Franklin D. Roosevelt   This 1933 photograph shows the outgoing and incoming presidents on the way to FDR's inauguration. By this time, the two men detested each other, a sentiment that, in this photograph, FDR concealed better than his predecessor.

By the time Roosevelt assumed office in March 1933, the economy lay in shambles. From 1929 to 1932, industrial production had fallen by 50 percent, while new investment had declined from $16 billion to less than $1 billion. In those same years, more than 100,000 businesses went bankrupt. In early 1933, with the nation's banking system on the verge of collapse, 34 states had ordered all the banks in their jurisdictions to close their doors. No one seemed to be able to bring the unemployment rate under control. Some Americans feared that the opportunity for reform had already passed.

Not Roosevelt. "This nation asks for action, and action now," Roosevelt declared in his inaugural address. Roosevelt was true to his word. In his first Hundred Days, from early March through early June 1933, Roosevelt persuaded Congress to pass 15 major pieces of legislation to help bankers, farmers, industrialists, workers, homeowners, the unemployed, and the hungry. He also prevailed on Congress to repeal Prohibition. Not all of the new laws helped relieve distress and promote recovery, but, in the short term, that seemed to matter little. Roosevelt had brought excitement and hope to the nation. He was confident, decisive, and defiantly cheery. "The only thing we have to fear is fear itself," he declared.

Legislation Enacted During the "Hundred Days," March 9–June 16, 1933

Date	Legislation	Purpose
March 9	Emergency Banking Act	Provide federal loans to private bankers
March 20	Economy Act	Balance the federal budget
March 22	Beer-Wine Revenue Act	Repeal Prohibition
March 31	Unemployment Relief Act	Create the Civilian Conservation Corps
May 12	Agricultural Adjustment Act	Establish a national agricultural policy
May 12	Emergency Farm Mortgage Act	Provide refinancing of farm mortgages
May 12	Federal Emergency Relief Act	Establish a national relief system, including the Civil Works Administration
May 18	Tennessee Valley Authority Act	Promote economic development of the Tennessee Valley
May 27	Securities Act	Regulate the purchase and sale of new securities
June 5	Gold Repeal Joint Resolution	Cancel the gold clause in public and private contracts
June 13	Home Owners Loan Act	Provide refinancing of home mortgages
June 16	National Industrial Recovery Act	Set up a national system of industrial self-government and establish the Public Works Administration
June 16	Glass-Steagall Banking Act	Create Federal Deposit Insurance Corporation; separate commercial and investment banking
June 16	Farm Credit Act	Reorganize agricultural credit programs
June 16	Railroad Coordination Act	Appoint federal coordinator of transportation

Source: Arthur M. Schlesinger Jr., *The Coming of the New Deal* (Boston: Houghton Mifflin, 1959), pp. 20–21.

Roosevelt used the radio to reach out to ordinary Americans. On the second Sunday after his inauguration, he launched a series of radio addresses known as "fireside chats," speaking in a plain, friendly, and direct voice to the forlorn and discouraged. In his first chat, he explained the banking crisis in simple terms but without condescension. "I want to take a few minutes to talk with the people of the United States about banking," he began. An estimated 20 million Americans listened.

To hear the president speaking warmly and conversationally—as though he were actually there in the room—was riveting. An estimated 500,000 Americans wrote letters to Roosevelt within days of his inaugural address. Millions more would write to him and to **Eleanor Roosevelt** over the next few years. Many of the letters were simply addressed to "Mr. or Mrs. Roosevelt, Washington, D.C." Democrats began to hang portraits of Franklin Roosevelt in their homes, often next to a picture of Jesus or the Madonna.

Roosevelt was never the benign father figure he made himself out to be. He skillfully crafted his public image. Compliant news photographers agreed not to show him in a wheelchair or struggling with the leg braces and cane he used to take even small steps.

His political rhetoric sometimes promised more than he was prepared to deliver in actual legislation. This was not simply a strategy meant to confuse his opponents and to sustain his own appeal. Roosevelt was struggling to keep together a party that was divided over a variety of issues. At the same time, he was attempting to establish a strong federal government in a polity that had long been hostile to that idea. Not only did Roosevelt have to overcome ideological opposition to a centralized state, but he had to find individuals able to run federal agencies in a nation in which that kind of administrative experience was in short supply.

Saving the Banks

Roosevelt's first order of business was to save the nation's financial system. With so many of the nation's banks already closed by inauguration day, Roosevelt's first act was to order the rest of the country's banks to cease all business—a bold move he brazenly called a "bank holiday." At his request, Congress rushed through the Emergency Banking Act (EBA), which made federal loans available to private bankers, and followed that with the Economy Act (EA), which committed the government to balancing the budget.

Both the EBA and the EA were fiscally conservative programs that Hoover had proposed. The EBA made it possible for private bankers to retain financial control of their institutions, and the EA announced the government's intention of pursuing a fiscally prudent course. Only after the financial crisis had eased did Roosevelt turn to the structural reform of banking. A second Glass-Steagall Act (1933) separated commercial banking from investment banking. It also created the Federal Deposit Insurance Corporation (FDIC), which assured depositors that the government would protect up to $5,000 of their savings. The Securities Act (1933) and the Securities Exchange Act (1934) imposed long-overdue regulation on the New York Stock Exchange, both by reining in buying on the margin and by establishing the Securities and Exchange Commission (SEC) to enforce federal law.

Economic Relief

Roosevelt understood the need to temper financial prudence with compassion. Congress responded swiftly in 1933 to Roosevelt's request to establish the Federal Emergency Relief Administration (FERA), granting it $500 million for relief to the poor. To head FERA, Roosevelt appointed a brash young reformer, Harry Hopkins, who disbursed $2 million during his first two hours on the job. Roosevelt next won congressional approval for the Civilian Conservation Corps (CCC), which put more than 2 million single young men to work planting trees, halting erosion, and otherwise improving the environment. The following winter, Roosevelt launched the Civil Works Administration (CWA), an ambitious work-relief program, also under Harry Hopkins's direction, which hired 4 million unemployed people at $15 per week and put them to work on 400,000 small-scale government projects. For middle-class Americans threatened with the loss of their homes, Roosevelt won Congressional approval for the Homeowners' Loan Corporation (1933) to refinance mortgages. These direct subsidies to millions of jobless and home-owning Americans lent credibility to Roosevelt's claim that the New Deal would set the country on a new course.

Agricultural Reform

In 1933, Roosevelt expected economic recovery to come not from relief, but through agricultural and industrial cooperation. He regarded the Agricultural Adjustment Act, passed in May, and the National Industrial Recovery Act (NIRA), passed in June, as the most important legislation of his Hundred Days. Both were based on the idea that curtailing production would trigger economic recovery. By shrinking the supply of agricultural and manufactured goods, Roosevelt's economists reasoned, they could restore the balance of normal market forces. As demand for scarce goods exceeded supply, prices would rise and revenues would climb. Farmers and industrialists, earning a profit once again, would increase their investment in new technology and hire more workers, and prosperity and full employment would be the final result.

To curtail farm production, the **Agricultural Adjustment Administration (AAA)**, which was set up by the Agricultural Adjustment Act, began paying farmers to keep a portion of their land out of cultivation and to reduce the size of their herds. The program was controversial. Many farmers were skeptical of a government offer to pay more money for working less land and husbanding fewer livestock, but few refused to accept payments. As one young Kansas farmer reported:

> There were mouthy individuals who seized every opportunity to run down the entire program . . . condemning it as useless, crooked, revolutionary, or dictatorial; but . . . when the first AAA payments were made available, shortly before Christmas, these same wordy critics made a beeline for the courthouse. They jostled and fell over each other in their mad scramble to be the first in line to receive allotment money.

The AAA had made no provision, however, for the countless tenant farmers and farm laborers who would be thrown out of work by the reduction in acreage. In the South, the victims were disproportionately black. A Georgia sharecropper wrote Harry Hopkins of his misery: "I have Bin farming all my life But the man I live with Has Turned me loose taking my mule [and] all my feed. . . . I can't get a Job so Some one said Rite you." New Dealers within the Department of Agriculture, such as Rexford Tugwell and Jerome Frank, were sympathetic to the plight of sharecroppers, but they failed during the First New Deal to extend to them the government's helping hand.

The programs of the AAA also proved inadequate to Great Plains farmers, whose economic problems had been compounded by ecological crisis. Just as the depression rolled in, the rain stopped falling on the plains. The land, stripped of its native grasses by decades of excessive plowing, dried up and turned to dust. And then the dust began to blow, sometimes traveling 1,000 miles across open prairie. Dust became a fixed feature of daily life on the plains (which soon became known as the Dust Bowl), covering furniture, floors, and stoves, and penetrating people's hair and lungs. The worst dust storm occurred on April 14, 1935,

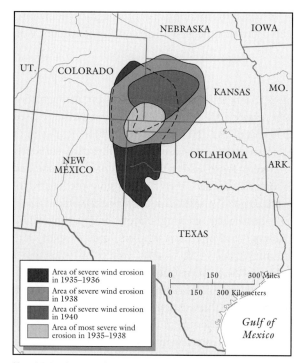

Map 25.2 Dust Bowl, 1935–1940 This map shows the areas in six states—Texas, New Mexico, Oklahoma, Colorado, Kansas, and a bit of Nebraska—claimed by the Dust Bowl between 1935 and 1940. The light shading in the center shows the area where the winds caused the worst damage.

when a great mass of dust, moving at speeds of 45 to 70 miles per hour, roared through Colorado, Kansas, and Oklahoma, blackening the sky, suffocating cattle, and dumping thousands of tons of topsoil and red clay on homes and streets.

The government responded to this calamity by establishing the Soil Conservation Service (SCS) in 1935. Recognizing that the soil problems of the Great Plains could not be solved simply by taking land out of production, SCS experts urged plains farmers to plant soil-conserving grasses and legumes in place of wheat. They taught farmers how to plow along contour lines and how to build terraces—techniques that had been proven effective in slowing the runoff of rainwater and improving its absorption into the soil. Plains farmers were open to these suggestions, especially when the government offered to subsidize those willing to implement them. Bolstered by the new assistance, plains agriculture began to recover.

Still, the government offered little assistance to the rural poor—the tenant farmers and sharecroppers. Nearly 1 million had left their homes by 1935, and another 2.5 million would leave after 1935. Most headed west, piling their belongings onto their jalopies, snaking along Route 66 until they reached California. They became known as Okies, because many, although not all, had come from Oklahoma. Their dispossession and forced migration disturbed many Americans, for whom the plight of these once-sturdy yeomen became a symbol of how much had gone wrong with the American dream.

In 1936, the Supreme Court ruled that AAA-mandated limits on farm production constituted an illegal restraint of trade. Congress responded by passing the Soil Conservation and Domestic Allotment Act, which justified the removal of land from cultivation for reasons of conservation rather than economics. This new act also called on landowners to share their government subsidies with sharecroppers and tenant farmers, although many landowners managed to evade this and subsequent laws that required them to share federal funds.

Searching for a Better Life   Scenes like this one were common in the 1930s as farm families in Oklahoma and Texas who had lost their land began heading to California. Here a family's entire belongings are packed onto a truck, and the mother tends to her baby on an isolated road. The woman's fur collar suggests that this family had once known better times.

The use of subsidies, begun by the AAA, did eventually bring stability and prosperity to agriculture, but at high cost. Agriculture became the most heavily subsidized sector of the U.S. economy, and the Department of Agriculture grew into one of the government's largest bureaucracies. The rural poor, black and white, never received a fair share of federal benefits. Beginning in the 1930s, and continuing in the 1940s and 1950s, they would be forced off the land and into the cities of the North and West.

Industrial Reform

American industry was so vast that Roosevelt's administration never contemplated paying individual manufacturers direct subsidies to reduce, or even halt, production. Instead, the government decided to limit production through persuasion and association—techniques that Hoover had also favored. To head the **National Recovery Administration (NRA)**, authorized under the National Industrial Recovery Act, Roosevelt chose General Hugh Johnson, a participant in industrial planning experiments during the First World War. Johnson's first task was to persuade industrialists and businessmen to agree to raise employee wages to a minimum of 30 to 40 cents per hour and to limit employee hours to a maximum of 30 to 40 hours per week. The limitation on hours was meant to reduce the quantity of goods that any factory or business could produce.

Johnson launched a high-powered publicity campaign. He distributed NRA pamphlets and pins throughout the country. He used the radio to exhort all Americans to do their part. He staged an NRA celebration in Yankee Stadium and a parade down New York City's Fifth Avenue. He sent letters to millions of employers asking them to place a "blue eagle"—the logo of the NRA—on storefronts, at factory entrances, and on company stationery to signal their participation in the campaign to limit production and restore prosperity. Blue eagles soon sprouted everywhere, usually accompanied by the slogan "We Do Our Part."

Johnson understood, however, that his propaganda campaign could not by itself guarantee recovery. So he brought together the largest producers in every sector of manufacturing and asked each group (or conference) to work out a code of fair competition that would specify prices, wages, and hours throughout the sector. He also asked each conference to restrict production.

In summer and fall 1933, the NRA codes drawn up for steel, textiles, coal mining, rubber, garment manufacture, and other industries seemed to be working. The economy

© Bettmann/CORBIS

Selling the NRA Through Sex and Sunburn   Americans were asked to display their support for the NRA by pasting eagles onto their factory entrances, storefronts, and even clothes. The young women in this photo dispensed with pasting, choosing instead to allow the sun to burn their bare backs around a stenciled blue eagle and NRA lettering, which were being applied by the woman in the white gown.

improved, and hard times seemed to be easing. But in winter and spring 1934, economic indicators plunged downward once again, and manufacturers began to evade the code provisions. Government committees set up to enforce the codes were powerless to punish violators. By fall 1934, it was clear that the NRA had failed. When the Supreme Court declared the NRA codes unconstitutional in May 1935, the Roosevelt administration allowed the agency to die.

Rebuilding the Nation's Infrastructure

In addition to establishing the NRA, the National Industrial Recovery Act launched the Public Works Administration (PWA). The PWA had a $3.3 billion budget to sponsor internal improvements that would strengthen the nation's infrastructure of roads, bridges, sewage systems, hospitals, airports, and schools. The labor needed for these construction projects would shrink relief rolls and reduce unemployment, but the projects could be justified in terms that conservatives approved: economic investment rather than short-term relief.

The PWA authorized the building of three major dams in the West—Boulder, Grand Coulee, and Bonneville—that opened up large stretches of Arizona, California, and Washington to industrial and agricultural development. It funded the construction of the Triborough Bridge in New York City and the 100-mile causeway linking Florida to Key West. It also appropriated money for the construction of thousands of new schools.

The TVA Alternative

One piece of legislation passed during Roosevelt's First New Deal specified a strategy for economic recovery significantly different from the one promoted by the NIRA. The Tennessee Valley Authority Act (1933) called for the government—rather than private corporations—to promote economic development throughout the Tennessee Valley, a vast river basin winding through parts of Kentucky, Tennessee, Mississippi, Alabama, Georgia, and North Carolina. The act created the **Tennessee Valley Authority (TVA)** to control flooding on the Tennessee River, harness its water power to generate electricity, develop local industry (such as fertilizer production), improve river navigability, and ease the poverty and isolation of the area's inhabitants. In some respects, the TVA's mandate resembled that of the PWA, but the TVA enjoyed even greater authority. The extent of its control over economic development reflected the influence of Rexford Tugwell and other New Dealers who were committed to a government-planned and government-operated economy. Although they rarely said so, these reformers were drawn to socialism.

The accomplishments of the TVA were many. It built, completed, or improved more than 20 dams, including the huge Wheeler Dam near Muscle Shoals in Alabama. At several of the dam sites, the TVA built hydroelectric generators and soon became the nation's largest producer of electricity. Its low electric rates compelled private utility companies to reduce their rates as well. The TVA also constructed waterways to bypass non-navigable stretches of the river, reduced the danger of flooding, and taught farmers how to prevent soil erosion and use fertilizers. **(See Map 25.3, Tennessee Valley Authority, in the color insert following page 1056.)**

Although the TVA was one of the New Deal's most celebrated successes, it generated little support for more ambitious experiments in national planning. For the government to have assumed control of established industries and banks would have been quite a different matter from bringing prosperity to an impoverished region. Like Roosevelt, few members of Congress or the public favored the radical growth of governmental power that such programs would have entailed. Thus, the thought of replacing the NRA with a nationwide TVA, for instance, made little headway. The New Deal never embraced the idea of the federal government as a substitute for private enterprise.

The New Deal and Western Development

As the TVA showed, New Deal programs could make an enormous difference to a particular region's welfare. Other regional beneficiaries of the New Deal included the New York City area, which prospered from the close links of local politicians to the Roosevelt administration. The region that benefited most from the New Deal, however, was the West. Between 1933 and 1939, per capita payments for public works projects, welfare, and federal loans in the Rocky Mountain and Pacific Coast states outstripped those of any other region.

Dam building was central to this western focus. Western real estate and agricultural interests wanted to dam the West's major rivers to provide water and electricity for urban and agricultural development, but the costs were prohibitive, even to the largest capitalists, until the New Deal offered to defray the expenses with federal dollars. Western interests found a government ally in the Bureau of Reclamation, a hitherto small federal agency (in existence since 1902) that became, under the New Deal, a prime dispenser of funds for dam construction, reservoir creation, and the provision of water to western cities and farms. Drawing on PWA monies, the bureau oversaw the building of the Boulder Dam (later renamed Hoover Dam), which provided drinking water for southern California, irrigation water for California's Imperial Valley, and electricity for Los Angeles and southern Arizona. It also authorized the Central Valley Project and the All-American Canal, vast water-harnessing projects in central and southern California meant to provide irrigation, drinking water, and electricity to California farmers and towns. The greatest construction project of all was the Grand Coulee Dam on the Columbia River in Washington, which created a lake 150 miles long. Together with the Bonneville Dam (also on the Columbia), the Grand Coulee gave the Pacific Northwest the cheapest electricity in the country and created a new potential for economic and population growth. Not surprisingly, these two dams also made Washington state the largest per capita recipient of New Deal aid.

These developments attracted less attention in the 1930s than the TVA because their benefits did not fully materialize until after the Second World War. Also, dam building in

Improving the Nation's Infrastructure   The federal government built several major dams in the West to boost agricultural and industrial development. This is a photograph of the mammoth Boulder Dam (later renamed the Hoover Dam) on the Colorado River.

the West was not seen as a radical experiment in government planning and management. Unlike the TVA, the Bureau of Reclamation hired private contractors to do the work. Moreover, the benefits of these dams were intended to flow first to large agricultural and real estate interests, not to the poor; they were intended to aid private enterprise, rather than bypass it. In political terms, dam building in the West was more conservative than it was in the Tennessee Valley. Even so, this activity made the federal government a key architect of the modern American West.

Map 25.4   Federal Water Projects in California Built or Funded by the New Deal   This map demonstrates how much California cities and agriculture benefited from water projects—dams, canals, aqueducts, pumping stations, and power plants—begun under the New Deal. The projects extended from the Shasta Dam in the northern part of the state to the All-American Canal that traversed the Imperial Valley south of San Diego, and included the Colorado River Aqueduct that would bring vital drinking water to Los Angeles.

Political Mobilization, Political Unrest, 1934–1935

Although Roosevelt and the New Dealers quickly dismantled the NRA in 1935, they could not stop the political forces it had set in motion. Ordinary Americans now believed they could make a difference. If the New Dealers could not achieve economic recovery, then the people would find others who could.

Populist Critics of the New Deal

Some critics were disturbed by what they perceived as the conservative character of New Deal programs. Banking reforms, the AAA, and the NRA, they alleged, all seemed to favor large economic interests. Ordinary people had been ignored.

In the South and Midwest, millions listened regularly to the radio addresses of Louisiana Senator **Huey Long,** a former governor of that state and an accomplished orator. In attacks on New Deal programs, he alleged that "not a single thin dime of concentrated, bloated, pompous wealth, massed in the hands of a few people has been raked down to relieve the masses." Long offered a simple alternative: "Break up the swollen fortunes of America and . . . spread the wealth among all our people." He called for a redistribution of wealth that would guarantee each American family a $5,000 estate.

Long's rhetoric inspired hundreds of thousands of Americans to join the Share the Wealth clubs his supporters organized. Most came from middle-class ranks or from the ranks of skilled workers. Long's supporters worried that the big business orientation of New Deal programs would undermine their economic and social status. By 1935, Roosevelt regarded Long as the man most likely to unseat him in the presidential election of 1936. Before that campaign began, however, Long was assassinated.

Meanwhile, in the Midwest, **Father Charles Coughlin,** the "radio priest," delivered his stinging critique of the New Deal to a weekly radio audience of between 30 and 40 million listeners. Like Long, Coughlin appealed to anxious middle-class Americans and to privileged groups of workers who believed that middle-class status was slipping from their grasp. A devoted Roosevelt supporter at first—he had once called the New Deal "Christ's Deal"—Coughlin had become, by 1934, a harsh critic. He charged that the New Deal was run by bankers and the NRA aimed to resuscitate corporate profits without concern for the average working man. Coughlin called for a strong government to compel capital, labor, agriculture, professionals, and other interest groups to do its bidding. He founded the National Union of Social Justice (NUSJ) in 1934 as a precursor to a political party that would challenge the Democrats in 1936. Coughlin increasingly admired dictators such as Italy's Benito Mussolini, who built their power and programs through decree rather than through democratic consent. If necessary, he admitted in 1936, he would "'dictate' to preserve democracy."

As Coughlin's disillusionment with the New Deal deepened, a strain of anti-Semitism became apparent in his radio talks, as in his accusation that Jewish bankers were masterminding a world conspiracy to dispossess the toiling masses. Although Coughlin was a compelling speaker, he failed to build the NUSJ into an effective political force. Its successor, the Union Party, attracted only a tiny percentage of voters in 1936. Embittered, Coughlin moved further to the political right. By 1939, his denunciations of democracy and Jews had become so extreme that some radio stations refused to carry his addresses. Still, millions of Americans continued to put their faith in the "radio priest."

Another popular figure was Francis E. Townsend, a California doctor who claimed that the way to end the depression was to give every senior citizen $200 per month with the stipulation that seniors would spend those dollars, thus putting more money in circulation and reviving economic demand. Townsend also pushed hard for a pension program to ease the plight of the nation's elderly. While the Townsend movement did not last long, it did prod a nervous Roosevelt administration to make relief for the elderly—a program that Roosevelt would label Social Security—an important component of the New Deal.

Labor Protests

The attacks by Long, Coughlin, and Townsend on the New Deal deepened popular discontent and inspired other insurgent movements. The most important of them was the labor movement. Workers began joining unions in response to the National Industrial Recovery Act, and especially its Clause 7 (a), which granted workers the right to join labor unions of their own choosing, and obligated employers to recognize unions and bargain with them in good faith. Union members made quite modest demands at first: (1) they wanted employers to observe the provisions of the NRA codes; (2) they wanted to be treated fairly by their foremen; and (3) they wanted employers to recognize and negotiate with their unions.

Few employers, however, were willing to grant their employees any say in working conditions. Many ignored the NRA's wage and hour guidelines altogether and used their influence over NRA code authorities to thwart worker requests for wage increases and union recognition. Workers flooded Washington with letters addressed to President Roosevelt, Labor Secretary Frances Perkins, and General Hugh Johnson, asking them to force employers to comply with the law. A Rhode Island textile worker who had been fired for joining a union asked why the NRA had neither responded to his complaint nor punished the company that had fired him. "If people can be arrested for violating certain laws," he wondered, "why can't this company?"

When their pleas went unanswered, workers began to take matters into their own hands. In 1934, they staged 2,000 strikes, some of which escalated into armed confrontations between workers and police. In Toledo, Ohio, in May, 10,000 workers surrounded the Electric Auto-Lite plant, declaring that they would block all exits and entrances until the company agreed to shut down operations and negotiate a union contract. Two strikers were killed in an exchange of gunfire. In Minneapolis, unionized truck drivers and warehousemen fought police, private security forces, and the National Guard in a series of street battles from May through July that left four dead and hundreds wounded. In San Francisco in July, skirmishes between longshoremen and employers killed two and wounded scores of strikers. This violence provoked a general strike in San Francisco that shut down the city's transportation, construction, and service industries for two weeks. In September, 400,000 textile workers at mills from Maine to Alabama walked off their jobs. Attempts by employers to bring in replacement workers triggered violent confrontations that caused several deaths, hundreds of injuries, and millions of dollars in property damages.

Anger at the Polls

By late September, textile union leaders had lost their nerve and called off the strike, but workers took their anger to the polls. In Rhode Island, they broke the Republican Party's 30-year domination of state politics. In the South Carolina gubernatorial race, working-class voters rejected a conservative Democrat, Coleman Blease, and chose instead Olin T. Johnston, a former mill worker and an ardent New Dealer. In the country as a whole, Democrats won 70 percent of the contested seats in the Senate and House. The Democrats increased their majority, from 310 to 319 (out of 432) in the House, and from 60 to 69 (out of 96) in the Senate. No sitting president's party had ever done so well in an off-year election.

The victory was not an unqualified one for Roosevelt and the First New Deal, however. The 74th Congress would include the largest contingent of radicals ever sent to Washington: Tom Amlie of Wisconsin, Ernest Lundeen of Minnesota, Maury Maverick of Texas, Vito Marcantonio of New York, and some 30 others. Their support for the New Deal depended on whether Roosevelt delivered more relief, more income security, and more political power to farmers, workers, the unemployed, and the poor.

Radical Third Parties

Radical critics of the New Deal also made an impressive showing in state politics in 1934 and 1936. They were particularly strong in states gripped by labor unrest. In Wisconsin, for example, Philip La Follette, the son of Robert La Follette (see chapter 21), was elected governor in 1934 and 1936 as the candidate of the radical Wisconsin Progressive Party. In Minnesota, discontented agrarians and urban workers organized the Minnesota Farmer-Labor (MFL) Party and elected their candidate to the governorship in 1930, 1932, 1934, and 1936. In Washington, yet another radical third party, the Commonwealth Builders, elected both senators and almost half the state legislators in 1932 and 1934. And in California, the socialist and novelist Upton Sinclair and his organization, End Poverty in California (EPIC), came closer to winning the governorship than anyone had expected.

A widespread movement to form local labor parties offered further evidence of voter volatility, as did the growing appeal of the **Communist Party.** The American Communist Party (CP) had emerged in the early 1920s with the support of radicals who wanted to adopt the Soviet Union's path to socialism (see chapter 23). The CP began to attract attention in the early 1930s, as its organizers spread out among the poorest and most vulnerable populations in America—homeless urban blacks in the North, black and white sharecroppers in the South, Chicano and Filipino agricultural workers in the West—and mobilized them into unions and unemployment leagues. CP members also played significant roles in strikes described earlier, and they were influential in the Minnesota Farmer-Labor Party and in Washington's Commonwealth Builders. Once they stopped preaching world revolution in 1935 and began calling instead for a "popular front" of democratic forces against fascism (a term used to describe the new kinds of dictatorships appearing in Hitler's Germany and Mussolini's Italy), their ranks grew even more. By 1938, approximately 80,000 Americans were thought to have been members of the Communist Party.

Although the Communist Party proclaimed its allegiance to democratic principles beginning in 1935, it nevertheless remained a dictatorial organization that took its orders from the Soviet Union. Many Americans feared the growing strength of the CP and began to call for its suppression. The CP, however, was never strong enough to gain power for itself. Its chief role in 1930s politics was to channel popular discontent into unions and political parties that would, in turn, force New Dealers to respond to the demands of the nation's poor.

The Second New Deal, 1935–1937

Focus Question
What was "underconsumptionism," and how did it inform the legislation of the Second New Deal? How was the Second New Deal different from the first?

The labor unrest of 1934 had taken Roosevelt by surprise. For a time, he kept his distance from the masses mobilizing in his name, but in spring 1935, with the 1936 presidential election looming, he decided to place himself at their head. He called for the "abolition of evil holding companies," attacked the wealthy for their profligate ways, and called for new programs to aid the poor and downtrodden. Rather than becoming a socialist, as his critics charged, Roosevelt sought to reinvigorate his appeal among poorer Americans and turn them away from radical solutions.

Philosophical Underpinnings

To point the New Deal in a more populist direction, Roosevelt turned increasingly to a relatively new economic theory, **underconsumptionism.** Advocates of this theory held that a chronic weakness in consumer demand had caused the Great Depression. The path to recovery lay, therefore, not in restricting production, as the architects of the First New Deal had tried to do, but in boosting consumer expenditures through government support for strong labor unions (to force up wages), higher social welfare expenditures (to put more money in the hands of the poor), and ambitious public works projects (to create hundreds of thousands of new jobs).

Underconsumptionists did not worry that new welfare and public works programs might strain the federal budget. If the government found itself short of revenue, it could always borrow additional funds from private sources. These reformers, in fact, viewed government borrowing as a useful antidepression tool. Those who lent the government money would receive a return on their investment; those who received government assistance would have additional income to spend on consumer goods; and manufacturers would profit from increases in consumer spending. Government borrowing, in short, would stimulate the circulation of money through the economy, increase consumer demand, and end the depression. This fiscal policy, a reversal of the conventional wisdom that government should always balance its budget, would in the 1940s come to be known as Keynesianism, after John Maynard Keynes, the British economist who had been its most forceful advocate.

Many politicians and economists rejected the notion that increased government spending and the deliberate buildup of federal deficits would lead to prosperity. Roosevelt was not easily convinced that he should put aside his concern for fiscal restraint and balanced budgets, but in 1935, as the nation entered its sixth year of the depression, he was willing to give the new ideas a try. Reform-minded members of the 1934 Congress were eager for a new round of legislation directed more to the needs of ordinary Americans than to the needs of big business.

Legislation

Congress passed much of that legislation in January to June 1935—a period that came to be known as the Second New Deal. Two of the acts were of historic importance: the **Social Security Act** and the National Labor Relations Act. The Social Security Act, passed in May, required the states to set up welfare funds from which money would be disbursed to the elderly poor, the unemployed, unmarried mothers with dependent children, and the disabled. It also enrolled a majority of working Americans in a pension program that guaranteed them

Selected WPA Projects in New York City, 1938

Construction and Renovation	Education, Health, and Art	Research and Records
East River Drive	Adult education: homemaking, trade and technical skills, and art and culture	Sewage treatment, community health, labor relations, and employment trends surveys
Henrik Hudson Parkway		
Bronx sewers	Children's education: remedial reading, lip reading, and field trips	Museum and library catalogs and exhibits
Glendale and Queens public libraries	Prisoners' vocational training, recreation, and nutrition	
King's County Hospital		Municipal office clerical support
Williamsburg housing project	Dental clinics	Government forms standardization
School buildings, prisons, and firehouses	Tuberculosis examination clinics	
Coney Island and Brighton Beach boardwalks	Syphilis and gonorrhea treatment clinics	
Orchard Beach	City hospital kitchen help, orderlies, laboratory technicians, nurses, doctors	
Swimming pools, playgrounds, parks, drinking fountains	Subsistence gardens	
	Sewing rooms	
	Central Park sculpture shop	

Source: John David Millet, *The Works Progress Administration in New York City* (Chicago: Public Administration Service, 1938), pp. 95–126.

a steady income upon retirement. A federal system of employer and employee taxation was set up to fund the pensions. Despite limitations on coverage and inadequate pension levels, the Social Security Act of 1935 provided a sturdy foundation on which future presidents and congresses would erect the American welfare state.

Equally historic was the passage, in June, of the National Labor Relations Act (NLRA). This act delivered what the NRA had only promised: the right of every worker to join a union of his or her own choosing and the obligation of employers to bargain with that union in good faith. The **NLRA,** also called the **Wagner Act** after its Senate sponsor, Robert Wagner of New York, set up a National Labor Relations Board (NLRB) to supervise union elections and to investigate claims of unfair labor practices. The NLRB was to be staffed by federal appointees with power to impose fines on employers who violated the law. Union leaders hailed the act as their Magna Carta.

Congress also passed the Holding Company Act to break up the 13 utility companies that controlled 75 percent of the nation's electric power. It passed the Wealth Tax Act, which increased tax rates on the wealthy from 59 percent to 75 percent, and on corporations from 13.75 percent to 15 percent; and it passed the Banking Act, which strengthened the power of the Federal Reserve Board over its member banks. It created the Rural Electrification Administration (REA) to bring electric power to rural households. Finally, it passed the huge $5 billion Emergency Relief Appropriation Act. Roosevelt funneled part of this sum to the PWA and the CCC and used another part to create the National Youth Administration (NYA), which provided work and guidance to the nation's youth.

Roosevelt directed most of the new relief money, however, to the **Works Progress Administration** (WPA) under the direction of Harry Hopkins, now known as the New Deal's "minister of relief." The WPA built or improved thousands of schools, playgrounds, airports, and hospitals. WPA crews raked leaves, cleaned streets, and landscaped cities. In the process, the WPA provided jobs to approximately 30 percent of the nation's jobless.

By the time the decade ended, the WPA, in association with an expanded Reconstruction Finance Corporation, the PWA, and other agencies, had built 500,000 miles of roads, 100,000 bridges, 100,000 public buildings, and 600 airports. The New Deal had transformed America's urban and rural landscapes. The awe generated by these public works projects helped Roosevelt retain popular support at a time when the success of the New Deal's economic policies was uncertain. The WPA also funded a vast program of public art, supporting the work of thousands of painters, architects, writers, playwrights, actors, and intellectuals. Beyond extending relief to struggling artists, it fostered the creation of art that spoke to the concerns of ordinary Americans, adorned public buildings with colorful murals, and boosted public morale.

Victory in 1936: The New Democratic Coalition

Roosevelt described his Second New Deal as a program to limit the power and privilege of the wealthy few and to increase the security and welfare of ordinary citizens. In his 1936 reelection campaign, he excoriated the corporations as "economic royalists" who had "concentrated into their own hands an almost complete control over other people's property, other people's money, other people's labor—other people's lives." He called on voters to strip the corporations of their power and "save a great and precious form of government for ourselves and the world." American voters responded by handing Roosevelt the greatest victory in the history of American presidential politics. He received 61 percent of the popular vote; Alf Landon of Kansas, his Republican opponent, received only 37 percent. Only two states, Maine and Vermont, representing a mere eight electoral votes, went for Landon.

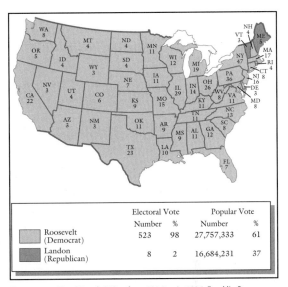

		Electoral Vote		Popular Vote	
		Number	%	Number	%
	Roosevelt (Democrat)	523	98	27,757,333	61
	Landon (Republican)	8	2	16,684,231	37

Map 25.5   Presidential Election, 1936   In 1936, Franklin D. Roosevelt's reelection numbers were overwhelming: 98 percent of the electoral vote, and more than 60 percent of the popular vote. No previous election in American history had been so one-sided.

The 1936 election won the Democratic Party its reputation as the party of reform and the party of the "forgotten American." Of the 6 million Americans who went to the polls for the first time, many of them European ethnics, 5 million voted for Roosevelt. Among the poorest Americans, Roosevelt received 80 percent of the vote. Black voters in the North deserted the Republican Party—the "Party of Lincoln"—calculating that their interests would best be served by the "Party of the Common Man." Roosevelt also did well among white middle-class voters, many of whom stood to benefit from the Social Security Act. These constituencies would constitute the "Roosevelt coalition" for most of the next 40 years, helping to solidify the Democratic Party as the new majority party in American politics.

Rhetoric Versus Reality

Roosevelt's 1935–36 anti-corporate rhetoric was more radical than the laws he supported. The Wealth Tax Act took considerably less out of wealthy incomes and estates than was advertised, and the utility companies that the Holding Company Act should have broken up remained largely intact. Moreover, Roosevelt promised more than he delivered to the nation's poor. Farm workers, for example, were not covered by the Social Security Act or by the National Labor Relations Act. Consequently, thousands of African American sharecroppers in the South, along with substantial numbers of Mexican American farm workers in the Southwest, missed out on protections and benefits brought by these laws. The sharecroppers were shut out because southern Democrats would not have voted for an act

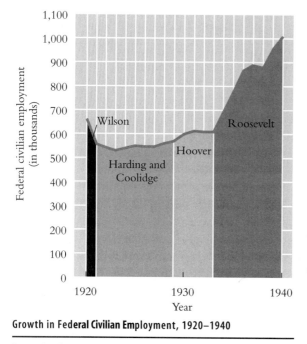

Growth in Federal Civilian Employment, 1920–1940

Source: Data from *Historical Statistics of the United States, Colonial Times to 1970* (White Plains, N.Y.: Kraus International, 1989), p. 1102.

that was seen as improving the economic or social condition of southern blacks. For the same reason, the New Deal made little effort to restore voting rights to southern blacks or to protect their basic civil rights. White supremacy lived on in New Deal democracy.

Roosevelt's 1935–36 populist stance also obscured the support that some capitalists were giving the Second New Deal. In the West, Henry J. Kaiser headed a consortium of six companies that built the Hoover, Bonneville, and Grand Coulee dams; and in Texas, building contractors Herman and George Brown were bankrolling a group of elected officials that included a young Democratic congressman named Lyndon Johnson. In the Midwest and the East, Roosevelt's corporate supporters included real estate developers, mass merchandisers (such as Bambergers and Sears, Roebuck), clothing manufacturers, and the like. These firms, in turn, had financial connections with recently established investment banks such as Lehman Brothers and Goldman Sachs, competitors of the House of Morgan and its allies in the Republican banking establishment, and with consumer-oriented banks such as the Bank of America and the Bowery Savings Bank. They tolerated strong labor unions, welfare programs, and high levels of government spending in the belief that these developments would strengthen consumer spending, but they had no intention of surrendering their own wealth or power. The Democratic Party had become, in effect, the party of the masses and one section of big business. The conflicting interests of these two constituencies would create tensions within the Democratic Party throughout the years of its political domination.

Men, Women, and Reform

The years 1936 and 1937 were exciting ones for academics, policy makers, and bureaucrats who designed and administered the rapidly growing roster of New Deal programs and agencies. Fueled by idealism and dedication, they were confident they could make the New Deal work. They planned and won congressional approval for the Farm Security Administration (FSA), an agency designed to improve the economic lot of tenant farmers,

Rates of Unemployment in Selected Male and Female Occupations, 1930

Male Occupations	Percentage Male	Percentage Unemployed
Iron and steel	96%	13%
Forestry and fishing	99	10
Mining	99	18
Heavy manufacturing	86	13
Carpentry	100	19
Laborers (road and street)	100	13
Female Occupations	**Percentage Female**	**Percentage Unemployed**
Stenographers and typists	96%	5%
Laundresses	99	3
Trained nurses	98	4
Housekeepers	92	3
Telephone operators	95	3
Dressmakers	100	4

Source: U.S. Department of Commerce, Bureau of the Census, *Fifteenth Census of the United States, 1930, Population* (Washington, D.C.: Government Printing Office, 1931).

sharecroppers, and farm laborers. They drafted and passed laws that outlawed child labor, set minimum wages and maximum hours for adult workers, and committed the federal government to building low-cost housing. They investigated and tried to regulate concentrations of corporate power.

Although they worked on behalf of "the people," the New Dealers constituted a new class of technocrats. The prospect of building a strong state committed to prosperity and justice fired their imaginations. They delighted in the intellectual challenge and the technical complexity of social policy. They did not welcome interference from those they regarded as less intelligent or motivated by obsolete ideologies.

This was particularly true of the men. Many had earned advanced degrees in law and economics at elite universities such as Harvard, Columbia, and Wisconsin. Not all had been raised among wealth and privilege, however, as was generally the case with earlier generations of reformers. To his credit, Franklin Roosevelt was the first president since his cousin Theodore Roosevelt to welcome Jews and Catholics into his administration. Some became members of Roosevelt's inner circle of advisers—men such as Thomas "Tommy the Cork" Corcoran, Jim Farley, Ben Cohen, and Samuel Rosenman. These men had struggled to make their way, first on the streets and then in school and at work. They brought to the New Deal intellectual aggressiveness, quick minds, and mental toughness.

The profile of New Deal women was different. Although a few, notably Eleanor Roosevelt and Secretary of Labor Frances Perkins, were more visible than women in previous administrations had been, many of the female New Dealers worked in relative obscurity, in agencies such as the Women's Bureau or the Children's Bureau (both in the Department of Labor). Women who worked on major legislation, as did Mary Van Kleeck on the Social Security Act, or who directed major programs, as did Jane Hoey, chief of the Social Security's Bureau of Public Assistance, received less credit than men in comparable positions. Moreover, female New Dealers tended to be a generation older than their male colleagues and were more likely to be Protestant than Catholic or Jewish. Many of them had known each other since the days of progressive-era reform and woman suffrage (see chapter 21).

The New Deal offered these female reformers little opportunity to advance the cause of women's equality. Demands for greater economic opportunity, sexual freedom, and full equality for women and men were put forward less often in the 1930s than they had been in the preceding two decades. One reason was that the women's movement had lost momentum after achieving the vote in 1920 (see chapter 24). Another was that prominent New Deal women, rather than vigorously pursuing a campaign for equal rights, chose to concentrate instead on "protective legislation"—laws that safeguarded female workers, whom they considered more fragile than men. Those who insisted that women needed special protections could not easily argue that women were the equal of men in all respects.

Even so, feminism was hemmed in on all sides by a male hostility that the depression had only intensified. Many American men had built their male identities on the value of hard work and the ability to provide economic security for their families. For them, the loss of work unleashed feelings of inadequacy. Male vulnerability increased as unemployment rates of men—most of whom labored in blue-collar industries—rose higher than those of women, many of whom worked in white-collar occupations less affected by job cutbacks. Many fathers and husbands resented wives and daughters who had taken over their breadwinning roles.

This male anxiety had political and social consequences. Several states passed laws outlawing the hiring of married women. New Deal relief agencies were reluctant to authorize aid for unemployed women. The labor movement made protection of the male wage earner one of its principal goals. The Social Security pension system left out waitresses, domestic servants, and other largely female occupations. Some commentators even proposed ludicrous gender remedies to the problem of unemployment. Norman Cousins of the *Saturday Evening Post,* for example, suggested that the depression could be ended simply by firing 10 million working women and giving their jobs to men. "Presto!" he declared. "No unemployment, no relief rolls. No Depression."

Many artists introduced a strident masculinism into their painting and sculpture. Mighty *Superman,* the new comic-strip hero of 1938, reflected the spirit of the times. Superman was depicted as a working-class hero who, on several occasions, saved workers from coal mine explosions and other disasters caused by the greed and negligence of villainous employers.

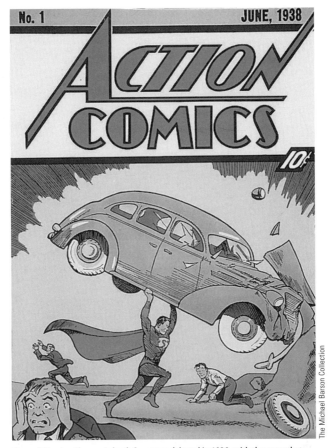

Man of Steel   The comic book *Superman* debuted in 1938, with the cover that appears in this reproduction. The character Superman partook of the New Deal's commitment to help ordinary Americans in need while offering men a fantasy about unconquerable male power.

Superman's greatest vulnerability, however, other than kryptonite, was his attraction to the sexy and aggressive *working* woman, Lois Lane. He could never resolve his dilemma by marrying Lois and tucking her away in a safe domestic sphere, because the continuation of the comic strip demanded that Superman be repeatedly exposed to kryptonite and female danger. But the producers of male and female images in other mass media, such as the movies, faced no such technical obstacles. Anxious men could take comfort from the conclusion of the movie *Woman of the Year,* in which Spencer Tracy persuades the ambitious Katharine Hepburn to exchange her successful newspaper career for the bliss of motherhood and homemaking. From a thousand different points, 1930s politics and culture made it clear that a woman's proper place was in the home. Faced with such obstacles, it is not surprising that women activists failed to make feminism a major part of New Deal reform.

Labor in Politics and Culture

In 1935, John L. Lewis of the United Mine Workers, Sidney Hillman of the Amalgamated Clothing Workers, and the leaders of six other unions that had seceded from the American Federation of Labor (AFL) cobbled together a new labor organization. The Committee for Industrial Organization (**CIO**—later renamed the Congress of Industrial Organizations) aspired to organize millions of unskilled and semiskilled workers whom the AFL had largely ignored. In 1936, Lewis and Hillman created a second organization, Labor's Non-Partisan League (LNPL), to develop a labor strategy for the 1936 elections. Although professing the league's nonpartisanship, Lewis intended from the start that the LNPL's role would be to channel labor's money, energy, and talent into Roosevelt's reelection campaign. Roosevelt welcomed the league's help, and labor would become a key constituency of the new Democratic coalition. The passage of the Wagner Act and the creation of the NLRB in 1935 enhanced the labor movement's status and credibility. Membership in labor unions climbed steadily, and, in short order, union members began flexing their new muscles.

In late 1936, the United Auto Workers (UAW) took on General Motors, widely regarded as the most powerful corporation in the world. Workers occupied key GM factories in Flint, Michigan, declaring that their **sit-down strike** would continue until GM agreed to recognize the UAW and negotiate a collective bargaining agreement. Frank Murphy, the pro-labor governor of Michigan, refused to use National Guard troops to evict the strikers, and Roosevelt declined to send federal troops. A 50-year-old practice of using soldiers to break strikes ended, and General Motors capitulated after a month of resistance. Soon, the U.S. Steel Corporation, which had defeated unionists in the bloody strike of 1919 (see chapter 23), announced that it was ready to negotiate a contract with the newly formed CIO steelworkers union.

The labor movement's public stature grew along with its size. Many writers and artists, funded through the WPA, depicted the labor movement as the voice of the people and the embodiment of the nation's values. Murals sprang up in post offices and other public buildings featuring portraits of blue-collar Americans at work. Broadway's most celebrated play in 1935 was Clifford Odets's *Waiting for Lefty,* a raw drama about taxi drivers who confront their bosses and organize an honest union. Audiences were so moved by the play that they often spontaneously joined in the final chorus of "Strike, Strike, Strike," the words that ended the play. *Pins and Needles,* a 1937 musical about the hopes and dreams of garment workers, performed by actual members of the International Ladies Garment Workers Union, became the longest-running play in Broadway history (until *Oklahoma!* broke its record of 1,108 performances in 1943).

Similarly, many of the most popular novels and movies of the 1930s celebrated the decency, honesty, and patriotism of ordinary Americans. In *Mr. Deeds Goes to Town* (1936) and *Mr. Smith Goes to Washington* (1939), **Frank Capra** delighted movie audiences with fables of simple, small-town heroes vanquishing the evil forces of wealth and decadence. Likewise, in *The Grapes of Wrath,* the best-selling novel of 1939, John

Steinbeck told an epic tale of an Oklahoma family's fortitude in surviving eviction from their land, migrating westward, and suffering exploitation in the "promised land" of California. In 1940, John Ford turned Steinbeck's novel into one of that year's highest-grossing and most acclaimed movies. Moviegoers found special meaning in the declaration of one of the story's main characters, Ma Joad: "We'll go on forever . . . 'cause we're the people." In themselves and in one another, Americans seemed to discover the resolve they needed to rebuild a culture that had surrendered its identity to corporations and business.

John Steinbeck wrote about the Okie migrants to California as an outsider. But the Okies produced a writer and musician of their own who became, in the late 1930s, a popular folk singer. Born in 1913 in Okemah, Oklahoma, Woody Guthrie grew up in nearby Pampa, Texas. He wasn't born poor—his father was a small businessman and a local politician—but by the time he reached his twenties, Guthrie had known a great deal of hardship: his father's business failed, three family homes burned down, one sister died from burns, and then the drought and dust storms struck. In the 1930s, Guthrie joined the large migration of Okies to California. There, his musical gifts were discovered, chiefly because radio stations, in particular, were keen to put "singing cowboys" on the air. Guthrie had emerged from a country music tradition in Texas and Oklahoma and found an audience among the many people from those states who had gone to California.

But Guthrie quickly developed a broader appeal as he cast himself as the bard of ordinary Americans everywhere. He loved America for the beauty of its landscape and its people, sentiments he expressed in one of his most popular songs, "This Land Is Your Land," which he wrote in 1940 in response to Irving Berlin's "God Bless America" (a song Guthrie did not like because of the false sense of complacency he thought it induced). Guthrie did not possess a refined singing voice, but his "hillbilly" lyrics, melodies, and humor were inventive and often inspiring. He would become a powerful influence on subsequent generations of musicians, including such major figures as Bob Dylan and Bruce Springsteen.

Guthrie traveled ceaselessly in the 1930s, from Los Angeles to New York and from Texas to Washington state. The more he learned about the hardships of individual Americans, the angrier and more politically active he became. He drew close to the labor movement and to the Communist Party, and increasingly, in his writings and songs, he criticized the industrialists, financiers, and their political agents who, he believed, had brought the calamity of the Depression on America. But Guthrie always associated his criticism with the hope that the working people of America, if united, could take back their land—which is the message he meant to convey when he sang "This Land Is Your Land"—and restore its greatness. The optimism of his message underscored how much the cultural mood had changed since the early 1930s. In his focus on ordinary working Americans, in his hope for the future, and in his fusion of dissent and patriotism, Guthrie was emblematic of the dominant stream of culture and politics in the late 1930s.

America's Minorities and the New Deal

Focus Question
Which minority groups in American society benefited the most from the New Deal and which benefited the least?

Reformers in the 1930s generally believed that issues of capitalism's viability, economic recovery, and the inequality of wealth and power outweighed problems of racial and ethnic discrimination; only in the case of American Indians did New Dealers pass legislation specifically designed to improve a minority's social and economic position. Because they were disproportionately poor, most minority groups did profit from the populist and pro-labor character of New Deal reforms, but the gains were distributed unevenly. Eastern and Southern European ethnics benefited the most, and African Americans and Mexican Americans advanced the least.

Eastern and Southern European Ethnics

Eastern and Southern European immigrants and their children had begun mobilizing politically in the 1920s in response to religious and racial discrimination (see chapter 24). Roosevelt understood their political importance well, for he was a product of New York Democratic politics, where men such as Robert Wagner and Al Smith had begun to organize the ethnic vote even before 1920 (see chapter 21). He made sure that a significant portion of New Deal monies for welfare, building and road construction, and unemployment relief reached the urban areas where most European ethnics lived. As a result, Jewish and Catholic Americans, especially those descended from Eastern and Southern European immigrants, voted for Roosevelt in overwhelming numbers. The New Deal did not eliminate anti-Semitism and anti-Catholicism from American society, but it did allow millions of European ethnics to believe, for the first time, that they would overcome the second-class status they had long endured.

Eastern and Southern European ethnics also benefited from their strong working-class presence. Forming one of the largest groups in the mass-production industries of the Northeast, Midwest, and West Coast, they formed a large part of the labor movement's new membership. Roosevelt accommodated himself to their wishes because he understood and feared the power they wielded through their labor organizations.

African Americans

The New Deal did more to reproduce patterns of racial discrimination than to advance the cause of racial equality. African Americans who belonged to CIO unions or who lived in northern cities benefited from New Deal programs, but most blacks lived in the rural South, where they were barred from voting, largely excluded from AAA programs, and denied federal protection in their efforts to form agricultural unions. The CCC ran separate camps for black and white youth. The TVA hired few blacks. Those enrolled in the

CWA and other work-relief programs frequently received less pay than whites for doing the same jobs. Roosevelt consistently refused to support legislation to make lynching a federal crime.

This failure to push a strong civil-rights agenda did not mean that New Dealers were racist. Eleanor Roosevelt spoke out frequently against racial injustice. In 1939, she resigned from the Daughters of the American Revolution when the organization refused to allow black opera singer **Marian Anderson** to perform in its concert hall. She then pressured the federal government into granting Anderson permission to sing from the steps of the Lincoln Memorial. On Easter Sunday, 75,000 people gathered to hear Anderson and to demonstrate their support for racial equality. The president did not attend.

Roosevelt did eliminate segregationist practices in the federal government that had been in place since Woodrow Wilson's presidency. He appointed Mary McLeod Bethune, Robert Weaver, William Hastie, and other African Americans to important second-level posts in his administration. Working closely with each other in what came to be known as the Black Cabinet, these officials fought hard to end discrimination in New Deal programs.

Roosevelt, however, refused to support the Black Cabinet if it meant alienating white southern senators who controlled key congressional committees. He believed that pushing for civil rights would cost him the support of the white South. Meanwhile, African Americans and their supporters were not yet strong enough as an electoral constituency or as a reform movement to force Roosevelt to accede to their wishes.

Mexican Americans

The Mexican American experience in the Great Depression was particularly harsh. In 1931, Hoover's secretary of labor, William N. Doak, announced a plan for repatriating illegal aliens (returning them to their land of origin) and giving their jobs to American citizens. The federal campaign quickly focused on Mexican immigrants in California and the Southwest. The U.S. Immigration Service staged a series of highly publicized raids, rounded up large numbers of Mexicans and Mexican Americans, and demanded that each detainee prove his or her legal status. Those who failed to produce the necessary documentation were deported. Local and state governments pressured many more Mexicans into leaving. The combined efforts of federal, state, and local governments created a climate of fear in Mexican communities that prompted 500,000 to return to Mexico by 1935. This total equaled the number of Mexicans who had come to the United States in the 1920s. Los Angeles lost one-third of its Mexican population. Included in repatriate ranks were a significant number of legal immigrants who were unable to produce their immigration papers, the American-born children of illegals, and some Mexican Americans who had lived in the Southwest for generations.

The advent of the New Deal in 1933 eased but did not eliminate pressure on Chicano communities. New Deal agencies made more money available for relief, thereby lightening the burden on state and local governments. But federal laws, more often than not, failed to dissuade local officials from continuing their campaign against Mexican immigrants. Where Mexicans gained access to relief rolls, they received payments lower than those given to "Anglos" (whites) or were compelled to accept tough agricultural jobs that paid less than living wages.

Life grew harder for immigrant Mexicans who stayed behind. The Mexican cultural renaissance that had emerged in 1920s Los Angeles (see chapter 24) stalled. Hounded by government officials, Mexicans everywhere sought to escape public attention and scrutiny. In Los Angeles, where their influence had been felt throughout the city in the 1920s, they retreated into the separate community of East Los Angeles. To many, they became the "invisible minority."

Mexicans and Mexican Americans who lived in urban areas and worked in blue-collar industries, however, did benefit from New Deal programs. In Los Angeles, for example, Chicanos employed in canneries, in garment and furniture shops, and on the docks responded to the New Deal's pro-labor legislation by joining unions in large numbers and winning concessions from their employers. Most Chicanos, however, lived in rural areas and labored in agricultural jobs, and the New Deal offered them little help. The National Labor Relations Act did not protect their right to organize unions, and the Social Security Act excluded them from the new federal welfare system.

American Indians

From the 1880s until the early 1930s, federal policy had contributed to the elimination of American Indians as a distinctive population. The Dawes Act of 1887 (see chapter 18) had called for tribal lands to be broken up and allotted to individual owners in the hope that Indians would adopt the work habits of white farmers. But American Indians had proved stubbornly loyal to their languages, religions, and cultures. Few of them succeeded as farmers, and many lost land to white speculators. By 1933, nearly half the American Indians living on reservations whose land had been allotted were landless, and many who retained allotments held land that was largely desert or semidesert.

The shrinking land base in combination with a growing population deepened American Indian poverty. The assimilationist pressures on American Indians, meanwhile, reached a climax in the intolerant 1920s, when the Bureau of Indian Affairs (BIA) outlawed Indian religious ceremonies, forced children from tribal communities into federal boarding schools, banned polygamy, and imposed limits on the length of men's hair.

Government officials working in the Hoover administration began to question this draconian policy, but its reversal had to await the New Deal and Roosevelt's appointment of **John Collier** as the commissioner of the BIA. Collier pressured the CCC, AAA, and other New Deal agencies to employ Indians on projects that improved reservation land and trained Indians in land conservation methods. He prevailed on Congress to pass the Pueblo Relief Act of 1933, which compensated Pueblos for land taken from them in the 1920s, and the Johnson-O'Malley Act of 1934, which provided funds to the states for Indian health care, welfare, and education. As part of his campaign to make the BIA more responsive to American Indian needs, Collier increased the number of Indian BIA employees from a paltry few hundred in 1933 to a respectable 4,600 in 1940.

Collier also took steps to abolish federal boarding schools, encourage enrollment in local public schools, and establish community day schools. He insisted that American Indians be allowed to practice their traditional religions, and he created the Indian Arts and Crafts Board in 1935 to nurture traditional Indian artists and to help them market their works.

The centerpiece of Collier's reform strategy was the Indian Reorganization Act (also known as the Wheeler-Howard Act) of 1934, which revoked the allotment provisions of the Dawes Act. The IRA restored land to tribes, granted Indians the right to establish constitutions and bylaws for self-government, and provided support for new tribal corporations that would regulate the use of communal lands. This landmark act signaled the government's recognition that American Indian tribes possessed the right to chart their own political, cultural, and economic futures. It reflected Collier's commitment to "cultural pluralism," a doctrine that celebrated the diversity of peoples and cultures in American society and sought to protect that diversity against the pressures of assimilation. Collier hoped that the IRA would invigorate traditional Indian cultures and tribal societies and sustain both for generations. Cultural pluralism was not a popular creed in America during the depression years, which makes its acceptance as the rationale for the IRA all the more remarkable.

Collier encountered opposition everywhere: from Protestant missionaries and cultural conservatives who wanted to continue an assimilationist policy; from white farmers and businessmen who feared that the new legislation would restrict their access to Native American land; and even from a sizable number of Indian groups, some of which had embraced assimilation and others that viewed the IRA cynically, as one more attempt by the federal government to impose "the white man's will" on the Indian peoples. This opposition made the IRA a more modest bill than the one Collier had originally championed.

A vocal minority of Indians continued to oppose the act even after its passage. The Navajo, the nation's largest tribe, voted to reject its terms along with 76 other tribes. Still, 181 tribes, nearly 70 percent of the total, supported Collier's reform and began organizing new governments under the IRA. Although their quest for independence would suffer setbacks, these tribes gained significant measures of freedom and autonomy during the New Deal.

The New Deal Abroad

When he first entered office, Roosevelt seemed to favor a nationalist approach to international relations. The United States, he believed, should pursue foreign policies to benefit its domestic affairs, without regard for the effects of those policies on world trade and international stability. Thus, in June 1933, Roosevelt pulled the United States out of the World Economic Conference in London, a meeting called by leading nations to strengthen the gold standard and thereby stabilize the value of their currencies. Roosevelt feared that the United States would be forced into an agreement designed to keep the gold content of the dollar high and U.S. commodity prices low, which would frustrate New Deal efforts to inflate the prices of agricultural and industrial goods.

Soon after his withdrawal from the London conference, however, Roosevelt put the United States on a more internationalist course. In November 1933, he became the first president to recognize the Soviet Union and to establish diplomatic ties with its Communist rulers. In December 1933, he inaugurated a **Good Neighbor Policy** toward Latin America by formally renouncing U.S. rights to intervene in the affairs of Latin American nations. To back up his pledge, Roosevelt ordered home the Marines stationed in Haiti and Nicaragua, scuttled the Platt Amendment that had given the United States control over the Cuban government since 1901, and granted Panama more political autonomy and a greater administrative role in operating the Panama Canal (see chapter 22).

None of this, however, meant that the United States had given up its influence over Latin America. When a 1934 revolution brought a radical government to power in Cuba, the U.S. ambassador there worked with conservative Cubans to replace the government with a regime more favorable to U.S. interests. The United States did refrain from sending troops to Cuba. It also kept its troops at home in 1936 when a radical government in Mexico nationalized several U.S.-owned and British-owned petroleum companies. The United States merely demanded that the new Mexican government compensate the oil companies for their lost property, which Mexico eventually did. Although the United States was still the dominant power in hemispheric affairs, its newfound restraint inspired Latin American hopes that a new era had dawned.

The Roosevelt administration's recognition of the Soviet Union and embrace of the Good Neighbor Policy can be seen as an international expression of the liberal principles that guided its domestic policies. These diplomatic initiatives, however, also reflected Roosevelt's interest in stimulating international trade. American businessmen wanted access to the Soviet Union's domestic market. Latin America was already a major market for the United States, but one in need of greater stability. To win the support of American traders and investors, Roosevelt stressed how the Good Neighbor Policy would improve the region's business climate.

Roosevelt further expressed his interest in building international trade through his support for the Reciprocal Trade Agreement, passed by Congress in 1934. This act allowed his administration to lower U.S. tariffs by as much as 50 percent in exchange for similar reductions by other nations. By the end of 1935, the United States had negotiated reciprocal trade agreements with 14 countries. Roosevelt's emphasis on international trade—a move consonant with the Second New Deal's program of increasing the circulation of goods and money through the economy—further solidified support for the New Deal in parts of the business community, especially among those firms, such as United Fruit and Coca-Cola, with large overseas investments.

Actually increasing the volume of international trade was more difficult than passing legislation to encourage it. In Germany and Italy, belligerent nationalists Adolf Hitler

Unemployment, 1920–1945

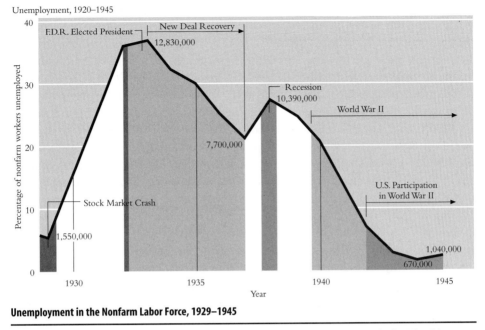

Unemployment in the Nonfarm Labor Force, 1929–1945

Source: Data from *Historical Statistics of the United States, Colonial Times to 1970* (White Plains, N.Y.: Kraus International, 1989), p. 126.

and Benito Mussolini told their people that the solution to their ills lay not in foreign trade but in military strength and conquest. Throughout the world, similar appeals to national pride proved more popular than calls for tariff reductions and international trade. In the face of this historical current, the New Deal's internationalist economic policies made little headway.

Stalemate, 1937–1940

By 1937 and 1938, the New Deal had begun to lose momentum. One reason was an emerging split between working-class and middle-class Democrats. After the UAW's victory over General Motors in 1937, other workers began to imitate the successful tactics of the Flint, Michigan, militants. Sit-down strikes spread to many industries and regions, a development that many middle-class Americans found disturbing.

The Court-Packing Fiasco

The president's proposal on February 5, 1937, to alter the makeup of the Supreme Court exacerbated middle-class fears. Roosevelt asked Congress to give him the power to appoint one new Supreme Court justice for every member of the court who was older than age 70 and who had served for at least 10 years. His stated reason was that the current justices were too old and feeble to handle the large volume of cases coming before them, but his real purpose was to prevent the conservative justices on the court—most of whom had been appointed by Republican presidents—from dismantling his New Deal. His proposal, if accepted, would have given him the authority to appoint six additional justices, thereby securing a pro–New Deal majority.

The president seemed genuinely surprised by the storm of indignation that greeted his **"court-packing"** proposal. Roosevelt's political acumen had apparently been dulled by his 1936 victory. His inflated sense of power infuriated many who had previously been New Deal enthusiasts. Although working-class support for Roosevelt remained strong, many middle-class voters turned away from the New Deal. In 1937 and 1938, a conservative opposition took shape, uniting Republicans, conservative Democrats (many of them southerners), and civil libertarians who were determined to protect private property and government integrity.

Ironically, Roosevelt's court-packing scheme may have been unnecessary. In March 1937, just one month after he proposed his plan, Supreme Court Justice Owen J. Roberts, a former opponent of New Deal programs, decided to support them. In April and May, the Court upheld the constitutionality of the Wagner Act and Social Security Act, both by a 5-to-4 margin. The principal reforms of the New Deal would endure. Roosevelt allowed his court-reform proposal to die in Congress that summer. Within three years, five of the aging justices had retired, giving Roosevelt the opportunity to fashion a court more to his liking. Nonetheless, Roosevelt's reputation had suffered.

The Recession of 1937–1938

Whatever hope Roosevelt may have had for a quick recovery from the court-packing fiasco was dashed by a sharp recession that struck the country in late 1937 and 1938. The New Deal programs of 1935 had stimulated the economy, prompting Roosevelt to scale back relief programs. Meanwhile, new payroll taxes took $2 billion from wage earners' salaries to finance the Social Security pension fund even though the government did not intend to begin paying benefits until 1941. Thus, the government substantially shrunk the volume of dollars it was putting into circulation. Starved for money, the economy and stock market crashed once again. Unemployment, which had fallen to 14 percent, shot back up to 20 percent. In the 1938 elections, voters vented their frustration by electing many conservative Democrats and Republicans who were opposed to the New Deal. These conservatives could not dismantle the New Deal reforms already in place, but they did block the passage of new programs.

Conclusion

Roosevelt first assumed the presidency in the same week that Adolf Hitler established a Nazi dictatorship in Germany. Some feared that Roosevelt, by accumulating more power into the hands of the federal government than had ever been held in peacetime, aspired to autocratic rule. Nothing of the sort happened. Roosevelt and the New Dealers not only strengthened democracy, they also inspired millions of Americans who had never before voted to go to the polls. Groups that had been marginalized— Eastern and Southern European ethnics, unskilled workers, American Indians—now believed that their political activism could make a difference.

Not everyone benefited to the same degree from the broadening of American democracy. Northern factory workers, farm owners, European American ethnics, and middle-class consumers (especially homeowners) were among the groups who benefited most. In contrast, the socialist and communist elements of the labor movement failed to achieve their radical aims. Southern industrial workers, black and white, benefited little from New Deal reforms; so did farm laborers. Feminists made no headway. African Americans and Mexican Americans gained meager influence over public policy.

New Deal reforms might not have mattered to any group if the Second World War had not rescued the New Deal economic program. With government war orders flooding factories from 1941 on, the economy grew vigorously, unemployment vanished, and prosperity finally returned. The architects of the Second New Deal, who had argued that large government expenditures would stimulate consumer demand and trigger economic recovery, were vindicated.

The war also solidified the political reforms of the 1930s: an increased role for the government in regulating the economy and in ensuring the social welfare of those unable to help themselves; strong state support of unionization, agricultural subsidies, and progressive tax policies; and the use of government power and money to develop the West and Southwest. In sharp contrast to progressivism, the reforms of the New Deal endured. Voters returned Roosevelt to office for unprecedented third and fourth terms, and these same voters remained wedded for the next 40 years to Roosevelt's central idea: that a powerful state would enhance the pursuit of liberty and equality.

SUGGESTED READINGS

T. H. Watkins, *The Great Depression: America in the 1930s* (1993), provides a broad overview of society and politics during the 1930s. No work better conveys the tumult and drama of that era than **Arthur M. Schlesinger Jr.'s** three-volume *The Age of Roosevelt: The Crisis of the Old Order* (1957), *The Coming of the New Deal* (1958), and *The Politics of Upheaval* (1960), but Schlesinger's work must now be supplemented with **David M. Kennedy, *Freedom from Fear: The American People in Depression and War, 1929–1945*** (1999). On Hoover's failure to restore prosperity and popular morale, see **David Burner, *Herbert Hoover: A Public Life*** (1979).

The most complete biography of FDR, and one that is remarkably good at balancing Roosevelt's life and times, is **Kenneth S. Davis, *FDR*** (1972–1993), in four volumes. For a vivid description of the political dangers confronting Roosevelt as he assumed office in 1933, see Jonathan Alter, *The Defining Moment: FDR's Hundred Days and the Triumph of Hope* (2006). On Eleanor Roosevelt, see **Blanche Wiesen Cook, *Eleanor Roosevelt,*** vol. 1 (1992). On the New Deal, see **William E. Leuchtenburg, *Franklin D. Roosevelt and the New Deal, 1932–1940*** (1963); **Anthony J. Badger, *The New Deal: The Depression Years, 1933–1940*** (1989); and **Steve Fraser and Gary Gerstle, eds.,**

The Rise and Fall of the New Deal Order, 1930–1980 (1989). **Ellis Hawley,** *The New Deal and the Problem of Monopoly* (1966), is essential to understand the First New Deal's industrial policy, while **Steven Fraser,** *Labor Will Rule: Sidney Hillman and the Rise of American Labor* (1991), examines the role of the labor movement in national politics.

Michael Denning, *The Cultural Front: The Laboring of American Culture in the Twentieth Century* (1996), is essential reading on the centrality of labor and the "common man" to literary and popular culture in the 1930s, as is **Lary May,** *The Big Tomorrow: Hollywood and the Politics of the American Way* (2000). For the economic and cultural ties between the New Deal and the rebirth of the labor movement, see **Lizabeth Cohen,** *Making a New Deal: Industrial Workers in Chicago, 1919–1939* (1990). **Irving Howe and Lewis Coser,** *The American Communist Party: A Critical History, 1919–1957* (1957), is still the best single-volume history of the Communist Party during the 1930s.

Harvard Sitkoff, *A New Deal for Blacks* (1978), is a wide-ranging examination of the place of African Americans in New Deal reform. **Abraham Hoffman,** *Unwanted Mexican Americans in the Great Depression: Repatriation Pressures, 1929–1939* (1974), analyzes the repatriation campaign, while the problems of illegal alienage created by that campaign are expertly analyzed in **Mae Ngai,** *Impossible Subjects: Illegal Aliens and the Making of Modern America* (2004). The importance of John Collier and the Indian Reorganization Act are treated well in **Lawrence C. Kelly,** *The Assault on Assimilation: John Collier and the Origins of Indian Policy Reform* (1983). **James T. Patterson,** *Congressional Conservatism and the New Deal* (1967), expertly analyzes the growing opposition to the New Deal in the late 1930s, while **Alan Brinkley,** *The End of Reform: New Deal Liberalism in Recession and War* (1995), provocatively examines the efforts of New Dealers to adjust their beliefs and programs as they lost support, momentum, and confidence in the late 1930s.

Visit the Liberty Equality Power Companion Web site for resources specific to this textbook: http://www.thomsonedu.com/history/murrin

Also find self-tests and additional resources at ThomsonNOW. ThomsonNOW is an integrated online suite of services and resources with proven ease of use and efficient paths to success, delivering the results you want—NOW!

www.thomsonedu.com/login/

America during the Second World War

The Second World War brought unprecedented destruction to much of the globe. The United States—whose own towns, farms, and cities would escape the impact of combat operations—lurched toward direct engagement in this conflict. Mobilization for war, already underway before formal U.S. entry in 1941, first lifted the nation out of the Great Depression and, then, transformed its economy. At war's end, the military might and productive capacity of the victorious United States—spurred by innovative technologies and new working relationships among government, business, labor, and scientific researchers—dwarfed that of all other nations. Franklin Roosevelt's wartime presidency, invoking military necessity as the justification, significantly expanded the power of the national government.

As the war proceeded, Americans came to reconsider how to understand liberty and equality. Although a government-directed publicity campaign initially stressed how wartime sacrifices would protect and preserve an "American way of life," the ongoing fight against fascist dictatorships overseas soon raised questions about what might—and should—change in the United States itself. Might the nation, while striving for military victory, also reorder its economy, rework its politics, and refashion the cultural and social patterns that had shaped racial, ethnic, and gender relationships during the 1930s? Could the interrelated tasks of reconstructing a war-ravaged world and strengthening forces for peace require the creation of new institutions, both at home and abroad?

The Road to War: Aggression and Response

Focus Question
How did events in Asia and in Europe affect debate within the United States over whether or not to embrace more interventionist policies overseas?

Tensions growing out of the First World War, heightened by a worldwide economic depression, fostered international instability during the 1930s. In Japan, Italy, and Germany, economic stagnation nurtured ultranationalist political movements that championed aggressive foreign policies. Elsewhere in Europe and in the United States, economic problems inclined governing majorities to turn inward, concentrating on promoting recovery and avoiding foreign entanglements.

CHRONOLOGY

1931	Japanese forces seize Manchuria
1933	Hitler takes power in Germany *1933*
1936	Spanish Civil War begins • Germany and Italy agree to cooperate as the Axis Powers
1937	Neutrality Act broadens provisions of Neutrality Acts of 1935 and 1936 • Roosevelt makes "Quarantine" speech • Japan invades China
1938	France and Britain appease Hitler at Munich
1939	Hitler and Stalin sign Soviet–German nonaggression pact • Hitler invades Poland; war breaks out in Europe • Congress amends Neutrality Act to assist Allies
1940	Paris falls after German *blitzkreig* (June) • Battle of Britain carried to U.S. by radio broadcasts • Roosevelt makes "destroyers-for-bases" deal with Britain • Selective Service Act passed • Roosevelt wins third term
1941	Lend-Lease established • Roosevelt creates Fair Employment Practices Commission • Roosevelt and Churchill proclaim the Atlantic Charter • U.S. engages in undeclared naval war in North Atlantic • Congress narrowly repeals Neutrality Act • Japanese forces attack Pearl Harbor (December 7)
1942	Rio de Janeiro Conference (January) • President signs Executive Order 9066 for internment of Japanese Americans (February) • General MacArthur driven from Philippines (May) • U.S. victorious in Battle of Midway (June) • German army defeated at Battle of Stalingrad (August) • Operation TORCH begins (November)
1943	Axis armies in North Africa surrender (May) • Allies invade Sicily (July) and Italy (September) • "Zoot suit" incidents in Los Angeles; racial violence in Detroit • Allies begin drive toward Japan through South Pacific islands
1944	Allies land at Normandy (D-day, June 6) • Allied armies reach Paris (August) • Allies turn back Germans at Battle of the Bulge (September) • Roosevelt reelected to fourth term • Bretton Woods Conference creates IMF and World Bank • Dumbarton Oaks Conference establishes plan for UN
1945	U.S. firebombs Japan • Yalta Conference (February) • Roosevelt dies; Truman becomes president (April) • Germany surrenders (May) • Hiroshima and Nagasaki hit with atomic bombs (August) • Japan surrenders (September) • United Nations established (December)

The Rise of Aggressor States

The first signs of another world war appeared in Asia. On September 18, 1931, Japanese military forces seized Manchuria, and Japan renamed the puppet state it created Manchukuo. This aggression by Japan violated the charter of the League of Nations, the Washington naval treaties, and the Kellogg-Briand Pact (see chapter 24). Focused on domestic matters, nations such as the United States hesitated to oppose Japan's move with military force. Instead, the Hoover-Stimson Doctrine (1931) announced a U.S. policy of "nonrecognition" toward Manchukuo, and the League of Nations merely condemned Japan's move. Japan simply ignored these rhetorical rebukes.

Two ultranationalist states in Europe also soon embarked on military aggression. **Adolf Hitler's** National Socialist (Nazi) Party, which came to power in Germany during 1933, announced a bold approach to addressing economic ills and political instability. Hitler created a one-party dictatorial state; denounced the Versailles peace settlement of 1919 as unfair to Germany; further blamed its problems on a Jewish conspiracy; claimed a genetic superiority for the "Aryan race" of German-speaking peoples; and promised a new Germanic empire, the **Third Reich.** His fascist regime also withdrew from the League of Nations in 1933 and, in a blatant violation of the Versailles treaty, dramatically boosted Germany's military budget.

Another, less powerful fascist government, headed by Benito Mussolini, had come to power in Italy during the 1920s. As Mussolini introduced authoritarian controls over Italy's domestic life, he launched his own military buildup and prepared for territorial expansion. Mussolini talked of making the Mediterranean an Italian-dominated sea. Building on earlier moves against Albania and Libya, Mussolini sent his armies, in 1935, into Ethiopia. After a brief and bloody conflict, Mussolini converted this previously independent African kingdom into an Italian colony and, then, began forging close ties with Hitler's regime in Germany.

U.S. Neutrality

In the United States, memories of involvement in the First World War helped justify efforts to isolate the nation from the foreign troubles of the 1930s. Antiwar books and movies, such as *All Quiet on the Western Front* (1931), implicitly portrayed President Woodrow Wilson's earlier call for making "the world safe for democracy" (see chapter 23) as part of a cynical power game directed by business and governmental elites. Appeals to noble ideals merely allowed corrupt power brokers to turn young soldiers into cannon fodder. During the mid-1930s, a U.S. Senate committee headed by Republican Gerald P. Nye of North Dakota elaborated on this view of recent history. After well-publicized hearings, the Nye Committee charged that bankers and munitions makers, in search of profits, had conspired with their counterparts in Britain and France to maneuver the United States into the First World War. An influential group of historians, endorsing different variations of this critique, charged Wilson with having ignored the U.S. national interest when plunging his nation into the war in 1915. Twenty years later, popular opinion polls suggested overwhelming opposition to a similar U.S. involvement in the foreign conflicts of the 1930s.

The U.S. Congress backed this stance with a series of **Neutrality Acts.** These measures aimed at keeping the United States free from the kind of entangling financial relationships that had supposedly pulled it into the First World War. Neutrality laws passed in 1935 and 1936 established an embargo on arms sales to **belligerent** nations, prohibited U.S. loans to any country at war, and curtailed travel by U.S. citizens on vessels belonging to any warring power. The **"cash-and-carry"** provision in the Neutrality Act of 1937 extended the earlier arms embargo to include any foreign trade with belligerents. It did allow nations at war to continue buying products in the United States if they paid in hard cash and transported goods away in their own ships, rather than on U.S. ships.

Critics of this neutrality legislation charged that foreswearing U.S. intervention actively aided expansionist powers such as Nazi Germany. In March 1936, Hitler's forces entered the Rhineland, an area of Germany from which the 1919 peace settlement had barred military installations. A few months later, Hitler and Mussolini began assisting General Francisco Franco, a fellow fascist seeking the overthrow of Spain's fragile Republic and the restoration of a monarchy closely tied to the Catholic Church and the Spanish military. Franco's opponents, including that nation's communist movement, appealed to nonfascist nations for assistance. Only the communist Soviet Union responded.

Fearing conflict in Spain could flare into a wider war, the governments of Britain, France, and the United States refused to become involved. The U.S. Congress extended its arms embargo to include civil wars, a move that blocked the Spanish Republic from obtaining weaponry in the United States and implicitly benefited General Franco's already well-armed fascist forces. As with the other pieces of neutrality legislation, President Roosevelt, who was personally sympathetic to more interventionist policies, signed this measure.

The Spanish Civil War, however, helped sharpen foreign policy debate in the United States. Conservative groups generally hailed General Franco as a staunch anticommunist who would promote social stability and religious values in Spain. In contrast, the political left saw the Spanish Republic being sacrificed to a fascist movement that threatened to spread repression all across Europe. Cadres of Americans, including members of an "Abraham Lincoln Brigade," crossed the Atlantic to fight alongside the anti-Franco forces in Spain. U.S. peace groups, which had generally presented a united front during the 1920s, differed over how best to avoid a wider war. Some advocated neutrality and isolation, but others argued that the threat of **fascism** now demanded a turn toward interventionism, beginning in Spain.

Roosevelt's administration did tilt in an interventionist direction, more overtly than before. Seeking to influence domestic debate, Roosevelt called for international cooperation against expansionist nations. In his controversial "Quarantine the Aggressors" Speech of October 1937, the president suggested the possibility of Congress modifying earlier neutrality measures. Still suspicious of foreign entanglements, a majority of legislators refused to budge, even if this meant a victory by Franco in Spain's civil war.

The Mounting Crisis

As Americans were weighing policies of maintaining strict neutrality against ones of opposing aggression overseas, expansionist forces in Japan seized the initiative. During the summer of 1937, after an exchange of gunfire between Japanese and Chinese troops at the Marco Polo Bridge near Beijing, Japanese armies mounted a full scale invasion of China. Japan's forces captured Shanghai, Nanjing, Shandong, and Beijing. Japan demanded that China accept economic and political direction from Tokyo. As the Nationalist Chinese government of Jiang Jieshi (formally spelled Chiang Kai-sheck) struggled to survive, Japan unveiled ambitious plans for an East Asian Co-Prosperity Sphere, a self-sufficient economic zone under Japanese leadership.

This expansionist vision, which Japan promised would liberate Asian nations from Western colonialism, worried the Roosevelt administration and heightened tensions between the United States and Japan. In late 1937, Japanese planes sank the *Panay*, a U.S. gunboat, as it was evacuating Americans from Nanjing. Japan's quick apology and promise to pay for damages defused a potential crisis. Still, the *Panay* incident and Japan's brutality in Nanjing, which took the lives of perhaps 300,000 Chinese civilians, further fueled interventionist efforts in the United States. President Roosevelt began consulting, secretly, with British leaders about how to respond to the threat of war in Asia, where Britain still held valuable colonies. In May 1938, FDR publicly announced a program of naval rearmament that went beyond treaty limits that Japan had already violated.

Meanwhile, in Europe, Germany continued on the march. In March 1938, Hitler used the threat of military action to engineer the annexation of Austria, a neighboring nation, into the Third Reich, and he soon suggested a similar plan for the Sudetenland, a portion of Czechoslovakia inhabited by 3.5 million people of German descent. French and British leaders, still hoping to avoid war, met with Hitler in Munich in September 1938. Without consulting the leaders of Czechoslovakia or those of the neighboring Soviet Union, they acquiesced to Germany's power play in the Sudetenland. In return, Hitler pledged to seek no more territory. Hailed by Britain's prime minister as a guarantee of "peace in our time," the arrangement soon became a symbol of what interventionists called the "appeasement" of aggression.

Any hope that the Munich Conference would guarantee peace faded quickly. In March 1939, German troops marched into the Czechoslovakian capital of Prague; within a few months, Hitler announced the annexation of the rest of Czechoslovakia. Then, in an August 1939 surprise, he protected his eastern flank by signing a nonaggression pact with the Soviet Union, supposedly his sworn enemy. In a secret protocol, Hitler and Soviet leader **Joseph Stalin** agreed on a plan to divide up Poland, Hitler's next target, and the Baltic States (Latvia, Lithuania, and Estonia), which were long coveted by the Soviet Union.

The Outbreak of War in Europe

When Hitler's armies stormed onto Polish soil on September 1, 1939, the Second World War officially began. Britain and France, the Allies, already pledged to defend the Polish government, declared war against Germany but could not mobilize in time to help Poland. Within weeks, Germany's war machine overran that nation. Then, as a brutal campaign of Nazi repression wracked Poland, an eerie calm—which observers called a *sitzkrieg*, or "sitting war"—settled over the rest of Europe during the winter of 1939–40.

Suddenly, in April 1940, a full-scale German **blitzkrieg**, or "lightning war," began. Employing massed tank formations, motorized infantry and artillery, and massive air support, German military forces moved swiftly. They raced through Denmark, Norway, the Netherlands, Belgium, Luxembourg, and into France. The speed of the Nazi advance shocked Allied strategists in Paris and London. Britain dramatically evacuated its troops, but not their valuable equipment, from the French coastal town of Dunkirk, just before it fell to a German onslaught. Early in June, Italy joined Germany and declared war on the Allies. Later in June, German troops marched into Paris.

Hitler declared France's western and northern regions to be occupied German territory and installed a pro-Nazi French government at Vichy in southern France. In an act of powerful symbolism, he staged France's formal surrender in the same railway car in which Germany had capitulated to France at the end of the First World War. General Charles DeGaulle, seeking safety in London, countered by proclaiming *France Libre* (Free France), an anti-Nazi government pledged to end the German occupation and topple the Vichy regime.

After only six weeks of combat, Hitler's military juggernaut gave Nazi Germany control of Europe's Atlantic coastline. Germany's sway extended from the North Sea south to Spain, where Franco's fascist government remained officially neutral but effectively in the camp of Germany and Italy, which after announcing their own formal alliance, became the Axis Powers. The Axis gained another member, in September 1940, when Japan joined them in signing the Tripartite Pact. Britain now loomed directly in Hitler's gun sights.

The U.S. Response to War in Europe

Meanwhile, alarmed at the Nazi surge, President Roosevelt pressured Congress to modify its neutrality legislation and called for other "measures short of war" to help Britain and France. Late in 1939, Congress lifted the ban on selling military armaments to belligerents and authorized arms sales to all buyers who could pay cash and use their own ships for transport. Because its naval forces dominated the Atlantic sea lanes, Britain primarily benefited from this revised cash-and-carry policy.

The United States took other steps toward intervention. Congress granted the White House's request for new military funding and for enactment of the Selective Training and Service Act of 1940, the first peacetime draft in U.S. history. Worried about Britain's precarious military and financial position, Roosevelt facilitated the shipment of military supplies, sometimes claimed to be "surplus," to Great Britain. He also added two distinguished, pro-interventionist Republicans to what now seemed a war cabinet. Henry Stimson became secretary of war and Frank Knox secretary of the navy. These appointments gave Roosevelt's foreign policy a bipartisan image, if not fully bipartisan support.

Hitler focused his attention on the British Isles. From August through October 1940, Germany's air force, the **Luftwaffe,** conducted daily raids on Britain's air bases and nearly knocked out its Royal Air Force (RAF). On the verge of a kayo, however, Hitler suddenly changed strategy and ordered, instead, the bombing of London and other British cities—first by day and, then, by night. In addition to allowing the RAF time to recover, Hitler's move steeled Britain's resolve and bolstered the interventionist argument in the United States. Use of German airpower against British civilians, in what became known as "the Battle of Britain," aroused sympathy in the United States for their plight. U.S. radio correspondents began reporting, nightly, during Nazi bombing raids. The dramatic radio broadcasts of CBS's Edward R. Murrow, observed the writer Archibald MacLeish, "skillfully burned the city of London in our homes, and we felt the flames."

Map 26.1   German Expansion at Its Height   This map shows the expansion of German power from 1938 through 1942. Which countries fell to German control? Why might Americans have differed over whether these moves by Germany represented a strategic threat to the United States?

The Roosevelt administration, in turn, inched closer to intervention. In September 1940, it announced the transfer of 50 naval destroyers, from the era of World War I, to the British navy. In exchange, Britain granted the United States the right to build eight naval bases in its colonial territories in the Western Hemisphere. This "Destroyers-for-Bases" deal infuriated Roosevelt's opponents. Senator Burton K. Wheeler of Montana mailed out, at governmental expense, more than a million anti-interventionist postcards, a move that Secretary of War Stimson condemned as approaching "very near the line of subversion . . . if not treason."

After deciding to seek an unprecedented third term as president in 1940, however, Roosevelt seemed to shift course. He certainly began to speak more circumspectly, dishonestly according to his critics, about intervention. With his New Deal domestic programs fading from view and his foreign policy controversial, he appeared likely to face a strong Republican challenge. The GOP, turning away from candidates opposed to interventionism, nominated Wendell Willkie, a lawyer and business executive with solidly pro-Allied and internationalist leanings, to oppose FDR. While generally supporting Roosevelt's policy toward the Allies, this former Democrat also charged that the president would soon carry the United States directly into battle. In response, Roosevelt courted anti-interventionist votes by assuring "American mothers" that "your boys are not going to be sent into any foreign wars." Although the Republicans did better than they had done in 1936, Roosevelt rather easily defeated Willkie, gaining nearly 55 percent of the popular vote, and FDR's Democratic Party retained control of Congress. Once safely reelected, Roosevelt unveiled an ambitious plan to support Britain's war effort.

The president's moves continued to generate significant opposition. The America First Committee, organized by the head of Sears, Roebuck, and Company, intensified its crusade against intervention. The aviator-hero Charles A. Lindbergh, its most famous member, flew to mass rallies, all across the country, and joined anti-Roosevelt politicians, such as Senators Wheeler and Nye, in denouncing aid to the Allies.

Interventionists came to label all of their opponents as "isolationists," a single, derogatory term that obscures the diversity within the uneasy coalition opposed to U.S. engagement in the Second World War. Pacifists within this broad constituency opposed all wars, even those against fascist regimes, as immoral and mutually destructive. Some political progressives such as Senator Wheeler condemned fascism but feared that U.S. entry into war would lead to centralization of governmental power at home. Other anti-interventionists, such as Lindbergh, praised the fascist states as bulwarks against communism, and some even covertly shared Hitler's anti-Semitism. Avowedly anti-Semitic and pro-fascist organizations, such as the German-American Bund, openly defended Hitler's racial policies and denounced the "Jew Deal," a reference to the presence of Jewish advisers in President Roosevelt's inner circle. During the fall of 1941, a special subcommittee of the U.S. Senate began "Propaganda Hearings" into whether or not the Hollywood film industry, with its many Jewish producers, calculatedly made movies, such as *Confessions of a Nazi Spy* (1939), which promoted interventionism.

The opposition to aiding the Allies, then, did tap anti-Semitic sentiment in the United States. In 1939, congressional leaders had quashed the Wagner-Rogers bill, which would have boosted immigration quotas to admit 20,000 Jewish children into the United States. Seemingly bowing to anti-Semitic prejudices, the United States adopted a restrictive refugee policy. The consequences of the U.S. stance became especially grave after June 1941, when Hitler established the death camps that would systematically exterminate millions of Jews, gypsies, homosexuals, and anyone else whom the Nazis deemed unfit for life in the Third Reich and its occupied territories.

The Fight Against Interventionism   The movement to keep the United States out of the Second World War mobilized powerful personalities, impassioned rhetoric, and colorful imagery. This emblem, for example, invokes nationalistic and patriotic imagery in the cause of avoiding, rather than engaging in, war.

© The Granger Collection, New York

Meanwhile, those who favored assisting the Allied cause mounted a popular campaign of their own. The most prominent group, the Committee to Defend America by Aiding the Allies, headed by William Allen White, a well-known Republican journalist, organized more than 300 local chapters in just a few weeks during the spring of 1940. These organizations, much like their opponents, gathered a diverse constituency. Interventionists agreed, however, that a fascist-dominated Europe would soon threaten the security and safety of the United States. Isolationists claimed to stand for "America First," according to a pro-interventionist folk song, but ignored the likelihood that the fascists already saw "America next."

An "Arsenal of Democracy"

Franklin Roosevelt now vigorously pressed the case for stronger anti-Axis measures. Recognizing the sorry state of Britain's finances, the president proposed that the United States would now "lend-lease," or loan rather than sell, munitions to the Allies. Making the United States a "great arsenal of democracy," FDR claimed, would "keep war away from our country and our people." Debate over a **Lend-Lease Act** became bitter, and a divided Congress narrowly passed this controversial measure, which carried the patriotic-sounding title of "House Resolution 1776," on March 11, 1941. Several months later, when Germany turned its attention away from Britain and suddenly attacked the Soviet Union, its recent ally, in violation of the 1939 nonaggression pact, Roosevelt extended lend-lease assistance to Joseph Stalin's communist government.

While proclaiming an official U.S. policy of nonbelligerence, Roosevelt next began coordinating his military strategy with that of Britain. He secretly pledged to follow a Europe-first approach if the United States ever found itself fighting a two-front war against Germany and Japan, its Axis partner in Asia. Publicly, Roosevelt deployed U.S. Marines to Greenland and Iceland, a move that freed up the British forces that had been protecting these strategic Danish possessions following Germany's 1940 conquest of Denmark.

In August 1941, Roosevelt and Winston Churchill, Britain's Prime Minister, met on a ship off the coast of Canada. They worked toward formalizing a wartime alliance and concluded their meeting by issuing an "Atlantic Charter," which disavowed territorial expansion, endorsed protection of human rights and self-determination, and pledged the postwar creation of a new world organization that would ensure "general security." Roosevelt also agreed to Churchill's request that the U.S. Navy provide convoys, as far as Iceland, to the ships that were carrying lend-lease supplies to Britain. Soon, in an undeclared war in the North Atlantic, the U.S. Navy engaged Germany's formidable **"wolf packs,"** groups of submarines that preyed on Allied shipping.

The White House now firmly believed that defeating Hitler would require formal U.S. entry into the war, but it lacked domestic support for making this move. Privately, the president likely hoped Germany would commit some provocative act in the North Atlantic that would swing U.S. popular opinion decisively behind intervention. The October 1941 sinking of a U.S. destroyer, the *Reuben James,* did convince a majority in Congress to back Roosevelt's calls for repealing the neutrality legislation of the 1930s. Still, the tone of debate became so bitter and the margin favoring repeal so slim that the White House acknowledged Congress would still not pass a formal declaration of war.

Hitler's military strategy in Europe only complicated Roosevelt's course. While avoiding a repetition of the *Reuben James* episode in the North Atlantic, Germany focused its military energies on the Soviet Union, the communist-led nation for which most Americans felt far less empathy than they did for Great Britain. As it turned out, however, conflict with Japan, rather than with Germany, would bring the United States formally into the Second World War.

Pearl Harbor

Relations between Japan and the United States had steadily worsened during the late 1930s and early 1940s. In response to Japan's 1937 invasion of China, the United States extended economic credits to the beleaguered Nationalist Chinese government and curtailed sales of equipment to Japan. In 1939, the United States abrogated its Treaty of Commerce and Navigation with Japan, an action that meant further restrictions on U.S. exports to that island nation. A 1940 ban on the sale of aviation fuel and high-grade scrap iron aimed at slowing military advances by Japan throughout much of Southeast Asia.

Measures of this kind failed to halt Japanese expansion, now aided by the conflict then engulfing Europe. The European war prevented France, the Netherlands, and Great Britain from supporting their colonies in Asia, and militarists in Japan saw an opportunity to enlarge their own East Asian Co-Prosperity Sphere. Japanese forces thus pushed deep into French Indochina, seeking the raw materials Japan could no longer buy from the United States. Military planners in Tokyo also secretly prepared plans for attacks against Singapore, the Netherlands East Indies (later Indonesia), and the Philippines, a U.S. colonial possession.

Roosevelt continued to maneuver. He expanded the trade embargo against Japan, promised further assistance to Nationalist China, and accelerated an ongoing U.S. military buildup in the Pacific. In mid-1941, the president played his most potent diplomatic card: He froze all Japanese financial assets held in the United States. This move effectively gave the Roosevelt administration control over all commerce between the two countries, including trade in petroleum, the vital commodity that fueled Japan's economy and its dreams for expansionism.

Japanese expansionists now squarely faced a fateful decision. Despite diminishing economic and military prospects, they refused to abandon their goal of creating an East Asian empire. Instead, they began planning a preemptive attack against the United States. In light of their nation's limited supplies of raw materials, especially oil, Japanese strategists saw little hope for winning a prolonged war but imagined that a crippling, surprise blow might limit U.S. military capabilities and even bring economic concessions from Washington. General Hideki Tojo, who became his nation's wartime prime minister, viewed Japanese strategy as something of a rash gamble: "Sometimes a man has to jump with his eyes closed," Tojo remarked.

On December 7, 1941, Japanese bombers swooped down on U.S. naval facilities at **Pearl Harbor,** in Hawaii. Specially modified to operate from aircraft carriers, the planes destroyed much of the U.S. Pacific Fleet. Altogether, Japan sank or severely damaged 19 ships; destroyed or disabled nearly 200 aircraft; and killed more than 2,200 Americans. The damage might have been worse. U.S. aircraft carriers, which were out to sea at the time of the attack, avoided the Japanese bombers, which also failed to take out Pearl Harbor's fuel storage tanks and repair facilities.

Japan's assault against Pearl Harbor brought the United States into war rather than bringing it to terms. In a dramatic message to Congress, broadcast over radio, on December 8,

Roosevelt decried the attack. Coining the phrase that would serve as a U.S. battle cry throughout the war, he called December 7 "a date which will live in infamy."

Pearl Harbor would also live on in historical debates. Roosevelt's most implacable critics quickly began asking, for example, why much of the U.S. Pacific Fleet at Pearl Harbor lay vulnerable and unprepared, rather than on a state of full alert. Could Roosevelt and his advisers really have been unaware of an impending attack? U.S. intelligence, it would later be revealed, had broken Japan's secret diplomatic code—calling the decrypted messages "MAGIC"—and enjoyed some insight into Japanese intentions. Other critics came to charge FDR with adopting a series of calculated policies that were designed to provoke Japan. Deliberately inciting a Japanese attack, in this view, provided Roosevelt with a way of opening a "back door" through which the United States could enter the Second World War.

Most historians, however, view the Roosevelt administration as more unlucky and confused than duplicitous and devious. Its plan for deterring Japanese expansion by increasing U.S. naval forces in the Pacific and stationing bombers in the Philippines, within striking distance of Japan, simply failed to work. U.S. intelligence, based on intercepted messages and visual sightings, did expect a major military move from Japan in late 1941, but one toward Singapore or other British or Dutch possessions in Asia rather than at Pearl Harbor. Moreover, strategists in Washington, including the president, doubted that Japan's military planners had the skill or daring that an attack on Pearl Harbor entailed.

Pearl Harbor disarmed the noninterventionist movement and brought the United States, officially, into the Second World War. On December 8, 1941, Congress declared war against Japan. Representative Jeanette Rankin, a longtime peace activist from Montana who had voted against entry into the First World War, now stood as a lone dissenter. Nothing in the Tripartite Pact specifically required Hitler, unaware of Japan's plans for Pearl Harbor, to support his Axis ally. Roosevelt's "date of infamy" speech never even mentioned Germany, but a presidential radio address, delivered a day later, bluntly accused all three Axis Powers of hatching a coordinated plan to attack the United States. Two days later, on December 11, Germany (soon joined by Italy) did declare war on the United States. Hitler mistakenly assumed that fighting Japan would keep the United States preoccupied in the Pacific and, therefore, out of any major combat operations across the Atlantic Ocean. Axis strategists drastically underestimated the United States's ability to mobilize swiftly and effectively.

Fighting the War in Europe

Focus Question
What military strategies did the United States and the Allies ultimately adopt when fighting in both the European and Asian theaters of the Second World War?

Initially, the war went badly for the Allies. Even as Hitler tried to consolidate his grip over Western Europe, his forces were rolling across North Africa, and his submarines were slashing away at Allied supply lines in the Atlantic Ocean. During the months that followed Pearl Harbor, German U-boats, according to U.S. General George Marshall, came to "threaten our entire war effort." U.S. officials concealed the actual toll, but German subs operating in Atlantic waters, sometimes within sight of the U.S. shoreline, sank nearly 400 ships in less than six months. In the Pacific, Japan seemed unstoppable. Its forces overran Malaya, the Dutch East Indies, and the Philippines; then, Japan moved against the British in Burma and the Australians in New Guinea.

New governmental bureaucracies quickly guided a crash program for U.S. mobilization. Establishing military priorities—acquiring naval bases, securing landing rights for aircraft, ensuring points for radio transmission, and gaining access to raw materials for military production—became the immediate order of business. Soon thereafter, a series of governmental agencies, often staffed by people from the business world, began to direct economic decision making.

At the same time, a newly formed Joint Chiefs of Staff, consisting of representatives from each of the armed services, oversaw military matters. In January 1943, after 16 months of around-the-clock work, builders completed the War Department's Pentagon complex, a giant five-story, five-sided building that symbolized the nation's new military might—and the new place of the military in American life. Technological breakthroughs assisted the U.S. military effort. In 1942, aircraft equipped with radar, a critical new technology developed in collaboration with Britain, proved effective against submarines. During 1943, Germany's U-boat threat faded "from menace to problem," in the words of one U.S. naval strategist.

A highly sophisticated Allied code-breaking operation also played a crucial role in changing the course of battle. Realizing the importance of radio communication to his war plans, Hitler's scientists had integrated the complex ENIGMA encryption machine, first introduced during the 1920s, into Germany's war effort. Experts initially considered Germany's ENIGMA messages immune to code-breaking efforts. The cipher keys changed daily and offered 150 million million million ways of encoding any message. Then a group of Polish mathematicians, who had escaped just before German armies subdued their country, brought key ideas for decoding ENIGMA's secrets to Britain. Their insights contributed to a successful and super-secret Allied code-breaking program headquartered at Bletchley Park in England. At its height, the Bletchley Park endeavor, not officially acknowledged until 1974, employed 4,000 people, including many from the United States.

The Allied code-breakers gradually perfected their operation. Decrypted German messages, called "ULTRA" for "ultra-secret," gave the Allies a crucial military advantage, beginning with the Battle of Britain and Germany's campaigns in North Africa. Amazingly, German commanders never discovered how many of their intercepted and decoded radio communications reached Allied commanders—sometimes even before making their way to their intended German recipients. In the postwar world, the code-breaking operation at Bletchley Park would contribute to the development of computer technology.

Campaigns in North Africa and Italy

The Allied Powers continually clashed over military strategy. Although other nations, such as China, joined the Allied ranks, the United States, Great Britain, and the Soviet Union dominated. These three nations agreed on making Europe the primary focus of their efforts, and Roosevelt and his military strategists established a unified command with their British counterparts. The Soviet Union's Stalin, his armies facing the bulk of Germany's forces in Eastern Europe, called for a second front in Western Europe, created by an invasion across the English Channel into France, to relieve pressure on the USSR. Many of Roosevelt's advisers agreed: If German troops succeeded in knocking the Soviet Union out of the war, Hitler could turn his full attention toward Britain. Churchill, however, urged instead the invasion of North Africa, garrisoned by German forces and officially under the colonial control of Vichy France, as a way of first nibbling away at the edges of Nazi power—and at areas he considered vital to maintaining Britain's colonial interests in the Mediterranean.

A North African campaign against German forces, code-named TORCH, began with Anglo-American landings in Morocco and Algeria in November 1942. Under the command of U.S. General **Dwight D. Eisenhower**, the initial invasion force included 400 ships, 1,000 planes, and more than 100,000 troops. To ease his way, Eisenhower signed an armistice agreement with Admiral Jean Darlan, a Nazi sympathizer and the person officially in charge of Vichy France's colonies in North Africa. This arrangement, which allowed Darlan and his colleagues to retain their political positions, outraged Eisenhower's Free-French allies, notably General Charles De Gaulle, and many people in the United States. When Darlan's opponents assassinated him, shortly after the beginning of TORCH, one of Eisenhower's aides called it an "act of providence." Even as TORCH, aided by the ULTRA intercepts, moved forward, Free French leaders, particularly De Gaulle, continued to nurture their resentments against their U.S. Allies.

At a meeting in Casablanca, Morocco, in January 1943, Roosevelt sided with Churchill. Arguing that a cross-Channel invasion of France still seemed too risky, they succeeded in postponing it to some indefinite future. Roosevelt hoped clear-cut Allied victories, in advance of any Channel crossing, could bolster his own sagging political popularity in the United States. To assuage Stalin's fear that Britain and the United States might sign a separate peace with Hitler, Roosevelt and Churchill promised to remain at war until Germany agreed to an "unconditional surrender." Continuing disagreement over the timing for opening the Second Front in France, however, still strained relations among the Allies.

Meanwhile, in Eastern Europe, Joseph Stalin's Red Army slowly turned the tide of battle with a decisive victory after more than five months of bloody warfare in and around the Soviet city of Stalingrad. Abandoning a largely defensive response to Hitler's offensive during the late summer of 1942, Stalin's forces finally counterattacked in early 1943. They cut off and, then, ground down an entire German army, more than 1 million soldiers, at Stalingrad, and sent other German forces reeling backward for the first time during the war.

Stalin's Allies could soon claim victories of their own. Although Hitler poured reinforcements into North Africa, he failed to stop either TORCH or a drive westward from

Egypt by British forces. Caught in between, nearly 200,000 Axis troops in North Africa surrendered to the Allies during the spring of 1943. Later that summer, the Allies followed up the North African campaign by overrunning the island of Sicily and then fighting their way, slowly, northward through Italy's rugged mountains. Allied successes did boost civilian morale in the United States and Britain, but the Italian campaign also diverted badly needed resources away from the upcoming cross-Channel invasion, without loosening the Nazi stranglehold over Western Europe.

Some U.S. officials increasingly worried about the postwar implications of the Roosevelt-Churchill strategy. Secretary of War Henry Stimson, for example, warned that the Allied campaigns through Africa and Italy might leave the Soviet Union as the dominant power in most of Europe. Unless the United States soon directly confronted German might, he colorfully argued, Germany could be left holding "the leg for Stalin to skin the deer," making "dangerous business for us at the end of the war." Finally heeding such advice, Roosevelt agreed to establish a firm date for the cross-Channel invasion the Allies had so long promised Stalin.

Operation OVERLORD

Named Operation OVERLORD and directed by General Dwight Eisenhower, the invasion began on June 6, 1944, D-day. During the preceding months, Allied commanders assembled, in England, one of the largest invasion forces in world history. German officials obviously knew about these preparations, but a disinformation campaign and diversionary tactics fooled them into expecting the Allied landing would come at the narrowest part of the English Channel rather than in the Normandy region of France. A new code-breaking machine, which dramatically increased the number of ULTRA intercepts, allowed Allied intelligence officers to confirm that their deceptions had worked.

After several delays, because of inhospitable weather, Allied commanders executed their daring plan. As naval gunner crews pounded the Normandy shore, three divisions of paratroopers dropped behind enemy lines and disrupted German communications. Finally, at dawn on June 6, more than 4,000 Allied ships began landing troops and supplies. The first U.S. forces to come ashore at Omaha Beach met especially heavy German fire and took enormous casualties, but waves of invading troops continued to land. Only three weeks after D-day, more than a million Allied personnel controlled the French coast, clearing the way for the long-awaited second front. (**See Map 26.2, Allied Advances and Collapse of German Power, in the color insert following page 1056.**)

Just as the 1943 Battle of Stalingrad had reversed the course of the war in the East, OVERLORD changed the momentum in the West. Within three months, U.S., British, and Free French troops entered Paris. After repulsing a desperate German counteroffensive in Belgium, at the Battle of the Bulge in December 1944 and January 1945, forces under Eisenhower's command swept eastward, crossed the Rhine River, and prepared to head toward Berlin to meet up with westward-advancing Soviet troops.

The Allies, not surprisingly, disagreed on how to orchestrate Germany's final defeat. British strategists urged a rapid advance, in hopes of meeting up with Stalin's troops in

Berlin or even farther to the east of that city. General Eisenhower dissented. He favored a strategy that would produce fewer casualties among his troops and might assuage the suspicious Soviets about the postwar intentions of their western Allies. Doubtful that his troops could beat the Soviets into Berlin anyway, Eisenhower decided that any attempt to race to Berlin would undermine chances for postwar cooperation between the United States and the Soviet Union.

Eisenhower's view prevailed. He moved his troops cautiously along a broad front and, then, halted them at the Elbe River, west of Berlin. This guaranteed that Soviet troops, who took staggering casualties while approaching Berlin, would enter the German capital first. Although Hitler took his own life in order to avoid capture, the majority of Germany's Nazi elite and its wartime leadership did fall into Allied hands.

As the war in Europe drew to a close, the horrors perpetrated by the leaders of the Third Reich became fully visible. Hitler's murderous campaign of extermination, now called the Holocaust, took the lives of more than 5 million Jews, roughly half of Europe's prewar population of 10 million. The Nazis also murdered hundreds of thousands of other people, including gypsies, homosexuals, intellectuals, communists, the physically and mentally challenged, and people from various other identity groups. Only Germany's defeat closed down Hitler's death camps, but the Allies might have saved at least some people if they had helped them escape and emigrate. Allied leaders, however, worried about how to deal with large numbers of refugees and claimed they could not spare scarce ships to transport people to sanctuary. In 1943, after officials in Romania proposed the evacuation of 70,000 endangered Jews from its territory, for instance, the Allies never seriously considered accepting the offer. With few places to go, people who might have been spared went off to Nazi death camps.

The attempt to respond to Nazi atrocities continued for years. In 1945 and 1946, the Allies first brought 24 of Germany's top officials to trial at Nuremberg for "crimes against humanity." After a series of subsequent trials, more than 10,000 former German officials stood convicted of war crimes. Large quantities of money, gold, and jewelry that Nazi leaders had stolen from victims of the Holocaust and deposited in Swiss banks, however, remained concealed for more than 50 years. Not until 1997 did groups representing Holocaust survivors and the U.S. government force an investigation of the Swiss banking industry's holdings of stolen "Nazi gold," an inquiry that finally prompted some restitution for the families who had been victimized.

Meanwhile, following Hitler's suicide in April and Germany's final surrender on May 8, 1945, the military foundations for a postwar European settlement fell into place. Soviet armies controlled Eastern Europe; British and U.S. forces predominated in Italy and the rest of the Mediterranean; the four European Allies divided up zones of occupation in Germany and Austria. Allied leaders also turned to the task of transforming these military-produced arrangements into a comprehensive postwar political settlement in Europe, even as the war in the Pacific, which had officially begun at Pearl Harbor, remained far from over.

The Pacific Theater

For six months after Pearl Harbor, Japan's forces steadily advanced. Singapore fell easily. Japan overwhelmed U.S. naval garrisons in the Philippines and on Guam and Wake islands. After taking heavy casualties, Filipino and U.S ground troops surrendered at Bataan and Corregidor in the Philippines. After a much larger Japanese fleet ravaged a U.S naval contingent in the Java Sea, Japan's naval forces headed southward to menace Australia and New Zealand and eastward to threaten Hawaii.

Seizing the Offensive in the Pacific

As the United States rapidly built up its combat capabilities, military strategists adopted, of necessity, a largely defensive strategy. Then, in May 1942, the first U.S. naval victory, at the Battle of the Coral Sea, relieved some of the Japanese pressure on Australia. In response, Japanese naval commanders decided to hit back hard. They amassed 200 ships and 600 planes to destroy what remained of the U.S. Pacific fleet and to take Midway Island, perhaps in preparation for an assault against Hawaii. U.S. Naval Intelligence, however, broke enough of the Japanese code to warn Admiral Chester W. Nimitz. Surprising the Japanese armada, U.S. planes sank four Japanese carriers and destroyed a total of 322 planes. The Battle of Midway, in early June 1942, preserved the presence of the U.S. Navy in the mid-Pacific. Nimitz's forces did suffer substantial losses at Midway, but the far greater ones that they inflicted prevented Japanese commanders from continuing their offensive in the Pacific.

Two months later, U.S. amphibious forces splashed ashore at Guadalcanal in the Solomon Islands and finally ended Japan's threat to Australia. Although bloody engagements in the Solomons continued for months, on both land and sea, they ultimately achieved their major objective: permanently seizing the military initiative in the Pacific. According to prewar plans, Europe was to have received the highest priority, but by 1943, the United States, now massively rearmed, could devote roughly equal resources to both theaters of the war.

Combat in the Pacific Theater became, in the historian John Dower's phrase, a "war without mercy." Battlefield conditions reinforced racial prejudices, and the brutality already evident during Japan's initial assault against China continued. Japanese militarists expected the war would confirm the superiority of the divine Yamato race. Japanese captors, particularly on the Asian mainland, mistreated prisoners in almost unimaginable ways. The Japanese army's infamous "Unit 731" tested bacteriological weapons in China and conducted horrifying medical experiments on live subjects. Following the surrender of U.S. and Filipino troops in 1942, Japanese commanders, in what became known as the "Bataan Death March," forced their captives to walk, on meager rations of food and water, more than 60 miles.

The United States exhibited its own signs of racially based behavior. Wartime imagery, in both the U.S. government publications and in popular culture, often portrayed all Japanese people as animalistic subhumans. On the battlefield, U.S. troops could, on occasion, rival their Japanese adversaries in disrespecting enemy dead and in killing opposing forces rather than taking prisoners. The longer the war in the Pacific lasted, the more brutal it became.

China Policy

U.S. policy makers continued to hope that China's Nationalist government might eventually mount an effective military opposition against Japan and emerge, after the war, to lead a strong and united nation. Neither hope seemed realistic.

The United States tried to bolster China's armed forces. General Joseph W. Stillwell, who had been advising Chinese commanders on military matters since the Japanese invasion of the late 1930s, continually clashed with Jiang Jieshi. Friction between the prickly "Vinegar Joe" and Jiang eventually prompted Roosevelt, who hoped the Nationalist leader could become an important U.S. ally, to withdraw Stillwell from China. Stillwell's departure, however, brought no improvement in the performance of Jiang's military forces.

China's political instability complicated matters. The U.S. officials most attuned to Chinese politics agreed with Stillwell: Incompetence and corruption riddled Jiang Jieshi's Nationalist government. It could avoid engaging the Japanese invaders but still make extravagant demands for U.S. military assistance. China's ongoing civil war, which Jiang's forces seemed to be losing, further worried U.S. officials. A powerful communist movement, led by Mao Zedong, clearly fought more effectively than the Nationalist government against China's Japanese invaders, but the White House continued to envision Jiang as the future leader of a noncommunist China. On this crucial matter, the Nationalist leader's powerful backers in the United States, members of the "China Lobby," successfully pressured FDR and other political leaders, particularly those in the Republican Party, to support the Nationalist cause. Roosevelt thus insisted that Nationalist China retain its status as a full member of the Allied Powers, and he convinced Stalin to support Jiang, rather than his fellow communist Mao. All the while, Japan's advance into Chinese territory continued.

U.S. Strategy in the Pacific

In contrast to the European Theater, no unified command guided the war in the Pacific. Consequently, makeshift, compromise military decisions actions often emerged. General Douglas MacArthur, who commanded U.S. Army forces, insisted on an offensive launched from his headquarters in Australia through New Guinea and the Philippines and on to Japan. In May 1942, Japan had humbled the haughty and imperious MacArthur by forcing him out of the Philippines, and he had pledged he would, one day, return in victory. He now claimed that controlling the Philippines at war's end would advance U.S. strategic interests in the postwar world. Admiral Nimitz, the hero of Midway, saw strategic calculations somewhat differently. He favored a direct advance toward Japan, across the smaller islands of the central Pacific. Taking this route meant that the drive against Japan would bypass MacArthur's beloved Philippines.

Unable to decide between the two strategies, the Joint Chiefs of Staff authorized both, which moved forward, amidst fierce fighting and heavy casualties. MacArthur's forces took

New Guinea, and those commanded by Nimitz liberated the Marshall Islands and the Marianas in 1943 and 1944. Supporting these efforts, a Marine platoon of Navajo Indians established a unique, highly effective radio communication system. Employing their own language in imaginative coded variations, which Japanese intelligence officers never cracked, the members of this **Navajo Signal Corps** ensured that U.S. troops could securely exchange messages.

By late 1944, U.S. military forces finally came within range of Japan. The fall of Saipan meant that U.S. bombers could easily reach Japanese targets. The capture of the islands of Iwo Jima and of Okinawa during spring 1945 further shortened the distance between U.S. bases and Japan's major population centers. The battle for Okinawa, however, also confirmed the human costs of the island-hopping strategy: 120,000 Japanese and 48,000 American soldiers died. After contemplating these numbers, U.S. military planners dreaded the prospect of invading Japan's home islands.

Increasingly, reliance on airpower looked more and more enticing. Key members of the U.S. military had long attributed almost magical qualities to aerial bombardment. Some had even insisted that the mere threat of bombing could provide a means of deterring war as well as a way of conducting it. Careful analyses of strategic bombing during the Second World War, though, suggested less sanguine assessments. The Nazi bombardment during the Battle of Britain, for example, had inflicted heavy damage but only appeared to strengthen civilian morale, while never giving Hitler the quick victory he had expected. Subsequent Allied bombing against Germany, including controversial campaigns against

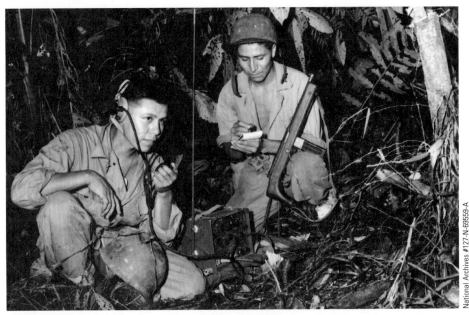

National Archives #127-N-69559-A

Navajo Signal Corps   Sending messages in their native language, which neither the Japanese nor the Germans could decipher, Navajo Indians in the Signal Corps made a unique contribution to preserving the secrecy of U.S. intelligence.

the civilian populations of Hamburg and Dresden, produced equally mixed results. Even as the Allies wreaked havoc on German cities, they endured losses in planes and pilots that seemed almost impossible to sustain over any length of time.

Nonetheless, U.S. strategists continued to see strategic bombing providing the crucial U.S. advantage in the Pacific. In February 1944, General Henry Harley ("Hap") Arnold devised a plan for firebombing major Japanese cities "not only because they are greatly congested but because they contain numerous war industries." Bombers added to the horror of war, Arnold conceded, but when used "with the proper degree of understanding" could become "the most humane of all weapons." President Roosevelt endorsed Arnold's air campaign, but it proved difficult to execute from bases in China.

In time, U.S. military victories opened the way for a more effective and lethal operation, run by General Curtis LeMay from Saipan in the Marianas. The blunt-talking LeMay, whom Arnold dubbed "the Babe Ruth of bombers," once summarized his strategy as "bomb and burn them until they quit." According to the official U.S. position, incendiary raids against Japanese cities constituted "precision" rather than "area" bombing. In actuality, as LeMay admitted, the United States measured the success of a mission by square miles of Japanese territory left scorched. According to a later estimate, the number of Japan's civilians who perished as a result of these raids exceeded the total of its troops killed in battle. Air attacks on Tokyo during the night of March 9–10, 1945, inaugurated the new policy. They leveled nearly one-quarter of the city and incinerated more than 100,000 people. **(See Map 26.3, Pacific Theater Offensive Strategy and Final Assault Against Japan, in the color insert following page 1056.)**

Meanwhile, as the war in the Pacific neared its end, a combined sea and air strategy emerged. The United States, under the agreement reached at the 1943 Casablanca Conference, still sought Japan's "unconditional surrender" by blockading its seaports, bombarding its cities from the air, and, perhaps, invading its home islands with U.S. combat units. Critics of the policy of unconditional surrender, which most Japanese assumed meant the death of their emperor, later suggested that it may have encouraged Japan's government to continue fighting, even when defeat seemed inevitable. This same stance also possibly prevented U.S. negotiators from more vigorously pursuing the peace feelers sent by some Japanese leaders. Anything less than unconditional surrender, its proponents counterclaimed, would have encouraged continued Japanese resistance. Whatever the case, the United States adopted a strategy of achieving total victory through massive destruction.

A New President, the Atomic Bomb, and Japan's Surrender

On April 13, 1945, newspaper headlines across the country announced: "PRESIDENT ROOSEVELT DEAD." After more than 13 years in office, an already frail FDR succumbed to a massive cerebral hemorrhage. Sorrow and shock spread through the armed forces, where many young servicemen and women could effectively remember no other president; through diplomatic conference halls, where Roosevelt's personal magnetism had often brought unity, if not always clarity; and among his many supporters, for whom Roosevelt had symbolized optimism during both economic depression and war.

Over the years, Roosevelt also accumulated a host of critics and enemies. His victory over Republican Thomas E. Dewey in 1944 rested on the smallest popular-vote margin in a presidential race since 1912. The GOP, extending gains it had made during the 1942 congressional elections, cut further into the once-overwhelming Democratic majorities in the Senate and House. Politically and physically weakened, Roosevelt fought to retain his dominant place in the political spotlight. Unaware of Roosevelt's precarious health, both Republican and Democrats assumed FDR would lead the United States into the postwar world.

Emerging from Roosevelt's shadow, the new president, **Harry S Truman,** initially seemed an unimposing presence. Born on a farm near Independence, Missouri, Truman had served in France during the First World War; become a U.S. Senator in 1934; and suddenly surfaced as Roosevelt's vice-presidential running mate in 1944. Roosevelt offered an upper-class image of well-practiced and worldly charm. The blunt-spoken Truman proudly presented himself as a "little man from Missouri." He also knew little about international affairs or about any informal understandings that Roosevelt may have made with Churchill and Stalin. During the period between Roosevelt's Fourth Inauguration in March 1945 and his death in mid-April, Truman met with FDR only three times.

Only after succeeding Roosevelt did Truman learn about events at Los Alamos, New Mexico. There, since the late 1930s, scientists from all across the world had been secretly working on a new weapon. Advances in theoretical physics suggested that the process of splitting atoms (fission) would release a tremendous amount of energy that could be packaged as a nuclear bomb. Fearful of Germany's outpacing the United States in this research, Albert Einstein, a Jewish refugee from Germany, had successfully implored Roosevelt to launch, on the basis of recent atomic knowledge, a crash bomb-building program. The government subsequently enlisted top researchers in the Manhattan Project, a huge, secret, military-directed operation. On July 16, 1945, the Project tested a workable atomic device at Trinity Site, near Alamogordo, New Mexico.

Truman and his top policy makers, eager to end the war quickly, decided to put the new weapon to immediate use. Planners agreed that any ground invasion of Japan's home islands would cost far too much in U.S. casualties. In addition, the Soviet Union, in a joint decision confirmed at a meeting of the Allies at the Potsdam Conference during the summer of 1945, would soon enter the Pacific Theater. Truman hoped to limit any advances that Soviet troops might make in the Far East as a way of curtailing Stalin's postwar influence there. Winston Churchill called the atomic bomb a "miracle of deliverance and a peace giver," and Truman, who always insisted it had been dropped on primarily military targets in Japan, later publicly claimed that he had never lost a night's sleep over its use.

Privately, he and other U.S. officials admitted to having greater qualms. Certainly, disagreement marked discussions over where and how to employ the new device. A commission of atomic scientists recommended a "demonstration" that would impress Japan with the bomb's destructive power without producing civilian casualties. General George C. Marshall suggested using it on purely military installations or only on manufacturing sites, after first warning away Japanese workers.

© Bettmann/CORBIS

© Bettmann/CORBIS

Total War: Dresden and Hiroshima The effects of "total war" are graphically illustrated in these photographs—of the devastation of Dresden, Germany (top), by the British Bomber Command and the U.S. 8th Air Force on February 13 and 14, 1945, and that of Hiroshima, Japan (bottom), by the U.S. 509th Composite Group on August 6, 1945. In the initial attack on Dresden, 786 aircraft dropped 5,824,000 pounds (2,600 long tons) of bombs on the city, killing an estimated 60,000 people and injuring another 30,000. An area of more than 2.5 square miles in the city center was demolished, and some 37,000 buildings were destroyed. To critics, the bombing of Dresden, a target that many argued was of little strategic value, exemplified the excessive use of airpower.

In sobering comparison, Hiroshima was devastated by one bomb weighing only 10,000 pounds (4.4 long tons)—an atomic bomb—dropped from one aircraft. The single U-235 bomb killed 68,000 people outright, injured another 30,000, and left 10,000 missing. (These figures do not include those who later developed diseases from deadly gamma rays.) The bomb obliterated almost five square miles of the city's center and destroyed 40,653 buildings. Truman reported the strike as "an overwhelming success." Many hailed the atomic bomb as a necessary step toward military victory; others worried about the dawn of the "nuclear age."

Ultimately, the Truman administration discarded these options. The United States needed, according to Secretary of War Henry Stimson, to make "a profound psychological impression on as many inhabitants as possible." In addition, LeMay's aerial bombardment of Japanese cities provided a powerful prologue to a nuclear attack. Many U.S. officials came to see the targeting of **Hiroshima** and Nagasaki, Japanese cities previously untouched by U.S. fire bombing, as a small departure from existing policy. "Fat Man" and "Little Boy," as the two atomic bombs dropped on August 6 and 9, 1945 were nicknamed, could seem merely larger and more lethal incendiary devices.

Stimson and most other observers soon acknowledged, however, that atomic weaponry introduced a new level of violence to world affairs. Colonel Paul Tibbets, who piloted the U.S. plane that dropped the first bomb on Hiroshima, reported that "the shimmering city became an ugly smudge . . . a pot of bubbling hot tar." Teams of U.S. observers who entered Hiroshima and Nagasaki in the aftermath of their bombing were stunned at the instantaneous incineration of both human beings and manmade structures, and shocked to contemplate the longer-lasting horror of radiation disease. Shortly after the atomic bombs fell on Japan, Stimson reconsidered his earlier view. He wrote Truman that atomic weaponry meant "a first step in a new control by man over the forces of nature too revolutionary and dangerous to fit into old concepts." The destruction of Hiroshima and Nagasaki inaugurated the "atomic age," one in which dreams of peace mingled with nightmares of destruction, potentially on a global scale.

During the late summer days of 1945, however, Americans who knew someone involved in the worldwide military effort invariably sighed with relief. News reports of August 15 heralded Japan's defeat. Those of September 2 reported its formal surrender, on "VJ Day," aboard the battleship *Missouri* in Tokyo Bay. Spontaneously, all across the nation, people flooded into the streets to celebrate the end of the Second World War.

The War at Home: The Economy

Focus Question
How did mobilizing for war produce political, economic, and social changes in the United States?

Securing military victory overseas depended on reviving, and then rapidly expanding, the domestic economy of the United States. Prewar production brought the Great Depression of the 1930s closer to an end, and wartime conditions quickly completed the recovery process. Moreover, innovations in wartime production processes promised to transform the nation's economic structure, its corporate and financial institutions, its labor force, and, perhaps, even the relationship between the economy and the national government.

Government's Role in the Economy

The federal bureaucracy grew, by one calculation, nearly 400 percent during the war. New governmental planning and regulatory agencies proliferated. The powerful War Production Board oversaw the conversion of factories to wartime production and, later, their expansion. It also planned resource usage and enforced production priorities and schedules. The War Labor Board adjudicated labor–management disputes, and the War Manpower Commission allocated workers to various industries. The Office of Price Administration regulated prices to control inflation and rationed scarce commodities such as gasoline, rubber, steel, shoes, coffee, sugar, and meat. Some observers who wished to expand on the New Deal of the 1930s imagined how the wartime system of economic controls might be adapted to peacetime conditions, while most of the Republicans and conservative Democrats in Congress looked forward to its postwar dismantlement.

From 1940 to 1945, the U.S. economy expanded rapidly, and the gross national product (GNP) rose, year-by-year, by 15 percent or more! When Roosevelt called for the production of 60,000 planes shortly after Pearl Harbor, skeptics sneered. Within a few years, though, the nation produced nearly 300,000 planes in a number of different designs. The Maritime Commission oversaw the construction of millions of tons of new ships. A once stagnant economy spewed out prodigious quantities of other supplies, including 2.5 million trucks and 50 million pairs of shoes. A worldwide war became one of "massed machines," the military journalist Hanson Baldwin observed.

In the cause of increasing production, most industries forged close relationships with governmental bureaucracies. Washington promoted, under the acronym of R&D, a coordinated plan for scientific and technological research and development. Greatly increased federal funding helped spawn new industries, such as electronics, and transform others, such as rubber and chemicals. Eventually, an Office of Scientific Research and Development contracted with universities and scientists for a variety of projects. Support from this governmental agency helped adapt radar and penicillin (initially British discoveries), rocket engines, and other new products for wartime use. The Manhattan Project provided the most dramatic example of the emergence of powerful new links between military-oriented R&D and the national government. In addition, this massive effort, which employed a number of people who had fled Nazi tyranny during the 1930s, demonstrated how much European-trained refuges might contribute to scientific and technological innovation.

Business and Finance

Washington pumped billions of dollars into the wartime economy. To finance the military effort, government spending rose from $9 billion in 1940 to $98 billion in 1944. In 1941, the national debt stood at $48 billion; at the end of the war, it would reach $280 billion. As production shifted from autos to tanks, from refrigerators to guns, the array of new consumer goods coming into the marketplace drastically shrank. In order to ensure that U.S. troops were adequately clothed, fed, and supplied, the government also set up an elaborate

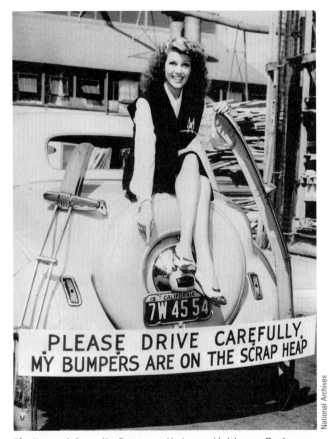

Rita Hayworth Scraps Her Bumpers   Movie stars aided the war effort by promoting the sale of war bonds and urging sacrifice. Here Hayworth urges Americans to scrap their unessential car parts.

system for rationing the amount of certain products—including foods, fabrics, and fuel—people could purchase. With fewer consumer products available, people invested in war bonds, turning their savings into tanks and planes. Sales of war bonds to ordinary people provided a relatively insignificant contribution to overall wartime spending, but bond drives helped raise personal saving to record levels and gave bondholders a direct stake, psychologically as well as economically, in the Allied cause.

Wartime conditions encouraged steps toward achieving greater economic equality. The rationing of items needed for the war effort overseas meant more equitable distribution of scarce goods at home. Increased taxes on wealthier Americans also helped redistribute income and narrow the gap in wealth between the very well-to-do and other people. Observers sympathetic to economic planning saw war bonds, rationing, and progressive taxation encouraging a sense of shared sacrifice and helping ease at least some of the domestic tensions evident during the 1930s.

At the same time, however, the war's emphasis on harmony helped Republicans and conservative Democrats make the case for sidetracking some of the earlier New Deal efforts, including controversial ones aimed at directly assisting the less affluent. The remarkable Republican surge in the off-year elections of 1942—the GOP gained 44 seats in the House and seven in the Senate—strengthened the anti–New Deal coalition in Congress. In 1943, legislators abolished the job-creation programs of the Works Progress Administration (WPA), the Civilian Conservation Corps (CCC), and the National Youth Administration (NYA) (see chapter 25). They also shut down the Rural Electrification Administration (REA) and Farm Security Administration (FSA), agencies most active in economically depressed rural areas. Moreover, as business executives flocked into government, to run the new wartime agencies, administrators in Washington began adopting a relatively cooperative stance toward large corporations.

Large businesses whose products seemed essential to wartime victory invariably flourished, often with governmental assistance. What seemed essential, of course, could become a matter of definition. Coca-Cola and the Wrigley chewing gum empire gained precious sugar allotments by arguing that GIs overseas needed to enjoy their products. The Kaiser Corporation, whose spectacular growth during the 1930s had been spurred by contracts for federal dam projects, now turned to building ships, aircraft, and military vehicles, including the famous "Jeep." By 1943, Kaiser controlled nearly one-third of the nation's military construction business, much of it taking place in Southern California, along the coastal corridor that stretched from San Francisco to San Diego. Elsewhere, federal subsidies and tax breaks enabled factories to expand and retool and corporations to prosper. The "cost-plus" provision, built into military contracts, guaranteed that manufacturers doing business with wartime Washington would gain a profit.

The Second World War also helped boost the economic power wielded by the largest corporations. After Roosevelt ordered his justice department to postpone enforcement of antitrust laws, government lawyers tucked away long-planned legal cases, such as one against America's great oil cartel. Congressional efforts to investigate possible collusion in the awarding of large government contracts and to increase assistance to small businesses made little headway. The top 100 companies, which had provided 30 percent of the nation's total manufacturing output in 1940, contributed 70 percent by 1943. Many smaller businesses, left to dealing in smaller niche markets only indirectly connected to war-related production, complained that Washington-based agencies short-changed them when allocating scare resources.

The Workforce

During the early years of the military buildup, people who had scrounged for jobs during the Great Depression began to find regular work. The primary job of governmental agencies, according to their leaders, involved obtaining employment for the people employers seemed most likely to hire. Thus, positions in heavy industry invariably went to men, and most of the skilled jobs to men of European descent. Initially, government-financed training centers also concentrated on white males and did much less for women and, particularly in the South, workers of color. As military service depleted the ranks of white males, however, other people became candidates for well-paid production jobs. In time, both private employers and public officials encouraged women to seek wartime work outside of their homes; African Americans from the rural South to move to industrial cities, including ones in the North and Far West; and Mexicans to enter the United States under the *Bracero* Agreement of 1942. In response to wartime necessities, then, the composition of the U.S. workforce changed significantly during the early 1940s.

Filling positions never before open to them, women became welders, shipbuilders, lumberjacks, and miners. Women won places in prestigious symphony orchestras, and one Major League Baseball owner financed creation of a separate women's league to give new life to the national pastime. Many employers hired married women who, before the war, would have been lucky to obtain a position even in traditionally "female occupations," such as teaching. Women of color moved into clerical and sales jobs, positions in which they had not previously been welcomed. Although wartime workplaces did generally remain segregated by sex—women usually working with other women and men alongside other men—the range of jobs open to women expanded.

The scope of unpaid labor, primarily provided by women, also expanded. Volunteer activities outside the home—such as Red Cross projects, civil defense work, and recycling drives—claimed more of the time of women, children, and older people. Government publications exhorted women to expand their homemaker routines: "Work in a garden this summer." "Save waste fats for explosives." "Wear it out, use it up, make it do, or do without." Both in the home and in the workplace, women's responsibilities and workloads increased.

The new labor market improved economic prospects for workers of color, especially African Americans. Many moved to labor-scarce cities in the North and West and into jobs previously closed to them. Despite the beginning of the northward migration earlier in the twentieth century, the prewar African American population had remained largely southern, rural, and agricultural; by the late 1940s, a substantial percentage of African Americans lived and worked outside of the South, in urban-industrial areas of the country. Although the war hardly eliminated discriminatory employment practices, twice as many African Americans held skilled jobs at the end of the conflict as at its beginning.

Washington did take some steps to address workplace discrimination. In June 1942, under pressure from African American union leaders led by A. Philip Randolph of the Brotherhood of Railway Porters, President Roosevelt issued an executive order creating the Fair Employment Practices Commission (FEPC). FDR charged this new governmental agency with attacking racial discrimination in hiring decisions. In 1943, the national government announced that it would not recognize as a collective bargaining agent any labor union that discriminated on the basis of race. In addition, the War Labor Board moved to outlaw the practice of paying different wages to whites and nonwhites for doing the same job.

For most of the people who found jobs, the war brought significantly higher wages and longer work hours. Although the government tried to limit wage increases during the war, the need to ensure rising production totals and the availability of overtime invariably meant larger paychecks. During the war, average weekly earnings for industrial workers rose nearly 70 percent. Farmers, who had suffered through many years of low prices and overproduction, doubled their incomes and then doubled them again.

The Labor Front

The labor union movement seemingly stood to benefit from the scarcity of home front workers during the war years. Membership rolls rose by 50 percent. Although women and workers of color joined unions in unprecedented numbers, white males, who still comprised the bulk of unionized workers, became the main beneficiaries of organized labor's new clout.

The commitment of most labor unions to their new female workers remained suspect. Not a single woman served on the executive boards of either the American Federation of Labor (AFL) or the Congress of Industrial Organizations (CIO). The International Brotherhood of Teamsters required its female members to accept revocation of their membership when the war ended. Unions did seek contracts stipulating equal pay for men and women who worked in the same position, but these helped only those women who could find a "male job." In addition, unions typically justified their stance on women employees as a way of ensuring employers would pay a "family wage," one on which a single male breadwinner could support a spouse and children. Union leaders seemed most interested in pressing for equal-pay provisions in order to maintain wage levels in jobs that they expected men to reclaim at war's end. It was also generally expected, when peace returned and employers trimmed workforces, that returning veterans, primarily men of European descent, would enjoy special preferences for the available job slots.

Some union leaders even resisted efforts to hire women and workers of color. Incorporating job-seekers from these groups, who were traditionally paid less than white males, into the wartime workforce might, they feared, jeopardize the gains unions had won during the hard-fought struggles of the 1930s. Early in the war, then, many union locals in the well-paying aircraft and shipbuilding industries flatly refused to enroll African Americans as members. After creation of the FEPC, some union leaders condemned governmental efforts to address racial discrimination as communist inspired. After greater numbers of African Americans managed to find jobs, racial tensions in the workplace sometimes led to direct confrontations. In various parts of the country—at a defense plant in Lockland, Ohio, at a transit company in Philadelphia, at a shipbuilding company in Mobile, for instance—white workers walked off the job to protest the hiring of African Americans. Management intended to use the war, protestors generally charged, as an excuse to erode union power by changing the composition of the workforce.

Other forms of grassroots labor militancy, although muted by a wartime no-strike pledge, persisted into the 1940s. Wildcat strikes erupted among bus drivers in St. Louis, assembly-line workers in Detroit, and streetcar conductors in Philadelphia. In the Motor City, a disgruntled group of aircraft workers, angry at increasing regimentation of the production process, fanned out across a factory floor and cut off the neck ties worn by supervisory personnel. Despite the no-strike assurance, the United Mine Workers called a walkout in the bituminous coal fields in 1943. A hard line by the War Labor Board against the union's demands only appeared to prolong the strike. Roosevelt's secretary of interior blasted both sides in the dispute and called the walkout "a black and stupid chapter in the history of the home front." A Congress increasingly hostile to union interests weighed in as well. In 1943, it passed the Smith-Connally Act, which empowered the president to seize plants or mines if strikes interrupted war production. The Second World War, then, may have quieted but never halted labor–management conflict.

Assessing Economic Change

Overall, the war had a substantial effect on the nation's political economy. During the conflict, most workplaces became more inclusive, in terms of gender and race, than ever before. So did labor unions. More people entered the paid labor force, and many earned more than rationing restrictions on consumer goods allowed them to spend. In a remarkable reversal of conditions during the Great Depression, savings piled up. Wartime production demands helped strengthen organized labor's place in the U.S. economy. By the end of the Second World War, union membership stood at an all-time high.

Perhaps most significantly, the Second World War helped accelerate long-term changes in the institutional scale of economic life. Big government, big business, and big labor all grew even larger. Scientific and technological innovations forged new links of mutual interest between governmental agencies and large corporations, particularly those directly involved in military-related production. An older United States—one marked by family farms, family-run businesses, and small towns—did not disappear, but urban-based, bureaucratized institutions were increasingly coming to dominate daily life, especially in most areas of the nation's burgeoning economy.

A New Role for Government?

The growth of governmental power during war years prompted new debate over the role of government in a postwar world. During the heyday of the New Deal during the 1930s, a relatively broad view of governmentally guaranteed "security" had enabled creation of programs such as the Social Security System and of federal agencies to secure home mortgages and personal savings accounts. At the same time, grassroots community-based groups, often working with labor unions, had begun building a set of cooperative social welfare and health institutions they hoped would create a vast, nonprofit security-safety net.

Although the New Deal had begun running out of political cards even before U.S. entry into the war, President Roosevelt and some of his advisers began to suggest new initiatives as military victory seemed increasingly likely. They talked of reharnessing the national government's power behind expanded efforts to enhance security in everyday life. Some dreamed, for example, of extending the government's wartime health care and day care programs into a more comprehensive social welfare system.

In 1944, FDR introduced his most ambitious domestic agenda in years: a "Second Bill of Rights." He called for measures to ensure that Americans could enjoy the right to a wide range of substantive liberties. These were to include regular employment, adequate food and shelter, appropriate educational opportunities, and guaranteed health care. Whenever people could not otherwise obtain these material conditions, the national government should use its power to ensure their availability. Translating this vision into reality, its proponents generally assumed, would require the national government to continue the kind of economic and social planning it was doing in wartime. The Second Bill of Rights, then, proposed that postwar politics and governance focus on guaranteeing individuals and families security in their everyday lives.

The vision of providing greater security appealed to more than hardcore New Dealers. Large insurance companies and some private businesses, recognizing the popularity of security-focused proposals, came forward with new private alternatives to governmental programs. Insurers expanded earlier efforts to market their own array of programs, directed toward individual policy holders, for providing security against sickness, disability, and unexpected death. At the same time, insurance companies worked with some large corporations to develop group insurance plans as substitutes and also as supplements to the kind of governmental programs already provided by the New Deal and imagined in the Second Bill of Rights.

The War at Home: Social Issues and Social Movements

The wartime years, along with the search for military victory overseas, highlighted a wide range of domestic social issues. Many people, ordered by their military superiors or attracted by new employment possibilities, moved away from the communities in which they had grown up. Mobilizing for military victory seemed to demand a willingness to change. At the same time, the wartime emphasis on preserving traditional ideals, including liberty and equality, helped spotlight how often social conditions in everyday life departed from idealized depictions.

Selling the War

The effort to sell a war overseas brought new attention to social issues at home. During the First World War, government propagandists had portrayed a struggle to end war and bring about a more democratic and peaceful world. Fighting for such idealistic goals, however, carried far less appeal during the 1940s. Only 20 years after Woodrow Wilson's "war to end all wars," after all, the United States found itself fighting a Second, and far wider, World War. Attuned to popular attitudes, the Roosevelt administration called on citizens to fight more for the preservation of a vague concept called the "American Way of Life" at home than for the transformation to a more democratic, peaceful world.

The work of the illustrator Norman Rockwell and of the movie director Frank Capra, masters of nostalgia, exemplified wartime image-making. Rockwell produced a set of iconic paintings that visualized President Roosevelt's "Four Freedoms": Freedom of Speech, Freedom of Worship, Freedom from Want, and Freedom from Fear. Using his neighbors in Arlington, Vermont, as models, Rockwell depicted these values as already comfortably rooted in small-town America. Originally published in the *Saturday Evening Post* magazine, Rockwell's "Four Freedoms" eventually adorned millions of posters distributed by the government.

Hollywood studios and directors eagerly answered the wartime call. "The American film is our most important weapon," proclaimed one Hollywood executive. The film factory produced both commercial movies with military themes, such as *Destination Tokyo* (1943), and documentaries, such as the *Why We Fight* series, directed by Frank Capra. During the 1930s, Capra's films had championed the decency and good sense of ordinary people (portrayed by stars such as Gary Cooper and Barbara Stanwyck) in movies such as *Mr. Deeds Comes to Town* (1936). Commissioned by Washington to dramatize why citizens should fight against the Axis, Capra put Rockwell-like characters in motion and contrasted the freedom of their daily routines with the tightly regimented lifestyles in the military-dominated dictatorships of Germany, Italy, and Japan.

Much of Hollywood followed Capra to war. Many of its shining stars and lesser players served in combat units, while most other Hollywood personalities sold war bonds, entertained the troops, and worked on documentaries for the Army's Pictorial Division. Darryl F. Zanuck of Twentieth Century Fox filmed Allied troops in North Africa and the Aleutian Islands, and the director-producer John Ford crafted powerful documentaries about Pearl Harbor and the Battle of Midway. Walt Disney's studio devoted most of its animation resources to the production of war-related cartoons and short features.

The advertising industry also contributed. The Roosevelt administration encouraged it to sell his "Four Freedoms," and most advertising professionals obliged. In their vision, freedom generally appeared in the form of new washing machines, improved kitchen appliances, streamlined automobiles, a wider range of lipstick hues, and other consumer products. Although wartime rationing prevented people from immediately acquiring these kinds of products, wartime ads promised that, once the fighting ended, technological know-how would transform the United States into a consumer's paradise. People could soon enjoy living in a bigger and better version of the prosperity-soaked world still associated, in popular memory and culture, with the 1920s (see chapter 24).

After initially resisting the idea of establishing a specific propaganda agency, Roosevelt finally did authorize, during the spring of 1942, creation of the Office of War Information (OWI). The OWI replaced an earlier, less aggressive effort, located in an Office of Facts and Figures. The President charged the OWI with coordinating a full range of informational initiatives. Many New Deal Democrats saw the OWI catering to advertisers who preferred

CASABLANCA (1942)

Directed by Michael Curtiz. Starring Humphrey Bogart (Rick Blaine), Ingrid Bergman (Ilsa Lund), Paul Henreid (Victor Lazlo), Conrad Veidt (Major Strasser), Claude Rains (Captain Renault), Dooley Wilson (Sam)

Casablanca, perhaps the most popular movie ever produced by the old Hollywood studio system, began as a rather modest wartime collaboration between Warner Brothers and the OWI. The studio provided the stars, the script, and the crew. The OWI offered guidance on how best to portray the Allied cause. It successfully urged, for example, that the role of "Sam," an African American piano player and singer, be related, more specifically than in earlier drafts of the script, to contemporary civil-rights issues.

Released in New York City at the same time, November 1942, that Allied forces were pursuing their TORCH campaign in North Africa, *Casablanca* contains numerous references to wartime themes and events. Most powerfully and pointedly, the film's own placement in cinematic time, December 1941, creates numerous opportunities to disparage isolationism. On several occasions, dialogue in the movie cleverly alludes to a real-life incident, the Japanese attack on Pearl Harbor, which will not happen until after *Casablanca*'s own narrative time frame ends. This technique, used in virtually every Hollywood film about familiar historical events, encourages viewers to take pride in their ability to spot historical references. Most important to *Casablanca*'s political agenda, these allusions to past events underscore its support for the necessity of U.S. involvement in the Second World War.

More often than not, though, *Casablanca* works to conceal its political messages by entangling them in a set of personal dilemmas faced by its male lead, "Rick Blaine," memorably played by Humphrey Bogart. Once an antifascist activist, who had "run guns to Ethiopia" and had fought fascism in Spain during the 1930s, Rick now only wants to isolate himself from larger causes and to preside over his gambling saloon in Casablanca. Remaining aloof from global politics, he watches refugees from fascism stream through this North African city on their way, hopefully, to freedom in the United States. For mysterious reasons, however, Blaine cannot or will not return home but, instead, runs "Rick's American Café," located at the edge of the North African frontier.

There seems little mystery, however, about the root cause of Rick's personal isolationism: a beautiful woman named "Ilsa Lund," portrayed by Ingrid Bergman. Before the Nazis stormed into Paris in 1939, Rick and Ilsa had planned to flee the city together, but she had left him waiting at the train station. Only when Ilsa unexpectedly resurfaces, two years later in Casablanca, does Rick learn why she had abandoned him. As she was preparing to leave Paris, news arrived that her husband, an antifascist crusader named "Victor Lazlo," had not perished, as she had thought, at the hands of the Nazis. Respecting her marriage vows, Ilsa had rushed to the injured Victor and nursed him back to health.

Trapped in Casablanca with a now-recovered Lazlo, Ilsa presents Rick with a series of personal and political dilemmas. She pleads with him, after her own husband's entreaties go unheeded, to help Victor escape to the United States, from where he can resume his antifascist activism. As long as Lazlo stays in Casablanca—nominally under the legal control of Vichy France but effectively under the thumb of a murderous Nazi officer, "Major Strasser"—his political reputation presumably protects him from immediate danger. At the same time, though, Lazlo's continued presence in North Africa makes him of little immediate value to the Allied cause, the one that the brooding Rick refuses to assist. Although Rick claims his noninterventionist policy stems from a commitment to political neutrality, the movie makes clear that personal considerations dominate his politics. Lazlo will only leave Casablanca with Ilsa, whom Rick suspects remains as romantically attracted to him as he still is to her.

Casablanca's script conveniently provides Rick with the means to help Ilsa and Lazlo—or Ilsa and himself—flee together: two blank "letters of transit," which have been hidden in Rick's Café. These documents, according to the movie's shaky legal logic, permit anyone, even Lazlo, to depart from Casablanca on the next plane flight. If Rick were to give the letters to Lazlo, he stands, once again, to lose Ilsa and to compromise his noninterventionist political principles. If he uses the documents to flee Casablanca with Ilsa, he will harm the Allied cause by preventing Lazlo from actively rejoining it. Will Rick, once a heroic activist, continue to remain uninvolved? Is there any way he can reconcile the conflicting demands he now confronts?

As *Casablanca* constructs Rick Blaine, Bogart's character can cut through all of these problems simply by embracing the role of a lone outlaw-hero, the iconic protagonist of so many of Hollywood's western movies. Blaine thus abandons his earlier reluctance to take a stance—along with the married woman he still loves—and takes the kind of decisive, if technically illegal, action that marks him as both manly and principled.

Symbolically structured as what film scholars call a "disguised western," *Casablanca* ends with Rick becoming a modern, North African version of an Old West gunfighter. At the point of a pistol, Blaine forces a duplicitous Vichy police officer, "Captain Renault," to sign the letters of transit over to Victor and Ilsa. Then, Rick turns his persuasive charms on Ilsa, who has mistakenly come to believe he will allow her to abandon Lazlo and leave Casablanca with him. These two lovers must set aside personal feelings, Rick implores her, and help her husband return to his antifascist work. When Major Strasser makes a last-ditch effort to stop Victor and Ilsa from boarding an outbound plane, Blaine simply guns him down. As the movie ends, Rick plans to light out, with Captain Renault rather than Ilsa as his traveling companion, for the North African frontier and join a Free French brigade—and the Allied cause.

Casablanca thus frames the fictional Rick Blaine's personal and political problems as symbolically parallel to those that the United States and its like-minded citizens faced before their own real-life entry into the Second World War. Seeing Humphrey Bogart make all the "correct" decisions, presumably, will help convince *Casablanca*'s wartime viewers that their political leaders, and they, are now working through the consequences of having made similarly appropriate ones. Watching *Casablanca* today, perhaps, helps convince viewers that people such as the fictional Rick Blaine really did make up America's "greatest generation."

One of Classical Hollywood's most powerful motion pictures, *Casablanca* (1943) highlighted the personal and political dilemmas raised by U.S. entry into the Second World War. Here, Rick (Humphrey Bogart), Ilsa (Ingrid Bergman), and Sam (Dooley Wilson) uneasily recall their past in pre-war Paris and ponder their wartime futures.

imagery extolling the future joys of consumerism rather than those promoting broader visions of liberty and equality. Interpreting OWI-sponsored images very differently, Republicans blasted the agency for cranking out crass political appeals for causes favored by Roosevelt's New Dealers. While fending off its critics, the OWI set up branch offices throughout the world, published a widely distributed magazine called *Victory,* and produced hundreds of films, posters, and radio broadcasts.

Gender Issues

Popular portrayals of why the nation was fighting the Second World War increasingly clashed with how wartime mobilization was changing everyday life. The gap between Rockwell-type imagery and daily demands became readily apparent in the range of social issues affecting women.

The wartime United States called on women to serve their country as more than wives and mothers. Some 350,000 women volunteered for military duty during the war, and more than a thousand became pilots for the Women's Air force Service Pilots (WASPs). Not everyone approved of the changes. One member of Congress asked, "What has become of the manhood of America?" Most of his colleagues, however, supported creation of a woman's corps in each branch of the military, an innovation proposed but never adopted during the First World War.

© CORBIS

Pin-up Girls   Male GIs often surrounded themselves with pin-up girls, images very different from that of the home front Rosie-the-Riveter.

Military service by women, together with their expanding roles in the wartime labor market, prompted debate over the possibility of enacting new legal-constitutional measures. Congress debated, without ever passing, a national equal-pay law and an Equal Rights Amendment (ERA) to the U.S. Constitution. Women's organizations disagreed among themselves over how to proceed. Groups claiming to speak for middle-class women, for example, strongly backed the ERA, but ones representing women who worked outside their homes, often for low wages, opposed its passage. They saw the ERA as a potential threat to the constitutionality of the array of special protective legislation, regulating hours and hazardous conditions, which reformers of the Progressive Era had struggled to obtain for women workers. Wartime conditions, then, helped refocus an earlier debate: Should working women continue to be accorded a protected status, in view of their vulnerability to exploitation in male-directed work environments, or would they ultimately benefit from gaining completely equal legal and constitutional status with men?

Even as wartime necessity helped alter older gender patterns in employment, widespread imagery frequently worked to frame the changes as temporary. Works of popular culture, for example, often portrayed the wartime participation of women in the workplace as a short-term anomaly and as a temporary sacrifice intended, ultimately, to preserve and protect their "natural" sphere in the home. Moreover, most wartime imagery tended to reinforce familiar ideals of femininity. A typical ad suggesting that women take on farm work declared: "A woman can do anything if she knows she looks beautiful doing it."

In some ways, the war may have even widened the symbolic gap between notions of femininity and masculinity. Male-dominated military culture seemed to foster the glamour-girl ideal. Service publications regularly featured pin-up sections and encouraged servicemen to decorate their wartime world—their sleeping quarters, their airplanes, even their tanks—with overt images of female sexuality. The home front entertainment industry, led by Hollywood, promoted its glamorous female stars as anxious to "please their boys" in the military. Some of the wartime popular culture came to associate masculinity with misogyny. Coming out of the war, the tough-guy genre, on prominent display in Hollywood's thrillers and in the author Mickey Spillane's series of "Mike Hammer" detective novels, portrayed female sexuality as both alluring and threatening to men.

Public policy making sometimes worked to reinforce gender divisions. The military assigned most of the women who joined the armed services to clerical and supply jobs, usually within the United States. The government and some private employers did provide, with differing degrees of enthusiasm and financial support, day care programs for mothers working outside of their homes. Although the thousands of centers set up during the conflict provided a precedent for future policy makers, the actual number of facilities met only a fraction of the child care need. Many centers, moreover, quickly shut their doors after the war's end. Meanwhile, social scientists often blamed mothers who worked outside of their homes during the war years for an apparent spike in rates of juvenile delinquency and divorce, and they pondered how new public policies might reverse these trends.

Racial Issues

The Second World War affected issues related to race as well as gender. The United States entered the global conflict as a nation in which many areas of daily life, particularly in the South and Southwest, featured highly visible signposts of racial and ethnic separatism. Citizens of African descent constantly negotiated an elaborate system of legalized segregation throughout southern states. Effectively disenfranchised politically in the South, African Americans in the rest of the country continued to experiment with how best to use the political power they had gained during the 1930s. In California and throughout the Southwest, residents who traced their ancestry back to Mexico, including many who had long resided in the United States, continued to work on addressing a wide range of issues involving employment, education, and housing.

After the United States formally entered the war, President Roosevelt refused to abandon the settled policy of racial segregation in the U.S. armed forces. Although the Army integrated Latino and American Indian soldiers, along with those from various European ethnic groups, into its combat units, military leaders refused to do the same for people of African and Japanese ancestry. Groups such as the NAACP pressed for integration, but Roosevelt's top advisers claimed that eliminating Jim Crow in the military could interfere with the nation's combat capabilities. The Red Cross and the U.S. Army even adopted the scientifically absurd practice of segregating donated blood into separate stores of "white" and "black" plasma.

Military officials often placed African Americans in inferior or highly dangerous support positions and initially excluded most of the segregated fighting units from combat duty. The White House deferred to these decisions, supported by white Democrats from the South who feared that permitting African Americans to join the fight for freedom abroad on an equal basis with other Americans might encourage attempts at desegregation at home. Toward the end of the war, when troop shortages forced the government to put segregated African American units into combat, these units invariably performed with distinction.

Wartime social tensions sometimes flared into open conflict. Within the military, for example, a 1944 explosion at an ammunition depot at Port Chicago, near San Francisco, killed 300 U.S. Navy dockworkers, all of them inadequately trained and most of African descent. When naval officers ordered other black sailors to similar duty, some refused, citing dangerous working conditions. The resulting court martial of 50 African Americans became the largest mass trial in naval history. A military court found all of them guilty of disobeying orders and imposed lengthy prison terms. After the war, the navy reduced the sentences and released the prisoners but refused requests to overturn their convictions. The Port Chicago incident remained a vivid memory among African Americans, and civil-rights groups continually pressed for redress. Finally, in 1999, one of the convicted sailors, Freddie Meeks, received a presidential pardon.

Meanwhile, on the wartime home front, a variety of volatile racial issues continued to simmer. As the wartime production system created more jobs, vast numbers of people from the rural South, including several hundred thousand African Americans, continued to move northward to cities such as Los Angeles and Detroit. The people already living in these areas often chafed at the influx of newcomers, who competed with them for jobs and housing and who placed greater demands on public services such as transportation, education, and recreational facilities.

Urban housing projects sometimes became sites of conflict. White residents of these facilities generally charged governmental agencies, when they attempted to challenge racial discrimination, with acting heavy-handedly, while persons of color criticized public officials for failing to move aggressively enough. In Buffalo, New York, threats of violence caused officials to cancel the construction of one housing project. In Detroit, in early 1942, that city's mayor deployed police officers in order to prevent clashes at the racially integrated Sojourner Truth site from escalating into something more serious.

The type of social strains evident early on in Detroit began to flare into violence. This escalation most often occurred in overcrowded urban spaces, where diverse populations and cultures already competed and clashed with one another. In Detroit, in June 1943, conflict between white and black youth at an amusement park rapidly spiraled into a multiple-day riot. Nearly 40 people, most of them African American, lost their lives before federal troops, dispatched by FDR at the request of the mayor of Detroit and the governor of Michigan, arrived in the Motor City. Critics of Detroit's police force charged it with not responding forcefully enough to the first disturbances, while the NAACP charged it with overreacting and with targeting black people, 17 of whom died as a result of deadly force used by officers. The violence in Detroit left hundreds injured and inflicted millions of dollars worth of damage to property. Federal troops remained in the city for six months after their initial deployment in June. The following month, Roosevelt sent another military force into New York City's Harlem to quell disturbances there.

Clashes extended beyond those between people of European and African descent. In Los Angeles, the "Zoot Suit Riots" of 1943 grew out of a complex set of social issues that had been roiling that fast-growing metropolis over the past several years. These included competition for control over contested public spaces, such as dance halls and jazz clubs; cultural-ethnic differences in dress and entertainment styles; and ethnic bitterness, especially growing out of the contentious 1942 "Sleepy Lagoon" murder case, which had produced controversial guilty verdicts (later reversed) against a group of Mexican American defendants. When social tensions finally produced violence, in late May and early June of 1943, the worst incidents initially pitted servicemen of European descent against young Mexican American men who were sporting **zoot suits.** This flamboyant outfit, which featured oversized coats and trousers, had come to exemplify ethnic pride and protest against wartime restrictions that seemed to fall hardest on communities of color.

For several days, increasingly larger groups of soldiers and sailors from nearby military bases entered the fray and stormed through parts of Los Angeles. Critics claimed that the city's police force did little to stop roving bands of servicemen, sometimes augmented by white residents of LA, who broadened their targets to include both African and Mexican Americans, whether zoot-suited or not. Police, the same critics charged, seldom hesitated to crack the heads of the young men who fought back. Largely ignoring the greater dimensions of what was going on in their city, members of the LA city council passed a resolution that made wearing a zoot suit a criminal offense. Finally, military authorities barred servicemen from coming into LA, a move that helped restore order.

Even when wartime tensions did not produce the kind of violence seen in Detroit and Los Angeles, the Second World War highlighted long-standing social issues. For many American Indians, for instance, the wartime years increased the pressures associated with longer-term patterns of migration and assimilation. Approximately 25,000 Indian men and several hundred Indian women served in the armed forces. Tens of thousands of other Indian men and women, many leaving their reservations for the first time, found wartime

© Universal Pictures/ Courtesy: Everett Collection

Zoot Suit Directed by Luis Valdez and based on his earlier stage play, the motion picture *Zoot Suit* (1981) recalled ethnic tensions in Los Angles during the Second World War. Starring Edward J. Olmos and Daniel Valdez, this innovative musical drama highlighted the struggles waged by Mexican Americans over space, identity, and legally protected rights. *Zoot Suit* explores, for example, how styles of masculine dress could become matters over which people would fight.

work in urban areas. Rapid City, South Dakota, near the Pine Ridge Reservation, attracted more than 2,000 Indians, most of whom settled in informal camps around city. Other cities with nearby reservations—such as Gallup, New Mexico; Flagstaff, Arizona; and Billings, Montana—became magnets for those seeking wartime work. Many people moved back and forth between city and reservation, where economic opportunities remained limited, and tried to juggle the problems produced by living in two significantly different worlds.

People of Japanese descent faced a unique set of social issues during the war. Shortly after the attack on Pearl Harbor, a powerful anti-Japanese political movement claimed to see signs of an impending sabotage campaign along the nation's West Coast, where most people of Japanese descent then lived. One military report claimed that a "large, unassimilated, tightly knit racial group, bound to an enemy nation by strong ties of race, culture, custom, and religion . . . constituted a menace" that justified extraordinary action.

Lacking evidence of any significant pockets of disloyalty, President Roosevelt nonetheless overrode objections from within his own administration and caved into political pressures. In February 1942, he issued Executive Order 9066, which directed the forced relocation of first- and second-generation Japanese Americans (called Issei and Nisei, respectively) and their internment in hastily constructed detainment camps located far away from West Coast areas. Significantly, in Hawaii, where the presumed danger of subversion should have been much greater, no similar mass internment took place. There, people of Japanese ancestry constituted nearly 40 percent of the population, and U.S. officials conceded their centrality to the local wartime economy.

The Roosevelt administration ultimately uprooted nearly 130,000 people of Japanese descent from their West Coast homes. Native-born U.S. citizens, including many young children, comprised two-thirds of the detainees. The relocation forced Japanese Americans to abandon their possessions and businesses or to sell them for a pittance before being transported to flimsy barracks surrounded by barbed wire and under armed guard. Many left behind thriving agricultural enterprises that were vital to wartime production. Civil libertarians generally condemned the internment program as militarily unnecessary and as unconstitutional, but a divided U.S. Supreme Court upheld its validity in *Korematsu* v. *U.S.* (1944). The Roosevelt administration closed the camps even before Japan's surrender, and in 1988, the U.S. Congress finally officially apologized for the internment. It also authorized payment of a cash indemnity to anyone who had been confined in the internment facilities.

Social Movements

The global fight against fascism proved helpful to the movements that were working for social change in America. German Nazism, with its doctrines of Aryan supremacy and racial inequality, helped expose the ugly underpinnings of older social science research. "The Huns have wrecked the theory of the master race with which we were so contented so long," lamented one pro-segregationist politician from Alabama. At the same time, the antifascist climate of the war years gave greater visibility to an expanding body of alternative research that saw racial difference as embedded in culture, rather than biology, and buttressed a growing conviction that a democracy could eliminate discrimination and bridge racial and ethnic gulfs.

The northward migration of African Americans contributed to efforts for social change. The nearly 750,000 African Americans who relocated to northern cities began to taste, for the first time in their lives, the real possibility of exerting political power. They found an outspoken advocate of civil rights within the White House. First Lady Eleanor Roosevelt repeatedly antagonized southern Democrats and members of her husband's administration by her advocacy of civil rights and her well-publicized participation in integrated social and political functions.

The *Amsterdam News*, a newspaper aimed at African Americans, called for a "Double V" campaign—victory at home as well as abroad. The labor leader A. Philip Randolph promised to lead tens of thousands of black workers in a march on Washington to demand more defense jobs and integration of the military forces. President Roosevelt feared the event would embarrass his administration and urged that it be canceled. Randolph's persistence ultimately forced Roosevelt to create the Fair Employment Practices Commission (FEPC). If this new agency gained little effective power over day-to-day events, its existence helped advance the ideal of nondiscrimination.

Particularly in urban areas such as Detroit and New York City, civil-rights groups, old and new, used the wartime years to construct a wider base from which to fight for jobs and political power. Founded in 1942, the inter-racial Committee (later, Congress) on Racial Equality (CORE) promised to find new, nonviolent ways of opposing discrimination. Testing a variety of strategies during the war, activists from CORE, led by Bayard Rustin, staged well-organized, well-publicized sit-ins. They called for integrating restaurants, theaters, and other public facilities, especially in wartime Washington, D.C.

The global dimension of the war effort proved of particular help to social movements addressing issues of importance to Mexican American communities. In California and throughout the Southwest during the war years, Latino organizations highlighted the irony of fighting overseas on behalf of a nation that denied equality at home and challenged the United States to live up to its democratic rhetoric. Approximately 500,000 Mexican Americans served, often with great distinction, in the military. Not wishing to anger this constituency, the Roosevelt administration, which also feared harm to its Good Neighbor Policy in Latin America, saw the 1943 zoot-suit incidents in LA as requiring a response from Washington. Consequently, the president's coordinator of Inter-American affairs, Nelson Rockefeller, allocated federal money to train Spanish-speaking workers for wartime employment, to improve education for Mexican Americans, and to provide high school graduates with new opportunities to enter college.

Organizations such as the League of United Latin American Citizens (LULAC) continually pressed for change. Although legal precedents in California and in Southwestern states formally classified Latinos as "white," actual practices usually discriminated against citizens and immigrants of Mexican descent. In Texas, Mexican American activists, working closely with the Mexican government, mounted several drives against discrimination. In

California, as the war was about to end in 1945, attorneys for LULAC backed an ambitious effort by several families to mount a legal challenge, grounded in the latest social science research, against cities in Orange County that segregated Mexican American children into separate and obviously unequal schools.

People of Japanese descent, despite the internment, also laid the basis for postwar campaigns to achieve greater equality for Asian Americans. The courage and sacrifice of Japanese American combat units, composed of volunteers from the stateside internment camps and from Hawaii, became legendary. Members of the 100th Battalion and the 442nd Regimental Combat Team, segregated units, suffered stunning causalities, often while undertaking extremely dangerous combat missions in Europe. In the Pacific Theater, 6,000 members of the Military Intelligence Service provided invaluable service against the same enemy their detractors once claimed they covertly supported.

Leaders of many social movements, then, came to see fighting for the American Way of Life as representing a commitment not to the past but to the future, one to be marked by new struggles on behalf of liberty and equality. After researching his influential study of racial relations, *An American Dilemma* (1944), the Swedish sociologist Gunnar Myrdal declared the need for "fundamental change." The African American novelist Richard Wright expressed a similar sentiment more tersely: The United States needed to address its "white problem."

In the face of divisive issues and new social movements, the OWI mounted informational campaigns that stressed national unity and contrasted America's "melting pot" ethos with the obsession in Germany and Japan about racial "purity." Many wartime motion pictures, plays, radio dramas, and musical pieces tried to foster a sense of national community by expressing pride in cultural diversity. As members of each of the nation's racial and ethnic groups distinguished themselves in the military, the claim to greater equality of condition— "Americans All," in the words of a wartime slogan—took on greater force. Governmental imagery extolling social solidarity and freedom provided another way in which the wartime years assisted the work of social activists.

Shaping the Peace

Focus Question
What major institutions and policies did the United States and the Allies adopt in their effort to shape the reconstruction of the postwar world?

Even before the war ended, U.S. policy makers began considering postwar peace arrangements. The Truman administration claimed to be building on Roosevelt's wartime conferences and agreements as it tried to shape a postwar framework for international relations.

Under Truman's leadership, the United States worked to establish the United Nations (UN), new international economic institutions, and other dispute-settling arrangements.

International Organizations

In the Atlantic Charter of 1941 and at a conference in Moscow in October 1943, the Allied powers pledged to create a replacement for the defunct League of Nations. Internationalist-minded Americans saw the new UN offering a more realistic version of Woodrow Wilson's earlier vision, one in which the United States would lead a world body that could deter aggressor nations and promote peaceful political change.

At the Dumbarton Oaks Conference in Washington in August 1944 and at a subsequent meeting in San Francisco in April 1945, the Allies worked out the UN's organizational structure. It included a General Assembly, in which each member nation would be represented and cast one vote. A smaller body, the Security Council, would include five permanent members from the Allied Coalition—the United States, Great Britain, the Soviet Union, France, and Nationalist China—and six rotating members. The Security Council would assume primary responsibility for taking action to maintain peace, but each of the permanent members could veto any council decision. A UN Secretariat, headed by a Secretary General, would handle day-to-day business, and an Economic and Social Council would sponsor measures to improve living conditions throughout the world.

The U.S. Senate, with only two dissenting votes, approved joining the UN in July 1945. This victory for internationalism contrasted sharply with the Senate's 1919 rejection of U.S. membership in the League of Nations. Opponents of Wilson's dream had then worried that the League would press internationalist policies that might limit the ability of the United States to pursue its own national interest. Following the Second World War, however, a newly powerful United States appeared able to dominate international organizations such as the UN. It seemed unlikely that decisions by it or other international bodies could seriously hamstring U.S. foreign policy. In addition, most U.S. leaders now saw the lack of a coordinated, international response to aggression during the 1930s as a major factor in the outbreak of the Second World War and wished to avoid reliving the "appeasement" policies of that era.

Eleanor Roosevelt, the former first lady and still a committed social activist, played a prominent role in promoting an internationalist agenda in the postwar period. A delegate to the first meeting of the UN's General Assembly, she chaired its Commission on Human Rights and guided the drafting of a Universal Declaration of Human Rights, adopted by the UN in 1948. The document set forth "inalienable" human rights and freedoms as cornerstones of international law.

A series of postwar economic agreements also illustrated a growing acceptance by U.S. leaders of the value of international organizations. At the Bretton Woods (New Hampshire) Conference of 1944, representatives from 45 nations created the International Monetary Fund (IMF), which they hoped could maintain a stable system of international exchange by ensuring the conversion of each nation's currency into that of every other at fixed and stable rates. The U.S. dollar, pegged at a value of $32 dollars for an ounce of gold, would provide the linchpin. Exchange rates could be altered only with the agreement of the IMF. This financial system, according to its architects, would facilitate smoothly flowing trade relationships and create the economic basis for preventing the kind of political instability that had paved the road to war during the 1930s.

Postwar U.S. planners participated in setting up other international economic organizations. At the Bretton Woods conference, they established the International Bank for Reconstruction and Development, later renamed the World Bank. Its creators envisioned it providing loans to war-battered countries and facilitating the resumption of world trade. In 1948, the United States also spearheaded implementation of the General Agreement on Tariffs and Trade (GATT). GATT established the institutional groundwork for subsequent meetings at which nations could come together and negotiate nondiscriminatory trade arrangements that would, in theory, operate freely and fairly throughout the world. Rather than confronting one another by raising protective tariffs or threatening military action over economic disputes, GATT would supposedly encourage nations to resolve their differences through cooperation, by engaging in a good-faith, internationally supervised bargaining process.

Spheres of Interest and Postwar Settlements

During their wartime negotiations, Stalin, Churchill, and Roosevelt had apparently assumed that the most powerful nations—their own—would enjoy special "spheres of influence" in the postwar world. As early as January 1942, the Soviet ambassador to the United States reported to Stalin that Roosevelt had tacitly assented to the Soviets exercising effective postwar control over the Baltic states of Lithuania, Latvia, and Estonia. In 1944, Stalin and Churchill agreed, informally and secretly, that Britain would continue to dominate Greece and that the Soviets could oversee Romania and Bulgaria. U.S. leaders, meanwhile, assumed that Latin America would remain within their sphere of influence. Roosevelt sometimes seemed to imply that he accepted Stalin's goal of having states friendly to the USSR on its vulnerable western border. At the Tehran Conference of November 1943, however, FDR also told Stalin that U.S. voters of Eastern European descent expected their homelands to be independent of Soviet control after the war.

Historians continue to differ on precisely how Roosevelt might have intended to reconcile his contradictory hints about the postwar Soviet sphere of influence. As long as the Soviet military remained essential to Germany's defeat—and Roosevelt also wanted the USSR to join the war against Japan—the ailing U.S. president struck a conciliatory tone with Stalin. After Roosevelt's death, however, the powerful position gained by the Soviets in Eastern Europe quickly became a focus of tensions between the United States and the USSR.

Early in the war, both nations did favor some plan for the dismemberment and deindustrialization of a defeated Nazi Germany. At a conference held at Yalta, Ukraine, in February 1945, the three major Allied powers agreed to divide Germany into four zones of occupation (with France's postwar government as the other occupying force). Later, as relations among the victors worsened, this temporary division of Germany hardened into a Soviet-dominated zone in the East and the other three zones to its west. The victors also divided Berlin, the German capital, into separate zones, even though the city lay uneasily within the Soviet-controlled portion of Germany.

Postwar differences also involved Poland. At the Yalta Conference, the Soviets agreed to hold elections in postwar Poland and to oversee creation of a government "responsible to the will of the people." Stalin also claimed, apart from these formalities, that the other Allied leaders tacitly acknowledged that the USSR would effectively dominate postwar Poland. Stalin apparently left Yalta expecting Poland would be in the USSR's sphere of influence, but many in the United States soon charged him with bad faith for failing to hold free elections and for not relinquishing Soviet control over Poland. Other critics, particularly powerful within Republican ranks, blamed Roosevelt and some of his key advisers for not bargaining harder or, even, for selling out to Stalin at Yalta. Observers more sympathetic to Roosevelt's problems with his allies, however, viewed the agreements reached at Yalta as inevitably ambiguous. With tough battles against Germany and Japan still looming on the horizon, British and U.S. leaders seemingly chose to sacrifice clarity in hopes of gaining further cooperation, especially on military matters, from Stalin.

In Asia, military projections likewise influenced postwar settlements. At a November 1943 conference in Tehran, and again at Yalta, Stalin pledged to send Soviet troops to Asia as soon as Germany surrendered. The first U.S. atomic bomb fell on Hiroshima, however, just one day before the Soviets were to enter the Pacific Theater of the war, and the United States assumed total charge of the occupation and postwar reorganization of Japan. After Soviet armies drove into the Korean Peninsula, the United States and the USSR divided Korea, which had been controlled by Japan, into separate zones of occupation. Here, as in Germany, these zones would later emerge as two antagonistic states, one beholden to the United States and the other to the Soviet Union (see chapter 27).

The fate of the European colonies seized by Japan in Southeast Asia provided another contentious issue. Most U.S. officials preferred to see the former British and French colonies become independent nations, but they also worried about the left-leaning politics of many anticolonial nationalist movements. As the Truman administration became more suspicious of the expansionist intentions of Stalin's Soviet regime, it became increasingly tempting to support British and French efforts to reassemble their colonial empires.

The United States maintained its own sphere of influence in the Pacific. In the Philippines, the Truman administration honored a long-standing pledge to grant independence. A government friendly to the United States, which agreed to respect American economic interests and accept U.S. military bases, took power in 1946. U.S. advisers from these bases soon began assisting the Philippine government in its campaign against leftist rebels, the Hukbalahaps, or Huks. In 1947, the United Nations designated the Mariana, Caroline, and Marshall Islands as the "Trust Territories of the Pacific" and authorized the United States to administer their affairs.

Although the nations of Latin America had been only indirectly involved in military conflict and peace negotiations, the Second World War encouraged Roosevelt to build on his Good Neighbor Policy of the 1930s (see chapter 25). Following the German invasion of Poland in 1939, Latin American leaders stood nearly united behind the Allies. After formal U.S. entry into the war, at a conference in Rio de Janeiro in January 1942, every Latin American country except Chile and Argentina broke diplomatic ties with the Axis governments. When naval warfare in the Atlantic severed commercial connections between Latin America and Europe, Latin American countries became critical suppliers of raw materials to the United States.

Wartime conferences avoided making many clear-cut decisions about the Middle East, especially about the founding of a Jewish state. The Second World War prompted survivors of the Holocaust and Jews from around the world to take direct action. **Zionism,** the international movement to found a Jewish state in Palestine, the ancient homeland of Jewish people, attracted thousands of Jews to the Middle East. They began efforts to carve out, against the wishes of Palestinians and other Arab people, a new Jewish state, Israel.

Conclusion

The world landscape changed dramatically during the Second World War. For the United States, wartime mobilization finally ended the Great Depression and focused most of the national government's attention on international concerns. The war brought not only victory over dictatorial, expansionist regimes but also left the United States as the world's preeminent economic and military power.

At home, the administration of President Franklin Roosevelt—concerned with successfully prosecuting a global war against fascism—embraced economic planning and assigned broad executive powers to governmental bureaucracies. Cooperative ties among government, business, and scientific researchers gradually took shape. These sectors worked together to provide the seemingly miraculous growth in the economic productivity that ultimately propelled the U.S. military effort.

Even as the war overseas went on, domestic debates over liberty and equality continued at home. Many Americans saw the Second World War as a struggle to protect and preserve the liberties they already enjoyed. Others, inspired by a struggle against racism and injustice abroad, insisted that a war for freedom should include efforts to advance social justice at home.

News of Japan's 1945 surrender prompted joyous celebrations throughout the United States. Still, most people seemed uncertain about postwar prospects. Internationally, could the United States maintain a cooperate relationship with its wartime Allies, especially the Soviet Union? Domestically, how would the wrenching dislocations of war affect both individuals and institutions? The nation, moreover, now faced the future without the charismatic leadership of Franklin D. Roosevelt.

SUGGESTED READINGS

On the United States and the coming of World War II, see **Robert Dallek, *Franklin D. Roosevelt and American Foreign Policy, 1932–1945*** (1979), and **Waldo H. Heinrichs, *Threshold of War: Franklin D. Roosevelt and American Entry into World War II*** (1988). On the isolationist coalition, see **Justus Doenecke, *Storm on the Horizon: The Challenge to American Intervention, 1939–1941*** (2003). For the war's military aspects, consult **John Keegan, *The Second World War*** (2005); **Gerhard L. Weinberg, *A World at Arms: A Global History of World War II*** (1994); and **Gerald F. Linderman, *The World within War: America's Combat Experience in World War II*** (1997). Few narrative histories can match the dramatic sweep of **Stephen Ambrose's** many works, such as ***D-Day: June 6, 1944: The Climactic Battle of World War II*** (1994). **Michael Beschloss, *The Conquerors: Roosevelt, Truman and the Destruction of Hitler's Germany, 1941–1945*** (2002) is also highly readable. The decision to drop atomic bombs on Japan is adroitly analyzed in **J. Samuel Walker, *Prompt and Utter Destruction: Truman and the Use of the Atomic Bombs against Japan*** (2005).

David Kennedy's *The American People in World War II: Freedom from Fear, Part II* (2003) is a recent overview of the wartime years. See also, **William L. O'Neill, *A Democracy at War: American's Fight at Home and Abroad in World War II*** (1993), and **Michael C. C. Adams, *The Best War Ever: America and World War II*** (1994). The superb synthesis by **John Morton Blum, *V Was for Victory: Politics and American Culture during World War II*** (1976) may be supplemented by the essays in **Lewis A. Erenberg and Susan E. Hirsch, eds., *The War in American Culture: Society and Consciousness during World War II*** (1996), and **Thomas Patrick Doherty, *Projections of War: Hollywood, American Culture, and World War II*** (1993). **Richard W. Steele, *Free Speech and the Good War*** (1999) examines governmental efforts to regulate dissent. **Karen Anderson, *Wartime Women: Sex Roles, Family Relations, and the Status of Women during World War II*** (1981) surveys women's roles during the war. **Ronald Takaki, *Double Victory: A Multicultural History of America in World War II*** (2000) is a good synthesis of issues related to race and ethnicity.

Visit the Liberty Equality Power Companion Web site for resources specific to this textbook: http://www.thomsonedu.com/history/murrin

Also find self-tests and additional resources at ThomsonNOW. ThomsonNOW is an integrated online suite of services and resources with proven ease of use and efficient paths to success, delivering the results you want—NOW!

www.thomsonedu.com/login/

The Age of Containment, 1946–1953

The Second World War, popularly portrayed as a struggle to preserve the "American Way of Life," ended up transforming much of it. The fight against fascism had propelled foreign-policy issues to the center of domestic politics, and postwar international tensions kept them there. As combat operations against the Axis powers gave way to conflict between the United States and the Soviet Union, U.S. leaders overhauled military strategy. They claimed a broad authority for the nation's commander in chief—and, hence, the office of the president—and the need for a global stand against communism. An aggressive campaign to shore up "national security," in addition, came to affect many areas of domestic life.

The early postwar years, between 1946 and 1953, raised questions about the reach of governmental power. What role should Washington, whose bureaucracies had undertaken extensive economic planning during the Second World War, play in the postwar economy? Could a more powerful national government help people enjoy greater security in their own daily lives? How might such a government affect liberty and equality? Debate over issues such as these marked the presidency of Democrat Harry Truman (1945–53), who struggled to implement his anticommunist agenda and to build upon social welfare measures from the New Deal era of the 1930s.

Creating a National Security State, 1945–1949

Focus Question
What major conflicts between the United States and the Soviet Union shaped the Cold War, and what were the principal elements of the foreign policy called containment?

The wartime alliance between the United States and the Soviet Union proved little more than a marriage of convenience. The shared goal of defeating the Axis had forced these two nations, capitalist and communist, to cooperate, but collaboration scarcely lasted beyond victory. Relations between the United States and the Soviet Union produced a **Cold War** marked by mutual suspicion and growing tension.

CHRONOLOGY

1946	Baruch plan for atomic energy proposed • Employment Act passed • Republicans gain control of Congress in November elections
1947	Truman Doctrine announced • HUAC begins hearings on communist infiltration of Hollywood • George Kennan's "Mr. X" article published • National Security Act passed (CIA and NSC established) • Marshall Plan adopted • Truman's loyalty order announced • Taft-Hartley Act passed over Truman's veto • Jackie Robinson and Larry Doby break major league baseball's color line
1948	Berlin Airlift begins • Truman wins reelection • The *Kinsey Report* and Dr. Benjamin Spock's *Baby and Child Care* published
1949	NATO established • China "falls" to communism • NSC-68 drafted • Soviet Union explodes atomic device • Truman unveils his Fair Deal
1950	Korean War begins • Senator Joseph McCarthy charges communist infiltration of State Department • McCarran Internal Security Act passed
1951	Truman removes General MacArthur as commander in Korea
1952	GI Bill of Rights passed • Dwight Eisenhower elected president

Onset of the Cold War

Historians have dissected the beginning of the Cold War from many different perspectives. The traditional interpretation focuses on Soviet expansionism. It sees a historical Russian appetite for new territory, an ideological zeal to spread international communism, or some interplay between these two desires. According to this view, the United States needed to check the expansionist designs of a malevolent USSR. Other historians—generally called revisionists—argue that the Soviet Union's obsession with securing its borders, an understandable response to the invasion of its territory during both world wars, dominated its foreign policy. The United States, in this view, might have tried harder to reassure the USSR, pursuing conciliatory policies instead of ones that intensified Soviet fears. Still other scholars maintain that assigning blame to one side or the other obscures how clashing interests and differing political cultures produced potentially dangerous confrontations, but never direct military conflict, between the two superpowers.

In every account, Harry Truman's administration plays a central role. The new U.S. president initially hoped that he could somehow deal with the Soviets but quickly came to distrust Soviet Premier Joseph Stalin. As differences between the former allies emerged, Truman turned to a group of hard-line, anti-Soviet advisers.

The atomic bomb provided an immediate source of U.S.-Soviet friction. At the Potsdam Conference of July 1945, Truman had casually told Stalin, without mentioning the atomic bomb, about a new U.S. weapon of "unusual destructive force." Well-informed by Soviet intelligence operations about the Manhattan Project, Stalin casually replied that Truman should make "good use" of this weapon. Less calmly, Stalin ordered his scientists to inten-sify the Soviet Union's own nuclear weapons program. Truman likely hoped that the bomb would scare the Soviets, and it did. Historians still debate whether it frightened the Soviets into more cautious behavior or made them more fearful and aggressive.

As atomic warfare against Japan gave way to atomic diplomacy with the Soviet Union, U.S. leaders clashed among themselves over how to proceed. A group that included Secretary of War Henry Stimson, predicting the Soviets would soon possess their own atomic weapons, urged Truman to share nuclear technology with the USSR, in hopes of forestalling a nuclear arms race. The president's more hard-line confidants, fearing Soviet intentions and doubting their nuclear knowledge, rejected this approach.

In 1946, Truman authorized Bernard Baruch, a special presidential representative at the United Nations, to explore ways of controlling the spread of atomic weapons. The Baruch Plan proposed that the United States would abandon its nuclear weapons, but only after the Soviets met certain conditions. Soviet leaders would have to agree to a process for outside monitoring and verification of their atomic energy program and would have to

© The Granger Collection, New York

Testing the Atomic Bomb at Bikini Atoll This atomic test, one of 23 detonations at Bikini Atoll in the Marshall Islands during the late 1940s, raised a column of water 5,000 feet high. Although Bikini islanders were evacuated from the blast sites, the radiation still affected nearby people, including U.S. service personnel, and the area's ecology for years to come. As nuclear-related imagery spread through Cold War culture, new "bikini" swimsuits for "bombshell" women became a fashion rage.

surrender veto power in the UN in cases regarding nuclear issues. Unwilling to submit to these conditions, Soviet leaders rejected the Baruch Plan. They counterproposed that the United States unilaterally destroy its atomic weapons as the initial step toward any final agreement. The United States opposed this idea, and both nations used the deadlock to justify seeking to outpace the other in developing nuclear weapons.

Additional sources of friction involved U.S. loan policies and Soviet domination of Eastern Europe. Under pressure from Republicans in Congress, Truman ended lend-lease assistance to the Soviet Union at the end of the war and, on advice from his own camp, linked extension of future reconstruction loans to signs of Soviet cooperation with the United States over the future of Europe. This linkage strategy never worked. The Soviet Union's need for capital and its suspicions about Western intentions provided excuses for an aggressive, hard-line stance. A repressive sphere of Soviet influence over Eastern Europe, which the USSR called defensive and the United States labeled expansionist, fell into place. By 1946, the two nations, once uneasy allies, seemed ready to become bitter adversaries.

Harry Truman increasingly placed his personal stamp on the presidency by pledging to stop the campaign of communist expansionism he claimed Moscow directed. Truman's anticommunist initiatives, in both foreign and domestic affairs, relied on new measures for extending the reach and power of the executive branch of the national government.

Containment Abroad: The Truman Doctrine

In March 1947, the president announced what became known as the Truman Doctrine. This pronouncement came during a speech to Congress about the civil war in Greece, a conflict in which communist-led insurgents appeared ready to topple a corrupt but pro-Western government. A war-weakened Britain had long considered Greece within its sphere of influence, but it could no longer maintain its formerly strong presence there or in other parts of the Middle East. Truman's advisers claimed that a leftist victory in Greece would expose nearby Turkey, a nation considered critical to the U.S. strategic position in the Mediterranean, to Soviet expansionism.

Seeking to justify U.S. aid to Greece and Turkey, Truman made his case to Congress in especially dramatic terms. Both the threat of communism and U.S. security interests, he said, now spanned the globe. The future of "free peoples" everywhere hung in the balance. Unless the United States aided those who were "resisting attempted subversion by armed minorities or by outside pressures," totalitarian communism would spread and, ultimately, threaten the United States.

The global vision of U.S. national security outlined in the Truman Doctrine encountered some skepticism. Henry Wallace, who had become Truman's most visible Democratic critic, chided the president for exaggerating the Soviet threat and urged a more conciliatory approach toward Moscow. Conservative Republicans, though firmly anti-Soviet, looked suspiciously at the increase of executive power and the vast expenditures the Truman Doctrine seemed to imply. If the president wanted to win support for his position, Republican Senator Arthur Vandenberg had already advised, Truman should "scare hell" out of people.

The rhetoric the president used when announcing the Truman Doctrine seemed to have followed this advice. Gaining backing from both Republicans and Democrats, Congress did approve Truman's request for $400 million in assistance to Greece and Turkey, most of it for military aid, in the spring of 1947. This vote signaled broad, if not unanimous, bipartisan support for a national security policy that came to be called **containment.**

The term *containment* first appeared in a 1947 article in the influential journal *Foreign Affairs* by **George Kennan,** the U.S. State Department's premier Soviet expert. Writing under the pseudonym "X," Kennan argued that the "main element" in any U.S. policy "must be that of a long-term, patient but firm and vigilant containment of Russian expansive tendencies." This article and the word containment quickly became associated, to Kennan's subsequent displeasure, with the urgent tone of the Truman Doctrine and with a military-dominated approach to world affairs.

Containment eventually came to provide a convenient catchphrase for the Truman administration's global, anticommunist national security policy. Although Kennan had envisioned containment primarily as a careful political strategy that tried to limit Soviet gains in Europe, the White House's rearticulation lacked Kennan's nuances and, instead, turned containment in militarized and globalized directions. Truman's version came to link all leftist insurgencies, wherever they occurred, to a **totalitarian movement** directed from Moscow. Soviet communism threatened the security of the United States by dangerous ideas as well as by military might. Even a relatively small gain by the Soviets in one part of the globe would, in this view, encourage them to extend, perhaps even accelerate, their aggressive initiatives. Although postwar debates over foreign policy did include sharp disagreements over precisely how and where to pursue containment, few U.S. leaders questioned the need for a global and activist foreign policy aimed against the spread of communism.

Truman's Loyalty Program

Only nine days after proclaiming the Truman Doctrine, the president issued Executive Order 9835. It declared there should be "a loyalty investigation" of every civilian employee "of any department or agency of the executive branch of the Federal Government." Newly established loyalty boards would determine whether or not there were "reasonable grounds" for concluding that a person working for the U.S. government belonged to an organization or held political ideas that might pose a "security risk." Any employees found to pose such a danger would lose their government jobs. The Truman loyalty program also authorized the attorney general's office to identify organizations it deemed **subversive,** and to place them on a special Attorney General's List.

The Truman Loyalty Program rested on a controversial assessment of Soviet espionage activity in the United States. Although knowledgeable observers consistently recognized that the Soviets had conducted spy operations inside the U.S. government during the 1940s, there has been sharp disagreement over their scope and success. Were the Soviets operating only at the fringes of government or had they penetrated its top levels? Were they simply collecting readily obtainable information or stealing vital national secrets?

Debate over questions such as these now takes place in light of evidence unavailable before the 1989 collapse of the Soviet Union. Previously closed Soviet archives and declassified files of U.S. surveillance agencies suggest both nations engaged in a wide range of spying activities. The wartime alliance had made it easier than ever before for the Soviet Union to obtain intelligence in the United States. By 1943, for instance, a super-secret U.S. Army counterintelligence unit had begun intercepting transmissions between Moscow and the United States. Called the "VENONA files" and not publicly revealed until 1995, these intercepted messages showed that the USSR helped finance America's Communist Party; placed informants in important U.S. governmental agencies; and began obtaining secret information about U.S. atomic work as early as 1944. U.S. officials, in short, justifiably saw Soviet espionage as a legitimate concern. Historians still differ, however, over the significance and reliability of specific pieces of evidence in the VENONA files and even over how much members of the Truman administration actually knew about information in these intercepts.

There can be little doubt, though, that the case Truman made on behalf of his loyalty policy failed to satisfy a diverse group of critics. The president claimed, in effect, that the United States faced relatively few security risks but that their potential for doing grave harm demanded a response unprecedented in peacetime. Many Republicans charged the Truman administration with underestimating the threat and warned that hundreds, perhaps thousands, of communists now worked in the federal bureaucracy. The Democrats, these Republicans argued, lacked the will to create the kind of aggressive loyalty program that could root them out. From a very different perspective, civil liberties groups saw a more limited threat and argued for a carefully calibrated response. Truman's approach, they insisted, failed to distinguish between, for example, an atomic scientist with ties to the Soviet Union and a politically outspoken clerical worker in the Interior Department. Truman's loyalty plan, therefore, angered both fervent anticommunists, who accused the president of doing too little to fight subversion at home, and civil libertarians, who charged him with whipping up fears that far exaggerated the menace and exceeded constitutional limitations on governmental power.

The National Security Act, the Marshall Plan, and the Berlin Crisis

Shaking off criticism from all sides, the Truman administration continued to pursue its anticommunist initiatives. It secured congressional passage of the National Security Act of 1947, which created several new governmental bureaucracies. The law began the process that transformed the old Navy and War Departments into a unified Department of Defense, finally established in 1949. It instituted another new arm of the executive branch, the National Security Council (NSC), and gave it broad authority over the planning and execution of foreign policy. It established the Air Force as a separate service alongside the Army and Navy, and it created, as a successor to the wartime Office of Strategic Services (OSS), a new Central Intelligence Agency (CIA).

The CIA, charged with gathering sensitive political information and conducting covert activities, proved to be the most flexible of the new national security bureaucracies.

Shrouded from public scrutiny and even close oversight by Congress, its secretly funded operations crisscrossed the globe. The CIA reached out, for example, to anti-Stalinist groups in Eastern Europe and even to some within the Soviet Union. It helped finance, in hopes of preventing the rise of communist-led organizations, pro-U.S. labor unions in Western Europe. It covertly intervened in overseas political campaigns, bolstering anti-communist parties in France and Japan. The CIA secretly claimed credit for preventing the Italian Communist Party from winning a nationwide electoral victory in 1948. The Truman administration came to see CIA operations as integral to its anticommunist foreign policy.

Truman's White House also considered its economic policies in Western Europe an important part of the containment effort. Concerned that Western Europe's severe economic problems might benefit communist-dominated movements, Secretary of State George C. Marshall hoped U.S. aid would quickly rejuvenate the region's economy. Under his 1947 Marshall Plan, the United States would extend funds designed to allow postwar Western European governments to coordinate a broad program of economic reconstruction. Between 1946 and 1951, the United States provided nearly $13 billion in assistance to 17 Western European nations.

The Truman administration consistently hailed the Marshall Plan, which Congress approved in early 1948, for complementing other national security initiatives. It credited aid from the United States for helping brighten the economic scene in Western Europe, where industrial production quickly rebounded. Improving standards of living, the White House claimed, enhanced political stability in Western Europe and undermined the appeal of communist-led movements. In response to conservative critics who complained of a "giveaway" program, supporters of the Marshall Plan insisted that U.S. economic aid expanded both markets and investment opportunities for U.S. firms wanting to do business in Western Europe.

The Truman administration also moved to beef up U.S. military resources, depleted as a result of an earlier postwar demobilization effort. After the USSR facilitated the installation of a pro-Soviet government in Czechoslovakia, during the spring of 1948, the president's key military advisers claimed Stalin likely intended a military strike against Western Europe. A brief war scare gripped Washington. Planners urged an immediate increase in across-the-board military spending and reinstitution of the military draft. Truman, addressing a joint session of Congress, declared that "moral God-fearing peoples . . . must save the world from Atheism" and from Soviet "totalitarianism."

U.S. policy makers viewed the future of postwar Germany, initially divided into four zones of occupation (see chapter 26), as crucial to the security of Western Europe. In June 1948, the United States, Great Britain, and France announced a currency-reform program as the first step toward integrating their separate sectors into the Federal Republic of Germany, popularly known as West Germany. Soviet leaders expressed alarm. Having twice been invaded by German armies during the preceding 35 years, they wanted, as a hedge against a third attack, any post-occupation Germany to remain economically enfeebled. Hoping to sidetrack

Western plans, in June 1948, the Soviets cut off all highways, railroads, and water routes linking Berlin, which was located within their own domain, to the western zones of occupation.

This Soviet attempt to seal off Berlin provided an opportunity for the newly created U.S. Air Force to display its capabilities. Under the direction of General Curtis LeMay, U.S. and British pilots began "Operation Vittles" or "the Berlin Airlift." Specially outfitted planes, flying around the clock, soared over the Soviet blockade and delivered virtually all of the items Berliners needed to continue their daily routines. The United States, hinting at a military response, also began negotiating for U.S. air bases in Western Europe and immediately stationed in Britain two squadrons of B-29s, reputably able to deliver atomic bombs to Soviet targets. Although these planes actually lacked nuclear capability, officials in the Pentagon began planning for an atomic attack, during some future confrontation, against the USSR. Once Stalin recognized the Berlin Airlift would continue, he abandoned his blockade, in May 1949, and moved to convert the Soviet-occupied sector of East Germany into the German Democratic Republic. The western portion of a divided Berlin, an anti-communist enclave inside East Germany, quickly became a prominent focus of Cold War tensions.

The Election of 1948

National security issues helped Harry Truman win the 1948 election. His victory capped a remarkable political story, one that featured a feisty incumbent president and a trio of challengers.

Truman faced significant political opposition that had been building since 1946. Dissident Democrats, who thought his containment policies too militant and his domestic ones too tame, began looking to an old Truman rival, former Vice-President (1941–45) Henry A. Wallace. After Wallace, whom Truman inherited from Roosevelt as his secretary of commerce, criticized U.S. policy toward the Soviet Union, the president ousted him from the cabinet in September 1946. This move angered those Democrats who saw Wallace, not Truman, as FDR's rightful successor. Later, the off-year national elections of November 1946 gave the Republicans control of Congress for the first time since 1928. GOP leaders saw this victory portending an end to their 20-year losing streak in presidential races. Although Truman's political fortunes did seem somewhat improved by late 1947, few political handicappers liked his chances in 1948.

Truman faced three prominent opponents. To his political left, a new Progressive Party, which nominated Henry Wallace for president, hoped to attract the disaffected Democrats who charged Truman with abandoning FDR's legacy. In addition, South Carolina's J. Strom Thurmond became the pro-segregationist candidate of a new States' Rights (or "Dixiecrat") party, and Thomas E. Dewey, the Republican who had run well during a losing race against Franklin Roosevelt in 1944, returned as the GOP nominee. Targeting Dewey, his most serious challenger, Truman called the GOP-controlled Congress into a special session and presented it with a list of domestic policy proposals that were abhorrent to most

Republicans. After GOP legislators predictably ignored Truman's wish list, the president targeted "that do-nothing, good-for-nothing, worst Congress."

Dewey helped Truman's cause by running an exceedingly cautious campaign. A pro-Democratic newspaper caricatured Dewey's standard speech as four "historic sentences: Agriculture is important. Our rivers are full of fish. You cannot have freedom without liberty. The future lies ahead." Ignoring critics, he remained confident of a November victory. When his campaign train, the "Victory Special," arrived in Truman's old political base of Kansas City, Dewey pointedly booked the same hotel suite the president used whenever he came to town.

Meanwhile, Truman mounted an energetic, tub-thumping effort. It featured blunt and caustic attacks on his opponents, most famously delivered from the back of his own campaign train. Dewey was plotting "a real hatchet job on the New Deal," the president charged, and the GOP, controlled by a cabal of "cunning men," was preparing for "a return of the Wall Street economic dictatorship." "Give 'em hell, Harry!" shouted his Democratic supporters. In November, Truman won slightly less than 50 percent of the popular vote but secured a solid majority in the Electoral College. The Democratic Party also regained control of Congress.

Truman's victory now seems less surprising to historians than it did to political analysts in 1948. Despite Republican victories in the 1946 congressional elections, the Democratic Party retained the core of its old New Deal base. In fact, Democratic congressional candidates who identified with Franklin Roosevelt rather than with his successor generally polled a higher percentage of the November vote in their districts than did Truman. Voter loyalty to the memory of Roosevelt and his New Deal coalition helped bring the Democrats their victory.

After accepting his party's call for new civil-rights measures, Truman survived the revolt of the Dixiecrats, disaffected white Southern Democrats, in 1948. Strom Thurmond had denounced Truman for backing a "civil wrongs" program and charged that "radicals, subversives, and reds" now controlled the national Democratic Party. He claimed that Dixiecrats did not oppose all civil-rights legislation but insisted that the U.S. Constitution required that state governments, not the federal government, possessed

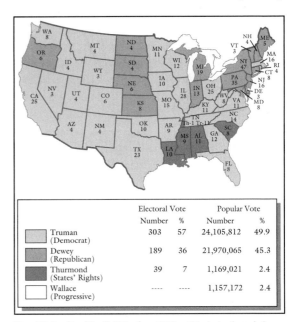

	Electoral Vote		Popular Vote	
	Number	%	Number	%
Truman (Democrat)	303	57	24,105,812	49.9
Dewey (Republican)	189	36	21,970,065	45.3
Thurmond (States' Rights)	39	7	1,169,021	2.4
Wallace (Progressive)	----	----	1,157,172	2.4

Map 27.1   Presidential Election, 1948   This electoral map helps show how, in this close election, Truman won the presidency with less than 50 percent of the popular vote.

the power to enact antidiscrimination measures. The Dixiecrat movement did portend longer-term political changes among southern whites, people who had loyally voted Democratic since Reconstruction. As a presidential candidate in 1948, however, Thurmond secured only the electoral votes of four Deep South states, while Truman carried all of the other states of the old Confederacy.

Truman's hard-line anticommunist rhetoric proved crucial to sidetracking Henry Wallace's once-promising campaign. Wallace and his supporters had never expected to win the presidency but hoped to do well enough to rekindle support for their vision of the New Deal and to build pressure for a less militantly anti-Soviet foreign policy. Eventually, though, many Democrats abandoned the Progressives because of their refusal to reject support from the U.S. Communist Party—a point that Truman contrasted with his own anticommunist stance. Henry Wallace received less than 3 percent of the popular tally and no electoral votes. The 1948 election left the Progressive Party in shambles and suggested a lesson for elections to come: Successful presidential candidates could never appear "soft" on national security issues if they hoped to gain the White House.

The Era of the Korean War, 1949–1952

Meanwhile, to carry out his containment policy, Truman continued to marshal the nation's economic and military resources. After a series of Cold War crises during 1949 and the outbreak of war on the Korean peninsula in 1950, he reaffirmed his administration's anticommunist stance.

NATO, China, and the Bomb

In April 1949, the United States, Canada, and 10 European nations formed the **North Atlantic Treaty Organization (NATO).** Under this "mutual defense" pact, each nation pledged that an attack against one would automatically be treated as a strike against all. Prominent critics, such as Republican Senator Robert Taft, called NATO a provocation to the Soviet Union, an "entangling alliance" that violated the traditional U.S. foreign policy, and a threat to the constitutionally guaranteed power of Congress to declare war. Because of NATO's mutual defense feature, Taft argued, the policies of other countries, rather than those of the United States, could bring the nation into a foreign conflict. The NATO concept prevailed, however, and the idea of pursuing containment through similar arrangements would expand during the 1950s. **(See Map 27.2, Divided Germany and the NATO Alliance, in the color insert following page 1056.)**

Meanwhile, events in China heightened Cold War tensions. Although the United States had extended billions of dollars in military aid and economic assistance to Jiang Jieshi's struggling Nationalist government, Jiang had steadily lost ground to the forces of Mao Zedong, who promised that a communist China would soon gain an important role in world affairs and that Chinese peasants would enjoy the fruits of a sweeping program of land reform. Experienced U.S. diplomats privately predicted Jiang's inevitable downfall.

Publicly, however, the Truman administration continued to portray Jiang as the capable and respected leader of a "free China." Then, in 1949, Mao's armies finally forced Jiang and his supporters to retreat from the Chinese mainland to the nearby island of Formosa (Taiwan). Mao's communist movement established the People's Republic of China, while Jiang's National Chinese government took root on Formosa. The two Chinas, like the two Germanys, became evocative symbols of a global Cold War.

Many people in the United States wondered how Mao's communist forces could have triumphed. Financed by conservative business leaders, the powerful "China lobby" excoriated Truman and his new secretary of state, Dean Acheson, for having "lost" China to the communists. Critics of Acheson's state department forced the removal of several analysts who had warned of Jiang's impending collapse or had merely emphasized his shortcomings. Although Acheson had once made some tentative, highly secret moves toward negotiating with the People's Republic, new international tensions and domestic political pressures ultimately convinced the Truman administration to embrace Jiang's regime on Taiwan and refuse to recognize or officially deal with Mao's "Red China." Nonrecognition remained U.S. policy for more than 20 years, even after the friction between communist China and the Soviet Union, which experienced "China hands" in the U.S. State Department had predicted, became evident.

In September 1949, Truman announced another event that reinforced his administration's anticommunist resolve. The Soviet Union, years earlier than many of the president's aides had expected, had conducted a successful "nuclear explosion." The USSR's crude atomic device, which ended the U.S. nuclear monopoly, increased concern about the threat posed by Soviet communism. Already besieged by domestic critics who saw recent history filled with Soviet gains and U.S. losses, Truman secretly pondered whether U.S. scientists should take the next step in nuclear weaponry: development of a hydrogen bomb. Acheson, who had once shared Henry Stimson's fears about a nuclear arms race, now threw the State Department's influence behind the H-bomb project.

NSC-68

In responding to events of 1949, the Truman administration began formally reviewing its foreign-policy assumptions. George Kennan, increasingly concerned about the emergence of a global, largely militarized redesign of his containment concept, resigned from the State Department's policy staff. As a result, the task of overseeing this review fell to Paul Nitze, a hard-liner who insisted on confronting the USSR throughout the world, lest small gains in one corner encourage more aggressive Soviet moves elsewhere. Nitze effectively dominated production of a policy paper identified as **NSC-68** (National Security Council Document 68), which provided a blueprint for both the rhetoric and the substance of future Cold War foreign policy. In the words of one of NSC-68's architects, the United States should "find every weak spot in the enemy's armor . . . and hit him with anything that comes to hand. Anything we do short of an all-out effort is inexcusable."

NSC-68 opened with an alarming account of a global ideological clash between "freedom," spread by U.S. power, and "slavery," promoted by the Soviet Union, the center of an international communist movement. Despairing of fruitful negotiations with the Soviets, NSC-68 urged a full-scale effort to expand U.S. influence. It endorsed covert action, economic pressure, propaganda campaigns, and a massive military buildup. Because some Americans might oppose larger military spending and budget deficits, the report cautioned, U.S. leaders should portray their actions as defensive and present greater military spending as a stimulus to the economy rather than as a potential drain on national resources. Although the details of NSC-68 remained classified for more than two decades, people in the United States certainly learned about its major assumptions. Led by Secretary of State Acheson, officials from the Truman administration stumped the country, preaching the key tenets of NSC-68 and popularizing its view of the Cold War as a global showdown between good and evil.

The Korean War

Supporters of NSC-68 could claim vindication in June 1950, when communist North Korea invaded South Korea. Truman characterized the attack as a simple case of Soviet-inspired aggression. According to a spokesperson for the State Department, the relationship between the USSR and North Korea resembled "that between Walt Disney and Donald Duck." President Truman invoked the rhetoric of containment and the domino-like vision of NSC-68: "If aggression is successful in Korea, we can expect it to spread through Asia and Europe to this hemisphere."

The situation on the Korean Peninsula, however, was more complicated. Japanese military forces had occupied all of Korea between 1905 and 1945, and Japan's defeat in the Second World War had encouraged most Koreans to hope they might reestablish their own independent nation. Instead, separate zones of occupation, resulting from separate wartime military operations by the United States and the Soviet Union, became two distinct states, with the 38th parallel providing the boundary between them. The Soviet Union supported North Korea's communist government, headed by the dictatorial Kim Il-sung. The United States backed the aging, American-educated Syngman Rhee to head up an unsteady, sometimes autocratic, government in South Korea. Separated by an arbitrary and militarized border, many Koreans saw themselves divided as much by internal political and religious differences as by Cold War considerations. Nonetheless, both Kim and Rhee recognized that patronage from the rival superpowers could help bolster their regimes and advance their conflicting plans for Korea.

As Rhee's policies, especially those favoring large landholders, generated internal opposition, Kim decided on unifying Korea under his control. He gambled that the United States would not, or could not, effectively intervene in Korea. At one point, after all, even the militantly anticommunist Dean Acheson had suggested the Korean peninsula fell outside the U.S. "defense perimeter." On June 25, 1950, Kim's communist troops moved across the 38th parallel into South Korea. Earlier, he had consulted Soviet and Chinese leaders and, after arguing for the likelihood of a quick North Korean victory, received their approval. His South Korean nation under attack, Syngman Rhee appealed to the Truman administration for military assistance. Over the strong opposition of General Omar Bradley, Head of the Joint Chiefs of Staff, supporters of U.S. intervention, led by Nitze and Acheson, prevailed.

The situation quickly escalated into a wider Cold War conflict, the **Korean War.** The Soviets, unaware of the details of Kim's plans, were boycotting the UN on the day North Korea launched its invasion and could not veto a U.S. proposal to send a UN military force, under U.S. command, to Korea. Under UN auspices, the United States rushed assistance to Rhee, who moved to quell dissent in the South as well as to repel the armies of the North.

U.S. leaders soon began debating their goal in Korea. Should they seek only to contain communism by driving North Korea's forces back over the 38th parallel? Or should they try to "roll back" communist power and reunify Korea under Rhee's leadership? Rollback initially seemed fanciful, as North Korean forces pushed rapidly southward. Within three months of their incursion, they took Seoul, the capital of South Korea, and probed into the southern tip of the Korean Peninsula. UN troops, most of them from the United States and under the command of General **Douglas MacArthur,** initially seemed unprepared. Soon, however, U.S.-supplied firepower took its toll on North Korea's elite troops and, later, on the untrained recruits Kim sent to replace them.

MacArthur then devised a plan that most other military commanders considered crazy: an amphibious landing behind enemy lines. Those stunned by his audacious proposal became even more astounded by its results. On September 15, 1950, a sizeable contingent of U.S. Marines landed at Inchon, suffered minimal casualties, and recaptured nearby Seoul in less than two weeks.

The shifting tide of battle devastated Korea. Many observers would call the Korean conflict a "limited" war, largely because it never spread off the Korean Peninsula or involved nuclear weapons. Intense bombing, however, preceded every U.S military move, and neither side seemed concerned about civilian casualties. Estimates of Koreans left dead and wounded reached perhaps one-tenth of the total population of both Koreas. While battling for control of Seoul, for example, rival forces reduced the city to rubble, with only the capitol building and a train station left standing.

As MacArthur's troops drove northward, Truman faced a crucial decision. Emboldened by success, the general urged moving beyond containment to an all-out war of "liberation" and the reunification of Korea. MacArthur's supporters in Washington saw an opportunity to demonstrate the feasibility of junking the policy of merely containing communism in favor of rolling it back. Other advisers warned, however, that Mao's China would likely retaliate if U.S. forces approached its border. After a joint meeting on Wake Island, far closer to MacArthur's home turf than to Truman's, the president did allow MacArthur to carry the war into North Korea but cautioned against provoking China.

Unimpressed by the threat of Chinese intervention, MacArthur advanced his forces to near the Yalu River on the Chinese-Korean border. China responded by sending at least 400,000 troops into North Korea, which forced retreating UN forces back across the 38th parallel. "We face an entirely new war," MacArthur admitted. Alarmists in Washington considered several possibilities: evacuating UN forces from Korea; employing atomic weaponry against China; or, perhaps, even mounting a preemptive nuclear strike against the USSR.

Truman pondered his options. After apparently wavering briefly, he made a crucial decision: It was not the time to employ atomic weapons, in Korea or anywhere else. Then, after MacArthur's troops stopped the Chinese advance and even regained the initiative, Truman also rejected any idea of further escalating the war in favor of settling for a military stalemate at the point where the 38th parallel bisected the Korean Peninsula. General MacArthur, directly challenging the president, argued publicly for an all-out offensive into North Korea—and, possibly, even into China as well. Invoking the principle that the U.S. Constitution made military officers subordinate to the president, the nation's commander-in-chief, a now-angry Harry Truman, summarily relieved MacArthur from his post in April 1951.

MacArthur returned home as a war hero and as a potential Republican presidential candidate. Opinion polls reported overwhelming opposition to Truman's decision to dump the popular general, now a hero of both the Korean and the Second World War. During U.S. Senate hearings on MacArthur's dismissal, however, equally distinguished military strategists dismissed his scenario for Korea as the "wrong war in the wrong place." MacArthur's once luminous image, along with his political ambitions, soon faded away.

Truman mobilized his remaining political resources behind an unsuccessful search for translating a temporary truce into a more permanent peace settlement for Korea. As negotiations stalled, another military hero, Dwight Eisenhower, whom Republicans tapped as their 1952 candidate for president, promised he would personally go to Korea, if elected, and accelerate the peace process. Harry Truman would leave office, in 1953, without securing a formal end to the Korean War.

Korea and Containment

Meanwhile, this conflict brought NSC-68's recommendations to life and spurred the Truman administration to expand its containment initiatives. It announced plans to rearm West Germany, scarcely five years after Nazi Germany's defeat, and to increase NATO's military forces. A proposal for direct U.S. military aid to Latin American governments, which legislators had voted down in the past, slid through Congress. In the Philippines, the United States stepped up military assistance to suppress the leftist Huk rebels. In 1951, the United States finally signed a formal peace treaty with Japan and inked a security pact that gave the United States the power to establish military bases on the Japanese island of Okinawa. The Truman administration acquired similar bases in the Middle East, bolstering the U.S. strategic position in that oil-rich area. The ANZUS mutual defense pact of 1952 linked the United States

Map 27.3   Korean War   This map shows the lines of battle and the armistice line that still divides the two Koreas. Note the advances made first by North Korea and then by UN (United States-led) troops.
View an animated version of this map or related maps at http://www.thomsonedu.com/history/murrin

strategically to Australia and New Zealand. And in French Indochina, Truman began assisting France's effort to prevent a communist-led independence movement from ousting its colonial regime.

Throughout the world, U.S. policy makers continued to oppose any movement whose political orientation seemed left-leaning and to give support to pro-United States parties and people. The U.S. occupation government in Japan, for example, increasingly restricted the activities of labor unions, suspended an antitrust program that American officials had earlier implemented, and barred communists from posts in the government and in the universities. As in Germany, the United States tried to convert a formerly fascist foe into an anticommunist ally by strengthening pro-U.S. elites and by promoting a U.S. model of economic growth.

In Africa, anticommunism prompted the United States to ally with South Africa. In 1949, that nation's all-white (and militantly anticommunist) Nationalist Party had instituted a legal-social system, called **apartheid,** based on elaborate rules of racial separation and subordination of blacks. Some officials in the State Department warned that any pact with South Africa, by implying support for apartheid, hardly presented the United States as an apostle of freedom, but the Truman administration nonetheless concluded an alliance with South Africa's white supremacist regime.

The Truman administration's anticommunism, again in line with NSC-68, included more than military moves. Truman's global "Campaign of Truth," an intensive informational and psychological offensive, used mass-media imagery and cultural exchanges to counter the Soviet's anticapitalist propaganda. A rhetoric that framed U.S. policy in terms of defending fundamental values took hold. As the Defense Department replaced the old War Department, U.S. policy makers increasingly talked about defending "national security" rather than advancing the "national interest."

Beginning with the Truman Doctrine of 1947, in short, the United States reinvented itself as a superpower with a global reach. In response to the specter of Soviet-led communism, the United States solidified its position within Iran, Greece, and Turkey, all once inside Britain's sphere of influence; initiated the Marshall Plan and NATO; transformed former enemies—Italy, Germany, and Japan—into anti-Soviet bulwarks; assumed control of hundreds of islands in the Pacific Ocean; launched research to develop an H-bomb; winked at apartheid to win an anticommunist ally in South Africa; solidified its sphere of influence in Latin America; acquired military bases around the world; and devised a master plan, NSC-68, for using military, economic, and covert action to advance far-flung national security goals.

As the Truman administration moved to fortify the U.S. strategic position overseas, its policies also produced what the historian Michael Sherry has called "the militarization of American life." With strong bipartisan support in Congress, the White House accelerated what would become a massive military buildup and, as a result, an increasing merger between military and economic policy making. The fight against communism and for greater security, at home and abroad, continually justified the expansion of the power of the governmental bureaucracies charged with protecting national security. Congress granted a new Atomic Energy Commission, for example, broad powers to oversee development of a U.S. nuclear power industry. To develop both the weaponry and the policies implied by a global security strategy, Congress created a think tank— **RAND,** an acronym for Research and Development. The Pentagon joined with aircraft manufacturers in an ultimately successful effort to develop surface-to-surface missiles. The Pentagon's soaring budget and its expensive contracts did worry cost-conscious members of Congress, but the prospect of governmental spending creating new jobs in their home districts helped mute opposition to a foreign policy that emphasized military initiatives.

Pursuing National Security at Home

Focus Question
How did the foreign policy of containment affect domestic policy and American life?

Although bipartisan support for Truman's national security measures overseas generally prevailed, the president's programs for containing subversive influences at home encountered bitter, sustained opposition. Militant anticommunists, sometimes taking their cue from Truman's own rhetoric, leveled increasingly alarming allegations about internal communist subversion and about his administration's unwillingness to respond appropriately. Civil libertarians, on the other hand, continued to complain about "witch-hunts" against people whose only apparent sin seemed dissent from prevailing policy choices. As the political climate became increasingly volatile, even some dedicated anticommunists began to worry that wild goose chases after unlikely subversives could discredit the government's effort to identify authentic Soviet agents. The widespread search for signs of subversion, which took place outside the control of the Truman White House, eventually touched many areas of postwar life.

Anticommunism and the U.S. Labor Movement

The issue of anticommunism, for example, helped unsettle the U.S. labor movement. After the end of the Second World War, militant workers had struck for increased wages and for a greater voice in workplace routines and production decisions. Labor strikes had brought both the auto and the electronics industries to a standstill. In Stamford, Connecticut, and Lancaster, Pennsylvania, general strikes had led to massive work stoppages that later spread to other U.S. large cities. After the president threatened to seize mines and railroads shut down by work stoppages and to order strikers back to work, labor militancy slowly began to subside.

Unimpressed, the Republican-controlled Congress effectively tapped anticommunist sentiment to pass the Labor-Management Relations Act of 1947. Opponents of the law, popularly known as the Taft-Hartley Act, charged that it seemed to have more to do with countering gains made by organized labor during the 1930s than with combating communism. It limited a union's power to conduct boycotts, to compel employers to accept "closed shops" in which only union members could be hired, and to conduct any strike that the president judged harmful to national security. In addition, the measure required that union officials sign affidavits stating that they did not belong to the Communist Party or to any other "subversive" organization. If a union refused to comply, it could lose some of the legal protections otherwise available under national labor laws. Truman vetoed Taft-Hartley, but Congress swiftly overrode him. By the end of the Truman era, some type of loyalty-security check had been conducted on about 20 percent of the U.S. workforce, more than 13 million people.

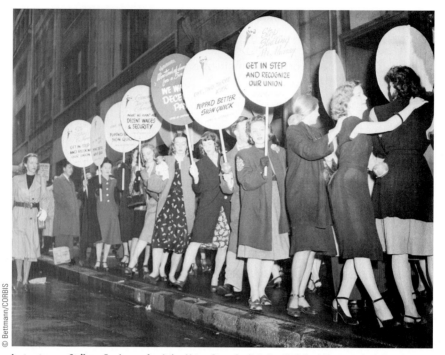

Instructors on Strike   Employees of an Arthur Murray Dance Studio in New York City demonstrate both the conga, a popular Latin American dance style in 1947, and their determination to form a union affiliated with Local 16 of the United Office and Professional Workers of America. During the immediate postwar period, workers in a wide range of occupations mounted strikes to secure higher wages, better conditions, and greater job security through unionization campaigns.

Anticommunism also affected both internal union politics and labor-management relations. Some workers had long charged communist organizers with displaying greater loyalty to the Communist Party than to their own unions or to the nation. Differences over whether to support the Democratic Party or Henry Wallace's Progressive effort in 1948 had embittered relations within the organized labor movement. During the years following Truman's victory, the Congress of Industrial Organizations (CIO) expelled 13 unions—a full third of its membership—for their political ties. In addition, outspoken labor activists discovered that their ideas about politics and economics, if they seemed to resemble communist tenets, could put their own jobs at risk. The anticommunist issue, forcefully invoked by businesspeople and conservative labor leaders, increasingly found its way into labor-management relations during the 1940s.

HUAC and the Search for Subversives

The entertainment industry attracted special attention. In 1947, only three days after Truman unveiled his famous Doctrine, the **House Un-American Activities Committee (HUAC)** opened hearings into subversive influences in Hollywood. Basking in the gaze of newsreel cameras, committee members seized on the refusal of a group of screenwriters, producers, and directors—all current or former members of the American Communist Party—to testify about their own politics and that of others in the film community. Known as "the Hollywood Ten," this group claimed that the First Amendment barred HUAC from scrutinizing political convictions. The federal courts upheld HUAC's investigative powers, however, and the Hollywood Ten eventually went to prison for contempt of Congress.

Studio heads also drew up a secret **blacklist,** a directory of alleged subversives whom they agreed not to hire. Movie moguls denied the existence of such a list, but their disavowals sounded unconvincing. As the staunchly anticommunist actor and producer John Wayne later conceded, "The only thing our side did that was anywhere near blacklisting was just running a lot of people out of the business." Leaders in other sectors of the entertainment industry, particularly television, adopted a similar policy. Although prominent celebrities such as the Hollywood Ten dominated media accounts of blacklisting activities, many anonymous labor union members, who worked behind the scenes in technical and support positions, also lost their source of livelihood in the entertainment business.

In time, hundreds of people charged with being subversives found their employment prospects resting on their willingness to appear as "friendly witnesses" before HUAC or some similar investigative committee. There, investigators would require witnesses to provide the names of other people who supposedly had attended a pro-communist meeting or event, usually at some point during an increasingly distant past. Some of those called to testify, such as the writer Lillian Hellman, refused to answer any questions. Others, such as the director Elia Kazan, cooperated and agreed to "name names." Individual decisions over whether to participate in the ritualistic process of naming names created personal anguish and political rancor that would divide members of the entertainment business and labor union movement for decades.

The search for subversives also created new political celebrities. Ronald Reagan, who served as president of the Screen Actors Guild and as a secret informant for the FBI (identified as "T-10"), eagerly testified before HUAC about communist influences within the movie industry. Richard Nixon, once an obscure member of Congress from California, began his rapid political ascent when he backed Whittaker Chambers, a journalist formally active in communist circles. Chambers, newly repentant and staunchly anticommunist, came before HUAC in 1948. He charged **Alger Hiss,** a prominent Democrat with a lengthy career in public service, with having been a party member who had slipped classified information to Soviet agents during the late 1930s.

The Hiss-Chambers-Nixon affair instantly sparked controversy. Hiss charged anticommunist zealots, expecially in the FBI, with framing him with bogus evidence, including documents Chambers had retrieved from a pumpkin patch on his farm. The federal government, legally barred from indicting Hiss on espionage charges, successfully prosecuted him for committing perjury while testifying before Congress. To Nixon and his supporters, the case of Alger Hiss, who had advised FDR during the Yalta Conference (see chapter 26), demonstrated the

It's Okay—We're Hunting Communists   This 1947 "Herblock" (Herbert Block) cartoon presents a critical view of the impact of HUAC's communist-hunting.

need for greater vigor in hunting down subversively inclined Democrats in Washington. Hiss and his supporters, however, would continue to stick to their frame-up story.

During the mid-1990s, the availability of long-classified documents prompted an extensive, extra-legal review of the Hiss controversy. A small group of scholars contended that the evidentiary trail left unsettled the key questions of what precise information Hiss might have revealed—and under what circumstances. Most observers, however, concluded that substantial evidence suggested that Hiss and several other high-ranking governmental officials had likely passed some information to the Soviets during the 1930s and 1940s and subsequently lied about their actions. Armed with an enhanced documentary record, then, historians continue to debate the details of individual causes, including that of Alger Hiss, into a new century.

Elaborating its own anti-subversive efforts, the Truman administration implemented its loyalty program and dismissed hundreds of federal employees. In addition, Truman's attorney general, Tom Clark (whom the president later appointed to the U.S. Supreme Court), authorized J. Edgar Hoover, head of the FBI, to compile a secret FBI file of alleged subversives whom the government could then detain, without any legal hearing, during a time of national emergency.

Fears that subversives from overseas might immigrate to the United States prompted Congress to pass the McCarran-Walter Act of 1952. It empowered U.S. immigration officials to deny entry to persons they determined could endanger national security by bringing dangerous ideas into the country. The law also authorized the deportation of immigrants, even those who had gained U.S. citizenship, if they belonged to organizations on the Attorney General's List.

At the same time, Hoover's FBI compiled its own confidential dossiers on a wide range of people. It often targeted artists and intellectuals, including some, such as Ernest Hemingway and John Steinbeck, with no ties to the Communist Party. The FBI and other federal agencies paid special attention to prominent African Americans. The FBI kept close tabs, for instance, on a wide range of civil-rights activists, including Bayard Rustin, a founder of CORE (see chapter 26). The U.S. State Department and immigration officials singled out Richard Wright (author of the acclaimed novel *Native Son*), W. E. B. Du Bois (the nation's most celebrated African American historian), and Paul Robeson (a well-known entertainer-activist) because of their links to the U.S. Communist Party and their identification with anti-imperialist and antiracist organizations throughout the world. In addition, suspicions of homosexuality could make people, including the only nominally closeted Rustin, into targets for governmental surveillance and discriminatory treatment.

Targeting Difference

Public signs of homosexual behavior, as the stance adopted by Bayard Rustin suggested, increased during the postwar era. Continuing a trend begun during the Second World War, more visible and assertive gay and lesbian subcultures emerged, particularly in larger cities such as New York and San Francisco. Dr. Alfred Kinsey's controversial research on sexual behavior—his first volume, on male sexuality, appeared in 1948—suggested that U.S. life included far more same-sex relationships than previous studies had ever imagined. Kinsey's volumes, which attracted considerable popular attention, claimed to find people pursuing a wide range of sexual behaviors, ranging from exclusively heterosexual to exclusively homosexual. In late 1952, the issue of transsexuality hit the headlines when the press revealed that, after a series of "sex-change" operations in Europe, George W. Jorgensen, Jr. had become a "blonde beauty," Christine Jorgensen.

By this time, in response to aggressive policing practices and to laws that criminalized homosexual behavior, a small "homophile" movement, aimed at combating legal discrimination, had emerged. Gays formed the Mattachine Society (in 1950), and lesbians later founded the Daughters of Bilitis, organizations that advocated equal rights for homosexuals. Why should the law of the land only protect sexual acts and social relationships generally viewed as "normal," these activists cautiously asked?

Meanwhile, an aggressive effort to contain these signs of homosexuality gained ground. *The Kinsey Report*'s implicit claim that homosexuality might be seen as simply another form of sexuality, alongside the discreet militancy of the Mattachine Society and the Daughters of Bilitis, helped fuel this campaign. The fact that several founders of the Mattachine Society had also been members of the Communist Party, coupled with the claim that Soviet agents could more easily blackmail homosexuals than heterosexuals, helped identify homosexuality as a threat to national security. "One homosexual can pollute a Government office," in much the same way as could a person with communist ideas, claimed a report from the U.S. Senate.

Now, historians of sexuality see a "Lavender Scare" about homosexuality accompanying the "Red Scare" about communism. Popular imagery, for example, portrayed both homosexuality and communism as subversive "diseases" that inwardly "sick" people, who seemed outwardly little different than other Americans, could spread throughout the body politic. It would take, according to this logic, sustained inquiries by knowledgeable experts to uncover all of the subversive communists and homosexuals working in sensitive positions in the U.S. government. Suspicion of "sexual deviance" became an acceptable basis for subjecting government employees to loyalty board hearings and, ultimately, denying them the same legal-constitutional protections enjoyed by heterosexuals.

The "Great Fear"

Some cultural historians view the search for subversives during the late 1940s and early 1950s unfolding against a backdrop of a widespread anxiety they call the "Great Fear." The very real events that energized the Truman administration, such as atomic tests by the Soviets, also heightened the emotional impact of stories about communist agents having stolen U.S. nuclear secrets or about gay subversives shaping U.S. foreign policy. A growing sense of insecurity, in turn, spurred even greater efforts to safeguard national security.

As this feeling of anxiety began to settle over U.S. politics, the U.S. Justice Department arrested, in 1950, several members of an alleged spy ring. Julius and Ethel Rosenberg, both members of the American Communist Party, became the central characters in this controversial episode.

The Rosenberg case, as with that of Hiss, became a Cold War melodrama. Their trial, the verdicts of guilty, the sentences of death, the numerous legal appeals, the worldwide protests, and their 1953 executions at Sing Sing Prison all provoked intense controversy. Could the Rosenbergs, the parents of two young children, have been involved in the theft of nuclear secrets? And if so, were their death sentences, on the charge of espionage, the constitutionally appropriate punishment? To their supporters, the Rosenbergs (who died maintaining their innocence) became symbols of how easily anticommunist hysteria could override rational analysis and legal-constitutional safeguards. Federal officials seemed primarily interested in calming the Great Fear by locating—and then sacrificing—convenient scapegoats. To others, however, the evidence presented at the couple's trial clearly showed that they had channeled nuclear information to the Soviets.

New cartloads of documents, including those that became available in the 1990s, have helped to focus, without quite ending, controversy over the Rosenberg case. The evidentiary record, as most historians now view it, demonstrates Julius Rosenberg's involvement in some kind of spying and Ethel Rosenberg's knowledge about his activities. Studies of other Cold War spy cases, however, also suggest that the U.S. government declined even to indict people who almost certainly had passed on important atomic-related information to the Soviets. In some instances, officials apparently feared a court trial would have revealed ongoing counter-espionage operations by the United States. Among all the people actually prosecuted for involvement with the Soviets, moreover, only Julius and Ethel Rosenberg faced a charge that carried the death penalty. Questions about precisely what information Julius Rosenberg helped convey to the USSR and how useful it actually proved to Soviet nuclear scientists also remain at issue.

The performance of the U.S. justice system during the Great Fear became another matter for sustained debate. How well did U.S. courts balance legitimate concerns about safeguarding national security with the protection of civil liberties? During the 1949 prosecution of leaders of the American Communist Party, for instance, the trial judge accepted Truman's Justice Department's claim that merely holding a leadership position in this political party helped further an international conspiracy against the United States and the larger "free world." The Marxist ideology of the American Communist Party and its theoretical publications, even in the absence of any proof of subversive *acts* by individual defendants, justified convicting the party's leaders of having committed the crime of sedition against the U.S. government.

This case eventually went to the U.S. Supreme Court and produced the landmark decision of *Dennis* v. *U.S.* (1951). Civil libertarians insisted that the government failed to present any evidence that Communist Party publications and speeches, by themselves, posed a "clear and present danger" to national security. In this view, the beliefs of the members of any political group, even an avowedly communist one, enjoyed the protection of the First Amendment. The government, in short, could only put actions, not ideas or political preferences, on trial. Although two dissenting Supreme Court justices adopted versions of this position, the majority modified the High Court's own "clear and present danger" doctrine and upheld the broader view of sedition-by-expression earlier advanced by the Truman administration and lower federal courts.

Even before the *Dennis* case reached the Supreme Court, however, the anticommunist credentials of Truman administration were drawing increased scrutiny from more zealous red-hunters. In Congress, most Republicans and many Democrats, denouncing Truman's initiatives as too limited, joined to pass the McCarran Internal Security Act of 1950. It authorized the detention, during any national emergency, of alleged subversives in special camps. It also created the Subversive Activities Control Board (SACB) to investigate organizations suspected of links to the Communist Party and to oversee registration of groups allegedly controlled by communists.

The Truman administration responded ambiguously. Although the president vetoed the McCarran Internal Security Act—a symbolic response that Congress quickly overrode—his administration authorized the FBI's J. Edgar Hoover to devise a secret detention program, which contained even fewer procedural safeguards than the one created by Congress, and continued to enforce its own loyalty program. Still, Truman could never defuse doubts about his anticommunist credentials and those of key members of his administration.

McCarthyism

Republican Senator Joseph McCarthy of Wisconsin eventually emerged as the Truman administration's primary accuser. An intelligence officer during the Second World War, McCarthy had entered national politics in the guise of a battle-hardened combat vet, "Tailgunner Joe." Enjoying a meteoric rise, which took him to the U.S. Senate in 1946, the rough-hewn McCarthy apparently preferred to be known as a brawler and boozer than as a legislator. The Great Fear, however, helped McCarthy refashion himself as a hard-driving, two-fisted anticommunist investigator, one who seemingly leaped out from the pages of a hard-boiled detective thriller.

In a famous 1950 speech at Wheeling, West Virginia, McCarthy charged Truman's State Department with employing hundreds of known communists. People rightly feared the future, according to McCarthy, "not because our only powerful potential enemy has sent men to invade our shores, but rather because of the traitorous actions of those who have been treated so well by this Nation." The people in this camp, according to McCarthy, included Secretary of State Acheson and his predecessor, General George C. Marshall.

A master of political imagery and sexual innuendo, McCarthy subtly linked together the Lavender and Red Scares. He portrayed anticommunists in Truman's administration as both overly privileged and insufficiently manly. Dean Acheson and his aides might pose as hard-headed realists who understood the dangers of communism, but McCarthy dismissed their claims. Lacking the all-around toughness of authentic anticommunists (such as the Wisconsin senator himself), people such as Acheson, who had been "born with silver spoons in their mouths," had degenerated into effete "enemies from within." To accentuate the secretary of state's supposed lack of manliness, McCarthy derided Acheson as the "Red Dean of fashion" and as the leader of the "lace handkerchief crowd."

By the final years of Truman's presidency, McCarthy seemed an unstoppable political force. Although McCarthy failed to substantiate most of his charges or to identify specific violations of the law, he lacked neither imagination nor potential targets. During the summer of 1950, a subcommittee of the U.S. Senate, after examining government files, concluded that McCarthy's charges against the State Department amounted to "the most nefarious campaign of half-truths and untruths in the history of this republic." McCarthy simply charged that the files had been "raped," and he went after Millard Tydings, the courtly Democratic senator who had chaired the subcommittee. The defeat of Tydings, whose opponents circulated a fabricated photograph linking him to pro-communist activities, in the November 1950 election seemed to confirm McCarthy's political clout and lack of scruples.

McCarthy's tactics produced considerable controversy. Despite his apparent reckless-ness, some influential people tolerated and even encouraged him. Conservative, staunchly anticommunist leaders within the Roman Catholic Church, for instance, embraced McCarthy, who was a Catholic. Leading Republicans welcomed McCarthy's assaults on their Democratic rivals. In contrast, the historically minded among the senator's oppo-nents saw him as the latest personification of a form of populist-style demagoguery, which became labelled **"McCarthyism."**

The National Security Constitution

Too much attention to the theatrics of McCarthyism, however, can obscure long-term political-constitutional shifts during the era of the Great Fear. Widespread concern about national security helped U.S. leaders refashion the nation's structure of governance. The sovereign people ratified only one addition to the formal, written Constitution during this era: The 22nd Amendment, adopted in 1951, responded to Roosevelt's election to third and fourth terms in the White House by limiting future presidents to two terms. But con-gressional legislation, especially the National Security Act of 1947 and the assumption of new powers by executive branch agencies—particularly the CIA, FBI, and the Pentagon—effectively changed the nation's constitutional structure and its approach to governance. The view that the presidency possessed only limited powers gave way to an opposing vision, which had been voiced during earlier times of perceived crisis such as the Second World War. Cold War conditions provided renewed justification for greatly extending the power of the national government, especially of the executive branch.

When Truman took the United States into a congressionally undeclared war in Korea, he encountered few constitutional obstacles. The idea of constitutional limitations only came into play after he asserted his presidential authority in 1952 and ordered his com-merce secretary to seize control of the domestic steel industry in order to prevent a threat-ened strike. Truman could have invoked the Taft-Hartley Act to obtain a 60-day "cooling off" period, but he resisted using a measure he had earlier (and unsuccessfully) vetoed. Truman claimed, in effect, that the Cold War had dramatically changed constitutional practice. The president, the nation's commander-in-chief, possessed virtually unlimited power whenever safeguarding national security required emergency action.

The "steel seizure case" (officially known as *Youngstown Sheet & Tube Company* v. *Sawyer*) quickly reached the U.S. Supreme Court. There, three justices, all Truman appointees, agreed with the president's claims of emergency executive powers. Six other justices, for differing reasons, rejected Truman's position as too broadly framed, but all expressed significant support, whenever national security issues came into play, for some-what less expansive views of presidential authority. Most constitutional scholars would come to see this 1952 case as a short-term defeat for Truman but hardly a long-term setback for national-security powers.

Truman's Fair Deal

Focus Question

What were the guiding assumptions of the Fair Deal, and which of its major initiatives seemed likely to pass through Congress? Which proposals seemed likely to stall there, and why?

Meanwhile, Harry Truman needed to operate within relatively narrow political boundaries when his administration left the national security arena and entered that of social welfare policy making. Truman's policy initiatives, which culminated in what the White House would call the Fair Deal, grew out of the Democratic Party's effort to frame a domestic agenda for the post-New Deal era.

Truman claimed to share much of Franklin Roosevelt's earlier vision. Many Democrats thus pressed him to embrace an expansive view, such as that set forth in FDR's Second Bill of Rights (1944) (see chapter 26), of how the national government might enhance the everyday security of ordinary citizens. Following the Second World War, after all, most Western European nations were creating or expanding their own "welfare states." These systems of governance, based on the principle and practice of using economic and social planning to guarantee all citizens certain substantive rights, such as access to adequate housing and medical care, featured an aggressive use of state power.

In the United States, however, proposals for governmental planning and new social welfare measures generally stalled. Critics had already assailed wartime Washington's extensive use of governmental power to regulate economic relationships as unnecessary and in conflict with the U.S. Constitution. During Truman's presidency, opposition to the kind of expansive social agenda suggested in FDR's Second Bill of Rights grew stronger. Any attempt to update the New Deal agenda for a postwar world, insisted most Republicans and some Democrats, could provide dangerous precedents for unconstitutionally trampling on private rights and erode traditional ideas about individual initiative and responsibility. Dixiecrat Democrats, for example, often joined with conservative Republicans to block any congressional legislation that might give Washington additional economic powers on the theory that such a move might imply analogous authority to begin dismantling white supremacy in the South. Weighing in on behalf of powerful business interests, the National Association of Manufacturers (NAM) consistently denounced the Truman administration as a menace to the nation's private, free-enterprise economic system.

The Employment Act of 1946 and the Promise of Economic Growth

The Truman administration, faced with this kind of opposition to economic planning and European-style welfare policies, sought an alternative vision of domestic social policy making. The 1946 debate over a "Full Employment Bill" provided it. This measure, as initially conceived, would have empowered Washington to ensure employment for all citizens seeking work. To the bill's opponents, the phrase "full employment" implied a step toward the European model of a welfare state, perhaps even toward socialism.

As the Democratic effort to enact this measure lost momentum, a scaled-back version moved forward. The law that Congress finally passed, renamed the Employment Act of 1946, called for "maximum" (rather than full) employment and specifically declared that private enterprise, not government, bore primary responsibility for economic decision making. The act nonetheless created a new executive branch body, the Council of Economic Advisers, to formulate long-range policy recommendations, and it thus signaled that the national government would assume some still undefined responsibility for the health and performance of the U.S. economy.

Moreover, the Employment Act of 1946 suggested that economic expertise now provided a vital national resource. The idea that *advice* from economic experts, as an alternative to government *planning,* could guarantee a constantly expanding economy helped muster crucial support for creating the Council of Economic Advisers. An influential group of economists, many of them disciples of Britain's John Maynard Keynes, pressed for this move. Their economic know-how, they claimed, could help government eliminate the boom-and-bust cycles that had long afflicted the nation's economy. Instead of abandoning the economy to the largely uncoordinated decisions of private individuals and corporations, economic expertise could help governmental and business leaders identify the policies most likely to produce growth.

The promise of economic expansion quickly came to dazzle postwar leaders. Using the relatively new measure of gross national product (GNP), economists claimed they could objectively calculate the nation's growing economic bounty. Developed in 1939, GNP—defined as the total dollar value of all goods and services produced in the nation during a given year—became the standard gauge of economic health. Corporate executives, who had generally feared that the end of the war would bring long-term labor unrest and trigger a deep recession, came to view a rising GNP as an important predictor of social stability. The Truman administration's domestic policy makers also welcomed the prospect of an expanding economy, which would automatically increase federal tax revenues and, thus, help remove some of the political obstacles blocking the financial path for the administration's domestic agenda. "With economic expansion, every problem is capable of solution," insisted one celebrant of economic growth. Another likened the promise of ongoing growth to finding the proverbial rainbow *and* the pot of gold at its end.

Truman and his advisers enthusiastically spread the gospel of governmentally stimulated economic growth. This new faith nicely dovetailed with the spending levels their national security plans required. The Cold War could serve as "an automatic pump primer" for the U.S. economy. At the same time, security-related assistance programs such as the Marshall Plan could create overseas markets and investment opportunities for U.S. businesses. The goal of sustained economic growth at home, in short, became linked to development in the world at large—and to the all-pervasive concern about protecting U.S. national security. Sharp increases in governmental spending for the Pentagon thus signaled a general economic policy that critical observers eventually began to call "military Keynesianism"—the practice of stimulating and regulating the economy through governmental spending in the military sector. *U.S. News and World Report*, a conservative weekly, suggested that government officials seemed to "have found the magic formula for almost endless good times."

Shaping the Fair Deal

In 1949, Truman unveiled a set of social welfare proposals he called the Fair Deal. He proposed extending popular New Deal programs, particularly Social Security and minimum wage laws; enacting legislation dealing with civil rights, national health care, and federal aid for education; and repealing the Taft-Hartley Act of 1947. The president also urged substantial spending on public housing projects, and his secretary of agriculture called for new governmental subsidies to support farm prices. The core assumption on which Truman built his entire Fair Deal—that sustained economic growth could finance enlarged government programs for specifically targeted groups—came to dominate policy planning. Changes to two prominent programs, both of which predated Truman's administration, illustrate the approach to domestic social policy that became standard procedure during the Fair Deal years.

The first, the so-called **GI Bill** (officially titled the Serviceman's Readjustment Act of 1944), provided a comprehensive social benefit package but only for those people who had served in the armed forces. Far more inclusive and clearly defined than programs for veterans of previous wars, the GI Bill gained crucial support from the conservative leadership of the American Legion. The law provided vets with financial assistance for college and job-training programs. Slightly more than 50 percent of veterans sought such funds, and during 1947, the year of peak enrollment, roughly half of the nation's entire college and university population received aid under the GI Bill. In addition, it gave veterans preferential treatment when applying for government jobs; favorable financial terms when borrowing money to purchase homes or businesses; and, eventually, comprehensive medical care in hospitals run by the Veterans Administration (VA). The Veterans Readjustment Assistance Act of 1952, popularly known as the GI Bill of Rights, extended these benefits to those who had served in the Korean War. The Truman administration never revived FDR's proposal for a Second Bill of Rights, but the Fair Deal did ensure that veterans would enjoy some of its key provisions.

The Social Security program also expanded during Truman's Fair Deal. Rebutting attacks against this New Deal measure by conservatives who denounced it as a poorly designed and unwarranted extension of federal power, advocates of Social Security stressed its carefully targeted provisions. Certainly, people who were disabled and blind deserved assistance, and older people had surely earned the "income security" provided by Social Security through their years of work and the monetary contributions withheld from their own paychecks. Under the Social Security Act of 1950, the level of benefits increased significantly; the retirement-related portions of the program became more flexible; and

The Postwar College Scene   This picture by the famed photojournalist Margaret Bourke-White shows veterans of the Second World War dominating available space in a classroom at the University of Iowa. Tapping financial support offered under the GI Bill (1944), more than 600 vets enrolled in 1946 at Iowa. Returning servicemen, who comprised more than 60 percent of this University's total enrollment, often taxed existing facilities here and at other universities throughout the country.

more than 10 million additional people, including agricultural workers, came into the Social Security system.

The Fair Deal's more expansive (and more expensive) proposals, however, either failed to gain congressional approval or passed in scaled-back form. Truman's plan for a comprehensive national health insurance program faced opposition from several different quarters. Consumer groups and labor unions, intent on creating nonprofit, community-run health plans, generally saw Truman's proposal for a centralized health system as a blueprint for unnecessarily bureaucratizing medical care. From a different perspective, the American Medical Association (AMA) and the American Hospital Association (AHA) opposed any direct governmental intervention in the traditional fee-for-service medical system and steered Congress toward a less intrusive alternative—expanding the federal financing of new hospitals under the previously enacted Hill-Burton Act (1946). In addition, large insurance companies, which were continuing to push their own private plans in cooperation with businesses (see chapter 26), also weighed in against the Truman plan. Opinion polls suggested that many voters, especially those who could enroll in affordable private health insurance plans such as the popular Blue Cross and Blue Shield systems, found themselves confused by or simply uninterested in Truman's initiative.

The Fair Deal's housing proposals met a similarly mixed reception. The severe postwar shortage of affordable housing in urban areas did stir some support for Washington's participation in home-building programs. Even some conservative Republicans, notably Senator Robert Taft of Ohio, supported the Housing Act of 1949 as a necessary response to a postwar housing pinch. Part of Truman's Fair Deal package, this measure authorized construction of 810,000 public housing units and provided federal funds for "urban renewal" zones, areas to be cleared of rundown dwellings and then rebuilt with new construction. The Housing Act of 1949 proclaimed ambitious goals but provided relatively modest funding, especially for its public-housing component. Private construction firms and realtors welcomed funding for urban renewal and for federal home loan guarantee programs such as those established under the GI Bill and those directed by the Federal Housing Administration (FHA). At the same time, they continually lobbied effectively against a more extensive program of publicly financed housing projects.

The Fair Deal, in short, proved most successful in advancing narrowly targeted social welfare measures. This meant the Truman administration provided significant assistance to veterans and to older Americans but failed to achieve its more ambitious goals of national health care and public housing construction. With opponents of the broader Fair Deal proposals dismissing them as "welfare schemes," the White House found it easier to advance the narrower initiatives that it could defend as fiscally sound "security" measures for specifically delineated groups of deserving recipients.

Civil Rights

The Truman administration also struggled to place at least some of the national government's power behind a growing civil-rights movement. A global struggle against the fascism of the Axis Powers had earlier assisted domestic campaigns against discrimination (see chapter 26), and subsequent efforts benefited from the postwar battle against communism. After returning to the home front, few service personnel of African, Latino, and Native American descent wished to remain passive bystanders when public laws and policing practices sometimes reduced them to second-class citizens. Moreover, people of color who had moved to larger cities, seeking to escape discrimination and find wartime employment, not only wanted to secure but to build on the social and economic gains they and their families had made during the earlier 1940s. Drives to translate the vision of liberty and equality on prominent display in FDR's Second Bill of Rights into reality also continued to animate some lawyers and grassroots activists during the immediate postwar period. The national government, from their perspectives, needed to mobilize its powerful resources to fight discrimination and injustice in the Cold War United States.

During his 1948 presidential campaign, Truman strongly endorsed the proposals of a civil-rights committee he had established in 1946. Its controversial report, entitled "To Secure These Rights," called for federal legislation against lynching; creation of a special civil-rights division within the Department of Justice; adoption of new initiatives against discrimination in employment, housing, and public facilities; and a plan for desegregating the U.S. military. These proposals had helped prompt the Dixiecrat revolt of 1948, but they also gained Truman significant support from African Americans and Latinos.

Truman continued to support the civil-rights cause. When successive congresses failed to enact legislation against lynching and poll taxes, which prevented most southern blacks from voting, leaders of the civil-rights movement turned to the White House and to the federal courts. The threat by A. Philip Randolph, head of the Brotherhood of Sleeping Car Porters, to work with activists such as Bayard Rustin in organizing a protest campaign, pushed Truman to issue an executive order, in 1948, which set in motion a gradual phasing out of the military's system of racial segregation.

Much as the antifascist environment of the Second World War had forced the Roosevelt administration to address some civil-rights issues, the Cold War climate helped energize Truman's Fair Dealers. Truman spoke candidly about how much legalized segregation tarnished the image of the United States in a Cold War world "which is 90 percent colored." Although the Cold War could help justify action against African American leaders whom governmental officials considered linked to subversive causes, it also made the federal government's tacit support of Jim Crow a foreign policy liability. Continuing efforts to preserve racialized segregation, spearheaded by Dixiecrats from the South, seemed in direct conflict with Washington's claim to represent liberty and equality in a world threatened by Soviet totalitarianism. The symbol of U.S. constitutional law still upholding racial separatism worked to the advantage of attorneys for the NAACP and for Latino groups such as LULAC, when they mounted court challenges against discriminatory measures, especially in the field of public education.

Lawyers from Truman's Justice Department appeared in court to support suits brought by civil-rights organizations. Working in concert, attorneys made the case against government-backed public school segregation and against "restrictive covenants" (legal agreements that prevented racial or religious minorities from acquiring real estate). In 1946, the Supreme Court declared restrictive covenants unconstitutional and began chipping away at the "separate-but-equal" principle, used since *Plessy* v. *Ferguson* (1896) to justify the legality of racially segregated public schools. A federal court in California, ruling on the case brought the previous year in Orange County by LULAC and the NAACP, held that segregating students of Mexican descent in separate, and unequal, schools violated their constitutional rights. According to one of the federal courts that heard this case—as *Mendez* v. *Westminster School District* in 1946—a separate school system could never pass constitutional muster, especially in a nation that had only recently emerged victorious over Nazi racism. The practice of "co-mingling" a diverse student body within the same educational institution "instills and develops a common cultural attitude," which would be "imperative for the perpetuation of American institutions and ideals," the court argued.

Subsequent court rulings cast further doubt on the future of the *Plessy* precedent. In 1948, a second federal court—with the case now entitled *Westminster School District* v. *Mendez*—agreed with the first: segregating Mexican-descended students violated their constitutional rights. Two years later, in cases involving students of African descent, the U.S. Supreme Court ruled unconstitutional, under the 14th Amendment, racial segregation in state-financed graduate and law schools. The familiar arguments used to legitimate racial segregation in other areas of public education now seemed ripe for successful constitutional challenges.

The years immediately after the Second World War, in sum, marked a turning point in domestic policy making. The New Deal's vision of comprehensive socioeconomic planning gave way to the Fair Deal's view: The nation could expect that uninterrupted economic growth would enable Washington to finance, through rising tax revenues, programs designed to assist specific groups. As one supporter of this approach argued, postwar policy makers were sophisticated enough to embrace "partial remedies," such as the GI Bill, rather than to wait for fanciful "cure-alls," such as FDR's Second Bill of Rights. Partisans of the Fair Deal hoped that at least some of these limited programs could be expanded in the years to come.

Signs of a Changing Culture

Focus Question
How did a resurgent civil-rights movement and a new suburban culture help signal changes in American life during the immediate postwar era?

The postwar years also accelerated the pace of cultural change. Encouraged by the advertising industry, most people seemed, at one level, to view most things new and novel as signs of progress. Yet, at another level, the speed and scope of cultural change generated widespread feelings of uneasiness and anxiety, which likely contributed to the Great Fear about subversion.

The Baseball "Color Line"

The complex interplay between celebrating and fearing change can be seen in the effort, during the 1940s and early 1950s, to desegregate the sport-entertainment business known as Organized Baseball. In 1947, the national pastime finally abandoned its policy of racial segregation when Jack Roosevelt (**Jackie**) **Robinson,** a multi-sport star at UCLA who had later played baseball in the Negro National League, took over first base for the Brooklyn Dodgers. Some ballplayers of European descent, including several in Robinson's own club, considered a boycott. Baseball's leadership, seeking new sources of on-field talent and seeing a steady stream of African American fans coming through the turnstiles, quickly displayed the power it could wield over its labor force. It squelched dissent by threatening to suspend any player who refused to play with or against Robinson.

Officially, Organized Baseball desegregated. Shortly after Robinson's debut, the Cleveland Indians acquired center fielder Larry Doby and, somewhat later, the already legendary hurler, Leroy (Satchel) Paige. Other top-flight players abandoned the Negro leagues for clubs in the American and National circuits. The skills of Robinson, named Rookie of the Year in 1947 and the National League's Most Valuable Player in 1949, and other players of African descent quickly carried the day. Although talented light-skinned Latinos had long passed through the racial barrier, Orestes ("Minnie") Minoso, a Cuban-born veteran of the Negro Leagues, became the first Afro-Latino to break into the Big Leagues in 1949. Close students of the game soon credited players such as Robinson and Minoso, fleet-footed and daring base runners, with reintroducing an aggressive style of play to a sport that had come to emphasize home runs and a base-to-base approach to scoring runs.

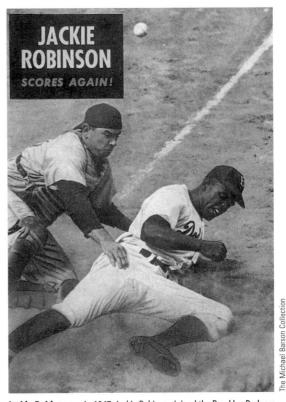

The Michael Barson Collection

Jackie Robinson In 1947, Jackie Robinson joined the Brooklyn Dodgers and became the first African American since the 19th century to play major league baseball. He had served as a lieutenant in the Army during the Second World War. Racial integration of the national pastime of baseball became a powerful symbol of progress in race relations.

Major League teams began fielding greater numbers of African American and Latino players, and some mounted extensive recruiting operations in Mexico and throughout the Caribbean. Years later, during the 50th anniversary of Robinson's debut, Major League Baseball would stage elaborate memorial ceremonies for Robinson, who had died in 1972, and would congratulate itself for having been at the forefront of the fight against racial prejudice during the Cold War years.

As historians generally note, however, baseball's Cold War leadership had unofficially limited its own desegregation effort. It allowed several teams—which claimed, improbably, that they could find no talented African American or Latino prospects—to wait years before integrating their rosters. More commonly, clubs restricted the number of African American and Latino players they would take on and adopted a Jim Crow policy for hiring managers, coaches, and front-office personnel. When age forced Jackie Robinson's retirement as a player, for instance, he found himself effectively shut out of the game he had earlier helped integrate.

Even many of the players who followed in Robinson's on-field footsteps confronted continuing obstacles. African American and Latino players, who faced subtle barriers while competing for a spot on a Major League roster, often encountered overt, off-the-field discrimination during the annual spring training period in the South and South-west. Young prospects endured similar problems while playing for minor league teams, generally located in relatively small towns with few services or businesses that catered to people of color. Spanish-speaking players faced special difficulties that extended beyond language. Even stars such as Minoso, accustomed to playing top-quality base-ball in the Negro Leagues and Caribbean winter leagues, struggled to convince man-agers, sportswriters, and teammates (African Americans as well as Caucasians) that they could "understand" the subtleties of either the "national pastime" or of the larger North American culture.

New Suburban Developments

The culture of postwar suburbia also showed how the celebration of cultural change and a resistance to its impact could coexist in an uneasy tension. Suburbs had long been part of the national landscape. During the late 1940s, however, suburban living came within the means of millions of families. The new Long Island town of Levittown, New York, which welcomed its first residents in October 1947, quickly became the preeminent symbol of postwar suburban culture.

Nearly everything about Levittown seemed unprecedented. Levitt & Sons, a construc-tion company that had mass-produced military barracks during the Second World War, claimed to be completing a five-room bungalow every 15 minutes. Architectural critics might sneer at these "little boxes," but potential buyers would brave long lines for a chance to purchase one. By 1950, New York's Levittown contained more than 10,000 homes and 40,000 residents, and bulldozers and construction crews were sweeping through similarly planned developments across the country.

To assist potential buyers, the national government continued to offer an extensive set of programs. The FHA, established during the New Deal, helped underwrite an elaborate lending system. Typically, people who bought FHA-financed homes needed only 5 percent of the purchase price as a down payment; they could borrow the rest and guarantee their loan with a long-term, government-insured mortgage. Military veterans enjoyed even more favorable terms under the GI loan program. This kind of public assistance to middle-income families made it cheaper for them to purchase a suburban house than to rent a sig-nificantly smaller apartment in most cities. Moreover, homeowners enjoyed another valu-able governmental subsidy. They could deduct the interest payments on their mortgages from their federal income tax.

The postwar suburb gained a reputation for being an ideal place in which to raise children, which U.S. families were having in unprecedented numbers. Toward the end of the Second World War, a number of demographic forces, including earlier marriages and rising incomes, had begun to fuel a **"baby boom"** that would last until the end of the 1950s. The baby boom generation, a key segment of the U.S. population for decades to come, made an immediate imprint on suburban culture. With houses generally occupying only about 15 percent of suburban lots, baby boomers could, with the help of their parents, convert the large lawns into lush, green private playgrounds. In addition, suburban children could claim credit for generating and consuming growing segments of the nation's GNP, especially those connected to entertainment, leisure, and public education. Suburban schools were as new as the homes, and school boards used their well-appointed facilities to attract both skilled, enthusiastic teachers and the children of other middle-income families.

In many respects, postwar suburban culture exuded a sense of optimism. Suburbia often symbolized new possibilities, confidence in the future, and acceptance of change. It also encouraged the vision of continued economic growth. Because the output of developers never caught up with the demand of buyers during the early Cold War era, suburbanites discovered they could often sell their existing home at a substantial profit and move up to a more spacious, more expensive dwelling in an even newer suburb. A suburban home, in short, became both a symbol of success and an important, highly liquid financial asset.

At the same time, some of the most noticeable markers of postwar suburban culture seemed to symbolize resistance to certain kinds of changes. As many contemporary observers noted, the new suburbs appeared to offer many of its residents a material and psychological refuge. Most obviously, buying a suburban home could provide many families of European descent a way of cushioning the impact of social and demographic change. As African American families continued to migrate to northern and western cities in search of jobs and greater opportunity,

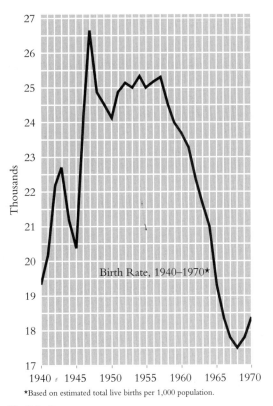

*Based on estimated total live births per 1,000 population.

The Baby Boom

white families began to see moving to the new suburbs as a way to avoid living in racially integrated communities. Governmental policies generally contributed to this trend through the financial incentives provided to homebuyers. Moreover, after the U.S. Supreme Court declared restrictive covenants unconstitutional, local officials rarely enforced the decision. Various informal and extralegal arrangements prevented, until well into the 1960s, any African American from buying a home in Long Island's Levittown.

Other policies and practices also helped segregate the new postwar suburbs. Although land and building costs would have been cheaper in these areas than in urban locales, most suburbanites jealously guarded their community's legal power to veto the building of public housing projects, whose units were likely to become racially and ethnically integrated. As a result, the federal government clustered housing projects on relatively expensive, high-density urban sites, a practice that helped make suburban living seem all that more desirable. At the same time, the lending industry generally channeled government-guaranteed loans for single-family homes toward the new suburbs, and private lenders routinely denied African Americans and Latinos the credit they needed to buy a newly built home. Their individual decisions, bankers insisted, rested purely on economic calculations. African American and Latino buyers invariably lacked the financial resources, lenders claimed, to qualify for a loan on a new suburban home. They needed to readjust their sights and seek housing within urban areas or in older suburbs. Any discrimination produced by this system, the housing-lending industry contended, flowed from the unintentional consequences of entirely race-blind, marketplace calculations.

The people who dominated the new suburban housing industry thus denied they were intentionally contributing to the spatial patterning of racial discrimination. William Levitt could proudly identify his private housing projects with the public crusade against communism. "No man who owns his house and lot can be a Communist," he remarked in 1948. "He has too much to do." Even as Levitt was claiming he could help solve the problem of housing—and perhaps even that of communist subversion—he was also resisting any suggestion that his firm's business-related choices bore any direct relationship to racial discrimination.

Similarly, developers saw the new suburbia's gender politics as the "natural" byproduct of larger marketplace forces. The financial industry, adopting a policy that resembled its approach to racial matters, extended the vast majority of its loan guarantees to men of European descent. Only rarely could single women, from any ethnic background, obtain loans. The FHA, a governmental agency, justified the gender tilt in its policies by insisting that men were the primary family breadwinners and that single women seldom made enough money to qualify as good credit risks.

Postwar Hollywood

Postwar Hollywood turned out powerful symbols of the Cold War era's fascination with— and fear of—cultural change. When the postwar era began, Hollywood still dominated the entertainment business. Enjoying the reopening of overseas markets and welcoming the return of their male stars from military service, the major studios expected to prosper during the postwar era. According to marketing studies, most people simply "went to the movies," giving little thought to what picture they might see. In 1946, Hollywood's attendance figures and profits reached all-time highs. As one historian later estimated, the average number of moviegoers in a single week, 90 million, amounted to nearly three-quarters of the people realistically able to reach a motion picture theater!

Hollywood, still congratulating itself for having cheered the nation through the Depression and the Second World War, expected to perform much the same service during the onset of the Cold War. Perhaps no movie genre seemed better designed to cheerlead than the Hollywood musical. Filled with lively stars, upbeat tunes, and flashy dance sequences, musicals invariably expressed optimism about the future. MGM's *On the Town* (1949), based on a 1944 Broadway smash and updated to the Cold War period, epitomized the early postwar musical. It saturated movie screens with hopeful imagery. During 24 hours of shore leave, three U.S. sailors sing and dance their way through New York City, sample the fruits of both elite and popular culture, and fall in love with three equally vibrant young women. Moving at a breakneck pace, *On the Town* suggested just how much three virile servicemen might accomplish in one day. Ending with a title card proudly proclaiming it had been filmed in "Hollywood, USA," this musical also seemed to herald the U.S. film industry's own bright future.

Even as *On the Town* arrived in movie theaters, however, Hollywood's fortunes were starting to change. By 1949, attendance figures—along with profits—began to plummet. During the next decade, Hollywood would lose fully half of its 1946 audience, and many studios would face bankruptcy.

Cultural historians once blamed television for keeping potential moviegoers at home, but Hollywood's difficulties set in even before TV became a serious rival. The same year MGM shot *On the Town*, for instance, the U.S. Supreme Court ruled that antitrust laws required the major studios to give up their highly profitable ownership of local movie theaters. This decision, the *Paramount Case* (1948), rocked Hollywood just as it faced labor strife, internal conflict over blacklisting, and soaring production costs. TV simply delivered another, albeit substantial, blow to an industry already reeling backward.

Meanwhile, as Hollywood struggled to adapt to changing times, images of fear and hopelessness began to pervade some of its own productions. An important cycle of 1940s motion pictures, first noticed by critics in France, came to be called *films noirs* or "dark cinema." The images of crime and of social behavior in many of these movies challenged established censorship limits, which the Hollywood studios had been enforcing under their Production Code since the mid-1930s. The industry, in fact, had refused to allow production of earlier versions of some of the noirish film scripts brought to the screen during the Cold War era. Nearly always filmed in black and white and often set at night in large cities, *films noirs* purported to peek into the dark corners of the American Way of Life. Noir characters continued to pursue dreams and hopes but with little chance of ever succeeding. Failure and loss, in *films noirs*, seemed to be the rule rather than the exception.

Most of Hollywood's *films noirs* conspicuously featured alluring *femmes fatales*, beautiful and dangerous women who challenge the prevailing order, particularly its gender hierarchies. Portrayed as in revolt against the popular injunction to support her man, the *femme fatale* character represented an image very different from that of the always faithful, and eternally nurturing, wife and mother. Usually unmarried or childless, amoral *femmes fatales* threaten both men, who were generally portrayed as weak and ineffectual, and other, less assertive women. Ultimately, however, Hollywood's *femmes fatales* fail to overcome the male-dominated forces they seek to challenge.

In *The File on Thelma Jordan* (1949), an archetypal *noir*, Barbara Stanwyck's title character cynically infiltrates the marriage of a weak-willed district attorney. Neither love nor even lust drives her illicit affair with him. Instead, she calculatedly seduces him as part of a cleverly ambitious, but ultimately unsuccessful, scheme to manipulate the criminal justice system. The postwar era's most prominent female stars—including Stanwyck, Joan Crawford, Rita Hayworth, and Lana Turner—achieved both popular and critical acclaim playing *femmes fatales*, women whose desire for radical change ultimately ends in failure.

In sum, developments in the national pastime of baseball, in the new suburbia, and in the Hollywood film industry provide three vivid examples of a more general cultural pattern: an ambivalent response to changes ushered in during the Cold War era. Alterations in supposedly settled cultural patterns could signal both the promise of living in the postwar United States and the potentially disastrous consequences of confronting changes that threatened to overwhelm both the daily lives of individuals and the cultural cohesion of the nation.

By the early 1950s, according to many contemporary observers, Cold War U.S. culture seemed in need, at the very least, of new symbols of stability. Particularly in the realms of politics and governance, there appeared a deeply felt desire for signs of reassurance. With a positive approval rating hovering under 30 percent, Harry Truman seemed to symbolize disarray, even despair. The "Little Man from Missouri" now seemed far too small a figure to lead the United States out of a time marked by ambiguous, even dire, signposts. Most people, including Truman, appeared to look forward to the end of his tenure in the White House.

From Truman to Eisenhower

Harry Truman refused even to consider running for another term in 1952. Still, his tumultuous years in the public spotlight put his Democratic Party on the defensive, and denunciations of communism and of Truman fueled an energetic Republican campaign.

The Election of 1952

Adlai Stevenson of Illinois, the Democratic presidential candidate in 1952, tried to take a hard line on national security. He warned that "Soviet secret agents and their dupes" had "burrowed like moles" into governments throughout the world. "We cannot let our guard drop for even a moment," he claimed. Stevenson approved of the conviction of the American Communist Party's leaders and the dismissal of schoolteachers who were party members. A solidly anticommunist stance, however, could not save Stevenson or the Democratic Party. The GOP's formula for electoral victory could be reduced to a simple equation, "K_1C_2": "Korea, corruption, and communism."

The Republicans first linked Stevenson's candidacy to the unpopular Truman presidency. They criticized Truman for mishandling the Korean War and highlighted revelations about some members of Truman's administration having solicited kickbacks in exchange for the granting of governmental contracts. The GOP's staunchly anticommunist vice-presidential candidate, Senator Richard Nixon of California, called Stevenson "Adlai the appeaser" and charged him with holding a Ph.D. from "Dean Acheson's Cowardly College of Communist Containment." Some Republicans even questioned the manliness of the Democratic contender, a soft-spoken lawyer-politician who remained unmarried following his 1949 divorce.

A Soldier-Politician

For their presidential candidate, Republicans looked to a hero of the Second World War, General Dwight David Eisenhower, popularly known as "Ike." Eisenhower had grown up in Kansas, graduated from West Point, ascended through Army ranks, and directed the Normandy invasion of 1944 as Supreme Allied Commander. He had served as Army Chief of Staff from 1945 to 1948 and, after an interim period as president of Columbia University, had become the commander of NATO, a post he held until May 1952. Eisenhower had never sought elective office, but a half-century of public service, most of it in the military, had taught him skills he found useful during his sudden plunge into partisan politics. Initially uncomfortable in the spotlight, Eisenhower fought through early difficulties and, with help from a bevy of consultants, developed an appealing media persona.

Eisenhower's personal appeal generally dazzled political insiders and commentators. Although Ike's partisan affiliations had long remained vague—hazy enough for some Democrats to have courted him as their own presidential nominee in 1948—he eventually emerged as the GOP's savior. Key Republicans, in turn, convinced Eisenhower that Senator Robert Taft, the likely GOP nominee if Ike declined to run, leaned too far to the right on domestic issues and lacked a firm commitment to containment policies overseas. Eisenhower, claiming to take a middle-of-the-road stance on controversial issues, appeared ready to direct the nation through the Cold War as skillfully as he had led it through a hot one. A generally adoring Washington press corps, grumbled Adlai Stevenson, embraced

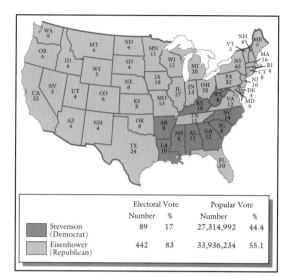

	Electoral Vote		Popular Vote	
	Number	%	Number	%
Stevenson (Democrat)	89	17	27,314,992	44.4
Eisenhower (Republican)	442	83	33,936,234	55.1

Map 27.4 Presidential Election, 1952 In this overwhelming victory for Eisenhower, Stevenson carried only a few states. Note that the so-called solid South remained largely Democratic. This trend would shift substantially over the next two decades.

the former war hero before learning "what his party platform would be" or "what would be the issues of the campaign." The Republican effort in 1952, the first to experiment with the possibilities of televised appeals, effectively tapped its presidential candidate's charisma. A popular GOP campaign simply announced: "I Like IKE!"

The first military leader to gain the presidency since Ulysses S. Grant (1869–77), Eisenhower achieved a great personal victory in 1952. The Eisenhower-Nixon ticket rolled up almost 7 million more popular votes than its Democratic opponents and dominated the Electoral College tally by a margin of 442 to 89. Despite Ike's trouncing of Stevenson, however, the Republican Party made relatively modest gains. It managed a single-vote majority in the U.S. Senate and an eight-vote edge over the Democrats in the House of Representatives. The Democratic coalition Franklin Roosevelt had forged during the 1930s thus survived. It did, however, show some signs of fraying, especially in the South. There, the votes of white southerners, many of which had gone to the Dixiecrats in 1948, began moving toward the Republicans. Eisenhower carried four states in the Democratic Party's once solid South.

Conclusion

An emphasis on aggressively safeguarding national security helped reshape national life during the years immediately following the Second World War. As worsening relations between the United States and the Soviet Union developed into a Cold War, the Truman administration pursued policies that expanded the power of the national government, particularly those of the executive branch. The militarization of foreign policy, presaged in the Truman Doctrine and solidified in NSC-68, intensified after the United States went to war in Korea in 1950.

The Cold War climate also affected the home front. People debated how best to protect national security, combat subversion, and calm cultural anxieties. The New Deal's vision, outlined in FDR's Economic Bill of Rights, faded, but Truman's Fair Deal offered a new view of social policy making. Fair Dealers promised that the wisdom of economic experts could guarantee economic growth and thereby provide the tax revenues to finance a set of effectively targeted social welfare programs. The Truman administration also pressed for national measures against racial discrimination.

The 1952 election of Dwight D. Eisenhower gave the Republicans the presidency for the first time in 20 years. Eisenhower's personal appeal, however, did not signal an imminent end to the power of the Democratic coalition that had held electoral sway since the 1930s. How would its vision of liberty and equality, as modified during the Fair Deal years, fare during the rest of the 1950s?

SUGGESTED READINGS

David Reynolds, *One World Divisible: A Global History since 1945* (2001) provides an international context for the emerging Cold War; Walter LaFeber, *America, Russia, and the Cold War, 1945–2002* (9th rev. ed., 2002) offers an expert interpretive synthesis of U.S. policies; and Melvyn P. Leffler and David Painter, eds., *The Origins of the Cold War: Rewriting Histories* (2005) presents accessible essays on Cold War controversies. Melvyn P. Leffler, *The Specter of Communism* (1994) is a brief, critical account of the onset of the Cold War. Leffler's *A Preponderance of Power: National Security, the Truman Administration, and the Cold War* (1992) offers more detail, as do Michael J. Hogan, *A Cross of Iron: Harry S. Truman and the Origins of the National Security State, 1945–1954* (1998), and Arnold A. Offner, *Another Such Victory: President Truman and the Cold War, 1945-1953* (2002). John Lewis Gaddis, *The Cold War: A New History* (2005) and his many other books present a less critical view. Alonso L. Hamby, *Man of the People: A Life of Harry S. Truman* (1995) provides an overview of Truman and his presidency.

On the Korean War, William Stueck, *Rethinking the Korean War: A New Diplomatic and Strategic History* (2004) and *The Korean War: An International History* (1995) provide overviews, while Bruce Cumings's many books, including *Korea: The Unknown War* (coauthored with Jon Halliday) (1988), provide a more critical view. Postwar reconstruction of former enemies is expertly treated in John Dower, *Embracing Defeat: Japan in the Wake of World War II* (2000), and Marc Trachtenberg, *A Constructed Peace: The Making of the European Settlement, 1945–1963* (1999).

On communism and anticommunism in America during this period, Allen Weinstein and Alexander Vassiliev, *The Haunted Wood: Soviet Espionage in America, the Stalin Era* (1999) examines Soviet espionage. Stanley I. Kutler, *American Inquisition: Justice and Injustice in the Cold War* (1982) and Ellen Schrecker, *The Age of McCarthyism* (2001) stress the excesses of anticommunist crusading.

The effect of the Cold War and containment on American culture is the subject of many excellent studies. Michael S. Sherry, *In the Shadow of War: The United States Since the 1930s* (1995), a broad synthesis, and Stephen Whitfield, *The Culture of the Cold War* (rev. ed., 1996) are good places to begin. Tom Englehardt, *The End of Victory Culture and the Disillusioning of a Generation* (1995) provides an influential interpretation. Paul Boyer, *By the Bomb's Early Light* (1985) and Alan Nadel, *Containment Culture: American Narrative, Postmodernism, and the Nuclear Age* (1995) examine diverse cultural effects of the atomic age. Lary May, *The Big Tomorrow: Hollywood and the Politics of the American Way* (2000) examines Hollywood film culture. Jessica Wang, *American Science in an Age of Anxiety: Scientists, Anticommunism, and the Cold War* (1999) stresses FBI pressure on scientists to support the

Cold War. Lizabeth Cohen, *A Consumer's Republic: Mass Consumption in Postwar America* (2003) critically highlights the convergence of a number of important Cold War-era social and political forces.

Visit the Liberty Equality Power Companion Web site for resources specific to this textbook: http://www.thomsonedu.com/history/murrin

Also find self-tests and additional resources at ThomsonNOW. Thomson-NOW is an integrated online suite of services and resources with proven ease of use and efficient paths to success, delivering the results you want—NOW!

www.thomsonedu.com/login/

28

Affluence and Its Discontents, 1953–1963

With the end of the fighting in Korea in 1953, Cold War tensions somewhat abated. A new U.S. president, Dwight David Eisenhower (1953–61), modulated the pitch of the anticommunist rhetoric coming from the White House. Yet he and his successor, John F. Kennedy (1961–63), pledged not only to continue a global anticommunist foreign policy but to take it in new directions.

At home, Ike and JFK supported, with differing degrees of enthusiasm, efforts to extend some of the domestic programs initiated during the 1930s and 1940s. Sustained economic growth during the late 1950s and early 1960s encouraged talk about an age of "affluence." It also generated concern about the spread of social conformity, the behavior and cultural tastes of young people, and the impact of commercial mass culture. At the same time, discussions about the distribution of the nation's economic bounty and movements to end racial discrimination triggered new debates over the ways in which the use of governmental power might affect how people understood—and enjoyed—liberty and equality.

Foreign Policy, 1953–1960

Focus Question
In what ways did the "New Look" reorient the foreign policy of containment?

The U.S. strategy for containing communism began shifting focus and direction during the 1950s. Bipolar confrontations between the United States and the Soviet Union over European issues continued alongside greater attention to building up nuclear arsenals and directing often-subtle power plays in the **Third World:** the Middle East, Asia, Latin America, and Africa.

Eisenhower Takes Command

Eisenhower honored a campaign pledge by personally traveling to Korea, in hope of speeding the end of U.S. military involvement there. Negotiations to conclude the Korean War temporarily broke down, however, over whether or not North Korean and Chinese prisoners of war (POWs) could choose to remain in South Korea. Anxious to conclude

CHRONOLOGY

1953	Korean War ends • Julius and Ethel Rosenberg executed • *Playboy* magazine debuts
1954	Joseph McCarthy censured by U.S. Senate • Communist Control Act passed • *Brown* v. *Board of Education of Topeka* decision issued • SEATO formed • Arbenz government overthrown in Guatemala • Elvis Presley releases first record on Sun label • Geneva Peace Accords in Southeast Asia signed
1955	Montgomery bus boycott begins • *National Review* founded • *Brown II* decision issued • U.S. deals with Suez Crisis • Anti-Soviet uprisings occur in Poland and Hungary • Federal Highway Act passed • Eisenhower reelected
1957	Eisenhower sends troops to Lebanon • Eisenhower sends troops to Little Rock, Arkansas • Congress passes Civil Rights Act, first civil-rights legislation in 80 years • Soviets launch *Sputnik* • Gaither Report urges more defense spending
1958	National Defense Education Act passed by Congress • *The Affluent Society* published
1959	Khrushchev visits United States
1960	Civil Rights Act passed • U-2 incident ends Paris summit • Kennedy elected president • Sit-in demonstrations begin
1961	Bay of Pigs invasion fails • Berlin Wall erected • Freedom rides begin in the South • Kennedy announces Alliance for Progress
1962	Cuban Missile Crisis brings superpowers to brink of war • Kennedy sends troops to University of Mississippi to enforce integration
1963	Civil-rights activists undertake march on Washington • Betty Friedan's The Feminine Mystique published • Kennedy assassinated (November 22); Lyndon Johnson becomes president

matters, Eisenhower began to hint about using nuclear weapons if diplomacy failed. Talks soon resumed, and on July 27, 1953, both sides signed a truce that established a commission of neutral nations to handle the POW issue. (The POWs were subsequently allowed to determine whether they wished to be repatriated to their own countries.) A conflict during which more than 2 million Asians, mostly noncombatants, and 53,000 Americans died finally ended. A formal peace treaty remained unsigned, however, and the 38th parallel, which divided North and South Korea, became one of the most heavily fortified borders in the world.

At home, Ike gradually wrested control of the national security issue from more militant anticommunists, including Senator Joseph McCarthy. A Republican-controlled Congress did exceed the wishes of the Eisenhower administration when it passed the Communist Control Act of 1954. This measure barred the American Communist Party from running candidates in elections and extended the registration provisions of the 1950 McCarran Act. With a GOP president and a former general in the White House, however, most Republicans began to inch away from aggressively confrontational styles of anticommunist politics.

Joe McCarthy finally careened out of control. While heading up a special Senate Subcommittee on Investigations, popularly known as the "McCarthy Committee," the senator enjoyed broad subpoena powers and legal immunity from libel suits. He could charge reluctant witnesses with selling out their country and lead sympathetic ones through stories about a vast Red Menace. After differences with military officials prompted McCarthy to speculate about subversives in the U.S. Army, a Senate committee conducted a televised investigation into his charges. Under the glare of TV lights, McCarthy allowed himself to play the role of a crude bully, who carelessly hurled wild slanders in every direction. In March 1954, the veteran journalist Edward R. Murrow devoted one of his "See It Now" TV programs to a dissection of McCarthy. Borrowing a tactic from McCarthy's own political playbook, other critics even hinted that the senator and his aides seemed lacking in "manliness." Finally, in late 1954, McCarthy's U.S. Senate colleagues approved, by a margin of 65 to 22, a resolution censuring him for "unbecoming" conduct. McCarthyism began receding to the fringes of domestic political culture, and McCarthy faded from the limelight. He would die, in 1957, while still a seldom-noticed member of the senate.

Meanwhile, the Eisenhower administration crafted its own national security agenda. Coming in the wake of the bombast of McCarthyism, its relatively low-key style of anticommunism could seem eminently reasonable and moderate. The apparent unreliability of legislators such as McCarthy strengthened the case for the White House when it asserted a constitutional privilege to withhold classified national security materials from Congress. Eisenhower generally refrained, however, from vigorously pressing claims about presidential power, as Truman had done in the "steel seizure case" of 1952, and avoided any serious legal-constitutional confrontations with the judiciary.

Relatively free from congressional and judicial oversight, the Eisenhower administration extended earlier programs of domestic surveillance and of covert action overseas. It also backed a secret program to develop new aerial surveillance capabilities; by 1956, intelligence photographs taken from the new **U-2 spy planes** provided U.S. strategists with a clear view of the Soviet arsenal.

Most historians have come to see Eisenhower, especially at the beginning of his presidency, as an adroit political strategist. He could aggressively press the power of his office while often seeming to be doing relatively little. In the words of one scholar, Eisenhower conducted a "hidden hand presidency." Mindful of how the pugnacious style of his predecessor had often dragged Harry Truman into partisan disputes and political scandals, Ike carefully guarded his personal popularity and reputation. To do this, he preferred to remain in the background of public controversies and project an air of calm steadiness, which sometimes bordered on the aloof. In foreign policy, he usually allowed John Foster Dulles, his secretary of state from 1953 to 1959, to take center stage. Ike also encouraged the idea that George Humphrey, his secretary of the treasury, and Sherman Adams, his chief of staff, looked after domestic matters.

The New Look, Global Alliances, and Summitry

Generally working behind the scenes, Eisenhower oversaw a refashioning of the nation's anticommunist foreign policy. To begin, he allowed Secretary of State Dulles to warn, repeatedly, that Washington would consider adopting measures to "rollback," rather than simply to contain, communism. This approach differed from one that international observers, such as Britain's Winston Churchill, suggested. In their view, the change of leadership in Moscow, following the 1953 death of Joseph Stalin, created opportunities for significantly reducing Cold War tensions. Nikita Khrushchev, who would eventually emerge as the new Soviet leader, did talk about "peaceful coexistence." Seeking to free up resources to produce more consumer goods, Khrushchev also inaugurated reductions in the USSR's armed forces.

Meanwhile, the Eisenhower administration undertook a review and a subsequent revision of U.S. military and strategic policies. The head of the Joint Chiefs of Staff urged cutting back the U.S. military budget and emphasizing nuclear weaponry and air power. Dubbed the "New Look," these changes dovetailed with Eisenhower's concern that spiraling military expenditures might eventually strangle economic growth. The president, despite his background in the Army, came to rely on advanced nuclear capabilities, to deemphasize costly ground forces, and to listen attentively to the Air Force's "bomber generals," such as Curtis LeMay, who headed the Strategic Air Command (SAC). In addition, advocates of the New Look stressed the value of covert action, cultural outreach, and economic pressure.

Under Eisenhower, the United States elevated psychological warfare and "informational" programs into major Cold War weapons. The government-run Voice of America extended the reach of its radio broadcasts and increased the number of languages in which it programmed. Washington also secretly funded Radio Free Europe, Radio Liberty (beamed to the Soviet Union), and Radio Asia, all ostensibly privately run ventures. In 1953, Eisenhower persuaded Congress to create the United States Information Agency (USIA), an executive-branch office that coordinated anticommunist informational and propaganda campaigns.

A key centerpiece of the New Look, the doctrine of **"massive retaliation,"** gambled that the threat of unleashing U.S. nuclear weaponry would check Soviet expansion. The administration publicly hinted that it would not hesitate, in any future confrontation involving communist military moves and U.S national security, to launch a nuclear attack against the USSR. Secretly, it drew up plans for such an eventuality. To extend the U.S. nuclear umbrella, the Eisenhower administration placed additional weapons under the direct control of military commanders, particularly those in SAC.

Eisenhower's administration also concluded a set of global military alliances. It expanded NATO to include West Germany in 1955 and added two other mutual defense pacts with noncommunist nations in Central and Southeast Asia. The Southeast Asia Treaty Organization (SEATO), formed in 1954, linked the United States to Australia, France, Great Britain, New Zealand, Pakistan, the Philippines, and Thailand. The Central

Treaty Organization (CENTO), created in 1959, aligned the United States with Pakistan, Iran, Turkey, Iraq, and Great Britain.

Simultaneously trying to soothe relations with the USSR, Eisenhower also stressed the importance of negotiations, including high-level "summit meetings," with the Soviets. In May 1955, U.S. and Soviet leaders decided finally to end the postwar occupation of Austria and to transform it into an independent and neutral nation. Two months later, the United States, the Soviet Union, Britain, and France met in Geneva, Switzerland, and agreed to inaugurate cultural exchanges as one way of reducing Cold War suspicions. Some optimistic observers even began to talk about the reconciliatory "spirit of Geneva." During the fall of 1959, as a way of healing recent rifts over the future of a still-divided Berlin, Khrushchev toured the United States. His most publicized stops included a farm in Iowa, a Hollywood studio, and Disneyland. Although a 1960 Paris summit meeting fell apart, amidst a bitter war of words, after the Soviets shot down a U-2 spy plane over their territory, the tone of Cold War rhetoric seemed to grow somewhat less strident during Eisenhower's eight years in office.

The two superpowers even began to consider how they might reduce their stockpiles of nuclear weaponry. Eisenhower's **"Open Skies"** initiative of 1955 proposed mutual reconnaissance flights over each other's territory to verify disarmament efforts. Always suspicious and hyper-secretive, the Soviet leadership balked at this idea, but the rival nations did make some progress toward limiting atomic testing. Responding to the health hazards of radioactive fallout, both slowed the pace of aboveground testing and even discussed a broader test-ban agreement.

For some Americans, however, these efforts came far too late. Government documents finally declassified in the 1980s confirmed suspicions that people who had lived "downwind" from nuclear test sites during the 1940s and 1950s had contracted a disproportionate number of atomic-related illnesses. Subsequent revelations also showed that the U.S. government had covertly conducted experiments with radioactive materials on unsuspecting citizens.

Meanwhile, events in Eastern Europe tested the likelihood of the United States and the USSR actually squaring off, militarily, there. By the mid-1950s, many of the Soviet-dominated "satellite" countries in that region resented their badly managed communist economies and detested their police-state regimes, ultimately supported by Moscow's military might. Seizing on hints of what appeared to be a post-Stalin relaxation of the USSR's heavy hand, insurgents in Poland staged a brief rebellion in June 1956. They forced the Soviets to accept Wladyslaw Gomulka, an old foe of Stalin, as Poland's head of state. Hungarians then rallied in support of Imre Nagy, another anti-Stalinist communist, who pledged to create a multiparty political system. After failed attempts at finding some accommodation, which would have preserved Moscow's power over Hungary, Soviet military forces moved against the new Hungarian government.

The Hungarian insurgents appealed to the United States for assistance. They apparently took seriously earlier U.S. calls, especially by Secretary of State Dulles, for "rolling back" Soviet power and "liberating" Eastern Europe. More cautious U.S. military strategists, however, recognized the danger of mounting a U.S. military operation in Eastern Europe, so close to Soviet territory. Soviet armies brutally crushed the Hungarian uprising, killing thousands of people, including Nagy. Anticommunist critics of rollback rhetoric suggested that the failed Hungarian Revolution showed how advocating a policy that moved beyond containment might secure political advantage at home but produce tragedy abroad.

Covert Action and Economic Leverage

Meanwhile, the U.S. campaign to contain communism shifted toward the Third World. As it did, covert action and economic pressure, less visible and less expensive than military deployments, became major policy tools. Using secretive operations and economic diplomacy in Africa, Asia, and Latin America, the Eisenhower administration reasoned, seemed less likely to provoke domestic political controversies or showdowns with the Soviets.

The CIA, headed by Allen Dulles, brother of the secretary of state, played a key role in U.S. policy in the Third World during the 1950s. In 1953, the CIA helped engineer the election of the strongly anticommunist Ramón Magsaysay as president of the Philippines. That same year, the CIA facilitated a coup in Iran, which overthrew Mohammed Mossadegh's constitutional government, after it threatened to nationalize Iran's oil industry, and restored Shah Reza Pahlavi to power. Increasingly dictatorial in his domestic policies, the Shah assured Eisenhower that Iran would remain a firm ally of Washington and a close friend to oil interests in the United States and Europe. (The Shah remained in power until ousted in 1979 in another coup, this time led by Islamic fundamentalists.)

The CIA continually expanded its global reach and its influence within the Eisenhower administration. In 1954, CIA operatives secretly helped topple President Jacobo Arbenz Guzmán's elected government in Guatemala. Officials in Washington and executives of the United Fruit Company desired the ouster of Arbenz, whose broad support included that of Guatemala's Communist Party. Using up-to-date informational strategies, including phony newscasts created by the U.S. advertising industry, the CIA undermined domestic support for Arbenz, who had promised a program to nationalize and redistribute large tracts of Guatemalan land owned by United Fruit.

Impressed by what the Iranian and Guatemalan operations appeared to suggest about the potential of covert action, the National Security Council secretly widened the CIA's mandate. By 1960, the CIA deployed approximately 15,000 agents around the world, compared to only 6,000 when Eisenhower took office.

Eisenhower also employed new economic strategies—trade and aid—to fight communism and win Third World converts to the U.S cause. Governmental economic initiatives sought to open new opportunities for U.S. enterprises overseas, discourage other countries from adopting state-directed economic systems, and encourage expanded trade ties. Those who supported these efforts credited U.S. policy with encouraging greater stability in

Map 25.3 **Tennessee Valley Authority** This map shows the vast scale of the TVA, and pinpoints the locations of 29 dams and 13 power plants that emerged from this project.

Map 26.2   Allied Advances and Collapse of German Power   This map depicts the final Allied advances and the end of the war in Germany. Through what countries did Soviet armies advance, and how might their advance have affected the postwar situation? How was Germany divided by occupying powers, and how might that division have affected postwar politics? View an animated version of this map or related maps at http://www.thomsonedu.com/history/murrin.

Map 26.3 Pacific Theater Offensive Strategy and Final Assault Against Japan This map suggests the complicated nature of devising a war strategy in the vast Pacific region. What tactics did the United States use to advance upon and finally prevail over the island nation of Japan?

The Cold War split Europe into two opposing alliances. Germany was divided into two countries: The Federal Republic of Germany (West Germany) and the German Democratic Republic (East Germany). Berlin, the former capital of Germany, was also divided. In 1949 NATO was formed, and in 1955 the Warsaw Pact came into existence.

NORWEGIAN SEA

ICELAND

NORWAY

SWEDEN

FINLAND

NORTH SEA

IRELAND

DENMARK

BALTIC SEA

UNITED KINGDOM

ATLANTIC OCEAN

NETH.

BELG.

Berlin

EAST GERMANY

POLAND

UNION OF SOVIET SOCIALIST REPUBLICS

LUX.

WEST GERMANY
(joined in 1955)

CZECHOSLOVAKIA

FRANCE

SWITZ.

AUSTRIA

HUNGARY

ROMANIA

PORTUGAL

ITALY

YUGOSLAVIA

BULGARIA

BLACK SEA

SPAIN
(joined in 1982)

ALBANIA

MEDITERRANEAN SEA

GREECE
(joined in 1952)

TURKEY
(joined in 1952)

MOROCCO

ALGERIA

CYPRUS

THE DIVISION OF BERLIN

	American Zone
	British Zone
	French Zone
	Soviet Zone

West Berlin

East Berlin

Berlin Wall (1961–1989)

(The American, British, and French zones were consolidated as West Berlin)

0   200   400 Miles
0   200   400 Kilometers

NATO Countries

Warsaw Pact Countries

Nonaligned Countries

LIBYA

EGYPT

Map 27.2   Divided Germany and the NATO Alliance   This map shows the geopolitics of the Cold War. Which countries aligned with the United States through NATO? Which aligned with the Soviet Union through the Warsaw Pact? Note how Berlin became a divided city, although it was located within East Germany.

recipient countries. Critics at home and abroad noted, however, that U.S. aid programs could seem heavy-handed and often alienated Third World leaders by equating "freedom" only with free-market economic policies that U.S. investors favored.

U.S. military aid to the Third World rose even more sharply than economic assistance. Under a Mutual Security and Military Assistance Program, the United States spent $3 billion annually, instructed Third World governments in anticommunist policies, trained their military forces, and advised their domestic police forces. The buildup of armaments in Third World nations did provide the United States with stronger anticommunist allies but also contributed to the development of military dictatorships.

The United States and Third World Politics, 1953–1960

In pursuing its policies in Third World areas, the Eisenhower administration employed a broad definition of "communist." In many nations emerging from colonialism, groups advocating labor rights and land redistribution sometimes did ally with local communist movements. Their domestic political opponents could thus hope to win U.S. support by mentioning the word *communist*, especially to people in Washington, D.C.

Latin America

In Latin America, the Eisenhower White House favored autocratic regimes that welcomed U.S. economic investment and opposed leftist political movements. Eisenhower publicly honored unpopular dictators in Peru and Venezuela and privately confessed admiration for the anticommunist politics of Paraguay's General Alfredo Stroessner, who sheltered German-Nazi fugitives and ran his country much as if it were a private fiefdom. Eisenhower's administration continued to cultivate close ties with Cuban dictator Fulgencio Batista. Batista also enjoyed strong support from U.S. crime syndicates, which controlled the Cuba's gambling industry, and from the CIA, which secretly trained his repressive security forces.

The backlash against U.S. policy boosted the appeal of **"yankeephobia"** in much of Latin America. Two important events of the late 1950s dramatized the growing unpopularity that U.S. policy makers now faced throughout much of the southern part of the Western Hemisphere.

When Vice-President Richard Nixon visited this region on a 1958 goodwill tour, he generally encountered ill will. Constantly escalating protest demonstrations reached their climax during Nixon's last stop, in Caracas, Venezuela. At one point, protestors surrounded the vice-president's motorcade, laid siege to his Cadillac limousine, and forced Nixon, hustled to safety by armed Secret Service agents, to take refuge in the U.S. Embassy.

Events in Havana, Cuba, the following year, added substance to the symbolism of Caracas. A relatively broad-based Cuban opposition movement, headed by a charismatic revolutionary named Fidel Castro, toppled Batista's pro-U.S. regime in December 1959. Once in control, Castro promised to reduce Cuba's dependence on the United States and to create a state-directed economic system, one he claimed would improve living conditions for most Cubans. These policies, together with Castro's own increasingly autocratic rule, prompted many of Cuba's more affluent citizens to depart for Florida, and the Eisenhower administration to impose an economic boycott against Cuba. Castro turned to the Soviet Union, declared his allegiance to Marxist doctrine, moved against political dissent at home, and pledged support for Cuban-style insurgencies throughout Latin America.

The Eisenhower administration began laying down a two-track response. First, it reconsidered U.S. policies that seemed to have been generating animosity and sparking anti-U.S. political movements throughout Latin America. This review ultimately recommended that Washington start encouraging democratic political processes, protection for human rights, and policies of economic growth. At the same time, Allan Dulles and the CIA were working on their own initiatives toward Cuba and Castro. Looking back at earlier operations and surveying current assets, including its contacts in organized crime, the CIA began planning how best to depose the Cuban leader, who was becoming an increasingly visible symbol of opposition to U.S. policies on the world stage.

The Middle East, Asia, and Africa

Meanwhile, a growing distrust of nationalism and neutralism shaped U.S. policy toward the Middle East. In 1954, after Colonel Gamal Abdel Nasser led a successful military coup in Egypt, against a corrupt monarchy closely tied to Great Britain, he promised to help rescue other Arab nations from European domination and guide them toward policies of "positive neutralism" in the Cold War. Nasser denounced Israel, boosted Egypt's economic and military power, extended diplomatic recognition to the People's Republic of China, and purchased advanced weapons from communist Czechoslovakia.

The Eisenhower administration viewed these policies as neither positive nor neutral. It quickly cancelled the U.S. loans intended to finance construction of the Aswan Dam, which Egypt hoped to make the centerpiece of a project designed to improve agriculture along the Nile River and to provide power for new Egyptian industries. Nasser responded, in July 1956, by seizing the British-controlled Suez Canal, which connected the Red Sea to the Mediterranean, as a way of gaining new revenues and prestige for Egypt. The Suez also remained of both economic and symbolic importance to Britain, and its forces, joined by those of France and Israel, attacked Egypt in October and quickly seized back the canal. Observers of the international scene talked about "the Suez Crisis."

Eisenhower distrusted Nasser, but he opposed Britain's blatant attempt to retain its imperial position in the Middle East. Denouncing the Anglo-French-Israeli action, which coincided with the Soviet Union's brutal campaign to shore up its communist empire by crushing Hungary, the U.S. president threatened to destabilize Britain's currency unless the invasion ended. Eventually, a plan supported by the United States and the UN gave Egypt control over the Suez Canal, but U.S. influence in the area still suffered, particularly after the Soviet Union took over the financing for the Aswan Dam.

With Nasser-style nationalism now seeming to lean toward the USSR, the Eisenhower administration came to fear the spread of "Nasserism" throughout the energy-rich Middle East. In spring 1957, the president's **"Eisenhower Doctrine"** pledged that the United States would defend Middle Eastern countries "against overt armed aggression from any nation controlled by international communism." When ruling elites in Lebanon and Jordan faced potential revolts by domestic forces friendly to Nasser, Eisenhower dispatched U.S. Marines to Lebanon, and Britain helped Jordan's King Hussein retain his throne.

The Eisenhower administration moved with similar determination elsewhere in the Third World. It remained steadfast in its policy of trying to squelch political movements it considered too closely tied to communism. In 1958, for example, the CIA furnished planes and pilots to rebels trying to overthrow Achmed Sukarno, leader of Indonesia, who drew support from that nation's large Communist Party. The rebellion failed, and Sukarno tightened his grip on power. CIA operatives also became involved in a plan to eliminate Patrice Lumumba in the Congo. Lumumba's opponents killed the popular black nationalist leader in January 1961, but scholars still debate the CIA's precise role in precipitating his death.

Vietnam

Eisenhower's effort to thwart communism and neutralism in the Third World set the stage for a more through commitment in Indochina. There, communist-nationalist forces led by Ho Chi Minh (born Nguyen Tat Thanh) continued to seek independence from France. Ho Chi Minh had studied in the Soviet Union and in France before returning to Indochina in 1941 to fight against the Japanese armies that had overrun this French colony. When Japan withdrew at war's end, Ho had appealed to the United States to back independence for Indochina. Despite wartime criticism of European colonialism, U.S. leaders supported the return of French rule. In 1946, Ho Chi Minh and his Vietminh forces went to war against France and its ally, Bao Dai, the Paris-educated Vietnamese emperor who had reigned since the 1920s.

Despite U.S. willingness to finance its military operations, France could not retain its hold over Indochina. A stunning 1954 Vietminh victory, orchestrated by General Vo Nguyen Giap, at the battle of Dien Bien Phu, convinced France to begin pulling out of Indochina. The Geneva Peace Accords of 1954, which the United States ultimately refused to sign, ended France's colonial regime and divided the old Indochina into three sovereign nations: Laos, Cambodia, and Vietnam. The accords further split Vietnam into two jurisdictions—North Vietnam and South Vietnam—until a future, nationwide election could create a government that would unify it as a single country.

Eisenhower's advisers feared that events in Vietnam, where Ho Chi Minh stood poised to win any electoral contest, could set off a geopolitical chain reaction. Using now-familiar Cold War language, the White House insisted that "the loss of any of the countries of Southeast Asia to Communist aggression" would ultimately "endanger the stability and security" of Europe and Japan, a formulation becoming known as the "domino theory." As

Ho Chi Minh's communist government consolidated control over North Vietnam, Eisenhower supported creation of a noncommunist state in South Vietnam.

Ike additionally ordered, in advance of the planned reunification election, covert operations and economic programs throughout South Vietnam. In late 1954, Washington dispatched to South Vietnam Colonel Edward Lansdale, who had directed the CIA's campaign against the leftist insurgency in the Philippines from 1950 to 1953. Lansdale helped oversee creation in Saigon, South Vietnam's capital city, of the pro-U.S. government headed by Ngo Dinh Diem, an anticommunist Catholic who had been educated in the United States. Lansdale also took charge of covert activities against anti-Diem factions, especially those loyal to Ho Chi Minh.

At first, the U.S.-directed effort at nation-building seemed to make headway. With Washington's concurrence, Diem's regime renounced the Geneva Peace Accords and refused to participate in any national election intended to establish a unified Vietnamese government. Diem extended his own government's authority over South Vietnam, redistributed land formerly owned by the French, augmented his military forces, and even launched an industrialization program.

Diem's authoritarian policies, together with opposition from North Vietnam, soon undermined the stability of his government. Diem alienated much of South Vietnam's predominantly Buddhist population, and his narrowing circle of political allies became best known for their notorious corruption. With encouragement and material support from North Vietnam, Vietminh loyalists in the South spearheaded opposition to Diem. As time passed, Diem grew increasingly isolated from key constituencies in his struggling nation and progressively more dependent on U.S. support. Early on, French officials had warned their U.S. counterparts of Diem's liabilities, but the Eisenhower administration could see no alternative. It sent billions of U.S. dollars and military advisers to prop up his government.

Eisenhower struggled to frame a coherent U.S. policy toward Vietnam. Ike had once claimed that U.S. military involvement there would be a "tragedy" and had rebuffed, in 1954, advisers who urged direct U.S. military intervention, including even the possible use of atomic weapons, on behalf of France. Following French withdrawal from Indochina, however, Eisenhower committed economic and military aid, along with America's international prestige, to Diem's shaky political fortunes. The decision of how far the United States might actually go in order to fulfill Eisenhower's commitment to South Vietnam would fall to his successors in the White House.

Affluence: A "People of Plenty"

Focus Question
How could economic growth seem to be both an opportunity and a problem during the 1950s?

President Eisenhower's "farewell address" of 1961 famously criticized the increasingly cozy relationship between the groups that directed nation's foreign policy and its economic system. The former general warned that a "military-industrial complex" threatened to so accelerate the costs of Cold War containment that the burden of military expenditures would eventually harm the U.S. domestic economy.

Eisenhower's warning contained several ironies. Most obviously, his administration, while trying to contain costs, had watched ever-larger sums of money flow to the national security establishment. Eisenhower's selection of Charles Wilson of General Motors in 1953 and Neil McElroy of Procter & Gamble in 1957 to head the Department of Defense, moreover, seemingly dramatized the same linkage Ike decried in his final address. Government spending on national security—what critics called "military Keynesianism" (see chapter 27)—pumped money into the general economy and stimulated key industries.

In addition, Eisenhower's warnings about possible dangers came after eight years during which his White House had praised the nation's continued economic growth. In 1945, the United States had still teetered on the brink of economic depression. By 1960, it could claim a GNP more than five times that of Great Britain and at least ten times that of Japan. The output of major U.S. corporations, such as General Motors, surpassed the GNP of many sovereign nations.

Economic Growth

The 1950s marked the midpoint of a period of generally steady economic growth that began during the Second World War and continued until the early 1970s. Writing in the mid-1950s, the historian David Potter called Americans a "people of plenty." Corporations turned out vast quantities of consumer goods and enjoyed rising profits. Investments and business ventures overseas boosted corporate profits at home. The domestic economy intersected with an international marketplace dominated by U.S.-based firms. The label "Made in America" announced both the quality of particular products and the economic power of the nation at large. A global national-security policy, in addition to making the Pentagon one of the nation's largest consumers, helped keep raw materials and energy flowing from the Third World. Abundant supplies of inexpensive oil and natural gas, in particular, lowered production costs and allowed U.S. industries to substitute less costly, and less polluting, foreign energy sources for domestically mined coal.

Newer U.S. industries, such as chemicals and electronics, quickly came to dominate the world marketplace. The Corning Glass Company reported that most of its sales during the mid-1950s came from products that had not even been on the market in 1940. General Electric proudly proclaimed that "progress is our most important product."

The newest suburbs—and the products their residents consumed—remained prominent emblems of this particular view of progress. Because these outlying areas lacked, at best, adequate mass transit, life revolved around the automobile. Initially, if the male breadwinner required the family car to commute to work, his spouse needed to spend her day near home. As the opportunities for buying automobiles on credit expanded during

© Bettmann/CORBIS

The "Mrs. America" Gas Kitchen   In 1959, the American National Exhibition in Moscow featured a "typical housewife" working in this RCA/Whirlpool "Mrs. America" gas kitchen, a symbol of the streamlined material progress of the postwar United States.

© Elliott Erwitt/Magnum Photos, Inc.

The Typical Housewife   This photograph depicts a different view of the "typical housewife" in her kitchen.

the mid-1950s, however, the two-car family and the new suburban shopping malls, surrounded by acres of free parking, became tangible symbols of economic growth. Widespread ownership of kitchen appliances, television sets, and automobiles marked those living in the United States, especially in the eyes of most of those in the rest of the world, as people of plenty.

Complaints about the limits of capitalism, widely expressed during the 1930s, all but disappeared from domestic political discourse. Capitalism seemed to work—and spectacularly well. Only a new vocabulary of superlatives, it seemed, could describe its wonders. In 1955, *Fortune* magazine hailed "The Changing American Market" and highlighted "The Rich Middle-Income Class" and "The Wonderful Ordinary Luxury Market." Harvard's celebrated economist John Kenneth Galbraith, who had simply entitled his 1952 study *American Capitalism,* gave his follow-up book a more grandiose-sounding title, *The Affluent Society* (1958). (This best seller actually took a far more critical look at the U.S. economy than Galbraith's first book; see following discussion.)

Words such as *plenty, abundance,* and ***affluence*** fit nicely with the dominant economic vision. The rate of growth and the burgeoning supply of consumer goods overshadowed all other economic indicators. Mainstream political discourse increasingly slid by what people *actually owned*—their accumulated wealth—to focus on their affluence—what they could, with the aid of generous credit terms, *consume.* From this perspective, observers could easily see the entire American Way of Life constantly improving. Some even predicted a leveling out of living standards between the top and the bottom levels of this growth-enabled consumer society. Any remaining gulf seemed not between people with cars and those without them, they announced, but between ones who drove Cadillacs and Lincolns and those who piloted Chevrolets and Fords. "Luxury has reached the masses," proclaimed *Fortune*.

Many economists claimed that greater government expenditures would generate even faster growth, but the Eisenhower administration demurred. Fearing that increased spending might fuel an inflationary spiral of rising prices and destabilize the economy, it kept expenditures for nonmilitary programs under tight control and remained committed, at least rhetorically, to restraining even the Pentagon's spending habits. As a result, by the late 1950s, the federal government began running balanced budgets.

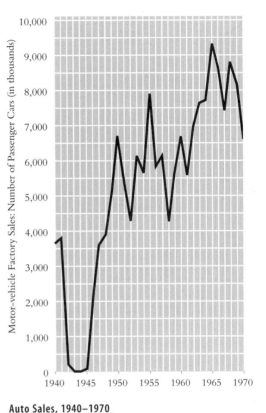

Auto Sales, 1940–1970

Highways and Waterways

The Eisenhower administration, after due deliberation, did endorse several costly new domestic programs. For one of these, the construction of an interstate highway system, it could invoke national-security considerations. Supposedly, during any military emergency, the government could rush supplies and personnel along federally financed superhighways. Creating a national tax on gasoline and other transportation-related products, the **Highway Act of 1956** authorized a national system of limited-access expressways. Touted as the largest public works project in world history, this program delighted the oil, concrete, and tire industries; provided steady work for construction firms and labor unions; and boosted the interstate trucking business. It also confirmed the victory of the automobile over competing modes of surface travel, including passenger trains, trolleys, and buses.

The White House also supported expensive water-diversion projects in the West. The Army Corps of Engineers and the Bureau of Reclamation—federal agencies with powerful supporters in business and Congress— spent billions of dollars on dams, irrigation canals, and reservoirs. Irrigation turned desert into crop land, and elaborate pumping systems even allowed rivers to flow uphill. No society in the history of the world had ever devoted *he Impala Convertible with Body by Fisher. Safety Plate Glass means better seeing in all new Chevies.*

YOU'LL HAVE PLENTY TO SHOW OFF *in the high-spirited performance of your* **NEW CHEVROLET.** *With its radical new Turbo-Thrust V8* and new action in all engines, it's so quick, agile and eager that once you take the wheel, you'll never want to leave it. You've got your hands on something really special!*

Your pride can't help showing just a bit when you slide behind the wheel of this new Chevrolet. You couldn't be sitting prettier—and you know it.

You're in charge of one of the year's most looked at, most longed for cars. Chevy's crisply sculptured contours and downright luxurious interiors are enough to make anybody feel like a celebrity.

Move your foot a fraction on the gas pedal and you feel the instant, silken response of a unique new kind of V8. You ride smoothly and serenely—cushioned by deep coil springs at every wheel. You can even have a real air ride*, if you wish.

See your Chevrolet dealer. . . . Chevrolet Division of General Motors, Detroit 2, Mich. **Optional at extra cost.*

CHEVROLET

Automobiles Symbolize a New Lifestyle This ad for a 1958 pink convertible shows off not only the nation's new economic productivity and consumer lifestyle but also suggests the dominant ideal of family "togetherness."

a similar portion of its resources to water projects. By 1960, much of the arid West enjoyed reliable access to trillions of gallons of water. Governmental expenditures laid the basis for new economic growth in states such as Texas, California, and Arizona.

These water projects came at a price. Technologically complicated and costly, they apparently needed similarly complex and expensive bureaucracies to sustain them. As a consequence, local communities lost power to governmental agencies and to the large-scale private entrepreneurs who pushed aside smaller farmers and ranchers. In addition, several American Indian tribes found significant portions of their land being flooded for large water reservoirs or being purchased by agribusinesses or large ranching interests. Moreover, these vast projects—which diverted surface waters, tapped into ground-water tables, and dotted the West with dams and reservoirs—also produced ecological problems. They disrupted and degraded critical habitats and contributed to the buildup of salt by-products in the water and the soil. Some scientists also began to warn about the consequences to animal and plant life from the overuse, especially by larger farming operations, of pesticides such as DDT.

Labor–Management Accord

Most corporate leaders, supportive of the kind of government involvement required to build the Interstate Highway System highways and water projects, were learning to live with labor unions as well. The auto industry, where management and labor leaders had negotiated a mutually acceptable contract in 1950, showcased what some economic observers saw as a tacit accord between the two sides.

At the end of the Second World War, more than 14 million U.S. workers, roughly 35 percent of those who worked in nonagricultural jobs, held union cards. Hoping to consolidate this base and to move forward cautiously, most union leaders saw closer cooperation with corporate management, rather than aggressive new organizing drives, as the safest way to guarantee employment stability and secure political influence for their unions.

The United Auto Workers (UAW), which had been one of the most militant Congress of Industrial Organizations (CIO) unions during the 1930s, helped lead the way. Unions such as the UAW dropped demands for greater involvement in "management prerogatives." These included organization of the daily work routine, introduction of new technologies, investment priorities, and, most important, decisions on where to locate new facilities. Unions continued to bargain aggressively but on a relatively narrow range of issues that immediately affected worker paychecks and benefits. Union leaders also assured management that rank-and-file workers would abide by their union contracts and disavow the wildcat tactics that had been used during the 1930s and 1940s. In another sign of declining militancy within the labor movement, the American Federation of Labor (AFL) and the CIO, long at odds, merged in 1955. Finally, to police this new labor–management détente in an even-handed manner, both sides looked to the federal government's National Labor Relations Board (NLRB). The 1950s thus seemed to signal an end to the kind of fierce labor–capital conflicts that had marked the 1930s and had continued through the 1940s.

Some union activists, however, expressed concern about the new direction of the labor movement. Although membership rolls stood at record highs, nearly two-thirds of all union-ized workers lived in only 10 states. Worse, there were already clear signs in some areas of union strength, such as the Northeastern United States, of companies beginning to move jobs elsewhere, beginning with states in the South. There, the union movement lacked strong roots, and the Taft-Hartley Act of 1947 allowed for state laws that frustrated new organizing drives, such as the ultimately underproductive effort known as "Operation Dixie."

Most business leaders, on the other hand, judged the new direction in labor–management relations as a substantial victory for their side. *Fortune* magazine noted that General Motors, while paying higher wages and shouldering costlier employee benefit packages, "got a bargain" on the larger issue of labor peace from its landmark 1950 contract with the UAW. To safeguard their control over decision making, corporations expanded their supervisory staffs, a practice that drove up consumer prices and curtailed worker partici-pation in planning the work process. The labor–management accord also helped divide industrial workers from one another: Those employed in the most profitable sectors of the economy, such as the auto industry, could bargain far more effectively than those who worked in less lucrative sectors.

To further consolidate management's power, many businesses expanded benefits for their workers. Companies such as Sears and Eastman Kodak encouraged a cooperative cor-porate culture, which included health and pension plans, profit-sharing arrangements, and social programs. Some even created private recreational parks for the exclusive use of their employees. Reaching out to workers, executives decided, would reduce the appeal of both aggressive unions and more extensive governmental welfare measures.

Between the end of the Second World War and the early 1960s, a large percentage of U.S. wage-earners came to enjoy at least some of the fruits of affluence. Real wages (what workers make after adjusting their paychecks for inflation) rose steadily, while job open-ings remained plentiful. The frequency of industrial accidents dropped; fringe benefits (what workers receive in the form of health insurance, paid vacation time, and retirement plans) invariably improved; and job security was generally high.

Political Pluralism

Economic growth also appeared to help sustain a stable political system. Observers of the domestic scene during the 1950s could not help but see their own times in terms of memories of the past and visions of the future. In contrast to the conflicts of the 1930s, the disruptions during the Second World War, and the Great Fear of the early Cold War period, the 1950s seemed an era of relative tranquility. Moreover, domestic life in the United States seemed less troubled and chaotic than that in other parts of the Cold War world, as the increasingly prosperous nation worked, fairly effectively, to mute conflict and solve domestic problems.

According to the dominant viewpoint, which political scientists called "pluralism" (or "interest-group pluralism"), U.S. politics featured a roughly equal bargaining process among well-organized interest groups. John Kenneth Galbraith, for example, coined the term "countervailing power" to describe the ability of labor unions, consumer lobbies, farm organizations, and other groups to check the appetites of giant corporations. No single group could hope to dictate to the others, celebrants of pluralism claimed, because so many interests felt securely empowered. Pluralists shrugged off signs of an apparent decline in political participation, clearly evident in how few citizens went to the polls on election days, by arguing that relatively low voter turnouts simply showed widespread satisfaction with how well existing processes worked.

In addition to praising the process, pluralists invariably praised the results. Public leaders, it seemed, could find a realistic solution to virtually every political problem. Short-term conflicts over specific issues might never disappear, but supporters of the pluralist vision pointed out how affluence could moderate political passions and point warring interests toward a viable long-term agreement on fundamental arrangements. As a professor at Harvard Law School put it, constant economic growth meant that "in any conflict of interest," it was "always possible to work out a solution" because continuing affluence appeared to guarantee that any settlement would leave all interests "better off than before."

A Religious People

The celebration of political pluralism accompanied the exaltation of the stabilizing role of religion. Signs of religious commitment seemed part of most people's weekly, sometimes daily, routine. Formal church membership grew at more than double the rate of the U.S. population during the 1950s. Moreover, public life appeared solidly anchored in religious values. As part of the crusade against "atheistic communism," Congress emphasized the role of religion by constructing a nondenominational prayer room on Capitol Hill, adding the phrase "under God" to the Pledge of Allegiance, and declaring the phrase "In God We Trust," emblazoned on U.S. currency for nearly a century, to be the official national motto.

At the same time, observers claimed that intense religious allegiances no longer divided people as much as they had in the past. President Eisenhower urged people to practice their own religious creed, whatever it might be. "Our government makes no sense," he declared, "unless it is founded in a deeply felt religious faith—and I don't care what it is." Tommy Sands, a young pop singer, advised his teenage fans that "all religions are the greatest."

Prominent religious leaders noted how a widespread "faith in faith" could bring people together. Rabbi Morris Kretzer, head of the Jewish Chaplain's Organization, reassured Protestants and Catholics that they and their Jewish neighbors shared "the same rich heritage of the Old Testament . . . the sanctity of the Ten Commandments, the wisdom of the prophets, and the brotherhood of man." A 1954 survey claimed that more than 95 percent of the population identified with one of the three major faiths, and religious commentators talked about the unifying power of a "Judeo-Christian tradition." The era's leading study of religion, Will Herberg's *Protestant-Catholic-Jew* (1955), argued that these three major faiths were really "saying the same thing in affirming the 'spiritual ideals' and 'moral values' of the American Way of Life."

The media elevated several religious leaders to celebrity status. Norman Vincent Peale, a Protestant minister who linked an embrace of religiosity to the achievement of individual peace of mind, sold millions of books containing the message that belief in a Higher Power could bring "health, happiness, and goodness" to daily life. Some close students of religion, such as Herberg, found Peale's most famous book, *The Power of Positive Thinking* (1952) to be a lightweight version of religious theology, but it remained a best seller throughout the 1950s. The Catholic Bishop Fulton J. Sheen hosted an Emmy-winning, prime-time television program called *Life Is Worth Living,* which continues to play in reruns on cable TV. The Baptist evangelist Billy Graham, a friend of Sheen's and eventually a confidant of President Eisenhower, achieved super-star status during the 1950s. The best-selling *Peace with God* (1953) offered the same message Graham preached to large crowds and over television: Only a spiritual rebirth, through a direct commitment to Jesus Christ, would bring salvation to individuals who lived in a world filled with so many signs of sin and corruption.

Although observers generally identified Peale, Sheen, and Graham with relatively conservative, anticommunist political causes, their differing approaches to religion shared a broadly pluralist stance. Billy Graham, for instance, scrupulously avoided the kind of anti-Semitic and anti-Catholic rhetoric that sometimes accompanied the sermons of other protestant evangelists, and his own ministry abandoned all forms of racial segregation during the mid-1950s.

Moreover, appeals to religious faith could be found all across the political spectrum. Dorothy Day, who had been involved in religiously based community activism since the early 1930s, continued to work with an interdenominational coalition of communitarians. Especially through the pages of her *Catholic Worker* magazine, she promoted programs for redistributing income and wealth in more equitable ways and for securing a more peaceful world. Church leaders and laypeople from all three major denominations supported

Split-Level Living This 1960 cartoon, by the *Washington Post's* "Herblock" (Herbert Block), illustrates the growing critique of Eisenhower-era social policy. While suburbanites enjoy new affluence in a split-level home, public services and distressed people remain underfunded.

efforts at addressing racial and religious discrimination, including the spiritually grounded efforts of Martin Luther King, Jr., and other civil rights leaders (see following discussion).

Discontents of Affluence

Celebrations of economic affluence, political pluralism, and religious commitment existed alongside a relatively vibrant body of social criticism. The widespread faith that the United States could deploy its abundant economic and political-social resources to solve virtually all of its remaining problems likely helped encourage this rich critical culture. The 1950s produced a sizeable and diverse body of literature that probed issues such as social conformity, unruly youth, mass culture, discrimination, and economic inequality.

Conformity in an Affluent Society

The sociologist William H. Whyte, Jr., gained a wide academic audience for *The Organization Man* (1956). This book indicted corporate culture for contributing to an unwanted by-product of affluence: social conformity. Criticizing the social, cultural, and psychological (although not the economic) role of large corporations, *The Organization Man* saw ordinary corporate employees deferring to the wishes and values of their bosses at the expense of their own individuality. Even among younger executives, Whyte's book claimed, the security of knowing what the corporate hierarchy desired—and when it wanted it—outweighed any concern about losing track of one's own sense of self.

The Lonely Crowd (1950) by another sociologist, David Riesman, offered an even broader critique of social conformity. This influential book claimed to see a shift from an "inner-directed" culture, in which people looked to themselves and to their immediate families for their sense of identity and self-worth, to an "other-directed" one, in which people constantly gazed at others for approval and measured their own worth against mass-mediated images. An other-directed society, in short, emphasized "adjustment" to the expectations of others rather than commitment to individual "autonomy."

Seeking to show how baby boomers would supposedly learn conformist values, *The Lonely Crowd* pointed to *Tootle, the Engine,* a popular children's book. After "Tootle" shows a preference for jumping the rails and frolicking in the nearby fields, people from his community use peer pressure to nudge him "back on the tracks." If he remains on the straight-and-narrow and follows lines laid down by others, Tootle learns, his future as a powerful and fast-moving streamliner will be assured. Riesman's book argued that this "modern cautionary tale," which stressed the importance of adjusting one's own path through life to the expectations of others, contrasted vividly with the self-reliant values served up in *Little Red Riding Hood* and other earlier conflict-filled fairy tales.

The critique of social conformity reached perhaps its widest audience through the best-selling books of journalist Vance Packard. *The Hidden Persuaders* (1957) argued that the advertising industry—especially through calculated appeals to the insecurities of consumers—encouraged conformist behavior, particularly in buying habits and cultural tastes. His book, Packard claimed, could help its readers "achieve a creative life in these conforming times," when so many people "are left only with the roles of being consumers or spectators."

If analysts looked hard enough, it seemed, evidence of conformity and loss of selfhood lurked nearly everywhere. Critics such as Whyte, Riesman, and Packard generally highlighted signs supposedly evident among middle-class men, but writers such as **Betty Friedan** warned about an analogous, although gendered, trend among many women, especially those with good educations and lively intellects who found themselves trapped in the new suburbia. Business corporations, for instance, expected that the wives of their male executives would help their husbands deal with the demands of corporate life, including the need for frequent dinner parties and occasional relocation moves. The organization man, it was said, should recognize that his ascent up the economic ladder could depend on how well an "organization woman," his spouse, conformed to her unpaid work for the greater good of the corporate world.

The affluent cultural climate of the 1950s, then, hardly discouraged social criticism, some of it occasionally quite pointed. Both the scholarly and more popular writings of the sociologist C. Wright Mills, for instance, denounced how corporate leaders and advertising executives operated as members of a "power elite." A relatively small coalition of the already powerful could set the agenda for public policy discussions, especially those involving national security and domestic spending priorities. This ruling elite, which also included military leaders and anticommunist politicians, shaped the crucial decisions on important policy issues. Moreover, its emphasis on generating sustained economic growth produced social problems that went far beyond the other-directedness analyzed in *The Lonely Crowd*. The much-vaunted American Way of Life, in Mills' view, featured increasingly regimented work routines and meaningless leisure-time activities that could never produce a true sense of satisfaction. Standing against the tide of pluralist accounts, Mills watched his claims undergo constant sifting and resifting. The numerous academics and journalists who espoused the pluralist faith during the 1950s invariably concluded that Mills, for all his passion and commitment, offered only simplistic "conspiracy theories." During the 1960s, however, his ideas about a "power elite" and a widespread sense of social "alienation" would circulate within a much more receptive cultural environment.

Restive Youth

Meanwhile, concern about young people, especially their cultural tastes and social behavior, intensified. At one point, in the mid-1950s, many criminologists linked a rise in the sale of comic books to a spike in reported rates of juvenile delinquency. *The Seduction of the Innocent* (1954), a popular study by the psychologist Frederick Wertham, blamed comics, especially those featuring images of sex and violence, for "mass-conditioning" children and for stimulating social unrest. Responding to regulatory legislation by some U.S. cities and to calls for additional measures by Congress, the comic book industry quickly embraced self-censorship. Publishers who adhered to new, industry-developed guidelines for portraying violence and deviant behavior began to display a seal of approval on their publications. The "great comic book scare" proved a relatively momentary fright.

Other worrisome signs, however, persisted. One of these, a former truck driver named **Elvis Presley,** rocked the pop music scene with several hits on the tiny Sun record label. Most of the major record distributors dismissed rock as a passing fad, but Sun's Sam Phillips detected something more substantial. As soon as Elvis began to make personal appearances, the overt sensuality that dominated his musical performance quickly validated Phillips' intuitions. Presley and other youthful (invariably male) rock stars—including Buddy Holly from West Texas, Richard Valenzuela (Richie Valens) from East Los Angeles, Frankie Lymon from Spanish Harlem, and "Little Richard" Penniman from Georgia—leaped over cultural and ethnic barriers. Rock derived new musical forms from older sources, especially African American rhythm and blues (R&B) and the "hillbilly" music of southern whites.

The first **rock 'n' rollers** seemingly spoke to the hopes and fears of millions of their youthful fans. They sang about the joy of "having a ball tonight," the pain of the "summertime blues," the torment of being "a teenager in love," and the promise of deliverance, through the power of rock, from "the days of old." Songs such as "Roll Over Beethoven" by Chuck Berry became powerful teen anthems.

Guardians of older, family-oriented forms of commercial culture found rock 'n' roll far more frightening than comic books. They denounced rock's sparse lyrics, pulsating guitars, and screeching saxophones as an assault on the very idea of music. Even the name of this music, it seemed obvious, played to raging teenage hormones. Religious groups thus denounced rock as the "Devil's music"; anticommunists detected a clever strategy by the Red Menace to corrupt youth; and segregationists saw its indebtedness to black musical forms as part of a sinister plot to encourage "race-mixing." Still a bellwether of conservative tastes, the FBI's J. Edgar Hoover saw rock music as "repulsive to right-thinking people" and as a social force that would soon have "serious effects on our young people." The danger of rock 'n' roll seemed abundantly evident in *The Blackboard Jungle* (1955), a hit movie (which featured "Rock Around the Clock" on its soundtrack) about a racially mixed group of sexually active students who, for good measure, terrorize teachers and mock any adult authority not "manly enough" to set limits on their excesses.

Eventually attentive to new turns in the product-centered culture of youth, the commercial entertainment industry soon recognized the potential breadth of rock 'n' roll's appeal. Its flexible cultural and musical vocabulary could attract its youthful audience with both critiques and celebrations of the consequences of material abundance. "Charlie Brown," for example, satirically contrasted pieties about staying in school with the bleak educational opportunities open to many students, especially those of African descent. Chuck Berry sang of a terminally bored teenager, riding around in his automobile, "with no particular place to go." The implied social criticism in songs such as these, which older listeners often failed to decode, anticipated the more overtly rebellious rock music of the 1960s.

At the same time, rock music and the larger youth culture of the 1950s could also merge seamlessly into that era's mass-consumption ethic. Sam Phillips, lacking the capital to distribute records to a rapidly expanding market, sold Presley's contract to RCA and watched the rest of his budding stars drift away from Sun to larger labels. The leading record companies and Top-40 radio stations saw middle-class teenagers, whose average weekly income/allowance reached $10 by 1958, as a market segment well worth targeting. In "Sweet Little Sixteen," Berry sang about an affluent teenager chasing after the latest fashions, the next rock 'n' roll show, and "about half-a million framed autographs." Record companies and disc jockeys began promoting a second generation of rock performers, such as the Beach Boys, and songs that exalted the pursuit of "fun, fun, fun," which apparently required the latest clothing fashions, late-model automobiles, and the top-selling rock 'n' roll records.

The Mass Culture Debate

Meanwhile, concern about social conformity and youth-oriented styles often joined a broader cultural debate over "mass culture." Much of the anxiety about the decline of individualism and the rise of disruptive young people encompassed deeper fears, especially among people who equated their own tastes with the future of civilization. From their perspective, the marketers who could apparently use standardized imagery to manipulate the cultural marketplace and sway the emotions of millions of people, those "hidden persuaders," also threatened to debase the fragile core of cultural life.

Cosmopolitan critics, connoisseurs of European-derived culture, decried the mass-marketed products flooding the newly affluent United States. They worried that the "bad"—such as comics and rock music—would soon purge anything "good" from the cultural marketplace and perhaps prevent future generations from even being able to distinguish between them. Moreover, they warned that a national mass media, by addressing millions of cultural consumers in the same manner, would obscure meaningful, and sometimes subtle, differences underneath a constant blur of pleasant, superficial imagery. After intensively studying a small town in upstate New York, for example, a team of sociologists claimed that mass-mediated images from outside this community seemed "so overwhelming that little scope is left for the expression of local cultural" forms.

Television, dominated by three large corporations (NBC, CBS, and ABC) and ultimately financed by revenues from national advertising accounts, provided a prominent target in the mass culture debate. Picturing millions of seemingly passive viewers gathered around "the boob tube," critics decried both the quality of television programming and its presumed impact on viewers. Network television, according to its critics, encouraged people to retreat into unreal, fabricated spaces, such as a mythical Old West or the fake competition on TV quiz shows. By the late 1950s, the television networks filled many of their prime-time hours with western-themed series (such as *Gunsmoke*) and quiz programs (such as the *$64,000 Question*), whose contestants had been supplied the answers they pretended to puzzle over. The head of the Federal Communications Commission (FCC) would later speak for the 1950s generation of TV critics when he denounced the entire medium as a "vast wasteland."

Social observers also noted how television even appeared to be recutting the fabric of everyday life. Architects rearranged living space within middle-class homes so that the TV set, serving as an electronic substitute for the traditional fireplace hearth, could become the focal point of family gatherings. New products—such as the frozen TV dinner, the TV tray, the recliner chair, and the influential magazine *TV Guide*—became extensions of a television-constructed culture.

The mass-produced cultural products that critics decried, however, also seemed inseparable from the pluralistic political system and the economic growth that these same observers generally celebrated. Was it possible to eliminate the curse of mass culture without sacrificing liberty and affluence? If, for example, Congress were to legislate against "dangerous" cultural products, might not such regulations shrink the boundaries for all legally protected expression? If local communities were to step in, as some had done with comics, the results might be even worse. The prospect of southern segregationists confiscating civil-rights literature or of local censorship boards rushing, unimpeded, to ban books by celebrated authors such as D. H. Lawrence hardly appealed to the cosmopolitan, well-educated critics of mass culture. Their critical diagnosis, in short, seemed short on viable remedies. Most important, the mass culture debate did nothing to halt the flood of products, especially TV programs, aimed at an ever-expanding audience.

Changing Gender Politics

Meanwhile, the 1950s saw the continuation of significant changes in how and where people lived and worked. This era particularly challenged ideas about the nature of gender relationships.

The New Suburbs and Gender Ideals

In middle-class homes, especially those located in the new suburbs, wives and mothers discovered just how "liberating" consumer technology might be. Colorful and chrome-plated appliances and "modern conveniences"—such as automatic clothes washers, more powerful vacuum cleaners, and home freezers—did ease old burdens but also created new ones. Clothes and floors now, according to advertisers, needed to be kept "spotlessly clean." Elaborate meals could be prepared in "a jiffy." Careful academic studies found that, contrary to what promoters of labor-saving devices promised, women could devote as much of their day to household tasks during the 1950s as had their grandmothers in the early 1900s. New household technologies did not so much reduce the time that women spent on domestic duties as shift it to different activities, ones requiring the household gadgets that accompanied the spread of affluence.

At first glance, the changing demands of housework fit into a broader pattern of "separate spheres." A set of clearly delineated and gendered barriers seemed to structure daily life, particularly in the newer suburbs. At its most rigid, the suburban lifestyle included a public sphere of work and politics dominated by men and a private sphere of housework and child care reserved for women. Because few businesses located in the suburbs, men began spending a good portion of their days commuting from home to work. Women who wanted to hold a job outside their homes initially found nearby employment opportunities about as scarce as child-care facilities. Consequently, mothers spent a great deal of time taking care of their baby-boomer children. In contrast to the urban neighborhoods or the rural communities in which many suburban housewives had grown up, the new suburbs of the 1950s contained few older relatives or younger single women who could assist with household and child-care duties.

Without mothers or grandmothers living close by, young suburban mothers turned elsewhere for child-rearing advice. Local Parents and Teachers Associations (PTAs), connected to neighborhood schools, offered the chance for women to exchange information with their neighbors, as did women's organizations such as the La Leche League. Increasingly, though, younger parents turned to an easily expandable shelf of child-care manuals. **Dr. Benjamin Spock's** *Baby and Child Care,* first published in 1946 with successive editions selling in the tens of millions, stood out from its competitors.

Following earlier advice books, Spock's book assigned virtually all child-care duties to women and underscored their nurturing role by stressing the need to constantly monitor a child's psychological growth. The future of the family—and the nation itself, Spock implied—depended on how well baby-boom-era mothers handled the daily responsibility of child-rearing. Other manuals picked up where Dr. Spock left off and counseled mothers on the care and feeding of teenagers.

The alarmist tone of many of these advice books reflected and helped generate a growing concern about teenage culture. A problem teen, according to one 1950s study, sprang from a "family atmosphere not conducive to development of emotionally well-integrated, happy youngsters, conditioned to obey legitimate authority." The ideal mother, from this perspective, did not work outside her home and devoted herself to rearing her own particular segment of the baby-boom generation. Women who desired careers outside of their home and marriage risked being labeled, in line with widespread psychological theories of the day, as maladjusted and deviant, real-life versions of the *femmes fatales* who populated *films noirs* (see chapter 27).

Slightly different versions of this message appeared nearly everywhere. Even the nation's most prestigious colleges for women assumed that their female students would pursue men and marriage instead of a career. In a 1955 commencement address at the prestigious, all-women Smith College, Adlai Stevenson, the Democratic Party's urbane presidential contender, reminded graduates that it was the duty of each to keep her husband "truly purposeful, to keep him whole." Popular magazines, psychology literature, and pop-culture imagery suggested that understanding, supportive wives and mothers held the keys to social stability. Conversely, women who desired alternative arrangements, either in their work or their sexual preferences, needed to be pressured, much as "Tootle, the Engine," to return to the straight and narrow path.

Competing portraits, however, painted different and more complicated pictures of gender arrangements. Most men told researchers that they preferred an active partner to a "submissive, stay-at-home" wife. Popular TV shows, such as "Father Knows Best" and "Leave It to Beaver," subtly suggested that middle-class fathers should become more engaged in family life than they normally seemed to be. Advice manuals still envisioned husbands earning their family's entire income but increasingly urged them to be "real fathers" at home. Parenting literature came to extol an ethic of "family togetherness," and institutions such as the Young Men's Christian Association (YMCA) began to offer courses on how to achieve this ideal.

The call for family togetherness seemed to be, in part at least, a response to what cultural historians have come to see as an incipient "male revolt" against "family values" and the "male breadwinner role." Hugh Hefner's *Playboy* magazine, which debuted in 1953, epitomized this rebellion. It ridiculed men who neglected their own happiness in order to support a wife and children as suckers rather than saints. *Playboy*'s first issue defiantly proclaimed: "We aren't a 'family magazine.'" Hefner advised women to pass *Playboy* "along to the man in your life and get back to your *Ladies Home Companion*." In this version of the good life, a man lived in his own "pad" rather than in the heavily mortgaged family home; drove a sports car rather than a four-door sedan or a station wagon; and courted the Playmate of the Month rather than the Mother of the Year.

Signs of Women's Changing Roles

Despite media images of homebound wives and mothers, greater numbers of women than ever before now worked outside of their homes. The rate of female employment, including that among married women, had begun to rise during the 1940s, and this trend continued throughout the 1950s. Women who were married often entered the labor force as part-time workers in the expanding clerical and service sectors. In 1948, about 25 percent of married mothers held jobs outside of the home; at the end of the 1950s, nearly 40 percent did. With the introduction of a new method of oral contraception in 1960, the birth control pill, women gained an additional measure of control over family planning and career decisions—and over decisions about their own sexual behavior. By 1964, one-quarter of the women who used contraception relied on "the pill." At the same time, women's groups began to press for an end to antiabortion laws that restricted the ability of women, particularly those without the means to travel overseas or to states that offered relatively liberal access to medical abortions, to find legal and relatively safe ways to terminate pregnancies.

Employment opportunities for women, especially when compared to those available to most men of European descent, still remained limited during the 1950s. Virtually all of the nation's nurses, telephone operators, secretaries, and elementary school teachers were women. Historically, pay scales in these areas lagged behind those for men in comparable fields; union jobs remained rare; and chances for rapid, or significant, advancement seemed elusive. As the number of low-paid jobs for women expanded during the 1950s, better-paid professional opportunities actually narrowed. Medical and law schools, along with most professional societies, admitted very few women. When Sandra Day (who would later become Justice Sandra Day O'Connor serving on the U.S. Supreme Court) graduated, with honors, from a prestigious law school during the 1950s, not a single private firm offered her a job, and she worked, without pay, in the public sector. The number of women on college and university faculties shrank during the 1950s, down from the already low levels of earlier decades.

The "family wage," as both ideal and practice, created a barrier to better-paying jobs for women. Employers still invoked the notion of a family wage to justify paying male workers higher wages and salaries than their female counterparts, even though significant numbers of women now needed to support not just themselves but also a family on their own paychecks. This was especially the case for women of color. By 1960, women headed slightly more than 20 percent of black families. Recognizing that idealized images of motherhood hardly characterized the lives of the many African American women who worked outside of their homes, *Ebony* magazine regularly celebrated black women who combined success in parenting and at work. It featured articles about educators and prominent entertainers, as well as about blue-collar workers, such as the only African American woman who worked as a mechanic at American Airlines.

Some of the mass-circulation magazines that targeted women of European descent also carried a relatively wide array of messages about gender roles. Although many social commentators continued to label a woman's desire to pursue activities outside of her home as "unnatural," popular publications increasingly featured stories about women successfully pursuing careers in public life and in business. The 1950s, in short, saw growing diversity in both the social roles that women were assuming and the ways in which commercial mass culture represented aspirations for further change.

The Fight against Discrimination, 1953–1960

Focus Question
How did the fight against discrimination raise new political issues and visions during the 1950s and early 1960s? How did the nation's political and social institutions respond to these issues?

When Dwight Eisenhower assumed the presidency in 1953, the U.S. Supreme Court was preparing to rehear a full-scale constitutional challenge to racially segregated educational systems. The NAACP and its chief legal strategist, Thurgood Marshall, spearheaded the attack on Jim Crow school arrangements. Before the rehearing took place, a vacancy in the Chief Justiceship allowed Ike to tap Earl Warren, a former Republican governor of California, to head the High Court. The Supreme Court, with Warren as its "Chief," entered the widening struggle against discrimination.

The Brown Cases, 1954–1955
The landmark Supreme Court case popularly known as "the *Brown* decision" actually included a series of constitutional challenges to school segregation. In 1954, Chief Justice Warren wrote a unanimous opinion (in **Brown v. Board of Education of Topeka**) striking down state-mandated segregation of public schools. This practice, according to Warren's relatively brief and broadly argued opinion, violated the constitutional right of African American students to equal protection of the law. A companion case, decided the same day (*Bolling* v. *Sharpe*), ruled against segregated schools in the District of Columbia. Although these decisions technically applied only to state-operated schools, they suggested that other segregated public facilities now lay open to constitutional challenge. In 1955, however, yet another Supreme

Court decision, known as *Brown II,* decreed that the process of public school desegregation should not go into effect immediately; it could, instead, move forward "with all deliberate speed."

Carrying out the broader implications of the *Brown* cases challenged the nation's political, social, and cultural institutions. A crucial part of the crusade against racial discrimination had long focused on the 16 states that the Census Bureau officially called "the South," but ongoing demographic changes ensured that the civil-rights struggle would not remain a regional matter.

During the 1950s, life in the South continued to become more like that in the rest of the country. New cultural forces, such as network television, penetrated this once relatively insular region, opening parts of it to ideas and practices that challenged the prevailing

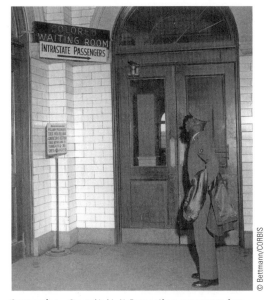

Segregation   Dressed in his Air Force uniform, a young man from New York City is faced with a "colored waiting room" in an Atlanta bus terminal in 1956. Before the civil-rights revolution of the 1960s, southern states maintained legally enforced segregation in most public facilities, a practice popularly called Jim Crow (see chapter 18).

racial patterns. Machine technologies continued to displace the South's predominantly black field workers, and the absence of strong labor unions and the presence of favorable tax laws attracted more national chain stores and northern-based businesses. In addition, an improved generation of air-conditioning units, for businesses and homes, helped transform work, leisure, and demographic patterns throughout the southern United States.

At the same time, the racial and ethnic composition of cities in the West, Midwest, and Northeast changed to look more like that in areas of the South. In 1940, more than three-quarters of the nation's African Americans lived in the South. Following earlier trends, African Americans continued to leave the rural South and become important political constituencies in Los Angeles, Chicago, New York, Cleveland, and other urban areas. In these locales, most Democrats and many Republicans generally supported efforts to end racial discrimination. As more African Americans came to cast Democratic ballots, however, the GOP sought to refocus its appeal, reaching out to white voters in what had long been the Democratic Party's solid South and in the new suburban neighborhoods, especially in the Mid and Far West. At the same time, the nation's Spanish-speaking population continued to grow and to become an increasingly important political force, particularly in the West and Southwest. **(See Map 28.1, Shifts in African American Population Patterns, 1940–1960, in the color insert following page 1248.)**

The most familiar stories about the civil-rights crusade during the 1950s have long concentrated on the South, but recent histories help underscore its nationwide scope. By 1963, efforts to change the entire spectrum of racially based patterns and practices affected local, state, and national politics. Civil rights activists outside the South, where people of African and Latin American descent already exercised some measure of political leverage, worked for better jobs, improved housing, stronger neighborhood institutions, and greater influence within the larger political system. Cultivating ties to sympathetic politicians and labor unions, a relatively broad movement to end segregation and racial discrimination emerged, especially among African Americans, in virtually every northern and western city.

These urban-based movements employed a variety of tactics on behalf of several different goals. They pressed "shop where you can work" campaigns, which urged African American consumers to patronize only businesses that would employ them as workers. They tried to bring more blacks into the labor union movement and the fast-growing public service sector, so that they could find jobs in police and fire departments as well as in all of the various agencies of state and local government. Leading attorneys, while still supporting lawsuits such as *Brown*, joined with black lawyers to concentrate on the ordinary day-to-day legal problems of clients in their own communities. Increasingly, though, gaining additional political leverage seemed crucial to making gains in other areas, including economic ones.

The search for political power became particularly contested and inexorably connected to the struggle to dismantle systems of officially sanctioned segregation throughout the South. Here, white segregationists pledged "massive resistance" to the *Brown* decisions. When the Supreme Court's "all deliberate speed" approach in *Brown II* seemed to give them time to maneuver, their lawyers went to court in pursuit of traditional and newly invented delaying tactics. In 1956, 100 members of the U.S. Congress signed a "Southern Manifesto," which condemned the Supreme Court's desegregation rulings as a "clear abuse of judicial power" and pledged support for any state that intended "to resist forced integration by any lawful means."

Defiance did not always remain within legal bounds, especially in the South. There, white vigilantes unfurled the banners and donned the robes of the Ku Klux Klan, and new racist organizations, such as the White Citizens Council, appeared on the scene. As a result, people who joined the civil-rights cause constantly risked injury and death. Even those who were only indirectly connected to the struggle could fall victim to racist violence. In August 1955, two white Mississippians brutally murdered 14-year-old Emmett Till, because they decided this black visitor from Chicago had acted "disrespectful" toward a married white woman.

Mamie Till Bradley insisted that her son's death not remain a private incident. She demanded that his maimed corpse be displayed publicly for "the whole world to see" and insisted that his murderers be punished. To the surprise of many observers, Mississippi officials did indict two men for Till's murder. When they came to trial, though, an all-white Mississippi jury quickly found the pair—who would subsequently confess their crime to a magazine reporter—not guilty.

The Montgomery Bus Boycott and Martin Luther King, Jr.

In response to the uncertainty of judicial remedies, the southern civil-rights movement began supplementing legal maneuvering with ever-more ambitious and larger campaigns of direct action. Following an earlier 1953 campaign that secured partial desegregation of the public transportation system in Baton Rouge, Louisiana, activists in Montgomery, Alabama, raised their own sights. After police arrested **Rosa Parks** for defying a local segregation ordinance, Montgomery's black community quickly mobilized and demanded a complete end to segregated buses. They coupled their demand with an ambitious boycott of city buses, which required organizing a system of private carpools as an alternative mode of transit. Joining with Rosa Parks, a longtime bastion of the local NAACP chapter, many other black women in Montgomery helped coordinate the complicated, months-long boycott. Responding to events in Montgomery, the U.S. Supreme Court extended the premise of the *Brown* decisions on education and specifically declared segregation of public buses to be unconstitutional.

After a campaign lasting more than a year, the effort succeeded. City officials, saddled with continued financial losses and legal defeat in court, agreed to end Montgomery's separatist

Montgomery Bus Boycott The drive to desegregate municipal buses in Montgomery, Alabama, required an elaborately organized and skillfully coordinated effort. It primarily relied on the talents and commitment of volunteers, particularly women. African American residents of Montgomery shared automobile transportation, coordinated by the boycott movement, while avoiding city buses, such as the one standing vacant across the street.

transit policy. Events in Montgomery suggested that other local black activists, even in the legally segregated South, could effectively mobilize—and then organize—community resources to fight against racial discrimination.

The Montgomery boycott of 1955–56 also vaulted **Dr. Martin Luther King, Jr.,** one of its leaders and its primary spokesperson, into the national spotlight. Born, raised, and educated in Atlanta, Georgia, with a doctorate in theology from Boston University, King joined with other black ministers to follow up the victory in Montgomery by forming the Southern Christian Leadership Conference (SCLC). Increasingly able to mobilize against segregated public facilities and racial discrimination, the SCLC turned to the more difficult task of organizing an ongoing sociopolitical movement that could work for permanent change in other areas of race relations.

The relatively young male ministers in the SCLC tapped advice from across generational and gender divides. They turned, for example, to Bayard Rustin, who had been involved in civil-rights activism since the 1940s, and to Ella Baker, another veteran organizer with experience in CORE and the NAACP. Aided by Rustin's tactical advice and Baker's organizational skills, Dr. King thrived as the titular leader of the SCLC's ambitious effort to register African American voters throughout the South.

King and his associates relied on nonviolent direct action. Following in the footsteps of Rustin and CORE (see chapter 27), they espoused a moral, religiously grounded ethic. The civil-rights crusade, in this sense, intended to be more than just another pluralist interest group that sought a place at the bargaining table. According to Dr. King's well-publicized sermons and writings, nonviolent direct action would dramatize, through both word and deed, the evil of racial discrimination. The civil-rights crusade promised to bring "redemption and reconciliation" to the entire nation.

King's powerful presence and religiously rooted rhetoric, which attracted all national media, played especially well on television. The people who directed this commercial medium began to recognize how news coverage, especially when focused on easily dramatized examples of conflict, could swell their audience and boost their journalistic stature. Media accounts of events in the South emphasized the roles played by King and his followers, helping to elevate their specific activities in the broader, constantly volatile drama of civil rights. The southern-based activists who looked to Dr. King, however, comprised only one part of a much broader, highly diverse movement that reached throughout the nation and into the world.

The Politics of Civil Rights: From the Local to the Global

All across the country, civil-rights activists pressed forward. Shortly after the conclusion of the **Montgomery bus boycott,** for example, New York City passed the nation's first "open housing" ordinance, a model for other local and state measures intended to end racial discrimination in the sale and rental of homes and apartments. In other cities and states outside the South, civil-rights groups enjoyed considerable success in obtaining legislation to outlaw racial discrimination in hiring. The majority of people in a 1944 opinion poll had agreed that workers of European descent "should have the first chance" at any job opportunity, but subsequent surveys showed a steady erosion of this sentiment during the 1950s.

Efforts to obtain laws aimed at ending discrimination in housing, however, faced tougher going than those focused on the workplace. Typically, white homeowners in those urban and older suburban neighborhoods where African Americans or Latinos might hope to buy or rent tried to adopt the same exclusionary strategies used so effectively by their counterparts in the new suburbs.

In a number of instances, civil-rights groups continued to work, however, with sympathetic allies. In 1958, for example, a labor and civil-rights coalition in California, joining under slogans such as "Keep Mississippi Out of California" and "Fight Sharecropper Wages," defeated an anti-union "right-to-work" proposal. Such a measure, its opponents claimed, threatened to drive down pay for workers, of both European and non-European descent, to levels found in the antiunion, pro-segregationist states of the Deep South. Buoyed by this success, the same coalition began aggressively lobbying members of the California legislature to enact a statewide opening housing measure.

Political institutions in Washington, D.C., also felt pressure to act on civil-rights matters. The Supreme Court lent its support at crucial times, such as the Montgomery bus boycott, but the Constitution did not grant the federal judiciary the power to provide the on-the-ground policing required to translate its definitions of liberty and equality into everyday practices. Congress, with the ability to enact enforcement legislation, remained deeply divided on racial issues. With southern segregationists, all members of the Democratic Party's majority, holding key posts on Capitol Hill, antidiscrimination measures faced formidable congressional obstacles.

Even so, Congress did pass its first civil-rights measure in more than 80 years. **The Civil Rights Act of 1957** established new procedures for expediting lawsuits by African Americans claiming illegal abridgement of their right, under the 15th Amendment, to vote. Generally credited to the tactical wizardry of Lyndon Johnson of Texas, the Democratic leader in the Senate, this legislation also created a permanent Commission on Civil Rights, a largely advisory body empowered only to study alleged violations and recommend additional remedies. In 1960, again after crucial maneuvering by Johnson, a second civil-rights act expanded the legal remedies available to blacks who were being barred from voting in the South. These civil-rights measures, passed in the face of fierce opposition from southern Democrats, dramatized the difficulty of getting even relatively limited measures through Congress and clearing the obstacles segregationists could throw in the way of civil-rights legislation.

The office of the president, which theoretically possessed the constitutional power to enforce legislation and court orders, appeared reluctant, under Dwight Eisenhower, to take action. Lobbied by Republicans from the Northeast and West, Ike did support the Civil Rights Act of 1957 but held back when these same Republicans urged a dramatic presidential step, perhaps issuing an executive order barring racial discrimination on construction projects financed by federal funds. A confirmed gradualist, Eisenhower saw the fight against segregation as primarily a state and local matter, and he expressed doubts about political leaders in Washington being able to change the attitudes of people who were opposed to the integration of public facilities or job sites.

During the fall of 1957, however, events in Little Rock, Arkansas, finally forced Eisenhower's hand. In response to a federal court order, which demanded desegregation of the city's Central High, the state's governor, Orval Faubus, had promised fellow segregationists that black students would never enter the school building. Ike's initial temporizing allowed Faubus time to play to the white supremacist galleries of Arkansas, and the governor eventually deployed his state's National Guard to prevent any move toward desegregation. Confronting this direct challenge to national authority, Eisenhower took command of the Arkansas National Guard and sent members of the U.S. Army to Little Rock. Black students, escorted by armed troops, finally entered Central High. The primary issue at stake, Eisenhower insisted, involved the defiance of the law of the land rather than the specific politics of school desegregation.

The confrontation in Little Rock also underscored, as the Eisenhower administration conceded, the international dimension of civil-rights politics in the United States. Washington often found itself on the defensive when foreign critics pointed to the U.S. record on civil rights. The Soviet Union delighted in reminding people around the world, particularly those in the Third World, how racial discrimination showed "the façade of the so-called 'American democracy.'" Secretary of State Dulles warned that racial conflict at home was "not helpful to the influence of the United States abroad." Events in Arkansas seemed to reaffirm the image, carried throughout the world by the Eisenhower administration's informational campaign, of the United States as a powerful nation that supported liberty and equality. When the U.S. Supreme Court, in *Cooper* v. *Aaron* (1958), unanimously invalidated an Arkansas law intended to block further integrationist efforts, newspapers around the globe highlighted its action.

American Indian Policy

The Eisenhower administration also struggled with the politics of American Indian policy. It attempted to implement two programs, "termination" and "relocation," that were already underway before it took office. The first called for Washington to terminate the status of Indians as "wards of the United States" and grant them all the "rights and privileges pertaining to American citizenship." This policy, to be pursued on a tribe-by-tribe basis, aimed at abolishing Indian reservations, liquidating tribal assets, and curtailing the social services offered by the Bureau of Indian Affairs (BIA). In 1954, a year after Congress proposed this general approach, legislators enacted six specific bills of termination, which would change the legal status of more than 8,000 American Indians and affect the ownership of more than 1 million acres of tribal land.

Under the relocation program, which had begun in 1951, the government financed incentive packages intended to entice Indians to leave rural reservations and seek jobs in urban areas. In 1954, the BIA intensified its relocation efforts, with Minneapolis, St. Louis, Dallas, and several other cities joining Denver, Salt Lake City, and Los Angeles as relocation sites. Both relocation and termination rested on the assumption—widespread in the social-science literature of the day—that governmental planners could re-chart the lives of American Indians and that the nation's social and cultural systems could quickly assimilate all Indian people into the mainstream of U.S. life.

The initiatives, however, faced fierce criticism. After Congress enacted several more termination bills during the 1950s, almost 12,000 people lost their status as tribal members, and land formally held by tribes continued to fall into the hands of commercial, non-Indian developers. Indians from terminated tribes stood to forfeit both their exemption from state taxation and the social services provided by the BIA. In return, they gained relatively little, especially in economic benefits. Relocation went no better than termination. Even as this process weakened the links between migrants and communal life on the reservations they left, most relocated Indians complained of finding only low-paying, dead-end jobs and racial discrimination away from their tribal homes.

American Indian activists and their supporters mobilized against the **termination and relocation** policies. By 1957, their efforts forced the U.S. government to scale back the initial congressional timetable, which had called for liquidating every tribe within five years. Continued protests led both Republicans and Democrats to repudiate termination in their party platforms of 1960. Two years later, Congress finally ended the program. Despite the criticism it produced, the relocation program continued until 1967. By then, almost half of the nation's Indians lived in relocation cities. This policy, critics constantly noted, neither touched the deep-rooted problems that many Indians confronted, including a life expectancy only two-thirds that of whites, nor provided significantly better opportunities for employment or education.

The Growth of Spanish-Speaking Populations

Millions of Spanish-speaking people, many of whom had recently arrived in the United States, also began mobilizing in hopes of realizing the nation's commitments to liberty and equality. Despite the prospect of discriminatory practices in the U.S. job and housing markets, large numbers of Puerto Ricans began moving from their island commonwealth to the mainland during the 1950s. By 1960, New York City's Puerto Rican population was nearly 100 times greater than it had been before the Second World War. Large numbers of Puerto Ricans also settled in Chicago, Boston, and Hartford, Connecticut, during the 1950s. The commonwealth government of Puerto Rico promoted immigration as a way of easing population pressures, but it also encouraged migrants to maintain cultural ties with the island. Officially U.S. citizens, most of the newcomers spoke only Spanish, and the formation of social and cultural clubs helped connect them with the Puerto Rican communities they had left behind.

At the same time, Puerto Ricans also began to form organizations that could help address conditions in the United States. The Puerto Rican–Hispanic Leadership Forum, organized in 1957, presaged the emergence of groups that looked more to social and economic conditions—and, ultimately, greater political clout—in the United States than to cultural affinities with Puerto Rico.

Meanwhile, large numbers of Spanish-speaking people from Mexico continued moving to California and the Southwest. There they settled, sometimes uncomfortably, into already established Mexican American communities. In 1940, Mexican Americans had been the most rural of all the major ethnic groups; by 1950, in contrast, more than 65 percent of Mexican Americans were living in urban areas, a figure that would climb to 85 percent by 1970. As a result of this fundamental demographic shift, Mexican Americans began to become an important political force in many western and southwestern cities.

Controversy over continued immigration from Mexico intensified during the early 1950s. Beginning in 1942 and continuing until 1967, the U.S. government sponsored the *bracero* (or farmhand) program, which brought nearly 5 million Mexicans across the U.S.–Mexican border, theoretically on short-term contracts, to fill agricultural jobs. Many *braceros* and their families remained in the United States, however, after these agreements expired. Legal immigrants from Mexico, along with growing numbers of people who filtered across the border, joined them.

"Operation Wetback," an ongoing U.S. government dragnet of the early 1950s, targeted undocumented immigrants from Mexico. The choice of a term of ethnic derision, which implied that all people of Mexican ancestry had illegally swum across the Rio Grande River to reach the United States, hardly built support for this program in Mexican American communities. During a five-year period, the U.S. government claimed to have rounded up and deported to Mexico nearly 4 million people, allegedly all undocumented immigrants. This operation, its critics charged, not only swept up some people who lacked ready documentation but served to stigmatize longtime citizens of Mexican heritage and to justify discriminatory treatment by local and state governments and by employers.

Groups representing Mexican Americans gradually broadened older struggles, which traced back to the 1930s (see chapter 25), against discrimination. Labor organizers, often defying efforts by employers and FBI personnel to label their efforts as "communist inspired," sought higher wages and better working conditions in the factories and fields. Unions with left-leaning political reputations and large Mexican American memberships, such as the United Cannery, Agricultural, Packing and Allied Workers of America (UCAPAWA), faced ongoing harassment from the FBI, other governmental agencies, and private businesses. A lengthy strike in New Mexico by Mexican American zinc miners, who were affiliated with a union that had been expelled from the CIO in 1950, became the subject of the motion picture *Salt of the Earth* (1954). Pressure from Washington, the film industry, and anti-communist labor unions prevented, throughout the 1950s, popular distribution of this independent production, a collaboration among blacklisted filmmakers, striking miners, and their families.

At the same time, organizations representing Mexican American professionals, such as LULAC and the Unity League, parlayed their legal resources into lawsuits seeking the desegregation of schools and other public facilities in Southern California and throughout the Southwest. When preparing to go to court, however, lawyers for these groups immediately faced a strategic dilemma. Legal challenges brought on behalf of plaintiffs of African descent, as in the *Brown* cases, relied on the claim that state laws separating "whites" and "coloreds" violated guarantees of legal equality. Most states, though, classified persons whose ancestors came from Mexico—people who, theoretically, could be of "mixed" ancestry, including European, Indian, African, and even Asian—as legally "white." In the area of education, as earlier cases such as *Westminster* had shown (see chapter 27), school officials in states such as California and Texas segregated students of Mexican descent on the basis of real and alleged "language deficiencies," rather than on that of "race." The "other white" legal status of Mexican Americans, in other words, complicated the ability of organizations such as LULAC to frame court challenges. In practice, it also prevented lawyers from automatically relying on precedents involving "white-against-black" discrimination.

Urban-Suburban Issues

The ongoing expansion of suburbia during the 1950s focused increasing attention on public policies related to cities. A variety of measures, adopted by both governmental and private institutions and organizations, for example, continued to shift resources away from cities, especially from neighborhoods with significant numbers of Latinos and African Americans. Continuing the now-familiar policy of **red-lining**, many banks and loan institutions denied funds for home-buyers and businesses in areas they considered "decaying" or "marginal." Using the same supposedly neutral criteria employed for suburban loans, the lending industry saw these blighted areas as "bad risks." They contained aging buildings, densely clustered homes, and growing numbers of low-income people, many of whom were of non-European descent. The FHA and other governmental agencies thus concentrated their activities in the newer suburbs. In 1960, for example, the FHA failed to put up a single dollar for home loan guarantees in Camden or Paterson, New Jersey, cities in which minority populations were growing, while it focused on the recently built, largely all-white suburbs that surrounded them.

"Urban renewal" programs, authorized by the Housing Act of 1949 (see chapter 27), according to numerous social-science studies, too often seemed aimed at "urban removal." Although the law called for "a feasible method for the temporary relocation" of persons displaced by urban renewal projects, lax enforcement meant that developers could generally ignore the needs of these people. Throughout the 1950s, Robert Moses, who dominated the planning and execution of New York City's vast construction projects, effectively concealed the number of people dislocated by his urban renewal and highway building programs. Although this unelected planner-bureaucrat always had his defenders, who insisted his vision ultimately encompassed the greater good of all residents, maps of New York City's always changing landscape showed office buildings, freeways, and relatively expensive housing complexes inexorably replacing the older living units that people with low-income jobs could afford.

Roughly similar debates over goals and results—along with the same general patterns in building—marked the histories of other large cities during the 1950s. Plans for new, federally built public housing, for example, quickly faltered in most areas of the United States. Newer suburban areas with their middle-income homeowners used their political clout and local zoning laws to freeze out government-sponsored housing projects. In addition, private housing interests lobbied to limit the number of public units actually constructed, invariably on relatively expensive and already densely populated urban sites, and to deny them amenities, such as closets or closets with doors, that could be found in most private apartments. Publicly built facilities, originally conceived as short-term alternatives for families who would soon move to their own homes, became stigmatized as "the projects." They gained reputations for being housing of last resort, reserved for people with chronically low incomes and meager prospects for economic advancement. In addition to disrupting urban housing patterns, renewal-removal projects also helped disperse industries that had long provided entry-level jobs for semi- and unskilled workers.

The urban-suburban policies of the 1950s, in short, seemed to be in need of major repair. In 1960, both the Democratic and Republican parties pledged to create a new cabinet office for urban affairs and to reconsider Washington's role in addressing the cycle of continued suburban growth and onrushing urban decay.

Debating the Role of Government, 1955–1960

Discussion of urban-suburban issues during the late 1950s accompanied a broader debate over how the national government in Washington might deal with a wide range of socioeconomic matters. Although Eisenhower sometimes hinted that he favored rolling back domestic programs established during the 1930s and 1940s, he possessed neither the political support nor the personal will to do so. Actually, his administration presided over a modest expansion of earlier initiatives: a larger Social Security system, a higher minimum wage, better unemployment benefits, and a new Department of Health, Education, and Welfare (HEW). Eisenhower denied that this record suggested the White House favored "big government," and insisted his approach represented a "moderate Republicanism."

The New Conservatives

Eisenhower's self-professed moderation on domestic issues angered a growing group of people who soon became known as the "new conservatives." Conservatives within the GOP's ranks conceded Eisenhower's popularity—and the fact that he was the first Republican president since Herbert Hoover—but they also complained that his administration seldom represented the conservative principles for which the Republican Party supposedly stood. From their perspective, the Republicans who voted in support of domestic social programs looked as bad as the Northern Democrats with whom they often allied.

The most popular conservative Republican of the 1950s, Arizona's Barry Goldwater, often voiced his doubts about the programmatic and regional shape of the national GOP. Ruggedly handsome and militantly anticommunist, Goldwater won election to the U.S.

Senate in 1952. Once in Washington, he quickly emerged as the spokesperson for those Republicans who viewed Eisenhower's policies as insufficiently conservative and too indebted to GOP constituencies on the East Coast. Goldwater once quipped that his party—and the nation—might be better off if someone could magically saw off the northern part of the eastern seaboard and let it drift out into the Atlantic, presumably toward a socialist-minded Europe.

Still, Goldwater took care to distinguish his conservatism from that of the "radical right," whose attacks against Eisenhower sometimes veered into anti-Semitic diatribes and claims of Ike being a conscious agent of Moscow. Carefully framed and largely ghost-written, Goldwater's *The Conscience of a Conservative* (1960) helped popularize his conservative critique. By refusing to seriously consider stronger military measures against the Soviet Union and by not making "victory the goal of U.S. policy," he argued, Eisenhower had likely endangered national security with his version of containment. Goldwater also portrayed almost all domestic programs, including federal civil-rights legislation, as grave threats to individual liberty. The Eisenhower administration seemed largely content to follow the Democratic Party's "New Deal antics" in its own domestic policy making, the Arizona senator alleged.

While Goldwater was pressing the GOP to reject Eisenhower's moderate Republicanism, others, such as the publisher William F. Buckley, Jr., used the 1950s to frame a broadly conservative message for the 1960s. Buckley, who grew up in a wealthy, cosmopolitan, and fervently conservative family, first gained national attention while still in his twenties. In *God and Man at Yale* (1952), the devoutly Roman Catholic Buckley attacked what he saw as a "collectivist" and antireligious tilt in higher education. Most Ivy League educators, he claimed, would defend neither capitalism nor Christianity. Known for wrapping his brickbats in humor, Buckley once claimed that he would rather be governed by the first 2,000 names in the Boston phone book than by the faculty of Harvard.

Buckley helped found the *National Review* in 1955. This weekly magazine attracted a talented group of writers and avoided positions, particularly the anti-Semitism of some old-line conservatives and the hysterical anticommunism of groups such as the John Birch Society, which Democrats and members of the media could label as extremist. Buckley and his *National Review* colleagues, recognizing they could not refashion conservatism quickly, adopted strategies for the long run. To this end, they established Young Americans for Freedom (YAF) in 1960, several years before similar college-based political organizations emerged from the New Left (see chapter 29).

Adopting another long-term approach, called "fusionism," to building a conservative movement, Buckley's group avoided any strict litmus test. As a result, the *National Review* initially even provided a sounding board for Joe McCarthy's embattled followers and for some southern segregationists. Relatively quickly, however, the magazine—and the larger movement it hoped to create—came to feature creative tension coming from three broad, not-always-compatible constituencies. This threesome included "traditionalist" conservatives, who insisted that social stability depended on jettisoning all notions of equality and allowing the educated-talented few, people such as themselves, to dominate the nation's institutions. The magazine also published pieces by "libertarians," people who rejected the hierarchical, anti-egalitarian vision of more traditional conservatives but who favored reducing the power of government and enlarging the liberties of capitalist entrepreneurs. Finally, the *National Review* consistently featured staunch anticommunists, such as Barry Goldwater, who insisted that national power be used, far more aggressively than either Democratic or Republican administrations had done, to oppose Soviet-led communism.

Meanwhile, a different style of conservative activism emerged, at the grassroots, especially within many new suburban areas. Barry Goldwater's brand of conservatism proved especially appealing to suburbanites in the "Sunbelt states" that stretched from California, across the Southwest, eastward through Texas, and over to Florida. Fiercely anticommunist, the "suburban warriors" from these areas, beginning with California, also framed a militantly conservative domestic agenda. It focused on keeping both state and national officials from using their power to infringe on what these conservative suburbanites considered liberties constitutionally reserved to their own local communities. They called for maintaining grassroots control of local school curricula, tough zoning laws, and the lowest possible rates of taxation, especially on real estate.

Advocates of a More Active Government

While the new conservative movement mobilized and, then, organized, in hopes of scaling back domestic social policies, an even more eclectic group tried to make the case for expanding governmental programs. Many of these commentators began by calling for greater activism from the office of the president.

The initial indecision by the White House during the 1957 situation at Little Rock's Central High School suggested, at least to these critics, that Dwight Eisenhower held an unsteady grasp of domestic issues. The national election of 1956 had given him (and Vice President Nixon) another landslide victory over a Democratic ticket, headed again by Adlai Stevenson, but Eisenhower's continued personal popularity had done even less for the Republican Party, which had failed to regain control of Congress, than in the 1952 contest. (The GOP would shed additional congressional seats—as well as state legislatures and governors' mansions—in the mid-term races of 1958. After this election, Democrats outnumbered Republicans by nearly 2-to-1 margins in both the U.S. Senate and the House of Representatives.) Meanwhile, Eisenhower, who had rebounded from a mild heart attack before the 1956 election, seemed progressively enfeebled, physically as well as politically.

After the president suffered a second heart attack and a mild stroke during his second term, critics intensified calls for more vigorous leadership from the White House. Social activists criticized the reluctance to use Washington's power to attack racial discrimination, and many economists, pointing to an economic downturn in 1958–59 when unemployment figures rose precipitously, ridiculed the Eisenhower administration's commitment to a balanced budget. Even after economic conditions improved, economists such as John Kenneth Galbraith urged significant deficit spending by Washington as a spur to further growth. Eisenhower's advisers stoutly resisted this advice.

Many of these critics, while avoiding the rhetoric of conservatives such as Goldwater, also found the Eisenhower administration's national security moves to be insufficient. The 1957 Gaither Report, prepared by Paul Nitze and other people who had been associated with the NSC-68 document of 1950 (see chapter 27), savaged New Look policies. The Gaither Report claimed that the Soviet Union's GNP was growing even more quickly than that of the United States and that a rapidly expanding military sector accounted for much of this expansion. The Gaither Report urged an immediate increase of about 25 percent in the Pentagon's budget and a crash program for building fallout shelters. It also called for developing intercontinental ballistic missiles (ICBMs) and expanding conventional military forces. Another report, largely written by a young political scientist named Henry Kissinger and issued by the prestigious Rockefeller Foundation, argued that the New Look, by relying on massive nuclear retaliation and downplaying non-nuclear options, actually undermined national security. It joined the Gaither Report in seeking greater U.S. spending for a wide range of defense initiatives.

Eisenhower, who remained far more attentive to foreign policy than domestic issues, reacted cautiously. Although the White House agreed to accelerate the development of ICBMs, it opposed any significant effort to build fallout shelters or to expand existing capabilities for fighting limited, non-nuclear wars. In fact, the Eisenhower administration reduced the size of several army and air force units and kept its defense budget well below the levels critics had proposed. Eisenhower felt confident in pursuing this course because super-secret U-2 surveillance flights over the USSR revealed that the Soviets were lagging behind, rather than racing ahead of, the United States in military capability.

Concerns about national security and calls for greater government spending also affected U.S. educational policies. Throughout the 1950s, the more traditionalist educators had often complained about schools imparting "life adjustment" skills—getting along with others and adapting to social change—instead of teaching traditional academic subjects. Rudolf Flesch's best-selling *Why Johnny Can't Read* (1956) anticipated books that asked why Johnny and his classmates couldn't add or subtract very well either and why they lagged behind their counterparts in the Soviet Union in science. Washington's help in funding K–12 instruction seemed an obvious way to upgrade educational performance. Simultaneously, the nation's leading research universities sought greater federal aid. In summer 1957, a committee of prominent scientists implored the Defense Department to expand its support for basic scientific research. "Research is a requisite for survival" in the nuclear age, it declared.

The case for increased federal spending suddenly became more compelling. On October 4, 1957, the Soviet Union orbited the world's first artificial satellite, a 22-inch sphere called **Sputnik,** and seemingly soared far beyond the United States in both space exploration and military capabilities. The USSR could use the same missile technology needed to launch *Sputnik,* argued Eisenhower's critics, to rain down nuclear weapons on U.S. cities. Effectively safeguarding U.S. national security, therefore, appeared to demand rebuilding, as rapidly as possible, the nation's military arsenal, its educational institutions, and its research capabilities.

The specter of the original *Sputnik,* along with that of a second and much larger Soviet satellite, improved chances that a wide range of institutions, and not simply the Pentagon, would now obtain federal funding. Phrases such as "national security" and "national defense" seemed to clear the way for financial resources to flow more freely out of Washington. In 1958, Congress passed the National Defense Education Act, which funneled aid to college-level programs in science, engineering, foreign languages, and the social sciences. This law marked a milestone in the long battle to overcome congressional opposition to federal funding of public education, especially from southern representatives who feared that aid from Washington could increase pressure for racial integration. Legislators also created another R&D effort, to be overseen by a new National Aeronautics and Space Administration (NASA). This governmental agency pledged to harness U.S. educational and technological know-how so that the United States could counter the Soviet Union's successes with its *Sputnik*s and preserve outer space for the benefit of "all mankind."

Many people also hoped that domestic social welfare programs would become the beneficiaries of increased federal spending. Galbraith's *The Affluent Society* (1958) saw a dangerous tilt in the "social balance," away from support for development of "public goods" and toward satisfaction of private desires. Already affluent families could afford to vacation in their own chrome-encrusted automobiles, but they would speed through shabby cities, motor along litter-filled roadsides, and gaze out at unsightly billboards. The researcher who developed a new carburetor is well rewarded, but anyone "who dreams up a new public service is [labeled] a wastrel," Galbraith's book sardonically noted.

Galbraith's critique seemed mild when compared to that of Michael Harrington. His passionate essays about the persistence of poverty recalled his apprenticeship at Dorothy Day's *Catholic Worker*. In 1959, *Commentary,* one of several influential national magazines featuring social criticism, published an article, which was immediately noticed in policy-making circles. In this essay, Harrington insisted that the need to address economic inequality remained as urgent as it had been during the 1930s. At least one-third of the nation's people—living in rural areas, small towns, and cities—barely subsisted in a land of supposed abundance and affluence. Avoiding the usual trappings of economic analysis, Harrington crafted dramatic stories about how economic deprivation ravaged the bodies and spirits of people whose lives had been largely untouched by the economic growth of the 1940s and 1950s.

During the 1960s, when addressing social and economic issues became a priority among policy makers drawn to Washington, pundits such as Galbraith and Harrington became political celebrities. These same people had honed their critiques, however, within the vibrant political culture of the late 1950s. The brief presidency of **John F. Kennedy** would, in fact, feature calls for more active foreign and domestic policies that had first emerged during the 1950s.

The Kennedy Years: Foreign Policy

Focus Question
What foreign and domestic policies did the Kennedy administration champion?

John Fitzgerald Kennedy's wealthy, politically ambitious father, Joseph P. Kennedy, claimed to have groomed his son for the White House. The young Kennedy graduated from Harvard in 1940, won military honors while serving in the Navy during the Second World War, won a 1946 election to represent his home district in Massachusetts in the lower house of Congress, and captured a Senate seat in 1952. Once in Washington, Kennedy became better known for his social life than for his command of legislative details, but he quickly parlayed his charm and youthful good lucks into political stardom. His 1953 marriage to Jacqueline Bouvier added yet another dash of glamour. A favorite of the media, Jackie won plaudits for her cultural tastes, choice in fashions, and fluency in several languages. After John Kennedy narrowly missed winning the Democratic vice presidential nomination in 1956, he immediately took aim at gaining the top spot on his party's 1960 ticket.

The Election of 1960

JFK, often accompanied by Jackie and by his brothers, Robert and Edward ("Ted") Kennedy, barnstormed across the country. This early presidential campaigning, along with a talented staff and his family's vast wealth, helped Kennedy overwhelm his Democratic challengers, including Senators Hubert Humphrey of Minnesota and Lyndon Johnson of Texas. By pledging to separate his Roman Catholic faith from his politics and by confronting those who appealed to anti-Catholic prejudice, Kennedy tried to defuse the religious issue that had doomed the candidacy of Al Smith in 1928 (see chapter 24).

Richard Nixon, running as the Republican standard bearer, spent much of the 1960 presidential campaign on the defensive. A widespread perception that the still-popular Eisenhower remained unenthusiastic about a Republican candidate who had served as his vice-president for eight years hardly cheered Nixon. Still, he tried to counter Kennedy's charisma with images of his own seasoned leadership, gained while at Ike's side. Nixon seemed notably off-balance during the first of several televised debates in which a cool, tanned Kennedy emerged, according to surveys of TV viewers, with a clear victory over a pale, nervous Nixon. (People who listened on radio assigned Nixon considerably higher marks.) Despite chronic and severe health problems, which Kennedy's entourage effectively concealed, JFK projected vigor and energy, if not experience.

Kennedy's 1960 campaign highlighted issues from the 1950s that, taken together, morphed into an agenda JFK would call the "New Frontier." Although Senator Kennedy's civil-rights record had been mixed, candidate Kennedy declared his support for new congressional legislation.

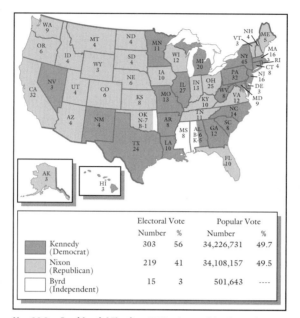

	Electoral Vote		Popular Vote	
	Number	%	Number	%
Kennedy (Democrat)	303	56	34,226,731	49.7
Nixon (Republican)	219	41	34,108,157	49.5
Byrd (Independent)	15	3	501,643	----

Map 28.2 Presidential Election, 1960   In one of the closest elections in American history in terms of the popular vote, Kennedy only narrowly outpolled Nixon. Kennedy's more commanding victory in the electoral vote produced some discussion about the consequences if the electoral college one day produced a president who had failed to carry the popular vote, a situation that occurred in the election of 2000.

In an important symbolic act, he dispatched aides to Georgia to assist Martin Luther King, Jr., who was facing jail time for a minor traffic violation. Kennedy also promised to use the president's executive authority, which Eisenhower had refused to do, to fight against job discrimination and to press for new social welfare programs to rebuild rural communities, increase educational opportunities, and improve urban conditions.

Kennedy's New Frontier also recalled two other central issues of the late 1950s: promoting greater economic growth and conducting a more aggressive foreign policy. Dismissing Eisenhower's economic policies as overly timid and largely ineffectual, Kennedy proposed using tax cuts and deficit spending to juice the economy. On foreign policy, he criticized Eisenhower for failing to rid Latin America, and Cuba, of Fidel Castro and for allowing a "missile gap" to develop between the United States and the Soviet Union. By spending more on defense, Kennedy claimed, the United States could respond, more flexibly, against communism, especially in the Third World. The "American people are tired of the drift in our national course . . . and they are ready to move again," Kennedy proclaimed.

The closely contested 1960 presidential election defied easy analysis. Despite his early problems, Nixon ran a skilled campaign, and Kennedy outpolled him by only about 100,000 popular votes. Kennedy's victory in the Electoral College, moreover, rested on razor-thin margins in several states, including Illinois. Many Republicans urged Nixon to challenge Kennedy's suspicious vote total there, but the vice president chose to accept the disputed result. JFK's triumph owed a great debt to his vice presidential running mate, Lyndon Baines Johnson. A tireless campaigner, LBJ gained credit for the Democratic ticket carrying the Deep South and his home state of Texas. Democrats remained the majority party in Congress and across the country, but this did not translate into a groundswell of support for Kennedy or his New Frontier.

JFK and Jackie achieved their earliest success by riveting media attention on the White House. They hobnobbed with movie stars and hosted prominent intellectuals. Kennedy's debut as president featured designer clothing, a poignant appearance by the aged poet Robert Frost, and an oft-quoted inaugural speech in which JFK challenged people to "ask not what your country can do for you; ask what you can do for your country." The "best and the brightest," the name a journalist later bestowed (tongue in cheek) on the hard-driving people who joined Kennedy's administration, promised to launch exciting and difficult crusades, even one to the frontier of outer space. Implicitly recalling the Soviet's 1957 triumph with its *Sputniks*, JFK promised that the United States would beat the USSR in the ultimate event in the space race, landing a manned craft on the surface of the moon, before the end of the 1960s.

Kennedy's Foreign Policy Goals

Kennedy promised an aggressive national security stance, which would include new **flexible-response** capabilities. Although Secretary of Defense Robert McNamara quickly found that the alleged missile gap between the United States and the USSR had never existed, the Kennedy administration still boosted the defense budget. It strongly supported military assistance programs, informational initiatives, and covert-action planning. In one of his most popular innovations, the president created the Peace Corps, a volunteer program that would prepare Americans, especially young people, to assist struggling people in nations around the world. Once overseas, they would work on various projects aimed at improving living conditions and, additionally, undercutting the appeal of left-leaning, procommunist movements.

The Kennedy administration also repackaged Eisenhower's effort to reorient U.S. Latin American policy. Kennedy's "Alliance for Progress" elaborated on Ike's earlier desire to move away from reliance on dictators and to support broadly conceived socioeconomic programs. Unveiled in spring 1961, in hopes of checking the spread of anti-Americanism and Castro-like insurgencies, the Alliance for Progress promised $20 billion in loans over a 10-year period to Latin American countries that would undertake land reform and economic development measures. Most Latin Americans judged Kennedy's Alliance, which underestimated obstacles to social and economic innovation, as more of a symbolic gesture than a substantive blueprint for change in their region.

Cuba and Berlin

The first serious setback for the Kennedy presidency, an ill-conceived 1961 CIA mission against Cuba, also had its roots in the Eisenhower administration. The CIA, looking to earlier covert actions against anti-American governments in Iran and Guatemala as models, had worked out a secret, Eisenhower-endorsed invasion to oust Fidel Castro. Overriding dissent from some of his advisers, Kennedy reaffirmed White House support for this plan. On April 17, 1961, however, when U.S.-backed and-trained forces (mainly anticommunist Cuban exiles) landed at the Bahia de Cochinas (the **Bay of Pigs**) on the southern coast of Cuba, the popular uprising, which the CIA had predicted, failed to materialize.

Instead, forces loyal to Castro quickly surrounded and captured the invaders. Confronting a badly planned and poorly executed operation, Kennedy rejected any additional steps, including last-minute U.S. air strikes that CIA operatives had apparently misled their Cuban allies into believing were part of the plan. The White House initially tried to deny any U.S. involvement in the Bay of Pigs invasion, but the CIA's role quickly became public knowledge. A new wave of anti-Yankee sentiment swept across much of Latin America, and Castro used the invasion as justification for further tightening his grip over Cuban life and strengthening his ties to the Soviet Union.

Kennedy responded to the Bay of Pigs by admitting error and by devising new anti-Castro strategies. "I have made a tragic mistake," Kennedy told one adviser. "Not only were our facts in error, but our policy was wrong." Stung by the failed invasion, the White House continued to target Castro with a covert program, "Operation Mongoose." It included efforts to destabilize Cuba's economy and, in concert with organized crime figures, to assassinate the Cuban leader.

Meanwhile, two other dramatic confrontations began unfolding, more slowly, in Berlin and in Cuba. In June 1961, Nikita Khrushchev and Kennedy met in Vienna, Austria, where the Soviets proposed ending the Western presence in Berlin and reuniting the city as part of East Germany. Khrushchev's initiative responded to the steady flow of immigrants from East Germany into West Berlin, a migration that was both politically embarrassing and economically draining to the German communist regime. Kennedy refused to abandon West Berlin, and in August 1961, with Soviet approval, East Germany began to erect first a barbed-wire fence and then a concrete barrier to separate East from West Berlin. This "Berlin Wall" became a symbol of communist repression. Kennedy's assertion, *"Ich bin ein Berliner,"* delivered in front of the wall to a cheering crowd of West Berliners, provided a memorable moment in his presidency.

Superpower confrontation escalated to a potentially lethal, even catastrophic, level during the **Cuban Missile Crisis** of October 1962. Responding to pleas from Fidel Castro and seeing Kennedy, especially after their personal meeting in Vienna, as an inexperienced bungler, Khrushchev took a bold gamble: He began sending advanced Soviet armaments to Cuba. After a U-2 spy plane showed missile-launching sites in Cuba, the Kennedy administration announced it would not allow the Soviet Union to place nuclear warheads so close to U.S. soil. It demanded that the Soviets dismantle the missile silos and turn back its supply ships, presumably containing the warheads, then heading for Cuba.

The Cuban Missile Crisis began in earnest. After tense strategizing sessions with his top advisers, Kennedy rejected calls by some military leaders, notably General Curtis LeMay, for a strike against Cuba. JFK thus heeded warnings that any such rash action risked escalating into nuclear warfare between the United States and the Soviet Union. Instead, Kennedy ordered the U.S. Navy to "quarantine" Cuba. The president did authorize Strategic Air Command (SAC) to go on full alert, in preparation for a possible nuclear conflict. Secretary of Defense Robert McNamara later recalled leaving a presidential conference during the 13-day crisis, looking up at the sky, and wondering if the world would still be there 24 hours later. Reflections of this kind encouraged both the United States and the USSR to engage in secret diplomatic maneuvers to forestall a military showdown.

Delicate maneuvering by both governments (and several private go-betweens) finally ended the standoff. On October 28, 1962, Khrushchev ordered the Soviet missiles in Cuba to be dismantled and the supply ships to sail for home; Kennedy pledged not to invade Cuba and secretly promised to complete a previously ordered withdrawal of U.S. missiles from Turkey. When researchers finally gained access to Soviet archives during the mid-1990s, they discovered that the Missile Crisis had been even more dangerous than U.S. officials had ever imagined. Unknown to anyone in the Kennedy administration in 1962, the Soviets had already placed in Cuba tactical nuclear weapons, which could have been launched against U.S. targets in retaliation for any air strike.

The Missile Crisis underscored how easily the United States and the USSR could careen toward nuclear conflict, and the dangers of October 1962 encouraged the two nuclear superpowers to begin moving with greater caution. To prevent a similar confrontation or an accident involving nuclear weapons, they established a direct telephone hotline between Moscow and Washington, D.C. Later, during a spring 1963 commencement address at American University, Kennedy underscored the importance of the United States working to promote world peace. Some Kennedy watchers, then as well as now, have argued that this American University speech portended what a second JFK administration would have attempted to achieve in foreign policy.

Southeast Asia and "Flexible Response"

Meanwhile, though, in Southeast Asia, Kennedy continued earlier U.S. attempts to preserve a noncommunist state in South Vietnam. After the Bay of Pigs fiasco, in which the attempt to overthrow an already established communist government had failed, JFK seemed more determined than before to prevent any communist-led "war of national liberation" from ever succeeding.

Even so, the odds against preserving a pro-U.S. government in South Vietnam seemed to grow ever longer as Kennedy's own presidency lengthened. Opposition to the regime of Ngo Dinh Diem, who had been in power since 1954, had now coalesced in the National Liberation Front (NLF). Formed in December 1960, the NLF included nationalist factions that resented Diem's dependence on the United States, communists who demanded more extensive land reform, an array of political leaders who were fed up with Diem's corruption and cronyism, and groups beholden to Ho Chi Minh's communist government in the North. North Vietnam began sending additional supplies and, then, thousands of its own troops to the South to support the NLF.

The Kennedy administration saw Vietnam as a test case for its anticommunist strategy, especially the doctrine of flexible response. Although it accepted a 1962 deal that created a technically neutral but communist-influenced government in Laos, the White House appeared determined to hold the line in South Vietnam. Washington trained elite U.S. troops, the Green Berets, in counterinsurgency tactics; sent teams of social scientists, charged with nation building, to advise South Vietnam on socioeconomic policies; and dispatched other experts to train that nation's internal security forces. Finally, the Kennedy administration deployed, in ever larger increments, nearly 11,000 U.S. troops who would supposedly only advise, rather than actively fight alongside, South Vietnamese forces.

These U.S. moves seemed to create only new opportunities for corruption and greater distrust between South Vietnam's government and its citizens. When U.S. officials became aware that disgruntled South Vietnamese military officers were planning to topple Diem's already tottering regime, they gave them a green light to continue orchestrating their plan. In November 1963, the conspirators routed Diem—an act that could hardly have surprised the Kennedy administration—from his presidential palace and—in a genuine shock to U.S. officials—summarily murdered him. This coup d'état, which brought a military regime to power in Saigon, appeared to create even greater political instability in South Vietnam. The NLF and North Vietnam, in turn, ratcheted up their military pressure on the new government in Saigon.

The Southeast Asian policy of Kennedy's administration seemed no more coherent than that of Eisenhower's. The overall goal, to be sure, remained consistent: prevent communist forces from toppling any anticommunist government in Saigon. The United States could not afford to "lose" South Vietnam. Although some in JFK's inner circle urged sending U.S. combat forces into battle, the president continued to reject this option. On several occasions, the White House even talked about withdrawing some of its combat-ready advisers, perhaps as a substantive shift in policy or as a public relations move. As with his domestic agenda, Kennedy's presidency ended, unexpectedly, with its future direction in Vietnam in a state of flux or, perhaps, even disarray.

The Kennedy Years: Domestic Policy

Kennedy hesitated to follow up on his campaign proposal of increasing federal spending to speed economic growth. He feared that federal budget deficits might cost him support among fiscal conservatives and business leaders. Relations with corporate leaders, nevertheless, did turn temporarily ugly in 1962, when Kennedy clashed with the president of U.S. Steel over that company's decision to raise its prices beyond the guidelines suggested by the White House. Recoiling from this imbroglio, the Kennedy administration hoped to chart a steadier domestic course. Events did not always cooperate.

Policy Making During the Early 1960s

In 1962, the White House staff finally sat down with key members of Congress to discuss lowering tax rates as a means of promoting economic growth. The economy had nicely rebounded from its downturn of 1957–58, but proponents of a tax cut promised even more rapid growth. Lower tax rates for everyone and special deductions for businesses that invested in new plants and equipment, the tax-cutters argued, would spur investment in facilities and jobs. Despite opposition from those Democrats who thought these changes tilted toward corporations and the wealthy, the tax bill seemed headed for passage in the fall of 1963.

Most of Kennedy's ideas about social welfare policy recalled earlier proposals. There was talk of raising the federal minimum wage rate and of new urban rebuilding programs. Under the programs begun during the 1940s, Kennedy-era bulldozers continued to raze large parts of urban America, still at the expense, critics charged, of people who desperately needed affordable housing. One new departure, the Area Redevelopment Bill of 1961, called for directing federal grants and loans to areas, such as Appalachia, that the economic growth of the 1940s and 1950s had largely bypassed.

The Civil-Rights Movement, 1960–1963

Although JFK had talked about supporting new civil-rights legislation, he also tried to placate the segregationist wing of his Democratic Party. Initially, the Kennedy administration assigned greater priority to the fight against organized crime than the one against racial discrimination. The president and his brother, Robert, whom he had appointed attorney general, listened sympathetically when J. Edgar Hoover, director of the FBI, falsely warned of continuing links between Martin Luther King, Jr., and members of the American Communist Party. To monitor King's activities and gather information that Hoover would later use to smear the civil-rights leader, the FBI intensified surveillance, illegally tapped King's phone conversations, and placed "bugs" in his hotel rooms.

Meanwhile, in early 1960, African American students at North Carolina A&T, a historically black college in Greensboro, sat down at a drugstore lunch counter and politely asked to be served in the same manner as white customers. This "sit-in" marked an intensification of direct action. Young activists directly challenged local segregation laws by acting as if these measures simply did not exist. Targeting locations in both the South and the North, demonstrators staged nonviolent sit-ins at restaurants, bus and train stations, and other public facilities.

The courage and commitment of these demonstrators brought new energy—and media attention—to the antidiscrimination movement. Singing anthems such as "We Shall Overcome" and "Oh, Freedom" to promote solidarity, young people pledged their talents, their resources—indeed, their lives—to the civil-rights struggle. In 1961, an inter-racial group of activists from CORE and a new group that had emerged from the **sit-in movement, the Student Nonviolent Coordinating Committee (SNCC)**, risked racist retaliation by conducting "freedom rides" across the South. The **freedom riders** were challenging the Kennedy administration to enforce the federal court decisions that had declared state laws requiring segregation on interstate buses (and in bus stations) to be unconstitutional.

This grassroots activism forced the Kennedy administration into action of its own. It first dispatched U.S. marshals to protect the freedom riders from racist violence. In 1962 (and again the following year), the White House called on National Guard troops and fed-eral marshals to prevent pro-segregationist mobs from halting court-ordered integration at several educational institutions in the Deep South, including the Universities of Mississippi and Alabama. In November 1962, Kennedy issued a long-promised executive order that banned racial discrimination in federally financed housing. The following February, he sent Congress a civil-rights bill that called for faster trials in lawsuits seeking to tear down barriers designed to prevent African Americans in the South from voting. Events of the early 1960s, especially in the South, however, always seemed to outpace the Kennedy administration's initiatives.

The racist violence that convulsed Birmingham, Alabama, in 1963 highlighted this dynamic. Birmingham's all-white police force unleashed dogs and high-pressure water hoses on African Americans, including young children, who were peacefully demonstrating on behalf of desegregating that city's public facilities. White supremacists later murdered four young girls and injured twenty other people when they bombed the Sixteenth Street Baptist Church, a center of the civil-rights campaign in Birmingham. After thousands of angry African Americans rallied in protest—and two more children were killed, this time by police officers—the Kennedy administration finally moved to staunch the bloodletting.

By this time, however, the determination and courage of civil-rights activists in defying the violence in Birmingham had produced another real-life, televised drama for the entire world to watch. Kennedy finally entered the picture. During an emotion-filled national television address, the president pleaded for a national commitment to the battle against discrimina-tion. Recent events in Alabama, he declared, had raised "a moral issue . . . as old as Scrip-tures and . . . as clear as the Constitution." The time for "patience" and "delay," Kennedy announced, had passed. Racial strife was already "retarding our Nation's economic and social progress and weakening the respect with which the rest of the world regards us." Against the backdrop of a televised battle line that seemed to stretch across the South, the issue of civil rights dominated national politics during the last six months of Kennedy's presidency.

The White House still hoped it might influence the direction and moderate the pace of change. It crafted additional legislation designed to dampen the enthusiasm for civil-rights demonstrations, without further inflaming white segregationists. Its proposed bill called for a ban against racial discrimination in public facilities and housing and for new measures to pro-tect the voting rights of African Americans in the South. When the administration recognized that its legislative proposals would not derail a "March on Washington for Jobs and Freedom," planned for the late summer of 1963, it belatedly endorsed the event, sponsored by a coalition of civil-rights and labor organizations.

On August 28, 1963, an integrated group of more than 200,000 people marched through the nation's capital to the Lincoln Memorial. There, Martin Luther King, Jr., delivered his famous "I Have a Dream" speech. Most other speakers generally applauded Kennedy's latest initiatives, but some urged a broader agenda. Demands included a higher minimum wage and a federal program to guarantee new jobs. Well-organized and smoothly run, this one-day demonstration received overwhelmingly favorable coverage from the national media, especially television, and put even greater political pressure on the White House and Congress to lend their assistance to the movement.

Women's Issues

The seeds of a resurgent women's movement were also being sown, although more quietly, during the early 1960s. All across the political spectrum, women began speaking out more forcefully and visibly than they had during the 1950s. The energy of suburban warriors on the political right nurtured the grassroots of their movement. Phyllis Schlafly, whose book *A Choice, Not an Echo* (1964) became one of the leading conservative manifestos, suggested how women could blend careers in politics with ones as wives and mothers. African American activists such as Bernice Johnson Reagon (whose work with the Freedom Singers combined music and social activism) and Fannie Lou Hamer (who spearheaded the organization of a racially integrated Freedom Democratic Party in Mississippi) fought discrimination based on both race and gender. Female union leaders pushed for greater employment opportunities and more equitable workplace environments. Chicana farm workers became key figures in union organizing efforts in California. Women also played an important role through organizations such as the Committee for a Sane Nuclear Policy (SANE) and the Women's Strike for Peace in orchestrating opposition to the U.S.–Soviet arms race.

During Kennedy's final year in office, 1963, Betty Friedan published *The Feminine Mystique*, which observers soon credited for helping to revive organized feminist activity in the United States. Friedan's book drew on her own social criticism from the late 1950s. Decrying the narrow confines of domestic life and the lack of public roles available to well-educated women, it resonated with the many middle-class women who became standard-bearers for "Second Wave Feminism."

Anxious to address women's concerns, Kennedy appointed a Presidential Commission on the Status of Women, chaired by Eleanor Roosevelt. Negotiating differences between moderate and more militant members, the commission issued a report that documented discrimination against women in employment opportunities and wages. Kennedy responded with a presidential order designed to eliminate gender discrimination within the federal civil service system. His administration also supported the Equal Pay Act of 1963, which made it a federal crime for employers to pay lower wages to women who were doing the same work as men.

The Assassination of John F. Kennedy

During fall 1963, the Kennedy White House, although still struggling to reframe both its domestic and foreign policies, expected JFK would rather easily win reelection in 1964. Then, around noontime, on November 22, 1963, the president was shot dead as his motorcade moved through Dealey Plaza in Dallas. Vice President Lyndon Johnson, who had accompanied Kennedy to Texas, hurriedly took the oath of office and then rushed back to Washington. Equally quickly, the Dallas police arrested Lee Harvey Oswald and pegged him as JFK's assassin. Oswald had loose ties to organized crime, had once lived in the Soviet Union, and had a bizarre set of political affiliations, including shadowy connections with groups interested in Cuba. Oswald, who declared his innocence, never faced trial. Jack Ruby, whose Dallas nightclub catered to powerful underworld figures, killed Oswald, on national television, while the alleged gunman was in police custody. A hastily conducted investigation by a special commission headed by Chief Justice Earl Warren concluded that both Oswald and Ruby had acted alone.

The Warren Commission's account of a lone gunman, Lee Harvey Oswald, came under intense scrutiny. Competing theories about the number of shots, the trajectory of the bullets, the nature of Kennedy's wounds, and the identity of his assassins began to proliferate. Over time, a myriad of conspiratorial scenarios—including ones pointing toward the CIA, high-ranking governmental officials, Castro's Cuba, anti-Castro Cubans, organized crime, and even Lyndon Johnson—took flight. Oliver Stone's *JFK* (1991) refocused attention on obvious shortcomings in the Warren Commission Report.

Kennedy's life and presidency remain topics of lively historical debate and tabloid-style speculation. Researchers have provided new details about his poor health, reliance on exotic medications, and dalliances with women, all of which his loyal aides and a compliant press had once kept from public view. As historians speculate about how such revelations might have affected Kennedy's ability to make crucial decisions, they continue to debate older questions, particularly what JFK might have done in Vietnam and on the domestic front had he won the 1964 presidential election. The passage of time, in short, has diminished neither scholarly nor popular interest in John F. Kennedy and his 1,000-day presidency.

Conclusion

After 1953, conflict between the United States and the Soviet Union increasingly migrated to the Third World, where conflict over Cuba, in 1962, brought the two superpowers to the brink of nuclear war. Even on those occasions, such as after the Missile Crisis, when signs of tension with the USSR seemed to subside, the United States continued to chart a determinedly anticommunist course. It pursued the buildup of nuclear weapons, new forms of economic pressure, and expanded abilities to conduct covert activities. Developments in the Third World, particularly in Cuba and Southeast Asia, became of growing concern to U.S. policy makers.

At home, the economy grew steadily between 1953 and 1963. A cornucopia of new consumer products encouraged talk about an age of affluence and abundance but also produced apprehension about conformity, unruly youth, and mass culture. At the same time, the millions of people sidelined by economic inequality and often disadvantaged by racial and ethnic discrimination moved to the center of public debate over liberty and equality. Some critics charged that the Eisenhower administration seemed overly cautious in using the power of government to spread affluence more widely or to fight discrimination. More quietly, particularly in the political and cultural arenas, a new conservative movement also began to take shape. These critics from the right claimed that Eisenhower and JFK used the power of government too much, not too little.

The policy initiatives of the Kennedy administration grew, in large part, from the political, social, and cultural criticism of the 1950s. Although Kennedy preferred to focus on matters of foreign policy, the press of events, particularly those associated with the civil-rights movement, forced the president to consider how the power of his office might be used to address the issues of liberty and equality at home.

The post-Kennedy era would continue to highlight questions about liberty, equality, and power. Was the United States encouraging freedom in the Third World, particularly in Vietnam? Was it sufficiently active in supporting equalitarian movements at home? The troubled era of "America's longest war," 1963–74, would turn on how different people attempted to respond to these questions.

SUGGESTED READINGS

James T. Patterson, *Grand Expectations: The United States, 1945–1974* (1996) provides a good overview of the years from 1953 to 1963. For accounts of Eisenhower's presidential leadership, begin with **Fred I. Greenstein,** *The Hidden-Hand Presidency: Eisenhower as Leader* (rev. ed., 1994). **Chester Pach, Jr. and Elmo Richardson,** *The Presidency of Dwight D. Eisenhower* (1991) presents a useful, brief history. On JFK, see **Robert Dallek,** *An Unfinished Life: John F. Kennedy, 1917–1963* (2003); **Richard Reeves,** *President Kennedy: Profile of Power* (1994); and **Seymour Hersh,** *The Dark Side of Camelot* (1997).

There are many studies of Eisenhower's foreign policy, but a good sense of the issues and scholarly debates can be gleaned from **Robert R. Bowie and Richard H. Immerman,** *Waging Peace: How Eisenhower Shaped an Enduring Cold War Strategy* (2000). **John Prados,** *Presidents' Secret Wars: CIA and Pentagon Covert Operations from World War II through the Persian Gulf* (1996), and **Zachary Karabell,** *Architects of Intervention: The United States, the Third World, and the Cold War, 1946–1962* (1999) put an important aspect of policy in a broad perspective. **Walter L. Hixson,** *Parting the Curtain: Propaganda, Culture, and the Cold War, 1945–1961* (1997) argues that cultural initiatives provided weapons in the Cold War. **Lawrence Freedman,** *Kennedy's Wars: Berlin, Cuba, Laos, and Vietnam* (2000) illuminates the major international crises of the Kennedy years.

For events on the home front, **James B. Gilbert,** *A Cycle of Outrage: America's Reaction to the Juvenile Delinquent in the 1950s* (1986) discusses cultural fears; **Karal Ann Marling,** *As Seen on TV: The Visual Culture of Everyday Life in the 1950s* (1994) stresses the importance of visual imagery; and **James B. Gilbert**, *Redeeming Culture: American Religion in an Age of Science* (1997) examines another aspect of America's changing culture. **W. T. Lhamon, Jr.**, *Deliberate Speed: The Origins of a Cultural Style in the American 1950s* (2002) advances a provocative interpretation. The highly readable examination of the struggle against racial discrimination by **Taylor Branch**, *Parting the Waters: America in the King Years, 1954–1963* (1988) may be augmented by **James Patterson**, *Brown v. Board of Education: A Civil Rights Milestone and Its Troubled Legacy* (2001); **Robert O. Self**, *American Babylon: Race and the Struggle for Postwar Oakland* (2003); **John D'Emilio**, *Lost Prophet: The Life and Times of Bayard Rustin* (2003); and **David L. Chappell**, *A Stone of Hope: Prophetic Religion and the Death of Jim Crow* (2004).

On women and families during the 1950s, **Elaine Tyler May**, *Homeward Bound: American Families in the Cold War Era* (rev. ed., 1999) stresses the new emphasis on domestic life and the family wage. Consult also, the relevant pages of **Ruth Rosen**, *The World Split Open: How the Modern Women's Movement Changed America* (2000). **Leila J. Rupp**, *Survival in the Doldrums: The American Women's Rights Movement, 1945 to the 1960s* (1987); **Joanne Meyerowitz**, ed., *Not June Cleaver: Women and Gender in Postwar America, 1945–1960* (1994); **Stephanie Coontz**, *The Way We Never Were: American Families and the Nostalgia Trip* (1992); and **Martin Meeker**, *Contacts Desired: Gay and Lesbian Communications and Community, 1940s to 1970s* (2006) work against that grain.

Visit the Liberty Equality Power Companion Web site for resources specific to this textbook: http://www.thomsonedu.com/history/murrin

Also find self-tests and additional resources at ThomsonNOW. ThomsonNOW is an integrated online suite of services and resources with proven ease of use and efficient paths to success, delivering the results you want—NOW!

www.thomsonedu.com/login/

America during Its Longest War, 1963–1974

The years from 1963 to 1974 brought political, social, and cultural upheaval to most areas of the world, including the United States. Lyndon Baines Johnson promised to finish what John Kennedy had begun, but popular memory has come to recall LBJ's troubled presidency (1963–69) more negatively than Kennedy's. When looking at foreign policy, Johnson faced a critical question: Should the United States deploy its own combat forces to prop up South Vietnam, its beleaguered ally? When surveying the domestic scene, where Johnson hoped to focus his attention, he already knew what he would do: mobilize the federal government's power to promote greater liberty and equality. Very quickly, however, Johnson saw his domestic dreams begin to vanish in the face of the ongoing foreign nightmare in Vietnam and turmoil at home. By 1968, the United States was politically polarized and awash in both foreign and domestic crises.

The polarization so much in evidence during 1968 seemed to worsen during the years that followed. By 1974, when a series of political scandals, known as the "Watergate Crisis," forced Richard Nixon to leave the presidency under pressure of impeachment, the nation's political and social fabrics looked very different from those of 1963.

The Great Society

Focus Question
How did the Johnson administration define Great Society goals, and how did it approach problem solving? Why did the Great Society produce so much controversy?

Lyndon B. Johnson lacked Kennedy's media-friendly charisma, but he possessed other political assets. As a member of the House of Representatives during the late 1930s and early 1940s and as majority leader of the U.S. Senate during the 1950s Johnson mastered the art of interest-group horse trading. Few legislative issues, it appeared, defied an LBJ-forged consensus. Every significant interest group could be flattered, cajoled, or threatened into lending this towering Texan its support. During Johnson's time in Congress, his wealthy Texas benefactors gained valuable oil and gas concessions and lucrative construction contracts, while Johnson acquired his own personal fortune. Johnson's skill in gaining federal funding for

CHRONOLOGY

1963	Johnson assumes presidency and pledges to continue Kennedy's initiatives
1964	Congress passes Kennedy's tax bill, the Civil Rights Act of 1964, and the Economic Opportunity Act • Gulf of Tonkin Resolution gives Johnson authority to conduct undeclared war • Johnson defeats Barry Goldwater in presidential election
1965	Johnson announces plans for the Great Society • Malcolm X assassinated • U.S. intervenes in Dominican Republic • Johnson announces significant U.S. troop deployments in Vietnam • Congress passes Voting Rights Act • Violence rocks Los Angeles and other urban areas
1966	Black Power movement emerges • *Miranda* v. *Arizona* decision guarantees rights of criminal suspects • Ronald Reagan elected governor of California • U.S. begins massive air strikes in North Vietnam
1967	Large antiwar demonstrations begin • Beatles release *Sgt. Pepper's Lonely Hearts Club Band*
1968	Tet offensive accelerates debates over war (January) • Martin Luther King, Jr. assassinated (April) • Robert F. Kennedy assassinated (June) • Violence rocks Democratic national convention in Chicago • Civil Rights Act of 1968 passed • Vietnam peace talks begin in Paris • Richard Nixon elected president
1969	Nixon announces "Vietnamization" policy • Reports of My Lai massacre become public
1970	U.S. troops enter Cambodia • Student demonstrators killed at Kent State and Jackson State • First Earth Day observed • Environmental Protection Act passed • Clean Air Act passed
1971	*Pentagon Papers* published • White House "Plumbers" formed • Military court convicts Lieutenant Calley for My Lai incident
1972	Nixon crushes McGovern in presidential election
1973	Paris peace accords signed • *Roe* v. *Wade* upholds women's right to abortion • Nixon's Watergate troubles begin to escalate
1974	House votes impeachment, and Nixon resigns • Ford assumes presidency
1975	Saigon falls to North Vietnamese forces

ambitious building projects brought economic growth to cities such as Dallas and Houston and to much of the Southwest.

Kennedy's death gave Johnson, who had been frustrated by his limited job description while serving as JFK's vice president, the opportunity to display his political skills on the presidential stage. Confident of being able to forge a national consensus behind a bold program for social and economic change, Johnson began his presidency by asking Congress to honor JFK's memory. He urged passage of legislation that Kennedy's administration had proposed and bombarded legislators with much grander proposals of his own. Between January 8, when he delivered his first State of the Union address, until August 27, 1964, when he accepted the Democratic Party's presidential nomination, Johnson concentrated on three domestic issues: tax cutting, civil rights, and economic inequality.

Closing the New Frontier

Even as Johnson closed JFK's New Frontier, he staked out additional political territory. In May 1964, during an address at Michigan University, Johnson declared it was time to "move upward to the Great Society," which rested on "liberty and abundance for all." The Great Society, according to LBJ, would not provide Americans with "a safe harbor, a resting place, a final objective, a finished work," but rather "a challenge constantly renewed, beckoning us toward a destiny where the meaning of our lives matches the marvelous products of our labor."

To stimulate the economic growth needed to produce the Great Society's abundance, Johnson had first, several months earlier in his presidency, emphasized the importance of cutting taxes. Intensively lobbying members of Congress who opposed the budget deficits that tax reductions would produce, he secured passage of the $10 billion tax-cut package JFK had earlier proposed. Its supporters hailed the measure as the guarantor of continuing economic growth. Although economists continue to disagree as to how much this tax measure actually contributed to the economic boom of the mid-1960s, it *appeared* to work. GNP rose 7 percent in 1964 and 8 percent the following year, unemployment dropped, and inflation remained low.

Advocating greater liberty and equality, Johnson pushed a more extensive version of Kennedy's civil-rights proposal through Congress. In early February 1964, the House of Representatives passed its own civil-rights bill. It included an amendment, Title VII of the measure eventually signed into law, that barred discrimination based not simply on "race" but on "sex" as well. Some southern Democrats had hoped that such a provision might scuttle the entire bill, but other House members saw the addition as a welcome victory for women. This provision would soon assist an already resurgent women's movement.

Although Johnson was championing the civil-rights bill as another memorial to Kennedy, he fully recognized that southerners in the Democratic Party would continue trying to block it. Consequently, he and his allies in the U.S. Senate courted crucial Republican support for curtailing a southern-led filibuster, for hammering out compromises on key provisions, and for reconciling the differing bills passed by the two houses of Congress.

Johnson finally obtained the **Civil Rights Act of 1964,** a truly bipartisan measure, in July 1964. It strengthened existing federal remedies, to be monitored by a new Equal Employment Opportunity Commission (EEOC), against job discrimination. More controversially, the act's "public accommodations" provision, which resembled an 1875 civil-rights law that an earlier Supreme Court had invalidated, prohibited racial discrimination in all facilities—such as hotels, motels, and restaurants—in any way connected to the flow of interstate commerce. Opponents of this section saw it as an overextension of federal power and an attack on the personal liberties of property owners. Its proponents predicted, correctly as it turned out, that the current Supreme Court would reject these constitutional claims.

Finally, Congress responded favorably to Johnson's third domestic priority, legislation to deal with socioeconomic inequality. A month after passage of the Civil Rights Act of 1964, under constant prodding from the White House, legislators adopted another landmark measure, the Economic Opportunity Act (EOA). Coming only six months after Johnson had called for "an unconditional war on poverty in America," during his January 1964 State of the Union address, the EOA provided LBJ with the means to launch a multifront campaign.

A new executive agency, the Office of Economic Opportunity (OEO) would coordinate a variety of different initiatives. LBJ charged the OEO, first headed by R. Sargent Shriver, a member-by-marriage of the Kennedy family, with eliminating "the paradox of poverty in the midst of plenty." In addition to establishing the new agency, the EOA mandated federal-government loans for rural and small-business development; established a work-training program called the Jobs Corps; created Volunteers in Service to America (VISTA), a domestic version of the Peace Corps; provided low-wage, public service jobs for young people; and began the "work-study" program to assist college students. In addition, it authorized grassroots social initiatives, Community Action Programs (CAPs), to be planned by local community groups but funded by Washington.

Meanwhile, however, Lyndon Johnson and the rest of the nation could already see signs that conflict would surely accompany change, particularly on the issue of civil rights. During the same summer that Congress passed the Civil Rights Act of 1964 and created the OEO, violence connected to racial issues broke out in different parts of the country. In New York City, tensions between police officers and African American demonstrators, protesting policing practices that had led to the fatal shooting of a black youth, flared into confrontations during mid-July.

At almost the same time, a different kind of violence rolled through those parts of Mississippi where a coalition of civil-rights groups was sponsoring what it called **"Freedom Summer."** This campaign to register black voters, by an interracial group of young volunteers including white northern college students, produced a murderous backlash from some segregationists. At least six civil-rights workers met violent deaths during that blood-soaked Mississippi summer. In the most notorious incident, whose legal fallout would last into the 21st century, KKK members and law-enforcement officials from Neshoba County, Mississippi, conspired to kidnap and brutally murder three volunteers—James Chaney, Michael Schwerner, and Andrew Goodman.

Other activists pressed forward, only to see the grassroots organizing of that summer frustrated by Lyndon Johnson and a majority of the national Democratic Party. Pressured by LBJ, the 1964 Democratic convention voted to seat Mississippi's "regular" all-white delegates, people who clearly intended to desert LBJ and the national party during the fall election. Democratic leaders gave only token recognition to members of the alternative, racially diverse "Freedom Democratic Party" (FDP). This rebuff prompted people, such as Fannie Lou Hamer, who had risked their lives to create the FDP, to recall earlier suspicions about Lyndon Johnson. Although LBJ seemed more committed to civil rights than John Kennedy had been, where would Johnson—and Hubert Humphrey, his handpicked vice presidential running mate—stand after the 1964 election? During a bittersweet meeting with Humphrey, Fannie Lou Hamer pointedly wondered if a willingness to reject the FDP signaled that this longtime supporter might soon abandon the civil-rights cause altogether.

The Election of 1964

By the fall of 1964, changes occurring within GOP ranks made Democratic support seem especially important to civil-rights forces. After a series of bitterly contested primary contests, the Republicans nominated Senator Barry Goldwater of Arizona, the hero of conservatives from the South and Far West, to challenge Lyndon Johnson. Strategists for Goldwater predicted that an aggressive campaign, based on an unabashedly conservative platform, would stir the hearts of the millions of voters who presumably rejected both Democratic policies and Dwight Eisenhower's moderate Republican ones. Goldwater denounced Johnson's foreign policy for tolerating communist expansion and attacked his domestic agenda, including strong support for civil rights, for destroying individual liberties. One of only eight Republican senators who had opposed the 1964 Civil Rights Act, Goldwater denounced the measure as an unwarranted extension of national power to meet the kind of problem, discrimination, which only state and local governments could remedy.

As the presidential campaign heated up, Goldwater's well-documented tendency for making ill-considered pronouncements haunted his candidacy. Goldwater once suggested that people who feared nuclear war were "silly and sissified." He wondered, out loud, if Social Security should become a voluntary program. His proclamation, at the 1964 Republican convention, that "extremism in the pursuit of liberty is no vice" and "moderation in the pursuit of justice is no virtue," fed Democratic claims that Goldwater represented political "extremism" rather than Republican, or even principled conservative, values. In time, Democrats succeeded in denying Goldwater one of his primary assets, his refusal to temporize on most controversial issues. Instead, they successfully portrayed the blunt-speaking Goldwater as wildly mercurial, perhaps even fanatical or mentally unbalanced. Republicans, for their part, leveled equally outsized charges against LBJ. One anti-Johnson tract, *A Texan Looks at LBJ* (1964), accused him of everything from stuffing ballot boxes to plotting murderous violence against political opponents.

As fantastical name-calling of this kind marked the 1964 campaign trail, a significant bloc of normally Republican voters deserted Goldwater, whose candidacy seemed to have strayed too far from middle-of-the-road signposts. The senator from Arizona led the GOP to a spectacular defeat in November. Johnson carried 44 states and won more than 60 percent of the popular vote; the Democrats also gained 38 additional seats in Congress. On the surface the 1964 election seemed a triumph for Lyndon Johnson's vision for using governmental power to change domestic life.

In retrospect, however, the 1964 election signaled important political changes that would soon rebound against Johnson and, in time, the national Democratic Party. During the Democratic primaries, Alabama's segregationist governor, George Wallace, had run strongly as a "protest candidate" against the president in several states. Already well-positioned as an opponent of the civil-rights movement, Wallace began to broaden his message, denouncing

LBJ'S 1964 Campaign against Barry Goldwater In this television ad from the 1964 campaign, Lyndon Johnson's supporters exploited Republican Barry Goldwater's image as a far-right extremist who might take the nation into a nuclear war.

any kind of "meddling" by Washington in local affairs. The 1964 election proved the last in which the Democratic Party would capture the White House by proposing to expand the domestic reach of the national government.

The GOP's 1964 effort, in contrast, merely provided a refueling stop for the conservative political machine that had propelled Goldwater's candidacy. His staff pioneered several innovative campaign tactics, such as direct-mail fundraising. While working to refine these techniques, conservative strategists insisted that 1964 would mark the beginning, not the end, of the Republican Party's movement to the right.

Goldwater's stand against national civil-rights legislation, his supporters noted, helped him carry five southern states. These victories—along with George Wallace's earlier appeal during the Democratic primaries—suggested just how much the GOP might gain by opposing additional civil-rights measures. After many years of tentative courtship, the Republican Party finally seemed ready to win over southern whites who had once been solidly Democratic. In an important sign of desertions to come, Senator J. Strom Thurmond of South Carolina announced during the 1964 campaign that he was permanently leaving the Democratic Party and joining the GOP.

Less-noticed voting trends in California provided conservatives with another sign of how racial issues were continuing to reshape political alignments. Although the Johnson-Humphrey ticket easily carried California, winning more than 60 percent of the popular vote, a coalition of real-estate interests and suburban activists sponsored a successful referendum, "Proposition 14." It repealed the state's recently enacted "Rumford Act," which prohibited racial discrimination in the sale or renting of housing. To overturn this statewide open housing measure, proponents of Proposition 14, which gained 65 percent of the vote throughout the state and much higher percentages in newer suburban areas, downplayed racial issues. Instead, they denounced the Rumford Act—because it regulated what property owners could do with their homes and apartment buildings—for trampling on personal liberties and constitutionally guaranteed freedoms.

The Goldwater campaign of 1964, especially in California and the Sunbelt states, also introduced an important group of conservative activists to national politics. Ronald Reagan—previously a radio personality, Hollywood actor, labor leader, corporate spokesperson, and Roosevelt Democrat—proved such an effective campaigner in 1964 that conservative Republicans in California began grooming him for electoral politics. Younger conservatives, such as William Rehnquist and Newt Gingrich, entered the national arena by working for Goldwater. Historians now generally credit Goldwater's 1964 candidacy for helping to refashion conservatism as a political force capable of dismantling the Democratic coalition that had dominated national politics since the 1930s.

Lyndon Johnson's Great Society

During the fall of 1964, however, the Democratic ranks seemed stronger than they had been in decades. Confident of his political support, Lyndon Johnson hoped to move quickly. Detailing plans he had hinted at during his 1964 campaign, Johnson fully unveiled a domestic vision designed, in his words, to "enrich and elevate our national life."

Some parts of LBJ's **Great Society** seemed constructed on top of the designs of his Democratic predecessors. Nationally funded medical coverage for the elderly (Medicare) and for low-income citizens (Medicaid) appeared to be capstones to efforts begun during the New Deal and Fair Deal eras. Similarly, an addition to the president's cabinet, the Department of Housing and Urban Development (HUD), built on earlier plans for improving coordination and execution of urban revitalization programs. This new cabinet post, LBJ promised, would prevent urban renewal from becoming urban removal (see chapter 28).

In 1965, Congress enacted two other milestone measures, both of which addressed matters long discussed—and long avoided. A new immigration law, the first measure ever directed through the Senate by newly elected Edward Kennedy, finally abolished the geographically discriminatory "national origins" quota system established in 1924. Henceforth, all nationalities of people wishing to immigrate to the United States faced roughly the same set of hurdles. This change, in practice, removed some of the previous barriers to people coming from regions outside of Europe (see chapter 31). **The Voting Rights Act of 1965,** which created a federal oversight system to monitor election procedures in the South, capped a long-term effort to end racial discrimination at the ballot box.

Other Great Society proposals rested on the economic growth that seemed, during the mid-1960s, destined to go on forever. Even an increasingly costly war in Southeast Asia could not dampen Johnson's optimism. Continuing prosperity would provide the tax dollars the president needed to underwrite his bold expansion of national power.

The array of Johnson-sponsored initiatives that rolled through Congress in 1965 and 1966 heartened LBJ's supporters and appalled his conservative critics. By one count, legislators passed nearly 200 new laws. The "Model Cities Program" offered smaller-scale alternatives to urban renewal efforts. Rent supplements and an expanded food stamp program went to help feed low-income families. Head Start provided educational opportunity for children who came from backgrounds social scientists labeled "disadvantaged." New educational programs targeted federal funds for upgrading classroom instruction, especially in low-income neighborhoods, and the Legal Services program promised government lawyers for clients who could not afford private attorneys. Planners of the Great Society stressed that measures such as these would provide social services that could help people fight their own way out of economic distress. This service-based approach to domestic social policy, Johnson insisted, would give people a "hand up" rather than a "handout."

The CAP initiative, part of the earlier EOA legislation, took a significantly different tack. Although drawing on social-science expertise, which had guided and informed other Great Society measures, this initiative ultimately sought to free ordinary citizens from the dictates and directions of social-service bureaucracies. CAP proposed to empower grassroots activists, working through neighborhood organizations rather than through political channels dominated by local city hall establishments, to design community-based projects. The most promising of these, EOA legislation promised, could gain funding from Washington.

Those who embraced CAP hailed its potential for redistributing power. It offered local communities the leverage that came from enjoying adequate financial resources while still allowing them, rather than outside bureaucracies, the political power to make crucial decisions about their own needs and priorities. By promoting "maximum feasible participation" by ordinary citizens rather than relying entirely on the expertise of social planners or on the political clout of party leaders, the architects of CAP hoped to grow new varieties of grassroots democracy that could change U.S. political culture from the bottom up.

Evaluating the Great Society

How did the Great Society—most of which initially enjoyed large, sometimes bipartisan majorities in Congress—become so controversial, so quickly? Most obviously, programs that further extended Washington's influence rekindled old debates about the use of the powers of the national government, as both an issue of constitutional law and a matter of pragmatic policy making. The Great Society, in this sense, gave an already well-positioned conservative movement another set of convenient targets. In addition, Johnson's extravagant rhetoric, such as promising to win an "unconditional" victory over poverty, raised expectations that no administration could possibly satisfy within the time frames voters normally use to judge the success or failure of governmental initiatives.

Perhaps most importantly, the expectation that continued economic growth would generate tax revenues sufficient to finance new social programs faded as the nation's economic engine began to sputter. Facing financial worries of their own, many people who had initially been willing to accept the Great Society became receptive to the argument, first popularized by George Wallace and the Goldwater campaign, that bureaucrats in Washington were taking their hard-earned dollars and wasting them on flawed social experiments. Worsening economic conditions, exacerbated by the escalating cost of the war in Vietnam, made federal expenditures on domestic social welfare measures more controversial than at any time since the 1930s.

Although historians agree about how Johnson's domestic programs lost support, there has been considerable disagreement about the Great Soiety's impact on daily life. Charles Murray's influential *Losing Ground* (1984) framed one powerful view. This study first charged that LBJ's social programs encouraged antisocial behavior. It argued that too many people, lured by what they could gain from Great Society measures, abandoned the goals of marrying, settling down, and seeking employment. Moreover, the money given over to Great Society programs created government deficits that slowed economic growth. Had ill-advised social spending not undermined personal initiative and disrupted the nation's economy, continued economic growth could have provided virtually all workers with a comfortable lifestyle. This conservative argument portrayed the Great Society as the cause of, not the solution for, economic distress and social disarray.

Most other close students of social policy treated the Great Society slightly more kindly. They found scant evidence, as opposed to colorful anecdotes, for the claim that most people preferred receiving welfare to seeking meaningful work. They generally blamed spending in the military sector because of the U.S. commitment in Vietnam, rather than outlays for domestic social programs, for generating the soaring budget deficits and a burgeoning national debt. Funds actually spent on Great Society programs, in this view, neither matched Johnson's promises nor reached the lavish levels claimed in conservative studies such as *Losing Ground*.

From a different perspective, many antipoverty activists faulted the Great Society for not seriously challenging the prevailing distribution of political and economic power in the United States. The Johnson administration, they argued, remained closely wedded to large-scale bureaucratic solutions, forged and then directed by people connected to Washington elites and entrenched interest groups. The White House jettisoned, for example, the CAP model for grassroots empowerment after local political officials complained about having to compete with activist groups for federal funds. In addition, by assuming that economic growth would continue to underwrite the financing of most federal initiatives, the people who planned the Great Society had also failed to consider revision of the tax code and other measures designed to redistribute income and wealth more equitably. Proponents of this critique concluded that the Johnson administration never seriously tried to fulfill its own domestic promises.

Most economists and historians have come to agree that the Great Society signaled a significant, though not revolutionary, break with the past. The national government, for the first time in several decades, devoted substantial new funding to social welfare programs. Washington's financial outlay on the domestic front increased more than 10 percent during every year of LBJ's presidency. According to one study, federal spending on social welfare in 1960 constituted 28 percent of total governmental outlays; by 1970, this figure had risen to more than 40 percent. Moreover, some Great Society programs produced significant change. Medicaid, the legal services program, and job training initiatives gave many low-income families access to things that more affluent families had long taken for granted. Civil-rights laws, even if they failed to eliminate all forms of discrimination, did use federal power to expand legally protected freedoms.

The Great Society, however, proved a political failure, unable to retain the popular support it had claimed in 1964–65. Variations on the severe evaluation framed in *Losing Ground* came to dominate popular memory and political culture. Continued allegiance to the Great Society agenda, as a matter of political pragmatism, could become a serious liability for nearly all Republican and most Democratic politicians during the late 1960s and early 1970s. Over time, as a highly critical view of the Great Society's flaws and failures helped energize the conservative wing of the GOP, fewer Democrats would risk stepping forward to defend Lyndon Johnson's vision. In short, Johnson's domestic policies helped inflame political passions, which soon turned against LBJ and his Great Society. A new generation of Democrats eventually came to dismiss "big government" as a relic of the past (see chapter 32).

Escalation in Vietnam

Focus Question

Through what incremental steps did the Johnson administration involve the United States ever more deeply in the war in Vietnam? What seemed to be the goal of its policies?

Meanwhile, Lyndon Johnson's ultimately divisive crusade to build a Great Society at home found its counterpart abroad. His pledge to preserve South Vietnam as a noncommunist, pro-U.S. enclave demanded ever more of his nation's resources. Even as Johnson's policies in Vietnam strained the U.S. economy, they polarized its politics and culture.

The Gulf of Tonkin Resolution

Immediately after John Kennedy's assassination, Johnson hesitated to widen the war in Southeast Asia. A committed Cold Warrior, however, LBJ hated the thought that his political associates—let alone the general electorate—might judge him "soft" on communism. He soon accepted the recommendation of his military advisers: Only the use of air strikes against targets in North Vietnam could save the South Vietnamese government from imminent collapse. He prepared a congressional resolution authorizing such an escalation of hostilities.

Events in the Gulf of Tonkin, off the coast of North Vietnam, provided the rationale for taking this resolution to Capitol Hill. On August 1, 1964, the U.S. destroyer *Maddox,* while on an intelligence-gathering mission in disputed waters that North Vietnam claimed as its own, exchanged gunfire with North Vietnamese ships. Three days later, the *Maddox* returned to the same area, accompanied by the *Turner Joy.* During severe weather, which distorted radar and sonar readings, U.S. naval commanders reported what possibly could have been signs of a failed North Vietnamese torpedo attack.

Although the *Maddox*'s commander later radioed that the episode needed further analysis, Johnson immediately denounced "unprovoked aggression" by North Vietnam against the United States and appealed to Congress for support. (A subsequent study concluded that the initial attack had likely occurred, but that reports of hostile fire on the second occasion lacked credible supporting evidence.) Congress quickly, and overwhelmingly, authorized the president to take "all necessary measures to repel armed attack." Johnson treated this **"Gulf of Tonkin Resolution"** as tantamount to a congressional declaration of war and cited it as legal justification for all subsequent U.S. military action in Vietnam.

Despite his vigorous response to events in the Gulf of Tonkin, Lyndon Johnson successfully positioned himself as a cautious moderate during the presidential campaign of 1964. When Barry Goldwater demanded stronger measures against North Vietnam and even hinted at possible use of tactical nuclear weapons, Johnson's campaign managers cited Goldwater's proposed strategies as further evidence of his extremist bent. One notorious TV ad even portrayed the Republican candidate as a threat to the survival of civilization. Johnson seemed to promise he would not commit U.S. combat troops to any land war in Southeast Asia.

Soon after the election, however, Johnson decisively deepened the U.S. involvement there. More than a year after the 1963 coup against Diem (see chapter 28), South Vietnam faced continued political chaos. The incompetence of successive governments in Saigon was still fueling popular discontent, and South Vietnamese troops were still deserting at an alarming rate. In January 1965, another Saigon regime collapsed, and factional discord stalled the emergence of any viable alternative.

Lacking an effective ally in South Vietnam, Johnson once more pondered his options. His close aides offered conflicting advice. National Security Adviser McGeorge Bundy predicted Saigon's defeat unless the United States greatly increased its own military role. Arguing for this same option, Walt W. Rostow assured Johnson that once North Vietnam recognized the United States would never abandon its commitment, this small nation could only conclude that it would never overrun South Vietnam. Undersecretary of State George Ball, by contrast, warned that the introduction of U.S. combat troops could not preserve South Vietnam. He wrote that "no one has demonstrated that a white ground force of whatever size can win a guerrilla war . . . in jungle terrain in the midst of a population that refuses cooperation to the white forces." Senate Majority Leader Mike Mansfield, who held an advanced degree in Asian history, urged Johnson to find some way of reuniting Vietnam as a neutral country. The Joint Chiefs of Staff, afflicted by interservice rivalries, provided conflicting readings of the current military situation and no clear guidance on how Johnson might proceed.

Although privately doubting U.S. chances of preserving an anticommunist South Vietnam, Johnson became obsessed about the political and diplomatic consequences of a U.S. pullout. He feared that the domestic reaction to anything resembling a communist victory—such as Washington's acceptance of a coalition government in Saigon that included the NLF—would enrage conservative activists in the United States and thereby endanger his

Great Society programs. Moreover, Johnson accepted the familiar Cold War proposition that a U.S. withdrawal would undoubtedly set off a "domino effect," toppling noncommunist governments in Asia. A pullback there would, then, encourage communist-leaning insurgencies in Latin America, increase Soviet pressure on West Berlin, and damage U.S. credibility around the world. Both Eisenhower and Kennedy, before him, had staked U.S. prestige on preserving a noncommunist South Vietnam. Johnson either had to abandon that commitment, by allowing South Vietnam's government to collapse, or chart an uncertain course by employing U.S. power to prop it up.

While remaining pessimistic about the results of his decision, Johnson chose the second option: dramatically expanding U.S. military involvement in Southeast Asia. He ordered a sustained campaign of bombing in North Vietnam, code-named "Rolling Thunder." He also deployed U.S. ground forces in order to help the government in Saigon regain lost territory, expanded U.S.-directed covert operations, and stepped up economic aid to the beleaguered South Vietnamese government. Only six months after the 1964 presidential election, with his advisers still divided, Johnson decided the United States had no choice but to wage a wider war.

The War Continues to Widen

The war grew more intense during 1965. Hoping to break the enemy's will, U.S. military commanders sought to inflict ever-increasing casualties. The Johnson administration authorized use of **napalm,** a toxic chemical that almost instantly charred both foliage and people, and allowed the Air Force to bomb new targets. Additional U.S. combat troops also arrived in South Vietnam, but every U.S. escalation seemed to require a further one. After North Vietnam rejected a Johnson-sponsored peace plan, which it viewed as little more than an offer for Hanoi to surrender, the United States once again stepped up its military effort. North Vietnam's leader, Ho Chi Minh, who was now pursuing a long-term strategy of attrition, became convinced that Johnson could not continue to find public or congressional support in the United States to fight such a costly war so far from U.S. shores.

In April 1965, Johnson applied his Cold War, anticommunist foreign policy closer to home. Responding to exaggerated reports about a communist threat to the government of the Dominican Republic, Johnson sent U.S. troops to unseat a left-leaning, but legally elected, president and to install a Dominican government eager to support U.S. interests. This U.S. incursion into the Dominican Republican violated a long-standing "good neighbor" pledge, by the United States, to avoid military intervention in Latin America. Although Johnson's action angered critics throughout the hemisphere, the overthrow of a leftist government in the Dominican Republic seemed to steel the White House's determination to hold the line against communism in Vietnam.

Later that same spring as yet another government, the fifth since Diem's 1963 murder, appeared in Saigon, U.S. strategists continued to wonder how they might stabilize South Vietnam. General William Westmoreland, who directed the U.S. military effort there, recommended moving even more aggressively and sending additional numbers of U.S. troops on "search and destroy" missions against communist forces. In July 1965, Johnson publicly announced he would send 50,000 additional military personnel to Vietnam. Privately, LBJ pledged that the Pentagon could have another 50,000, and he left open the possibility of sending even more. To supplement the search-and-destroy strategy, he also approved "**saturation bombing**" in the South Vietnamese countryside and an intensified air campaign against North Vietnam. **(See Map 29.1, Vietnam War, in the color insert following page 1248.)**

Some advisers urged Johnson to admit candidly the greatly expanded scope of the U.S. effort. They recommended seeking an outright declaration of war by Congress or at least legislation allowing the executive branch to wield the economic and informational controls that previous presidential administrations had used during wartime. But Johnson worried about arousing greater protests in Congress and from a growing antiwar movement. Rather than risk debates that could ramp up dissent against his policies, Johnson decided to stress the administration's willingness to negotiate and to act as if the war the United States was now fighting was not really a war. As the Johnson administration talked of seeing "light at the end of the tunnel" in Vietnam, it apparently hoped that most people in the United States would remain largely in the dark.

Over the remaining years of Lyndon Johnson's presidency, U.S. involvement steadily grew. By late 1965, the number of U.S. combat troops in Vietnam totaled more than 200,000; three years later, this figure had more than doubled, to about 535,000. The level of violence escalated as well. In pursuit of "Operation RANCHHAND," an effort to eliminate the natural cover for enemy troop movements, the United States dropped huge quantities of herbicides, scorching South Vietnam's croplands and defoliating roughly half of its forests. Approximately 1.5 million tons of bombs—more than all the tonnage dropped during the Second World War—pounded North Vietnamese cities and pummeled villages and hamlets in the South. Still, Johnson carefully avoided bombing close to the North Vietnamese–Chinese border or doing anything else that might provoke either China or the Soviet Union to go beyond supporting and supplying North Vietnam.

Despite all of the troops and violence, Vietnam remained a "limited" war. The U.S. strategy concentrated on straining the NLF and North Vietnam by continually escalating the cost they would pay, in lost lives and bombed-out infrastructure. Once the price of continuing to fight became too high, the Johnson administration reasoned, the other side would finally stop its effort to displace a pro-U.S., anticommunist government in South Vietnam.

The weekly "body count" of enemy purportedly killed became the primary measure for gauging U.S. progress in South Vietnam. Pentagon estimates that a kill ratio of 10 to 1 would force North Vietnam and the NLF to pull back not only encouraged the U.S. military to unleash more firepower but also to inflate enemy casualty figures. This same calculation provided an automatic justification for more U.S. troops: Whenever the number of enemy forces seemed to increase, the Pentagon required additional U.S. troops to maintain the desired kill ratio. Johnson, whose notorious temper flared at the first hint of bad news, welcomed improving kill statistics as a tangible sign that victory was around the corner. North Vietnam, assisted by the Soviet Union and China, however, managed to

AP Images/Eddie Adams

An Image That Shocked This 1968 photo, widely reproduced because of the absence of formal governmental censorship during the Vietnam conflict, shows a South Vietnamese military officer summarily executing a suspected Viet Cong leader on the streets of Saigon. The prevalence of images such as this one complicated the U.S. government's attempt to portray its support of South Vietnam as a fight for freedom and the rule of law.

match every U.S. escalation. Conscripting younger fighters and employing more women in support positions, the North Vietnamese continued to funnel troops and supplies into the South, using a shifting network of roads and paths called the "Ho Chi Minh Trail." By the end of 1967, several of Johnson's key aides, most notably Secretary of Defense Robert McNamara, decided that the United States could not sustain, from any reasonable costs versus benefits perspective, its seemingly open-ended commitment to South Vietnam. The majority of Johnson's advisers, however, refused to accept such a gloomy assessment.

Meanwhile, the destruction wreaked by U.S. forces was giving NLF, North Vietnamese, Chinese, and Soviet leaders a decided advantage in what had become an international war of images. Critics of the U.S. effort, in the United States and around the world, highlighted pictures showing the results of Johnson's strategy. Demonstrations against the United States became especially prominent features of political life in Western Europe. Antiwar protestors hounded LBJ and members of his administration, everywhere they went, and the president began complaining of becoming a prisoner in his own White House.

In addition, the United States failed to find an attractive, or even very effective, ally in South Vietnam. The devastation of the countryside, the economic destabilization caused by the flood of U.S. dollars, and the corruption in Saigon took their toll. The "pacification" and "strategic hamlet" programs, which gathered Vietnamese farmers into tightly guarded villages, sounded viable in Washington but created greater chaos by uprooting at least one-quarter of the South Vietnamese citizenry from its villages and ancestral lands. Buddhist priests persistently demonstrated against foreign influence. When, in 1967, two generals, Nguyen Van Thieu and Nguyen Cao Ky, after having sustained a military regime longer than any of their predecessors, tried to legitimate their rule with a nationwide election, the effort fell short. A voting process marked by corruption only highlighted the precariousness of their political position and underscored their dependence on support from Washington.

The Media and the War

Johnson continually gave presidential lectures about the necessity for upholding the nation's honor and diplomatic commitments, but dissent slowly mounted. During the Second World War and the conflict in Korea, presidential administrations had restricted media coverage. Hoping to avoid the controversy that overt censorship would surely have caused, the Johnson administration employed informal ways of managing the flow of information about Vietnam. Many of the print reporters sent to Southeast Asia seemed content, at first, to accept the reassuring reports handed out by U.S. officials in Saigon. Only a relatively few, such as David Halberstam, ventured into the South Vietnamese countryside, where they saw a different conflict than the one being described back at U.S. headquarters. Even before media pundits started talking about television making Vietnam a **"living room war"**—one that people in the United States could watch in their own homes—Johnson kept three sets playing in his office in order to monitor what viewers might be seeing. Most of what he saw, early on, he liked.

Antiwar activists continually assailed what they viewed as the U.S. media's uncritical reporting about events and policies in Vietnam. According to a common complaint, too many media executives appeared willing to accept story frames constructed by the White House, and too many journalists seemed to base their stories on official handouts. During the early years of U.S. involvement, few print publications or TV reports contained stories that dissected either the U.S. military effort or the travails of Washington's South Vietnamese ally.

In time, however, the tone and substance of media coverage changed. Images of unrelenting destruction came across television screens. After gazing at his TV sets, LBJ began telephoning network executives, castigating them for critical broadcasts and urging them to root for the United States, not its communist enemies. Print journalists generally outpaced their TV counterparts in breaking away from the government line, and some followed Halberstam in forthrightly challenging U.S. officials in Saigon. Gloria Emerson's grim reports portrayed the U.S. effort as one in which poor and disproportionately nonwhite troops seemed to be fighting, and dying, so that wealthy families, many with "fortunate sons" who held draft exemptions, might reap war-related profits. In 1966 and 1967, Harrison Salisbury of the *New York Times* sent back stories from North Vietnam that highlighted the impact U.S. bombing missions exacted on civilian targets. Accounts by younger journalists, such as those published by Michael Herr in *Esquire,* represented the war as a violent, amoral, and drug-drenched venture into the surreal.

As the conflict dragged on, the media began to talk about a "war at home" that paralleled the one in Vietnam. TV and most print media adopted a stark, bipolar story frame: It pictured **"hawks"**—those who wanted to fight, as long and as hard as necessary, until the United States defeated the communist forces—fighting against **"doves"**—those who, whatever their earlier views, now desired to end U.S. involvement in Vietnam as quickly as possible. In response to those who called for an even greater use of military force, President Johnson insisted his administration was following time-tested containment policies. His secretary of state, Dean Rusk, warned doves of the dangers of "appeasement." But an increasing number of influential U.S. politicians, led by J. William Fulbright of Arkansas, dissented. This influential head of the powerful Senate Foreign Relations Committee warned of misplaced priorities and of an "arrogance of power." Meanwhile, the antiwar movement merged into several other movements, many of which were coming to challenge the larger direction of U.S. politics and culture.

The War at Home

Focus Question

What domestic social movements emerged during America's longest war? How did they seek to change U.S. political culture and the direction of public policy? What role did commercial media play in the "movement of movements"?

Millions came to oppose the war in Southeast Asia, and support for the Great Society at home began to erode. By 1968, tensions escalated into confrontation, violence, and one of the most divisive presidential election campaigns in U.S. history.

The Movement of Movements

Popular memories generally will recall the 1960s as the time of a "youth revolt." Young people from a "New Left," most of them college students, protested against the war in Vietnam and in favor of social change, especially in race relations. Other imagery from the 1960s displays the colorful signs of a **"Counterculture,"** again viewed as a preoccupation of the college-aged population. Devotees of this Counterculture urged people to expand their minds, often with a little help from drugs and rock music, and to seek alternative ways of seeing, and then living out, their everyday world. Another set of iconic images from this time represents new forms of racial and ethnic consciousness, beginning with the **"Black Power"** movement. Now more easily accessible than ever before, all of this memorable imagery has etched pictures of life during America's longest war deeply into historical memory.

Increasingly, though, historians look beyond individual pictures of separate movements, each of which can claim its own background and trajectory, to a kaleidoscopic panorama composed of what one historian calls a "movement of movements." All across the political and cultural spectrum—not simply on some New Left or among the young or African Americans or cultural dissenters—people joined movements that aimed to challenge key parts of the established order. Activists from a wide variety of different backgrounds and circumstances placed their energies at the active service of one movement or another.

The combined energy produced by this movement of movements tended to tilt, albeit in different ways, against two dominant ideals of the 1950s and early 1960s: the faith in political (or interest group) pluralism and the parallel conviction that deeply held spiritual beliefs ultimately united, rather than divided, the nation and its diverse people (see chapter 28). As the war in Vietnam dragged on, people increasingly doubted that the

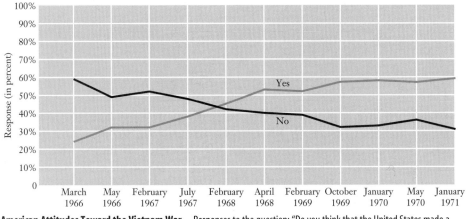

American Attitudes Toward the Vietnam War   Responses to the question: "Do you think that the United States made a mistake in sending troops to fight there?"

existing political system could actually solve problems. At the same time, disparate movements based on deeply held values—involving issues such as war and peace, race relationships, gender politics, the environment, and sexuality—appeared headed in different directions or on collision courses.

Ultimately, this movement of movements produced political, social, and cultural polarization. No one group, say a New Left or a youth culture, could lay exclusive claim to the historical era often called "the Long Sixties," the period from roughly 1963 to 1974, which coincided with America's longest war. Numerous social movements sought to redirect national life down different paths, often with no clear maps.

Most movements could not avoid dealing with commercial, particularly visual, media. Media imagery did not create or manufacture, for popular consumption, this movement of movements. Activists recognized, however, that even the briefest of time in the media spotlight could help them display their deep personal commitments and demonstrate their passionate disdain for policies they opposed. Often beginning with posters and pamphlets, movements such as the one pressing for a rapid U.S. withdrawal from Vietnam began to produce increasingly sophisticated imagery and to stage media-catching public demonstrations.

Television, in particular, offered these social movements a potentially vast audience. Some movement activists became media celebrities. In a 1965 internal memo, the then-head of SNCC referred to himself, tongue in cheek, as "Mr. Stokely Carmichael (star of stage, screen, and television)." Behind the scenes, less famous activists worked both to sustain their movements as viable organizations and to help script the kind of political performances that could attract media attention.

Four of the earliest and most prominent of the movements that accompanied America's longest war involved the New Left, the Counterculture, "Black Power," and antiwar protest.

Movements on College Campuses: A New Left

Colleges and universities became important sites for mobilizing students and organizing them as forces for social change. Only a relatively small number of college students ever became active in social movements, but their activities set the tone for campus politics, attracted extensive media interest, and eventually generated popular controversy.

In 1962, two years after conservatives had already formed the YAF (see chapter 28), students at the left end of the political spectrum established Students for a Democratic Society (SDS). Young men, mostly of European descent and eager to link their grand ideals to specific political activities, dominated the early SDS effort. Beginning with a call for mobilizing the power of government to expand liberty and promote equality, SDS endorsed measures, such as civil-rights laws, that seemed little different from those that Lyndon Johnson would soon champion.

SDS attracted far greater attention, however, for the more spiritual and personalized style of its politics. The "Port Huron Statement" of 1962, SDS's founding manifesto, pledged opposition to the "loneliness, estrangement, isolation" that supposedly afflicted so many people. It charged that arrogant political elites, immersed in the techniques of interest-group pluralism, ignored underlying moral values. These insiders allegedly prized the expertise of bureaucrats over active engagement by ordinary citizens and favored policies promoting economic growth over opportunities for meaningful work. SDS claimed to speak for alternative visions. In politics, it called for "participatory democracy"—grassroots political activities and small-scale institutions responsive to the needs of local communities.

Students from North Carolina A&T University had earlier sparked the sit-in movement of 1960 (see chapter 28), and college students continued to play important roles in many of the civil-rights dramas that followed. Localized struggles in communities throughout the South, such as those waged during Freedom Summer in Mississippi, seemed tangible examples of participatory democracy. They appeared to promise a regeneration of the nation's politics and a reorientation of its moral compass. Organizing efforts in the Deep South thus attracted idealistic white students from schools in the North. Only partially aware of the violence and social challenges they would face, these activists left their own campuses to work alongside those from historically black institutions, such as Tuskegee, who were trying to register African American voters and organize them for political action. Some of these students remained in the South; others turned their energies to neighborhood-based political projects in northern cities; and some brought their experiences in the South back to their own campuses.

New Left activists insisted on a constantly expanding view of what counted as "politics." Political practice should be broadly participatory, but active participation by large numbers of ordinary people only provided the starting point. Although voter registration drives in the South did seek greater access to the existing political process, New Left activists placed far greater emphasis on alternative, often disruptive political forms, such as sit-ins and demonstrations.

Their emerging vision of politics favored action over contemplation, improvisation over careful advance planning, and personal feelings over extended political analysis. As Mario Savio, a Berkeley graduate student who had participated in the Mississippi Freedom Summer, proclaimed in 1964, the dominant political machinery sometimes "becomes so odious" that "you can't even tacitly take part" in its operations. Instead, people needed to put their own "bodies upon the gears" and try "to make it stop." Later, a prominent Jewish rabbi, Abraham Herschel, offered a similar formulation of this basic political ideal: "Mere knowledge or belief" could sometimes be "too feeble a cure," and the "only remedy was the kind of personal sacrifice" exemplified by activists such as Martin Luther King, Jr.

Students attracted to an expansive concept of personalized politics saw their own campuses as centers for testing new political styles more than as places for ingesting the wisdom of the past. Seeing older academic-activists, such as C. Wright Mills, as attractive role models, these college students viewed their generation as uniquely situated to confront a political system dominated by powerful and entrenched interests. Although a worldview focused on personally expanding the range of political options seemed to appeal more to students in the humanities and social sciences than to those in the "hard" sciences, business, or engineering, plenty of potential recruits remained. The rapid expansion of higher education, along with the Baby-Boom population bulge, greatly swelled the number of young people who enrolled in colleges and universities during the early 1960s.

Students who embraced movement politics, following in the footsteps of academics such as Mills, saw activism and intellectualism as complementary pursuits. They denounced courses and research projects that appeared irrelevant to the pressing issues of the day. They confronted administrators who tried to impose lifestyle restrictions, such as sex-segregated living arrangements and dorm hours, on students that state laws otherwise treated as adults. Far worse, these politically active students argued, giant universities, accepting funding from the Pentagon and corporations, seemed oblivious to the social and moral implications of their war-related research. Although accounts of campus activism once highlighted only a few institutions, such as the University of California at Berkeley, recent histories have shown most schools, some even earlier than Berkeley, played host to social and political movements. Still, events at a few select schools, including Berkeley, dominated the media spotlight.

Initially working to mobilize around domestic issues such as civil rights, student-led movements at Berkeley became generational lightning rods. Protests on and around the Berkeley campus, which began in earnest in 1964, over restrictions against on-campus political activity, provided some of the most prominent, and lasting, symbols of what media pundits came to call "the war on campus." After organizing a "Free Speech Movement," in opposition to limits on political expression, students and sympathetic faculty mounted the "Berkeley Revolt." This effort included sit-ins, boycotts of classes, contention among faculty members, and intermittent clashes between dissenting students and law enforcement officials. Activists demanded an end to any cultural divide, let alone legal regulations, which tried to separate activism on campus from that in the wider world.

The Counterculture

Berkeley also came to symbolize the interrelationship, however uneasy, between political movements associated with a New Left and the vertiginous energies of a Counterculture. The Counterculture of the 1960s has always seemed a difficult "movement" to identify, especially since one of its self-defining slogans proclaimed "Do Your Own Thing." It elected no officers, held no formal meetings, and maintained no central office to issue manifestos. Bursting into view in low-income neighborhoods, such as San Francisco's Haight-Ashbury area, and along thoroughfares bordering college campuses, such as Berkeley's Telegraph Avenue, the Counterculture maintained a vague sense of unity through a loose infrastructure of small shops, restaurants, and overcrowded living units. People who claimed to speak for the Counterculture espoused values, styles, and institutions hailed as both "utopian" and as "realistic" alternatives to those of the prevailing or "straight" culture. Countercultural groups such as San Francisco's Diggers, a commune that mixed improvisational street-theater productions with social-service projects, distanced themselves from Great Society organizations.

Dissenting cultural ventures did not spring up spontaneously but drew on earlier models, such as the "Beat movement" of the 1950s. A loosely connected group of writers and poets, the Beats had denied that either the material abundance or conventional spiritual ideals of the 1950s fulfilled the promise of liberty. Rejecting the "people of plenty" credo, the Beats claimed that an overabundance of consumer goods, a commercialized culture industry, and oppressive technologies condemned most people to wander through alienated lives that seemed oppressive, emotionally crippling, or just plain boring.

Beat writers such as Jack Kerouac, author of *On the Road* (1957), praised the rebels of their generation. They saw nonconformists like themselves challenging settled social routines and seeking more instinctual, more sensual, and more authentic ways of living. The Beat poet Allen Ginsberg, in works such as *Howl* (1956), decried soulless materialism and puritanical moral codes for tempting a culture already awash in alienation to acts of madness and despair. In search of alternative visions and oppositional lifestyles, Ginsberg's poetry celebrated the kind of liberty that drugs, Eastern mysticism, and same-sex love affairs could supposedly provide. Beats such as Ginsberg, in contrast to critics who merely condemned conformity (see chapter 28), seemed commited to testing the possibilities of liberty by seeking to live their everyday lives beyond conventional boundaries.

Many of the Beats, especially Ginsberg, nonetheless had recognized how conventional commercial media might play to their advantage. Media exposure, respectful and (more often) disdainful, helped the Beats sustain bohemian-style communities in San Francisco's North Beach and New York City's Greenwich Village. In time, as influential cultural critics and college professors praised the Beats, young people began encountering their writings and poetry in humanities courses and literary-minded bookstores. Ginsberg's status as a dissenting celebrity continued to grow, especially on college campuses, and he eagerly promoted his iconic status as a link between the Beat movement of the 1950s and the Counterculture of the 1960s.

This Counterculture—perhaps best seen as a collection of alternative subcultures rather than a single impulse—left its imprint on a wide range of movements. These included nonprofit urban cooperatives, radical strains of feminism, **environmentalism,** and the fight against restrictions, especially involving sexuality, on lifestyle choices.

Mass media of the 1960s, however, initially treated the Counterculture as a source for titillating stories about longish and unkempt hair styles, flamboyant clothing, and uninhibited sexuality. The media also liked to portray countercultural lifestyles, among young people who came to be known as **"hippies,"** as being on the cutting edge of a supposedly massive, fun-filled youth rebellion. Observers of this Counterculture also highlighted its use of drugs, particularly marijuana and LSD, and its preference, often because of financial necessity, for communal living arrangements.

New musical stylings, such as the folk-rock of The Byrds and the acid-rock of The Grateful Dead, also helped identify the Counterculture. The singer-songwriter Bob Dylan, who had abandoned acoustic folk music and "gone electric" in 1965, gained unwanted recognition as the Counterculture's prophet-laureate. Fusing musical idioms used by African American blues artists such as Muddy Waters with poetic touches indebted to the Beats, Dylan's "Like a Rolling Stone" (1965) exploded onto both the Top-40 charts of AM radio and the freewheeling play lists of the alternative FM stations and college radio stations linked to the Counterculture. Publications primarily aimed at college students, including the magazine *Rolling Stone,* dispatched youthful journalists to report on—and also participate in—the countercultural scene.

The more traditional commercial marketplace also welcomed images and products from the Counterculture. The ad agency for Chrysler Motors, alert to the appeal of countercultural imagery, urged car buyers to break away from older patterns, purchase a youthful-looking 1965 model, and thereby join the "Dodge Rebellion." The clothing industry marketed colorful countercultural-looking styles as the latest in "hip" fashions. For women, this generally meant expensive versions of bohemian-style garb, which typically displayed a considerable amount of skin (as with the miniskirt) and avoided restrictive foundation garments (as in the braless look). Marketers urged men seeking a more youthful appearance to exchange white shirts and regimental neckties for more colorful and more casual clothing styles.

Recognizing the appeal of bands such as San Francisco's Jefferson Airplane, the popular music industry saw profits to be made from the sound, as well as the look, of the Counterculture. An early countercultural happening, "the Human Be-In," organized by community activists from San Francisco in early 1967, provided a model for subsequent, commercially dominated music festivals such as Monterrey Pop (later in 1967) and Woodstock (in 1969).

Back on college campuses, some of the students and faculty attracted to New Left political movements seemed baffled by the Counterculture. The novelist and LSD-guru Ken Kesey, for example, shocked a 1965 political demonstration at Berkeley with a style of politics indebted to the theatrics of the Counterculture. Accompanied by veterans from the Beat movement and youthful members of his communal group, "the Merry Pranksters," Kesey ridiculed other speakers. They were playing the same tired political game—parsing the details of alternative foreign policies—as Lyndon Johnson. Between singing choruses of "Home on the Range," Kesey advised pursuing pleasurable activities of genuine interest to oneself and, ultimately, of real help to others. Everyone should abandon conventional politics and pursue a more personalized political agenda, one focused on revolutionizing, especially through drugs such as LSD, how they lived their own lives.

African American Social Movements

Meanwhile, this movement of movements—and changing ideas about the nature of politics— also reshaped specific efforts to achieve freedom and equality for people of African descent. Initiatives that still looked to Dr. Martin Luther King, Jr., faced growing criticism for embracing too limited a vision of political action. Moreover, as with other areas of movement politics, the battle against discrimination involved differences over how to address the ever-present commercial mass media.

Early on, Dr. King tacitly acknowledged how much SCLC campaigns depended on commercial media, especially the weekly news magazines and television. Network TV images of the violence directed against his 1965 voter registration drive in Selma, Alabama, substantially aided his cause. In a moment that dramatically framed the politics at stake in Selma, ABC television interrupted the network premiere of *Judgment at Nuremberg,* an anti-Nazi movie, in favor of pictures showing all-white squads of Alabama state troopers beating peaceful voting-rights marchers. Lyndon Johnson also recognized the power of these images. Going on television several nights later, to urge Congress to speed passage of the landmark Voting Rights Act of 1965, he promised that "we shall overcome" the nation's "crippling legacy of bigotry and injustice," supposedly evident to people looking at TV images from Selma.

At the same time, however, other people interpreted such TV images differently. Growing numbers of people saw direct-action movements for liberty and equality as subversive agitation and demanded a renewed commitment to conventional forms of politics and to measures restoring law and order.

Less than a week after congressional passage of the Voting Rights Act, six days of violent conflict devastated parts of Los Angeles. The violence apparently began with an altercation, near the largely African American community of Watts, between a white California highway patrol officer and a black motorist. A growing crowd, additional law-enforcement officers, long-standing differences over policing practices in LA, and deep-seated grievances within Watts soon spiraled into what some called a "riot," others an "insurrection" or an "uprising." By whatever name, burning and looting swept over Watts and edged into other areas of south-central Los Angeles. Thirty-four people died; fires consumed hundreds of businesses and homes; heavily armed National Guard troops patrolled the city's streets; and platoons of television camera crews carried images from LA across the nation and around the world.

What should be the response to events in Watts, people immediately asked? Most local political leaders, including LA's mayor and police chief, denied any responsibility for the violence, blamed civil-rights "agitation" for the troubles, and sought additional resources for the LAPD. Dr. King rushed to the scene, preaching the politics of nonviolence, only to

Malcolm X (1992)

Directed by Spike Lee. Starring Denzel Washington (Malcolm X), Angela Bassett (Betty Shabbaz), Al Freeman, Jr. (Elijah Muhammad).

Spike Lee, the U.S. film industry's best-known African American director, campaigned aggressively to make a movie about Malcolm X. For nearly 25 years, Hollywood moguls had been trying to portray the Black Power leader who was gunned down in 1965 and whose *Autobiography* became a literary classic. Delays in obtaining financing, crafting a script, and finding a director always stymied production plans.

Lee, who had denounced the Hollywood establishment for passing over his celebrated (and controversial) *Do the Right Thing* (1989) for an Academy Award nomination, insisted that only he could do justice to the story of Malcolm X. Initially buoyed by a $34 million budget, Lee eventually encountered problems of his own, including his insistence on releasing a movie that ran for more than three hours. Lee called *Malcolm X* "my interpretation of the man. It is nobody else's."

Denzel Washington stars as Malcolm X.

Everett Collection

The finished film displays Lee's desire to show the presence of the past in the present. Produced by Lee's own independent production—whose name, "Forty Acres and a Mule," recalls the land-distribution program advanced by advocates of Radical Reconstruction after the Civil War—the movie argues for Malcolm X's continuing relevance to social and racial politics.

The segments that begin and end the movie employ collages of iconic images that underscore this aim. Against the backdrop of the Warner Brothers logo, the soundtrack introduces the actual voice of Malcolm X, decrying U.S. history as a story of racist actions. Malcolm's accusations continue as a giant American flag, perhaps a reference to the popular film *Patton* (1970), appears on screen. Then, the image of the flag is cut into pieces by jagged images from the homemade videotape of the 1991 incident in which Los Angeles police officers beat an African American man named Rodney King. Next, the flag begins to burn until, revealed behind it, a giant "X," adorned with remnants of the flag, dominates the film frame. The ending uses substantial archival footage of Malcolm, along with images of South African freedom fighter Nelson Mandela, while the soundtrack features the voice of Ossie Davis, the celebrated African American actor, giving a eulogy to Malcolm X.

Released near Thanksgiving, the film opened to packed houses and took in considerably more money than Oliver Stone's *JFK* had garnered when it had debuted only one year earlier. Despite a multimedia publicity blitz, *Malcolm X*'s box-office revenues steadily declined. Reviewers and industry spokespeople reported that the lengthy, episodic movie seemed to tax the patience and attention span of most filmgoers.

Watching *Malcolm X* on video or DVD, however, can allow a viewer to concentrate on its many stunning sequences, speeding by ones that seem to drag, and returning to ones that may seem unclear at first viewing. *Malcolm X* remains a fascinating cinematic history of the early Black Power movement and, more generally, of the social ferment that gripped the nation during its longest war.

encounter, as he had expected, anger from both LA's political establishment and local black organizations. Only aggressive, sometimes even violent, forms of political action, some black activists were insisting, could get the attention of Californians who ignored racial inequalities in jobs, housing, and law enforcement. Only the previous year, white suburbanites had voted overwhelmingly to scrap the Rumford Act, the hard-won open-housing law. Lyndon Johnson, stunned by what he saw on his trio of TV sets, quickly responded through the kind of politics he understood best. Even as fires continued to burn, LBJ ordered up new social-welfare resources for LA: "Let's move in—money, marbles, and chalk." Groups more attuned to participatory democracy began reorganizing local movements and creating new ones, such as the Watts Writers' Workshop, convinced that changing times dictated shifting forms of response.

Among African Americans, new movement initiatives had been appearing throughout the 1950s and 1960s (see chapter 28). Some of the most recent looked to Malcolm X, a charismatic African American minister whose February 1965 death amplified, rather than silenced, his powerful voice. While still calling himself Malcolm Little, he had engaged in petty criminal activities, served time in prison, and reoriented his life by joining the Nation of Islam during the 1950s. As Malcolm X, he soon became a leader of this North American–based group, popularly known as the "Black Muslims," which had emerged during the 1930s.

Malcolm X's fiery denunciations of the civil-rights movement, which gained him a lurid reputation in commercial media, found a receptive grassroots audience in many urban black neighborhoods in the North and West. Dr. King's gradualist, nonviolent campaign for new civil-rights laws, Malcolm X charged, simply ignored the everyday problems of most African Americans and the undesirability—indeed, the impossibility—of integration. "White America" would never accept persons of African descent as equals, and dark-skinned people should thus work, as the Nation of Islam and other "black nationalist" groups had long urged, to build and strengthen their own communities. Although he never advocated initiating confrontation, Malcolm X strongly endorsed self-defense, "by any means necessary."

Although mainstream media continued to portray Malcolm X as a dangerous subversive, he offered more than angry rhetoric. He called for pride in African American cultural practices and for economic reconstruction. He urged African Americans to "recapture our heritage and identity" and "launch a cultural revolution to unbrainwash an entire people." Seeking a broader movement, one that could forge multiracial coalitions, Malcolm X eventually broke from the Black Muslims and established his own Organization of Afro-American Unity. Murdered by enemies from the Nation of Islam, Malcolm X soon became, especially after the posthumous publication of his *Autobiography* (1965), a source for black-oriented political and cultural visions.

These visions, which reshaped many older movements and inspired new ones, diverged from the political perspectives that dominated Lyndon Johnson's administration. Officially committed to additional civil-rights legislation, particularly a national open-housing law and to new Great Society programs, the president was also coming to sense that many federal laws ignored the root causes of current conflicts. He began listening to members of his administration who suggested social programs, which would later be called "affirmative action" measures, specifically intended to assist African Americans. In a 1965 speech, he suggested that centuries of racial discrimination against people of African descent had produced "wounds" and "weaknesses" that had become "the special handicaps of those who are black in a Nation that happens to be mostly white."

Although Johnson intended his words to soothe, they tended to inflame. African Americans who now viewed empowering black communities as a major civil-rights goal, for example, wondered if the president's subliminal message might be that laws could not adequately advance liberty and equality because black culture and society seemed, from his perspective, "inadequate"? Could Johnson be hinting that differences in America arose because of "superior" and "inferior" societies and cultures?

Disparate answers from different movements to questions such as these—along with growing opposition to specific Johnson administration policies—became evident during the fall of 1965. When the president invited several hundred black leaders to the White House for a "racial summit," two veteran activists, A. Philip Randolph and Bayard Rustin, used the occasion to lobby for their "Freedom Budget," an implicit indictment of LBJ's funding priorities. They called for a 10-year plan for spending $100 billion on infrastructure projects in low-income neighborhoods. Other critics denounced a recent study written by Daniel Patrick Moynihan, a social scientist who had worked for both JFK and LBJ. The *Moynihan Report,* apparently intended as a prelude to new White House proposals but widely seen as a response to Watts, argued that social conditions within African American communities often made laws mandating equality largely irrelevant. It singled out the prevalence of families headed by single women. "The harsh fact is that . . . in terms of ability to win out in the competition of American life," this report concluded, African Americans were simply "not equal to most of the groups with which they will be competing."

People such as Rustin, who focused on pocketbook issues and on brick-and-mortar matters, dismissed this "black family debate" as a distraction. Most younger movement activists, however, argued that Moynihan's single report spoke volumes about the Johnson administration's paternalistic mindset. Accustomed to dealing with competing interests from which he could cobble a consensus, Lyndon Johnson privately denounced movement leaders for using, in reference to the Freedom Budget, *his* summit to start "raising unshirted hell and saying it's got to be a 100 billion."

Meanwhile, events in the South also highlighted the increasingly frenetic—and the also gradually more effective—movement-of-movements phenomenon. SNCC and Dr. King's SCLC continued to press forward, though often along separate paths. Their movements constantly faced the threat of violence and death and confronted state and local legal systems seemingly unable to restrain or punish vigilantes who attacked, or even killed, civil-rights workers. White southern legal officials, moreover, appeared no better at overseeing electoral contests. Charging that vote-counters had robbed of victory a SNCC-sponsored slate in a local election in Lowndes County, Alabama, Stokely Carmichael began to organize, against the advice of King's SCLC, an all-black political organization in that locale. To symbolize the militancy of this third-party movement, the "Lowndes County Freedom Organization," SNCC commissioned a special logo: a coiled black panther.

The following spring, SNCC joined other movements in a well publicized foray into Mississippi. In June 1966, a KKK gunman shot James Meredith, who was conducting a one-person "March against Fear" from Memphis, Tennessee, to Jackson, Mississippi. Convinced of the need to defy violence, representatives from most of the individual movements that comprised the wider antidiscrimination cause hastily gathered in Mississippi. Although state officials provided only minimal protection and armed KKK vigilantes assembled at almost every crossroad, most activists, including Stokely Carmichael and Dr. King, remained determined to stay on course.

An enlarged March against Fear became the first large-scale movement project—in contrast to the 1963 March on Washington or the 1965 voting-rights campaign in Alabama—that did not seek new civil-rights legislation. In this sense, it seemed an effort to demonstrate that movements for liberty and equality now also emphasized struggles for dignity, pride, and empowerment. Moreover, highly symbolic political activities of the kind coming into prominence obviously relied on media visibility, and Meredith's shooting had already focused national news coverage on Mississippi. Considerations such as these seemingly justified a difficult and dangerous group effort to complete the quixotic crusade one person had begun. Displaying a remarkable degree of solidarity—if not always unanimity—the March Against Fear ended with an interracial crowd of 15,000 people, most of whom had arrived in Mississippi just before the finale, marching into Jackson in late June.

This march also underscored differences, in rhetorical and programmatic emphases, among (and within) various movements. As Stokely Carmichael played to the omnipresent TV cameras, Dr. King, an old hand at this political art form, admiringly acknowledged the younger activist's shrewd grasp of media routines. After being hauled off to jail, during one of the local voter registration campaigns that accompanied the march, an enraged Carmichael claimed he would never again, passively and nonviolently, submit to arrest.

Carmichael now explicitly urged that the struggle not remain just one for "Freedom," the byword of the SCLC, but also for "Black Power." As different movements within this march's ranks chanted "Black Power," others called for "Freedom." During one lengthy debate among the marchers, Carmichael rejected a compromise slogan, "Black Equality," and insisted that Black Power best described the kind of politics that direct-action movements such as SNCC should now embrace.

Black Power did not magically spring forth from the March against Fear. Always a slippery concept to grasp, especially when applied to constantly shifting political values and strategies, Black Power provided an apparently inflammatory label for a sometimes commonsensical set of claims. At different times and places during the 1960s, African American activists determined that they should seek greater on-the-ground power both in—and for—their own communities. If black-led movements in cities such as LA and Oakland, for example, could not count on their state's hard-won open-housing law to remain in force or if local political establishments could block federal funding of CAP initiatives, seeking greater power for a grassroots black politics seemed a logical, if politically uncertain, move.

Operating from this perspective, in 1966, several college students from Oakland, who were already active in community-based projects, announced formation of a new Black Power organization. Taking its name, the "Black Panther Party," from SNCC's earlier effort in Lowndes County, this movement issued a platform that employed militant rhetoric on behalf of 10 objectives, many already familiar to local civil-rights groups. These included greater economic opportunities—for housing, education, and employment—and greater legal protections, especially against police misconduct and flawed legal proceedings. The group also created its own grassroots social programs, including ones to improve health and nutrition in low-income black neighborhoods.

The Panthers quickly became a media phenomenon. Adapting quasi-military symbols and organizational forms from Third World revolutionary movements, a trio of media-savvy young men—Huey Newton, Bobby Seale, and Eldridge Cleaver—quickly gained national attention for the Black Panthers. A 1967 rally on behalf of the Second Amendment right to use firearms for self-defense, against what armed demonstrators called "fascist pig" police officers, attracted the notice of J. Edgar Hoover. The FBI head eventually made destroying the Black Panther Party, by almost any available means, a key goal.

Far less flamboyantly than the Black Panthers, other groups and movements extended Black Power ideals to a wide range of issues. Fully embracing the word *black* and a cultural agenda that stressed racial identity, they asserted their power to pursue separate, African American–directed routes not just toward liberty and equality but, sometimes, "liberation" from the prevailing U.S. political culture. Receiving a more generous hearing from commercial media than Malcolm X had gained during his lifetime, many Black Power efforts, more importantly, forged political links and cultural networks within African American communities. "Black Is Beautiful" became a watchword. James Brown, the "Godfather" of soul music, captured this new spirit with his "Say It Loud, I'm Black and I'm Proud" (1968).

Against this rapidly changing backdrop, the U.S. Congress passed the **Civil Rights Act of 1968.** A central provision of this omnibus measure, the last *new* civil-rights legislation of the 20th century, sought to eliminate racial discrimination in the real estate market. This section of the law, popularly known as the "Fair Housing Act," provided a national version of open housing legislation. Its initial proponents, however, considered the final version shot through with exemptions and plagued by enfeebled enforcement mechanisms. Moreover, another section of the same Civil Rights Act declared it a crime to cross state lines in order to incite a "riot." Supporters hailed this provision as a law-and-order measure, while critics insisted it illegally targeted specific political activists, especially ones espousing Black Power. Whenever tested in federal court, though, this section passed constitutional scrutiny.

The Antiwar Movement

Meanwhile, one movement began to overshadow all others. Even as campus-centered ferment, countercultural activities, and African American empowerment efforts continued—and other movements, such as environmentalism and second-wave feminism, began to emerge—the one that sought to pressure Lyndon Johnson into abandoning his crusade in Vietnam dominated U.S. politics and culture.

The antiwar movement, as with the broader movement-of-movements impulse, never fell into neat categories. The dominant media frame of the day, hawks against doves, failed to account for the diverse coalition that came to oppose the Johnson administration. Some of the strongest "antiwar" sentiment, for example, blamed LBJ for not prosecuting the war *aggressively enough*. Convinced that he would never strive for a clear-cut victory, some people in this camp decided to oppose continued U.S. involvement, at least on Johnson's terms. At the other end of the antiwar spectrum, as the White House and its supporters constantly noted, were small movements that called for a North Vietnam–NLF victory. "Ho, Ho, Ho Chi-Minh/NLF's Gonna Win" went a chant that enraged Johnson and distressed many members of the antiwar coalition.

The broad middle ground of the anti-Johnson, antiwar alliance could never fully agree on many issues. A diverse constituency, in another concrete example of participatory democracy, continually debated how and why the United States had ever become committed to preserving a noncommunist South Vietnam. They also split over how and if the antiwar movement could change LBJ's course. In addition, the antiwar cause faced the same questions as all other movements of the 1960s: What kind of politics best expressed the ethical and spiritual values of its supporters? And how might mass-mediated images of this movement's activities represent its politics to a broader audience?

By 1967, the issue of Vietnam had become *the* controversy on most college campuses. At a series of "teach-ins," supporters and opponents of the war had already debated their positions. Later, these events had given way to street demonstrations, in both local communities and in Washington, D.C., against Johnson's Vietnam policies. Most male students possessed a direct stake in such activities. Their local draft boards normally granted them educational deferments, but these expired at graduation and could be revoked or denied, sometimes because of a young man's view of Johnson's policies. Many students, joining the less fortunate sons who did not attend college, complied with draft regulations, and a good number volunteered for service in Vietnam. A strong draft-resistance movement, often symbolized by the burning of draft cards and sometimes marked by the flight to foreign countries, especially Canada, also emerged. During October 1967, campus protests against war-related activities passed a crucial threshold when a pitched, bloody battle broke out between antiwar demonstrators and police at the University of Wisconsin in Madison.

That same year, 1967, saw two other important antiwar milestones. Long critical of the war, Dr. Martin Luther King, Jr. now faced intensive pressure, especially from activists among the clergy, to spell out his moral and spiritual position. At the same time, many of his civil-rights allies warned against doing anything that might break his already severely strained relationship with the Johnson White House and escalate attacks from enemies such as J. Edgar Hoover. Speaking in early April 1967, at New York's Riverside Church, Dr. King boldly laid out his views. In an analysis similar to that of Black Power spokespeople and of critical journalists such as Gloria Emerson, Dr. King noted a black-and-white truth. African American troops, mostly from low-income communities, served and died in numbers far greater than their proportion of the U.S. population "for a nation that has been unable to seat them together in the same schools" with the white soldiers now at their side in Vietnam. The immoral "madness" in Vietnam "must cease," Dr. King thundered, but he also wondered if "the world now demands a maturity of America that we may not be able to achieve."

This speech provided an important gauge of both the growing antiwar movement and the expanding polarization within the country. Although Dr. King had expected a backlash, he failed to anticipate that voices from all across the political-media spectrum would condemn his address. Although the editorial board of the *New York Times* did not, as some commentators did, call King a "traitor," it read his antiwar pronouncement through the familiar frame of narrowly imagined interest groups. The *Times* charged him with seeking media attention and with damaging the civil-rights cause by expounding on a matter about which he likely knew little and on which he might lack the political credentials to comment intelligently. Why should people give his foreign policy opinions more weight than those of the boxer Muhammad Ali, who had been widely condemned for his antiwar statements?

The same interrelated issues raised by King's speech—the nature of politics and the role of the media—also surrounded popular discussion of a massive 1967 antiwar demonstration in Washington, D.C. This event underscored how the politics of the New Left and the spirit of the Counterculture marched together, at least when in opposition to Lyndon Johnson's policies in Vietnam.

Noting the visual media's voracious appetite for pictures of political and cultural dissent, a small group of experienced activists decided to feed media outlets a uniquely prepared supply of imagery. To do this, they invented a kind of "nonmovement movement," which bypassed the hard work of mobilization and organization in favor of hoping media images would do the mobilizing and organizing for them. Two members of this group, Abbie Hoffman and Jerry Rubin, proclaimed themselves leaders of a (nonexistent) "Youth International Party"—or "YIPPIE!"—and simply waited for media coverage to surround their activities, as they knew it would.

Hoffman and Rubin raised the curtain on a neo-vaudevillian, countercultural style of politics. In one famous incident, they tossed fake money onto the floor of the New York Stock Exchange. Invoking the sit-in movement, they joked about staging department-store "loot-ins" to strike at "the property fetish that underlies genocidal war" in Vietnam. Even more audaciously, they announced their contribution to the 1967 antiwar march would be a separate trek to the Pentagon. There, they claimed, marchers chanting mystical incantations would levitate this five-sided head of the military-industrial complex several hundred feet into the air.

Although the Pentagon remained firmly planted, events around its perimeter generated eye-catching TV footage and gained novelist Norman Mailer a National Book Award for his first-person report. According to Mailer's admirers, his book *Armies of the Night* (1968), by interweaving Mailer's personal politics with a journalistic account of a public event, reinvented orthodox political reporting in a way that seemed to parallel how activists were reinventing what counted as politics.

1968

Other observers of events at the Pentagon and harsher critics of *Armies of the Night*'s journalistic style dissented. Might not media images of colorful quipsters such as Hoffman and Rubin be helping to fuel cultural polarization rather than to provide new models of useful political action? Might the media's taste for spectacular demonstrations be trivializing underlying issues, including moral ones? Questions such as these became even more pressing during the tumultuous 12 months of 1968, a year that saw violence and upheaval span most of the globe.

Turmoil in Vietnam

January of 1968 had not even concluded when Lyndon Johnson's crusade in Vietnam, though not the violence accompanying it, effectively ended. Late that month during a truce declared in observance of Tet, the Vietnamese lunar New Year celebration, NLF and North Vietnamese forces suddenly went on the attack throughout South Vietnam. One group even temporarily seized the grounds of the U.S. embassy in Saigon. U.S. strategists had fully expected some violation of the Tet truce, but they never anticipated the breadth and ferocity of the communist offensive.

The Johnson administration tried to assess the fallout. Militarily, U.S. forces emerged victorious from this **Tet offensive.** After regrouping, they inflicted heavy casualties on NLF and North Vietnamese troops, who gained relatively little territory at considerable cost. Supporters of the war in the United States soon blamed media imagery for exaggerating the effect of the early attacks, ignoring NLF and North Vietnamese losses, and thereby turning "victory" into "defeat." Critics of the war countered that the Tet offensive had initially caught U.S. military commanders ill-prepared and, later, highlighted their inability to effectively pursue the badly mauled enemy forces.

In any case, Tet proved a defeat for the Johnson administration. Events seemed to belie its constant assurances of improving fortunes and imminent victory. Walter Cronkite, the esteemed CBS-TV anchor, returned from a post-Tet tour of Vietnam and proclaimed, to a national television audience, that the United States would never prevail militarily on the battlefield and needed to consider negotiating its withdrawal. Reportedly, Lyndon Johnson mused that if he had lost the celebrity anchor then known as "the most trusted person in America," he had also lost much of the rest of the country.

LBJ received more bad news when he summoned his most trusted advisers and a distinguished group of elderly statespeople, the so-called wise men, to consider General Westmoreland's request for an additional 206,000 U.S. troops. To Johnson's surprise, a majority advised against another massive infusion of U.S. troops. If South Vietnam were to survive, its own forces needed to shoulder more of the military burden. Johnson capitulated to this argument, conceding that another large increase in U.S troops, even if forces could have been spared from other duties, would have further fanned opposition to his policies.

The Tet offensive threw Lyndon Johnson's own political future into question. Faced with open revolt by antiwar Democrats, who rallied behind a presidential bid by Senator

Eugene McCarthy of Minnesota, Johnson reconsidered, for the final time, his political options. Although LBJ controlled enough party-selected delegates to bury McCarthy's candidacy at the Democratic national convention, McCarthy's primary campaigns against Johnson, which attracted youthful volunteers and abundant media coverage, revealed how little political capital the president now possessed.

Eugene McCarthy, who was athletic enough to have considered a professional baseball career and sufficiently academic to have been a college professor, had always seemed uncomfortable with the path he did choose, electoral politics. After serving, capably but as if on autopilot, in both houses of Congress, McCarthy suddenly achieved instant political fame as an unorthodox presidential hopeful. LBJ technically defeated McCarthy in the 1968 New Hampshire primary, but the antiwar message of "Clean Gene" (as media pundits dubbed him) resonated both with voters who favored the United States bombing its way to victory and with those who favored a speedy withdrawal.

With McCarthy poised to defeat LBJ in the Wisconsin primary, Johnson surprised all but his closest aides and reconfigured the diplomatic and political landscapes. On March 31, 1968, he went on TV to declare a halt to the U.S. bombing of North Vietnam, to announce an offer to begin peace negotiations, and to proclaim he would not seek reelection. Deprived of his greatest asset, not being LBJ, Eugene McCarthy pledged to continue his fight for the Democratic nomination, He prepared to square off against his former senatorial colleague from Minnesota and Johnson's ever-loyal vice president, Hubert H. Humphrey.

Turmoil at Home

Among the many former LBJ supporters gladdened by the turn in political events, was Dr. Martin Luther King., Jr. He hoped that the Democratic Party would reject Humphrey and embrace an antiwar candidate, preferably Senator Robert Kennedy (RFK) of New York, JFK's younger brother, who had belatedly entered the presidential sweepstakes after Johnson's surprise announcement.

Less than a week after seeing glimmers of political hope, on April 4, 1968, King met the violent death he had long anticipated. While visiting Memphis, Tennessee, in support of a labor strike by African American sanitation workers, the civil-rights leader received an almost instantly fatal head wound, as he stood on the balcony of the Lorraine Motel. Law enforcement officials soon identified (and eventually apprehended) the alleged shooter: James Earl Ray, a drifter with a lengthy criminal record. Ray quickly pleaded guilty to having assassinated King, waived a jury trial, and received a 99-year sentence. Subsequently, though, Ray recanted and claimed to have been a pawn in some larger white supremacist conspiracy. Ray died in 1998, still insisting on his innocence, a claim that intrigued several members of the King family but convinced very few legal observers or historians.

As news of King's murder spread, violent protests swept through urban neighborhoods. More than 100 cities and towns witnessed outbreaks; 39 people died; 75,000 regular and National Guard troops were called to duty. When President Johnson proclaimed Sunday,

© UPI-Bettmann/Corbis.

Martin Luther King, Jr.'s Funeral Cortege   Martin Luther King, Jr.'s assassination in 1968 sparked both violent protests and solemn mourning for the slain civil rights leader. Thousands of his grieving supporters followed the cart, drawn by mules, which carried King's body through the streets of his native Atlanta.

April 7, as a day of national mourning for the slain civil-rights leader, parts of the nation's capital city, including neighborhoods near the White House, remained ablaze.

Claiming he would devise policies to end violence at home and in Vietnam, Robert Kennedy mounted a nonstop campaign for the Democratic presidential nomination. Unwilling to risk a test of his personal popularity, Humphrey stayed out of the Democratic primaries, inheriting most of the nonelected delegates previously pledged to LBJ and leaving RFK and McCarthy to fight over the rest. His celebrity-assisted campaign recalling memories of JFK's, Robert Kennedy sought to convince Democrats pledged to Humphrey or favoring McCarthy that only another Kennedy could win the presidency in November.

Then, on June 5, after besting Eugene McCarthy in California's primary, RFK fell victim to an assassin's bullets. Bystanders immediately grabbed Sirhan Sirhan, a Palestinian-born immigrant, who was later charged and convicted of killing Kennedy. Television coverage of Kennedy's body being returned to Washington, D.C., and of his funeral provided poignant, and disturbing, reminders of Dr. King's recent murder and of the assassination of JFK five years earlier. Was there, some people wondered, some "sickness" afflicting U.S. political culture? Did "government by gunplay" rather than political pluralism best describe the prevailing system of governance?

The violence of 1968 continued. During the Republican national convention in Miami, presidential candidate **Richard Nixon** promised to restore law and order. Inside the convention hall, he unveiled a surprise choice as his running mate, Governor Spiro Agnew of Maryland, an outspoken critic of movement activists. Outside, in a largely African American section of Miami, clashes broke out between police and citizens, during which four people lost their lives. Later that summer, in Chicago, thousands of people, drawn from a cross-section of the antiwar movement, converged on the Democratic Party's convention to protest the nomination of Hubert Humphrey, who was still loyally supporting Johnson's policy in Vietnam. Responding to acts of provocation by some demonstrators, including Abbie Hoffman and Jerry Rubin, police officers struck back. Some used indiscriminate force against antiwar activists and members of the media. Although an official report later talked about a "police riot," opinion polls showed that most people approved of how police officers had acted in Chicago. Humphrey easily captured the Democratic presidential nod, but differing views over Johnson's Vietnam policy and over the meaning of the violence in Chicago left his party bitterly divided.

The Election of 1968

Both Humphrey and Nixon worried about the candidacy of Alabama's George Wallace. After adroitly organizing a third-party run, Wallace stumbled badly by tabbing retired general Curtis LeMay, who immediately hinted at the possibility of using nuclear weaponry against North Vietnam, as a running mate. With his own views in favor of victory in Vietnam and against civil rights well established, Wallace could play to opinion polls that suggested growing sentiment against the Counterculture and the antiwar movement. If any "hippie" protestor ever blocked his motorcade, Wallace once announced, "it'll be the last car he'll ever lay down in front of." Declaring his independence from the interest groups that supposedly controlled the political process, Wallace also courted voters who saw themselves as captive to "tax-and-spend" bureaucracies in Washington.

George Wallace never expected to gain the presidency. He hoped, however, to secure enough electoral votes to deny Humphrey or Nixon a majority. Then, as the U.S. Constitution prescribed, the selection of a president would rest with the House of Representatives, where Wallace might act as a power broker on behalf of his favorite issues and his own political fortunes.

Nixon narrowly prevailed in November. Hinting at a secret plan to honorably end the war in Vietnam, Nixon also promised to restore tranquility at home. Although the former vice president won 56 percent of the electoral vote, he outpolled Humphrey in the popular vote by less than 1 percent. Humphrey had benefited when Johnson ordered a pause in the

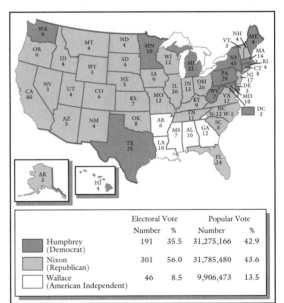

	Electoral Vote		Popular Vote	
	Number	%	Number	%
Humphrey (Democrat)	191	35.5	31,275,166	42.9
Nixon (Republican)	301	56.0	31,785,480	43.6
Wallace (American Independent)	46	8.5	9,906,473	13.5

Map 29.2   Presidential Election, 1968   George Wallace's independent, third-party candidacy influenced the election of 1968. Compare this map with ones of earlier and later election years to see how the southern states gradually left the Democratic column and, in time, became a base of Republican power.

bombing of North Vietnam and pledged to begin peace talks in Paris, an initiative that Nixon secretly worked to undermine through back-channel negotiations with the South Vietnamese government. In the end, Humphrey carried only Texas in the South. George Wallace picked up 46 electoral votes, all from states in the Deep South, and 13.5 percent of the popular vote nationwide. Nixon won five crucial southern states and claimed the support, from all across the country, of those whom he called "the forgotten Americans, the non-shouters, the non-demonstrators."

The Nixon Years, 1969–1974

Focus Question
What new domestic and foreign policies did the Nixon administration initiate?

Raised in a modest Quaker home in southern California, Richard Nixon campaigned for the presidency in 1968 as the kind of leader who could restore domestic tranquility. The beginning of Richard Nixon's presidency, however, coincided with more, rather than less, turmoil.

Lawbreaking and Violence

A handful of people on the political fringe, such as those in a tiny group known as the "Weather Underground," openly embraced violence. According to one assessment, authorities logged approximately 40,000 bomb threats, most unfounded, during the first 18 months of Nixon's first term. There were, though, nearly 200 actual and attempted bombings on college campuses during the 1969–70 academic year, with an explosion at the University of Wisconsin claiming the life of a late-working grad student. Nonlethal attacks rocked other targets, including the Bank of America, the Chase Manhattan Bank, and even the U.S. Congress. On one highly publicized occasion in 1970, three members of the Weather Underground blew themselves apart when their own bomb factory exploded.

At the same time, governmental officials stepped up their use of force. Several prominent Black Power figures, including Fred Hampton of the Black Panthers and the celebrated prison activist George Jackson, died under circumstances their supporters likened to political assassination but public officials considered normal law enforcement activities. J. Edgar Hoover's FBI went beyond shadowing members of entirely peaceful antiwar and women's organizations to harass activists, plant damaging rumors, and even operate as *agent provocateurs,* urging protestors to undertake actions that officials might later prosecute as criminal offenses. After a lengthy investigation of COINTELPRO—a once-secret FBI program aimed at disrupting a wide range of activist groups—a congressional committee concluded that the FBI had illegally ruined careers, severed friendships, besmirched reputations, bankrupted businesses, and even endangered lives. The Bureau terminated COINTELPRO in 1971, only after documents stolen by antiwar activists from an FBI office in Pennsylvania revealed its existence.

State and local officials stepped up their own efforts to restore order. During the fall of 1971, for instance, New York's Governor Nelson Rockefeller suddenly broke off negotiations with representatives for more than a thousand prison inmates, who had seized several cell blocks and taken a number of guards hostage while protesting what they considered to be intolerable living conditions at Attica State Prison. Rockefeller then ordered heavily armed state troopers and National Guard forces into the complex. When this "Attica Uprising" finally ended, 29 prisoners and 11 guards lay dead. At the same time, on college campuses, local officials and administrators seemed increasingly ready to employ force against demonstrators, a course praised by law-and-order advocates and decried by civil libertarians.

A New President

Richard Nixon continued to insist that his vast public experience made him the ideal president for such troubled times. After graduating from Whittier College, Nixon had studied law at Duke University and served in the Navy during the Second World War. He then enjoyed a meteoric political career that took him to the House of Representatives in 1946, the Senate in 1950, and the vice presidency in 1952. His 1960 presidential defeat, at the hands of John Kennedy, began an equally rapid descent. After his failure, in 1962, to win the California governorship, Nixon denounced media commentators and announced his retirement from politics.

Nixon, however, seemed to thrive on confronting a constant series of personal challenges. He entitled an early memoir of his political life *Six Crises*. The defeat of Goldwater, for whom Nixon had doggedly campaigned in 1964, and Johnson's problems resurrected the former vice president's political fortunes. He emerged from the 1968 election more confident than ever before, it seemed, of his leadership abilities.

Once in the White House, Nixon even expected to tame a media that had long bedeviled him. Although his staff remained suspicious of media figures, and eventually clashed with many of them, the president and his key aides felt they possessed more skill than Johnson's administration in the image-making arts. Media personalities might be considered "con artists," Nixon once mused, but politicians could expend "energy to try to rig the news . . . their way." Public officials and media reporters entered "the ring together, each trying to bamboozle the other." Nixon's close advisers, many with backgrounds in advertising and in Southern California's image-driven popular culture, threw themselves into the sport of shaping media portrayals of the Nixon White House.

The Economy

One area in which Nixon seemed less prepared to act almost immediately threatened to upset his political plans. Nixon's presidency coincided with economic problems that would have been unthinkable only a decade earlier. No single cause can account for these difficulties, but most economic analyses begin with the war in Vietnam. This expensive military commitment, along with increased domestic spending and a volatile international economy, began curtailing economic growth.

Lyndon Johnson, determined to stave off defeat in Indochina without cutting Great Society programs or raising taxes, had concealed the true costs of the war, even from his own economic advisers. Nixon inherited a deteriorating (although still favorable) balance of trade and rising rate of inflation. Between 1960 and 1965, consumer prices grew an average of only about 1 percent per year; by 1968, this figure exceeded 4 percent.

By 1971, just as the Nixon administration began planning for the 1972 election, economic conditions worsened, with the unemployment rate topping 6 percent. According to conventional wisdom, expressed in a technical economic concept called "the Phillips curve," when unemployment increases, prices should stay flat or even decline. Yet *both* unemployment and inflation remained on the rise. Economists coined the term **stagflation** to describe this puzzling convergence of economic stagnation and price inflation. Stagflation contributed to another disturbing trend: U.S. exports becoming less competitive in international markets. For the first time in the 20th century, the United States ran a trade deficit in 1971, importing more products than it exported.

With his plans for a two-term presidency perhaps in jeopardy, Richard Nixon faced yet another of his crises. Long opposed to governmental regulation of the economy but now fearful of the political consequences of stagflation and trade imbalances, he needed a quick cure for the nation's economic ills. Suddenly, in what one observer likened to a religious conversion, Nixon proclaimed his belief in governmentally imposed economic controls and announced, in August 1971, his "new economic policy." It included a 90-day freeze on any increases in both wages and prices, to be followed by government monitoring to detect "excessive" increases in either.

Seeking to address the trade deficit, Nixon radically revised the relationship between the United States and the world monetary structure. Dating from the 1944 Bretton Woods agreement (see chapter 26), the United States had tied the value of its dollar to that of gold, at the rate of $35 per ounce of the precious metal. To guarantee stability in currency markets, the United States stood ready to exchange, at this rate, its dollars for gold whenever any other nation's central bank requested it to do so. As dollars piled up in foreign banks because of trade deficits and military spending abroad, however, the fixed value of the U.S. dollar came under pressure from the threat that foreign banks might suddenly demand massive gold conversion. There had been a brief flurry of this kind of activity toward the end of LBJ's presidency, prompting Johnson to institute a "tax surcharge," but gold again steadily poured out of the United States under Nixon's watch.

The president had little choice but to abandon the fixed gold-to-dollar ratio in August 1971. Henceforth, the U.S. dollar would "float" in world currency markets. This meant its value, no longer pegged to a fixed price in gold, could fluctuate in relationship to that of all other currencies. The U.S. dollar, consequently, quickly devalued, and the Nixon administration expected U.S. goods would become cheaper, and thus more competitive, in global markets.

Social Policy

At the urging of Daniel Patrick Moynihan, the Democrat who had written the controversial 1965 report on black family structures, Nixon also proposed an equally dramatic overhaul of social welfare policy. A special presidential adviser on domestic issues, Moynihan suggested Nixon could sponsor truly "radical" changes because his popular political image as a "conservative" would help deflect criticism from within his own Republican party and from southern Democrats.

Following Moynihan's lead, Nixon advanced a "Family Assistance Plan" (FAP). Under FAP, every family would be guaranteed an annual income of $1,600. FAP also proposed scrapping most existing welfare measures, particularly the controversial and increasingly costly Aid to Families with Dependent Children (AFDC), which provided government payments to cover basic care for low-income children who had lost the support of a bread-winning parent. Moynihan touted FAP as advancing equality because it would replace existing arrangements, which assisted *only* those with special circumstances (such as mothers eligible for AFDC), with a system that aided *all* low-income families. The sheer simplicity of FAP, Nixon also promised, would allow for significantly trimming back federal bureaucracies

The FAP proposal debuted to tepid reviews. Conservatives decried the prospect of governmental income supplements for families with regularly employed, albeit low-paid, wage earners. From this perspective, FAP looked too costly—and too much like "socialism." People with a more favorable view of assistance programs, in contrast, argued that FAP's income guarantee seemed too miserly. The U.S. House of Representatives approved a modified version of FAP in 1970, but a curious alliance of senators who opposed Nixon's proposal for very different public policy reasons blocked its passage. In time, Nixon seemed to lose interest in pressing his own plan, and the nation's welfare system would not be overhauled until the 1990s.

Meanwhile, however, the Nixon White House and Congress agreed on several significant changes in domestic policy. In one important move, Congress passed the president's revenue-sharing plan, part of Nixon's "new federalism." It returned a portion of federal tax dollars to state and local governments in the form of **"block grants."** Instead of Washington specifying how these funds could be used, the block grant concept allowed state and local officials, within general guidelines, to spend the funds as they saw fit. In some areas, such as the construction of low-income housing, Nixon's new federalism provided state and local governments with significantly more federal money than they had earlier received under Great Society programs.

A Democratic-controlled Congress and a Republican White House also cooperated on other social-welfare matters. Although Nixon vetoed a congressional measure that would have established federally funded day-care centers for use by women who worked outside of their homes, he endorsed a less comprehensive bill that provided tax benefits for those who used existing facilities. The two branches of government also agreed to increase funding for many Great Society initiatives, including Medicare, Medicaid, rent subsidies for low-income people, and Supplementary Security Insurance (SSI) payments to those who were elderly, blind, or disabled. Moreover, in 1972, Social Security benefits were "indexed," which meant they would increase along with the inflation rate.

The reach of federal social-welfare programs actually *expanded* during Nixon's presidency. According to one estimate, the amount spent for nondefense programs grew nearly

50 percent during the years between Lyndon Johnson's last budget and Richard Nixon's 1971–72 one. In addition, the percentage of people living below the governmentally defined "poverty line" dropped during Nixon's first term as president. After reflecting on Nixon's domestic record, a prominent political scientist suggested, only partly in jest, that this Republican chief executive might well be called "the last Democratic president" of the 20th century.

Environmentalism

A new environmental movement became a significant political force during Nixon's presidency. Landmark legislation of the 1960s—such as the Wilderness Act of 1964, the National Wild and Scenic Rivers Act of 1968, and the National Trails Act of 1968—had already protected large areas of the country from commercial development. During the early 1970s, a broader environmental movement focused on people's health and on ecological balances. Accounts such as **Rachel Carson's** *Silent Spring* (1962) had raised concern that the pesticides used in agriculture, especially DDT, threatened bird populations. Air pollution in cities such as Los Angeles had become so toxic that simply breathing became equivalent to smoking several packs of cigarettes per day. Industrial processes, atomic weapons testing, and nuclear power plants had prompted fear of cancer-causing materials. The Environmental Defense Fund, a private organization formed in 1967, went to court in an effort to limit use of DDT and other dangerous toxins. "Earth Day," a festival-like event first held in 1970 and growing out of countercultural movements, aimed at raising popular awareness about the hazards of environmental degradation.

Although the Nixon administration did not sign up to help sponsor Earth Day, it did take environmental issues seriously. The White House supported creation of the **Environmental Protection Agency (EPA),** and Nixon signed several major pieces of congressional legislation. These included the Resources Recovery Act of 1970 (dealing with waste management), the Clean Air Act of 1970, the Water Pollution Control Act of 1972, the Pesticides Control Act of 1972, and the Endangered Species Act of 1973. National parks and wilderness areas were expanded, and a new law required that "environmental impact statements" be prepared in advance of any major government project.

The new environmental standards brought both unanticipated problems and significant improvements. The Clean Air Act's requirement for taller factory smokestacks, for example, moved pollutants higher into the atmosphere, where they produced a dangerous by-product, "acid rain." Still, the act's restrictions on auto and smokestack emissions cleared smog out of city skies and helped people with respiratory ailments. This law would reduce six major airborne pollutants by one-third in a single decade. Lead emissions into the atmosphere would soon decline by 95 percent.

Controversies over Rights

New legislation on social and environmental concerns accompanied political struggles over constitutionally guaranteed rights. The struggle to define these rights embroiled the U.S. Supreme Court in controversy.

A majority of justices, supporters of the Great Society's political vision, had stood ready to announce an expanding list of constitutional rights. As this group had charted the Court's path during the 1960s, two Eisenhower appointees, Chief Justice Earl Warren and Associate Justice William Brennan, often led the way. Although nearly all of the Warren Court's decisions involving rights issues drew critical fire, perhaps the most emotional cases involved persons entangled in the criminal justice system.

Miranda v. *Arizona* (1966) had held that the Constitution required police officers to advise persons suspected of having committed a felony offense of their constitutional rights to remain silent and to consult an attorney, with the government providing a lawyer to people without money to hire their own. Defenders of this decision, which established the famous "Miranda warning," saw it as the logical extension of precedents involving liberty and equality. The Court's critics, in contrast, accused its majority of inventing liberties not found in the original Constitution or in any of its amendments. Amid rising public concern over crime, political conservatives made *Miranda* a symbol of the judicial coddling of criminals and the Warren Court's supposed disregard for constitutional limits on its own power.

Richard Nixon had campaigned for president as an opponent of the Warren Court and promised to appoint federal judges who would "apply" rather than "make" the law. Apparently worried about a Nixon victory, Earl Warren announced, prior to the 1968 election, his intention to retire as Chief Justice. A Republican–Southern Democratic alliance in the Senate, however, blindsided Lyndon Johnson and blocked his plan to anoint Associate Justice Abe Fortas, an LBJ confidante, as Warren's successor. Consequently, the victorious Nixon could appoint a Republican loyalist, Warren Burger, to replace Earl Warren. Subsequent vacancies, including one produced by the resignation of a scandal-plagued Fortas, allowed Nixon to bring three additional Republicans—Harry Blackmun, William Rehnquist, and Lewis Powell—onto the High Court.

This new "Burger Court" faced controversial rights-related cases of its own. Lawyers sympathetic to the Great Society vision advanced claims of a constitutionally protected right to receive federal economic assistance sufficient to provide an adequate living standard. The Supreme Court, however, rejected this claim when deciding *Dandridge* v. *Williams* (1970). It held that states could limit the amount they paid to welfare recipients and that payment schedules could vary from state to state without violating the constitutional requirement of equal protection of the law.

Rights-related claims involving health-and-safety legislation generally fared better. A vigorous consumer movement, drawing much of its inspiration from Ralph Nader's exposé about auto safety (*Unsafe at Any Speed*, 1965), joined with environmentalists to gain laws that recognized rights to workplace safety, consumer protection, and nontoxic environments. Overcoming opposition from many business groups, their efforts found congressional expression in such legislation as the Occupational Safety Act of 1973 and stronger consumer and environmental protection laws. The Burger Court invariably supported the constitutionality of these measures.

At the same time, a newly energized women's rights movement pressed another set of issues. It first sponsored an **"Equal Rights Amendment" (ERA)** to the Constitution. This measure, initially proposed during the 1920s and supported by both Republicans and Democrats, promised to explicitly guarantee that women possessed the same legal rights as men. Easily passed by Congress in 1972 and quickly ratified by more than half the states, the ERA suddenly stalled. Conservative women's groups, such as Phyllis Schlafly's "Stop ERA," charged that this constitutional change would undermine traditional "family

Women's Rights Demonstrators, August 16, 1970   Activists, who have gathered in Washington, D.C., to demonstrate on behalf of women's rights, take time to rest. Symbolically, they effectively "occupy" a statue erected in honor of a 19th-century military hero, Admiral David G. Farragut.

values" and expose women to new dangers, such as those they would encounter when serving in the U.S. military on a equal basis with men. The ERA failed to attain approval from the three-quarters of states needed to ratify any amendment to the Constitution. Ultimately, women's groups abandoned the ERA effort in favor of using the judicial system to adjudicate equal rights claims on a case-by-case, issue-by-issue basis.

One of these issues, whether a woman possessed a constitutional right to terminate a pregnancy, became far more controversial than the ERA. In *Roe* **v. Wade** (1973), the Burger Supreme Court narrowly ruled, with Republican Harry Blackmun writing the key opinion, that a state law making abortion a criminal offense violated a woman's "right to privacy." The *Roe* decision outraged antiabortion groups, which countered with their own rights-based arguments on behalf of unborn fetuses. This "Right-to-Life" movement soon provided important new sources of support, especially from religious groups, for the still expanding conservative wing of the Republican Party. On the other side, movements organizing on behalf of women's issues made the rights of privacy and individual liberty, especially as related to reproductive decisions, central rallying calls.

Outside of the Supreme Court spotlight, Richard Nixon's administration pressed forward, often relatively quietly, on several rights-related matters. With little controversy, the president signed a bipartisan congressional extension of the Voting Rights Act of 1965. Another Nixon-approved measure, popularly known as "Title IX," banned sexual discrimination in higher education. In time, it became the legal basis for pressing colleges to adopt "gender equity" in all areas of their programming, including intercollegiate athletics. In addition, Republican appointees of the Nixon administration, who assumed leadership positions in agencies such as the EEOC, successfully pressed for small policy changes that expanded the federal government's role in monitoring and enforcing laws barring both gender and racial discrimination in employment.

Perhaps most surprisingly, members of Nixon's administration refined the "affirmative action" concept, which had surfaced during Lyndon Johnson's presidency. Beginning with the limited "Philadelphia Plan" of 1969, which was applicable to a single city, the White House built on a campaign pledge to give African Americans tangible economic assistance. Ultimately, Nixon's Department of Labor required that all hiring and contracting that depended on federal funding take "affirmative" steps to enroll, without being held to any bright-line quota, greater numbers of African Americans as union apprentices. When Nixon's critics claimed to detect a clever plan to unsettle labor–union politics, other political observers noted how an important group in the Nixon administration hoped to chart a political course that could gain the GOP new support from African Americans.

Foreign Policy under Nixon and Kissinger

In 1968, while campaigning for the White House, Richard Nixon had promised an administration that would "bring us together." Instead, as it struggled with the issue that had brought down Lyndon Johnson, U.S. policy in Vietnam, Nixon's administration found itself making decisions that seemed to promote greater violence in Indochina and more divisiveness on the home front.

Even as it wrestled with domestic policy concerns, the Nixon White House appeared far more interested in international matters. Henry Kissinger, Nixon's national security adviser and then secretary of state, laid out a grand, three-part strategy: (1) **"détente"** with the Soviet Union, (2) normalization of relations with China, and (3) disengagement from direct military involvement in South Vietnam.

Détente and Normalization

Although Richard Nixon had built his early political career on a hard-line version of anti-communism, he and Kissinger considered themselves "realists" who favored flexibility when trying to advance the interests of the United States in the international arena. By seeking to ease tensions with the Soviet Union and China, the Nixon-Kissinger team expected that improving relations could lead these two major communist nations to reduce their support to North Vietnam, thus increasing chances for a successful U.S. pull-back from the war in Southeast Asia.

Arms-control talks took top priority in U.S.–Soviet relations. In 1969, the two super-powers opened the Strategic Arms Limitation Talks (SALT); after several years of high-level diplomacy, they signed an agreement (SALT I) that limited further development of both antiballistic missiles (ABMs) and offensive intercontinental ballistic missiles (ICBMs). SALT I's impact on the arms race proved relatively limited because it said nothing about the number of nuclear warheads that a single missile might carry. Still, the ability to conclude any arms-control pact signaled the possibility of improving relations between Washington and Moscow.

Nixon's overtures toward the People's Republic of China brought an even more dramatic break with the Cold War past. Secret negotiations, often conducted personally by Kissinger, led to a slight easing of U.S. trade restrictions and, then, to an invitation from China for U.S. table-tennis players to compete against Chinese teams. This much-celebrated "ping-pong diplomacy" presaged more significant exchanges. Most spectacularly, in 1972 Nixon visited China, with the U.S. media firmly in tow. TV crews pictured the president, once a bitter foe of "Red China," talking with communist leaders, including Mao Zedong, and strolling along China's Great Wall. A few months later, the UN admitted the People's Republic as the sole representative of China, and in 1973 the United States and China exchanged informal diplomatic missions.

Vietnamization

In Vietnam, the Nixon administration decided to speed withdrawal of U.S. ground forces, the policy called **"Vietnamization."** Putting this move, which had quietly begun under Johnson, in a grander frame, the president announced, in July 1969, a "Nixon Doctrine." It pledged that the United States would extend military assistance to anticommunist governments in Asia but would require them to supply their own combat forces. From the outset, Vietnamization imagined the removal of U.S. ground troops without accepting a coalition between the NLF and the government in Saigon or permitting North Vietnamese forces to defeat those of South Vietnam. While officially adhering to Johnson's 1968 bombing halt over the North, Nixon and Kissinger accelerated both the ground and air wars by launching new offensives inside South Vietnam. In 1970, they approved a controversial military invasion of Cambodia, an ostensibly neutral country, through which North Vietnam had been sending troops and military supplies into the South. A quick strike into Cambodia, the White House gambled, would buy further time for executing its Vietnamization strategy.

The 1970 Cambodian invasion, which gained the United States a scant military payoff, set off a new wave of protests around the world and in the United States. As the campus antiwar movement revived, many colleges and universities exploded in angry demonstrations. Bomb threats prompted some schools, which were besieged by student protestors, to begin the 1970 summer vacation earlier than originally planned. White police officers fatally shot two students at the all-black **Jackson State College** in Mississippi, and National Guard troops at **Kent** State University in Ohio opened fire on unarmed protestors, killing four students. As antiwar demonstrators descended on Washington, President Nixon seemed personally unnerved by the domestic furor surrounding his Vietnam policies.

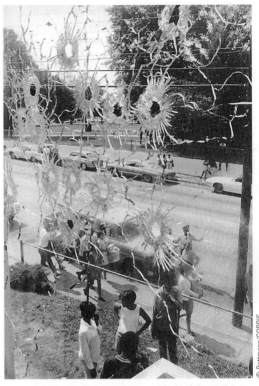

Jackson State   In 1970, the violence associated with America's longest war came home. In May, police gunfire killed two students and wounded 15 others at Jackson State University in Mississippi. This picture was taken through a bullet-riddled window in a women's dorm.

© Bettmann/CORBIS

The continuing controversy over the "My Lai incident" further polarized sentiment over continuing the war. Shortly after the 1968 Tet episode, troops had entered the small Vietnamese hamlet of My Lai and murdered more than 200 civilians, most of them women and children. After a bungled cover-up, news of this massacre became public in 1969 and refocused debate over U.S policy. Military courts convicted only one officer, Lieutenant William Calley, of any offense. This controversial decision prompted charges that higher-ups had offered Calley up as a scapegoat for a failed strategy that emphasized body counts and lax rules of engagement. (Nearly forty years later, researchers found evidence of many other smaller-scale incidents resembling that at My Lai.) Injecting the White House into the Calley controversy, Nixon ordered that the young lieutenant, pending the results of his appeal, be confined to his officer's quarters rather than imprisoned. Ultimately, a higher military court ordered that Calley, because of procedural irregularities, be released from custody.

Meanwhile, the Nixon administration widened its operations to include Laos as well as Cambodia. Although the United States denied waging any such campaign, its bombing ravaged large areas of these largely agricultural countries. As the number of refugees in Cambodia swelled and food supplies dwindled, the communist guerrilla force there—the Khmer Rouge—became a well-disciplined army. The Khmer Rouge eventually came to power and, in a murderous attempt to eliminate dissent, turned Cambodia into a "killing field." It slaughtered more than a million Cambodians. While Nixon continued to talk about U.S. troop withdrawals and to conduct peace negotiations with North Vietnam and the NLF in Paris, the **Vietnam War** broadened into a conflict that seemed to be destabilizing all of Indochina.

Even greater violence was yet to come. In spring 1972, a North Vietnamese offensive approached within 30 miles of Saigon, and U.S. generals warned of imminent defeat. Nixon responded by resuming the bombing of North Vietnam and by mining its harbors. Just weeks before the November 1972 election, though, Kissinger again promised peace and announced a ceasefire. After Nixon's reelection, when peace negotiations again stalled, the United States unleashed even greater firepower. During the "Christmas bombing" of December 1972, the heaviest bombardment in history, B-52 planes pounded military and civilian targets in North Vietnam around the clock.

By this time, however, the Nixon administration found it increasingly difficult to carry out its war policies. Support, all across the political spectrum, seemed to grow ever thinner. Critics condemned the violence in Asia and the administration's effort to expand its domestic power when responding to dissent at home. Perhaps most importantly, sagging morale among troops in the field began to undermine the U.S. effort. An increasing number of soldiers questioned the purpose of their sacrifices; some refused to engage the enemy; and a few openly defied their own superiors. At home, Vietnam Veterans against the War (VVAW), a new organization, joined the antiwar coalition.

Running out of options, Nixon proceeded toward full-scale Vietnamization. In January 1973, the United States signed peace accords in Paris that provided a timetable for the withdrawal of U.S. troops. As U.S. ground forces departed, an increasingly demoralized and ineffectual South Vietnamese government, headed by Nguyen Van Thieu, continued to fight with U.S. support. In spring 1975, nearly two years after the Paris accords and with Nixon's successor in office, South Vietnam's army and Thieu's government would collapse as North Vietnamese armies entered the capital of Saigon. America's longest war ended in defeat.

The Aftermath of War

Between 1960 and 1973, approximately 3.5 million American men and women served in Vietnam: 58,000 died, 150,000 were wounded, and 2,000 were classified as missing. In the aftermath of this costly, divisive war, people struggled to understand why the United States failed to prevail over a small, barely industrialized nation. Those who supported the war to the end argued that it had been lost on the home front. They blamed an irresponsible media, a disloyal antiwar movement, and a Congress afflicted by a "failure of will." The war, they still insisted, had been for a laudable cause. Politicians, by setting unrealistic limits on the Pentagon, had prevented military strategists from attaining victory.

By contrast, others doubted the possibility of any U.S. "victory," short of devastating North Vietnam and risking a wider war with China. These analysts stressed the overextension of U.S. power, the misguided belief in national omnipotence, and the miscalculations of decision makers. Many concluded that the United States had waged a war in the wrong place for the wrong reasons. The conflict's human costs, to the United States and the people of Indochina, outweighed any possible gain from preserving a pro-U.S., noncommunist South Vietnam.

Regardless of their positions on the war, most Americans seemed to agree on a single proposition, which carried different meanings: There should be "no more Vietnams." For most national leaders, this meant the United States should not undertake another substantial military operation unless it involved clear and compelling political objectives, sustained public support, and realistic means to accomplish a goal that clearly advanced the national interest. Eventually, however, the people who wanted to aggressively reassert U.S. power in the world, worried that what they called "the Vietnam syndrome" might shape a timid and ineffective foreign policy.

Expanding the Nixon Doctrine

Meanwhile, Nixon and Kissinger extended the premise of the Nixon Doctrine to the entire world. The White House made it clear that the United States would not dispatch its own troops to quash insurgencies but would generously aid anticommunist governments or factions willing to fight their own battles.

During the early 1970s, U.S. Cold War strategy came to rely on supporting staunchly anticommunist regional powers. These included nations such as Iran under Shah Reza Pahlavi, South Africa with its apartheid regime, and Brazil with its repressive military dictatorship. All of these countries built large, U.S.-trained military establishments. U.S. military assistance, together with covert CIA operations, also incubated and protected anticommunist dictatorships in South Korea, the Philippines, and much of Latin America. U.S. arms sales to the rest of the world skyrocketed. In one of its most controversial foreign policies, moreover, the Nixon administration employed covert action against the elected socialist government of Salvador Allende Gossens in Chile in 1970. After Allende took office, Kissinger pressed for the destabilization of his government. On September 11, 1973, the Chilean military overthrew Allende, immediately suspended democratic rule, and announced that Allende had committed suicide.

Subsequent debates about U.S. foreign policy under Nixon and Kissinger often highlighted events in Chile in order to illustrate broader claims. Democratic Senator Frank Church, for example, directed Senate hearings during the mid-1970s that suggested policies toward Chile exemplified how the Nixon administration, in the name of anticommunism, often had wedded the United States to questionable covert activities and military dictators. Supporters of Nixon and Kissinger, in contrast, praised the pair for conducting a pragmatic foreign policy that combined détente directed toward the communist giants, the USSR and China, with containment directed toward the spread of revolutionary movements, including that of Allende's government in Chile.

The Wars of Watergate

Focus Question
What political and legal controversies entrapped the Nixon administration, and how did Watergate-related events ultimately force Nixon's resignation?

Nixon's presidency ultimately collapsed as a result of fateful decisions made in the Oval Office. Nixon and his closest aides came to Washington with a view of politics that was as expansive as that espoused by many of the social movements the Nixon White House abhorred. The "new Nixon" endorsed a "new politics"—evidenced in his foreign policy moves toward China and the Soviet Union and in his short-lived enthusiasm for FAP.

At the same time, reminders of the "old Nixon" constantly surfaced. Long known as a political loner, who ruminated about taking revenge against his enemies, Nixon often seemed to be his own greatest foe. Even as his administration publicly built a domestic record that often seemed sympathetic to matters of liberty and equality, it secretly pressed the power of the presidency in constitutionally suspect, and often simply foolish, ways. It ordered the Internal Revenue Service (IRS) to harass prominent Democrats with expensive audits, placed antiwar and Black Power activists under illegal surveillance, and conducted risky covert activities on the domestic front. Some of these activities even rattled the constitutional sensibilities of an old Nixon ally, J. Edgar Hoover, who rarely worried about legal niceties when his own FBI swung into action. The Nixon administration prosecuted leading antiwar activists for allegedly impeding the Selective Service process and on various conspiracy charges. It also encouraged Vice President Spiro Agnew to assail media commentators for daring to criticize White House policies.

Largely isolated from political give-and-take, with a close-knit group of advisers, Nixon eventually created his own secret intelligence unit, which set up shop in the White House. The Nixon administration planned to use this group to undertake secret presidential missions against selected enemies. Its first job, to plug "leaks" of information about Vietnam to the media, soon provided the unit with a name, "the **Plumbers**."

During the summer of 1971, stories in the *Washington Post* and, later, the *New York Times* enraged the president. These papers had culled their revelations about deceptions and miscalculations by previous presidential administrations from a top-secret history of U.S. involvement in the Vietnam War, popularly known as the *Pentagon Papers*. Daniel

Ellsberg, an antiwar activist who had once worked in the national security bureaucracy, had sent photocopies of this lengthy, classified document, commissioned in 1967 by Robert McNamara, to selected media outlets.

Although the material in the *Pentagon Papers* concerned events that preceded Nixon's presidency, his administration responded angrily. It became determined to make an example of what would happen to anyone else who trafficked in leaked and classified documents. The administration's legal counterattack failed when the Supreme Court rejected, by a 6-3 margin, an attempt to halt through court injunction all media publications based on the *Papers*. More ominously, the White House unleashed its "plumbers." Seeking information that might discredit Ellsberg, this clandestine unit burglarized his psychiatrist's office. Thus began a series of **"dirty tricks"** and outright crimes, sometimes financed by funds solicited for Nixon's 1972 reelection campaign, which would culminate in the constitutional crisis that became known as **"Watergate."**

The Election of 1972

Because Republicans had fared rather poorly in the mid-term elections of 1970, Nixon's political strategists worried that domestic and foreign troubles might deny the president another term. Creating a campaign organization separate from that of the Republican Party, with the ironic acronym of "CREEP" (Committee to Re-elect the President), they secretly raised millions of dollars, much of it from illegal contributions.

As the 1972 presidential campaign took shape, Nixon's chances for reelection dramatically improved. An assassin's bullet crippled George Wallace. Senator Edmund Muskie of Maine, initially Nixon's leading Democratic challenger, made a series of blunders (some of them, perhaps, precipitated by Republican dirty tricksters) that derailed his campaign. Eventually, Senator George McGovern of South Dakota, an outspoken opponent of the Vietnam War but a lackluster campaigner, won the Democratic nomination.

McGovern never seriously challenged Nixon. Early on, opinion pollsters suggested, a majority of voters decided that McGovern

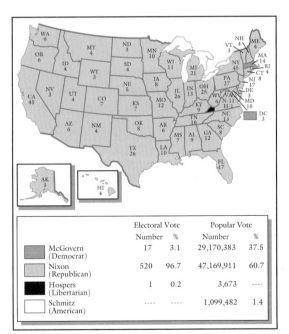

Map 29.3   Presidential Election, 1972   This map shows what is commonly called a landslide election. Less than two years later, however, Nixon would resign from the presidency to avoid facing impeachment charges connected to his role in the Watergate burglary and other "dirty tricks" associated with his presidency.

	Electoral Vote		Popular Vote	
	Number	%	Number	%
McGovern (Democrat)	17	3.1	29,170,383	37.5
Nixon (Republican)	520	96.7	47,169,911	60.7
Hospers (Libertarian)	1	0.2	3,673	----
Schmitz (American)	----	----	1,099,482	1.4

seemed too closely tied to the antiwar movement, New Left activists, and the Countercul-ture. His key issues—a call for higher taxes on the wealthy, a guaranteed minimum income for all Americans, amnesty for Vietnam War draft resisters, and the decriminalization of marijuana—fell outside of what most potential voters considered the "political main-stream." In foreign policy, McGovern urged deep cuts in defense spending and an immedi-ate peace initiative in Vietnam. Nixon successfully portrayed these proposals as signs of the South Dakota senator's "softness" on communism and "weakness" on foreign policy.

Nixon won an easy victory in November. He received the Electoral College votes of all but one state and the District of Columbia. Although the 26th Amendment, ratified one year before the election, had lowered the voting age to 18, a surprisingly small number of newly enfranchised voters cast ballots. Never seriously interested in helping other GOP candidates, Nixon watched the Democrats retain control of Congress.

Nixon Pursued

In achieving victory, the president's supporters left a trail of crime and corruption. In June 1972, a surveillance team with links to both CREEP and the White House Plumbers had been arrested while fine-tuning eavesdropping equipment in the Democratic Party's head-quarters in Washington's Watergate office complex. Apparently, Nixon and his aides feared that Democratic leaders possessed documents that might hinder the president's reelection drive. In public, Nixon's spokespeople initially dismissed the Watergate break-in as a "third-rate burglary" and, then, as an unseemly incident unconnected to anyone of substance at the White House. Privately, though, the president and his inner circle imme-diately launched a cover-up campaign, which gradually unraveled. They paid hush money to the Watergate burglars and ordered CIA officials to misinform the FBI that any investi-gation by that agency would jeopardize national security operations. The White House succeeded in limiting the political damage until after the 1972 election, but events soon overtook their efforts.

While reporters from the *Washington Post* pursued the taint of scandal around the White House, Democrats in Congress and federal prosecutors sought evidence of illegal activities during the 1972 campaign. In 1973, Judge John Sirica, a Republican appointee presiding over the trial of the Watergate burglars, pushed for additional information, and Senate leaders convened a special, bipartisan Watergate Committee. Headed by North Carolina's conservative Democratic senator Sam Ervin, it enjoyed broad power to investigate election-related issues, including the Watergate break-in. Then, prosecutors uncovered evidence that seemed to link key administration figures, including John Mitchell, Nixon's former attorney general and later the head of CREEP, to illegal activities.

During the spring of 1973, one of the Watergate burglars and other witnesses testified before the Senate's Watergate Committee about various illegal activities committed by CREEP and the White House. Senator Ervin called Nixon's closest aides, though not the president, before the committee, and the televised hearings became a daily political drama that attracted a large and loyal viewer audience. Ultimately, testimony from John Dean, who had been the president's chief legal counsel, linked Nixon to attempts to conceal the Watergate episode and to other seemingly illegal activities. The president steadfastly denied Dean's charges.

Along the way, though, Senate investigators discovered that Nixon had ordered installation of voice-activated taping machines, which had recorded every conversation in his Oval Office. These tapes (now housed at the National Archives) opened the way to determining whether the president or Dean, Nixon's primary accuser, was lying. While maintaining he was not "a crook," Nixon also claimed an "executive privilege" to keep the tapes from being released to either Congress or federal prosecutors, but Judge Sirica, Archibald Cox (a special, independent prosecutor in the Watergate case), and Congress all demanded access to the tapes.

If Nixon's own problems were not enough, his outspoken vice president resigned in October 1973, after pleading no contest to charges of income-tax evasion. Spiro Agnew agreed to a plea-bargain arrangement to avoid prosecution for having accepted illegal kickbacks, which he had not reported as income, while in Maryland politics. Acting under the 25th Amendment (ratified in 1967), Nixon appointed—and both houses of Congress confirmed—Representative **Gerald Ford** of Michigan, a Republican Party stalwart, as the new vice president.

Nixon's Final Days

Nixon's clumsy efforts to protect himself, while retaining his tapes, backfired. During the fall of 1973, Nixon ordered the Justice Department to dismiss Archibald Cox, a move intended to prevent the special prosecutor's office from gaining access to the White House tapes. When Cox's firing only seemed to confirm suspicions of a Nixon cover-up, political pressure forced the president to agree to the appointment of an equally tenacious and independent replacement, Leon Jaworski. Nixon's own release of edited transcripts of some Watergate-related conversations delivered another self-inflicted wound. These flawed documents only helped strengthen the case for independent ears hearing the original recordings. Finally, by proclaiming that he would obey only a "definitive" Supreme Court decision, Nixon all but invited the justices, including ones he had appointed, to deliver a unanimous ruling on the question of the tapes. On July 24, 1974, the Court did just that in the case of *U.S.* v. *Nixon*. A claim of executive privilege could not override the refusal to release evidence required in an ongoing criminal investigation.

Meanwhile, the Democratic-controlled Congress, with support from some Republican members, began steps to impeach Nixon and remove him from office. After televised deliberations, a bipartisan majority of the House Judiciary Committee voted three formal articles of impeachment against the president—for obstruction of justice, violation of constitutional liberties, and refusal to produce evidence. Nixon promised to rebut these accusations before the Senate, the body authorized by the Constitution (Article I, Section 3) to render a verdict of guilty or not guilty after impeachment by the House.

Nixon's aides, however, were already orchestrating his departure. One of his own attorneys had discovered that a tape Nixon had been withholding contained the long-sought "smoking gun," clear evidence of a criminal offense. This recording confirmed, during a 1972 conversation, that Nixon had helped hatch the plan by which the CIA would advance its fraudulent claim of national security in order to stop the FBI from investigating the Watergate break-in. At this point, Nixon's own secretary of defense ordered military commanders to ignore any order from the president, the constitutional commander-in-chief, unless the secretary countersigned it. Now abandoned by almost every prominent Republican, most notably Barry Goldwater, and confronted with enough Senate votes to convict him of the impeachment charges, Nixon capitulated. He went on television on August 8, 1974, to announce his resignation. On August 9, Gerald Ford, who had never even been elected to the vice presidency, became the nation's 38th president.

The events that ended Nixon's presidency have helped to highlight some of the dynamics of historical memory. Shortly after Nixon's departure, most people told pollsters they considered the "Watergate Crisis" to be one of the gravest threats by unchecked power to constitutional liberty in the long history of the republic. As time passed, though, the details of Watergate faded away. Opinion polls conducted on the 20th anniversary of Nixon's resignation suggested that most people already only dimly recalled what had prompted Nixon to leave office.

What specific forces could account for this change? One of these might be that Nixon avoided being prosecuted for his actions. Although nearly a dozen members of his administration—including its chief law enforcement officer, John Mitchell—were convicted or pleaded guilty to having committed criminal offenses, Nixon received an unconditional pardon from his successor. Gerald Ford claimed he wanted to spare the nation another media spectacle: one featuring a former president undergoing a lengthy trial process. Ford's action, however, also prevented any authoritative accounting, in a court of law, of a traumatic political-legal episode.

Another reason for changing memories may be the media's habit of affixing the Watergate label to nearly every political scandal of the post-Nixon era. The suffix-*gate* became attached to apparently grave constitutional episodes and to obviously trivial political events. As the Nixon presidency receded in time, many people came to consider "Watergate" a synonym for "politics as usual." Finally, the specific images of what the historian Stanley Kutler calls the "wars of Watergate" have tended to blend into the broader pictures of the political, social, economic, and cultural turmoil that accompanied U.S. involvement in the nation's longest war.

Conclusion

Attempts to extend the power of the national government marked the years between 1963 and 1974. Lyndon Johnson's Great Society provided a blueprint for waging a War on Poverty, and his administration dramatically escalated the war in Vietnam. This use of governmental power prompted divisive debates that helped polarize the country. During Johnson's presidency, both the war effort and the economy faltered, top leaders became discredited, and Johnson abandoned the office he had so long sought. His Republican successor, Richard Nixon, became implicated in abuses of power that ultimately drove him from the White House. The hopes of the early 1960s—that the U.S. government could aggressively promote liberty and equality both at home and throughout the rest of the world—ended in frustration.

The era of America's longest war was also a time of changing ideas about politics, cultural and racial patterns, and definitions of patriotism. It saw the slow convergence of a wide array of social movements, a veritable movement of movements. As different groups invoked different explanations for the failures of both the Great Society and the war effort, divisions from this era would shape U.S. politics and culture for years to come. Many people became skeptical, some even cynical, about enlarging the power of the federal government in the name of expanding liberty and equality.

SUGGESTED READINGS

On Lyndon Johnson, see **Robert J. Dallek**, *Flawed Giant: Lyndon Johnson and His Times, 1961–1973* (1998), **Irving Bernstein**, *Guns or Butter: The Presidency of Lyndon Johnson* (1996), and **Randall B. Woods**, *LBJ: Architect of American Ambition* (2006).

The many outstanding overviews of U.S. involvement in Vietnam include **George Herring**, *America's Longest War: The United States and Vietnam, 1950–1975* (rev. ed., 2001); **Robert D. Schulzinger**, *A Time for War: The United States and Vietnam, 1941–1975* (1997); **David Kaiser**, *American Tragedy: Kennedy, Johnson, and the Origins of the Vietnam War* (2000); **Frederick Logevall**, *The Origins of the Vietnam War* (2001); **James Mann**, *A Grand Delusion: America's Descent into Vietnam* (2001); and **James H. Willbanks**, *Abandoning Vietnam: How America Left and South Vietnam Lost its War* (2004). *Working-Class War: American Combat Soldiers and Vietnam* (1993) and *Patriots: The Vietnam War Remembered from All Sides* (2003), both by **Christian Appy**, provide a wide range of perspectives. See also, **Odd Arne Wested**, *The Global Cold War* (2005) and **Jussi Hanhimaki**, *The Flawed Architect: Henry Kissinger and American Foreign Policy* (2004). **Jeffrey Kimball**, *The Vietnam War Files: Uncovering the Secret History of Nixon-Era Strategy* (2004) collects and skillfully organizes a revealing set of documents. Finally, **David Maraniss**, *They Marched into Sunlight: War and Peace; Vietnam and America October 1967* (2003) moves back and forth, between Vietnam and the home front, during a single crucial month.

The "movement of movements" during the 1960s can be surveyed, from diverse vantage points, in **David W. Levy**, *The Debate over Vietnam* (rev. ed., 1994); **Lynn Spigel and Michael Curtain**, *The Revolution Wasn't Televised: Sixties Television and Social Conflict* (1997); **Maurice Isserman and Michael Kazin**, *America Divided: The Civil War of the 1960s* (1999); and **Edward K. Spann and David L. Anderson**, eds., *Democracy's Children: The Young Rebels of the 1960s and the Power of Ideals* (2003).

On the civil-rights movement and its larger context, **Taylor Branch** concludes his multivolume history with *Pillar of Fire: America in the King Years, 1963–1965* (1998), and *At Canaan's Edge: America in the King Years, 1965–1968* (2006). **William L. Van Deburg**, *New Day in Babylon: The Black Power Movement and American Culture, 1965–1975* (1992), along with **Kathleen Cleaver and George Katsiaficas**, eds., *Liberation, Imagination, and the Black Panther Party: A New Look at the Panthers and their Legacy* (2001) offer useful overviews, while **Robert Self,**

American Babylon: Race and the Struggle for Postwar Oakland (2003) provides a superb local study, as does **Gerald Horne, *Fire This Time: The Watts Uprising and the 1960s*** (1995). See also, **Robin D.G. Kelley, *Freedom Dreams: The Black Radical Tradition*** (2002).

On the late 1960s and early 1970s, begin with the opening portions of **Bruce J. Shuman, *The Seventies: The Great Shift in American Culture, Society, and Politics*** (2001) and **Andreas Hillen, *1973 Nervous Breakdown: Watergate, Warhol, and the Birth of Post-Sixties America*** (2006). The year of 1968 is the subject of numerous volumes, including **Carole Fink, Philipp Gassert, and Detlef Junker, eds, *1968: The World Transformed*** (1998); **Tariq Ali and Susan Watkins, *1968: Marching in the Streets*** (1998); **Mark Kurlansky, *1968: The Year that Rocked the World*** (2003); and the broader account by **Jeremy Suri, *Power and Protest: Global Revolution and the Rise of Détente*** (2003).

On the riddle that was Richard Nixon, see **Richard Reeves, *President Nixon: Alone in the White House*** (2001); **David Greenberg, *Nixon's Shadow: The History of an Image*** (2003); and **Mark Feeney, *Nixon at the Movies*** (2004). **Stanley I. Kutler, ed., *Abuse of Power: The New Nixon Tapes*** (1997) provides evidence of Nixon's approach to politics and constitutional limits, in his own words, along with commentary that updates Kutler's own *The Wars of Watergate* (1992). **John D. Skrentny, *The Minority Revolution*** (2002) details the bureaucratic activism that expanded rights during the Nixon years, while interpretations of activism on the Supreme Court can be found in **Morton J. Horwitz, *The Warren Court and the Pursuit of Justice*** (1999) and in **Lucas A. Powe, Jr., *The Warren Court and American Politics*** (2000).

Visit the Liberty Equality Power Companion Web site for resources specific to this textbook: http://www.thomsonedu.com/history/murrin

Also find self-tests and additional resources at ThomsonNOW. ThomsonNOW is an integrated online suite of services and resources with proven ease of use and efficient paths to success, delivering the results you want—NOW!

www.thomsonedu.com/login/

30

Power and Politics, 1974–1992

Following the onset of the Great Depression of the 1930s and the Second World War, the national government continually expanded its power. Most people supported domestic programs intended to cushion against economic downturns and to assist families in distress, and they endorsed national security measures designed to upgrade U.S. military and intelligence capabilities.

Events of the 1960s and early 1970s, particularly the failed intervention in Vietnam and Watergate, shook people's faith in government. Secrecy, corruption, and economic problems bred further disillusionment. During the 1970s and 1980s, people debated questions they did not need to ask a generation earlier: How should the federal government respond to an aging industrial economy, a ballooning federal deficit, and a beleaguered social welfare system? Might conditions improve, as conservatives had long contended, if Washington reduced, rather than continued to enlarge, its role? Emotionally charged issues such as abortion, environmental regulation, and taxation policy also created controversy over the use of governmental power.

Disagreement extended to foreign policy. Should the United States place less emphasis on anticommunism to pursue other goals, as Democratic president Jimmy Carter (1977–1981) initially urged? Or should it wage the Cold War even more vigorously, as his successor, Republican Ronald Reagan (1981–1989), advocated? Had the U.S. extended its power too far or not far enough? After 1989, when the Cold War ended unexpectedly, the United States needed to forge a foreign policy for a post–Cold War world, a task that fell to the post-Reagan generation of national leaders.

Meanwhile, the "movement of movements," a legacy of the 1960s, refused to fade away. Along with a "New Right" movement, activism associated with women's rights, gay pride, and racial and ethnic identities influenced policy discussions and how people defined themselves.

The Caretaker Presidency of Gerald Ford (1974–1977)

Focus Question
How did the legacies of the Vietnam War and Watergate help shape the presidencies of Gerald Ford and Jimmy Carter?

CHRONOLOGY

1968	Indian Bill of Rights enacted by Congress
1969	The Stonewall Inn raid inaugurates a new phase in gay and lesbian activism
1970	Congressional Black Caucus organized
1973	*Roe* v. *Wade* decision upholds women's right to abortion
1974	Nixon resigns and Ford becomes president; Ford soon pardons Nixon
1975	South Vietnam falls to North Vietnam • Ford asserts U.S. power in *Mayaguez* incident • National Conservative Action Political Committee formed
1976	Jimmy Carter elected president • OPEC sharply raises oil prices
1978	Carter helps negotiate Camp David peace accords on Middle East
1979	Soviet Union invades Afghanistan • *Sandinistas* come to power in Nicaragua • U.S. hostages seized in Iran
1980	Reagan elected president • U.S. hostages in Iran released
1981	Reagan tax cut passed
1983	U.S. troops removed from Lebanon • U.S. troops invade Grenada • Reagan announces SDI ("Star Wars") program
1984	Reagan defeats Walter Mondale
1986	Tax Reform Act passed • Reagan administration rocked by revelation of Iran-*contra* affair
1988	George H. W. Bush defeats Michael Dukakis in presidential election • Congress enacts Indian Gaming Regulation Act
1989	Communist regimes in Eastern Europe collapse; Berlin Wall falls • Cold War, in effect, ends
1990	Bush angers conservative Republicans by agreeing to a tax increase
1991	Bush orchestrates Persian Gulf War against Iraq • Clarence Thomas confirmation hearings highlight issue of sexual harassment
1992	Bill Clinton defeats Bush and third-party candidate Ross Perot in presidential race

When Richard Nixon resigned in August 1974, Gerald R. Ford, his vice president, moved from one office to which voters had never elected him to another, the presidency. Emphasizing his long career in the House of Representatives, Ford promised he possessed the experience to "heal the land," but his administration always seemed a stopgap one. This former college football star preferred that the fight song of his alma mater, the University of Michigan, rather than "Hail to the Chief," accompany his public entries. Genial and unpretentious, Ford never attracted the kind of media criticism that enraged Lyndon Johnson and Richard Nixon. Recurrent images of a string of minor presidential mishaps, including tumbles down a ski slope and off an airplane ramp, however, helped reinforce perceptions of Ford as a bumbling, unsteady leader.

Trying to Whip Inflation

Ford's plan to present his administration as an updated version of the moderate Republicanism of the 1950s quickly foundered. His pardoning of former president Nixon, in September 1974, proved widely unpopular, and his appointment of Nelson Rockefeller as vice president infuriated GOP conservatives. Ford's approval rating began skidding downward.

Economic problems dominated the domestic side of the 865-day Ford presidency. Quick-fix policies had helped Nixon win reelection in 1972, but they left his successor with the underlying problems. Ford touted a program called "Whip Inflation Now" (WIN), which included a one-year surcharge on income taxes and cuts in federal spending as his solutions. After both unemployment and prices still crept higher, Ford conceded WIN to be a loser. During 1975, unemployment reached 8.5 percent, and the inflation rate topped 9 percent.

The president continually clashed with the Democratic-controlled Congress. Ford, who vetoed nearly 40 spending bills while in office, finally agreed to a congressional economic package. It included a tax cut, an increase in unemployment benefits, an unbalanced federal budget, and limited controls on oil prices. Democrats charged that Ford could not implement coherent programs of his own, and many Republicans complained that he would not stand up to congressional Democrats.

Foreign Policy

Upon assuming office, Ford pledged a renewal of U.S. military support to the government in South Vietnam, if North Vietnam ever directly threatened its survival. A mood of war weariness in the United States and battlefield conditions that favored North Vietnam, however, made fulfilling this commitment impossible. North Vietnam's armies stormed across the South in March 1975. Congress, relieved that U.S. troops had finally been withdrawn after the 1973 Paris peace accords (see chapter 29), rejected any suggestion of reintroducing them. Conducting their last mission in Vietnam, U.S. helicopters scrambled to airlift U.S. officials and top-ranking South Vietnamese officers off the American embassy's rooftop.

Spring 1975 brought new communist victories in Indochina. In early April, Khmer Rouge forces drove a U.S.-backed government from the Cambodian capital of Phnom Penh, and on April 30, 1975, North Vietnamese troops overran Saigon, renaming the former South Vietnamese capital Ho Chi Minh City. Contention over the history of U.S. policy in Indochina became especially heated in the months that followed.

Operating within this contentious atmosphere, Ford tried to demonstrate U.S. military power. In May 1975, a contingent of Khmer Rouge boarded a U.S. ship, the *Mayaguez*, taking its crew hostage. Henry Kissinger, now Ford's secretary of state, declared that the United States needed to "look ferocious" and convinced the president to order bombing strikes against Cambodia and a rescue operation. This military response, coupled with Chinese pressure on the Khmer Rouge, secured the release of the *Mayaguez* and its crew.

Although the *Mayaguez* rescue cost more lives than it saved, Ford's approval ratings briefly shot up. His other initiatives, which included extending Nixon's policy of détente with the Soviet Union and pursuing peace negotiations in the Middle East, achieved little. Gerald Ford increasingly appeared to be a caretaker president.

The Election of 1976

Ford nearly lost the GOP presidential nomination in 1976. Conservative Republicans rallied behind **Ronald Reagan,** who finally ignited a sputtering campaign by offering himself as a "true conservative" who, unlike Ford, owed nothing to Washington insiders. The president had already won just enough delegates during the early primaries, however, to eke out a narrow first-ballot victory at the Republican Party's national convention. Speaking to this gathering, Reagan accurately predicted, "I shall rise and fight again."

The Democrats, a party in far more disarray than the GOP, did turn to an outsider, **James Earl (Jimmy) Carter.** A retired naval officer, engineer, peanut farmer, and former governor of Georgia, Carter campaigned by stressing personal character. He highlighted his small-town roots and his Southern Baptist faith. To balance the ticket, he picked Senator Walter Mondale of Minnesota as his running mate. In November, Carter won a narrow victory over Ford.

Carter's election rested on a diverse, transitory coalition. Reversing recent Democratic fortunes, this native of the South carried every southern state except Virginia. He ran particularly well among white voters who regularly attended fundamentalist and evangelical churches and among African Americans. Carter also courted former antiwar activists by promising presidential pardons for most Vietnam-era draft resisters. Walter Mondale's appeal to old-line Democratic interests, especially in the labor–union movement, helped Carter narrowly carry New York, Pennsylvania, and Ohio. The final tally remained close, however, and voter turnout sank to its lowest mark, 54 percent of those eligible, since the end of the Second World War.

Jimmy Carter's One-Term Presidency (1977–1981)

Jimmy Carter's lack of a popular mandate and his outsider status proved serious handicaps in Washington. He delighted the inaugural-day crowd and TV viewers by leaving his presidential limousine and walking, hand-in-hand, with his wife Rosalyn down Pennsylvania Avenue. This stroll would remain one of the highpoints of the Carter presidency. After leaving government, Carter reflected on his difficulties: "I had a different way of governing. . . . I was a southerner, a born-again Christian, a Baptist, a newcomer." Moreover, Carter became caught between advisers who claimed that the national government already exercised too much power and those who argued that Washington still did too little to address domestic and foreign problems. The Carter administration, a reflection of a divided Democratic Party in this regard, often seemed unsure of how to view governmental power.

Welfare and Energy Initiatives

Carter puzzled over welfare policy. His own staff differed over whether to increase funding for social-welfare assistance to low-income families or to create several million public service jobs, underwritten by additional federal spending. Ultimately, Carter proposed a compromise that failed to pass Congress, and the impulse to overhaul the nation's social-welfare system continued to flounder.

The president had little choice but to push harder on energy-related issues. The United States obtained 90 percent of its energy from fossil fuels, much of it from imported petroleum. In 1976, as it had in 1973, the Organization of Petroleum Exporting Countries (OPEC), a cartel dominated by oil-rich nations in the Middle East, dramatically raised the price of crude oil and precipitated acute worldwide shortages. As gasoline became expensive and in short supply, drivers in the United States denounced high prices and long lines at the pumps. Carter promised to make the nation less dependent on imported petroleum.

The president charged James Schlesinger, head of a new department of energy, with developing a plan. Schlesinger outlined four ambitious goals to decrease U.S. reliance on foreign sources: (1) use tax incentives and deregulation to increase domestic energy production; (2) raise the federal gasoline tax to discourage consumption; (3) foster conservation; and (4) promote nonpetroleum energy sources, especially coal and nuclear power. Neither Carter nor Schlesinger consulted Congress or even some members of the president's own administration when drawing up these key proposals. Instead, in April 1977, Carter announced that the energy crisis represented "the moral equivalent of war," and he advanced a complicated battle plan, which ultimately included more than 100 interrelated provisions.

Congress quickly rebuffed the president. Gas and oil interests opposed higher taxes. Consumer activists helped block deregulation. Environmentalists charged that greater use of coal would increase air pollution. Carter continued to press for energy conservation, for development of renewable sources, such as solar and wind-generated energy, and for greater use of nuclear power.

The nuclear option generated especially sharp controversy. In theory, nuclear reactors could provide inexpensive, almost limitless amounts of energy. The actual cost of building and maintaining them, however, far exceeded original estimates, and antinuclear activists warned of grave safety risks. In 1979, a serious reactor malfunction at Three Mile Island, Pennsylvania, along with a popular movie about a similar event (*The China Syndrome*), appeared to confirm the worst fears. A nuclear-reactor meltdown at a single facility seemed capable of producing massive environmental damage and substantial casualties. Responding to growing concerns, power companies canceled orders for new reactors, and the nuclear power industry's expansion halted. Meanwhile, OPEC oil prices continued to skyrocket, from $1.80 per barrel in 1971 to nearly $30 a decade later, at the end of Carter's presidency.

A Faltering Economy

Rising oil prices and a lingering case of stagflation, legacies of the Nixon and Ford years, heightened the nation's economic woes. Carter pledged to lower both unemployment and inflation, to rekindle economic growth, and to balance the federal budget (which showed a deficit of about $70 billion in 1976). He ultimately settled on tax cuts and increased public-works spending as the best ways to accomplish these objectives. In addition, the Federal Reserve Board increased the supply of money in circulation and kept the prime interest rate relatively low.

These measures, however, only further aggravated matters. By 1980, government statistics showed virtually no economic growth; unemployment numbers, after temporarily dipping, continued to rise; and the inflation rate topped 13 percent. Stagflation, in turn, brought high interest rates, discouraged investment, and ate away at consumer confidence. Many voters told pollsters that Carter's time in office had coincided with deterioration of their own economic fortunes.

Economic distress spread beyond individuals. New York City, beset by long-term economic problems and short-term fiscal mismanagement, faced bankruptcy. A group of private bankers and public officials managed to secure congressional bailout legislation, which granted special loan guarantees to the nation's largest city. Its troubles were hardly unique. According to one estimate, Chicago lost 200,000 manufacturing jobs during the 1970s. Bricks salvaged from demolished buildings in St. Louis became one of that city's leading products. Soaring unemployment, rising crime rates, deteriorating downtowns, and shrinking tax revenues afflicted most urban areas, even as inflation further reduced the public services that cash-strapped city budgets could afford to finance.

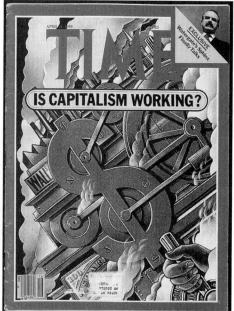

© Time & Life Pictures/Getty Images

"Is Capitalism Working?"   In 1980, *Time* magazine wondered about the economic future of the United States. Persistent economic problems, especially high rates of inflation and unemployment, dominated the Ford and Carter presidencies.

Conservative economists and business interests charged that domestic programs favored by most congressional Democrats contributed to this economic distress. Increasing the minimum wage and vigorously enforcing safety and antipollution regulations, they argued, drove up the cost of doing business and forced companies to raise prices to consumers.

During its last two years in Washington, the Carter administration seemed to agree with some of this analysis. Defying many Democrats in Congress, the president cut spending for some social programs, sought to reduce capital-gains taxes to encourage investment, and began deregulating various industries, beginning with the financial and transportation sectors.

Negotiating Disputes Overseas

In foreign, as in domestic policy, Carter came to Washington promising new directions. As a symbol of letting go of the Vietnam War issue, he immediately fulfilled his pledge of granting amnesty to most Vietnam-era draft resisters. He soon declared that his presidency would press human-rights issues and would avoid any "inordinate fear of communism."

Pulled in divergent directions, the Carter administration's foreign policy appeared to waffle. Although Carter was a hard worker and a quick study, he possessed little background in foreign-policy issues. Furthermore, his top aides—Cyrus Vance as secretary of state and Zbigniew Brzezinski as national security adviser—advocated (and sometimes tried to pursue) very different agendas. Vance preferred quiet diplomacy and avoidance of confrontations, while Brzezinski favored a hard-line, anti-Soviet policy with an emphasis on military muscle. Carter favored settling disputes through negotiation, rather than military force, and promoting human rights overseas as a major priority.

Carter's faith in negotiations and his personal skills as a facilitator yielded some successes. On the issue of the Panama Canal, the object of diplomatic negotiations for 13 years, Carter secured treaties that granted Panama increasing authority over the waterway and, then, full control in 2000. Carter personally lobbied key members of the U.S. Senate, where he needed a two-thirds majority to ratify any treaty, and finally convinced enough skeptics that ownership of the canal was no longer economically or strategically crucial to the United States.

The "Camp David Peace Talks" of 1978 highlighted Carter's personal diplomatic touch. Relations between Egypt and Israel had been strained since the Yom Kippur War of 1973, when Israel repelled an Egyptian attack and seized the Sinai Peninsula and territory along the "West Bank" (of the Jordan River). Reviving earlier Republican efforts to broker a peace settlement, Carter brought Menachem Begin and Anwar Sadat, leaders of Israel and Egypt, respectively, to the presidential retreat at Camp David. After 13 days of difficult bargaining, the three leaders announced a framework for further negotiations and a peace treaty between Egypt and Israel. Tensions in the Middle East hardly vanished, but these Camp David Accords kept alive high-level discussions, lowered the level of acrimony between Egypt and Israel, and bound both nations to the United States through Carter's promises of economic aid.

In Asia, the Carter administration built on Nixon's initiative, expanding economic and cultural relations with China. The United States finally established formal diplomatic ties with the People's Republic on New Year's Day 1979.

Campaigning for Human Rights Abroad

Carter's foreign policy became best known for its emphasis on human rights. Carter argued that Cold War alliances with unpopular, repressive dictatorships, even in the name of anticommunism, had undermined the international reputation and influence of the United States.

Carter's human-rights policy, however, proved difficult to implement. Judged by its own standards, it appeared that his administration continued to support some dictatorial regimes, such as that of Ferdinand Marcos in the Philippines, when it seemed expedient to do so. Moreover, Carter's critics, especially Republicans, complained that his rhetoric about human rights helped justify uprisings against long-standing pro-American dictators in Nicaragua and Iran. Revolutions in these countries, partially fueled by resentment against the United States, brought anti-American regimes to power and presented Carter with difficult choices.

In Nicaragua, the revolutionary *Sandinista* movement in 1979 toppled the dictatorship of Anastasio Somoza, whom the United States had long supported. The *Sandinistas*, initially a coalition of moderate democrats and leftists, soon veered toward a militant Marxism and began to expropriate private property. Consequently, Carter's opponents at home charged his policies with having given a green light to Marxist-style insurrections throughout Central America, and some pledged to seek the overthrow of the *Sandinistas*.

Confronting Problems in Iran and Afghanistan

If events in Nicaragua marred Carter's foreign-policy reputation, those in Iran and Afghanistan battered it. The United States had steadfastly supported the autocratic Shah Reza Pahlavi, who had reigned in oil-rich Iran since the American-supported coup of 1953. The shah's own ouster in January 1979, by a revolutionary movement dominated by Islamic fundamentalists, signaled a repudiation of the U.S. presence in Iran. When the White House agreed that the deposed shah could enter the United States for medical treatment in November 1979, a militant group of Iranians, acting at the behest of their nation's revolutionary government, seized the U.S. embassy, along with 66 American hostages, in Teheran. They demanded the United States return the shah to Iran in exchange for release of the hostages.

Carter responded with uncharacteristic aggressiveness. He replaced human-rights rhetoric with tougher talk and announced economic sanctions against Iran. Over the objections of Cyrus Vance (who subsequently resigned in protest), Carter also sent a military rescue mission into Iran. When this effort ended in an embarrassing failure, Carter's critics cited the on-going "hostage crisis" as proof of his incompetence. (Diplomatic efforts would finally free the hostages, after Carter's defeat in the 1980 presidential election, but the United States and Iran would remain bitterly at odds.)

Criticism of Carter also focused on the Soviet Union's 1979 invasion of Afghanistan, a move primarily sparked by the Kremlin's fear of the growing influence of Islamic fundamentalists along and within the borders of the USSR. Carter tried to respond in nonmilitary ways. He halted grain exports to the Soviet Union (angering his farm constituency), organized a boycott of the 1980 Summer Olympic Games in Moscow, withdrew a new Strategic Arms Limitation Treaty (SALT) from the U.S. Senate, and revived registration for military service. Still, Republicans (along with some conservative Democrats) charged Carter with allowing U.S. power and prestige to decline.

For a time, after Senator Edward Kennedy of Massachusetts entered the 1980 Democratic presidential primaries, it seemed as if Carter's own party might deny him a second term.

Although Kennedy's campaign challenge eventually fizzled, it popularized anti-Carter themes that Republicans would gleefully embrace. "It's time to say no more hostages, no more high interest rates, no more high inflation, and no more Jimmy Carter," went Kennedy's standard stump speech.

A New Right

By 1976, the idea of preventing another Carter *or* another Kennedy presidency animated a diverse coalition of conservatives: a "New Right." A broadly based movement, this new conservatism succeeded in holding together several different constituencies. The already disparate group that had initially gathered around William F. Buckley's *National Review* during the 1950s provided one of these constituencies. Even as Buckley continued to use his magazine to push conservative ideas, he reached out to new converts through television. His long-running interview show, *Firing Line*, debuted on PBS in 1971 (and ran for another 28 years). The economist Milton Friedman—a frequent Buckley guest, a 1976 Nobel laureate, and creator of a PBS series touting free-market economic principles—provided another important link between the conservatism of the 1950s and that of the 1970s. In addition, many of the then-youthful conservatives who had energized Barry Goldwater's 1964 presidential campaign, such as Patrick Buchanan, came to the New Right after having worked in Richard Nixon's administration.

In contrast, the "neoconservative" (or "neocon") wing of the New Right of the 1970s had generally identified with Democrats, rather than Republicans, during the 1950s and much of the 1960s. Fiercely anticommunist, writers and academics such as Norman Podhoretz, Gertrude Himmelfarb, Jeane Kirkpatrick, and Irving Kristol saw too many Democrats criticizing Lyndon Johnson and, then, rallying behind George McGovern and his theme of "Come Home America." Fearful that the Democratic Party might abandon a strong anticommunist stance, **neoconservatives** also viewed most domestic movements of the 1960s, particularly those displaying countercultural values, as threatening the social stability and intellectual values they admired. This initial generation of neoconservatives, often the offspring of European-Jewish immigrants, also complained that U.S. foreign policy, even under Richard Nixon and Henry Kissinger, failed to support Israel strongly enough. This claim tended to anger some older "paleo-conservatives," those who had never quite shed the anti-Semitism that Buckley's *National Review* had urged all conservatives to abandon.

Conservative business leaders provided another important New Right constituency. Convinced that anticorporate professors and students dominated most colleges and universities, business magnates such as Joseph Coors, of the Colorado brewing family, placed at least some of their fortunes at the service of their convictions. In their view, new regulatory legislation accepted by the Nixon administration, especially measures dealing with workplace safety issues and environmental concerns, threatened "economic freedom" and "entrepreneurial liberty." If colleges and universities could not provide intellectual support for conservative perspectives, then businesses should create counter-institutions in the form of right-leaning think tanks. Conservative business leaders and their philanthropic foundations generously funded research institutions, such as the American Enterprise

Institute (founded in 1943), and created new ones, such as The Heritage Foundation (established in 1973).

Money from New Right businesspeople also financed lobbying efforts, such as those mounted by their own Business Roundtable (created in 1973) and The Committee on the Present Danger (CPD). This bipartisan group, which took its name and much of its leadership from a similarly named group of the 1950s, argued that the foreign-policy establishment of the 1970s, including "realists" such as Henry Kissinger, underestimated the threat that the Soviet Union still posed to the United States. The CPD's successes included persuading Gerald Ford's appointee as CIA director, George H. W. Bush, to order a review of the CIA's assessment of the communist menace by a group of outside analysts. Ultimately known as "Team B" and dominated by people close to the CPD, this panel warned of CIA complacency in the face of Soviet aggressiveness.

Groups such as the CPD also operated effectively outside of the Washington, D.C., beltway. In 1975, activists who had worked for Goldwater's 1964 campaign formed the National Conservative Political Action Committee (NCPAC), the first of many similar movement organizations aimed at mobilizing and organizing at the grassroots. Initiatives such as NCPAC backed conservative political candidates and advocated a wide range of policies. Forging a political strategy aimed at defending "family values," they opposed policies identified with feminist movements, such as legalized abortion, and LGBT (lesbian, gay, bisexual, transgender) lifestyles.

The New Right of the 1970s also attracted grassroots support from Protestants in fundamentalist and evangelical churches. People from these religious groups had generally stayed clear of overtly partisan politics since the 1920s but continued to express concern, exemplified in the work of Billy Graham's organization, about public issues that involved spiritual and social matters. Already angered by Supreme Court decisions that seemed to eliminate sectarian prayers from public schools, many expressed greater outrage over *Roe* v. *Wade* (1973), the landmark abortion ruling. Reaching out to antiabortion Catholics, people whom most members of southern Protestant congregations would have shunned a generation earlier, a "Religious Right" slowly took shape. The Reverend Jerry Falwell of the Thomas Road Baptist Church and *The Old Time Gospel Hour* television ministry declared *Roe* showed the necessity of fighting back on the political front because antireligious elites in Washington "have been imposing morality on us for the last fifty years."

Leaders of the Religious Right insisted that sacred values should actively shape political policy making. The clear separation between church and state, a guiding principle of constitutionalism during the era of Earl Warren's Supreme Court, struck the Religious Right as a violation of a right specifically mentioned in the First Amendment: the "free exercise of religion." Particularly in the South, conservatives embarked on a lengthy legal crusade to prevent the Internal Revenue Service from denying tax-exempt status to the private Christian colleges and academies that opposed racial integration. Challenging older constitutional precedents against state aid to religious institutions, they also urged that government should use tax monies to help fund church-centered education and "faith-based" social programming. Most spokespeople for the Religious Right championed foreign policies that maximized the use of U.S. military power, especially on behalf of Israel. Protestants who embraced "dispensational pre-millennialism," the belief that the Second Coming of Christ would occur in their lifetimes, saw the survival of a Jewish state in the Middle East as crucial to the future they expected to unfold according to Biblical prophesy.

Especially in the South, the process of a political switch to the GOP could almost seem comparable to that of a religious conversion. In 1976 most **evangelicals** and **fundamentalists** from the South, including Jerry Falwell, supported Jimmy Carter. His religious values made him seem less committed to the *Roe* decision than Gerald Ford, whose spouse, Betty Ford, often identified herself with women's issues. Very soon, however, Falwell and others on the Religious Right began realigning their politics with those of the GOP's conservative bloc and embracing a political messiah, Ronald Reagan.

Ronald Reagan (1981–1989)

Focus Question
To what extent did Ronald Reagan's administration represent a victory for the New Right agenda in both domestic and foreign policy?

Ronald Reagan increasingly seemed the best hope of conservative Republicans. Most right-of-center activists had viewed Nixon and Gerald Ford as Eisenhower-style moderates, who only vaguely understood, let alone reliably adopted, conservative perspectives. Their search for a dedicated movement conservative seemed especially urgent after Ford tabbed Nelson Rockefeller, whom many conservative members of the GOP viewed as a crypto-Democrat, as his vice president. "I could hardly have been more upset if Ford had selected Teddy Kennedy," one outraged conservative claimed.

Popular memory now recalls Reagan, particularly after his 2004 death, in glowing terms. Even people who disliked his political ideas and programs often credited him with possessing the presidential aura of FDR, the movie-land charisma of JFK, and the persuasive powers of LBJ. In striking contrast, when Reagan had first run for elective office in 1966, observers from outside the conservative fold tended to dismiss him as a "flake," a washed-up or never-was movie actor, and an intellectual lightweight. Throughout Reagan's entire political career, the tendency to denigrate or, more commonly, underestimate his talents and intellect generally worked to his advantage.

After Reagan had steamrollered a two-term Democratic incumbent to become governor of California in 1966, many political watchers expected he would create havoc once in office. He had campaigned as a political leader who would restore order on university campuses by encouraging police to crack heads—which he *did* do—and as someone who would tear down the state's social-welfare system—which he *did not* do. During his own eight years as California's chief executive, Reagan pursued a moderately conservative path on most issues and generally won praise for a governing style that one historian would later describe as combining "visionary rigidity" with "tactical flexibility."

Still, despite Reagan's promise that the failed 1976 effort to push aside Ford would not mark his last political hurrah, most political observers again discounted his presidential prospects as 1980 approached. Surely, as he neared age 70, Reagan could never redebut in national politics, commentators generally predicted. As Carter's presidency seemed to wander, however, Reagan reemerged as a fresh, new face—an outsider like Carter, but one with better political instincts and a personality that promised to wear well. Using his most obvious asset, the well-practiced ability to communicate across virtually all media, Reagan recorded nearly 1,500 nationally syndicated radio addresses, which he personally drafted in longhand. His domestic priorities well known, Reagan focused many of these speeches on national defense, concentrating on the implications of his major claim: that U.S. leaders had simply stood idly by while the USSR conducted the "biggest military buildup in the history of mankind."

Meanwhile, back in California, angry conservative taxpayers were organizing a grassroots effort to slash the state's property taxes by a ballot initiative labeled Proposition 13. (Ironically, Reagan's agreement to tax hikes during his time as governor had helped fuel the Proposition 13 movement.) This measure, a testament to how effectively conservative activists could mobilize grassroots volunteers and corporate contributors, passed by a large margin in 1978. Always ready to denounce high taxes, Reagan shrewdly elevated the already important tax-cutting issue to a central place in his 1980 presidential campaign.

Still, some on the diverse New Right continued to wonder about Reagan. Where, precisely, did this divorced, one-time Democrat stand on issues such as abortion and school prayer? Pragmatists in the New Right movement, including those with strong ties to the GOP establishment, ultimately viewed Reagan, whether or not he really qualified as a true conservative, as the most conservative presidential hopeful with the best chance of actually winning the White House in 1980.

The Election of 1980

Easily capturing the Republican nomination, and anointing one of his defeated rivals, George H. W. Bush, as a running mate, Ronald Reagan never doubted he could defeat Jimmy Carter. Employing his well-practiced media skills and well-honed message, Reagan sought to transfer his own optimistic vision of a rejuvenated America to the electorate. His standard speech, punctuated with quips inspired by Hollywood movies, stressed opposition to domestic social spending, commitment to significant cuts in federal taxes, and renewed support for the post-Vietnam Pentagon, supposedly short-changed by Democrats and moderate Republicans alike. Speaking before a pro-military audience, Reagan insisted the USSR had surged so far ahead in nuclear capabilities that, during any confrontation with the Soviets, the United States would face a stark choice: "surrender or die." Looking at opinion polls about how people linked their own declining economic circumstances to those of the entire nation during Carter's presidency, Reagan repeatedly asked a simple public policy question: "Are you better off now than you were four years ago?" Quickly offering his own answer, Reagan cited a homemade economic statistic, the "misery index," which added the rate of inflation to that of unemployment.

Reagan also seized issues that the Democratic Party had long regarded as its own—economic growth and increased personal consumption. In 1979, one of Jimmy Carter's advisers had gloomily portrayed the nation's economic problems as so severe that there was "no way we can avoid a decline in our standard of living. All we can do is adapt to it." In contrast, Reagan promised that sharp tax cuts and budget trimming would bring about the return, for the first time since the late 1960s, of robust economic expansion.

The Reagan-Bush team swept to victory. Although it gained only slightly more than 50 percent of the popular vote because John Anderson, a middle-of-the-road Republican, running as an independent, won about 7 percent of the total—the GOP ticket captured the Electoral College tally by a 489 to 49 margin. Carter conceded defeat even before West Coast voting booths had officially closed. Moreover, Republicans took away 12 Democratic Senate seats, including those of George McGovern and Frank Church, widely visible opponents of the foreign-policy vision championed by Reagan. For the first time since 1954, Republicans controlled the U.S. Senate, though not the House of Representatives.

Ronald Wilson Reagan had reinvented himself during the 1960s, supposedly a time dominated by youth. At 70 years of age, he promised to do the same for a nation that seemed to have not yet recovered from the years of polarization.

A "New Morning in America"

Even after his 1980 victory, many political observers continued to underestimate Reagan. Once people experienced President Reagan's actual policies and administrative ineptitude, went a common argument among Democrats, his finely buffed image and well-practiced media skills would count for little. His detractors, with some justification, saw the presidential election representing more of a referendum against Jimmy Carter than a groundswell for Ronald Reagan.

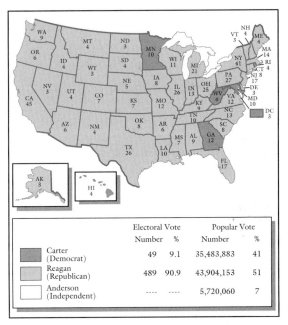

Map 30.1   Presidential Election, 1980   Compare this map with the one showing the election of Jimmy Carter four years earlier. What factors might explain such a sudden downturn in Democratic fortunes?

Although conservative think tanks deluged the Reagan administration with policy suggestions, the president and his closest aides focused on three major priorities: (1) cutting federal taxes, (2) reducing the governmental regulatory structure, and (3) boosting national-security capabilities. Implicitly hedging their bets on the depth of their political support and recognizing the desirability of moving quickly, they prepared to take Washington by storm, ironically using FDR's first "100 days" as their model for an anti–New Deal agenda.

Taxes, Supply-Side Economics, and the "Reagan Revolution"

To justify cutting taxes, Reagan continued to endorse a theory widely known as "**supply-side economics.**" In this view, the approach that Democrats had favored since the Second World War used ever-increasing tax revenues to finance programs that propped up spending by consumers, thus focusing on the "demand side." Supply-siders leaned in the other direction. Reducing the tax burden on those who paid the most, they argued, would stimulate economic growth by putting more money in the hands of people who supplied the capital needed to stimulate production and increase investment. During the run-up to the 1980 election, a number of top Republican conservatives had pressed this approach, once denounced by Reagan's own Phi Beta Kappa vice president, when he was a rival candidate, as "voodoo economics."

Reagan's administration claimed to support this approach wholeheartedly. The president immediately pressed for a 30 percent reduction in federal taxes, 10 percent in each of the next three years. Dismissing claims that this would produce huge federal deficits, the White House predicted that reductions gained from cutting wasteful programs, and the additional revenues generated by renewed economic growth, would guard against any serious deficit. Lobbying intensely and skillfully with sympathetic Democrats, who had supported limited tax reductions during Carter's presidency, and suspicious old-style Republicans, who were devoted to balanced budgets, Reagan pushed a less ambitious tax-reduction plan through Congress in 1981. He coupled this with a budget bill that aimed at cutting expenditures for social programs.

In the short run, "Reaganomics" appeared to produce a bust rather than a boom. A severe economic downturn in 1981 and 1982, one of the worst since the Great Depression of the 1930s, sent economic indicators and Reagan's approval rating, which reached a low of 35 percent, hurtling downward. Republican losses in the off-year 1982 elections cut into the gains of 1980.

Then, the U.S. economy dramatically rebounded and entered a vibrant period of non-inflationary growth that lasted, without any interruption, until the end of the 1980s. According to one study, the economy added nearly 17 million new jobs; figures on real income, after having declined throughout the 1970s, began to rise; and inflation dropped from double digits to around 2 percent. Although unemployment figures did not fall as sharply, Reagan's supporters would come to talk about a "Reagan Revolution."

This economic resurgence and its precise causes, however, proved controversial. Fiscal conservatives often complained that Reagan failed to match tax cuts to budget reductions, ballooning the U.S. deficit right along with production figures. Reagan constantly inveighed against deficits and "big spenders," but his eight years in Washington, even after he once again displayed his pragmatism by agreeing to a rollback of the initial tax reduction package, saw annual deficits triple to nearly $300 billion. Reagan's own financial guru, David Stockman, later dismissed supply-side economics as more of a rhetorical turn than a prescription for policy. To finance its deficit spending, the United States borrowed abroad and piled up the largest foreign debt in the world. Any Reagan Revolution, critics often charged, brought recovery for the 1980s by courting a long-term budget crisis for the 1990s.

Other economic observers, focusing on the crucial issue of inflation, argued that the policies of the Federal Reserve Board (FRB) under Paul Volcker, a Carter appointee, counted for more than anything done by the White House. By steadfastly keeping interest rates high and the money supply low, from this perspective, Volcker's FRB spearheaded the economic boom through its monetary moves.

© Eve Arnold/Magnum Photos, Inc.

Selling off the Farm　Hard economic times during the early 1980s forced the liquidation of many small, family-run farms. Here, neighbors gather at a farm where everything, including a well-used pitchfork, headed to the auction block.

Moreover, a number of critics, especially from Democratic Party ranks, denounced the policies of both the Reagan administration and the FRB as unfair. Partisans of the Reagan Revolution always argued that its effects would ultimately "trickle down" and benefit everyone. In a battle of metaphors, however, its detractors countered that too many people continued to fall through the holes of Reagan's "Swiss-cheese" economy. Reagan's critics noted that farmers in the Midwest, who were holding high-interest loans from the inflation-ridden 1970s, watched falling crop prices hamper their ability to service their debt loads during the early 1980s. A wave of mortgage foreclosures, reminiscent of the 1930s, hit the farm states, and the ripple effect washed over the always vulnerable economies of nearby towns. In urban areas, many of the jobs created during the boom of the 1980s came in the service sector and offered low wages and, at best, meager fringe benefits. The minimum wage, when adjusted for inflation, declined in value throughout the 1980s.

The surge of the Reagan era, then, brought prosperity to many, upward mobility for some, and growing distress for others. If critics desired to emphasize low-wage jobs in the service sector, the so-called McJobs (as at McDonald's and other fast-food outlets), the celebrants of the Reagan Revolution could reply by highlighting the many more well-paid ones for managers and technicians in fields such as electronics and computers. People with solid educational backgrounds and marketable skills generally made significant economic gains during the 1980s.

The number of African American families earning a solid middle-class income, for example, more than doubled between 1970 and 1990. A greater percentage of black women and men completed college than ever before, with black women earning postsecondary degrees at a higher percentage rate than either black men or women of European descent. African American college graduates could expect incomes comparable to those of their white classmates, partly as a result of the Reagan administration's reluctance to overturn affirmative-action hiring plans put in place by the Nixon and Carter administrations. More African American professionals could afford to live in gentrified urban neighborhoods or in suburban areas such as Dekalb County, Georgia. The Reagan administration hailed people, such as Clarence Thomas, who headed the EEOC, as evidence that blacks could not only thrive as Republicans but take pride in being "black conservatives."

The situation looked very different, however, for people who remained persistently un- or underemployed, especially those who lived in declining urban centers or older suburbs. As the construction crews moved in to rehabilitate their urban neighborhood, some financially embattled African American homeowners lost their houses at fire-sale prices. At the end of the 1980s, one-third of all African American families lived in poverty, and the number with an annual income of less than $15,000 per year had doubled since 1970. In inner cities, fewer than half of African American children were completing high school, and more than 60 percent were unemployed. The gap between the very well-off and what one prominent sociologist called the "truly disadvantaged" widened during the 1980s.

Cutting Regulations and Welfare Measures

Meanwhile, Reagan pursued his second major goal: cutting back on the federal regulatory structure. A movement to decrease federal regulations had already taken hold before Reagan ever reached Washington. An early Reagan move, defying the elaborate structure of federal labor law and summarily firing the nation's air traffic controllers, after their union refused to halt a nationwide strike, immediately gladdened conservatives.

Reagan had entered office promising to break OPEC's oil monopoly by eliminating regulations that discouraged development of new sources of supply. Ignoring calls to decrease U.S. dependence on fossil fuels by promotion of renewable sources, the Reagan administration pursued a "cheap oil" policy. The tapping of new oil fields at home and abroad during the 1980s, together with rivalries among OPEC's members, weakened the cartel's hold on the world market and reduced the relative cost of energy.

To encourage conservative interpretations of existing regulatory measures, the Reagan administration worked to place a New Right stamp on the federal legal system. Almost immediately, Reagan nominated a Supreme Court justice, Sandra Day O'Connor (the first woman to sit on the Court), who initially appeared to be a staunch conservative. With the Republican Party controlling the U.S. Senate until 1986, Reagan enjoyed a relatively free hand naming prominent conservative jurists, such as Robert Bork and Antonin Scalia, to lower federal courts. The Senate Judiciary Committee, chaired by Strom Thurmond of South Carolina, gained a reputation for streamlining the confirmation process for White House-favored nominees. An informal network of conservative professors and law students, which had become a feature of every major law school during the 1970s, helped identify right-of-center lawyers for possible appointment to the federal bench. It selected a large number of Catholic jurists, many of whom seemed strong social conservatives. Although the Reagan administration appointed about the same number of women as had that of Jimmy Carter, it found few African American nominees.

This effort at judicial recruitment joined a larger Reagan-era effort to modify, if not overrule, the Warren-era Supreme Court rulings that had consistently supported rights claims. Civil libertarians soon faced the prospect of the federal courts becoming less hospitable to legal arguments made by criminal defendants, labor unions, and political dissenters. By 1990, because of retirements, about half of all federal judges had reached the bench during Ronald Reagan's presidency. His administration also sought out avowedly conservative lawyers for nonjudicial appointments. It staffed the Reagan justice department with young attorneys, such as John Roberts and Samuel Alito, who expressed a desire to assist conservative judges whittle back Warren-era judicial precedents.

On environmental issues, Reagan appointed James Watt, an outspoken critic of governmental regulation, as his first secretary of the interior. Born in Wyoming, Watt supported the so-called sage-brush rebellion, in which entrepreneurs from the Far West demanded fewer governmental restrictions on the use of public lands, especially if they could be used for grazing or tapped for mining and oil-drilling operations. Many people living in the timber-rich states of the Pacific Northwest opposed, with equal vigor, efforts to protect endangered species, such as rare bird populations, if regulations interfered with lumber-related opportunities. Reagan's first two appointees to the Department of Energy actually proposed eliminating the cabinet office they headed—an idea that Congress blocked. Through its appointments to both the interior and energy departments, the

White House achieved some relaxation of the enforcement of safety and environmental regulations.

Overall, however, the Reagan administration pruned rather than clear-cut the regulatory forest. Despite its efforts, most conservatives expressed some disappointment that the Reagan administration had not rolled back even more federal regulations.

Conservatives also pressed the Reagan administration to decrease more drastically its funding for various kinds of public-benefit programs, particularly AFDC. These reductions in food stamps and other programs increased poverty rates and disproportionately affected female-headed households and children. By the end of the 1980s, one of every five children was being raised in a household whose total income fell below the official poverty line.

Reagan, though, steadfastly rejected any suggestion of completely eliminating the basic set of New Deal programs that he called a "social safety net," and he consistently refused to push ideas for revising the popular Social Security program. During the 1970s, Congress had indexed Social Security payments, mandating they would automatically increase along with the rate of inflation. While supporting this practice, the Reagan White House also agreed to congressional legislation raising the payroll taxes for both Social Security and Medicare. Larger Social Security checks, along with continued Medicare benefits, enabled millions of Americans over the age of 65 to do relatively well during the Reagan years. By the end of Reagan's two-term presidency, what the federal government spent on social-welfare programs roughly equaled the amount it had laid out when he entered office.

Despite sometimes sharp debate, especially over the soaring federal deficit and widening income and wealth gaps, Reagan became steadily more popular than he had been in 1980. His genial optimism seemed unshakable. He even appeared to rebound quickly—although close observers noted a perceptible decline in his energies and ability to concentrate—after being shot by a would-be assassin in March 1981. No matter what problems beset other members of his administration, criticism never stuck to Reagan, whom one frustrated Democrat dubbed the "Teflon president."

Routing the Democrats, 1984

Still, many traditional Democrats continued to underestimate Reagan's appeal—a miscalculation that doomed their party's 1984 presidential effort. Walter Mondale, Jimmy Carter's former vice president, ran on a platform that seemed to offer something for nearly everyone. It called for "the eradication of discrimination in all aspects of American life" and for an expansion of national social-welfare programs. Mondale bravely called for higher taxes, while providing few details about from where the revenue might come and to whom it might be channeled. In addition, he chose as his running mate Representative Geraldine Ferraro of New York, the first woman to stand for president or vice president on a major party ticket.

Republican campaign ads—often framed by the slogan "It's Morning Again in America"—portrayed a glowing landscape of bustling small towns and lush farmlands. They attacked Mondale's support from labor unions and civil-rights groups, along with his selection of Ferraro, as a vestige of the "old politics" of "special interests." They labeled his promise to raise taxes as a return to the "wasteful" policies popularly associated with stagflation and the misery index during the 1970s. The 1984 presidential election ended with Mondale carrying only his home state of Minnesota and the District of Columbia.

Reagan's Second Term

Conservatives would eventually almost unanimously hail Ronald Reagan as a giant of their movement, but not during his second term. Then, many activists on the New Right looked balefully at his domestic record, especially on social issues such as abortion and school prayer. His record on judicial politics drew additional criticism. The 1986 resignation of Warren Burger allowed Reagan to elevate William Rehnquist to the position of chief justice and appoint Antonin Scalia, an even more outspoken conservative, to replace Rehnquist as an associate justice. After the 1986 off-year elections gave the Democrats control of the Senate again, however, this body rejected Reagan's 1987 nomination of Robert Bork, a legal and cultural conservative who had become a particular favorite of the New Right, to the High Court.

Bork's lengthy record of legal opinions and scholarly articles, his opponents argued, clearly showed a jurist whose views fell outside the "legal mainstream." To them, Bork not only seemed out of step on current issues such as abortion rights but apparently on settled ones such as the constitutional validity of the 1954 desegregation decision in *Brown*. Some angry conservatives blamed Reagan for not expending his political capital on behalf of his nominee, thereby allowing Democrats and a few apostate Republicans to "Bork" him with a barrage of negative attacks. The battle over the Bork nomination provided a model for the brass-knuckles politics, from both parties, that would become more prevalent during the years that followed.

Meanwhile, many from the Religious Right chafed at what they considered Reagan's halfhearted support of their crusades against abortion and in favor of sectarian prayer in public schools. Many complained that the president and his wife Nancy, who apparently advised on many sociocultural issues, brought some of Tinsel Town's toleration for personal differences, as well as Hollywood-style glamour, with them to Washington. Religious conservatives became increasingly determined to find Republican candidates who would pledge unwavering support for their values.

Although economic growth continued, corruption and mismanagement in the financial industry increasingly loomed as toxic by-products of Reaganomics. The deregulation of financial institutions, supported by Democrats and Republicans alike, had allowed savings and loan (S&L) institutions to assume more risky investments, especially in real estate, using depositors' funds. By 1985, alarmed prognosticators foresaw an impending S&L meltdown, but both the Reagan administration and most members of Congress, hoping to duck the matter until after the 1988 election, ignored obvious warning signs.

Not until 1989 would Congress adopt a bailout plan. It saved some tottering S&Ls and transferred assets from already-failed institutions to still-solvent ones. The arrangement proved astronomically expensive, and taxpayers footed the bill. Meanwhile, the process by

THE FIRST MOVIE-STAR PRESIDENT

Ronald Reagan began his presidency in Hollywood. The political career of the "great communicator" built on, rather than broke away from, his days in the entertainment industry. His media advisers could count on directing a seasoned professional. Reagan always knew where to stand, how to deliver lines effectively, how to convey emotions through both body language and dialogue, and when to melt into the background so that other players in the cast of his presidency might carry a crucial scene.

Several of Reagan's actual movies provided rehearsals for roles he would play in the White House. Initially, Reagan's opponents had predicted that his old film parts, particularly in *Bedtime for Bonzo* (1947), in which he co-starred with a chimpanzee, would become political liabilities. Instead of disavowing his days in Hollywood, Reagan accentuated his fluency with film-related imagery. His efforts to cheer on the nation during the 1980s consciously invoked his favorite film role, that of the 1920s Notre Dame football star, George Gipp, whom Reagan played in *Knute Rockne, All American*

(1940). Similarly, when tilting with a Democratic-controlled Congress over tax policy, Reagan invoked Clint Eastwood's famous screen character "Dirty Harry," promising to shoot down any tax increase. "Go ahead, make my day," he taunted. On another occasion, he cited *Rambo* (1982), an action thriller set in post-1975 Vietnam, as a possible blueprint for dealing with countries that had seized U.S. hostages. As he freely drew from Hollywood motion pictures, Reagan occasionally seemed unable to separate "reel" from "real" life. During one session with reporters, he referred to his own dog as "Lassie," the canine performer who had been Reagan's Hollywood contemporary during the 1940s and 1950s.

Life in Hollywood also provided a prologue to President Reagan's conservative policies. Early in his film career, Reagan appeared in four films as the same character, a government agent named "Brass Bancroft." In these B-grade thrillers, Reagan developed an image that he later deployed in politics: an action-oriented character who could quickly distinguish (good) friends from (evil) foes. *Murder in the Air* (1940), one of the Brass Bancroft

which large, well-connected commercial banks purchased the remaining assets of bankrupt S&Ls at bargain-basement prices reeked of corruption and scandal. As a result of the S&L debacle of the 1980s, many people lost at least a portion of their savings, and the banking industry went through a sudden, unplanned consolidation.

Meanwhile, the White House and Congress claimed to have boldly addressed several other domestic issues. First, the Tax Reform Act of 1986 simultaneously lowered the IRS bill of some and raised that of others, with only accountants and tax attorneys being able to determine this complex measure's precise impact on specific individuals and groups. It thus utterly failed to satisfy a major aim of most people: greater simplicity in the tax code. Second, in the 1985 Gramm-Rudman-Hollings Act Congress set a series of targets designed to achieve a balanced federal budget by 1991. (Neither Congress nor the White House, however, seemed to take this goal very seriously, and the government deficit continued to soar.)

Ronald Reagan as the "Gipper" in *Knute Rockne, All American*.

Second World War, but he served long hours as an Army Air Corps officer, making movies in support of the war effort. He appeared in several films, such as *For God and Country* (1943), and more often provided upbeat voiceovers, once even sharing a soundtrack with President Franklin Roosevelt. He also starred, on loan from the Air Corps, in *This Is the Army* (1943), one of the most successful of wartime Hollywood's military-oriented musicals. After the war, Reagan increasingly directed his energies toward Cold War politics in the film capital. His tenure as the anticommunist president of the Screen Actors Guild—and as a secret FBI informant—likely speeded his conversion from New Deal Democrat to right-leaning Republican. In his final onscreen roles, Reagan usually portrayed the kind of independent, rugged individualist—often in westerns such as *Law and Order* (1953)—whom he would later lionize in his political speeches.

Nancy Reagan, who co-starred with her spouse in *Hellcats of the Navy* (1957) and later as the nation's First Lady, offered her close-up view of the relationship between Reagan the actor and Reagan the politician: "There are not two Ronald Reagans." During the 1980s, the cultures of Hollywood and Washington, D.C. became embodied in the same character, Ronald Wilson Reagan.

movies, even featured a science-fiction-style "death ray" that resembled SDI (Star Wars) armaments that President Reagan would champion more than 40 years later.

Subsequent film roles refined his Hollywood image. Poor eyesight kept Reagan out of combat during the

Finally, Congress passed the Family Support Act of 1988. Largely the work of Daniel Patrick Moynihan (then a Democratic senator from New York), it encouraged states to inaugurate work-training programs and to begin moving people, including mothers receiving AFDC payments, off welfare rolls. Although the measure actually contributed to *raising* federal welfare costs, a pragmatically conservative President Reagan ignored his more ideologically conservative advisers and signed the measure.

Despite complaints from some on the New Right about the White House's often lackadaisical interest in issues such as abortion, the Reagan administration helped change the nation's political vocabulary to the benefit of the larger conservative movement. "Democratic Party programs," to a degree unthinkable in Lyndon Johnson's time, no longer suggested governmental initiatives to stimulate the economy, promote greater equality, and advance liberty for all. Instead, Republicans made "liberal Democrat" a code word for someone devoted to ill-considered social experiments, devised by bureaucrats from a bloated federal government, which gouged hardworking people and squandered their dollars. The term "conservative," as used by New Right Republicans, was coming to stand for economic growth through the curtailment of governmental power; equal treatment for all, rather than "special entitlements" for some; and reverence for traditional sociocultural values. The once-dominant Democratic coalition, forged during the New Deal era, seemed to confront an uncertain future.

Renewing the Cold War

Reagan had campaigned, between 1977 and 1980, on a pledge to reassert U.S. power on the global stage and thus reverse what he characterized as Jimmy Carter's failure to protect national security. Harkening back to the Vietnam War era, Reagan suggested that the U.S. effort had been a "noble cause" and that politicians had refused to allow the Pentagon to win. Renewing the moralistic rhetoric of the early Cold War era and jettisoning the realism of Henry Kissinger, Reagan promised to confront the Soviets with a massively rearmed United States and, soon, denounced the USSR as an "evil empire."

The Defense Buildup

Although tax cuts were reducing federal revenues, the Reagan administration pressed for dramatic increases in military spending. Its initial budget called for increasing military expenditures nearly 30 percent in four years. It allowed the Pentagon to enlarge the Navy and expand strategic nuclear forces, deploying additional missiles throughout Western Europe. At the height of Reagan's military buildup, which contributed significantly to budget deficits, the Pentagon was purchasing about 20 percent of the nation's manufacturing output.

In 1983, Reagan suggested perhaps the most ambitious, and expensive, military system in history. He proposed an elaborate defense shield that would protect the United States against any incoming missiles. Beginning as a vague hope, this **"Strategic Defense Initiative" (SDI)**, soon could claim its own Pentagon agency, which initially sought $26 billion, over five years, just in research costs.

Controversy immediately swirled around SDI. Skeptics ridiculed it as something out of the movie *Star Wars*. Budget analysts trained in cost-benefit calculations shuddered at its astronomical costs, especially after most scientists dismissed the plan as impossible to implement effectively. Reagan succeeded in launching, however, a national security initiative that subsequent GOP leaders would loyally follow: faith in the feasibility of constructing, rather than simply imagining "out in the blue," a defensive shield that would eliminate any nuclear threat to the United States. Some in Reagan's administration also suggested that, as the Soviet Union struggled to compete with the United States in the accelerating arms race, the increased burden on the USSR's fragile economy could trigger an economic-political meltdown behind the Iron Curtain. Once proposed, SDI altered strategic debates at home and arms talks with the Soviet Union.

Reagan's foreign-policy agenda also included numerous nonmilitary initiatives. In a new "informational" offensive, the administration funded conservative groups around the world and established Radio Martí, a Florida-based station beamed at Cuba and aimed at discrediting Fidel Castro's communist government. When the Reagan administration and its allies in Congress detected an anti-American tilt in **UNESCO** programs, they simply cut off U.S. contributions that went to fund this UN agency. In addition, the White House championed the benefits of a free and open international marketplace, pressing other nations to minimize tariffs and restrictions on foreign investment. Its "Caribbean Basin Initiative," for example, rewarded with U.S. aid small nations in the Caribbean region that adhered to free-market principles.

The CIA, under the aggressive leadership of Reagan-appointee William Casey, stepped up its covert activities. Some became so obvious they hardly qualified as covert. It seemed no secret, for instance, that the United States was sending aid to anticommunist forces in Afghanistan, many of them radical Islamic fundamentalist groups, and to the opponents of the *Sandinista* government in Nicaragua, the ***contras.***

Deploying Military Power

In renewing the global Cold War, Reagan promised military support to "democratic" revolutions anywhere. This move seemed designed to contain, or even roll back, the Soviet Union's sphere of influence in Third World areas. Reagan's neoconservative ambassador to the UN, Jeane Kirkpatrick, famously wrote that "democratic" forces included almost any movement, no matter how autocratic, committed to opposing communism. The United States thus funded opposition forces in many countries aligned with the Soviet Union. In addition to Afghanistan and Nicaragua, these nations included Ethiopia, Angola, South Yemen, El Salvador, Guatemala, and Grenada. Reagan sometimes called the participants in such anticommunist insurgencies "freedom fighters," although some displayed no visible commitment to such values.

The Reagan administration, on occasion, directly deployed U.S. military power, initially in southern Lebanon in 1982. Here, Israeli troops faced off against Islamic groups supported by Syria and Iran. Alarmed by radical Islamic influence within Lebanon, the Reagan administration convinced Israel to withdraw and sent 1,600 U.S. marines as part of an international "peacekeeping force" to restore stability. Islamic militias, however, turned against the U.S. forces. After a massive truck bomb attack against a military compound killed 241 U.S. troops, mostly marines, in April 1983, a majority in the Reagan administration, overriding dissenting opinions, decided to end this ill-defined undertaking. In February 1984, Reagan ordered the withdrawal of U.S. troops and disengaged from Lebanon.

Meanwhile, another military intervention accomplished its goal. In October 1983, Reagan sent 2,000 U.S. troops to the tiny Caribbean island of Grenada, where a socialist leader appeared to be tilting ever closer to Castro's Cuba. After a brief military operation, which analysts subsequently judged to have been rather ineptly planned and executed, U.S. troops swept aside Grenada's left-leaning government and installed one friendlier to U.S. interests.

Buoyed by events in Grenada, some in the Reagan administration fixed their sights on Nicaragua. Here, the Marxist-leaning *Sandinista* government, seeking to break Nicaragua's historic dependence on the United States, became the target. The Reagan administration marshaled economic pressure, mounted an anti-*Sandinista* informational campaign, and pledged greater military and financial assistance to the *contras*. These early initiatives stirred considerable controversy. Soon, charges by human-rights groups against the *contras*, which highlighted evidence of their corruption and brutal tactics, produced further political discord at home and criticism around the world. Finally, Democrats in Congress successfully pressed to bar additional military aid to the *contras*, a group the president had once compared to America's own "Founding Fathers." Although his administration encouraged wealthy U.S. conservatives and friendly foreign governments to donate money to the *contra* cause, Reagan rebuffed calls to send U.S. troops to Nicaragua.

Violence continued to escalate, meanwhile, throughout the Middle East. As the Israeli-Palestinian conflict remained unresolved and Israel continued its presence in Lebanon, militant Islamic groups increased attacks against Israel and Western powers. Bombings and kidnappings of Westerners became more frequent. Seeing Libya's Muammar al-Qaddafi and Iranian leaders encouraging such activities, the White House attempted, during the spring of 1986, what looked like a long-range assassination attempt against a foreign leader, an action outlawed by Congress. The United States launched an air strike against Qaddafi's personal compound. It killed his young daughter, but Qaddafi and his government survived. Polls suggested broad support at home for using strong measures against nations that sponsored terrorism and those who aided and abetted hostage taking.

The Iran-Contra Controversy

During the 1980 campaign, Reagan had portrayed the hostages held in Iran as tangible symbols of how weak the United States had become under Jimmy Carter's leadership. When Iranian-backed groups continued to kidnap Americans during Reagan's own presidency, members of his administration began seeking clandestine ways to recover hostages. In November 1986, a small Lebanese magazine reported that the Reagan administration was selling arms to Iran in order to secure the release of Americans being held hostage by militants who looked to Iran's Islamic Republic for inspiration and, perhaps, direction. These alleged deals seemingly violated the Reagan administration's own pledges against selling arms to Iran or rewarding hostage-taking by negotiating for the release of captives.

As Congress began to investigate, the story became even more bizarre. The Reagan administration revealed that it had not only sold arms to Iran but had funneled profits from these back-channel deals to the *contra* forces in Nicaragua, thereby circumventing the congressional ban on U.S. military aid for the controversial anti-*Sandinista* forces. Lieutenant Colonel Oliver North, an aide in the office of the national security adviser, directed the effort, working with international arms dealers and private go-betweens. North's covert machinations seemingly violated both the stated policy of the White House and the will of Congress.

Despite its colorful cast of characters, evidence of illegality, and apparent zaniness, the **"Iran-*contra* affair"** played far less visibly in popular political culture than had the earlier Watergate scandal. Oliver North destroyed so many documents and left so many false paper trails that even congressional investigators struggled to compile a simple narrative of his activities. In contrast to Richard Nixon, Ronald Reagan stepped forward and testified, through a deposition, asserting he could not recall any details about either the release of hostages or the funding of the *contras*. His management and oversight skills might deserve criticism, Reagan admitted, but he had never intended to break any laws or presidential promise. Vice President George H. W. Bush, whom a special independent prosecutor personally considered linked to some of North's machinations, also claimed ignorance.

Unable to uncover evidence directly implicating the president or vice president, federal prosecutors pursued others. They secured felony convictions, for offenses that included falsifying documents and lying to Congress, against North and several others in Reagan's administration, but appellate courts later overturned these verdicts on procedural grounds. Finally, in 1992, just a few days before the end of his presidency, George H. W. Bush would pardon six former Reagan-era officials connected to the Iran-*contra* controversy.

The Beginning of the End of the Cold War

After beginning with a renewal of Cold War confrontations, Reagan's presidency ended with a sudden thaw in U.S.–Soviet relations. The economic cost of superpower rivalry was burdening both nations. Moreover, political change swept the Soviet Union and eliminated reasons for continued confrontation.

Mikhail Gorbachev, who became general secretary of the Communist Party in 1985, promised a new style of Soviet leadership. He understood that his isolated country faced economic stagnation and environmental problems brought on by decades of poorly planned industrial development. To redirect his nation's course, he withdrew Soviet troops from Afghanistan, reduced economic commitments to Cuba and Nicaragua, proclaimed a policy of **glasnost** ("openness"), and began to implement **perestroika** ("economic liberalization") at home. Recognizing Gorbachev as a Soviet leader with whom he could deal, Reagan seemed reenergized and worked diligently to forge good relations with the person whom U.S. media often called "Gorby."

Gorbachev's policies gained him acclaim throughout the West. Summit meetings with the United States yielded breakthroughs in arms control. At Reykjavik, Iceland, in October 1986, President Reagan shocked both Gorbachev and his own advisers by proposing a wholesale ban on nuclear weapons. Although negotiations at Reykjavik stumbled over Soviet insistence that the United States abandon SDI, Gorbachev later dropped that condition. Finally, in December 1987, Reagan and Gorbachev signed a major arms treaty that reduced each nation's supply of intermediate-range missiles and allowed for on-site verification, which the Soviets had never before permitted. The next year, Gorbachev scrapped the policy that forbade nations under Soviet influence from renouncing communism. In effect, he declared an end to the Cold War. Within the next few years, the Soviet sphere of influence— and the Soviet Union itself—would cease to exist. Ronald Reagan's final presidential triumph, according to his admirers, was leading the United States to victory in the Cold War.

Reagan's personal imprint on the 1980s, the "Reagan era," has emerged as a mixed one. Even before Reagan sought the presidency and through much of his time in Washington, many people seemed to judge him, apart from his role as "the great communicator," in light of the rather low expectations he had long engendered. Many early accounts of his administration generally adopted an even harsher frame. Most described a remarkably passive, often detached president—the kind of chief executive Reagan admitted to having been while some of his national security advisers were hatching the Iran-*contra* scheme.

After the mid-1990s, as the effects of Alzheimer's kept Reagan out of the public eye, however, other memoirists and biographers offered a more laudatory view. In addition to painting portraits of a public leader who could inspire by personal example, their works expanded on Reagan's own Farewell Address. When leaving office in 1989, Reagan had judged his two greatest accomplishments to have been "economic recovery" and "the recovery of our morale. America is respected again in the world and looked to for leadership."

The First Bush Presidency (1989–1993)

Focus Question
What forces and events contributed to the end of the Cold War? How did the Cold War's end affect U.S. foreign policy?

The Reagan presidency, particularly its initatives in foreign policy, boosted the 1988 presidential prospects of Reagan's heir-apparent, his own vice president, George Herbert Walker Bush. Bush easily secured the Republican nomination.

The Election of 1988

Born into a wealthy Republican family and educated at Yale, Bush had prospered in the Texas oil business, adopted Houston as his home, served in the U.S. House of Representatives, and headed the CIA. To court the New Right, which was decidedly lukewarm to his candidacy, Bush chose Senator J. Danforth (Dan) Quayle, a youthful conservative from Indiana who vaguely resembled the movie star Robert Redford, as a running mate. Quayle, already considered a better golfer than a legislator by most Senate colleagues, quickly acquired a reputation, especially among comedians who specialized in political humor, for off-the-wall comments about issues whose nuances and contexts he apparently failed to grasp.

Governor Michael Dukakis of Massachusetts emerged as the Democratic presidential candidate. After reevaluating Walter Mondale's disastrous effort of 1984 and crediting early polls showing him defeating Bush, Dukakis avoided talk of new domestic programs and higher taxes. Apparently short on larger ideas of any kind, Dukakis engendered little enthusiasm when promising to bring competence and honesty to a White House recently marked by the Iran-*contra* affair. Later, Dukakis seemed genuinely adrift when the GOP launched a series of negative attacks, reminiscent of the infamous LBJ daisy ad of 1964, on his character and gubernatorial record.

Bush emerged the winner, but Democrats retained control of both houses of Congress. Exit polls suggested that neither Bush nor Dukakis thrilled large numbers of potential voters, and the turnout recorded in November seemed to confirm this. It was the lowest, percentage wise, for any national election since 1924.

Once in the White House, Bush began losing crucial support. He angered many New Right Republicans by agreeing to an increase in the minimum wage and by failing to veto a seemingly noncontroversial civil-rights measure, which critics from the New Right charged with establishing "quotas" for the "preferential hiring" of women and people of color. Most importantly, Bush broke a pledge, "no new taxes," on which most conservatives had come to judge his worthiness as Reagan's successor. After the White House and congressional Democrats agreed to an "upward revision" in tax rates, in hopes of dealing with the still-rising federal deficit, activists on the New Right bitterly denounced this accord as one that raised taxes by another name.

Meanwhile, the Democratic-controlled Congress and the Republican-occupied White House deadlocked over how to address several key domestic issues. These included reorganization of the health care and the social-welfare systems. Worse for the president's political future, the economic growth of the Reagan years began to slow, while the budget deficit continued to grow. George H. W. Bush's chances for a second term seemed to depend on his record in foreign, rather than domestic, policy.

The End of the Cold War

During the first Bush presidency, communist states began toppling as if dominoes. In 1989, Poland's anticommunist labor movement, Solidarity, sparked the ouster of the pro-Soviet regime. The pro-Moscow government in East Germany fell in November 1989, and both West and East Germans hacked down the Berlin Wall and, then, began the difficult process of building a reunified Germany. Popular movements similarly forced out communist governments throughout Eastern Europe. Yugoslavia quickly disintegrated, and warfare ensued as rival ethnic groups re-created separate states in Slovenia, Serbia, Bosnia, and Croatia. In the Baltic region, Latvia, Lithuania, and Estonia, all of which had been under Soviet control since the Second World War, declared their independence.

Most dramatically, the major provinces that had anchored the Soviet Union assumed self-government. The president of the new state of Russia, Boris Yeltsin, put down a coup by hard-line communists in August 1991, and he soon solidified his political position. In December 1991, Yeltsin brokered a plan to abolish the Soviet Union and to replace it with 11 separate republics, loosely joined in a commonwealth arrangement. **(See Map 30.2, Collapse of the Soviet Bloc, in the color insert following page 1248.)**

In response, the Bush administration set about redefining U.S. national security in a post–Cold War era. The collapse of the Soviet Union weakened support for the leftist insurgencies in Central America that had so worried many members of the Reagan administration. Nicaraguans voted out the *Sandinistas*, who became just another faction, rather than a revolutionary movement, in a multiparty political system. The Pentagon pondered

Berlin Wall, 1989 Berliners celebrated the end of the Cold War by chiseling away at the Berlin Wall, which the communist East German state had erected in 1962 to prevent the flow of refugees to West Berlin. Pieces of the Berlin Wall became coveted symbols of the fall of communism.

new military missions, imagining rapid, sharply targeted strikes by specially trained forces rather than lengthy, conventional campaigns. The U.S. armed forces might even serve in the "war against drugs," an effort that George H. W. Bush had suggested during his 1988 presidential campaign.

Fighting the drug menace provided a major justification for toppling General Manuel Noriega, the dictatorial president of Panama. Long suspected of being deeply involved in the drug trade, Noriega had continued ruling Panama despite a U.S. indictment against him for international narcotics trafficking, secured earlier by the Reagan administration.

Confronting Noriega posed a potentially embarrassing problem for the Bush administration. The anticommunist general had been recruited as a CIA "asset" during the mid-1970s, when Bush had headed the Agency. Nevertheless, the White House decided the United States needed a friendly, stable, and more competent government in Panama when it completed the transfer of the Panama Canal to Panamanian sovereignty in 2000. Bush decided to topple the mercurial Noriega in "Operation Just Cause." Broadcast live on television, U.S. Marines landed in Panama in December 1989, and they laid siege to the president's headquarters, surrounding it with U.S. troops and round-the-clock ear-splitting rock music. Noriega soon surrendered, faced successful extradition to Florida, and went to prison after a 1992 conviction for trafficking in cocaine.

The Panamanian operation carried major implications. Unilaterally deposing the leader of a foreign government by U.S. military action seemingly raised thorny questions of international law, but this effort, which involved 25,000 U.S. troops and few casualties, provided a new model for post–Cold War strategy. The Pentagon firmed up its plans for creating highly mobile, rapid deployment forces that could undertake similar missions. A partial test of its new strategy came during the Persian Gulf War of 1991.

The Persian Gulf War

On August 2, 1990, Iraq's dictator Saddam Hussein ordered his troops to occupy the neighboring oil-rich emirate of Kuwait. Having been caught off guard about Kuwait, U.S. intelligence analysts now warned that Iraq's next target might be Saudi Arabia, the largest oil exporter in the Middle East and a longtime U.S. ally.

Moving swiftly, President George H. W. Bush orchestrated a multilateral, international response. Four days after Iraq's invasion of Kuwait, he launched "Operation Desert Shield" by sending several hundred thousand U.S. troops to Saudi Arabia. Bush convinced the Saudi government, with which he enjoyed close personal ties, to set aside concerns among some Islamic fundamentalists, including a wealthy businessman named Osama bin Laden, about allowing Western troops on sacred Islamic soil. Saudi Arabia's ruling family finally decided it feared Saddam Hussein more than the Islamic outcry against a U.S. military presence. After consulting with European leaders, Bush approached the UN, which denounced Iraqi aggression, ordered economic sanctions against Iraq, and authorized the United States to lead an international force to Kuwait if Saddam Hussein's troops did not immediately withdraw.

Following the advice of his military strategists, particularly General Colin Powell, Bush then assembled a massive coalition force. Ultimately, it included nearly 500,000 troops from the United States and some 200,000 from other countries. Bush claimed a moral obligation to rescue Kuwait, but his policy makers also spoke frankly about the economic threat that Hussein's aggression posed for the oil-dependent economies of the United States and its allies. These arguments persuaded Congress, after heated debate in the Senate, to approve a resolution backing the use of force.

In mid-January 1991, coalition planes attacked Iraqi targets. After a relatively brief but devastating aerial bombardment, General Norman Schwarzkopf directed a February ground offensive against Iraqi forces. Coalition troops, enjoying air supremacy, decimated Saddam Hussein's armies in a matter of days. U.S. casualties were relatively light (148 deaths in battle). Estimates of Iraqi military casualties, in stark contrast, ranged from 25,000 to 100,000 deaths. Although the entire conflict had lasted scarcely six weeks, it took an enormous toll on highways, bridges, communications, and other infrastructure facilities in both Iraq and Kuwait.

In a decision that aroused dissent from neoconservatives within his own administration, Bush stopped short of ousting Saddam Hussein. The UN had never approved such a step, and U.S. military planners worried about being able to control a post-Saddam Iraq. Instead, the Bush administration, backed by the UN, maintained its economic pressure against Saddam Hussein's regime and ordered the dismantling of its programs for nuclear and biological warfare. In addition, U.S. planes enforced "no-fly" zones over northern and southern Iraq to help protect the Kurds and, less successfully, Shi'a Muslims from continued persecution by Saddam Hussein. The Persian Gulf War temporarily boosted George H. W. Bush's popularity.

Bush's direction of economic foreign policy, although less visible than his leadership during the Iraq war, became of considerable importance. The president pressed, for instance, measures that would assist international economic integration. During the mid-1980s, huge debts owed by Third World nations to U.S. institutions had threatened the international banking system, but most of these obligations had been renegotiated by the early 1990s. Market-based economies, which replaced centrally planned ones, began to emerge in the former communist states; Western Europe moved toward economic integration; and most nations of the Pacific Rim experienced steady economic growth. The president supported (but could not obtain congressional passage of) a North American Free Trade Agreement (NAFTA), which proposed eliminating tariff barriers and joining Canada, the United States, and Mexico together in the largest free-market zone in the world.

When Bush ran for reelection in 1992, however, most potential voters judged even his administration's record on foreign affairs as something of a muddle. The White House had organized an international coalition against Iraq, constructively assisted post–Cold War Russia and Eastern Europe, and embraced global economic integration. On other issues, though, the Bush administration seemed less decisive. The United States remained on the sidelines as full-scale warfare erupted among the states of the former Yugoslavia, with Serbs launching a brutal campaign of territorial aggrandizement and "ethnic cleansing" against Bosnian Muslims. In Africa, after a severe famine wracked Somalia, Bush ordered U.S. troops to secure supply lines for humanitarian aid, but popular opinion in the United States remained wary of this mission in a country without a stable government. After the longtime goal of containing the Soviet Union became irrelevant, George H. W. Bush never succeeded in effectively articulating a new overall vision to guide policy.

The Election of 1992

The inability to portray coherence in either his domestic or foreign policies threatened Bush's reelection. In response, the White House made a series of concessions to the New Right. Vice President Dan Quayle, although clearly a political liability outside of his conservative constituency, returned as Bush's running mate. The president allowed New Right activists, who talked about "a religious war" against Democrats for "the soul of America" and on behalf of "family values," to dominate the 1992 Republican national convention. Conservative Democrats and independents, who had supported Ronald Reagan and Bush in the previous three presidential elections, found the rhetoric of the GOP convention somewhat unsettling.

Bush's Democratic challenger, Governor **William Jefferson ("Bill") Clinton** of Arkansas, stressed economic issues and images of his relative youth. Calling himself a "New Democrat," one who promised fewer governmental programs than had Walter Mondale and who offered more pizzazz than had Michael Dukakis, Bill Clinton promised to create new jobs, reduce the federal deficit, and restructure the nation's health-care system. Sometimes sounding as if he were running as a Republican, Clinton also pledged to shrink the size of government and to "end this [welfare] system as we know it." "People who can work ought to go to work, and no one should be able to stay on welfare forever," he insisted. Rhetoric of this kind frustrated Bush's attempts to label Clinton as a proponent of "big government."

The Democratic focus on the economy also helped deflect attention from sociocultural matters, including rumors of extramarital affairs, on which Clinton seemed vulnerable. As a college student, he had avoided service in Vietnam and, while in England as a Rhodes scholar, had participated in antiwar demonstrations. When Bush, a decorated veteran of the Second World War, challenged the patriotism of his Democratic challenger, Clinton countered by emphasizing, rather than repudiating, his roots in the 1960s. He appeared on MTV, which was promoting a "rock-the-vote" effort aimed at its relatively young audience, and talked about his devotion to (relatively soft) rock music. In addition, he chose Senator Albert Gore of Tennessee, a Vietnam veteran, as his running mate.

The 1992 election brought Clinton a surprisingly easy victory. The self-financed presidential campaign of Ross Perot—a Texas billionaire who spent more than $60 million on a third-party run that emphasized the federal deficit and the necessity for fiscal prudence—probably hurt Bush more than Clinton. With Perot in the race, Clinton garnered only 43 percent of the popular vote but won 370 electoral votes by carrying 32 states and the District of Columbia. Bush gained a majority only among white Protestants in the South. In contrast, Clinton carried the Jewish, African American, and Latino vote by large margins and even gained a plurality among people who had served in the Vietnam War. He also ran well among independents who had supported Reagan and Bush during the 1980s. Perhaps most surprising, about 55 percent of eligible voters went to the polls in 1992, a turnout that reversed 32 years of steady decline in voter participation.

Movement Activism

Focus Question
How did social movements of the post-1960s era affect social life, culture, and the ways people saw their own personal identities during the 1970s and 1980s?

Popular memory often recalls the years between the 1974 resignation of Richard Nixon and the 1992 election of Bill Clinton as ones when social movements of the kind generally associated with the 1960s faded away, sometimes in spasms of self-destructive violence. A few small fringe groups, such as the "Weather Underground" and the "Symbionese Liberation Army" (SLA), did embrace fantasies of revolutionary liberation. The SLA, for instance, briefly made headlines in 1974 by kidnapping Patricia Hearst, the daughter of a wealthy San Francisco newspaper publisher, and committing, sometimes with Hearst's participation, a string of robberies, bombings, and shootings. By the 1980s, the only sociocultural activists still hard at work, from this perspective, toiled for the New Right or for nostalgic and marginal efforts that only vaguely recalled the halcyon days of the 1960s.

Popular pundits constantly looked for symbols of how the 1960s had given way to very different eras, the 1970s and the 1980s. In one popular formulation, the emphasis on social transformation and political empowerment, particularly among people who found well-paying employment, had devolved into a focus on transforming and empowering one's own mind and body. The 1970s, in this view, became the "Me Decade." Extending this story, other observers talked about the "hippies" and "Yippies" of the 1960s morphing, by the mid-1980s, into "Young Upwardly mobile Professionals," or "Yuppies." Self-absorbed, Yuppies supposedly cared little about social values and a great deal about their personal consumption habits.

Recent historical and sociological studies, however, have come to place greater emphasis on the continuation of the kinds of social activism associated with the 1960s. Take, for example, the labor movement. Although contemporary media accounts during the 1970s and early 1980s generally stressed Republican efforts to peel blue-collar workers away from the Democratic Party, the 1960s had spawned a new militancy, particularly among younger workers. As the number of labor strikes reached a postwar high, between 1968 and 1974, dissidents among the rank-and-file also looked askance at their own unions. A number of movements sought to bring the spirit of participatory democracy into union politics.

Grassroots activism would remain a feature of the larger union movement, but the nationwide economic problems of the later 1970s and 1980s eventually acted as a powerful damper on this kind of pressure from below. Ronald Reagan's action against striking air traffic control workers portended aggressive antiunion strategies that both his administration and business interests would pursue during the 1980s. The percentage of unionized workers, by the end of Reagan's presidency, fell to just 16 percent. Seeing the balance of power tilting against them, workers increasingly turned away from strikes as an economic weapon.

Other grassroots movements, however, became more firmly embedded in the daily life of the post-1960s United States. The proliferation of locally based activism, often focused on particular neighborhood-related projects, such as safer streets and cleaner parks, prompted one historian to see a "backyard revolution" taking place during the 1970s and 1980s. Even the U.S. Congress, hardly an institution inclined to fund domestic revolutions, recognized the value of locally based activism and created, in 1978, the National Consumer Cooperative Bank. Legislators charged it with providing loans to support grassroots, cooperative enterprises. Many other public initiatives displayed the influence of activists who represented a constituency or goal that had first become visible during the era of America's longest war, the 1960s.

Mass demonstrations, reminiscent of earlier ones against U.S. policies in Vietnam, remained a feature of the post-1960s movement environment. Both antiabortion and pro-choice forces, for example, regularly demonstrated in Washington, D.C., and in local communities. During the 1980s, the Clamshell Alliance movement conducted a campaign of civil disobedience against a nuclear reactor being built in Seabrook, New Hampshire, and a coalition of West Coast activists waged a lengthy, unsuccessful struggle to close the University of California's Lawrence Livermore National Laboratory, a site for developing nuclear weapons. In nearly every major city and many smaller towns, women's groups staged "Take Back the Night" rallies to call attention to the danger of sexual assaults.

National media, especially network television, however, tended to ignore demonstrations that lacked prominent celebrities or violent conflict. In 1991, for example, 30,000 Korean Americans staged a march for racial peace in Los Angeles. Although it was the largest demonstration ever conducted by any Asian American group, even most local media failed to give it any significant attention. Only C-Span, the niche TV network devoted to public-affairs programming, seemed committed to covering demonstrations intended to dramatize social and political issues.

Women's Issues

In this environment, women's groups adopted a range of methods to rally new supporters and reenergize their core constituencies. Struggles over gender-related issues had emerged within the labor, civil-rights, and antiwar movements of the 1960s. Initially, many of the men involved in these causes complained that issues of gender equality interfered with broader fights to redirect labor, racial, or foreign policies. Women from these movements invariably insisted, though, on calling attention to gender politics, including their own second-class status, in movements that claimed to be egalitarian.

Throughout the 1970s, women continued to promote "consciousness-raising" sessions. These intense personal discussions helped participants consider how *political* empowerment for women often seemed inseparable from *personal* power relationships. The popularity of the birth control pill, for example, allowed greater control over reproductive choices but also complicated the meaning of "sexual freedom." Consciousness-raising also tackled personal-political issues such as sexual preferences, household work routines, child-rearing responsibilities, and economic independence. "The personal is political" became a watchword for many women, especially those who called themselves "feminists."

Although many women kept their distance from overtly feminist organizations, the number of movements addressing issues of concern to women continued to expand during the post-1960s era. The National Organization for Women (NOW), founded in 1966, remained identified with the rights-based agenda of the mainstream of the Democratic Party and the Supreme Court justices who had produced decisions such as *Roe* v. *Wade* of 1973. African American women began forming separate organizations, which emphasized issues of cultural and racial identity. Similarly, Chicana groups coalesced within and alongside most Mexican American organizations. Lesbians also organized their own groups, often allying with an emerging gay rights movement. Organizations in the United States also joined with groups in other nations on behalf of international women's rights.

If particular agendas inevitably varied along lines of race, ethnicity, religion, and economic circumstance, women with differing perspectives also worked together to build new institutions and networks. Their efforts included battered-women's shelters, health and birthing clinics specializing in women's medicine, rape crisis centers, economic development counseling for women-owned businesses, union-organizing efforts led by and directed toward women, organizations of women in specific businesses or professions, women and gender studies programs in colleges and universities, and academic journals and popular magazines devoted to women's issues. Organized pressure for gender equity also affected existing institutions. Country clubs and service organizations began admitting women members. Many Protestant denominations came to accept women into the ministry, and Reform Judaism placed women in its pulpits.

Efforts at empowering women to gain economic self-sufficiency proved an important common concern. By 1990, only about 15 percent of all U.S. households consisted of a fully employed husband and a mother who only worked on tending to home and children. Around twice that percentage consisted of two parents who drew paychecks. Moreover, as the number of single women, including ones heading families, increased, reliance on a male breadwinner, as both ideal and practice, became less viable than ever before. Women wanted—and needed—to find employment that would allow them to support themselves or a family, or to provide additional purchasing power for a multi-income household. The steadily growing number of women entering the paid-labor market helped account for the impressive job-creation statistics of the 1980s.

The labor market these women entered, however, remained laced with inequalities. The average income for women employed full-time continued to lag behind that for men: women earning around 75 cents, in 1990, for every dollar taken home by men. Although this gap largely closed when comparison involved men and women with similar credentials, the overall differential suggested persistent structural inequalities, in educational opportunities and at the entry points to the labor market, that prevented many women from earning a family wage. In addition, professional and business women complained of informal "glass ceilings," gender-based barriers that effectively limited their chances for advancement. And any woman with small children who worked outside her home immediately confronted the two persistent problems of locating and paying for adequate child-care facilities.

The gender gap in pay contributed to another trend—a "feminization of poverty." Homeless shelters, which once catered almost exclusively to single men, began taking in women and children. Women who relied on governmental assistance faced declining prospects. Increases in AFDC payments and expansion of the food stamp program had helped sustain single mothers with children during the 1960s, but economic dislocations of the 1970s and political trends of the 1980s undercut the value, measured in constant dollars, of governmental benefits such as AFDC. Proposals for reshaping the pattern of governmental support through welfare reform, after the failure of Nixon's FAP initiative, generally focused on how to limit direct governmental payment. They also emphasized moving women, even those with young children, into the paid labor force.

Sexual harassment on the job became another highly visible political issue. Most women's groups pressed government and private employers to curtail sexually charged behaviors, which they saw primarily as moves aimed at demeaning women and at further empowering male supervisors and coworkers. The Supreme Court finally ruled in a 1986 decision that sexual harassment constituted a form of discrimination under the Civil Rights Act of 1964.

Several years later, differences over this issue gained national attention when Anita Hill, an African American law professor, testified during 1992 U.S. Senate hearings on the nomination of Clarence Thomas, another African American, to the U.S. Supreme Court. Hill accused Thomas of having sexually harassed her when both had worked in the Reagan administration. Noting how rarely sexual harassment became a public issue, some observers wondered if male senators would have even listened to Hill had Thomas not been otherwise a controversial nominee. Supporters of Thomas, in turn, criticized Hill for being overly sensitive or, perhaps, a "scorned and jealous" woman. In response, feminists denounced the all-male senate judiciary committee for failing even to understand, let alone investigate seriously, the issue of sexual harassment. Although the Senate narrowly approved Thomas for the High Court, political observers credited Hill's testimony with helping women's groups mobilize female voters and with electing four women as U.S. senators in the 1992 elections.

Sexual harassment also became a controversial issue within the U.S. military, which began to recruit women more actively. The service academies accepted female cadets, and women found places within the military hierarchy. Soon, however, revelations about harassment and even sexual assaults against female naval officers by male comrades soon surfaced. Attempts by Navy officials to cover up sexual harassment during the 1991 "Tailhook" convention provoked outrage, and several high-ranking officers were forced to step down.

Sexual Politics

Movements pressing issues involving gays and lesbians also became more public and political as the 1960s turned into the 1970s. In 1969, New York City police raided the Stonewall Inn, an unlicensed bar in Greenwich Village with a largely homosexual clientele. Seeing the liquor license issue as simply a pretext for harassing patrons of the Stonewall, a group of gay and transgendered people in the bar resisted arrest. The resultant confrontation spilled over into the neighborhood and pitted local activists, who viewed themselves as recurring targets for police harassment, against law enforcement officials.

Historians of sexuality have come to criticize what they call "the Stonewall Narrative," a story in which an event at a single Greenwich Village bar ignited what would become known as the Lesbian-Gay-Bisexual-Transgendered (LGBT) movement. Recent studies emphasize that LGBT activism did not suddenly emerge in 1969 but, instead, grew out of earlier movements, such as the Mattachine Society, and cultural communities, including those of the Beats (see chapter 29). Two years before Stonewall, for example, the ACLU reversed its previous stance and declared that legal guarantees of equality prevented authorities from singling out same-sex behaviors as objects for criminal prosecution.

Still, the 1969 events at the Stonewall Inn, because of the prominence they received in mainstream and alternative media, marked an important benchmark in the history of sexual politics. Gay and lesbian activism, though neither nonexistent nor entirely invisible earlier, became an important part of the larger "movement of movements" that continued during the 1970s and 1980s. A number of advocacy and support groups, such as New York City's Gay Activist Alliance (GAA), sprang up. As many individuals "came out of the closet," newspapers, theaters, nightspots, and religious groups proudly identified themselves as activists. LGBT communities emerged, particularly in larger cities, helping to create, and also benefiting from, the general relaxation of legal and cultural controls over the portrayal and the more open practice of a wide range of sexual choices. Activists demanded that law enforcement officials treat attacks against people identifying themselves with an LGBT agenda no less seriously than ones against all other citizens. They also asserted constitutional claims to equal access to housing, jobs, and fringe benefits for partners.

The results of these efforts initially disappointed LGBT activists. In some locales, counter-activism from movements associated with the New Right resulted in battles over the fate of so-called gay rights ordinances. Gradually, during the 1980s, a few states— beginning with Wisconsin and Massachusetts—began enacting statewide antidiscrimination laws. Results at the federal level proved less encouraging to LGBT advocates. Although the EEOC extended the reach of civil-rights laws mandating equality to other "minorities," it refused to do so in response to complaints from LGBT groups. It did not, for example, hold that the refusal to grant spousal benefits between heterosexuals to gays and lesbians violated federal law.

Moreover, in *Bowers* v. *Hardwick* (1986), a divided Supreme Court upheld a Georgia law that made it a crime to engage in sodomy. The majority stressed the lack of any specific mention of sexual liberty in the U.S. Constitution and the long tradition of such measures. LGBT activists took some solace from the recognition that many states had repealed anti-sodomy statutes, that law enforcement officials in other states rarely enforced them, and that opinion polls suggested a majority opposed the sociocultural premises of the *Bowers* decision. (Indeed, in 2003, another divided U.S. Supreme Court would cast aside *Bowers* and declare that state laws criminalizing sodomy violated the Constitution.)

LGBT communities, in contrast, found less comfort when confronting another issue, one with international implications. During the 1970s, public health officials began seeing an apparently new, highly contagious human immunodeficiency virus (HIV). It produced an acquired immunodeficiency syndrome (AIDS), which could become a fatal disease for which medical science offered virtually nothing in the way of cure or treatment. The virus could be transmitted through the careless use of intravenous drugs, tainted blood supplies, and unprotected sexual intercourse. At first, the incidence of **HIV-AIDS** in the United States appeared primarily limited to gay men, and some spokespeople for the New Religious Right viewed HIV-AIDS as a divine judgment against homosexuals. LGBT activists charged

© Reuters/CORBIS

Aids "ACT-UP" Campaign   Health-care issues increasingly galvanized grassroots activists in the late 20th century. In 1989, members of ACT-UP, a group that embraced direct action, protested what they saw as the federal government's inattention to the issue of AIDS during the 1980s.

that the Reagan administration's support from cultural and religious conservatives inclined it to place a low priority on funding efforts to understand the causes of HIV-AIDS, check its spread, or devise viable medical responses.

The AIDS controversy galvanized empowerment efforts among LGBT organizations, such as the "Aids Coalition to Unleash Power" (ACT-UP). Non-LGBT groups joined the effort. Within a relatively short time, new research projects took shape. With the development of prevention programs and drugs that could combat HIV-AIDS, most public figures came to support new efforts both at home and overseas, particularly in Africa, to address HIV-AIDS. Still, it remained a modern scourge that threatened economic advancement and social stability in many parts of the world, but its specific identification with LGBT rights faded.

Race, Ethnicity, and Social Activism

Use of specific group identity as a fulcrum for wider social activism became especially strong within racial and ethnic communities. Building on the model of Black Power activism during the 1960s, groups emphasized pride in their distinctive traditions and insisted cultural differences should be affirmed rather than ignored or merely tolerated. The influx of new immigrants from Third World areas helped focus additional attention on social movements that addressed the question of "multiculturalism."

Activism Among African Americans

African American activists had developed a strong sense of cultural identity during the civil rights and Black Power struggles of the 1960s (see chapters 28 and 29), and activism during the following decades continued to stress pride in African American cultural life. The emphasis on racial pride, for example, showed in Spike Lee's film *Malcolm X* (1991), in rap and hip-hop music, and among educators who advocated an "Afrocentric" curriculum. The Black Entertainment Television network (BET) aimed its programming specifically to African American viewers, attracting a broader audience in the process.

Academics such as Henry Lewis Gates, Jr., who became head of Harvard's Afro-American Studies Department in 1991, sought to integrate study of the black culture into wider frames. In the view championed by Gates and other black scholars, cultural works produced by African Americans should not be seen as "a thing apart, separate from the whole, having no influence on the shape and shaping of American culture." Gates praised African American authors, such as Toni Morrison (who would win the Nobel Prize for Literature in 1993) and Alice Walker, as writers who took "the blackness of the culture for granted" and used this as "a springboard to write about those human emotions that we share with everyone else." The cultural works of African Americans, in short, could simultaneously be seen as unique and different, *and also* be viewed in relationship to broader cultural traditions.

Issues of equal treatment, especially in the legal and criminal justice systems, remained an important part of the agenda for African American activists. Repeated studies suggested, for instance, that police detained African Americans as criminal suspects and stopped black motorists far more often than members of any other ethnic group. Criminologists called this practice **"racial profiling,"** while activists talked about being arrested for a DWB, "driving while black." (In Hispanic communities, DWB came to stand for "driving while brown.") Profiling seemed a reminder, both symbolic and real, of the days of legally sanctioned discrimination and suggested the difficulty of translating formal guarantees of equality into practice.

In addition, differences in the sentencing patterns for convicted felons raised a broader concern. Courts imposed harsher sentences for crimes, for instance, involving crack cocaine, a drug consumed in some African American neighborhoods, than for those involving the more expensive, illegal coca-based products favored by white and suburban drug abusers. Statistical evidence also indicated that African American men in their late twenties were about 10 times more likely than their white counterparts to be imprisoned. Similar statistics showed African Americans who had been convicted of potential capital crimes were far more likely to receive the death penalty than were prison inmates from other ethnic and racial backgrounds.

Other practices viewed as symbolizing the institutionalized racism of the past became the target of activist movements. At the beginning of the 1990s, for instance, the battle flag of the Confederate States of America still flew over public buildings and institutions throughout much of the South. Groups that defended this practice insisted it honored the people who had supported the southern cause during the mid-19th century and said nothing about the system of chattel slavery. Critics, including many African American organizations, wondered how the Confederate cause could ever be separated from the defense of slavery and noted the more recent use of the Confederate flag to symbolize resistance to the civil-rights movement. Was officially displaying the Flag of the Old Confederacy, constitutional lawyers asked, a kind of expression akin to sexual harassment, or was it the sort of symbolic political speech that the First Amendment obviously protected?

African American activists increasingly saw the symbolic politics associated with Confederate flags closely related to efforts at greater empowerment within the country's major political institutions. Symbol and substance, in this view, went together. Beginning about 1970, when less than 1,500 African Americans held elective office in the United States, the number of African Americans in such positions began to increase dramatically. By 1992, there were more than 8,000. In 1970, 13 African American members of Congress established the **"Congressional Black Caucus" (CBC)** as a means of presenting a common front on a wide range of foreign and domestic issues. Picking up the mantle of A. Philip Randolph and Bayard Rustin's "Freedom Budget," the CBC would issue a hypothetical "Alternative Budget," which sought to redirect federal spending toward social initiatives. It also campaigned on behalf of better relations between the United States and African nations.

Activism Among American Indians

American Indians mounted activist movements along two broad fronts. Indians had long-standing identities based on their tribal affiliation, and many issues, particularly those involving land and treaty disputes, turned on specific, tribal-based claims. Other questions, which seemed to require strategies that extended beyond a single tribe or band, became identified as "pan-Indian" in nature.

American Indian activism had burst into the national media, in November 1969, when a group calling itself "Indians of All Tribes" began an extended occupation of the former federal prison on Alcatraz Island in San Francisco harbor. These activists, many of whom had attended colleges in the San Francisco Bay area, hoped to dramatize a history of broken treaty promises. This effort, which lasted for nearly two years, initially attracted extensive media attention.

Expanding on this direct-action tactic, the American Indian Movement (AIM), which had been created in 1968 by young activists from several Northern Plains tribes, adopted even more confrontational approaches. In 1973, they seized control of the small community of Wounded Knee, on South Dakota's Pine Ridge Reservation. This had been the site of a notorious 1890 massacre of Indian people by the U.S. Army, and 83 years later, members of AIM clashed with both federal officials and older American Indian leaders during a military-style standoff that finally ended after several months. In response, federal officials targeted members of AIM with illegal surveillance and a series of controversial criminal prosecutions. The most celebrated trial, which took place in St. Paul, Minnesota, ended after a federal judge dismissed all charges against two AIM members because of improper conduct by governmental officials.

Meanwhile, important social and legal changes had been taking place. A number of tribal Indian organizations, tapping federal funds first made available during the War on Poverty, began a process of empowerment from the grassroots. The U.S. Congress and the White House, pressured by Indian organizations and their supporters, moved to undo the termination and relocation policies of the 1950s. The multipart Civil Rights Act of 1968, for example, contained several sections that became known as the "Indian Bill of Rights." In these, Congress extended most provisions of the constitutional Bill of Rights to American Indians living on reservations, while reconfirming legitimacy of specifically tribal laws and powers.

Federal legislation and several Supreme Court decisions in the 1970s subsequently reinforced the constitutional principle of "tribal self-determination." In 1973, a campaign sparked by supporters of the Menominee tribe, which had been officially disbanded under

© Andre Jenny/The Image Works

Gaming at Potawatomi Casino During the 1980s, casino style gaming began to emerge as one of the nation's leading entertainment enterprises. Native Americans embraced casinos, such as this one located near Milwaukee, Wisconsin, as important ways to generate jobs and capital on Indian reservations. The Potawatomi complex, which opened in 1991, now juxtaposes traditional style sculptures, an Indian heritage center and gift shop, an imaginatively designed building, more than 1000 slot machines, and a cabaret-style dinner theater patterned after ones in Las Vegas.

the termination policy, succeeded in getting Congress to begin the process of reversing the earlier action. Confirming tribal identification often required extensive legal activity. As litigation proceeded, the federal government came to officially recognize a steadily increasing number of separate tribes and bands.

Tapping the expertise of the Native American Rights Fund (NARF), tribes pressed demands that derived from treaties between tribes and the U.S. government. Some sought recognition of tribal land claims, which could often be traced back to treaty agreements that the U.S. officials had subsequently broken. Others dealt with fishing and agricultural rights. Some of these efforts provoked resistance and resentment among non-Indians, who argued that state and local laws that incidentally affected Indian tribes should not give way to special claims based on federal treaty authority and tribal self-determination. Courts invariably held these state and local laws in conflict with the U.S. Constitution, which established the supremacy of federal treaties. Indians also sued to protect tribal water rights and traditional religious ceremonies, some of which included the ritualistic use of drugs such as peyote. In 1990, responding to pressure from an activist coalition, Congress passed the Native American Graves Protection and Repatriation Act, which required universities and museums to return human remains and sacred objects to tribes who requested them.

Claiming exemption from state gaming laws, many American Indian tribes also began to cash in on self-determination. They opened bingo halls and, then, full-blown, Las Vegas–style gambling casinos. In 1988, the U.S. Supreme Court ruled that states lacked any power to prohibit gambling operations on tribal land, and Congress responded with the Indian Gaming Regulatory Act. As gambling began to emerge as one of the most lucrative sectors of the nation's entertainment business, Indian-owned casinos thrived, generating substantial employment and profit. Ironically, the glitzy, tribal-owned casinos often financed tribal powwows and other efforts to nurture older cultural practices.

To forestall the disappearance of native languages, American Indian movements emphasized the importance of bilingualism and gave renewed attention to tribal rituals. In a related initiative, a 1978 congressional measure provided federal funding for Indian-run educational institutions, which would build job skills and preserve tribal cultures. Indian activists, especially those from AIM, also denounced the use of stereotypical nicknames, such as "Chiefs" and "Redskins," and Indian-related logos in amateur and professional sports.

A steady and substantial increase in the nation's American Indian population provided perhaps the most tangible sign of the renewal of cultural pride: This surging growth rate came not from any increase in birth rates but from a dramatic rise in the number of people of Indian descent who, for the first time in their lives, sought enrollment with a tribe or band and identified themselves as American Indian on the U.S. Census form.

Activism in Spanish-Speaking Communities

Census data showed that the fastest-growing ethnic group in the United States spoke Spanish. Many Spanish-speaking people, especially in the Southwest, came to prefer the umbrella term "Latino," whereas others, particularly in Florida, favored "Hispanic." At the same time, people whom the U.S. Census began (in 1980) labeling "Hispanic" more frequently identified themselves according to the specific Spanish-speaking country or commonwealth from which they or their ancestors had immigrated. People who employed Spanish as their first language, often in the workplace and in their communities as well as at home, thus highlighted the diversity and complexity of identity.

Mexican Americans, members of the oldest and most numerous Spanish-speaking group, could tap a long tradition of political and social activism. The late 1960s saw an emerging spirit of **Chicanismo,** a populist-style pride in a heritage that could be traced back to the ancient civilizations of Middle America. Young activists made "Chicano/a," terms of derision that older Mexican Americans had generally avoided in the past, into symbolic affirmations of their particular heritage. "Crusade for Justice," an organization that first took root in Denver, Colorado, provided a model for other local movements that emphasized getting young people through school and training them for careers in business, education, and social activism. At the same time, many of these groups espoused a view of the past that stressed how, long before the arrival of the Spanish conquistadores and the subsequent incorporation of large parts of an independent Mexico into the United States, the ancestors of *chicanos* and *chicanas* of the 1960s had once controlled vast amounts of land and determined their own destiny. Some even began to talk about regaining control of parts of this territory, which they called *Aztlan*.

Other activists expressed more interest in future politics than old land claims. Beginning in the late 1960s, political and cultural visions of *Chicanismo* gained considerable influence in cities in the Southwest. Members of La Raza Unida, a movement founded in 1967, began to win local elections. At the same time, Mexican American communities experienced a cultural flowering. New Spanish-language newspapers and journals reinforced a growing sense of pride, and many churches sponsored festivals that featured ethnic dancing, mural painting, poetry, and literature. Mexican Americans successfully pushed for programs in Chicano/a Studies at colleges and universities.

The labor organizer Cesar Chavez gained wider media (and, later, historical) attention than any other Mexican American activist, but urban-based movements likely exerted a greater impact on far more people than Chavez's United Farm Workers union (UFW). Developments in San Antonio, Texas, a city with a large Mexican American population, suggested the potential fruits of grassroots political organizing. In the 1970s, Ernesto Cortes, Jr., took the lead in founding Communities Organized for Public Service (COPS), a group that brought the energy and talents of Mexican Americans, particularly women, out of specific neighborhoods and into the city's larger public arena for the first time. Mexican American activists worked with Anglo business leaders and with Democratic politicians such as Henry Cisneros, who became the city's mayor in 1981.

In addition, representatives from the older, political-legal movements, often feeling pressure from younger people who admired the energy of activists such as Cortes and Chavez, embraced new forms of activism. Established organizations such as LULAC, the American GI Forum, and the Mexican American Political Association (MAPA) began demanding that the EEOC take a more proactive approach to job-related issues. In 1967, a multimillion-dollar grant from the Ford Foundation facilitated creation of a Mexican American Legal Defense and Education Fund (MALDEF). This activist legal group gradually abandoned the "other white" due process litigation strategy, used during the 1940s and 1950s (see chapter 27), and began filing lawsuits that charged discrimination against Mexican-descended people, including the kind found in public schools, violated constitutional requirements of equality.

Over time, Mexican American activism became increasingly diverse. After some successes, the UFW confronted greater resistance from growers. It managed to survive, especially as a cultural presence centered on Caesar Chavez and his legacy, but could claim fewer and fewer organizing victories. MALDEF emerged as perhaps the most visible national group, one ready to lobby or litigate. At the local level, organizations formed on the model of COPS, such as United Neighborhood Organization (UNO) in Los Angeles, worked on community and citywide concerns. Mexican Americans, both women and men, often spearheaded urban-based labor-organizing efforts, particularly in the rapidly expanding service sector. Professional women could join organizations such as the National Network of Hispanic Women.

Social activism among Puerto Ricans in the United States emerged more slowly. Many stateside Puerto Ricans focused much of their political energy on the persistent "status"

Mural Art in Chicago   Themes in Mexican history and culture, inspired by the great Mexican muralists, appeared in Mexican American communities throughout the country.

© Ralf-Finn Hestoft/CORBIS

question—that is, whether Puerto Rico should seek independence, strive for statehood, or retain a commonwealth connection to the mainland. New York City's Puerto Rican Day Parade became the city's largest ethnic celebration and an important focus of cultural pride. A 1976 report by the U.S. Commission on Civil Rights, however, concluded that Puerto Ricans remained "the last in line" for government-funded benefits and opportunity programs. In the 1980s, the Puerto Rican Legal Defense and Education Fund and allied groups helped Puerto Ricans surmount obstacles to the ballot box and to political office.

Cuban Americans who had begun arriving in southern Florida during the 1960s, fleeing from Fidel Castro's Cuba, quickly established an important local presence, particularly in Miami. The earliest arrivals generally enjoyed greater access to education and higher incomes than did most Latinos who came later, even from Cuba. This initial wave of Cuban immigrants also tended to be more politically conservative, generally voted Republican, and lobbied for a hard line toward Castro's communist government back in Cuba. This generation created institutions that, taken together, amounted to a government in exile, located in Miami. During the early 1990s, polls consistently revealed that as many as one-fifth of Cubans living in South Florida claimed they would immediately return to Havana once Castro left the scene. Other Cuban Americans, especially the generations born in the United States, became active in Florida politics and civic affairs. Some increasingly questioned their elders' persistent "exile mentality," which took much of its identity and spirit from anti-Castro activities.

Beneath a common Spanish language, then, lay great diversity in terms of economic status, national and cultural identification, political affiliation, and activist goals and organizations. Established communities that identified with Mexico, Puerto Rico, and Cuba developed a wide range of mobilizing and organizing styles.

Activism Among Asian Americans

Americans of Chinese, Japanese, Korean, Filipino, and other backgrounds began to create an Asian American movement. Organizations such as the Asian Pacific Planning Council (APPCON), founded in 1976, lobbied to obtain government funding for projects that benefited Asian American communities. The Asian Law Caucus, founded during the early 1970s by opponents of U.S. intervention in Vietnam, and the Committee against Anti-Asian Violence, created a decade later in response to a wave of racially motivated attacks, mobilized to fight a wide range of legal battles. During the 1970s, Asian American studies programs also took shape at colleges and universities on the West Coast. By the early 1980s, Asian American political activists enjoyed growing influence, especially within the Democratic Party, and began getting elected to public office.

Emphasizing a broad, Asian American identity, however, raised questions of inclusion, exclusion, and rivalry. Filipino American activists, members of the second largest Asian American group in the United States, according to the 1990 Census, often resisted the Asian American label because they believed that Chinese Americans or Japanese Americans dominated groups such as APPCON. Many people of Filipino descent focused on specific goals, particularly an effort to obtain citizenship and veteran's benefits for former soldiers of the Second World War who had fought against Japan in the Philippines. Japanese American groups also lobbied on behalf of specific issues, and in 1988, Congress formally apologized and voted to pay $20,000 in reparations to every living Japanese American who had been confined in internment camps during the Second World War. Similarly, Hmong and Vietnamese groups began pursuing special concerns, many of which stemmed back to the anticommunist ties that had connected the first generation of immigrants to the United States during the Vietnam War era.

Socioeconomic and cultural differences made it impossible to frame a single Asian American agenda. Although many groups showed remarkable upward educational and economic mobility during the late 1980s and early 1990s, for example, others such as Hmong immigrants and Chinese American garment workers struggled to find jobs that paid more than the minimum wage.

The Dilemmas of Antidiscrimination Efforts

How might governmental power best advance the cause of equality? Between the end of the Second World War and about the mid-1960s, antidiscrimination movements and the courts had demanded that the government not categorize individuals according to group identities based on race or ethnicity. On matters such as education, housing, or employment, the law must remain "color-blind" and treat people equally.

Gradually, however, new social-activist agendas envisioned that governmental power should do more than simply eliminate discriminatory barriers to *individual* opportunity. It should take **"affirmative action"** so that *groups* that had historically faced discrimination on the basis of their shared identity could begin to receive an equitable share of the nation's jobs, public spending, and educational programs. Affirmative action, supporters argued, would help compensate for past discrimination and for continued, perhaps hidden, prejudices that laws guaranteeing formal equality failed to reach.

Affirmative action sparked intense controversy. Some beneficiaries of compensatory programs complained that the derogatory label of "affirmative action applicant" tended, inevitably, to throw into question their individual talents and capabilities. More broadly, critics charged that programs to "set aside" jobs or openings in educational institutions for certain racial or ethnic groups smacked of "quotas" and thereby violated the principle of equality. Moreover, was not affirmative action *on behalf of* people in some groups inevitably also "reverse discrimination" *against* those in others? The claim of reverse discrimination became particularly emotional when members of one ethnic group, despite lower scores on aptitude or admissions exams, received preferences for employment or for entry into educational institutions. Supporters of these programs insisted that *any* process of selection would inevitably "affirm" some qualities, such as family or old school lineages, at the expense of others. Efforts at undoing years of discrimination, in this view, required complicated views of what counted as "equality."

The nation's courts struggled to square new affirmative action programs with older antidiscrimination precedents. They tended to strike down as unconstitutional affirmative action plans that contained inflexible quotas and to uphold less rigid ones that made group identity only one of several criteria for making hiring or educational decisions. In the controversial Supreme Court decision of 1978, popularly known as "the *Bakke* case," a majority of the High Court implicitly endorsed the importance of multiculturalism. Affirmative action programs in educational settings could gain constitutional legitimacy because they aimed at redressing past discrimination *and* because they promoted "diversity," a desirable quality that enriched any learning environment. Movements opposed to affirmative action efforts, strongest among people and groups within the broad New Right, redoubled their efforts, in the wake of *Bakke*, to curtail this practice through further litigation and legislative action.

On the local level, the Religious Right mobilized and organized to influence school boards. These activists charged educational bureaucrats from outside their communities with seeking to indoctrinate school children with what they considered anti-Biblical ideas such as feminism, multiculturalism, and evolution. Many rallied behind the ideas of "vouchers" and charter schools, both methods by which financing could be shifted from the public schools and directed toward private educational alternatives. On a wide range of issues, conservative activists wanted tax dollars to directly support the religious and cultural values held by their churches and families.

The New Right also opposed innovations associated with the 1960s in college curricula and in cultural life. It saw colleges contributing to "the closing of the American mind" (the title of a best-selling 1987 book by Allan Bloom) by exposing students only to what was trendy and "politically correct" (PC). Educational conservatives associated with the Reagan administration, most notably William Bennett and Lynn Cheney, warned about what they considered the debasement of intellectual life by trendy and shallow changes masked as innovations. The government-funded National Endowment for the Humanities (NEH) and the National Endowment for the Arts (NEA) came under the New Right's fire when they backed nontraditional projects.

The New Right continued to master the art of publicizing its positions. Well-funded conservative organizations sponsored academic conferences, popular gatherings, and radio and television programs. Pat Robertson, a lawyer turned evangelist, built a multimedia empire, including his popular *700 Club,* a TV program that adeptly merged evangelical religion with New Right politics. Conservative broadcasters such as Rush Limbaugh attracted significant audiences to the talk-radio genre. Not coincidentally, Limbaugh's program became national in 1988, the year after the deregulation movement of the 1980s had led to the Federal Communications Commission (FCC) eliminating the "Fairness Doctrine," a rule requiring broadcasters to provide "equal" time for a diversity of viewpoints and opinions.

The New Right, much like other activist groups, hardly moved in lockstep. More traditional members of the New Right coalition, such as the journalist and sometime presidential candidate Patrick Buchanan, decried a new generation of neocons, such as William

Kristol, for hijacking and undermining the conservative movement. Buchanan and his followers denounced the free trade policies and the global military strategy that other conservatives promoted.

While remaining a coalition of disparate parts, the New Right became a powerful force in American life. It successfully challenged the once-dominant political agenda of the Democratic Party, propelled the mainstream of the Republican Party decidedly rightward, established a strong foothold in public-policy and media discussions, and succeeded in re-imagining the nation's cultural and informational landscape.

Conclusion

The "Reagan Revolution" of the 1980s rested on a conservative movement that had been taking shape since the 1950s. New Right Republicans distrusted extending federal government power, advocated sharp tax cuts, and stressed a sociocultural agenda emphasizing traditional values. The dozen years of Republican dominance of the White House, from 1980 to 1992, helped shift the terms of political debate in the United States. In foreign policy, Reagan's military buildup coincided with—and contributed to, according to his admirers—the last years of the Cold War.

Meanwhile, U.S. society seemed to fragment into specialized identifications. Social activism often organized around sexual, ethnic, and racial identities. Celebrants of multiculturalism generally welcomed this fragmentation, while others, especially on the New Right, worried about the nation becoming disunited into warring, even "alien" factions. The New Right's stress on limiting the power of government and promoting conservative social and cultural values increasingly set the terms for public debate, reconfiguring discussions about how government power could best promote liberty and equality.

SUGGESTED READINGS

For differing views of the political trends that came together during the 1980s, see **Garry Wills,** *Reagan's America: Innocents at Home* (rev. ed., 2000); **Burton J. Kaufman,** *The Presidency of James Earl Carter* (1993); **Douglas Brinkley,** *The Unfinished Presidency: Jimmy Carter's Journey to the Nobel Peace Prize* (1998); **John W. Sloan,** *The Reagan Effect: Economics and Presidential Leadership* (1999); **Frances Fitzgerald,** *Way Out There in the Blue: Reagan and Star Wars and the End of the Cold War* (2000); **Lisa McGirr,** *Suburban Warriors: The Origins of the New American Right* (2001); **John Schoenwald,** *A Time for Choosing: The Rise of Modern American Conservatism* (2001); **W. Carl Biven,** *Jimmy Carter's Economy: Policy in an Age of Limits* (2002); **W. Elliott Brownlee and Hugh Davis Graham, eds.,** *The Reagan Presidency: Pragmatic Conservatism and Its Legacies* (2003); **Gil Troy,** *Morning in America: How Ronald Reagan Invented the 1980s* (2005); **John Ehrman,** *The Eighties: America in the Age of Reagan* (2005); **Richard Reeves,** *President Reagan: The Triumph of Imagination* (2005); and **Mark Bowden,** *Guests of the Ayatollah, The First Battle in America's War with Militant Islam* (2006). See also, **Bruce J. Schulman,** *The Seventies: The Great Shift in American Culture, Society, and Politics* (2001) and **James T. Patterson,** *Restless Giant: The United States from Watergate to Bush vs. Gore* (2005).

Suggestive studies relevant to themes of social and cultural activism include **Juan P. Garcia,** ed., *Mexican Americans in the 1990s* (1997); **John D'Emilio, William B. Turner, and Urvashi Vaid, eds.,** *Creating Change: Sexuality, Public Policy, and Civil Rights* (2000); **Ellen Messer-Davidow,** *Disciplining Feminism: From Social Action to Academic Discourse* (2002); **Frank Wu,** *Yellow: Race in America Beyond Black and White* (2002); **Larry Nesper,** *The Walleye War: The Struggle for Ojibwe Spearfishing and Treaty Rights* (2002); **Sara Evans,** *Tidal Wave: How Women Changed America at Century's End* (2003); **Van Gosse and Richard Moser, eds.,** *The World the 60s Made: Politics and Culture in Recent America* (2003); **David Carter,** *Stonewall: The Riots that Sparked the Gay Revolution* (2004); **Laura Pulido,** *Black, Brown, Yellow & Left: Radical Activism in Los Angeles* (2006); and **Andreas Hillen,** *1973 Nervous Breakdown: Watergate, Warhol, and the Birth of Post-Sixties America* (2006).

Visit the Liberty Equality Power Companion Web site for resources specific to this textbook: http://www.thomsonedu.com/history/murrin

Also find self-tests and additional resources at ThomsonNOW. ThomsonNOW is an integrated online suite of services and resources with proven ease of use and efficient paths to success, delivering the results you want—NOW!

www.thomsonedu.com/login/

Economic, Social, and Cultural Change in the Late 20th Century

The late 20th and the early 21st centuries brought sweeping changes to American life. A dramatic increase in immigration, along with movements of people throughout sprawling metropolitan areas and into states in the West and South, altered U.S. demographic patterns. The continuing transformation away from employment in the manufacturing sector of the economy changed the workplace for many Americans. A digital revolution transfigured systems of information in business and other areas of national life. A vast entertainment-informational complex, with an increasing emphasis on professional sports, also emerged. At the same time, religious life in America became more diverse, more devout, and more intertwined with the nation's politics.

A Changing People

Focus Question
What major demographic trends characterized the post-1970 United States? How did they contribute to changing daily life?

The demographic makeup of the United States changed significantly during the final three decades of the 20th century. The nation's people became older, more metropolitan, and more ethnically and racially diverse. Moreover, important centers of power continued shifting away from the Northeast and toward the South and West.

An Aging, Shifting Population

During the 1950s, the height of the Baby Boom, the population had grown by 1.8 percent per year; after 1970, even with new waves of immigration and longer life expectancies, the growth rate slowed to about 1 percent per year. Younger people generally delayed marriage until well into their 20s, most raised smaller families than had their parents, and more remained unmarried for much of their life. The number of households with at least one child under 18 continually shrank. In 1960, nearly 50 percent fell into this category; by 1999, only about one-third of U.S. households contained even one person under the age of 18. Consequently, by the mid-1980s, people in the 25-to-44 age range constituted a larger slice of the U.S. population than any other category, and the number of those between their teens and early twenties was relatively small.

CHRONOLOGY

1965	Congress passes Immigration Act of 1965
1980	Microsoft licenses its first personal computer software
1981	MTV and CNN debut
1985	Supreme Court rules that home taping of TV programs does not violate copyright law
1986	Immigration Reform and Control Act toughens laws against employing undocumented immigrants
1988	Fox television network debuts
1990	Immigration Act revises conditions for admittance • Census designates "Asian or Pacific Islanders" as single, pan-Asian category
1991	Catch-phrase "surfing the Internet" is coined
1993	Cesar Chavez dies • Number of Internet sites passes the 100,000 mark
1995	Dial-in Internet services begin
1996	Fox News Networks debuts
1997	First Harry Potter book published
1998	E-commerce begins in earnest • German Daimler buys out Chrysler Motors
1999	E-commerce and dot-com stocks surge
2000	Last census of 20th century conducted • Many dot-com enterprises collapse
2001	People classified as "non-Hispanic whites" no longer a majority of California's population • America Online merges with Time-Warner
2005	Final theatrical release in *Star Wars* series

The steady rise of the median age of the population brought public policy, as well as personal, dilemmas. As aging Baby Boomers pondered retirement options, for example, policy makers worried that the projected Social Security and Medicare payouts would bequeath a staggering burden of costs to the smaller post–Baby Boom generations of workers. Trend watchers of the 1960s had talked of a "youth revolt." At the beginning of the 21st century, their counterparts pondered the "graying of America."

Significant change also occurred in the geographic distribution of population, and these transformations helped to shift the regional distribution of political and economic power. After 1970, the vast bulk of the nation's population growth occurred in the South and the West. Nevada, California, Florida, and Arizona became the fastest-growing states, and by 2000, more than one in ten Americans lived in California. Between 1990 and 2001, California gained eight seats in the U.S. House of Representatives, Florida added six, New York lost five, and several other northeastern states lost two or three. Presidential politics increasingly turned on results from Florida, Texas, and California.

Many reasons account for this demographic shift: affordable air-conditioning, the expansion of tourism and new retirement communities in **Sun Belt** areas, businesses attracted by lower labor costs, the absence of strong unions, and the development of high-tech industries connected to military-related spending and the computer revolution. **(See Map 31.1, Population Shifts Toward the Sunbelt, in the color insert following page 1248.)**

The governmentally financed space program, directed by NASA installations in Texas and Florida, symbolized the geographic shift in the research and technology sectors. In 1961, President Kennedy had announced plans for the manned Apollo program, and in July 1969, astronaut Neil Armstrong had stepped from a spacecraft onto the lunar surface. Apollo flights continued until 1972, when NASA began to develop a space station. In the 1980s, NASA started operating **"space shuttles,"** manned craft that served as scientific laboratories in outer space and could be flown back to Earth for reuse. In early 1986, a *Challenger* shuttle craft exploded as it was about to take off, and the program stalled for a few years. Still, the accelerating ripple effect of space and defense spending continued to stimulate technological innovation and population growth in Sunbelt areas.

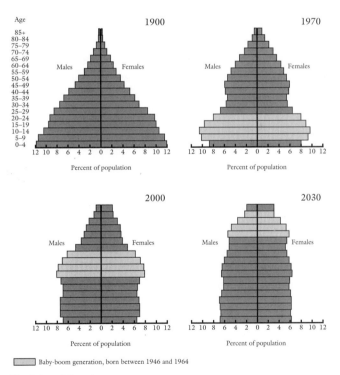

Baby-boom generation, born between 1946 and 1964

The Aging of America

Source: U.S. Census Bureau. Adapted from C. L. Himes, "Elderly Americans," *Population Bulletin 2002*, 56(4): p. 4.

New Immigration

A dramatic increase in immigration from countries mostly to the south and west of the United States accounted for much of the U.S. population growth, particularly in the southern and western parts of the country. The vast bulk of post-1970 immigration came from Asia, Oceania, Latin America, and Africa rather than from Europe, the primary source of immigrants from the 1790s to 1924. In 2000, roughly 12 percent of the U.S. population had been born outside of the United States, compared to the all-time high of 15 percent in 1890.

The largest number of non-European immigrants came from Mexico. Responding to labor shortages in the United States and poor economic prospects at home, both legal and undocumented immigration from Mexico rose substantially during the last 30 years of the 20th century. Many immigrants from Mexico arrived as seasonal agricultural workers or temporary laborers, but most soon formed permanent communities. According to the 2000 census, 90 percent of all Mexican Americans lived in the Southwest, primarily Texas and California.

Most immigrants from Puerto Rico settled around New York City, but sizable Puerto Rican communities developed in Chicago and in cities in New England and Ohio as well. Economic problems on the mainland during the 1970s prompted some to return to the island, but the flow reversed again after about 1980. By 2000, the Puerto Rican population on the U.S. mainland totaled about 3 million, compared to slightly less than 4 million in Puerto Rico.

Cubans had begun immigrating in large numbers in response to Fidel Castro's revolution. After the U.S. Congress, in 1962, designated people fleeing from Castro's Cuba as "refugees" eligible for admittance, more than 800,000 Cubans from every strata of society came to the United States during the next 20 years. They gradually moved northward into many major American cities, but the greatest impact came in south Florida. An agreement with Castro in 1995 brought the first U.S. restrictions on the flow of immigrants from Cuba. In 2000, however, about half of all the people residing in Miami were of Cuban descent.

By the early 21st century, the number of Spanish-speaking people in the United States totaled more than in all but four countries of Latin America. Los Angeles became the second largest "Mexican city" in the world, trailing only Mexico City, and LA's Salvadoran population just about equaled that of San Salvador. More Puerto Ricans lived in New York City than in San Juan, and the Big Apple's Dominican population rivaled that of Santo Domingo.

Changes in immigration patterns began with the landmark **Immigration Act of 1965,** which spurred not only population growth but diversity as well. Since the 1920s, the nature of immigration to the United States had been determined by quotas based on national origins (see chapter 24). The 1965 act abolished these. Instead, it placed a ceiling of 20,000 immigrants for every country, gave preference to those with close family ties in the United States, and accorded priority to people with special skills and those classified as refugees. Although largely unforeseen at the time, this legislation laid the basis not only for a resumption of high-volume immigration but also for a substantial shift in the countries of origin.

International events also affected U.S. immigration policy. In the aftermath of the Vietnam War, for example, U.S. officials facilitated the admittance of many Vietnamese, Cambodians, Laotians, and **Hmong** (an ethnically distinct people who inhabited lands extending across the borders of these three Asian countries). The goal was to resettle people who had allied with the United States during the war and whose families were consequently in peril.

In response to the growing number of people seeking admission to the United States, Congress later passed the **Refugee Act of 1980.** It specified that political refugees, "those fleeing overt persecution," could be admitted more easily but that people seeking simply to improve their economic circumstances could not. In practice, U.S. officials interpreted the terms "political" and "economic" so that they generally admitted people leaving communist regimes but not those fleeing right-wing dictatorships. For example, Cubans and Soviet Jews invariably qualified under the Refugee Act, but Haitians often did not. (The number of undocumented Haitians entering the United States, however, rose rapidly.) Many Guatemalans and Salvadorans, hoping to escape repres-

Chinatown, San Francisco People navigating many U.S. cities found decoding bilingual signage a useful, if not necessary, skill.

sive military governments backed by the United States during the 1980s, stood little chance of being admitted as legal immigrants. Thousands of undocumented immigrants from all over Central America, however, entered the United States to look for work.

Immigration soon began generating political controversy. As proponents and opponents of restrictions offered conflicting perspectives on how new immigrants, both legal and undocumented, were affecting domestic life, partisan differences emerged. In general, Democrats favored less restrictive policies than their GOP counterparts. Although many congressional Republicans hoped President Ronald Reagan would weigh in on their side, he played a minimal role in the passage of the Immigration Reform and Control Act of 1986. This measure, at first glance, looked fairly restrictive. It granted full residency status to recent immigrants who could prove that they had been living in the United States since 1982, but it included stricter penalties on businesses employing undocumented workers. Lacking effective means of enforcing its penalties on employers, however, the new law did little to halt the flow of immigrants, especially during a time when jobs in the United States remained plentiful.

As a result, the debate over immigration grew more acrimonious and increasingly polarized. Another congressional act, in 1990, raised the number of immigrants who could legally be admitted on the basis of special job skills or the investment capital they could bring to the United States. A 1996 report, by a special congressional Commission on Immigration Reform, called for lowering the total of official immigration slots and for tightening restrictions against undocumented workers, but a wide range of political and social movements opposing such changes blocked such a response by Congress.

Conflicting demands and contradictory claims about the economic impact of immigrant workers helped stalemate further change in policy. Most business interests favored relatively

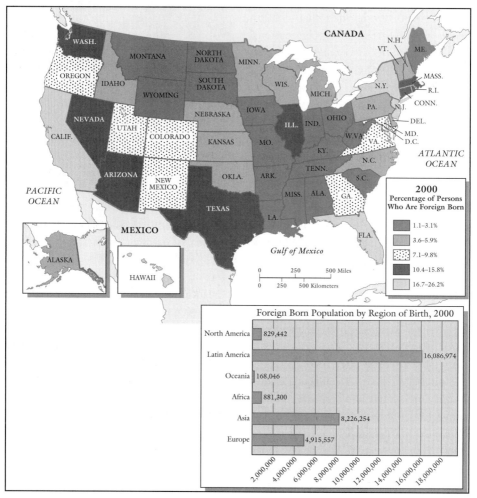

Map 31.2   New Americans: Percentage of Persons Who Are Foreign Born and Foreign-Born Population by Region of Birth, 2000   This map and chart illustrate the wave of new immigration into the United States. Which regions of the world contributed the most immigrants? Which states received the most, and the least, immigration?

Source: U.S. Census Bureau, Census 2000 Summary File 3, Matrix P21; U.S. Census Bureau, Census 2000 American Indian and Alaska Native Summary File, Matrices PCT43, PCT46, and PCT48.

open immigration policies and opposed strict enforcement of rules against hiring undocumented workers. They supported the claim that immigrants, both the highly educated and the skilled, along with those at the entry level, filled job slots that would otherwise remain open. Opponents, on the other hand, cited figures that suggested immigrants were assuming jobs formerly held by U.S. citizens, especially ones with minimal education and job training, and driving down wage rates. Data to sustain any claim about the precise impact of immigration remained thin and highly contested. Moreover, political debate generally turned on reciting emotionally charged, largely anecdotal evidence rather than on closely analyzing available economic numbers.

The new immigration likely changed California more than any other state. (States along the southwestern border of the United States also felt the impact of immigration from Mexico but never experienced the same high level of Asian immigration as did California.) In the Golden Gate State, the counties of Los Angeles and Orange seemed microcosms of world culture. By 2000, fewer than half of schoolchildren in LA could claim proficiency in English, and no single ethnic group comprised a majority of the city's population. As with the earlier surges of immigration, the wave that began during the 1970s produced not only problems and ethnic-based rivalries but also cooperation and hopes for the benefits of multiculturalism.

The Metropolitan Nation

Urban-suburban demographics, too, remained in a state of flux. At the end of the 20th century, more than 80 percent of Americans lived in vast metropolitan areas. With the overall population growing, though more slowly than during the 1950s and 1960s, the relationship between central cities and adjacent suburbs continued to change. Many once-distinct suburban areas melded into **"urban corridors,"** or "metropolitan strips," which ran along freeway links between older cities such as Seattle and Tacoma or Washington and Baltimore. Outlying areas also sprouted "edge cities," shopping and business complexes such as the Tyson's Corner area, just outside of Washington, D.C. Edge cities competed with older urban centers for businesses, jobs, and residents. People living in these new areas, studies showed, rarely found the need to visit the nearby center cities.

Demographic patterns in suburbia also changed. First, greater numbers of people from non-European backgrounds began moving to suburbs, just as more Americans of European descent were relocating in cities. As a result, the percentage of African Americans residing in urban centers steadily declined, and the percentage living in suburbia increased, especially after 1990. With a number of immigrant groups settling outside central cites, some suburbs—even in midsized urban areas such as Minneapolis-St. Paul, Minnesota—came to contain more people identified with non-European ethnic groups than the central cities they surrounded.

Second, many new suburbs sprouted up farther away than ever from either edge or core cities. A frenzy of new construction transformed more and more farmland and small towns into a series of sprawling housing developments, which demographers called "exurbs." Built on relatively inexpensive land, exurbs allowed cost-conscious home buyers, many of them drawn to the tax-cutting policies of the Republican Party, to purchase more space for less money. At the same time, exurban areas of the early 21st century, as had the new suburbs of the mid-20th century, offered families with young children newly built schools and freshly constructed playgrounds. They also, however, allowed anyone commuting to work the opportunity to spend up to several hours every day trapped inside a car, inching in and out of exurban areas.

Meanwhile, the nation's urban cores underwent continual transformation. During the 1970s and much of the 1980s, as manufacturing jobs began leaving urban areas and retail shopping continued to shift to outlying malls, cities focused on becoming financial, administrative, and entertainment centers. Distinct areas in most large cities also faced rising rates of homelessness, crime, and infrastructure deterioration, especially in their sewer and water systems. Big-city mayors complained that the government in Washington did little to address urban problems. Federal funding decreased from $64 per urban resident in 1980 to less than $30 by 1993.

During the late 1980s and 1990s, however, parts of most central cities underwent a stunning revival that reversed the declines of the 1970s. A building boom brought new office towers, residential buildings, and sports and arts complexes to downtowns across the country. Moreover, the population drain away from cities, at least in part, shifted into reverse. People with money to invest in housing and to spend at restaurants and on entertainment began returning to selected areas, which thus became labeled as "gentrified," in most cities.

Many different sources fed the gentrification movement. During the economically troubled 1970s, affluent young people in the rapidly expanding 25-to-44 age category rediscovered cities as interesting, relatively inexpensive places in which to live. Older homes and neighborhoods, which their parents had rejected, suddenly looked potentially "quaint" and "charming," especially when properly renovated. Encouraged by federal laws that provided funds and tax breaks for refurbishing historic buildings, developers and ordinary people looked for workers skilled in dry-walling, tuck-pointing, and kitchen remodeling. During the 1980s and 1990s, the relatively healthy national economy helped the urban revival continue. Innovative urban design schemes skillfully integrated diverse architectural styles with new green spaces and revitalized river- and lakefronts.

At the turn of the 21st century, many U.S. cities seemed to be emerging as exciting, transnational spaces. Community development corporations (CDCs), grassroots efforts indebted to movement cultures of the 1960s and early 1970s, helped finance affordable housing, child-care facilities, and employment opportunities. The Community Reinvestment Act, which obliged banks to invest in low-income areas, stimulated economic activity. Community policing, a trend toward harsher sentencing, and an aging population lowered urban crime rates. Moreover, commuters frustrated by increasingly clogged freeways discovered that they could save both time and money by moving from distant suburbs to revitalizing downtowns. In addition, new immigrants, many bringing marketable skills and significant amounts of capital, also repopulated once-declining neighborhoods, refurbishing property and reviving commercial zones.

Economic Change

Focus Question
What were the most important, post-1970 technological and economic changes? How did technological change create both new problems and new possibilities?

Most people living in the United States at the turn of the 20th century oriented their lives around technologies that were either unavailable or only in their infancy 30 years earlier. The most technologically sophisticated could awake to some kind of digital device; pop breakfast into a microwave; telecommute to work, at home, on a portable computer; and talk to friends or colleagues over a cell phone. They could interrupt work, or follow it up, by listening to music downloaded from the Internet; watching a movie or television program recorded earlier; and going online to seek information, entertainment, or companionship. The pace of post-1970 technological change, in short, brought astonishing transformations in work routines and the rhythms of daily life.

New Technologies

Some of the most noteworthy technological changes occurred in biotechnology, in high-performance computing machines and software, and in other communications systems.

In one of the most important research projects of the late 20th century, scientists announced in June 2000 that they had successfully mapped the entire human genetic code. This **Human Genome Project** paved the way for new techniques of gene transfer, embryo manipulation, tissue regeneration, and even cloning. Breakthroughs in biotechnology promised new approaches to the treatment of cancer and other diseases. Genetic manipulation in plants seemed able to revolutionize food production, waste conversion, and toxic cleanup. Large food companies heralded the use of genetically modified crops as an extension of the earlier "green revolution," which had boosted agricultural yields.

Serious questions about the role of science in manipulating genetic codes and altering reproductive processes, however, soon arose. Controversy swirled around the impact of genetically modified foods on the planet's biodiversity. Research on fetal stem cells, which could be used to regenerate human tissue, raised a highly politicized religious-ethical debate over the definition of life.

The computer revolution entered a new phase during the 1970s. The introduction of **microchips** boosted the hardware capability and reduced the size and cost of computers. Powerful memory capacities and parallel processors, which allow many operations to run simultaneously, transformed industrial and informational systems, lowering labor costs and making production schedules more flexible. "Artificial intelligence" (AI) capabilities emerged, along with voice interaction between people and machines.

New communications technologies, such as fiber-optic networks and satellite transmission, and the computer revolution also fueled an **"information revolution."**

Libraries replaced card catalogs with computer networks. Voice-mail, fax transmissions, e-mail, and text-messaging came to supplement or simply replace posted mail and conventional telephone conversations. Cellular phone calls became more common than those using land-lines. The speed and accessibility of information thus changed patterns of human interaction. The simple act of "talking to a real person" or to a consumer representative who lived in the same community or even the same country became an increasingly rare occurrence.

Big Business

Other forms of computerized communications helped transform business operations. Although the practice of buying on credit had become increasingly common since the 1920s, vast computer systems greatly assisted the rapid expansion of bank-issued credit cards. Other innovations—automated teller machines (ATMs), automatic depositing, debit cards, and electronic bill payment—moved Americans closer to a cashless economy. Congressional deregulation of financial industries during the 1980s and 1990s, which prompted the Savings & Loan crisis, also permitted banking institutions and brokerage houses to offer similar financial services, accelerating competition among the financial giants that sold stocks, lent money, and offered insurance.

Franchises and chain stores also changed consumption and workplace patterns. McDonald's and Holiday Inn had pioneered nationwide standardization in the fast-food and travel industries during the late 1950s. Other chains soon copied their models. Starbucks elevated a simple beverage into pricey designer commodities. The Arkansas-based Wal-Mart chain became the country's largest private employer. By the early 21st century, one of about every 120 workers and nearly one of every 20 workers in the retail sector received their paycheck from Wal-Mart. Such chains often brought a greater array of merchandise and lower prices, but critics charged them with crushing local, independent retailers in thousands of midsized and small towns.

U.S. chain businesses expanded overseas as well. After the end of the Cold War, McDonald's opened to great fanfare in Moscow and Budapest, while the Hilton chain quickly placed new hotels in Eastern European capitals. Pepsi and Coke carried their "cola wars" into foreign markets. Starbucks created a controversy when it opened a branch in Beijing's imposing Forbidden City.

Amazon.com led another branch of innovation—e-commerce, or the practice of buying and selling products over the Internet. At the end of the 1990s, a wave of new "dot-com" businesses promised to move more and more purchasing to the Internet and set off a short-term bubble in dot-com stocks. During 2000, stock prices for these enterprises collapsed as dramatically as they had risen. Buying and selling on the Web, however, remained an important new feature of consumer culture. Amazon and eBay, the online auction site, became models for doing business in cyberspace.

Production, as well as consumption, turned global. U.S. automakers, for example, increasingly moved their procurement and assembly work offshore, even as foreign car

© Keren Su/CORBIS

Lattes in Shanghai   American chain businesses spread throughout the world, part of the controversial process known as globalization.

manufacturers established new assembly plants in the United States. Moreover, the trend toward privatization (the sale of government-owned industries to private business) in many economies worldwide provided U.S. based firms with new opportunities for overseas acquisitions. Conversely, foreign interests purchased many U.S. companies and real estate holdings. In the early 1990s, RCA, Doubleday, Mack Truck, and Goodyear were just some of the traditionally American brands owned by foreign-based corporations. So many industrial giants had become global by the early 21st century that it was difficult to define what constituted a U.S. company or a foreign one.

Postindustrial Restructuring

New technologies and economic globalization helped change the American business structure and the workforce. In the 1970s, citing pressure from international competition and declining profits, many companies began cutting back their workforce and trimming their management staff, moves known as "downsizing." Major steel plants closed, and the auto industry laid off thousands of workers. In the 1980s and 1990s, the steel and auto industries temporarily regained profitability, but other sectors took their turns at downsizing. Business restructuring, together with the government's deregulation of major industries, touched off a merger boom. During the prosperity of the late 1990s, huge mergers, with acquisitions totaling more than $1.6 trillion per year, brought a concentration in corporate power unseen since the 1890s.

Meanwhile, the kinds of jobs held by Americans shifted. As employment in traditional manufacturing and extractive sectors (such as mining) decreased, jobs in the service sector, high-tech fields, and the information and entertainment areas increased. In 1960, the production of goods, as opposed to services, had engaged roughly one-quarter of the U.S. workforce. By the early 21st century, the comparable figure stood at about 15 percent. Moreover, according to one estimate, more than 40 percent of U.S. corporate profits came from the financial services sector, while only about 10 percent came from manufacturing. Financial services, computing, and other high-tech sectors offered relatively high salaries—astronomical ones for top management—but most jobs in the rapidly expanding service sector—such as clerks and cleaners—remained low paying, part-time, and nonunionized.

Many individuals and families maintained their lifestyles by incurring rising levels of personal debt. In addition to discussing the "U.S. deficit," economists began analyzing "the household deficit," the difference between what U.S. households earned and what they actually spent. As late as 1980, the rate of indebtedness for households, though higher than that during the 1950s, still remained lower than it had been during the 1920s. The 1980s, however, inaugurated a trend that would accelerate into the next century: People living in the United States assumed ever-larger financial obligations enabled through various credit arrangements. As more people shouldered greater debt, the number of personal bankruptcies increased. Conversely, opportunities for accumulating one's own rainy day fund declined. The rate of personal savings in the United States fell to the lowest in the industrialized world.

In turn, the nation's business structure came to include a complex set of greatly expanded, often politically influential, financial institutions. (Financial institutions, benficiaries of deregulation, constituted the largest contributors to political parties.) Some pundits called these, taken together, the "Debt and Credit-Industrial Complex" or the "Borrower-Industrial Complex." A wide range of businesses—from international "super banks," such as Citigroup and the Bank of America, to street corner institutions, such as Check 'n' Go and Moneytree, to pawn-shop chains, such as Pawn America, right on down to illegal loan sharking operations—profited from people who never seemed able to balance their personal books. Many neighborhood loan sharks, cynics quipped, operated with only slightly less regulation, while providing more cordial service, than large banking chains. Federal court decisions and regulatory rulings during the 1990s effectively gave credit-card issuers a green light when charging interest rates and imposing other terms. Banks competed for customers from all across the spectrum but placed increasing importance on spreading "plastic" among the college-age population, for whom personal indebtedness was soaring. Observing the growth of a financial sector reined in by fewer and fewer governmental regulations, the head of the U.S. Senate's banking committee rejected any calls for re-regulation. Greater competition among lenders, he claimed, rather than greater oversight by government, provided the best solution to questionable banking practices: We "believe freedom is the answer," he insisted.

As important business sectors, particularly the financial one, flourished, virtually every part of the labor union movement suffered as membership rolls continued to shrink. During the 1950s, more than 30 percent of the U.S. workforce belonged to a union; in the early 1970s, the figure had declined only slightly, to about 29 percent; by 1991, it stood at slightly above 16 percent. By the early 21st century, it slipped further, to around 13 percent. Some unions suffered greater attrition than others. Unions that represented workers in the "needle trades," such as the fabled International Ladies' Garment Workers Union, lost two-thirds of their membership during the last three decades of the 20th century.

Efforts to organize agricultural workers on the West Coast, who were largely of Mexican and Filipino descent, dramatized some of the difficulties of expanding the union movement. **Cesar Chavez,** a charismatic leader who emulated the nonviolent tactics of Martin Luther King, Jr., vaulted the United Farm Workers (UFW) into public attention during the early 1970s. As the union's president and iconic symbol, Chavez undertook personal hunger strikes and instituted well-publicized consumer boycotts of lettuce and grapes to pressure growers to bargain with the UFW. During the later 1970s and the 1980s, however, the UFW steadily lost ground. Strong antiunion stands by growers and the continued influx of new immigrants who were eager for work undercut the UFW's efforts. When Chavez died in April 1993, his union was struggling to recruit new members and to retain those already on its rolls.

The broader union movement faced only slightly less difficulty making inroads into new sectors of the economy. The major growth for organized labor came among government employees and health care workers. Unions launched ambitious organizing drives among clerical, restaurant, and hotel workers, but businesses adamantly fought back. Employers also continued to cut the health and retirement benefits that the leading U.S. firms had once proudly offered.

The system of fringe benefits found in the United States, which many companies had greatly expanded after the Second World War, came under increasing pressure toward the end of the 20th century. An attractive benefit package had once provided an employer, in the relatively competitive job market of the 1940s and 1950s, a way of attracting workers without paying dramatically higher wages and salaries. Moreover, the amount of money a company paid toward its share of a health plan did not count, under federal law, as part of an employee's taxable compensation. Everyone thus stood to gain, it had seemed, from relatively generous benefit programs.

Things had begun to change, however, during the 1960s as U.S. companies faced both increasing foreign competition and rising domestic health care costs. In 1960, only about 5 percent of the entire U.S. GDP went for health care; some 45 years later, the comparable figure reached more than 15 percent, a greater percentage than people paid for food. The annual cost of providing health care for a family, according to most estimates, came to about what a full-time, minimum-wage worker would earn over a year and twice the pay of the average Wal-Mart employee. Any U.S. company facing domestic or foreign competition, such as the large auto manufacturers, found it increasingly difficult to maintain extensive benefit packages that included health care for an aging workforce.

As early as the 1980s, economists warned that the shift to a globalizing "postindustrial" economy was "deskilling" the labor force and eroding living standards in the United States. Critical observers expressed alarm over statistical evidence that so many of the new jobs created in the U.S. economy offered low wages and few benefits. Did the widening gulf between highly paid, highly skilled positions and minimum-wage jobs threaten to undermine the middle-class nature of American society? Wal-Mart, for example, actively resisted the unionization of its enormous workforce, which earned an average of $7 to $8 per hour in 2003 and enjoyed limited or no fringe benefits. Moreover, manufacturers wanting to lower costs to attract the huge Wal-Mart purchasing contracts moved their plants into countries with the least expensive labor costs. This trend further contributed to the disappearance of relatively better-paid manufacturing jobs from the United States.

Other economists painted a different picture. They acknowledged that internationalization and corporate downsizing might temporarily mean lost jobs for some people but insisted that gains in productivity and new jobs generated by innovative industries would eventually translate into lower consumer prices and rising living standards for all. Celebrants of change pointed to many success stories, especially in high-tech industries, where innovation paved a broad avenue of upward economic mobility for those with computer-age skills. Real wages did begin to rise during the 1990s, but this trend would reverse as the economy softened after 2000, and the gap between the highest and lowest income levels continued to grow.

At the beginning of the 20th century, skilled workers had tended to stick to one profession or place of employment throughout their working life. By century's end, even many highly educated professionals likely faced the prospect of switching occupations several times before reaching retirement age. The need for training and retraining programs that served people of all ages, many observers noted, demanded a transformation in the relationship among education, job training, and employment.

The Sports-Entertainment Complex

What might be called a sports-entertainment complex inexorably expanded after 1970. Metropolitan areas competed vigorously to bring a home team to their locale—or retain the ones already located there. Lucrative TV contracts and generous tax write-offs attracted business entrepreneurs, such as George Steinbrenner of the New York Yankees, who decided they might also be interested in running their own sports team. The generation of owners who had relied on revenues from a sports franchise for their primary livelihood, such as the Griffith family in baseball or the Halas family in football, began disappearing. Even professional wrestling, which still bore the imprint of its carnival origins during the 1970s, finally became part of the sports-entertainment complex. During the 1980s, Vince McMahon, Jr., transformed his late father's World Wrestling Federation (later World Wresting Entertainment or WWE) into a multimillion-dollar, worldwide name brand.

Although still unofficially "the national pastime," baseball faced numerous challenges during the post-1970 era. Seeking a better fit with emerging economic, demographic, and social forces, baseball's own leadership tinkered with the structure of their operation. By relocating franchises to burgeoning metropolitan areas, Major League Baseball (MLB) could acquire a fresh supply of fans, advantageous TV deals, and stadiums financed by public money. If moving existing franchises made sense, creating new ones seemed an even shrewder option. In the single decade of the 1970s, for instance, MLB moved teams out of and back into Milwaukee; into, out of, and finally back into Seattle; and out of, back in, and then out again of Washington, D.C.

This kind of franchise reshuffling paled by comparison to that in professional football and basketball, sports that initially claimed greater growth than MLB. The National Football League (NFL) and the National Basketball Association (NBA) had both prospered during the 1960s, in large part because of national television coverage and franchise expansion, especially into the West and South. The NFL's leadership began citing surveys that showed more sports fans narrowly preferred professional football over the slower-moving product of MLB.

Just in time for the 1970 season, the NFL merged with an upstart rival, the American Football League (AFL), with which it had been playing a "Super Bowl" since 1967. Dividing its TV revenues equally, this revamped NFL ensured that a small-market team, such as the Green Bay Packers, enjoyed a secure financial base and the opportunity to compete, over the long run, on a roughly level playing field with larger-market franchises. During the 1970s, ABC began televising an NFL game during prime-time hours, and the instant success of *Monday Night Football* signaled how important sporting events had become to TV and to the nation's popular culture. Noting the obvious, a group of TV entrepreneurs launched, toward the end of the 1970s, ESPN, a new cable network devoted to nothing but sports. In 2006, the flagship *Monday Night Football* offering moved to ESPN.

The NBA rounded out the big three of the sports entertainment business. With its relatively small court making this sport even more TV-friendly than football, professional basketball could expand into new locales and broaden its television coverage. As the NBA's revenues grew, it came to feature high-profile African American stars, such as Julius ("Dr J") Irving, more prominently than either the NFL or MLB. At century's end, the NBA led the sports-entertainment world in promoting African Americans, including its greatest star Michael Jordan, into coaching and management positions.

Promoters aggressively marketed other sports-entertainment operations. These included a greatly expanded National Hockey League (NHL) and revamped tours of the men's Professional Golfing Association (PGA) and a tour for women (LPGA). The nation's love affair with the automobile helped to speed the growth of auto racing. The Indianapolis 500 initially vied with the Super Bowl for recognition as the most spectacular one-day event in sports, but stock-car competition eventually overtook Indy-style racing, expanding from its traditional base in the South. John Kennedy had tried to soft-pedal his fascination with sports, in favor of emphasizing more cerebral pursuits, but later political figures eagerly sought the glamour coming to surround big-time sports. Political candidates rushed to sign up prominent athletes for their campaign squads, and some, including former star quarterback Jack Kemp, successfully made the transition from the sports to the political field. In addition to tapping his family connections, George W. Bush used his part-ownership of the Texas Rangers baseball team as an entrée into electoral politics.

With the business of sports booming, it seemed inevitable that its legal foundations would also begin shifting. Professional players had long complained of receiving a disproportionately small share of profits, but the laws governing sports operations invariably favored owners. A new generation of athletes, armed with union advisers, challenged the old order. In 1970, baseball's owners celebrated when the U.S. Supreme Court narrowly rejected a suit challenging MLB's key contractual arrangement, the reserve clause that bound a player to a team year-after-year, as an unconstitutional form of involuntary servitude. Subsequent rulings, however, created slightly different systems of "free agency" throughout every team-sport enterprise. As a consequence, talented athletes could auction off their services in the marketplace. (The super-talented, such as Bo Jackson, even played off one professional sport against another.) Although some fans grumbled, especially when highly paid players failed to perform up to expectations, owners discovered that steadily rising revenues from TV, tax breaks, and favorable stadium deals could support the new salary structures. Perhaps the most successful examples of unionization in the post-1970 era came in the sports-entertainment field, where labor strikes remained a viable option for unions. Knowledgeable fans found themselves needing to become conversant with labor relations as well as more traditional sports-world matters.

Sports and legal questions also became intertwined with social issues. Feminists condemned big-time sports for promoting sexism—pointing, for example, to the emphasis the NFL placed on female cheerleading squads that resembled Las Vegas chorus lines—and urged inclusion of more opportunities and better financial rewards for women athletes. Colleges and universities, mandated by Title IX of the Educational Amendments of 1972 to achieve equality in sports activities, faced difficult decisions about how to finance and promote women's sports. In women's sports where professionalism prevailed, such as tennis and golf, the trend was unabashedly toward emulating the male model. Prize money, endorsement contracts, and media coverage for women athletes all steadily escalated during the last decades of the 20th century.

As the importance that cultural commentators assigned to Jackie Robinson's struggle to desegregate MLB during the 1940s had underscored, the sports-entertainment complex had long provided a cultural mirror. Sports supposedly reflected and represented larger themes. How much opportunity the sports-entertainment complex really offered to people of non-European descent, a question that had been raised dramatically by a Black Power protest at the 1968 Summer Olympics, remained a persistent issue. By the early 21st century, the number of African Americans playing MLB was declining, while that of Latino ballplayers was soaring. Similarly, as NBA scouts identified talented international players, especially from Eastern Europe, some observers began to fear that the strong African American presence might disappear from professional basketball courts.

As the sports-entertainment complex grew in wealth and visibility, traditionalists inevitably saw signs of decline. Sporting events, such as the Winter and the Summer Olympic Games, no longer amateur competitions in any meaningful sense, seemed awash in commercialism and on-field corruption. Similarly, the surge of interest in MLB at the end of the 20th and the beginning of the next century appeared to owe a great deal to the prodigious feats of homerun hitters, led by Mark McGwire, Sammy Sosa, and

Barry Bonds. It soon became evident, however, that consumption of greater quantities of performance-enhancing drugs was helping players drive balls out of MLB parks. The super-knowledgeable sports fan, it seemed, not only needed a background in legal but now in pharmaceutical matters as well.

Media and Popular Culture

Focus Question
How did new forms of media change the ways in which people received information and entertainment?

A greater range of knowledge could prove handy for fans of all popular culture. New technologies significantly altered how people received and used books, movies, TV, music, and informational resources. By the early 21st century, virtually every home or apartment had at least one television and VCR or DVD player, and about 60 percent had a personal computer. People looked to the Internet for access to newspapers, books, music, and movies. E-mail and text-messaging increasingly became the first choice for contacting friends. The omnipresent video screen, which became ever more portable, seemed the preeminent symbol of American culture.

The Video Revolution

At the beginning of the 1970s, TV broadcasters could still expect a hit program to draw more viewers in a single evening than a hit motion picture attracted over an entire year. The three networks could promise advertisers that a rough cross section of the American public would be in front of their TV sets watching their sales pitches.

During the 1970s, however, the networks found themselves increasingly forced to embrace the strategy called "narrowcasting," fragmenting the viewing audience into carefully targeted segments. CBS replaced several highly watched programs, such as *The Beverly Hillbillies,* with shows aimed toward viewers under the age of 40, those coveted by advertisers because research studies identified them as more likely than older viewers to spend money on products and services. CBS also introduced "edgier" programming. *All in the Family,* a sitcom about a blue-collar family's intergenerational conflicts associated with the 1960s, made its bigoted protagonist, Archie Bunker, a lightning rod for issues involving race and gender. Although *The Mary Tyler Moore Show* rarely took overtly feminist positions, its cleverly constructed storylines and sharp dialogue consistently addressed the personal politics of working women. Other CBS shows, such as the antiwar sitcom *M*A*S*H,* also merged comedy and social commentary.

With CBS leading the way, the entire TV industry prospered during a nearly 10-year period beginning in the mid-1970s. ABC found its niche among high-school and college-age viewers, emphasizing sex-and-action programs (*Charlie's Angels*), mildly risqué sitcoms

(*Three's Company*), and shows about teen life (*Happy Days*). NBC brought the barbed humor of the 1960s Counterculture to network television by nurturing *Saturday Night Live*. At the end of the 1970s, nine of every ten television sets were tuned to a network program during prime-time viewing hours.

A decade later, however, network programmers faced a harsher TV landscape. NBC could claim two now-classic hits, *The Cosby Show* (featuring an affluent African American family) and *Cheers* (set in a Boston tavern where "everybody knows your name"), but its other prime-time programs garnered disappointing ratings. Facing a similar situation, the other two networks joined NBC in slashing budgets and staff, especially in their news-gathering divisions. At the same time, local stations, which formerly limped along without a network affiliation, suddenly thrived. These independents programmed older Hollywood films, sporting events, and reruns of canceled, prime-time shows now being syndicated to individual stations. Several hundred independent television stations debuted during the 1980s.

Capitalizing on the rise of these independents, the Fox television network went on the air in 1988. Using a pattern that was later imitated by other would-be networks, Fox offered a limited schedule to previously nonaffiliated stations. Fox's first big hit, *The Simpsons,* an animated send-up of the standard family sitcom, became a pop cultural phenomenon and mass-marketing bonanza. In 1993, Fox outbid CBS for the rights to carry professional football games. The WB, UPN, and Fox networks featured programs, such as *Buffy the Vampire Slayer, That 70s Show,* and *Malcolm in the Middle,* for audiences that contained more minority, young, and urban viewers than those of the three older networks.

New technologies, which promised viewers greater choice, challenged all of these networks. The remote control, an innovation of the 1960s that finally caught on during the 1980s, created a television aesthetic called "channel surfing," in which viewers flipped rapidly from program to program. Videocassette recorders (VCRs), introduced during the 1980s, became the first of the record-and-view-later technologies allowing viewers even greater control over their television offerings.

The initial challenge to the networks came from cable television (CATV), which was in nearly 75 percent of the nation's homes by 2000. The arrival of CATV accelerated the fragmentation of TV's audience. Atlanta's Ted Turner introduced the Cable News Network (CNN), several movie channels, and an all-cartoon network before his communication empire merged with that of Time-Warner. Companies selling direct satellite transmission challenged both the networks and cable, but the lack of a standard reception format slowed the expansion of this competing medium. By the early 21st century, the percentage of viewers watching prime-time network programs had fallen from 90 percent to under 60 percent. At the 2003 Emmy awards ceremonies, shows initially running on CATV received, for the first time, more awards than those carried on the traditional networks.

The "New Hollywood"

New technologies and changing business practices during the 1970s produced a "New Hollywood." With movie attendance in 1970 about the same as it had been in 1960, Hollywood studios needed to change their mode of operation. They began raising ticket prices, betting

The Family Guy As the once mass U.S. TV audience began to fragment, animated shows increasingly found exceedingly loyal niche markets, especially on cable channels. The FOX network debuted *The Family Guy* in 1999 but canceled the series in 2000 and, again, in 2002. After noting the popularity of *The Family Guy* in re-runs and the strong DVD sales, FOX began producing new episodes for the Cartoon Network. Although the inept anti-hero of the series, "Peter Griffin," recalls "Fred Flintstone" and "Homer Simpson," aficionados of this series prefer to consider his antics and *The Family Guy's* references to popular culture several cuts above those found on *The Flintstones* and *The Simpsons*.

on a few blockbuster films, such as the highly profitable *Star Wars* series (1977–2005), and hoping for a surprise hit, such as *My Big Fat Greek Wedding* (2002). Yet for every blockbuster or unexpected success, there was a super-expensive flop such as *Gigli* (2003).

Volatility in the movie market encouraged most filmmakers to play it safe. Many movie makers recycled titles and special effects that had made money in the past. They transferred popular stories, such as *How the Grinch Stole Christmas* (2000), and TV shows, such as *The Brady Bunch* (1995), to the big screen and produced sequels for any movie, such as *Pirates of the Caribbean* (2003), which even approached blockbuster status. In addition, Hollywood expanded the older practice of targeting younger viewers with movies such as *Ferris Bueller's Day Off* (1986). Meanwhile, celebratory stories that tapped themes in popular history, such as *Braveheart* (1995) and *Titanic* (1997), impressed both ticket buyers and industry insiders.

At the same time, however, relatively small-scale movies also began to flourish. Woody Allen became one of the first U.S. filmmakers to specialize in movies, such as *Crimes and Misdemeanors* (1989) and *Scoop* (2006), which borrowed techniques and themes from European cinema. The actor-director Robert Redford launched the Sundance Film Institute in the hopes of encouraging "offbeat" examples of screenwriting and direction. Held in Park City, Utah, the annual Sundance Festival began attracting Hollywood moguls who sought the next "small" movie, such as *The Blair Witch Project* (1999), which might find a large audience. The CATV lineup soon included several outlets, including the Sundance Channel, for independent films, and the Landmark movie chain featured films that seemed unlikely to play in the multiplex mall theaters. Some major studios even created special divisions, such as Paramount Classics, to specialize in so-called independent films. Moviemakers also experimented with digital technology, and by 2007, digital movies played regularly in commercial theaters, a trend traditionalists condemned for degrading the visual richness of cinematic imagery.

The New Hollywood became increasingly intertwined with the changing television establishment—once its feared rival—and with the emerging VCR, DVD, and iPod industries. Hollywood gained badly needed revenue by licensing its offerings to TV and for VCR and DVD distribution. During the 1980s and early 1990s, before a few chain operations cornered the market, the United States had claimed more video rental outlets than movie theaters. Constantly updated technologies gave viewers improved visual imagery, bonus attractions, such as footage cut from the theatrical release, wide-screen prints, and the kind of expert commentary and analysis hitherto only available at a film school. As Hollywood studios discovered that DVD sales easily matched theatrical receipts, they sought action films with elaborate special effects that promised to sell well on DVD. They also confronted, however, new "pirating" technologies that allowed their movies to appear in illegal, bootlegged editions at virtually the same time they debuted in theaters.

The Changing Media Environment

CATV, VCRs, and digital technology transformed the entire media-entertainment environment, including the pop music industry. The Music Television channel (MTV), initially offering a 24-hour supply of rock videos, debuted in 1981. Critics immediately charged it with portraying women as sex objects and excluding artists of color. Eventually, however, MTV defused complaints, especially after featuring Michael Jackson's 29-minute video based on his hit single "Thriller" (1983). By the early 21st century, MTV and other CATV channels programmed videos that represented the increasingly multiethnic nature of the music industry.

Musical performers of the 1980s, such as Madonna, used MTV to forge a new relationship between music and visual imagery, the "MTV aesthetic." This fast-paced visual style played with traditional ideas about time and space, recycled images from movies and TV programs, and often carried a sharp, satirical edge. The hit series *Miami Vice,* revived as a feature film in 2006, helped introduce the MTV aesthetic to a broader audience. During the 1990s, MTV abandoned its initial all-video format and developed a wide range of youth-oriented programming. Its cult classic, *The Real World,* anticipated the run of "reality" shows that quickly became staples on other CATV channels and on the networks.

Entertainment conglomerates began marketing music in a variety of ever newer formats. The 45-rpm record and the long-play album (LP), associated with the musical revolutions of the 1950s and 1960s, all but disappeared. Digital compact discs (CDs) and iPods changed not only the technology through which pop music was delivered but also the nature of the product and the listening experience. The classic LPs of the late 1960s and early 1970s had featured 10 to 12 songs, split between the two sides and often organized around a core theme. The turn-of-the-21st-century CD player or iPod, by contrast, could hold a hodge-podge of songs, with themes, if any, established by the listener, not the producer.

Taken together, the Internet and digital technology permitted people to obtain, pre-serve, and exchange music in entirely new ways. The commercial music industry and most artists complained about people using the Internet to pirate copyrighted material. After years of legal sparring, while the practice of Internet file swapping soared, the music indus-try tried a carrot-and-stick approach. It began selling songs online and filed an unprece-dented number of lawsuits for copyright infringement against ordinary people who were sharing music files from their personal computers.

The New Mass Culture Debate

New trends in mass commercial culture predictably generated popular controversy. In 1975, the Federal Communications Commission (FCC) ordered the television networks to dedicate the first 60 minutes of prime-time each evening to "family" programming free of violence or "mature" themes. Eventually, federal courts struck down this family-hour requirement as a violation of the First Amendment's guarantee of free expression. Demands that Congress regulate rock lyrics and album covers also ran afoul of complaints that this kind of legislation would be unconstitutional. Eventually, TV programmers, record pro-ducers, and new Internet gaming companies, following the example of the Hollywood film industry, adopted "warning labels" that supposedly informed parents about products with violent and sexually explicit imagery.

Meanwhile, works of commercial culture were attracting serious aesthetic analysis. Unlike the critics of the 1950s, who had dismissed mass culture as trivial and degenerate, analysts who gravitated to the new academic field of Cultural Studies, and its various spin-offs in the journalistic world, often seemed to be unabashed fans of the commercial prod-ucts they studied. Most consequently jettisoned the distinction between lowbrow and highbrow. The music of The Beatles could be studied along with that of Beethoven, and Bob Dylan's lyrics along with poetic classics. The careers of manufactured celebrities such as Britney Spears and Tom Cruise attracted the attention of entertainment journalists and academics. They sought to understand what the popularity of these iconic figures pur-portedly signified about American life. The Cultural Studies approach rejected the elitist-sounding criticism of the 1950s, which had seen consumers as cultural "dupes" who pas-sively soaked up worthless products. Instead, it stressed how people could interact creatively with commercial culture. Scholarly studies of *Star Trek,* for example, examined how, through self-produced magazines (called "fanzines"), conventions, and the Internet, "Trekkies" had created a grassroots subculture that used the TV series of the 1960s and its spin-offs to launch and sustain discussions about social and political issues.

The Cultural Studies approach tended to embrace multiculturalism. It highlighted, and often celebrated, works produced by women, political outsiders, and non-Western writers and artists. It also encouraged students to see traditional texts within their political and historical contexts rather than as timeless works. Traditionalists condemned this "cultural turn" as a legacy of the counterculture of the 1960s and blamed it for eroding settled ideas of artistic quality and value.

Some of the fiercest debates over an alleged decline in the popular arts involved the emergence of an "infotainment" complex, especially on television. An imprecise cultural category, infotainment signaled that the always-delicate balance between informing and merely amusing audiences was now tilting decisively toward the latter side of the equation. TV news operations, for instance, seemed to have headed in this direction with the 1981 retirement of revered CBS newscaster Walter Cronkite, long considered the "most trusted" person in the country. None of Cronkite's successors, including his replacement at CBS, Dan Rather, ever gained his elevated reputation and credibility.

At the same time, the invention and expansion of CATV news brought strains of infotainment to the gathering and dissemination of news about the United States and the world. Images and commentary, to be sure, reached far more households and ran 24/7 on Cable Network News (CNN), which debuted in 1980. None of the anchors or reporters who worked for this path-breaking operation, however, achieved the oracle-like aura that people such as Cronkite had earlier supplied. As initially directed by Ted Turner, the mercurial CATV visionary, CNN sometimes pursued a "hard-news" agenda, from camera crews and correspondents stationed around the globe, but increasingly stressed programs, such as its one-time signature offering *Firing Line*, that relied on the in-studio pyrotechnics of verbally dueling pundits. Its eventual rival, the Fox News Channel (FNS), created in 1996 as a right-leaning alternative to CNN, retrofitted the *Firing Line* approach and used it in much of its programming, which came to feature a recognizable stable of attractive, verbally quick personalities with conservative views.

Moreover, in contrast to the old TV network format, which aimed at a "big-tent" audience, public affairs coverage on CATV adopted an avowedly narrowcasting strategy. With talk- and news-radio, local TV news programs, and most Internet sites offering much the same approach, critics of the new trends stressed how narrowly informed, according to polling data, consumers of the wide array of public affairs programming seemed to be. Infotainment seemed intent on reconfirming the existing perspectives of its core constituencies. In this same vein, public-opinion data suggested that two popular "fake" news programs, *The Daily Show* and *The Colbert Report,* themselves testaments to the Comedy Central network's own limited audience strategy, likely produced—or simply attracted—viewers who were more broadly informed about issues than aficionados of the "real" news programs.

Another "Great Awakening"

The 1960s, according to most cultural historians, ushered in another religious **Great Awakening.** By employing this term, they did not mean that the nation's diverse people suddenly became roused to spiritual enthusiasm. Religiosity had long been a far more powerful component of cultural life in the United States than in European nations. The last decades of the 20th century, however, witnessed the further intensification of always intense religious sentiments. People drawn to the **Religious Right** became particularly vocal about their commitment to seeing the world through religious teachings, but this perspective was hardly limited to political conservatives. Polls taken during the 1990s revealed that more than 75 percent of Americans believed in a divine being who performed miracles on earth.

This latest Great Awakening emerged within a culture of greater religious diversity than the nation had ever witnessed. During the 1950s, for example, Will Herberg could confidently expect his book entitled *Protestant-Catholic-Jew* (1955) to characterize the religious dimensions of the "American Way of Life." A half-century later, however, these three faiths represented only some of the religious dominations in the United States.

The cultural ferment of the 1960s, for example, affected the nation's religious landscape. Popular memory still identifies the 1960s with cultlike movements, such as the "Jesus People," loosely associated with the Counterculture. Embracing a strategy used by earlier groups that aimed at religious purification, some countercultural groups withdrew from secular institutions and sought to create communal retreats organized around religious principles and teachings. Many people drawn to alternative cultures during the 1960s also embraced spiritual and religious impulses outside of the Protestant-Catholic-Jewish triad. Asian-inspired spiritual traditions, such as Transcendental Meditation and Buddhism, also proved appealing. Looking out from his own Harvard University campus into his local community during the mid-1970s, a religion professor claimed to find more than 40 Asian religions being practiced.

More importantly, the Immigration Act of 1965 enabled larger numbers of immigrants from a variety of places—and religious backgrounds—to come to the United States. By the early 1990s, as the array of different faiths continually expanded, the weekly directory of religious services in LA's leading newspaper noted times and places for nearly 600 different denominations.

Immigration swelled the numbers of people in particular religious faiths, especially Islam, which had held only a minimal presence in the United States prior to about 1970. The Black Power impulse had attracted some new converts to the homegrown Nation of Islam during the 1960s, and later immigration from countries with large Islamic populations brought to the United States several million people who practiced more traditional versions of Islam. According to careful estimates—the official U.S. Census does not track religious affiliations—the number of U.S. residents who practiced Islam by the year 2000 surpassed that of Judaism or of individual mainline Protestant denominations such as Presbyterian and Episcopalian.

Gradually adapting to U.S. cultural conditions, mosques began making Sundays, rather than the traditional Friday, the week's major Islamic holy day. In a similar spirit, leading Islamic institutions such as the Islamic Center of Southern California and the Muslim Community Center in Chicago came to offer a variety of religious and nonreligious services for their congregations. They also sought to inform non-Muslims about their faith, which claimed more followers worldwide than any other religion, and to present an organized front against acts of discrimination.

Similar growth spurts came among Protestant evangelicals and Mormons, both of which grew faster than the U.S. population as a whole. Between the 1960s and the 1990s, the Southern Baptist Convention, moving outside of its regional base in the South, added 6 million new members. The Church of Jesus Christ of the Latter Day Saints (the Mormon faith) added more than half that many. In addition to augmenting their membership rolls in the United States, many of these groups greatly expanded their international missionary activities.

Although the fundamentalist and evangelical faiths associated with the Religious Right flourished, religious allegiance varied considerably all across the political spectrum. A number of evangelical groups such as the Sojourners, for example, embraced sociopolitical positions almost diametrically opposed to those espoused by the New Right.

© Rebecca Cook/Reuters/CORBIS

The Islamic Center of America, Dearborn, Michigan Opened in the spring of 2005, this 70,000 square-foot facility dramatized the growing presence of Islam in the United States. It features building materials imported from throughout the world, a gold dome, twin minarets, and a prayer hall that can accommodate a thousand worshippers.

Moreover, many evangelicals began to embrace the cause of environmental stewardship, a policy once associated more with the political left.

Most organized religious groups struggled with questions about the relationship between spiritual faith and the lifestyles celebrated by LGBT movements. Some leaders of the Religious Right, such as Jerry Falwell, mobilized and organized against what they saw as moral decay. In 1979, he and other like-minded fundamentalist ministers formed the Moral Majority, an activist movement devoted to encountering, as Falwell once put it, enemies of Judeo-Christian values "face-to-face and one-on-one" and to bringing "them under submission to the gospel of Christ." Orthodox Judaism, Islam, and Catholicism also considered same-sex relationships as sinful. In stark contrast, a minority of churches, synagogues, and temples—especially in larger cities—reached out to welcome LGBT members. A few accepted gays and lesbians as ministers and rabbis, and recognizable bodies of "gay theology," grounded in reinterpretations of Biblical passages as well as on general principles of religious tolerance, began to emerge.

Religious divisions emerged over foreign policy questions. During America's longest war, devoutly religious people from virtually every denomination spoke out, from seemingly every possible perspective, about the religious implications of U.S. involvement in Vietnam. If many spiritual leaders and lay people, during the post-1960s era, tended to express foreign policy perspectives comparable to the militant anticommunism that dominated the Religious (and the larger New) Right, a somewhat smaller, and equally devout, number of people believed their religious values impelled them to oppose some U.S. initiatives.

The movement to contain the spread of—and, ultimately, to eliminate—nuclear weapons attracted the support of a number of religious groups, including leaders of the U.S. Catholic Church. After prolonged internal debate among differing factions, Catholic bishops in the United States issued a pastoral letter entitled "The Challenge of Peace" (1983). It joined statements

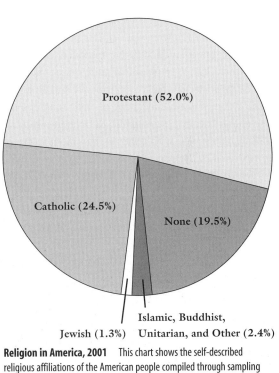

Religion in America, 2001   This chart shows the self-described religious affiliations of the American people compiled through sampling techniques.

Source: Data adapted from *The American Religious Identification Survey,* Graduate Center, City University of New York.

by several Protestant movements and, in effect, declared the nuclear policies of the United States to be in conflict with religious teachings. At about the same time, some Catholic priests joined Protestant congregations in offering sanctuary to undocumented refugees from Latin America, particularly El Salvador and Guatemala, who were fleeing from U.S.-supported military regimes and, once they reached the United States, from immigration authorities.

Three prominent religious figures who entered partisan politics exemplified the diversity of religion's relationship to political action. Father Robert F. Drinan, while a member of the U.S. House of Representatives from 1971 to 1981, generally embraced positions associated with George McGovern's rather than Jimmy Carter's wing of the Democratic Party and, on issues such as abortion, often stood against the pronouncements of his own Roman Catholic Church. Eventually, apparently largely in response to Drinan's political positions, the Church hierarchy ordered that no priest should hold a political office. Espousing political perspectives similar to those of Drinan, the Reverend Jesse Jackson, a Baptist, made two serious bids, in 1984 and in 1988, for the Democratic presidential nomination. He presented himself as part of a "Rainbow Coalition." This movement style of politics looked back, in some ways, to the religious fervor of the civil-rights movement and forward, in other ways, to the secular multiculturalism of post-1960s politics. In contrast, the Protestant evangelist Pat Robertson used his links to the Religious Right to mount an aggressive presidential bid. He hoped to wrest the 1988 GOP presidential nomination away from George H. W. Bush and place it more firmly in the hands of the New Right.

The political campaigns of Jackson and Robertson inevitably revisited charges of corruption that had touched both of their religious movements—and several others as well. The charges against Jackson and Robertson—generally involving sloppy bookkeeping, payrolls heavily staffed with relatives, and ineptly phrased political pronouncements—paled in comparison to the controversies that swamped two other religious movements during the 1980s. Jim and Tammy Faye Bakker of the "Praise the Lord" (PTL) crusade and Jimmy Lee Swaggart, all of whom were prominent celebrities in "the electronic church," saw their multimillion-dollar, multimedia empires collapse when tabloid headlines revealed their well-publicized lapses into the kind of sexual and financial values against which their TV ministries preached. Jim Bakker went to jail, and Swaggart eventually found his TV ministry relegated to public-access CATV channels rather than the top-ranked independent stations on which he once starred.

Far broader and deeper in its appeal than some detractors initially allowed, however, the Religious Right succeeded in establishing itself within the nation's religious-cultural landscape. The crusade led by Billy Graham avoided any hint of financial or moral malfeasance, and Graham remained one of the nation's most admired—and officially nonpartisan—citizens. The Religious Right created cultural-spiritual networks that included publishing enterprises, bookstores, radio and TV outlets, Christian academies and other "charter" schools, an expanded set of religiously affiliated colleges and seminaries, and even schools of law and of public policy.

Emerging early on from this milieu, Hal Lindsey's *The Late, Great Planet Earth* (1970), a best-selling book of the 1970s and 1980s (though not one found on lists compiled by mainstream bookstores and media), prepared the way for other successful apocalyptic novels, particularly the blockbuster *Left Behind* series. Conceived by the Reverend Tim LaHaye, a founder of the Moral Majority, and written by Jerry Jenkins, its 16 entries (1995–2007) featured page-turning tales about Earth's "final days" before the Rapture that would carry true believers to heaven. The actor-director Mel Gibson's *The Passion of the Christ* (2004), a blockbuster movie made outside of the Hollywood studio system, also highlighted the commercial potential of cultural products that tracked the theological-political doctrines of the Religious Right.

This broad movement succeeded in developing a powerful narrative about the history of the United States and of the entire planet, one that could be used to bolster its work on this earth. As articulated by the historian-theologian Francis Schaeffer, a committed evangelical, the people who believed that Christian teachings should shape civil society and the realm of governance had become political outsiders since the Renaissance. In this view of history, the Enlightenment had given birth to **"secular humanism,"** which wrongly separated the secular state from religious values and thus marginalized the true faith. The Religious Right embraced Schaeffer's books, such as *How Should We Then Live* (1976) and *The Christian Manifesto* (1981), as revelatory texts that pointed toward a politics that could reunite the sacred and the secular.

The Republican Party, first in opposition to President Bill Clinton and then in support of George W. Bush, became the primary electoral vehicle of the Religious Right. Religious activists persuaded some state Republican organizations, including that in Texas, to adopt a "Christian" platform that called for curtailing the separation of church and state and radically reorienting the activities of the national government. Also mobilizing and organizing at the local level, the Religious Right created movements that sought to influence the decisions of city and county school boards. From the grassroots to the White House, then, the Religious Right after 1992 played an increasingly important role in an American political culture that revolved around images of hope and fear.

Conclusion

Sweeping changes occurred in demographics, economics, culture, and society during the last quarter of the 20th century. The nation aged, and more of its people gravitated to the Sun Belt. Sprawling urban corridors challenged older central cities as sites for development. Rapid technological change fueled the growth of globalized industries and the restructuring of the labor force to fit a postindustrial economy.

The most prominent development in American popular culture was the proliferation of the video screen. Television, motion pictures, and the Internet increasingly targeted specific audiences, and the fragmented nature of cultural reception was exemplified by the rise of new, particularistic media ventures.

SUGGESTED READINGS

The economic ferment of the late 20th and early 21st centuries may be surveyed, from differing perspectives, in **Daniel Yergin**, *The Commanding Heights: The Battle between Government and the Marketplace That Is Remaking the Modern World* (1998); **Randall E. Stross**, *Eboys: The First Inside Account of Venture Capitalists at Work* (2001); **Kevin Phillips**, *Wealth and Democracy: A Political History of the American Rich* (2003); **Joseph Stiglitz**, *The Roaring Nineties: A New History of the World's Most Prosperous Decade* (2003); and **Paul Krugman**, *The Great Unraveling: Losing Our Way in the New Century* (2003).

An overview of major demographic and social issues can be gleaned, from very different viewpoints, in studies such as **David Hollinger**, *Post-Ethnic America: Beyond Multiculturalism* (1995); **David M. Reimers**, *Unwelcome Strangers: American Identity and the Turn against Immigration* (1998); **Debra L. DeLaet**, *U.S. Immigration Policy in an Age of Rights* (2000); **Joseph Nevins**, *Operation Gate-Keeper: The Rise of the "Illegal Alien" and the Remaking of the U.S.-Mexico Boundary* (2001); **Alice O'Connor**, *Poverty Knowledge: Social Science, Social Policy, and the Poor in Twentieth-Century U.S. History* (2001); and **Hugh Davis Graham**, *Collision Course: The Strange Convergence of Affirmative Action and Immigration Policy in America* (2002).

The much-contested cultural scene comes into view in **Lawrence Grossberg**, *We Gotta Get Out of This Place: Popular Conservatism and Postmodern Culture* (1992); **Fred Goodman**, *Mansion on the Hill: Dylan, Young, Geffen, Springsteen, and the Head-On Collision of Rock and Commerce* (1997); **Robert Kolker**, *Cinema of Loneliness: Penn, Kubrick, Scorsese, Spielberg, Altman* (rev. ed., 2000); **Diana L. Eck**, *A New Religious America* (2003); **Patrick Allitt**, *Religion in America Since 1945: A History* (2003); **Virginia Postel**, *The Substance of Style: How the Rise of Aesthetic Value Is Remaking Commerce, Culture, and Consciousness* (2003); **Sam Roberts**, *Who We Are Now: The Changing Face of America in the Twenty-First Century* (2004); **Reynold Farley** and **John Haaga**, eds., *The American People: Census 2000* (2005); and **Jon C. Teaford**, *The Metropolitan Revolution: The Rise of Post-Urban America* (2006).

Visit the Liberty Equality Power Companion Web site for resources specific to this textbook: http://www.thomsonedu.com/history/murrin

Also find self-tests and additional resources at ThomsonNOW. ThomsonNOW is an integrated online suite of services and resources with proven ease of use and efficient paths to success, delivering the results you want—NOW!

www.thomsonedu.com/login/

Politics of Hope and Fear, 1993–2007

The 1990s brought an eight-year economic boom, the longest in U.S. history. As the stock market moved steadily, and then swiftly, upward, some economic observers began to talk about a new, depression-proof economy. Others warned, accurately as events turned out, that the good times would eventually end. Still, as the federal deficit began to shrink and, then, to disappear, the administration of Bill Clinton took considerable pride in—and credit for—the unprecedented economic growth.

The first Democratic president in 12 years, Clinton successfully urged his party to limit, rather than expand, social-welfare spending. Meanwhile, however, the conservative wing of the Republican Party regrouped behind an effort to reduce federal programs even more than "New Democrats" such as Clinton desired. Political polarization between the two parties intensified during the 1990s, emblemized by the only impeachment trial of a 20th-century U.S. president and the bitterly disputed 2000 presidential election. Once in office as the nation's 43rd president, George W. Bush pushed the economic and social agenda that the New Right had been advocating, especially on tax cuts.

Both the administrations of Clinton and Bush, following in the wake of Bush's own father, tried to chart foreign policies for a post–Cold War world. Clinton pushed initiatives, sometimes against opposition from within his own Democratic Party, consistent with his view of the inevitability of the "globalization" of economic relationships. Clinton's attempt to address other matters, particularly the use of U.S. military power, produced Republican complaints about the lack of any consistent purpose or clear guideposts in his policy making. Following the attacks of September 11, 2001, the Bush White House found a clear focus for its foreign policy: fighting a "war against terrorism" and attempting to prevail in a war in Iraq.

The Presidency of Bill Clinton (1993–2001)

Focus Question
How did President Bill Clinton seek to reshape the Democratic Party's domestic appeal? How did he try to redesign foreign policy for a post–Cold War world?

William Jefferson Clinton brought images of youth, vitality, and cultural diversity to Washington. The inaugural celebration included different balls, including one broadcast live on MTV, for different musical tastes. Clinton's initial cabinet included three African

CHRONOLOGY

1993	Congress approves North American Free Trade Agreement (NAFTA)
1994	Republicans gain control of both houses of Congress and pledge to enact their Contract with America • Special prosecutor Kenneth Starr takes over the investigation of Whitewater allegations
1995	World Trade Organization (WTO) created
1996	The Personal Responsibility and Work Opportunity Reconciliation Act becomes the first major overhaul of the national welfare system since the 1930s • Clinton defeats Robert Dole in the presidential race
1997	Congress and the White House agree on legislation aimed at reducing taxes and rolling back the federal deficit
1998	Republicans lose House seats in off-year election • Republican-controlled House impeaches Clinton
1999	Senate fails to convict Clinton on impeachment charges • Clinton orders bombing campaign against Serbia
2000	Longest economic expansion in U.S. history continues • George W. Bush defeats Gore in close, hotly disputed election decided by U.S. Supreme Court decision
2001	Large tax cuts passed • al-Qaeda terrorists crash passenger airplanes into World Trade Center and Pentagon on September 11 • USA PATRIOT Act passed • U.S. military campaign ousts Taliban from power in Afghanistan
2002	Midterm elections increase Republican majorities in House and Senate
2003	U.S. invades Iraq and overthrows Saddam Hussein • Huge federal budget deficits return • U.S. Supreme Court overturns *Bowers* v. *Hardwick* • Medicare Drug benefit passes
2004	George W. Bush defeats Democratic nominee John Kerry • Allegations of torture at Abu Ghraib revealed
2005	Price of oil soars • Hurricane devastates U.S. Gulf Coast region, especially New Orleans • Permanent Iraqi Government created
2006	U.S. Supreme Court invalidates Bush administration's trial procedure for Guantanamo detainees

Americans and two Latinos; three cabinet posts went to women. His first nominee to the Supreme Court was Ruth Bader Ginsburg, who subsequently became only the second woman to sit on the High Court. As U.S. representative to the United Nations, Clinton named Madeleine Albright, who would later become the country's first female secretary of state during his second term.

Clinton's First Two Years

Emulating Ronald Reagan, Clinton tried to move quickly on domestic issues. An executive order ended the Reagan era's ban on abortion counseling in federally funded family planning clinics. The White House pushed a family leave plan for working parents through Congress; established "Americorps," a program that allowed students to repay college loans through community service; and secured passage of the "Brady Bill," which instituted restrictions on handgun purchases. (The U.S. Supreme Court would later rule a part of this measure exceeded the constitutional authority of Congress.)

Clinton's 1993 deficit-reduction plan also passed, after Vice President **Al Gore** cast a tie-breaking vote in the Senate. To stimulate economic growth, this measure featured a tax increase and spending-cut package aimed at reducing the federal deficit and thereby eventually lowering interest rates. It also expanded an existing governmental program, called the earned tax credit, which assisted low-income workers with children.

In 1994, Congress enacted a Clinton-sponsored anticrime bill that provided federal funds for placing more police officers on the streets. It also contained money for prison construction and a controversial "three strikes and you're out" provision, which mandated a lifetime prison sentence for a third felony conviction.

Clinton's run of domestic successes ended with an ill-fated effort to contain costs and fill gaps in the nation's health care system. First Lady **Hillary Rodham Clinton** led a task force that, by trying to incorporate existing institutions into a new structure, produced a plan so complex that assessments of its potential impact varied widely. The GOP used her proposal to paint both Clintons as "Big Government Democrats." Talk-radio shows by New Right personalities such as Rush Limbaugh featured nonstop criticism of Hillary Clinton and the White House. The Clinton health plan became a hot-button issue on the increasingly important cable news channels, especially CNN. Conservative pressure groups and many business associations lobbied heavily against the plan. Sick on arrival, the proposal died in Congress.

A Republican Congress, a Democratic White House

Congressional Republicans, energized by Representative Newt Gingrich of Georgia and other southerners, led the GOP to a dramatic, unexpected victory in the 1994 elections. For the first time in 40 years, the Republicans gained control of both houses of Congress, ousting 52 Democratic representatives and 10 senators. The GOP also won several new governorships, gained ground in most state legislatures, and made significant headway in many city and county elections, particularly across the South. Gingrich claimed a mandate for the GOP's "Contract with America," an ambitious 10-point program. It aimed at resuscitating the New Right agenda of the 1980s: drastically rolling back federal spending and reducing social-welfare programs and governmental regulations.

Congressional Republicans, however, overplayed their hand. Polls suggested that many people distrusted Gingrich, who became the speaker of the house, more than Clinton. When conflict between a GOP Congress and a Democratic president over budget issues forced two brief shutdowns of governmental agencies, most people blamed congressional Republicans rather than the White House, now advised by Dick Morris, a conservative who counseled Clinton to stress his independence from both parties.

Most importantly, the revived U.S. economy buoyed Clinton's presidency. Alan Greenspan, who had succeeded Paul Volker as head of the Federal Reserve Board during the Reagan administration, gained acclaim as "the Maestro" for helping, through adroit management of the money supply and interest rates, to keep inflation in check. Most economists credited low inflation, declining federal deficits, and increasing productivity with spurring economic growth and creating new jobs. Corporate profits rose, and the U.S. stock markets soared. Some observers talked about a "new economy," one virtually immune to the ups and downs that supposedly always afflicted market-based economies. Most people saw their own economic fortunes improving. Unemployment fell steadily, and statistics on real income began to grow for the first time in nearly 15 years.

The benefits of this Clinton-era expansion, however, seemed almost as inequitably distributed as had been those of the Reagan Boom of the 1980s. The agricultural economy continued to push smaller farmers off the land; the gap between earnings of corporate executives and ordinary workers grew steadily larger; and the wealthiest 10 percent of households owned 90 percent of the nation's stockholdings.

In addition, the corporate scandals of the 1980s mutated into equally virulent ones during what one economist later dubbed the "Roaring Nineties." A Texas-based corporation, Enron, subsequently became the poster firm for this decade's culture of corruption. Before falling into bankruptcy, Enron would manipulate deregulated energy markets, while its top executives skimmed off vast sums from a business with cooked books and inadequately secured pension funds. The role of deregulation in enabling corporate malfeasance and inflated stock values became a matter of heated debate between those who stressed entrepreneurial liberty and those who emphasized governmental power as an essential counterweight to the clout of private corporations.

Meanwhile, Clinton continued to pursue his new Democratic course. He used his 1996 State of the Union address, his last before having to stand for reelection, to declare that "the era of big government is over" and began working with congressional Republicans to fulfill his goal of overhauling the social-welfare system. The **Personal Responsibility and**

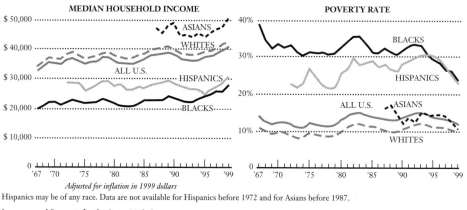

Adjusted for inflation in 1999 dollars

Hispanics may be of any race. Data are not available for Hispanics before 1972 and for Asians before 1987.

Income and Poverty in the Late 20th Century

Two reports by the Census Bureau in 2000 showed the economic expansion of the 1990s reaching all racial and ethnic groups.

Work Opportunity Reconciliation Act of 1996 (PRWORA) represented a series of compromises. Clinton voiced concern over cuts in the food stamp program and in benefits for recent immigrants, but he embraced the law's central feature. It replaced the AFDC program, which had long provided funds and services to poor families headed by single unemployed women, with a flexible system of block grants to individual states. The new program, entitled Temporary Assistance to Needy Families (TANF), allowed the 50 states to design, under general federal guidelines, their own welfare-to-work programs. Senator Daniel Patrick Moynihan, who had been the architect of Richard Nixon's FAP program, called PRWORA "the most brutal act of social policy" since the 19th century.

TANF, which replaced the national welfare system created during the New Deal and the Great Society eras, provoked especially bitter controversy outside Congress. Its proponents claimed that TANF would encourage states to experiment with programs to reduce welfare costs and encourage employment. Critics worried that its limitation of five years of government assistance over a person's lifetime and its authorization that states could suspend benefits if recipients failed to find employment within two years underestimated the difficulty faced by people without job skills. They also feared the impact on children, particularly in states with already minimal child care, nutrition, and medical care programs. By deferring protracted debate over these difficult issues, however, the new law effectively removed the call for welfare overhaul as a campaign issue in 1996, a turn that assisted Bill Clinton's reelection drive.

Victory and Impeachment

In 1996, Clinton and Gore defeated the Republican team of Robert Dole and Jack Kemp by about the same margin they had beaten that of George H. W. Bush and Dan Quayle in 1992. Ross Perot, although running a less aggressive, and less expensive, campaign than he had four years earlier, gained more than 8 percent of the vote, again denying the Democratic ticket a majority of the popular ballots cast. Still, Bill Clinton became the first Democratic president since Franklin Roosevelt to win back-to-back terms. Democrats held a majority of the seats in the 50 state legislatures, but Republicans retained control of Congress and gained several new governorships.

After the election, Clinton and congressional Republicans again cooperated, establishing a timetable for eradicating the federal deficit. The president's 1998 State of the Union address proclaimed that the United States had "a smaller government but a stronger nation," a result he attributed to his administration charting a "third way" between Republicans and most of its fellow Democrats. Clinton also secured a measure extending health care coverage to several million children from low-income families, tried to launch a "national conversation" about racial issues, and proposed programs to improve education. The White House even seemed poised, in early 1998, to work with congressional Republicans on reshaping the Social Security and Medicare programs.

During the rest of Clinton's presidency, however, domestic politics seemed to be geared toward the 2000 election and revolved around the president's personal behavior rather than legislative initiatives. The President and First Lady's joint financial dealings in

Arkansas—particularly those connected to a bankrupt S&L and a failed land development called "Whitewater"—increasingly intrigued critics on the New Right. A special investigation into Whitewater, which Republicans hoped could become this era's Watergate-like scandal, seemed headed nowhere until Kenneth Starr, a conservative Republican jurist, took it over in August 1994, and, then, expanded it to other matters.

Starr's inquiry, which would eventually cost $50 million, finally narrowed to the complex legal implications of a simple question: Had the president been concealing extramartial sexual encounters? Although Clinton unequivocally denied any wrongdoing, Republicans claimed his responses to Starr's inquiry amounted to obstruction of justice. Internet sites and 24/7 cable news channels competed with the print media and talk radio to ferret out the latest tidbits on the Clinton-Starr battle. Meanwhile, with economic statistics continuing to show solid growth, Clinton's approval ratings continued to rise, while Starr's steadily plummeted.

The president's denials crumbled, though, after Starr obtained irrefutable evidence of sexual encounters between Clinton and a young White House intern, Monica Lewinsky. The president, who was already a target for TV's political jokesters and Starr's investigative team, saw his legal problems dramatically escalate. Republicans insisted that Bill Clinton's public actions, particularly a deposition in a private lawsuit for sexual harassment, which a federal judge had already dismissed, justified his ouster. Most Democrats denounced Clinton's personal conduct but insisted that his private failings failed to merit, under constitutional standards, his removal from public office.

Clinton's approval rating, which remained consistently higher than those of his Republican critics, seemingly provided a formidable, nonconstitutional barrier against **impeachment proceedings.** After making Clinton the major issue during the mid-term elections of 1998, in fact, the GOP actually lost five seats in the House of Representatives. Even worse for the New Right, the public revelation of the long-term extramarital affair of Newt Gingrich forced him from office. (Similar problems prompted Gingrich's successor to follow his mentor into retirement.) Even so, the outgoing Republican majority in the House of Representatives sent two articles of impeachment against Clinton, for perjury and obstruction of justice, to the Senate on December 19, 1998. After a dramatic, televised trial, another reminder of Watergate, neither article passed.

With opinion polls suggesting that the constitutional case against Clinton swayed few people not previously inclined to find him guilty, the president's popularity actually grew during and after the impeachment imbroglio. For the first time in more than 30 years, the unemployment rate dipped under 4 percent. The continuing economic expansion, which had begun toward the end of George H. W. Bush's presidency, produced 16 million jobs. Once reviled by Ronald Reagan as the party of the "misery index," the Democrats under Clinton seemed associated with economic growth, full employment, low inflation, and fiscal responsibility. Crime statistics dropped dramatically, and the welfare rolls shrank to one-seventh of their 1994 high, or 2.2 million families. The earned income tax credit provided crucial federal assistance to low-income wage-earners with families.

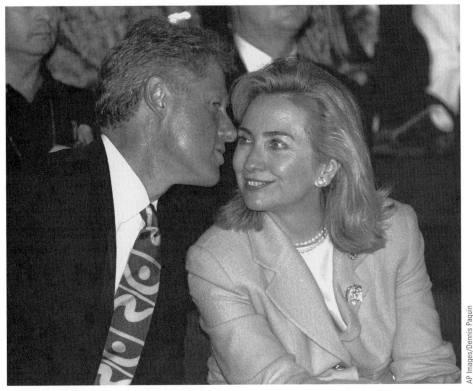

The Clintons, Bill and Hillary   Stories about personal and temperamental differences have always marked the controversial, interlocking public careers of Bill and Hillary Clinton. Still, the two have remained together, serving as political confidantes and as effective teammates.

On the eve of Clinton's departure from office, nearly 70 percent of poll respondents judged him an effective political leader. Generating bitter enemies, Clinton engendered equally fervent support, particularly among African Americans. Author Toni Morrison joked that Clinton, who had grown up in a multiracial community, might have been the nation's first "black president." The success of the earned income measure also allowed Clinton to retain a strong base among low-income families. Most surprisingly, polls even indicated that people, although disapproving of Clinton's personal behavior, became somewhat less cynical about the national government's performance during his presidency.

Environmental Policy

Clinton's years in office brought an expansion of environmental measures. His administration negotiated plans to manage and protect old-growth forests in the Pacific Northwest, to implement a conservation framework for nine national forests in the Sierra Nevada, and to handle the crowds of tourists in Yosemite National Park. In highly controversial moves, Clinton's secretary of the interior set aside 16 new national monuments and blocked road construction and logging in nearly 60 million acres of wild areas in national forests.

Building on the work of its Republican predecessors, Clinton's administration placed almost 6 million new surface and underwater acres under federal protection. Environmental managers often sought to promote change through incentives rather than penalties. In 1997, for example, the Conservation Reserve Program, a farm subsidy program that had previously paid farmers to remove land from tillage, now extended payment to those who would restore their wetlands, as a means of decreasing polluted runoff into streams and preserving wildlife habitat.

The Clinton administration also highlighted how the U.S. government had often been a flagrant polluter. Throughout the Cold War, governmental nuclear facilities had spewed toxic wastes and inadequately warned workers about the dangers of radiation. In 1993, Clinton's energy secretary released long-secret medical records relating to radiation and promised to inform and compensate victims. The legacy of other military-related pollutants also became evident after Congress ordered, during the 1990s, the shuttering of many of the nation's military installations.

The environmental movement of the 1990s increasingly focused on long-term ecological dangers, which its adherents saw threatening the entire planet. They warned of chlorofluorocarbons (CFCs) causing holes in the ozone layer, climate change associated with deforestation and desertification, pollution of the oceans and seas, the decline of biodiversity in plant and animal species, and, most ominously, "global warming," the gradual increase in temperatures, partly resulting from under-regulated industrial processes. Addressing problems such as these, according to environmentalists, required worldwide cooperation toward "sustainable development."

International meetings on environmental issues became more frequent. World leaders and environmental activists staged a 1992 "Earth Summit" in Brazil, and a convention, held in Japan, in 1997, produced the **"Kyoto Protocol."** This agreement pointed toward establishing international standards on emissions of CFCs and gases that most scientists identified as the primary cause of global warming.

Dissenters within the scientific community, warmly embraced by U.S. conservatives, questioned many of the studies cited by environmentalists. Was there really good scientific evidence *directly* linking environmental changes such as global warming to human causes? Or was a complex set of long-term, cyclical forces, many of them entirely "natural" in origin, producing climatic change? Claiming scientific data to be inconclusive, the New Right became increasingly insistent that environmental regulations limited the economic potential of the United States and disadvantaged the nation with foreign competition. Republicans thus made the Clinton administration's views on international environmental matters another complaint about Democratic foreign policy during the 1990s.

Post–Cold War Foreign Policy

For nearly half a century, anticommunism and rivalry with the Soviet Union had shaped U.S. foreign policy. The Clinton White House tried to articulate a new internationalist vision. It included working on global environmental and health concerns, promoting free-market policies, improving relations with the UN, expanding NATO, advancing human rights and democracy, and reducing nuclear threats.

One of the most perplexing issues facing the United States during the 1990s involved decisions about when, and how, to employ its own military power in localized conflicts. When Clinton took office, U.S. troops, under the umbrella of a UN mission, were already on the ground in Somalia. There, they were attempting to protect humanitarian efforts directed toward providing food and relief supplies in this heavily militarized, deeply divided African nation. After 18 American service personnel died—the result of the entire U.S. force becoming caught in the middle of Somalia's factional warfare—domestic criticism of U.S. involvement, which conservative critics derided as an attempt at "nation building," mounted. Clinton ordered a pullout from Somalia during the spring of 1994, a decision some of his critics would later condemn as an example of "cutting and running."

Somalia provided a backdrop to future U.S. decisions about dispatching military forces. The next year, recalling criticism of the Somalian effort, Clinton refused U.S. support for a UN peacekeeping effort in Rwanda, where 500,000 Tutsis would ultimately die during a genocidal civil war. In Haiti, however, Clinton ordered U.S. troops, in cooperation with the UN, to help reinstall the ousted elected president, Jean-Bertrand Aristide.

The United States, through NATO, also sent troops into the former Yugoslavia to stop Bosnian Serbs from massacring Bosnian Muslims. The U.S. military remained in Bosnia to oversee a cease-fire and peace-building process created in the U.S.-brokered Dayton (Ohio) accords of 1995. Four years later, Clinton supported a NATO bombing campaign to protect Albanian Muslims, nearly 90 percent of the population in the Serbian province of Kosovo, from the "ethnic cleansing" program of Serbia's president, Slobodan Milosevic. In June 1999, after 78 days of bombardment had decimated Serbia's infrastructure, Milosevic withdrew from Kosovo, and Serbs eventually elected a new president, supportive of multiethnic democracy and the West. As in Bosnia, U.S. and other allied troops remained as peacekeepers.

Clinton's actions overseas provoked intense partisan controversy. Republican critics accused the president of lacking clear guidelines for employing U.S. power. Suspicious of cooperating with UN forces, they denounced peacekeeping and nation-building, and demanded that any plan for the overseas deployment of U.S. troops include clear-cut exit strategies. Clinton's defenders, in contrast, continued to view flexibility and cooperation with international initiatives as the strengths, not the weaknesses, of his foreign policy.

Clinton's post–Cold War agenda included several other priorities. The White House successfully encouraged mediation of conflict in Northern Ireland. During the closing hours of his administration, Clinton personally brought Israeli and Palestinian leaders to Camp David but failed to broker a peace agreement. The Clinton administration also supported efforts to stop proliferation of nuclear weapons and ordered the dismantling of some of the U.S. nuclear arsenal. It increased economic aid to Ukraine, then the third greatest nuclear power in the world, in exchange for a pledge that this new nation would disarm the 1,600 Soviet-era warheads it had inherited when the USSR went out of business.

After promises of U.S. help, North Korea also agreed to begin halting its fledgling nuclear weapons program and permitting international inspections—agreements that it later repudiated. The White House successfully pressed for a new Nuclear Nonproliferation Treaty, during the spring of 1995, and three years later neared the brink of war with Iraq to maintain international inspections of **Saddam Hussein's** weapons programs. After enduring punishing air strikes, however, Iraq still expelled the investigators.

A wave of terrorist attacks by Islamic militants emerged as a pressing concern during the 1990s. Terrorists bombed the World Trade Center in New York City in 1993, U.S. embassies in Kenya and Tanzania in 1998, and a U.S. battleship, the *Cole,* docked in Yemen in 2000. These events raised alarm bells throughout the executive branch of government and prompted heightened security efforts, but produced no comprehensive U.S. plan—Clinton's critics would later emphasize—for responding to this new threat.

Globalization

The Clinton administration also pressed for lowering trade barriers and expanding global markets—the economic process called globalization. Implicitly endorsing Reagan-Bush policies, Clinton viewed globalization as boosting prosperity and fostering democracy around the world, to the ultimate benefit of the U.S. economy. A highly visible, emotionally impassioned antiglobalization movement, however, took root in most nations during the 1990s.

As part of his globalization emphasis, Clinton enthusiastically promoted the stalled **North American Free Trade Agreement (NAFTA)** among the United States, Canada, and Mexico and pushed it through Congress in late 1993. After a close vote that depended on Republican support, some of the fiercest residual opposition to NAFTA came from within Democratic, especially labor–union ranks. Then, in early 1995, Mexico's severe debt crisis and a drastic devaluation of its currency prompted Clinton to extend a $20 billion loan to Mexico. Unprecedented and controversial, the move stabilized the Mexican economy and, within a few years, had been repaid with $1 billion in interest. When Asian economies began faltering during 1998, Clinton successfully lobbied the International Monetary Fund (IMF) to provide emergency credits to shore up financial systems from Korea to Indonesia.

Clinton's administration, during the eight years it directed U.S. policy, signed more than 300 trade agreements. Promising that expanded trade ties would benefit all nations, trade negotiators completed the so-called Uruguay Round of the General Agreement on Tariffs and Trade (GATT) in late 1993. Then, in February 1994, the United States ended its own 19-year-old trade embargo against Vietnam. Early the following year, a more powerful **World Trade Organization (WTO)** replaced GATT. Anxious to move China toward a market economy, Clinton reversed his earlier position and backed China's entry into the WTO, in exchange for its promise to relax its trade policies. Everywhere he went, Clinton extolled the "New Century" in which freer trade would expand prosperity, and "liberty will spread by cell phone and cable modem."

The Presidency of George W. Bush (2001–2007)

Focus Question
How did the presidency of George W. Bush, especially in the wake of the attacks of September 11, 2001, seek to reorient both domestic and foreign-policy priorities?

Opinion polls showed Bill Clinton retaining his popularity as he neared the end of his second term. After one of the closest elections in U.S. history, however, his Republican successor soon began to take the country in different directions. **George W. Bush,** son of the nation's 41st president, seemed determined to move forward the New Right agenda of the 1980s, which the presidencies of his father and of Clinton had interrupted.

The Long Election

A retro aura surrounded the presidential campaign of 2000. Al Gore, Clinton's vice president for eight years, reappeared as the Democratic presidential nominee, and he selected Senator Joseph Lieberman of Connecticut, who practiced Orthodox Judaism, as his running mate. The Republican ballot, for the fifth time in the last six elections, bore the name of Bush. The younger Bush selected **Richard (Dick) Cheney,** a New Right stalwart who had served in his father's administration, as the GOP's vice presidential candidate. The presidential ballot also included a third-party challenger with a familiar name: Ralph Nader, the veteran activist. Running as the Green Party candidate, Nader attracted less than 3 percent of the popular vote, a far less impressive showing than Ross Perot's 1992 campaign or even Perot's less robust effort of 1996.

A listless presidential campaign stirred few passions. Bush claimed his record as the governor of Texas showed he could work with Democrats and might attract a following among African Americans and Hispanics. As president, he promised a "compassionate conservatism." While the Bush camp stayed "on message," Al Gore's disorganized campaign struggled to articulate any coherent theme. By distancing himself from Clinton, the vice president likely squandered two potential assets: Clinton's personal popularity and his record of presiding over eight years of economic prosperity. In contrast, New Right voters who reviled Clinton did turn out—and overwhelmingly favored Bush over Gore.

Barely 50 percent of the eligible voters went to the polls in 2000. Following a pattern evident since the Reagan era, the popular vote displayed discernible gender, racial, and ethnic imbalances. According to exit polls, Bush attracted 54 percent of the votes cast by men but only 43 percent of those from women. He received 38 percent of the votes from Latinos, 37 percent from Asian Americans, and 9 percent from African Americans.

The election of 2000 produced a near dead heat. Republicans narrowly maintained control of the House of Representatives, and the Senate ended up evenly split between the two parties. Gore carried the popular vote, however, by about 500,000 ballots. The only presidential tally that mattered, the one in the Electoral College, remained so close that the

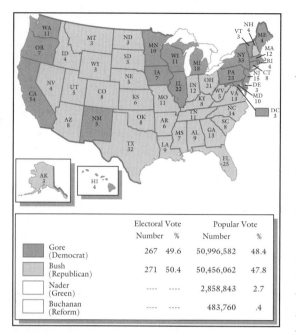

		Electoral Vote		Popular Vote	
		Number	%	Number	%
	Gore (Democrat)	267	49.6	50,996,582	48.4
	Bush (Republican)	271	50.4	50,456,062	47.8
	Nader (Green)	----	----	2,858,843	2.7
	Buchanan (Reform)	----	----	483,760	.4

Map 32.1 Presidential Election, 2000 Although Gore won the popular vote, Bush won the electoral vote after a bitter dispute involving ballots in Florida. Note the possible impact of third-party candidates.

identity of the next chief executive turned on the 25 electoral votes from Florida, where Bush's brother Jeb served as governor and Republicans controlled the legislature. The preliminary tally in Florida showed only about 1,000 popular votes separating the two candidates, but Fox Cable News, followed by NBC, soon declared Bush, on the basis of exit polls and samplings, to have been the winner there.

Partisan fervor, largely muted during the campaign, suddenly flared. For a month, no official winner emerged. After counting all absentee ballots, Republican officials in Florida declared, by a margin of 930 votes, that the state had gone for Bush. Democrats complained that many circumstances— including antiquated voting machines, deliberately confusing ballots, and apparent efforts to discourage voting by African Americans—had distorted the tally. They sued to force hand recounts in several counties from which Gore's totals seemed suspiciously low.

More than 50 lawsuits, by Democrats and Republicans alike, quickly dotted court dockets. Both parties, particularly the GOP, flooded Florida with cadres of lawyers and party activists. When the early recounts seemed to be reducing Bush's already slim margin, Republicans charged Democrats with trying to "steal" his "victory." A number of unofficial recounts later suggested Gore, not Bush, had carried Florida, but statisticians also generally advised that no procedure for hand-counting so many disputed ballots, in such a close election, could ever yield a universally agreed-upon result.

In any event, the U.S. Supreme Court, in two 5–4 opinions, chose the new president. The Court's more conservative Republicans (over the dissents of two other Republicans and two Democrats) declared, on December 12, 2000, that conducting recounts only in the contested Florida counties would violate constitutional guarantees of equality. In addition, the same justices insisted that the need of state officials to report to the Electoral College left no time for the alternative solution, a statewide recount. Legally outflanked, Gore conceded political defeat, and George W. Bush became the 43rd president of the United States.

A Conservative Domestic Agenda

As had Bill Clinton, Bush used the Reagan administration's high-octane entry into Washington as a model, one on which he and his advisers hoped to improve. New Right think tanks produced thousands of proposals for policy changes and assembled similar numbers of resumes of reliably conservative appointees. Bush chose a cabinet and White House staff that looked as diverse as Clinton's first one. It included Colin Powell in the key post of secretary of state, three women, two Asian Americans, and even a Democrat (Norman Mineta) who had served in Clinton's administration.

Bush's approach to executive branch operations, however, differed significantly from that of his predecessor. In contrast to Clinton, who reveled in loosely structured intellectual give-and-take, Bush desired brief, highly structured meetings that moved toward clearly delineated decisions. As Bush tacitly admitted and as former members of his administration detailed, this president displayed little interest in exploring, or sometimes even hearing or reading, ideas in conflict with his instincts and hunches. He allowed Vice

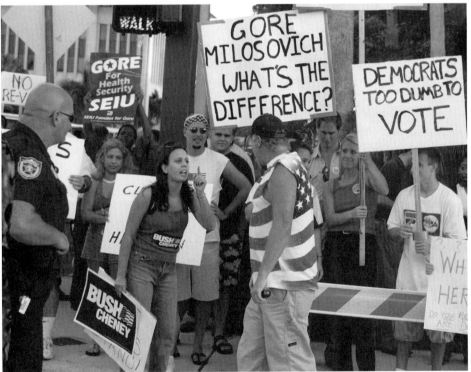

The 2000 Presidential Campaign, Phase 2　The inconclusive popular vote in Florida extended the 2000 presidential campaign for an additional month. Partisan activists, especially on the Republican side, became a familiar sight throughout much of Florida and on TV. GOP demonstrators insisted that George W. Bush had carried the Sunshine State and that the Democrats were conspiring to "steal" his victory.

President Dick Cheney and Secretary of Defense Donald Rumsfeld wide latitude to set policy directions. Finally, Bush unabashedly highlighted, especially to people who shared his spiritual views, how his born-again Christianity directly shaped his political outlook. During the 2000 campaign, in a response to a reporter's question about his intellectual roots, he pointedly identified Jesus as the philosopher who had most influenced his intellectual development.

An economic downturn, anticipated by most economists, provided the domestic backdrop to the early days of Bush's administration. Declining economic numbers, accompanied by a plunge in U.S. stock markets, which had been grossly overvalued and riddled with fraud, signaled the end of the 1990s boom. Revenue surpluses, at both the national and state levels, began dwindling and, then, turning into deficits. Consumer confidence slumped as revelations about apparently widespread corporate and accounting dishonesty rocked Wall Street and sent several major companies staggering toward eventual bankruptcy.

Unveiling its own agenda, the Bush administration advanced three controversial proposals, the first two of which the new president had promised while a candidate. First, Bush proposed a tax cut, which Democrats charged favored the wealthiest 1 percent of the population, to provide an economic stimulus. Second, he championed an educational program called "No Child Left Behind." It called for mandatory, nationwide testing of children as a means of determining which schools were teaching effectively. Finally, Vice President Cheney put together an ambitious energy plan, based on easing both restrictions on oil drilling and regulations on pricing. Democrats claimed this proposal, devised behind closed doors, would primarily benefit large oil and gas firms, especially ones headquartered in Texas, and do little to develop alternative sources of energy or encourage conservation.

Bush's initiatives, which seemed bolder than either his campaign rhetoric or his loss of the popular vote might have suggested, confronted a divided Congress and a suspicious public. Congress passed a revised tax plan, which mandated phasing-in substantial cuts gradually, in June 2001. It also enacted, with Democratic support, the No Child Left Behind program. Congressional opponents of the energy bill, however, blocked its passage until 2005. Foreign policy, an area in which Bush conceded his limited background, would soon push most domestic issues to the side.

Foreign Policy Changes Course

Initially, the White House seemed more intent on extracting the United States from existing international initiatives, awaiting ratification by the U.S. Senate, than in offering new proposals of its own. It announced that the United States no longer supported the Kyoto Protocol on global warming and several other international agreements, including a test ban treaty and one establishing an International Criminal Court.

As the White House sorted out its foreign-policy priorities, a small group of Islamic militants provided it with an overriding goal. On **September 11, 2001,** 19 suicide terrorists, divided into separate squads, took over four commercial jetliners, already airborne and loaded with highly flammable jet fuel, for use as high-octane, human-guided missiles. Two planes sliced into the Twin Towers of New York's World Trade Center, toppling them and several adjacent buildings; another ripped into one side of the Pentagon in Washington; and only the courageous actions of passengers on a fourth plane, which crashed in rural Pennsylvania, prevented a second attack in the nation's capital. Nearly five years later, when real-time audio- tapes from September 11 finally surfaced, they suggested disbelief, missed and mixed signals, and chaos among military and civilian officials who seemed mystified by the suicide strategy of the hijackers. The executive branch finally authorized Air Force pilots to shoot down any attacking planes, but its order did not go out until all four hijacked aircraft had hit the ground.

When the confusion ended and the initial shock passed, nearly 3,000 people, including several hundred passengers and an even larger number of police and fire officers in New York City, were dead. Various kinds of toxic materials, as later studies confirmed, covered large parts of lower Manhattan. For several days, activities not related to recovering from the attacks virtually stopped, as people watched wall-to-wall TV coverage.

George W. Shows Texas Style George W. Bush emerged victorious despite losing the popular vote to Democrat Al Gore.

Immediately compared to the 1941 Japanese attack on Pearl Harbor, September 11 rallied virtually every U.S. leader and citizen behind the White House. Three days after the attacks, Congress passed a resolution that declared the president, the nation's commander-in-chief, should "use all necessary and appropriate force" to protect the United States from another terrorist assault. In turn, Bush and other members of his administration insisted the nation now faced a very different, "post–September 11 world." Old policies and procedures, including those from the Cold War era and the Clinton years, required drastic revision. No longer facing another superpower, the now-collapsed Soviet Union, the United States could freely deploy its full power, as Clinton had supposedly refused to do— if not restricted by international agreements, other nations, or the UN. Offering himself as the determined leader of an embattled nation, George W. Bush promised to wage an all-out "war against terrorism."

To begin, the United States would retaliate militarily. Knowing the attacks had originated in Afghanistan and with Osama bin Laden, an Islamic fundamentalist from a wealthy Saudi Arabian family who headed a terrorist network called **al-Qaeda,** the Bush administration organized a multinational invasion force. In December 2001, U.S.-led troops toppled the fundamentalist Islamic regime of the Taliban, which had been dominating Afghanistan with bin Laden's help, and installed a pro-U.S. government in Afghanistan's capital city of Kabul. The Afghani effort failed, however, to secure that nation's countryside, which was divided among rival tribal factions, or to capture bin Laden and his top aides.

At the same time, President Bush began detailing other parts of his post–September 11 foreign policy. Denouncing all terrorist networks and any nation sponsoring terrorism or accumulating weapons of mass destruction, he proclaimed a "Bush Doctrine." The United States henceforth claimed the unilateral authority to use its military power for waging preemptive war against any force, including any foreign nation, that endangered its national security. In addition, congressional Democrats joined Republicans in passing legislation popularly known as the **"USA PATRIOT Act"** (Uniting and Strengthening America by Providing Appropriate Tools Required to Intercept and Obstruct Terrorism). This temporary measure gave the executive branch broad latitude to watch over and, then, detain people it considered threats to national security. The president's pre–September 11 approval ratings, which had hovered under 50 percent, soared. The off-year elections of 2002 gave the GOP secure control of the U.S. Senate and an even larger margin than before in the House of Representatives.

Although the White House clearly suggested that fighting a war on terrorism required a reconsideration of the balance between protecting national security and safeguarding civil liberties, it asked for few other sacrifices on the domestic front. Instead, it successfully pressed for adding a complicated—and very costly—prescription drug program, which critics denounced as a disguised subsidy for pharmaceutical companies, to the Medicare and Medicaid programs. The White House also argued for further tax cuts. Downplaying the record federal budget deficit (in part the result of the administration's previous tax reductions) and soaring defense expenditures, supporters of this measure claimed it would guarantee the return of prosperity. Again, Democrats condemned Bush's approach to tax cutting for tilting toward the already wealthy, now in an economy that had recently shed nearly 3 million jobs and in a nation that had seen the gap between rich and poor widen since the end of the 1990s. The partisan pitch of political rhetoric steadily increased, especially in the halls of Congress, on talk-radio, and on the 24/7 news channels.

As Osama bin Laden dropped from sight, the administration invoked the Bush Doctrine against Iraq. Dominated by the regime of Saddam Hussein, the old nemesis of the president's father, Iraq possessed some of the richest oil reserves in the world. It also posed a clear and immediate danger, claimed members of the Bush administration, to the United States. Long before the election of 2000, neo-conservatives who would later join the Bush administration had begun targeting Saddam Hussein. Many from this same group, especially Paul Wolfowitz, an aide to Donald Rumsfeld who had moved between Democratic and Republican administrations and academic life, had repeatedly called throughout the

1990s for "regime change" in Iraq. In this view, Iraq symbolized a broader challenge, one that included other anti-U.S. states such as Iran.

Safeguarding U.S. national security, according to neoconservatives such as Wolfowitz and those working for Vice President Dick Cheney, required the United States to go on the offensive. It could clear away threatening, repressive regimes, beginning with that of Saddam Hussein, and replace them with pro-U.S. democracies. Using its military power to spread liberty around the globe would not only advance U.S. strategic and economic goals but fulfill a moral mission as old as the American republic. Since "the United States is the beacon for freedom in the world," President Bush would later proclaim, it had a "responsibility to promote freedom" in the world that is "as solemn as the responsibility [to protect] the American people, because the two go hand-in-hand."

In addition to strategic-moral arguments, based on Iraq's oil reserves and on a U.S. mission to export democracy, the Bush administration offered two more immediate, pragmatic, and post–September 11 reasons for regime change in Iraq. It highlighted intelligence reports claiming Iraq already possessed, or was actively seeking, **"weapons of mass destruction" (WMDs).** Less strongly, it implied that there had been pre–September 11 ties between Saddam Hussein and al-Qaeda. Citing evidence that became increasingly controversial, the White House asked the UN and other nations to authorize military force for removing the danger Iraq supposedly posed to other nations.

Led by France, Germany, and Russia, most other UN members urged caution. They favored giving weapons inspectors, mandated after the 1991 Gulf War and readmitted into Iraq by Saddam Hussein, additional time to determine what, if any, WMDs Iraq possessed. Avoiding any conclusion to the inspection process and bypassing the UN, the Bush administration assembled, in early 2003, what Secretary of State Powell called a "coalition of the willing." It included small troop contingents from Poland, Italy, Spain, and several other countries, along with a sizeable contribution from Great Britain. Overriding some Pentagon projections, which estimated a need for at least 300,000 U.S. troops, the Secretary of Defense and the White House detailed only a little more than one-third of that total for duty in Iraq.

On March 20, a U.S.-directed air and ground operation, entitled "Iraqi Freedom," targeted Saddam Hussein's government. The White House apparently hoped a massive U.S. bombing campaign, an effort it called "shock and awe," would create physical and psychological confusion, allow British and U.S. troops to secure oil fields and other strategic locations, and permit an Iraqi opposition to organize a new government. Most of the U.S. media, which had rarely doubted the Bush administration's claims about Iraq's arsenal and intentions, enthusiastically covered this military effort, with TV reporters often "embedded" alongside U.S. forces. Far more than Vietnam had ever been, Iraqi Freedom became a "living-room war." After Iraqi troops melted away, to fight another day, Saddam Hussein's regime fell in less than two months.

On May 1, 2003, President Bush proclaimed, from the deck of the aircraft carrier *Abraham Lincoln*, the end of "significant combat" in Iraq. Shortly after this carefully crafted media event, however, it became evident that Iraqi insurgents intended to resist the

American-directed reconstruction, which aimed at creating a pro-U.S. government and an economic order closely tied to U.S. companies. Insurgents also attacked aid workers from the United Nations, the Red Cross, and other international relief agencies. What Americans had viewed as a joint American-Iraqi "liberation" and "reconstruction" effort soon floundered on opposition from Iraqi groups who saw U.S. troops as an unwelcome force of "occupation."

As U.S. officials and cooperating Iraqis worked to create a system of governance, every step in this slowly moving process faced an evolving insurgency that brought rising military and civilian casualties. In part, this carnage stemmed from Saddam Hussein's loyalists who continued to resist. More importantly, ethnic, religious, and regional divisions within Iraq spurred growing conflict. Under Saddam Hussein, Sunni Arabs who primarily lived in areas around Baghdad had dominated political power. The central government had treated Shi'a Arabs, a majority of the nation's population, concentrated in the South, and the northern Kurds, mostly Sunni but non-Arabs, as unwelcome outsiders. Shi'a groups and the Kurds (who had enjoyed de facto independence from Saddam Hussein's regime since the end of the 1991 Gulf War) now wanted a share of governmental power. Divisions also emerged between Iraqis who insisted any new government remain secular (as had been Saddam Hussein's) and those who desired one based on Islamic law. Moreover, Islamic terrorist groups from outside Iraq joined the insurgency to fight against their American enemy.

Struggles between diverse factions and the U.S. occupation often placed American troops, who had little knowledge of Iraq's socioreligious dynamics, in the middle of struggles they hardly understood. U.S. casualties mounted; the pace of military recruitment at home fell off; and the Joint Chiefs of Staff warned of the Iraqi occupation stretching its resources so thin that it might not be able to counter other threats around the globe. Moreover, the paucity of international support for U.S. action meant that, unlike the 1991 Persian Gulf War, U.S. taxpayers directly bore the rising costs of this operation.

Initially, the Bush administration had suggested that Iraqi oil revenues could pay for "liberating" Iraq, but it repeatedly asked Congress for additional billions of dollars to fund ongoing combat and occupation activities in Iraq and in Afghanistan. Iraqi oil revenues remained low; insurgents blew up infrastructure nearly as fast as it could be rebuilt; and unemployment in Iraq soared, further fueling the insurgency. Financial mismanagement, according to later audits, meant that U.S. officials could not account for considerable sums of money, which had been slated for Iraqi redevelopment and channeled to relatively few, politically well-connected U.S. companies.

Meanwhile, the Bush administration's public rationale for invading Iraq and its conduct of the war produced further controversy. Knowledgeable observers found no credible evidence of any significant connection between al-Qaeda and Saddam Hussein. Moreover, an exhaustive and official U.S. government report, issued in April 2005, concluded that Iraq had possessed no biological or nuclear weapons at the time of the U.S.-led invasion. In response to apparent failures in intelligence gathering and assessment, Congress placed existing efforts under a new umbrella agency and created a director of national intelligence as the key coordinating official. Partisans of the Bush administration, however, continued

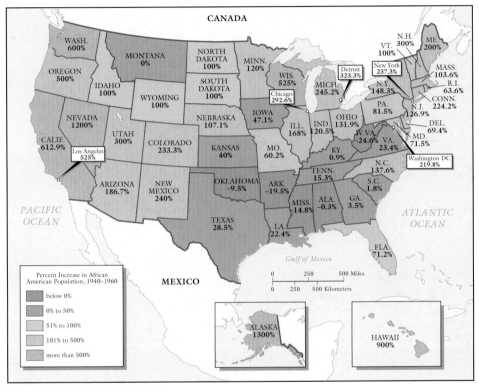

Map 28.1 Shifts in African American Population Patterns, 1940–1960 During and after the Second World War, large numbers of African Americans left the rural South and migrated to new locations. Which states had the largest percentage of outmigration? Which saw the greatest percentage of population increase? How might this migration have affected American life? View an animated version of this map or related maps at http://www.thomsonedu.com/history/murrin.

Map 29.1   Vietnam War   The war in Vietnam spread into neighboring countries as the North Vietnamese ran supplies southward along a network called the Ho Chi Minh Trail, and the United States tried to disrupt their efforts. Unlike the Korean War (see map on p. 1023), this guerrilla-style war had few conventional "fronts" of fighting.
View an animated version of this map or related maps at http://www.thomsonedu.com/history/murrin.

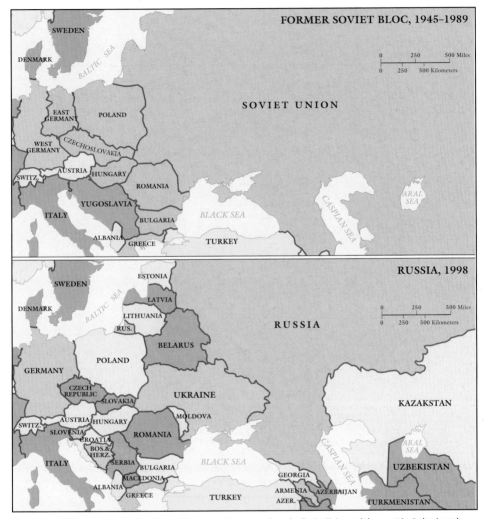

Map 30.2   Collapse of the Soviet Bloc   These contrasting maps show the Soviet Union and the countries it dominated before and after the fall of communist governments. What countries in Eastern Europe escaped Russian control after 1989? What new countries emerged out of the old Soviet Union?

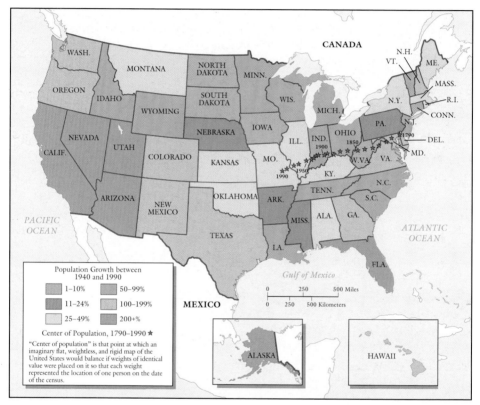

Map 31.1 **Population Shifts Toward the Sunbelt**   In the era after the Second World War, Americans gravitated toward the South and West. Which states grew the fastest? What might be some of the causes and consequences of such population shifts? View an animated version of this map or related maps at http://www.thomsonedu.com/history/murrin.

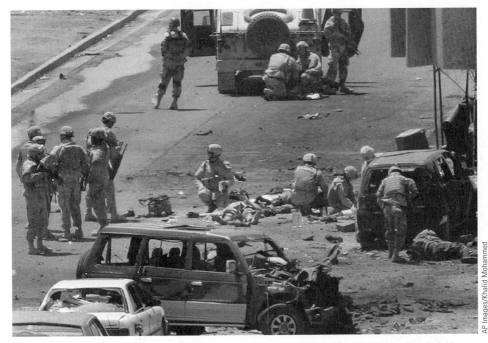

Baghdad, Iraq, 2006   Bomb attacks, aimed at both Iraqis and U.S. personnel, followed the fall of Saddam Hussein. In May 2006, a news crew from CBS fell victim to a bomb attack. This incident underscored the danger that journalists confronted whenever they left the relative safety of the U.S.-controlled "Green Zone" in central Baghdad in search of stories about the fate of pacification and reconstruction efforts.

to assert claims about Saddam Hussein's arsenal and his al-Qaeda connections. Opinion polls from 2006 suggested that nearly half of all respondents still erroneously believed that Iraq had been stockpiling WMDs and that a significant number also believed Saddam Hussein had somehow conspired in the September 11 attacks.

As the initial case for war came under fire, so did its conduct. Photographs showing abuse of detained Iraqis, especially at Baghdad's Abu Ghraib prison, and stories of a few U.S. troops deliberately killing civilians fueled domestic debate over the use and definition of "torture" and "war crimes" and over the wisdom of having U.S. forces occupy another country.

Activism at Home during the Second Term

In many ways, the ongoing conflict in Iraq proved a political asset to President Bush during the presidential campaign of 2004. Fine-tuned by consultant Karl Rove, White House political strategy portrayed "staying the course" in Iraq as central to the broader mission to fight terrorism and to spread liberty and democracy. The Democratic nominee, **Senator John Kerry** of Massachusetts, who had served in Vietnam during the 1960s before becoming an antiwar activist, used the Democratic National Convention to highlight his military background. On the campaign trail, Kerry supported the goals of the Iraqi operation but criticized the Bush administration's strategy and tactics. Kerry kept a careful distance from the relatively small antiwar movement.

A fiercely partisan campaign, a contrast to that of 2000, featured intensive use of the Internet and energetic efforts to mobilize key constituencies. The president's supporters attacked Kerry's Vietnam War record and warned that irresponsible dissent could endanger national security. Democrats charged Bush with misleading the country about Iraq, saddling future generations with a horrendous burden of debt, enabling a small percentage of the current generation to enjoy tax cuts, and having failed to show up for military service during the Vietnam years. The election prompted a large turnout and charges of fraud, especially in Ohio.

Bush defeated Kerry and his Democratic running mate, Senator John Edwards of North Carolina, by less than 3 percent of the popular vote and gained only 15 more electoral ballots. As in 2000, Bush did best in suburbia and small towns and among people who attended church regularly. Kerry failed to do as well as had Al Gore in 2000 among white voters, still more than three-quarters of the electorate, or to win enough middle-income people, whom the Democrats had contended were suffering from Bush's economic policies.

The White House immediately claimed a mandate and announced an ambitious second-term agenda. It included a radical overhaul of the Social Security system and a restructuring of the entire tax code. Bush barnstormed the country on behalf of these initiatives, but most people seemed wary. The economy was slowly recovering, but the yawning federal deficit and sharply rising energy prices appeared worrisome signs of greater problems to come. At the same time, a series of scandals also inclined some members of the GOP-controlled Congress to move carefully. Investigations of illegal contributions from lobbyists forced the resignations of several conservative Republican stalwarts, including Tom DeLay, the effective powerbroker in the House of Representatives. The conduct of these members of Congress eroded popular faith in the legislative branch, whose approval ratings fell below that of the Bush White House. Increasingly, activist movements, rather than the White House or the party leadership in

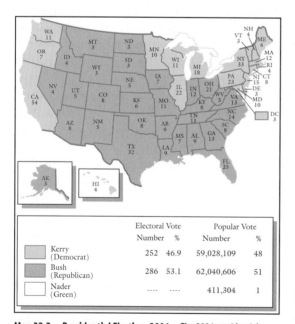

	Electoral Vote		Popular Vote	
	Number	%	Number	%
Kerry (Democrat)	252	46.9	59,028,109	48
Bush (Republican)	286	53.1	62,040,606	51
Nader (Green)	----	----	411,304	1

Map 32.2   Presidential Election, 2004   The 2004 presidential election proved almost as closely contested as that of 2000. Although the Republican ticket carried the popular vote, the Electoral College result turned on the GOP winning a narrow, and controversial, victory in Ohio.

Congress, seemed to be driving domestic politics, especially on several familiar social and cultural issues.

As immigrants had continued to enter the United States in near-record numbers during the 1990s, for example, their settlement patterns had begun to change. Increasing numbers of new arrivals, especially from Mexico, bypassed the western United States in favor of settling in cities and smaller towns elsewhere, particularly in the South. In response, movements that opposed current immigration laws and practices mobilized and organized in most parts of the country. Conservative radio commentators often helped facilitate their efforts. A few people, occasionally with tacit support from local and state officials, took direct action: They formed armed militia-style patrols, fanned out along the southwestern border, and prepared to turn back Mexicans trying to enter the United States. Other organizations mounted intensive lobbying efforts. They demanded new congressional legislation to restrict immigration, tighten border security, and strengthen measures against employing undocumented immigrants. Some also pressed local governments to pass restrictive ordinances.

Pro-immigrant organizations, particularly ones in California and in other states with large Mexican-descended populations, had already become equally active. Tapping the power of Spanish-language radio and TV stations, they staged temporary work stoppages and mounted large demonstrations, pointedly designed to demonstrate the economic importance of immigrant workers and the potential political power of the pro-immigration movement. Citing statistical studies, supporters challenged claims that immigrants "took away" jobs and depressed wage levels.

Political leaders responded cautiously. Republicans in the House, especially those from securely GOP districts, backed legislation favored by anti-immigration activists. Democrats, most of whom opposed these initiatives as too restrictive, gained enough Republican votes in the Senate to block any dramatic legislative response. Confusing matters further, the Bush White House finally promised to send National Guard troops to help secure the U.S.-Mexican border but also angered many congressional Republicans by endorsing some type of "guest worker" arrangement, a course strongly favored by most business organizations. Unable to assess how immigration legislation might affect electoral results in 2006, Republican congressional leaders backed away from taking any significant action.

Meanwhile, other activists pressed other topics. One of the most emotionally charged issues involved "gay marriage." As LGBT communities had gained greater visibility and political clout during the 1990s, some (though not all) activists sought to secure, for both symbolic and very practical reasons, legal recognition of long-term relationships they viewed to be every bit as permanent as heterosexual marriages. When the U.S. Supreme Court, in 2003, overruled its own *Bowers* v. *Hardwick* decision (in *Lawrence* v. *Texas*), its ruling hinted that the same constitutional logic that invalidated anti-sodomy laws might apply to bans against same-sex marriage. Opinion polls suggested sharply divided views about gay marriage but fairly broad support for civil unions or other legal arrangements that would recognize LGBT partnerships. In response to lawsuits supported by civil liberties and LGBT organizations, several courts held that the bedrock principle of legal-constitutional equality guaranteed gays and lesbians a "right to marry."

New Right activists responded vigorously. They tweaked existing marriage statutes and fine-tuned the legal arguments against gay marriage. In response, several judicial tribunals held that carefully drawn laws advanced legitimate public purposes, such as encouraging the best possible child-rearing practices, rather than simply discriminated against same-sex legal relationships. In addition, movements on the New Right sought an amendment to the U.S. Constitution, backed by the Bush White House, which specifically declared marriage as a "union between a man and a woman." During the spring of 2006, Democrats in the U.S. Senate narrowly turned back a GOP-sponsored effort to send such an amendment to the states for ratification.

Clashes between religious beliefs and scientific-medical knowledge also flared. Right-to-Life activists had, since the early 1990s, broadened their agenda beyond opposition to legalized abortion and the *Roe* decision. They condemned all practices that seemed inimical to a "culture of life." These included legislation, court decisions, and administrative rulings appearing to support any "unnatural" means for terminating a person's life, such as "assisted suicide" or removal of feeding tubes; anti-pregnancy drugs, such as "Plan B"; medical research that used stem cells from human embryos; and even regulations that targeted "global warming," considered a "hoax" by some on the New Right.

Differences over these issues encouraged a politics that joined deeply held ethical and spiritual values to media theatrics. In the most spectacular of these, Republicans in Congress and the Bush White House, responding to pressure from the Religious Right, backed an extraordinary 2005 legislative measure. It gave federal courts authority to intervene in a highly publicized Florida case, which involved removal from life-support systems of a young woman who had been in a vegetative state for years. As during the 2000 election controversy, activists from a variety of different movements rushed to the Sunshine State. Eventually, several federal courts refused the invitation to overrule local tribunals. Later, in July 2006, when Congress passed a measure in support of stem cell research, President Bush, standing on "culture-of-life" grounds, responded by issuing, on live television, the first veto of his presidency.

New Right activists and the Bush administration enjoyed perhaps their greatest domestic success in placing judicial nominees on the federal bench. Early in Bill Clinton's presidency, conservatives had begun worrying that an influx of new judges—exemplified by Ruth Bader Ginsburg and Steven Breyer, successfully nominated by Clinton for the U.S. Supreme Court—might cancel out the impact of Reagan-era appointees. Following the GOP surge of 1994, Senate Republicans had managed to block confirmation of a number of judges they considered "liberal activists." When campaigning for the White House in 2000, George W. Bush had declared Antonin Scalia and Clarence Thomas, two of the five Republican justices who would help ensure his presidency in *Bush* v. *Gore,* to be his favorite members of the High Court.

After 2001, the Bush White House and Republican senators seemed, according to their opponents, to want not only conservative judges but a key core of ultra-conservative ones.

Democrats charged several Bush appointees with holding views outside the "legal mainstream" and possessing scant judicial experience. Overriding such complaints, the White House mobilized movements on the New Right and adroitly lobbied wavering GOP and even some Democratic senators. The GOP leadership in the Senate also threatened to change long-standing rules that enabled filibusters, if Democrats continued to block Bush nominees.

These strategies worked. Despite an embarrassing misfire, when a Bush nominee for the Supreme Court, Harriet Miers, met determined opposition not from Democrats but from the New Right, conservative Republicans invariably succeeded in placing their favorites on the lower federal courts. In addition, the White House easily obtained Senate ratifications for two reliably, though reputedly not radically, conservative Supreme Court nominees—John Roberts to replace William Rehnquist as Chief Justice and Samuel Alito to succeed the retiring Sandra Day O'Connor. The Court seemed closer than ever before to having a five-Justice majority for overruling the *Roe* decision.

The Politics of National Security during the Second Term

Meanwhile, continuing its attempt to end the insurgency in Iraq, the Bush administration intensified efforts to create a new Iraqi government. In January 2005, Iraqis elected a 275-member national assembly, charged with establishing a temporary government and drafting a federal constitution. This body, dominated by Shi'a and Kurds, chose an interim prime minister and produced a constitution that, although opposed by many Sunnis, gained popular approval in October 2005. After several false starts and complicated maneuvering among the contending factions, Nouri al-Maliki, a Shi'a, finally emerged as a potentially viable prime minister. Coalition troops continued training Iraqi security forces, but the insurgency seemed to intensify.

Assurances from the Bush administration that U.S. troops would "stand down" whenever Iraq's security forces could "stand up" for Iraqi democracy downplayed obvious difficulties. One problem the White House did emphasize, the strong Iranian presence within Iraq, seemed especially worrisome for those neo-conservatives who had hoped the toppling of Saddam Hussein would increase U.S. power in the Middle East.

In addition, the Iraqi government included factions, such as that led by the fundamentalist Islamic cleric Moqtada al-Sadr, with a thin commitment to Western-style democratic processes and opposed to the American presence in Iraq. Movements such as al-Sadr's participated in electoral politics, held a crucial number of seats in Parliament, and also maintained their own well-armed private militias. This meant that other parliamentary factions could not expect Iraq's struggling central government to enforce policies that religious factions such as al-Sadr's strongly opposed. Contrary to the Bush Doctrine and other neoconservative blueprints, then, it seemed that encouraging democratization in places such as Iraq might not produce stable or pro-American governments, at least not for many years. During 2006, Pentagon officials conceded that Iraq seemed engulfed in what analysts could call a "civil war" and began a thorough review of U.S. tactics.

Elsewhere in the Middle East, the Bush administration confronted the rising power of neighboring Iran, a country whose influence a strong Iraq had once held in check. A new hard-line president, backed by fundamentalist Shi'a clerics, opposed to the United States and seemingly intent on developing nuclear capacities, dominated Iran's political system. Tensions escalated as the United States pressured the UN to adopt stronger measures against Iran. Then, in July 2006, fighting broke out in southern Lebanon between Israel, backed by the United States, and Hezbollah, a fundamentalist Islamic group armed with missiles provided by Iran. A more powerful version of the movement that had likely killed hundreds of the U.S. marines sent to Lebanon by Ronald Reagan in 1982, Hezbollah represented a militant Islamic movement that Lebanon's weak secular government, recently freed from Syrian domination, had lacked the power to control. This short war in Lebanon, ended through UN action, left southern Lebanon devastated and raised tensions throughout the region to new highs.

Previous U.S. administrations, including those as different as Jimmy Carter's and George H. W. Bush's, had seen a pro-Israel stance as consistent with actively facilitating peace arrangements whenever escalating conflict threatened to unhinge Middle Eastern politics. George W. Bush called for a solution that would both recognize Israel's right to exist and also provide for an independent Palestinian state, but, in contrast to his predecessors, he appeared to publicly position the United States as a firm partisan of Israeli policy.

By the end of 2006, meanwhile, military operations in Afghanistan and Iraq had claimed the lives of nearly 3,000 U.S. troops (with more than 15,000 others injured). Some estimates of casualties among Iraqi civilians, statistics that the United States neglected to collect, reached into the hundreds-of-thousands and continued to grow. Independent researchers estimated the monetary cost of the ongoing occupation, to the United States, at $6 billion per month. George W. Bush, who during the 2000 presidential campaign had denounced Democratic attempts at nation building abroad, made Iraq one of the greatest nation-building challenges in U.S. history. With Americans in sharp disagreement over both the justifications and handling of the conflict, popular support for U.S. policy in Iraq and the president's own approval rating dropped below 40 percent.

Hurricane Katrina, slamming into the U.S. Gulf Coast region in late August 2005, had also prompted an intense reevaluation, at least for a time, of nation building and national security on the home front. Local, state, and federal officials from both political parties bumbled through this massive disaster, the first post–September 11 emergency. The Department of Homeland Security, despite its sizable budget and staff, seemed unprepared to assist people in the path of the storm and those who suffered from its aftermath. Although the White House would claim no one had "anticipated the breach of levees" that supposedly protected New Orleans from flood waters, videotapes later showed members of the Bush administration, including the president, receiving precisely such a warning. Katrina exacted an especially heavy toll on the region's truly needy residents, especially those in low-lying—and low-income—neighborhoods of New Orleans. After failing to provide effective

Hurricane Katrina Hits New Orleans, 2005   This photo provides a birds-eye view of post-Katrina New Orleans. Katrina highlighted, at least temporarily, the domestic dimensions of "Homeland Security" and the apparent inadequacy of the social-economic "safety net" that different levels of government supposedly would extend to those in need.

aid to hundreds of thousands of people, authorities could not supply a precise figure, presumably in the several thousands, of those who had lost their lives as a result of Katrina.

Katrina prompted questions that went beyond the inadequacy of preparations for a single hurricane. The "safety net," intended to protect people who were already in distressed circumstances from falling, in this case literally, into desperate circumstances, seemed inadequate or, perhaps, even nonexistent.

More broadly, the Katrina episode raised questions about governmental power. People who expected private insurance companies to help pay for storm damage often discovered that the small print in their policies contained large exemptions. Subsequent studies also raised troubling hints that governmental under-funding for construction and inspection had saddled New Orleans with a badly flawed water-control system. Most controversially, Katrina revived the debate over whether or not global warming might represent the kind of national-security threat that merited, over the long term, a more substantial governmental commitment to remedial measures. Should government action provide appropriate and vital domestic social and public services that private institutions apparently could not provide?

When considering the potential power of the national government, the Bush administration increasingly looked toward expanding the capabilities of the executive branch. It pressed vigorously, and successfully, for a revised version of the "USA PATRIOT Act," which otherwise would have automatically expired in 2006. When a bipartisan coalition blocked the administration's controversial nomination of John Bolton to become ambassador to the UN, Bush placed him in this position through an unprecedented interim appointment, which did not require Senate confirmation. The White House also appointed two new CIA heads, presumably to increase its control over the Agency. On several other key issues, which the White House claimed involved national security and the president's role as commander-in-chief, Bush and his advisers seemed intent on circumventing limitations on the power of the office of the president. Vice President Cheney and Secretary of Defense Rumsfeld, who had served in the executive branch during the immediate post-Watergate era, appeared particularly eager that the Bush administration overcome congressional and judicial restrictions that had initially grown out of Richard Nixon's troubles during the 1970s.

Several constitutional controversies over the scope of presidential power marked Bush's second term. Initially, when dealing with alleged terrorists captured overseas, especially in Afghanistan, the Bush administration chose to operate outside of both domestic and international agreements and to detain hundreds of captives in Cuba, at newly constructed facilities inside the U.S. enclave at Guantanamo Bay. In a related issue, the Bush administration insisted on a loose definition of what constituted "torture" when intelligence operatives questioned people being detained. Later, the administration devised a special legal proceeding for trying detainees being held at "Gitmo," which the U.S. Supreme Court struck down, in a 5-3 decision, during the spring of 2006. In response to the various controversies over detainee treatment and the court's rebuke, the administration successfully pressed Congress in late 2006 to pass the Military Commissions Act of 2006. This act created new procedures for military commissions to try "unlawful enemy combatants" and adopted a controversial view of what constituted "torture."

In another hotly contested move, the Bush administration effectively ignored the Foreign Intelligence Surveillance Act of 1978 (FISA), which mandated special procedures before undertaking domestic wiretaps. The White House insisted the post–September 11 congressional resolution on fighting terrorism and the president's inherent powers as commander-in-chief allowed him to bypass FISA's provisions in order "to save lives."

Finally, and perhaps most strikingly, the White House, very quietly but also very publicly, asserted that all presidents possessed an independent constitutional power to interpret legislation and legal requirements. Invoking a constitutional theory called "the unitary executive," the White House inserted nearly 750 "signing statements" into the *Federal Register* during Bush's first six years in office—after the president had put his name on acts passed by Congress. Although other presidents had issued similar statements, no previous chief executive had done so on such a massive scale or in concert with such a sweeping constitutional vision of presidential authority.

The unitary executive thesis, as formulated by conservative jurists, relied on a section of Article II in the Constitution and the presidential oath of office. Both contain language about "faithfully executing " the duties of the presidency *and* the laws of the United States, magic words that some constitutional theorists read as justifying chief executives to inter-pret independently and, then, apply unilaterally U.S. laws, even against alternative inter-pretations by other branches of government. Bush's many signing statements, testaments to an indefatigable White House legal team, included presidential dissents against laws protecting governmental whistleblowers and ones limiting governmental oversight of fed-erally funded research projects.

On the eve of the 2006 mid-term election, the unpopularity of the war in Iraq, the controversies over executive power, several high-profile corruption cases, and schisms within the president's New Right coalition sapped Republican party strength. A re-energized Democratic party capitalized on popular discontent over all of these issues. In the 2006 midterm elections Democrats picked enough senate and house seats to capture control of Congress. Democratic candidates also unseated six Republican governors. In response, the White House announced the resignation of Donald Rumsfeld as secretary of defense.

Conclusion

The end of the 20th century and the beginning of a new one saw the United States seek-ing to develop domestic policies that could ensure continued economic growth. At the same time, this period witnessed the nation adjusting to the end of a global Cold War and the beginning of an equally broad struggle against terrorism.

Bill Clinton, styling himself a New Democrat, adopted a relatively conservative socioeconomic agenda that included slashing the federal deficit and reshaping the welfare system. During his presidency, Clinton sought to move the Democratic Party away from its big government image. At the same time, however, he supported other issues, such as environmental protection, that were heatedly opposed by many Republicans. Clinton's emphasis on aligning the United States with economic globalization seemed his most forceful attempt to address a post–Cold War world.

The first president to take office—and, then, win a second term—during the 21st century, George W. Bush recalled and promised to re-ignite the conservative surge of the Reagan years. After achieving one of its major domestic goals, tax-cutting, the Bush administration responded to the September 11 attacks with military actions overseas and claims of new exec-utive powers. Its major foreign-policy initiative, a preemptive strike against Saddam Hussein's Iraq, initially prompted widespread support and, later, produced growing controversy.

Clinton and Bush, who used very different images and media skills to become two-term presidents, inspired intense adoration and passionate dislike. Both tried to redraw the political landscape in his own party's favor, yet polling data suggested that the electorate, at the beginning of 2007, remained roughly evenly divided. Against the backdrop of insis-tent reminders, especially from the Bush White House, that the nation remained under constant threat, an increasingly diverse people continued to negotiate the difficult balances among liberty, equality, and power.

SUGGESTED READINGS

Very different perspectives on the Clinton years appear in **Bob Woodward**, *The Agenda: Inside the Clinton White House* (1994) and *The Choice* (1996); **Theodore Lowi and Benjamin Ginsburg**, *Embattled Democracy: Politics and Policy in the Clinton Era* (1995); **Kenneth Baer**, *Reinventing Democrats: The Politics of Liberalism from Reagan to Clinton* (2000); **Haynes Johnson**, *The Best of Times: America in the Clinton Years* (2001); **David Halberstam**, *War in a Time of Peace* (2001); **Sidney Blumenthal**, *The Clinton Wars* (2003); **John F. Harris**, *The Survivor: Bill Clinton in the White House* (2005); and **Joseph E. Stiglitz**, *The Roaring Nineties* (2003).

The electoral contest that elevated George W. Bush to the presidency is analyzed in **Jack M. Rakove**, ed., *The Unfinished Election of 2000* (2002) and **Jeffrey Toobin**, *Too Close to Call* (2001). For preliminary assessments of how Bush remained in the White House, see **William J. Crotty**, ed., *A Defining Moment: The Presidential Election of 2004* (2005).

The controversy surrounding George W. Bush's presidency, and especially its relationship to the attacks of September 11, is reflected in titles such as **Bob Woodward**, *Bush at War* (3 vols., 2002-6); **Craig Calhoun, Paul Price, and Ashley Timmer**, eds., *Understanding September 11* (2002); **David Frum**, *The Right Man: The Surprise Presidency of George W. Bush* (2003); **Stephen Hess and Marvin Kalb**, eds., *The Media and the War on Terrorism* (2003); **Gerald Posner**, *Why America Slept: The Failure to Prevent 9/11* (2003); **Joanne Meyerowitz**, ed., *History and September 11th* (2003); **Chalmers Johnson**, *The Sorrows of Empire: Militarism, Secrecy, and the End of the Republic* (2004); **Kevin Phillips**, *American Theocracy: The Peril and Politics of Radical Religion, Oil, and Borrowed Money in the 21st Century* (2006); **Michael R. Gordon and General Bernard E. Trainor**, *Cobra II: The Inside Story of the Invasion and Occupation of Iraq* (2006); **Thomas E. Ricks**, *Fiasco: The American Military Adventure in Iraq* (2006); **Ron Suskind**, *The One Percent Doctrine* (2006); and **Vali Nasr**, *The Shia Revival: How Conflicts within Islam Will Shape the Future* (2006).

James T. Patterson, *Restless Giant: The United States from Watergate to Bush v. Gore* (2005) offers an excellent overview of the era from 1974 to 2001. **Godfrey Hodgson**, *More Equal Than Others: America from Nixon to the New Century* (2004) is more impressionistic.

Visit the Liberty Equality Power Companion Web site for resources specific to this textbook: http://www.thomsonedu.com/history/murrin

Also find self-tests and additional resources at ThomsonNOW. ThomsonNOW is an integrated online suite of services and resources with proven ease of use and efficient paths to success, delivering the results you want—NOW!

www.thomsonedu.com/login/

Appendix

The Declaration of Independence

The Unanimous Declaration of the Thirteen United States of America

When in the Course of human events it becomes necessary for one people to dissolve the political bands which have connected them with another, and to assume among the Powers of the earth, the separate and equal station to which the Laws of Nature and of Nature's God entitle them, a decent respect to the opinions of mankind requires that they should declare the causes which impel them to the separation.

We hold these truths to be self-evident, that all men are created equal, that they are endowed by their Creator with certain unalienable Rights, that among these are Life, Liberty and the pursuit of Happiness. That to secure these rights, Governments are instituted among Men, deriving their just Powers from the consent of the governed. That whenever any Form of Government becomes destructive of these ends, it is the Right of the People to alter or to abolish it, and to institute new Government, laying its foundation on such principles and organizing its Powers in such form, as to them shall seem most likely to effect their Safety and Happiness. Prudence, indeed, will dictate that Governments long established should not be changed for light and transient causes; and accordingly all experience hath shewn, that mankind are more disposed to suffer, while evils are sufferable, than to right themselves by abolishing the forms to which they are accustomed. But when a long train of abuses and usurpations, pursuing invariably the same Object evinces a design to reduce them under absolute Despotism, it is their right, it is their duty, to throw off such Government, and to provide new Guards for their future security. Such has been the patient sufferance of these Colonies; and such is now the necessity which constrains them to alter their former Systems of Government. The history of the present King of Great Britain is a history of repeated injuries and usurpations, all having in direct object the establishment of an absolute Tyranny over these States. To prove this, let Facts be submitted to a candid world.

He has refused his Assent to Laws, the most wholesome and necessary for the public good.

He has forbidden his Governors to pass Laws of immediate and pressing importance, unless suspended in their operation till his Assent should be obtained; and when so suspended, he has utterly neglected to attend to them.

Text is reprinted from the facsimile of the engrossed copy in the National Archives. The original spelling, capitalization, and punctuation have been retained. Paragraphing has been added.

He has refused to pass other Laws for the accommodation of large districts of people, unless those people would relinquish the right of Representation in the Legislature, a right inestimable to them and formidable to tyrants only.

He has called together legislative bodies at places unusual, uncomfortable, and distant from the depository of their Public Records, for the sole Purpose of fatiguing them into compliance with his measures.

He has dissolved Representative Houses repeatedly, for opposing with manly firmness his invasions on the rights of the People.

He has refused for a long time, after such dissolutions, to cause others to be elected; whereby the Legislative Powers, incapable of Annihilation, have returned to the People at large for their exercise; the State remaining in the mean time exposed to all the dangers of invasion from without, and convulsions within.

He has endeavoured to prevent the Population of these States; for that purpose obstructing the Laws for Naturalization of Foreigners; refusing to pass others to encourage their migrations hither, and raising the conditions of new Appropriations of Lands.

He has obstructed the Administration of Justice, by refusing his Assent to Laws for establishing Judiciary Powers.

He has made Judges dependent on his Will alone, for the tenure of their offices, and the amount and payment of their salaries.

He has erected a multitude of New Offices, and sent hither swarms of Officers to harass our People, and eat out their substance.

He has kept among us, in times of peace, Standing Armies without the Consent of our legislatures.

He has affected to render the Military independent of and superior to the Civil Power.

He has combined with others to subject us to a jurisdiction foreign to our constitution, and unacknowledged by our laws; giving his Assent to their Acts of pretended Legislation:

For Quartering large bodies of armed troops among us:

For protecting them, by a mock Trial, from Punishment for any Murders which they should commit on the Inhabitants of these States:

For cutting off our Trade with all parts of the world:

For imposing Taxes on us without our Consent:

For depriving us in many cases, of the benefits of Trial by Jury:

For transporting us beyond Seas to be tried for pretended offences:

For abolishing the free System of English Laws in a neighbouring Province, establishing therein an Arbitrary government, and enlarging its Boundaries so as to render it at once an example and fit instrument for introducing the same absolute rule into these Colonies:

For taking away our Charters, abolishing our most valuable Laws, and altering fundamentally the Forms of our Governments:

For suspending our own Legislatures, and declaring themselves invested with Power to legislate for us in all cases whatsoever.

He has abdicated Government here, by declaring us out of his Protection, and waging War against us.

He has plundered our seas, ravaged our Coasts, burnt our towns, and destroyed the lives of our people.

He is at this time transporting large Armies of foreign Mercenaries to compleat the works of death, desolation and tyranny, already begun with circumstances of Cruelty and perfidy scarcely paralleled in the most barbarous ages, and totally unworthy the Head of a civilized nation.

He has constrained our fellow Citizens taken Captive on the high Seas to bear Arms against their Country, to become the executioners of their friends and Brethren, or to fall themselves by their Hands.

He has excited domestic insurrections amongst us, and has endeavoured to bring on the inhabitants of our frontiers, the merciless Indian Savages, whose known rule of warfare, is an undistinguished destruction of all ages, sexes and conditions.

In every stage of these Oppressions We have Petitioned for Redress in the most humble terms: Our repeated Petitions have been answered only by repeated injury. A Prince, whose character is thus marked by every act which may define a Tyrant, is unfit to be the ruler of a free People.

Nor have We been wanting in attentions to our British brethren. We have warned them from time to time of attempts by their legislature to extend an unwarrantable jurisdiction over us. We have reminded them of the circumstances of our emigration and settlement here. We have appealed to their native justice and magnanimity, and we have conjured them by the ties of our common kindred to disavow these usurpations, which, would inevitably interrupt our connections and correspondence. They too have been deaf to the voice of justice and of consanguinity. We must, therefore, acquiesce in the necessity, which denounces our Separation, and hold them, as we hold the rest of mankind, Enemies in War, in Peace Friends.

WE, THEREFORE, the Representatives of the UNITED STATES OF AMERICA, in General Congress, Assembled, appealing to the Supreme Judge of the world for the rectitude of our intentions, do, in the Name, and by Authority of the good People of these Colonies, solemnly publish and declare, That these United Colonies are, and of Right ought to be FREE AND INDEPENDENT STATES; that they are Absolved from all Allegiance to the British Crown, and that all political connection between them and the State of Great Britain, is and ought to be totally dissolved; and that, as Free and Independent States, they have full Power to levy War, conclude Peace, contract Alliances, establish Commerce, and to do all other Acts and Things which Independent States may of right do. And for the support of this Declaration, with a firm reliance on the protection of divine Providence, we mutually pledge to each other our Lives, our Fortunes and our sacred Honor.

The Constitution of the United States of America

We the People of the United States, in Order to form a more perfect Union, establish Justice, insure domestic Tranquility, provide for the common defence, promote the general Welfare, and secure the Blessings of Liberty to ourselves and our Posterity, do ordain and establish this Constitution for the United States of America.

Article I.

Section 1. All legislative Powers herein granted shall be vested in a Congress of the United States, which shall consist of a Senate and House of Representatives.

Section 2 The House of Representatives shall be composed of Members chosen every second Year by the People of the several States, and the Electors in each State shall have the Qualifications requisite for Electors of the most numerous Branch of the State Legislature.

No Person shall be a Representative who shall not have attained to the Age of twenty five Years, and been seven Years a Citizen of the United States, and who shall not, when elected, be an Inhabitant of that State in which he shall be chosen.

Representatives and direct Taxes[1] shall be apportioned among the several States which may be included within this Union, according to their respective Numbers, which shall be determined by adding to the whole Number of free Persons, including those bound to Service for a Term of Years, and excluding Indians not taxed, three fifths of all other Persons.[2] The actual Enumeration shall be made within three Years after the first Meeting of the Congress of the United States, and within every subsequent Term of ten Years, in such Manner as they shall by Law direct. The Number of Representatives shall not exceed one for every thirty Thousand, but each State shall have at Least one Representative; and until such enumeration shall be made, the State of New Hampshire shall be entitled to chuse three; Massachusetts eight; Rhode Island and Providence Plantations one; Connecticut five; New York six; New Jersey four; Pennsylvania eight; Delaware one; Maryland six; Virginia ten; North Carolina five; South Carolina five; and Georgia three.

When vacancies happen in the Representation from any State, the Executive Authority thereof shall issue Writs of Election to fill such Vacancies.

The House of Representatives shall chuse their Speaker and other Officers; and shall have the sole Power of Impeachment.

Section 3. The Senate of the United States shall be composed of two Senators from each State, chosen by the Legislature thereof, for six Years; and each Senator shall have one Vote.[3]

Text is from the engrossed copy in the National Archives. Original spelling, capitalization, and punctuation have been retained.

[1]Modified by the Sixteenth Amendment.

[2]Replaced by the Fourteenth Amendment.

[3]Superseded by the Seventeenth Amendment.

Immediately after they shall be assembled in Consequence of the first Election, they shall be divided as equally as may be into three Classes. The Seats of the Senators of the first Class shall be vacated at the Expiration of the second Year, of the second Class at the Expiration of the fourth Year, and of the third Class at the Expiration of the sixth Year, so that one third may be chosen every second Year; and if Vacancies happen by Resignation, or otherwise, during the Recess of the Legislature of any State, the Executive thereof may make temporary Appointments until the next Meeting of the Legislature, which shall then fill such Vacancies.[4]

No Person shall be a Senator who shall not have attained to the Age of thirty Years, and been nine Years a Citizen of the United States, and who shall not, when elected, be an Inhabitant of that State for which he shall be chosen.

The Vice President of the United States shall be President of the Senate, but shall have no Vote, unless they be equally divided.

The Senate shall chuse their other Officers, and also a President pro tempore, in the Absence of the Vice President, or when he shall exercise the Office of President of the United States.

The Senate shall have the sole Power to try all Impeachments. When sitting for that Purpose, they shall be on Oath or Affirmation. When the President of the United States is tried, the Chief Justice shall preside: And no Person shall be convicted without the Concurrence of two thirds of the Members present.

Judgment in Cases of Impeachment shall not extend further than to removal from Office, and disqualification to hold and enjoy any Office of honor, Trust or Profit under the United States: but the Party convicted shall nevertheless be liable and subject to Indictment, Trial, Judgment and Punishment, according to Law.

Section 4. The Times, Places and Manner of holding Elections for Senators and Representatives, shall be prescribed in each State by the Legislature thereof, but the Congress may at any time by Law make or alter such Regulation, except as to the Places of chusing Senators.

The Congress shall assemble at least once in every Year, and such Meeting shall be on the first Monday in December, unless they shall by Law appoint a different Day.[5]

Section 5. Each House shall be the Judge of the Elections, Returns and Qualifications of its own Members, and a Majority of each shall constitute a Quorum to do Business; but a smaller Number may adjourn from day to day, and may be authorized to compel the Attendance of absent Members, in such Manner, and under such Penalties as each House may provide.

Each House may determine the Rules of its Proceedings, punish its Members for disorderly Behaviour, and, with the Concurrence of two thirds, expel a Member.

---

[4]Modified by the Seventeenth Amendment.
[5]Superseded by the Twentieth Amendment.

Each House shall keep a Journal of its Proceedings, and from time to time publish the same, excepting such Parts as may in their Judgment require Secrecy; and the Yeas and Nays of the Members of either House on any question shall, at the Desire of one fifth of those Present, be entered on the Journal.

Neither House, during the Session of Congress, shall, without the Consent of the other, adjourn for more than three days, nor to any other Place than that in which the two Houses shall be sitting.

Section 6. The Senators and Representatives shall receive a Compensation for their Services, to be ascertained by Law, and paid out of the Treasury of the United States. They shall in all Cases, except Treason, Felony and Breach of the Peace, be privileged from Arrest during their Attendance at the Session of their respective Houses, and in going to and returning from the same; and for any Speech or Debate in either House, they shall not be questioned in any other Place.

No Senator or Representative shall, during the Time for which he was elected, be appointed to any civil Office under the Authority of the United States, which shall have been created, or the Emoluments whereof shall have been encreased during such time; and no Person holding any Office under the United States, shall be a Member of either House during his Continuance in Office.

Section 7. All Bills for raising Revenue shall originate in the House of Representatives; but the Senate may propose or concur with Amendments as on other Bills.

Every Bill which shall have passed the House of Representatives and the Senate shall, before it become a Law, be presented to the President of the United States; If he approve he shall sign it, but if not he shall return it, with his Objections to that House in which it shall have originated, who shall enter the Objections at large on their Journal, and proceed to reconsider it. If after such Reconsideration two thirds of that House shall agree to pass the Bill, it shall be sent, together with the Objections, to the other House, by which it shall likewise be reconsidered, and if approved by two thirds of that House, it shall become a Law. But in all such Cases the Votes of both Houses shall be determined by yeas and Nays, and the Names of the Persons voting for and against the Bill shall be entered on the Journal of each House respectively. If any Bill shall not be returned by the President within ten Days (Sundays excepted) after it shall have been presented to him, the Same shall be a Law, in like Manner as if he had signed it, unless the Congress by their Adjournment prevent its Return, in which Case it shall not be a Law.

Every Order, Resolution, or Vote to which the Concurrence of the Senate and House of Representatives may be necessary (except on a question of Adjournment) shall be presented to the President of the United States; and before the Same shall take Effect, shall be approved by him, or being disapproved by him shall be repassed by two thirds of the Senate and House of Representatives, according to the Rules and Limitations prescribed in the Case of a Bill.

Section 8. The Congress shall have power To lay and collect Taxes, Duties, Imposts and Excises, to pay the Debts and provide for the common Defence and general Welfare of the United States; but all Duties, Imposts and Excises shall be uniform throughout the United States;

To borrow Money on the credit of the United States;

To regulate Commerce with foreign Nations, and among the several States, and with the Indian Tribes;

To establish an uniform Rule of Naturalization, and uniform Laws on the subject of Bankruptcies throughout the United States;

To coin Money, regulate the Value thereof, and of foreign Coin, and fix the Standard of Weights and Measures;

To provide for the Punishment of counterfeiting the Securities and current Coin of the United States;

To establish Post Offices and post Roads;

To promote the Progress of Science and useful Arts, by securing for limited Times to Authors and Inventors the exclusive Right to their respective Writings and Discoveries;

To constitute Tribunals inferior to the supreme Court;

To define and punish Piracies and Felonies committed on the high Seas, and Offences against the Law of Nations;

To declare War, grant Letters of Marque and Reprisal, and make Rules concerning Captures on Land and Water;

To raise and support Armies, but no Appropriation of Money to that Use shall be for a longer Term than two Years;

To provide and maintain a Navy;

To make Rules for the Government and Regulation of the land and naval Forces;

To provide for calling forth the Militia to execute the Laws of the Union, suppress Insurrections and repel Invasions;

To provide for organizing, arming, and disciplining, the Militia, and for governing such Part of them as may be employed in the Service of the United States, reserving to the States respectively, the Appointment of the Officers, and the Authority of training the Militia according to the discipline prescribed by Congress;

To exercise exclusive Legislation in all Cases whatsoever, over such District (not exceeding ten Miles square) as may, by Cession of particular States, and the Acceptance of Congress, become the Seat of the Government of the United States, and to exercise like Authority over all Places purchased by the Consent of the Legislature of the State in which the Same shall be, for the Erection of Forts, Magazines, Arsenals, dock-Yards, and other needful Buildings;—And

To make all Laws which shall be necessary and proper for carrying into Execution the foregoing Powers, and all other Powers vested by this Constitution in the Government of the United States, or in any Department or Officer thereof.

Section 9. The Migration or Importation of such Persons as any of the States now existing shall think proper to admit, shall not be prohibited by the Congress prior to the Year one thousand eight hundred and eight, but a Tax or duty may be imposed on such Importation, not exceeding ten dollars for each Person.

The Privilege of the Writ of Habeas Corpus shall not be suspended, unless when in Cases of Rebellion or Invasion the public Safety may require it.

No Bill of Attainder or ex post facto Law shall be passed.

No Capitation, or other direct, Tax shall be laid, unless in Proportion to the Census or Enumeration herein before directed to be taken.

No Tax or Duty shall be laid on Articles exported from any State.

No Preference shall be given by any Regulation of Commerce or Revenue to the Ports of one State over those of another: nor shall Vessels bound to, or from, one State, be obliged to enter, clear, or pay Duties in another.

No Money shall be drawn from the Treasury, but in Consequence of Appropriations made by Law; and a regular Statement and Account of the Receipts and Expenditures of all public Money shall be published from time to time.

No Title of Nobility shall be granted by the United States: And no Person holding any Office of Profit or Trust under them, shall, without the Consent of the Congress, accept of any present, Emolument, Office, or Title, of any kind whatever, from any King, Prince, or foreign State.

Section 10. No State shall enter into any Treaty, Alliance, or Confederation; grant Letters of Marque and Reprisal; coin Money; emit Bills of Credit; make any Thing but gold and silver Coin a Tender in Payment of Debts; pass any Bill of Attainder, ex post facto Law, or Law impairing the Obligation of Contracts, or grant any Title of Nobility.

No State shall, without the Consent of the Congress, lay any Imposts or Duties on Imports or Exports, except what may be absolutely necessary for executing its inspection Laws: and the net Produce of all Duties and Imposts, laid by any State on Imports or Exports, shall be for the Use of the Treasury of the United States; and all such Laws shall be subject to the Revision and Controul of the Congress.

No State shall, without the Consent of Congress, lay any Duty of Tonnage, keep Troops, or Ships of War in time of Peace, enter into any Agreement or Compact with another State, or with a foreign Power, or engage in War, unless actually invaded, or in such imminent Danger as will not admit of delay.

Article II.

Section 1. The executive Power shall be vested in a President of the United States of America. He shall hold his Office during the Term of four Years, and, together with the Vice President, chosen for the same Term, be elected, as follows:

Each State shall appoint, in such Manner as the Legislature thereof may direct, a Number of Electors, equal to the whole Number of Senators and Representatives to which the State may be entitled in the Congress: but no Senator or Representative, or Person holding an Office of Trust or Profit under the United States, shall be appointed an Elector.

The Electors shall meet in their respective States, and vote by Ballot for two Persons, of whom one at least shall not be an Inhabitant of the same State with themselves. And they shall make a List of all the Persons voted for, and of the Number of Votes for each; which List they shall sign and certify, and transmit sealed to the Seat of the Government of the United States, directed to the President of the Senate. The President of the Senate shall, in the Presence of the Senate and House of Representatives, open all the Certificates, and the Votes shall then be counted. The Person having the greatest Number of Votes shall be the President, if such Number be a Majority of the whole Number of Electors appointed; and if there be more than one who have such Majority, and have an equal Number of Votes, then the House of Representatives shall immediately chuse by Ballot one of them for President; and if no Person have a Majority, then from the five highest on the List the said House shall in like Manner chuse the President. But in chusing the President, the Votes shall be taken by States, the Representation from each State having one Vote; A quorum for this Purpose shall consist of a Member or Members from two thirds of the States, and a Majority of all the States shall be necessary to a Choice. In every Case, after the Choice of the President, the Person having the greatest Number of Votes of the Electors shall be the Vice President. But if there should remain two or more who have equal Votes, the Senate shall chuse from them by Ballot the Vice President.[6]

The Congress may determine the Time of chusing the Electors, and the Day on which they shall give their Votes; which Day shall be the same throughout the United States.

No Person except a natural born Citizen, or a Citizen of the United States, at the time of the Adoption of this Constitution, shall be eligible to the Office of President, neither shall any Person be eligible to that Office who shall not have attained to the Age of thirty five Years, and been fourteen Years a Resident within the United States.

In Case of the Removal of the President from Office, or of his Death, Resignation, or Inability to discharge the Powers and Duties of the said Office, the Same shall devolve on the Vice President, and the Congress may by Law provide for the Case of Removal, Death, Resignation or Inability, both of the President and Vice President, declaring what Officer shall then act as President, and such Officer shall act accordingly, until the Disability be removed, or a President shall be elected.[7]

The President shall, at stated Times, receive for his Services, a Compensation, which shall neither be increased nor diminished during the Period for which he shall have been elected, and he shall not receive within that Period any other Emolument from the United States, or any of them.

---

[6]Superseded by the Twelfth Amendment.
[7]Modified by the Twenty-fifth Amendment.

Before he enter on the Execution of his Office, he shall take the following Oath or Affirmation:—"I do solemnly swear (or affirm) that I will faithfully execute the Office of President of the United States, and will to the best of my Ability, preserve, protect and defend the Constitution of the United States."

Section 2. The President shall be Commander in Chief of the Army and Navy of the United States, and of the Militia of the several States, when called into the actual Service of the United States; he may require the Opinion, in writing, of the principal Officer in each of the executive Departments, upon any Subject relating to the Duties of their respective Offices, and he shall have Power to grant Reprieves and Pardons for Offences against the United States, except in Cases of Impeachment.

He shall have Power, by and with the Advice and Consent of the Senate, to make Treaties, provided two thirds of the Senators present concur; and he shall nominate, and by and with the Advice and Consent of the Senate, shall appoint Ambassadors, other public Ministers and Consuls, Judges of the supreme Court, and all other Officers of the United States, whose Appointments are not herein otherwise provided for, and which shall be established by Law; but the Congress may by Law vest the Appointment of such inferior Officers, as they think proper, in the President alone, in the Courts of Law, or in the Heads of Departments.

The President shall have Power to fill up all Vacancies that may happen during the Recess of the Senate, by granting Commissions which shall expire at the End of their next Session.

Section 3. He shall from time to time give the Congress Information of the State of the Union, and recommend to their Consideration such Measures as he shall judge necessary and expedient; he may, on extraordinary Occasions, convene both Houses, or either of them, and in Case of Disagreement between them, with Respect to the Time of Adjournment, he may adjourn them to such Time as he shall think proper; he shall receive Ambassadors and other public Ministers; he shall take Care that the Laws be faithfully executed, and shall Commission all the Officers of the United States.

Section 4. The President, Vice President and all civil Officers of the United States, shall be removed from Office on Impeachment for, and Conviction of, Treason, Bribery, or other high Crimes and Misdemeanors.

Article III.

Section 1. The judicial Power of the United States, shall be vested in one supreme Court, and in such inferior Courts as the Congress may from time to time ordain and establish. The Judges, both of the supreme and inferior Courts, shall hold their Offices during good Behaviour, and shall, at stated Times, receive for their Services, a Compensation, which shall not be diminished during their Continuance in Office.

Section 2. The judicial Power shall extend to all Cases, in Law and Equity, arising under this Constitution, the Laws of the United States, and Treaties made, or which shall be made, under their Authority;—to all Cases affecting Ambassadors, other public Ministers and Consuls;—to all Cases of admiralty and maritime Jurisdiction;—to Controversies to which the United States shall be a Party;—to Controversies between two or more States;—between a State and Citizens of another State;[8]—between Citizens of different States,—between Citizens of the same State claiming Lands under Grants of different States, and between a State, or the Citizens thereof, and foreign States, Citizens or Subjects.

In all Cases affecting Ambassadors, other public Ministers and Consuls, and those in which a State shall be Party, the supreme Court shall have original Jurisdiction. In all the other Cases before mentioned, the supreme Court shall have appellate Jurisdiction, both as to Law and Fact, with such Exceptions, and under such Regulations as the Congress shall make.

The Trial of all Crimes, except in Cases of Impeachment, shall be by Jury; and such Trial shall be held in the State where the said Crimes shall have been committed; but when not committed within any State, the Trial shall be at such Place or Places as the Congress may by Law have directed.

Section 3. Treason against the United States, shall consist only in levying War against them, or in adhering to their Enemies, giving them Aid and Comfort. No Person shall be convicted of Treason unless on the Testimony of two Witnesses to the same overt Act, or on Confession in open Court.

The Congress shall have Power to declare the Punishment of Treason, but no Attainder of Treason shall work Corruption of Blood, or Forfeiture except during the Life of the Person attainted.

Article IV.

Section 1. Full Faith and Credit shall be given in each State to the public Acts, Records, and judicial Proceedings of every other State. And the Congress may by general Laws prescribe the Manner in which such Acts, Records and Proceedings shall be proved, and the Effect thereof.

Section 2. The Citizens of each State shall be entitled to all Privileges and Immunities of Citizens in the several States.

A Person charged in any State with Treason, Felony, or other Crime, who shall flee from Justice, and be found in another State, shall on Demand of the executive Authority of the State from which he fled, be delivered up, to be removed to the State having Jurisdiction of the Crime.

---

[8]Modified by the Eleventh Amendment.

No Person held to Service or Labour in one State, under the Laws thereof, escaping into another, shall, in Consequence of any Law or Regulation therein, be discharged from such Service or Labour, but shall be delivered up on Claim of the Party to whom such Service or Labour may be due.

Section 3. New States may be admitted by the Congress into this Union; but no new State shall be formed or erected within the Jurisdiction of any other State, nor any State be formed by the Junction of two or more States, or Parts of States, without the Consent of the Legislatures of the States concerned as well as of the Congress.

The Congress shall have Power to dispose of and make all needful Rules and Regulations respecting the Territory or other Property belonging to the United States; and nothing in this Constitution shall be so construed as to Prejudice any Claims of the United States, or of any particular State.

Section 4. The United States shall guarantee to every State in this Union a Republican Form of Government, and shall protect each of them against Invasion; and on Application of the Legislature, or of the Executive (when the Legislature cannot be convened) against domestic Violence.

Article V.

The Congress, whenever two thirds of both Houses shall deem it necessary, shall propose Amendments to this Constitution, or, on the Application of the Legislatures of two thirds of the several States, shall call a Convention for proposing Amendments, which, in either Case, shall be valid to all Intents and Purposes, as Part of this Constitution, when ratified by the Legislatures of three fourths of the several States, or by Conventions in three fourths thereof, as the one or the other Mode of Ratification may be proposed by the Congress; Provided that no Amendment which may be made prior to the Year One thousand eight hundred and eight shall in any Manner affect the first and fourth Clauses in the Ninth Section of the first Article; and that no State, without its Consent, shall be deprived of its equal Suffrage in the Senate.

Article VI.

All Debts contracted and Engagements entered into, before the Adoption of this Constitution, shall be as valid against the United States under this Constitution, as under the Confederation.

This Constitution, and the Laws of the United States which shall be made in Pursuance thereof; and all Treaties made, or which shall be made, under the Authority of the United States, shall be the supreme Law of the Land; and the Judges in every State shall be bound thereby, any Thing in the Constitution or Laws of any State to the Contrary notwithstanding.

The Senators and Representatives before mentioned, and the Members of the several State Legislatures, and all executive and judicial Officers, both of the United States and of the several States, shall be bound by Oath or Affirmation, to support this Constitution; but no religious Test shall ever be required as a Qualification to any Office or public Trust under the United States.

Article VII.

The Ratification of the Conventions of nine States, shall be sufficient for the Establishment of this Constitution between the States so ratifying the Same.

Done in Convention by the Unanimous Consent of the States present the Seventeenth Day of September in the Year of our Lord one thousand seven hundred and Eighty seven and of the Independence of the United States of America the Twelfth. In witness whereof We have hereunto subscribed our Names,

Articles in Addition to, and Amendment of, the Constitution of the United States of America, Proposed by Congress, and Ratified by the Legislatures of the Several States, Pursuant to the Fifth Article of the Original Constitution.

Amendment I [9]

Congress shall make no law respecting an establishment of religion, or prohibiting the free exercise thereof; or abridging the freedom of speech, or of the press; or the right of the people peaceably to assemble, and to petition the Government for a redress of grievances.

Amendment II

A well regulated Militia, being necessary to the security of a free State, the right of the people to keep and bear Arms shall not be infringed.

Amendment III

No Soldier shall, in time of peace, be quartered in any house, without the consent of the Owner, nor in time of war, but in a manner to be prescribed by law.

Amendment IV

The right of the people to be secure in their persons, houses, papers, and effects, against unreasonable searches and seizures, shall not be violated, and no Warrants shall issue, but upon probable cause, supported by Oath or affirmation, and particularly describing the place to be searched, and the persons or things to be seized.

---

[9]The first ten amendments were passed by Congress September 25, 1789. They were ratified by three-fourths of the states December 15, 1791.

Amendment V

No person shall be held to answer for a capital or otherwise infamous crime, unless on a presentment or indictment of a Grand Jury, except in cases arising in the land or naval forces, or in the Militia, when in actual service in time of War or public danger; nor shall any person be subject for the same offence to be twice put in jeopardy of life or limb; nor shall be compelled in any criminal case to be a witness against himself, nor be deprived of life, liberty, or property, without due process of law; nor shall private property be taken for public use, without just compensation.

Amendment VI

In all criminal prosecutions, the accused shall enjoy the right to a speedy and public trial, by an impartial jury of the State and district wherein the crime shall have been committed, which district shall have been previously ascertained by law, and to be informed of the nature and cause of the accusation; to be confronted with the witnesses against him; to have compulsory process for obtaining witnesses in his favor, and to have the Assistance of Counsel for his defence.

Amendment VII

In suits at common law, where the value in controversy shall exceed twenty dollars, the right of trial by jury shall be preserved, and no fact tried by a jury, shall be otherwise reexamined in any Court of the United States, than according to the rules of the common law.

Amendment VIII

Excessive bail shall not be required, nor excessive fines imposed, nor cruel and unusual punishments inflicted.

Amendment IX

The enumeration in the Constitution, of certain rights, shall not be construed to deny or disparage others retained by the people.

Amendment X

The powers not delegated to the United States by the Constitution; nor prohibited by it to the States, are reserved to the States respectively, or to the people.

Amendment XI[10]

The Judicial power of the United States shall not be construed to extend to any suit in law or equity, commenced or prosecuted against one of the United States by Citizens of another State, or by Citizens or Subjects of any Foreign State.

---

[10]Passed March 4, 1794. Ratified January 23, 1795.

Amendment XII[11]

The Electors shall meet in their respective States and vote by ballot for President and Vice-President, one of whom, at least, shall not be an inhabitant of the same State with themselves; they shall name in their ballots the person voted for as President, and in distinct ballots the person voted for as Vice-President, and they shall make distinct lists of all persons voted for as President, and of all persons voted for as Vice-President, and of the number of votes for each, which lists they shall sign and certify, and transmit sealed to the seat of the government of the United States, directed to the President of the Senate;—The President of the Senate shall, in the presence of the Senate and House of Representatives, open all the certificates and the votes shall then be counted;—The person having the greatest number of votes for President, shall be the President, if such number be a majority of the whole number of Electors appointed; and if no person have such majority, then from the persons having the highest numbers not exceeding three on the list of those voted for as President, the House of Representatives shall choose immediately, by ballot, the President. But in choosing the President, the votes shall be taken by states, the representation from each state having one vote; a quorum for this purpose shall consist of a member or members from two-thirds of the states, and a majority of all the states shall be necessary to a choice. And if the House of Representatives shall not choose a President whenever the right of choice shall devolve upon them, before the fourth day of March next following, then the Vice-President shall act as President, as in the case of the death or other constitutional disability of the President.—The person having the greatest number of votes as Vice-President, shall be the Vice-President, if such number be a majority of the whole number of Electors appointed, and if no person have a majority, then from the two highest numbers on the list, the Senate shall choose the Vice-President; a quorum for the purpose shall consist of two-thirds of the whole number of Senators, and a majority of the whole number shall be necessary to a choice. But no person constitutionally ineligible to the office of President shall be eligible to that of Vice-President of the United States.

Amendment XIII[12]

Section 1. Neither slavery nor involuntary servitude, except as a punishment for crime whereof the party shall have been duly convicted, shall exist within the United States, or any place subject to their jurisdiction.

Section 2. Congress shall have power to enforce this article by appropriate legislation.

Amendment XIV[13]

Section 1. All persons born or naturalized in the United States, and subject to the jurisdiction thereof, are citizens of the United States and of the State wherein they reside. No State shall make or enforce any law which shall abridge the privileges or immunities of citizens of

---

[11]Passed December 9, 1803. Ratified June 15, 1804.

[12]Passed January 31, 1865. Ratified December 6, 1865.

[13]Passed June 13, 1866. Ratified July 9, 1868.

the United States; nor shall any State deprive any person of life, liberty, or property, without due process of law; nor deny to any person within its jurisdiction the equal protection of the laws.

Section 2. Representatives shall be apportioned among the several States according to their respective numbers, counting the whole number of persons in each State, excluding Indians not taxed. But when the right to vote at any election for the choice of electors for President and Vice-President of the United States, Representatives in Congress, the Executive and Judicial officers of a State, or the members of the Legislature thereof, is denied to any of the male inhabitants of such State, being twenty-one years of age, and citizens of the United States, or in any way abridged, except for participation in rebellion, or other crime, the basis of representation therein shall be reduced in the proportion which the number of such male citizens shall bear to the whole number of male citizens twenty-one years of age in such State.

Section 3. No person shall be a Senator or Representative in Congress, or elector of President and Vice-President, or hold any office, civil or military, under the United States, or under any State, who, having previously taken an oath, as a member of Congress, or as an officer of the United States, or as a member of any State legislature, or as an executive or judicial officer of any State, to support the Constitution of the United States, shall have engaged in insurrection or rebellion against the same, or given aid or comfort to the enemies thereof. But Congress may by a vote of two-thirds of each House, remove such disability.

Section 4. The validity of the public debt of the United States, authorized by law, including debts incurred for payment of pensions and bounties for services in suppressing insurrection or rebellion, shall not be questioned. But neither the United States nor any State shall assume or pay any debt or obligation incurred in aid of insurrection or rebellion against the United States, or any claim for the loss or emancipation of any slave; but all such debts, obligations, and claims shall be held illegal and void.

Section 5. The Congress shall have the power to enforce, by appropriate legislation, the provisions of this article.

Amendment XV[14]

Section 1. The right of citizens of the United States to vote shall not be denied or abridged by the United States or by any State on account of race, color, or previous conditions of servitude—

Section 2. The Congress shall have power to enforce this article by appropriate legislation.

Amendment XVI

The Congress shall have power to lay and collect taxes on incomes, from whatever source derived, without apportionment among the several States, and without regard to any census or enumeration.

---

[14]Passed February 26, 1869. Ratified February 2, 1870.

Amendment XVII[15]

The Senate of the United States shall be composed of two Senators from each State, elected by the people thereof, for six years; and each Senator shall have one vote. The electors in each State shall have the qualifications requisite for electors of the most numerous branch of the State legislatures.

When vacancies happen in the representation of any State in the Senate, the executive authority of such State shall issue writs of election to fill such vacancies: *Provided,* That the legislature of any State may empower the executive thereof to make temporary appointments until the people fill the vacancies by election as the legislature may direct.

This amendment shall not be so construed as to affect the election or term of any Senator chosen before it becomes valid as part of the Constitution.

Amendment XVIII[16]

Section 1. After one year from the ratification of this article the manufacture, sale, or transportation of intoxicating liquors within, the importation thereof into, or the exportation thereof from the United States and all territory subject to the jurisdiction thereof for beverage purposes is hereby prohibited.

Section 2. The Congress and the several States shall have concurrent power to enforce this article by appropriate legislation.

Section 3. This article shall be inoperative unless it shall have been ratified as an amendment to the Constitution by the legislatures of the several States, as provided in the Constitution, within seven years from the date of the submission hereof to the States by the Congress.

Amendment XIX[17]

The right of citizens of the United States to vote shall not be denied or abridged by the United States or by any State on account of sex.

Congress shall have power to enforce this article by appropriate legislation.

Amendment XX[18]

Section 1. The terms of the President and Vice-President shall end at noon on the 20th day of January, and the terms of Senators and Representatives at noon on the 3d day of January, of the years in which such terms would have ended if this article had not been ratified; and the terms of their successors shall then begin.

Section 2. The Congress shall assemble at least once in every year, and such meeting shall begin at noon on the 3d day of January, unless they shall by law appoint a different day.

---

[15]Passed May 13, 1912. Ratified April 8, 1913.
[16]Passed December 18, 1917. Ratified January 16, 1919.
[17]Passed June 4, 1919. Ratified August 18, 1920.
[18]Passed March 2, 1932. Ratified January 23, 1933.

Section 3. If, at the time fixed for the beginning of the term of the President, the President elect shall have died, the Vice-President elect shall become President. If a President shall not have been chosen before the time fixed for the beginning of his term, or if the President elect shall have failed to qualify, then the Vice-President elect shall act as President until a President shall have qualified; and the Congress may by law provide for the case wherein neither a President elect nor a Vice-President elect shall have qualified, declaring who shall then act as President, or the manner in which one who is to act shall be selected, and such person shall act accordingly until a President or Vice-President shall have qualified.

Section 4. The Congress may by law provide for the case of the death of any of the persons from whom the House of Representatives may choose a President whenever the right of choice shall have devolved upon them, and for the case of the death of any of the persons from whom the Senate may choose a Vice-President whenever the right of choice shall have devolved upon them.

Section 5. Sections 1 and 2 shall take effect on the 15th day of October following the ratification of this article.

Section 6. This article shall be inoperative unless it shall have been ratified as an amendment to the Constitution by the legislatures of three-fourths of the several States within seven years from the date of its submission.

Amendment XXI[19]

Section 1. The eighteenth article of amendment to the Constitution of the United States is hereby repealed.

Section 2. The transportation or importation into any State, Territory, or possession of the United States for delivery or use therein of intoxicating liquors, in violation of the laws thereof, is hereby prohibited.

Section 3. This article shall be inoperative unless it shall have been ratified as an amendment to the Constitution by conventions in the several States, as provided in the Constitution, within seven years from the date of the submission hereof to the States by the Congress.

Amendment XXII[20]

No person shall be elected to the office of the President more than twice, and no person who has held the office of President, or acted as President, for more than two years of a term to which some other person was elected President shall be elected to the office of the President more than once.

---

[19]Passed February 20, 1933. Ratified December 5, 1933.
[20]Passed March 12, 1947. Ratified March 1, 1951.

But this Article shall not apply to any person holding the office of President when this Article was proposed by the Congress, and shall not prevent any person who may be holding the office of President, or acting as President, during the term within which this Article becomes operative from holding the office of President or acting as President during the remainder of such term.

Amendment XXIII[21]

Section 1. The District constituting the seat of Government of the United States shall appoint in such manner as the Congress may direct:

A number of electors of President and Vice President equal to the whole number of Senators and Representatives in Congress to which the District would be entitled if it were a State, but in no event more than the least populous State; they shall be in addition to those appointed by the States, but they shall be considered, for the purposes of the election of President and Vice President, to be electors appointed by the State; and they shall meet in the District and perform such duties as provided by the twelfth article of amendment.

Section 2. The Congress shall have power to enforce this article by appropriate legislation.

Amendment XXIV[22]

Section 1. The right of citizens of the United States to vote in any primary or other election for President or Vice President, or for Senator or Representative in Congress, shall not be denied or abridged by the United States or any State by reason of failure to pay any poll tax or other tax.

Section 2. The Congress shall have power to enforce this article by appropriate legislation.

Amendment XXV[23]

Section 1. In case of the removal of the President from office or of his death or resignation, the Vice President shall become President.

Section 2. Whenever there is a vacancy in the office of the Vice President, the President shall nominate a Vice President who shall take office upon confirmation by a majority vote of both Houses of Congress.

---

[21]Passed June 16, 1960. Ratified April 3, 1961.

[22]Passed August 27, 1962. Ratified January 23, 1964.

[23]Passed July 6, 1965. Ratified February 11, 1967.

Section 3. Whenever the President transmits to the President pro tempore of the Senate and the Speaker of the House of Representatives his written declaration that he is unable to discharge the powers and duties of his office, and until he transmits them a written declaration to the contrary, such powers and duties shall be discharged by the Vice President as Acting President.

Section 4. Whenever the Vice President and a majority of either the principal officers of the executive department or of such other body as Congress may by law provide, transmit to the President pro tempore of the Senate and the Speaker of the House of Representatives their written declaration that the President is unable to discharge the powers and duties of his office, the Vice President shall immediately assume the powers and duties of the office of Acting President.

Thereafter, when the President transmits to the President pro tempore of the Senate and the Speaker of the House of Representatives his written declaration that no inability exists, he shall resume the powers and duties of his office unless the Vice President and a majority of either the principal officers of the executive department or of such other body as Congress may by law provide, transmit within four days to the President pro tempore of the Senate and the Speaker of the House of Representatives their written declaration that the President is unable to discharge the powers and duties of his office. Thereupon Congress shall decide the issue, assembling within forty-eight hours for that purpose if not in session. If the Congress, within twenty-one days after receipt of the latter written declaration, or, if Congress is not in session, within twenty-one days after Congress is required to assemble, determines by two-thirds vote of both Houses that the President is unable to discharge the powers and duties of his office, the Vice President shall continue to discharge the same as Acting President; otherwise, the President shall resume the powers and duties of his office.

Amendment XXVI[24]

Section 1. The right of citizens of the United States, who are eighteen years of age or older, to vote shall not be denied or abridged by the United States or by any State on account of age.

Section 2. The Congress shall have power to enforce this article by appropriate legislation.

Amendment XXVII[25]

No law, varying the compensation for the service of the Senators and Representatives, shall take effect, until an election of Representatives shall have intervened.

---

[24]Passed March 23, 1971. Ratified July 5, 1971.
[25]Passed September 25, 1789. Ratified May 7, 1992.

Glossary

1919 steel strike Walkout by 300,000 steelworkers in the Midwest demanding union recognition and an eight-hour day. It was defeated by employers and local and state police forces, who sometimes resorted to violence.

40 acres and a mule Largely unfulfilled hope of many former slaves that they would receive free land from the confiscated property of ex-Confederates.

9th and 10th U.S. Cavalry African-American army units that played pivotal roles in the Spanish-American war.

abolitionism Movement begun in the North about 1830 to abolish slavery immediately and without compensation to owners.

abolitionist A person who wanted to abolish slavery.

abrogating a treaty Process of abolishing a treaty so that it is no longer in effect.

affirmative action Program or policy that attempted to compensate for past injustice or discrimination to ensure more employment and educational opportunities.

affluence Abundance of material goods or wealth.

Agricultural Adjustment Administration (AAA) 1933 attempt to promote economic recovery by reducing supply of crops, dairy, and meat produced by American farmers.

Aguinaldo, Emilio Anti-colonial leader who fought for independence of the Philippines first from Spain and then from the United States.

Alamo Battle between Texas revolutionaries and the Mexican army at the San Antonio mission called the *Alamo* on March 6, 1836, in which all 187 Texans were killed.

Albany Congress An intercolonial congress that met in Albany, New York, in June 1754. The delegates urged the Crown to assume direct control of Indian relations beyond the settled boundaries of the colonies, and they drafted a plan of confederation for the continental colonies. No colony ratified it, nor did the Crown or Parliament accept it.

Algonquians Indian peoples who spoke some dialect of the Algonquian language family.

alien Person from another country who is living in the United States.

American Anti-Slavery Society Organization created by northern abolitionists in 1833 that called for immediate, uncompensated emancipation of the slaves.

American Colonization Society Established by elite gentlemen of the middle and upper-south states in 1816, this organization encouraged voluntary emancipation of slaves, to be followed by their emigration to the West African colony of Liberia.

American System Program proposed by Henry Clay and others to foster national economic growth and interdependence among the geographical sections. It included a protective tariff, a national bank, and internal improvements.

Amerind The forerunner of the vast majority of Indian languages in the Americas.

amnesty General pardon granted to a large group of people.

anarchist Activist who called for the violent destruction of the capitalist system so that a new socialist order could be built.

Anasazi An advanced pre-Columbian cliff-dwelling culture that flourished for two centuries in what are now the states of Arizona, New Mexico, Utah, and Colorado before abandoning these sites in the late 13th century A.D.

Anderson, Marian Black opera singer who broke a color barrier in 1939 when she sang to an interracial audience of 75,000 from the steps of the Lincoln Memorial.

Anglican A member of the legally established Church of England, or that church itself.

Anglos English-speaking people.

anxious bench Bench at or near the front of a religious revival meeting where the most likely converts were seated.

apartheid Legal system practiced in South Africa and based on elaborate rules of racial separation and subordination of blacks.

armistice A temporary stop in fighting. Often in effect before a final peace treaty is signed.

Article X of the Covenant Addendum to the Treaty of Versailles that empowered the League of Nations to undertake military actions against aggressor nations.

artisan A skilled laborer who works with his hands. In early America, artisans often owned their own shops and produced goods either for general sale or for special order.

Association Groups created by the First Continental Congress in local committees to enforce its trade sanctions against Britain. The creation of these groups was an important sign that Congress was beginning to act as a central government.

associationalism Herbert Hoover's approach to managing the economy. Firms and organizations in each economic sector would be asked to cooperate with each other in the pursuit of efficiency, profit, and the public good.

astrolabe A device that permitted accurate calculation of latitude or distances north and south.

Atlantic slave trade A European commerce that led to the enslavement of millions of people who were shipped from their African homelands to European colonies in the Americas.

attrition A type of warfare in which an effort is made to exhaust the manpower, supplies, and morale of the other side.

Auburn system Prison system designed to reform criminals and reduce expenses through the sale of items produced in workshops. Prisoners slept in solitary cells, marched in military formation to meals and workshops, and were forbidden to speak to one another at any time.

Australian ballot (secret ballot) Practice that required citizens to vote in private rather than in public and required the government (rather than political parties) to supervise the voting process.

Aztec The last pre-Columbian high culture in the Valley of Mexico. It was conquered by the Spaniards in 1519–1521.

baby boom Sudden increase in births in the years after World War II.

backcountry Term used in the 18th and early 19th centuries to refer to the western settlements and the supposed misfits who lived in them.

Bacon's Rebellion The most serious challenge to royal authority in the English mainland colonies prior to 1775. It erupted in Virginia in 1676 after the governor and Nathaniel Bacon, the principal rebel, could not agree on how best to wage war against frontier Indians.

balance of trade The relationship between imports and exports. The difference between exports and imports is the balance between the two. A healthy nation should export more than it imports. This is known as a favorable balance of trade.

bandeirantes Brazilian frontiersmen who traveled deep into South America to enslave Indians. The slaves then were worked to death on the sugar plantations.

banknotes Paper money, issued by banks, that circulated as currency.

barrios Spanish-speaking urban areas, usually separate districts in southwestern towns and cities.

bateau A light, flat-bottomed boat with narrow ends that was used in Canada and the northeastern part of the colonies.

Battle of Lexington The first military engagement of the Revolutionary War. It occurred on April 19, 1775, when British soldiers fired into a much smaller body of minutemen on Lexington green.

Battle of Little Big Horn A battle in eastern Montana Territory on the bluffs above Little Big Horn River on June 25, 1876.

Bay of Pigs Site of an ill-fated 1961 invasion of Cuba by a U.S.-trained force that attempted to overthrow the government of Fidel Castro.

Beatles Preeminent musical group associated with the "British invasion" in the 1960s.

belligerent Country actively engaged in a war.

Beringia A land bridge during the last ice age across the Bering Strait between Siberia and Alaska. It was once an area where plants, animals, and humans could live.

bicameral legislature A legislature with two houses or chambers.

Bill of Rights First ten amendments to the Constitution, which protect the rights of individuals from abuses by the federal government.

Black Codes Laws passed by southern states that restricted the rights and liberties of former slaves.

Black Power Mid-1960s movement that called for modifying integrationist goals in favor of gaining political and economic power for separate black-directed institutions and emphasized pride in African-American heritage.

Black Republicans Label coined by the Democratic Party to attack the Republican Party as believers in racial equality. The Democrats used this fear to convince many whites to remain loyal to them.

blacklist In the postwar years, a list of people who could no longer work in the entertainment industry because of alleged contacts with communists.

blitzkrieg A "lightning war"; a coordinated and massive military strike by German army and air forces.

block grants Part of Nixon's new economic plan in which a percentage of federal tax dollars would be returned to state and local governments to spend as they deemed fit.

blockade runner A ship designed to run through a blockade.

blockade The closing of a country's harbors by enemy ships to prevent trade and commerce, especially to prevent traffic in military supplies.

blockhouse A wooden fort with an overhanging second floor. The white settlers of Kentucky used blockhouses to defend themselves against Indians.

blood sports Sporting activities emphasizing bloodiness that were favored by working-class men of the cities. The most popular in the early 19th century were cockfighting, ratting, dogfights, and various types of violence between animals.

bonanza farms Huge wheat farms financed by eastern capital and cultivated with heavy machinery and hired labor.

Bonus Army Army veterans who marched on Washington, D.C., in 1932 to lobby for economic relief but who were rebuffed by Hoover.

Boone, Daniel A pioneer settler of Kentucky, Boone became the most famous American frontiersman of his generation.

border ruffians Term used to describe proslavery Missourians who streamed into Kansas in 1854, determined to vote as many times as necessary to install a proslavery government there.

Boston Massacre The colonial term for the confrontation between colonial protestors and British soldiers in front of the customs house on March 5, 1770. Five colonists were killed and six wounded.

Boston Tea Party In December 1773, Boston's Sons of Liberty threw 342 chests of East India Company tea into Boston harbor rather than allow them to be landed and pay the hated tea duty.

bounty jumpers Men who enlisted in the Union army to collect the bounties offered by some districts to fill military quotas; these men would enlist and then desert as soon as they got their money.

Boxers Chinese nationalist organization that instigated an uprising in 1900 to rid China of all foreign influence.

braceros Guest workers from Mexico allowed into the United States because of labor shortages from 1942 to 1964.

Brown v. Board of Education 1954 case in which the U.S. Supreme Court unanimously overruled the "separate but equal" doctrine and held that segregation in the public schools violated the principle of equal protection under the law.

"broad" wives Wives of slave men who lived on other plantations and were visited by their husbands during off hours.

Brown, John Prominent abolitionist who fought for the antislavery cause in Kansas (1856) and led a raid to seize the Harpers Ferry arsenal in 1859.

Bryan, William Jennings A two-term Democratic congressman from Nebraska who won the party's presidential nomination in 1896 after electrifying delegates with his "Cross of Gold" speech. Bryan was twice more nominated for president (1900 and 1908); he lost all three times.

Bull Moosers Followers of Theodore Roosevelt in the 1912 election.

bulldozing Using force to keep African Americans from voting.

Burr, Aaron Vice President under Thomas Jefferson who killed Alexander Hamilton in a duel and eventually hatched schemes to detach parts of the west from the United States.

Bush, George H. W. Republican President (1989–1993) who directed an international coalition against Iraq in the Persian Gulf War.

Bush, George W. Republican president (2001–) elected in the highly disputed 2000 contest decided by the Supreme Court.

bushwhackers Confederate guerrilla raiders especially active in Missouri. Jayhawkers were the Union version of the same type of people. Both groups did a tremendous amount of damage with raids, arson, ambush, and murder.

Butternuts Democrats from the southern river-oriented counties of the Northwest region whose name came from the yellow vegetable dye with which they colored their homespun clothing.

Cahokia The largest city created by Mississippian mound builders. Located in Illinois near modern St. Louis, it thrived from A.D. 900 to 1250 and then declined.

californios Spanish-speaking people whose families had resided in California for generations.

camp meeting Outdoor revival often lasting for days; a principal means of spreading evangelical Christianity in the United States.

Capra, Frank Popular 1930s filmmaker who celebrated the decency, honesty, and patriotism of ordinary Americans in such films as *Mr. Deeds Goes to Town* and *Mr. Smith Goes to Washington.*

caravel A new type of oceangoing vessel that could sail

closer to a head wind than any other sailing ship and make speeds of from three to twelve knots per hour.

Carnegie, Andrew A Scottish immigrant who became the most efficient entrepreneur in the U.S. steel industry and earned a great fortune.

carpetbaggers Northerners who settled in the South during Reconstruction.

Carson, Rachel American marine biologist and author best known for *Silent Spring* (1962), a widely read book that questioned the use of chemical pesticides and helped stimulate the modern environmental movement.

Carter, Jimmy Democratic president (1977–1981) whose single term in office was marked by inflation, fuel shortages, and a hostage crisis.

cash and carry U.S. foreign policy prior to American entry into World War II that required belligerents to pay cash and carry products away in their own ships. This arrangement minimized risks to American exports, loans, and shipping.

Cavaliers Supporters of the Stuart family of Charles I during the civil wars.

changing system Elaborate system of neighborhood debts and bartering used primarily in the South and West where little cash money was available.

Chavez, Cesar Political activist, leader of the United Farm Workers of America, and the most influential Mexican American leader during the 1970s.

Cherokee War Between December 1759 and December 1761, the Cherokee

Indians devastated the South Carolina backcountry. The British army intervened and in turn inflicted immense damage on the Cherokee.

Chicanismo Populistic pride in the Mexican American heritage that emerged in the late 1960s. Chicano, once a term of derision, became a rallying cry among activists.

chinampas The highly productive gardens built on Lake Taxcoco by the Aztecs.

CIO The Committee (and then Congress) for Industrial Organization, founded in 1935 to organize the unskilled and semiskilled workers ignored by the AFL. The CIO reinvigorated the labor movement.

circuit court Court that meets at different places within a district.

circuit-riding preachers Methodist ministers who traveled from church to church, usually in rural areas.

Civil Rights Act of 1957 First civil-rights act since Reconstruction, aimed at securing voting rights for African Americans in the South.

Civil Rights Act of 1964 Bipartisan measure that denied federal funding to segregated schools and barred discrimination by race and sex in employment, public accommodations, and labor unions.

Civil Rights Act of 1968 Measure that banned racial discrimination in housing and made interference with a person's civil rights a federal crime. It also stipulated that crossing state lines to incite a riot was a federal crime.

Clay, Henry Speaker of the House, senator from

Kentucky, and National Republican presidential candidate who was the principal spokesman for the American System.

Clinton, Bill Democratic president (1993–2001) whose two-term presidency witnessed rapid economic growth but also a sexual scandal that fueled an impeachment effort, which he survived.

close-order assault Military tactic of attacking with little space between men. In the face of modern weapons used during the Civil War, such fighting produced a high casualty rate.

Clovis tip A superior spear point developed before 9000 B.C. It was in use nearly everywhere in North and South America and produced such an improvement in hunting ability that it contributed to the extinction of most large mammals.

Coercive (Intolerable) Acts Four statutes passed by Parliament in response to the Boston Tea Party, including one that closed the port of Boston until the tea was paid for, and another that overturned the Massachusetts Charter of 1691. The colonists called them the Intolerable Acts and included the Quebec Act under that label.

Cold War The political, military, cultural, and economic rivalry between the United States and the Soviet Union that developed after the Second World War and lasted until the disintegration of the Soviet State after 1989.

collective bargaining Negotiations between representatives of workers and employers on issues such as wages, hours, and working conditions.

Collier, John Activist head of the Bureau of Indian Affairs who improved U.S. policy toward Native Americans and guided the landmark Indian Reorganization Act through Congress.

colonial economy Economy based on the export of agricultural products and the import of manufactured goods; sometimes used to describe the dependence of the South on the North.

Columbus, Christopher The Genoese mariner who persuaded Queen Isabella of Spain to support his voyage of discovery across the Atlantic in 1492. Until his death in 1506, he believed he had reached East Asia. Instead he had discovered America.

Committee on Public Information U.S. Government agency established in 1917 to arouse support for the war and, later, to generate suspicion of war dissenters.

committees of correspondence Bodies formed on both the local and colonial levels that played an important role in exchanging ideas and information. They spread primarily anti-British material and were an important step in the first tentative unity of people in different colonies.

common law The heart of the English legal system was based on precedents and judicial decisions. Common-law courts offered due process through such devices as trial by jury, which usually consisted of local men.

common schools Tax-supported public schools

built by state and local governments.

Communist Party Radical group that wanted America to follow the Soviet Union's path to socialism. The CP organized some of the country's poorest workers into unions and pushed the New Deal leftward, but was never popular enough to bid for power itself.

commutation fee $300 fee that could be paid by a man drafted into the Union army to exempt him from the current draft call.

compensated emancipation Idea that the federal government would offer compensation or money to states that voluntarily abolished slavery.

competence Understood in the early republic as the ability to live up to neighborhood economic standards while protecting the long-term independence of the household.

Compromise of 1850 Series of laws enacted in 1850 intended to settle all outstanding slavery issues.

Congressional Black Caucus (CBC) Congressional group formed in 1969 that focused on eliminating disparities between African Americans and white Americans.

congressional caucus In the early republic, the group of congressmen who traditionally chose the party's presidential candidates. By the 1820s, the American public distrusted the caucus as undemocratic because only one party contested for power. The caucus was replaced by the national nominating convention.

conquistadores The Spanish word for conquerors.

Conscience Whigs A group of antislavery members of the Whig Party.

Conservation Movement that called for managing the environment to ensure the careful and efficient use of the nation's natural resources.

consumer durable Consumer goods that were meant to last, such as washing machines and radios.

containment Label used to describe the global anticommunist national-security policies adopted by the United States to stop the expansion of communism during the late 1940s.

contraband of war Term used to describe slaves who came within the Union lines.

contras Military force in Nicaragua, trained and financed by the United States, that opposed the Nicaraguan socialist government led by the Sandinista Party.

convention In England, a meeting, usually of the houses of Parliament, to address an emergency, such as the flight of James II to France in 1688. The convention welcomed William and Mary, who then restored the traditional parliamentary system. In the United States by the 1780s, conventions had become the purest expression of the popular will, superior to the legislature, as in the convention that drafted the Massachusetts Constitution of 1780.

cooperatives Marketing groups established by such groups as the Farmers Alliance that eliminated "middlemen" and reduced prices to farmers. The idea also was tried by some labor groups and

included other types of businesses, such as factories.

Copperheads Term used by some Republicans to describe Peace Democrats to imply that they were traitors to the Union.

corrupt bargain Following the election of 1824, Andrew Jackson and his supporters alleged that, in a "corrupt bargain," Henry Clay sold his support during the House vote in the disputed election of 1824 of John Quincy Adams in exchange for appointment as Secretary of State.

Cortés, Hernán The Spanish conquistador who vanquished the Aztecs.

cotton Semitropical plant that produced white, fluffy fibers that could be made into textiles.

Coughlin, Father Charles The "radio priest" from the Midwest who alleged that the New Deal was being run by bankers. His growing anti-Semitism discredited him by 1939.

counterculture Antiestablishment movement that symbolized the youthful social upheaval of the 1960s. Ridiculing traditional attitudes toward such matters as clothing, hair styles, and sexuality, the counterculture urged a more open and less regimented approach to daily life.

coureur de bois A French phrase interpreted as "a roamer of the woods," referring to French colonists who participated in the fur trade with the Indians and lived part of the year with them.

court-packing plan 1937 attempt by Roosevelt to appoint one new Supreme

Court justice for every sitting justice over the age of 70 and who had sat for at least 10 years. Roosevelt's purpose was to prevent conservative justices from dismantling the New Deal, but the plan died in Congress and inflamed opponents of the New Deal.

Covenant Chain of Peace An agreement negotiated by Governor Edmund Andros in 1677 that linked the colony of New York to the Iroquois Five Nations and was later expanded to include other colonies and Indian peoples.

covenant theology The belief that God made two personal covenants with humans: the covenant of works and the covenant of grace.

coverture A common-law doctrine under which the legal personality of the husband covered the wife, and he made all legally binding decisions.

Crazy Horse War chief of the Oglala Lakota (Sioux) Indians, who forged an alliance with Cheyenne chiefs to resist white expansion into the Black Hills in 1874–1875; led the attack on Custer's 7th Cavalry at Little Big Horn.

Credit Mobilier Construction company for the Union Pacific Railroad that gave shares of stock to some congressmen in return for favors.

crisis conversion Understood in evangelical churches as a personal transformation that resulted from directly experiencing the Holy Spirit.

crop lien system System of credit used in the poor rural South, whereby merchants in small country stores provided necessary goods on credit in return for a lien on the crop. As the price of crops fell, small farmers, black and white, drifted deeper into debt.

Cuban Missile Crisis (1962) Serious Cold War confrontation between the United States and the Soviet Union over the installation of Soviet missiles in Cuba.

Custer, George A. Civil War hero and postwar Indian fighter who was killed at Little Big Horn in 1876.

Davis, Jefferson Mississippi planter and prominent leader of the Southern Democrats in the 1850s, who later served as president of the Confederacy.

Dawes Plan 1924 U.S.-backed agreement to reduce German reparation payments by more than half. The plan also called on banks to invest $200 million in the German economy.

Debs, Eugene V. Leader of the Socialist Party who received almost a million votes in the election of 1912.

Declaration of Independence A document drafted primarily by Thomas Jefferson of Virginia; this document justified American independence to the world by affirming "that all men are created equal" and have a natural right to "life, liberty, and the pursuit of happiness." The longest section of the Declaration condemned George III as a tyrant.

deflation Decline in consumer prices or a rise in the purchasing power of money.

Deism Belief that God created the universe but did not intervene in its affairs.

Denmark Vesey Leader of a slave conspiracy in and around Charleston, South Carolina, in 1822.

deskilling Process in which the employment market produces jobs requiring fewer skills (and offering less income) than in the past.

détente An easing of tensions, particularly between the United States and the Soviet Union.

Dewey, John Philosopher who believed that American technological and industrial power could be made to serve the people and democracy.

direct election of senators Constitutional amendment that mandated the election of senators by the people rather than by selection by state legislatures.

dirty tricks Actions designed to destroy the reputation and effectiveness of political opponents of the Nixon administration.

disfranchisement Process of barring groups of adult citizens from voting.

dissenter Person who disagrees openly with the majority opinion.

Dix, Dorothea Boston reformer who traveled throughout the country campaigning for humane, state-supported asylums for the insane.

dollar diplomacy Diplomatic strategy formulated under President Taft that focused on expanding American investments abroad, especially in Latin America and East Asia.

domestic fiction Sentimental literature that centered on household and domestic themes that emphasized the toil and travails of women and children who overcame

adversity through religious faith and strength of character.

Douglas, Stephen A. Senator from Illinois who emerged as a leading Democrat in 1850 and led efforts to enact the Compromise of 1850.

doves Opponents of military action, especially those who wanted to end quickly U.S. involvement in the Vietnam War.

dower rights The right of a widow to a portion of her deceased husband's estate (usually one-third of the value of the estate). It was passed to their children upon her death.

dowry The cash or goods a woman received from her father when she married.

drawbacks Form of rebate offered to special customers by the railroads.

Dred Scott Missouri slave who sued for freedom on grounds of prolonged residence in a free state and free territory; in 1857, the Supreme Court found against his case, declaring the Missouri Compromise unconstitutional.

Du Bois, W. E. B. Leader of the NAACP, the editor of its newspaper, *The Crisis*, and an outspoken critic of Booker T. Washington and his accomodationist approach to race relations.

economy of scale Term used in both industry and agriculture to describe the economic advantages of concentrating capital, units of production, and output.

Eisenhower Doctrine Policy that stated that the United States would use armed force to respond to imminent or actual communist aggression in the Middle East.

Eisenhower, Dwight D. Supreme Commander of the Allied Forces in Europe, orchestrator of the Normandy Invasion, and President of the United States (1953–1961).

elect Those selected by God for salvation.

Electoral College The group that elects the president. Each state receives as many electors as it has congressmen and senators combined and can decide how to choose its electors. Every elector votes for two candidates, one of whom has to be from another state.

emancipation Refers to release from slavery or bondage. Gradual emancipation was introduced in Pennsylvania and provided for the eventual freeing of slaves born after a certain date when they reached age 28.

embargo Government order prohibiting the movement of merchant ships or goods in or out of its ports.

encomienda A system of labor introduced into the Western Hemisphere by the Spanish. It permitted the holder, or *encomendero*, to claim labor from Indians in a district for a stated period of time.

enfranchise To grant the right to vote.

Enlightenment The new learning in science and philosophy that took hold, at least in England, between 1660 and the American Revolution. Nearly all of its spokesmen were religious moderates who were more interested in science than religious doctrine and who favored broad religious toleration.

entail A legal device that required a landowner to keep his estate intact and pass it on to his heir.

enumerated commodities A group of colonial products that had to be shipped from the colony of origin to England or another English colony. The most important commodities were sugar and tobacco.

Environmental Protection Agency (EPA) Organization established in 1970 that brought under a single institutional umbrella the enforcement of laws intended to protect environmental quality.

environmentalism Movement with roots in earlier conservation, preservation, and public health movements that grew in power after 1970, when concern mounted over the disruption of ecological balances and critical habitats.

Equal Rights Amendment (ERA) Proposed amendment to the Constitution providing that equal rights could not be abridged on account of sex. It won congressional approval in 1972 but failed to gain ratification by the states.

Erie Canal Canal linking the Hudson River at Albany with the Great Lakes at Buffalo that helped commercialize the farms of the Great Lakes watershed and channel that commerce into New York City.

Espionage, Sabotage, and Sedition Acts Laws passed in 1917 and 1918 that gave the federal government sweeping powers to silence and even imprison dissenters.

established church The church in a European state or colony that was sustained by the government and supported by public taxes.

evangelical A style of Christian ministry that includes much zeal and enthusiasm. Evangelical ministers emphasized personal conversion and faith rather than religious ritual.

evangelicals Religious groups that generally placed an emphasis on conversion of non-Christians.

excise tax Internal tax on goods or services.

external taxes Taxes based on oceanic trade, such as port duties. Some colonists thought of them more as a means of regulating trade than as taxes for revenue.

factories A term used to describe small posts established for the early slave trade along the coast of Africa or on small offshore islands.

fall line A geographical landmark defined by the first waterfalls encountered when going upriver from the sea. These waterfalls prevented oceangoing ships from sailing further inland and thus made the fall line a significant early barrier. Land between the falls and the ocean was called the tidewater. Land above the falls but below the mountains was called the piedmont.

fascism Type of highly centralized government that used terror and violence to suppress opposition. Its rigid social and economic controls often incorporated strong nationalism and racism. Fascist governments were dominated by strong authority figures or dictators.

favorite son Candidate for president supported by delegates from his home state.

Federal Reserve Act Act that brought private banks and public authority together to regulate and strengthen the nation's financial system.

Federalists Supporters of the Constitution during the ratification process. Anti-Federalists resisted ratification.

feudal revival The reliance on old feudal charters for all of the profits that could be extracted from them. It took hold in several colonies in the mid-18th century and caused serious problems between many landowners and tenants.

fiat money Paper money backed only by the promise of the government to accept it in payment of taxes. It originated in Massachusetts after a military emergency in 1690.

filibuster Congressional delaying tactic involving lengthy speeches that prevent legislation from being enacted.

filibustering A term used to describe several groups that invaded or attempted to invade various Latin American areas to attempt to add them to the slaveholding regions of the United States. The word originated from *filibustero,* meaning a free-booter or pirate.

fire-eaters Southerners who were eager, enthusiastic supporters of southern rights and later of secession.

First Continental Congress This intercolonial body met in Philadelphia in September and October 1774 to organize resistance against the Coercive Acts by defining American rights, petitioning the king, and appealing to the British and American people. It created the Association, local committees in each community to enforce nonimportation.

Five-Power Treaty 1922 treaty in which the United States, Britain, Japan, France, and Italy agreed to scrap more than 2 million tons of their warships.

flappers Rebellious middle-class young women who signaled their desire for independence and equality through style and personality rather than through politics.

flexible response Kennedy's approach to the Cold War that aimed to provide a wide variety of military and non-military methods to confront communist movements.

Ford, Gerald A GOP member of the House of Representatives, Gerald Ford became the first person to be appointed Vice President of the United States. When Richard Nixon resigned in 1974, Ford became President.

Fort Sumter Fort in Charleston's harbor occupied by United States troops after the secession of South Carolina.

Fourteen Points Plan laid out by Woodrow Wilson in January 1918 to give concrete form to his dream of a "peace without victory" and a new world order.

free silver Idea that the government would purchase all silver offered for sale and coin it into silver dollars at the preferred ratio between silver and gold of 16 to 1.

Freedmen's Bureau Federal agency created in 1865 to supervise newly freed people. It oversaw relations between whites and blacks in the South, issued food rations, and supervised labor contracts.

freedom riders Members of interracial groups who traveled the South on buses to test a series of federal court decisions declaring segregation on buses and in waiting rooms to be unconstitutional.

Freedom Summer Summer of 1964 when nearly a thousand white volunteers went to Mississippi to aid in voter registration and other civil-rights projects.

free-labor ideology Belief that all work in a free society is honorable and that manual labor is degraded when it is equated with slavery or bondage.

Free-Soilers A term used to describe people who opposed the expansion of slavery into the territories. It came from the name of a small political party in the election of 1848.

French and Indian War Popular name for the struggle between Britain and France for the control of North America, 1754 to 1763, in which the British conquered New France. It merged into Europe's Seven Years' War (1756–1763) that pitted Britain and Prussia against France, Austria, and Russia.

Friedan, Betty Author of *The Feminine Mystique* (1963) and founder of the National Organization for Women (1966).

frontier An area on the advancing edge of American civilization.

fugitive slaves Runaway slaves who escaped to a free state.

Fulton, Robert Builder of the *Clermont,* the first practical steam-driven boat.

fundamentalists Religious groups that preached the necessity of fidelity to a strict moral code, individual commitment to Christ, and faith in the literal truth of the Bible.

funded national debt The state agreed to pay the interest due to its creditors before all other obligations.

Gabriel's rebellion Carefully planned but unsuccessful rebellion of slaves in Richmond, Virginia, and the surrounding area in 1800.

gang labor A system where planters organized their field slaves into gangs, supervised them closely, and kept them working in the fields all day. This type of labor was used on tobacco plantations.

Garvey, Marcus Jamaican-born black nationalist who attracted millions of African Americans in the early 1920s to a movement calling for black separatism and self-sufficiency.

gas and water socialists Term used to describe evolutionary socialists who focused their reform efforts on regulating municipal utilities in the public interest.

gentleman Term used to describe a person of means who performed no manual labor.

gentlemen's agreement (1907) Agreement by which the Japanese government promised to halt the immigration of its adult male laborers to the United States in return for President Theodore Roosevelt's pledge to end the discriminatory treatment of Japanese immigrant children in California's public schools.

GI Bill Officially called the Serviceman's Readjustment Act of 1944. It provided veterans with college and job-training assistance, preferential treatment in hiring, and subsidized home loans, and was later extended to Korean War veterans in 1952.

girdled trees Trees with a line cut around them so sap would not rise in the spring.

glasnost Russian term describing increased openness in Russian society under Mikhail Gorbachev.

Glorious Revolution The overthrow of King James II by Whigs and Tories, who invited William of Orange to England. William landed in November 1688, the army defected to him, James fled to France, and in early 1689, Parliament offered the throne to William and his wife Mary, a daughter of James. Contemporaries called the event "glorious" because almost no blood was shed in England.

gold bugs "Sound money" advocates who wanted to keep the United States on the international gold standard and believed the expanded coinage of silver was foolhardy.

Gompers, Samuel F. America's most famous trade unionist while serving as president of the AFL (1896–1924). He achieved his greatest success in organizing skilled workers.

Good Neighbor Policy Roosevelt's foreign policy initiative that formally renounced the right of the United States to intervene in Latin American affairs, leading to improved relations between the United States and Latin American countries.

governor-general The French official responsible for military and diplomatic affairs and for appointment of all militia officers in a colony.

graduated income tax Tax based on income with rates that gradually rise as the level of income rises.

Grangers Members of the Patrons of Husbandry (a farmers' organization) and a contemptuous name for farmers used by ranchers in the West.

Grant, Ulysses S. General-in-chief of Union armies who led those armies to victory in the Civil War.

Great American Desert The treeless area in the plains that most Americans considered unsuitable for settlement. It generally was passed over by settlers going to the Pacific Coast areas.

Great Awakening An immense religious revival that swept across the Protestant world in the 1730s and 1740s.

Great Depression Economic downturn triggered by the stock market crash in October 1929 and lasting until 1941.

Great Society Series of domestic initiatives announced in 1964 by President Lyndon Johnson to "end poverty and racial injustice." They included the Voting Rights Act of 1965; the establishment of the Department of Housing and Urban Development, Head Start, and job-training programs; Medicare and Medicaid expansion; and various community action programs.

Great White Fleet Naval ships sent on a 45,000-mile world tour by President Roosevelt (1907–1909) to showcase American military power.

Greeley, Horace Editor of the *New York Tribune*, one of the most influential newspapers in the country.

greenbacks Paper money issued by the federal government during the Civil War to help pay war expenses. They were called greenbacks because of their color.

Greene, Nathanael A general from Rhode Island whose superb strategy of irregular war reclaimed the Lower South for the American cause in 1780–1781.

Greenwich Village Community of radical artists and writers in lower Manhattan that provided a supportive environment for various kinds of radical ideals.

Grenville, George As head of the British government from 1763 to 1765, Grenville passed the Sugar Act, Quartering Act, Currency Act, and the Stamp Act, provoking the imperial crisis of 1765–1766.

Grimke, Sarah Along with her sister Angelina, this elite South Carolina woman moved north and campaigned against slavery and for temperance and women's rights.

gross national product (GNP) Total value of all goods and services produced during a specific period.

Gulf of Tonkin Resolution Measure passed by Congress in August 1964 that provided authorization for an air war against North Vietnam after U.S. destroyers were allegedly attacked by North Vietnamese torpedoes. Johnson invoked it as authority for expanding the Vietnam War.

Gullah A language spoken by newly imported African slaves.

Originally, it was a simple second language for everyone who spoke it, but it gradually evolved into modern black English.

habeas corpus Right of an individual to obtain a legal document as protection against illegal imprisonment.

haciendas Large, landed estates established by the Spanish.

Hale, Sarah Josepha Editor of *Godey's Ladies Book* and an important arbiter of domesticity and taste for middle-class housewives.

Half-Way Covenant The Puritan practice whereby parents who had been baptized but had not yet experienced conversion could bring their children before the church and have them baptized.

Hamilton, Alexander Secretary of the Treasury under Washington who organized the finances of the new government and led the partisan fight against the Democratic Republicans.

Hard Money Democrats Democrats who, in the 1830s and 1840s, wanted to eliminate paper money and regarded banks as centers of trickery and privilege.

Harlem Renaissance 1920s African-American literary and artistic awakening that sought to create works rooted in black culture instead of imitating white styles.

Harpers Ferry Site of John Brown's 1859 raid on a U.S. armory and arsenal for the manufacture and storage of military rifles.

hawks Supporters of intensified military efforts in the Vietnam War.

Haywood, William Labor organizer known as "Big

Bill," who led the radical union Industrial Workers of the World.

headright A colonist received 50 acres of land for every person whose passage to America he financed, including himself. This system was introduced in Virginia.

heathen A term used sometimes by Christians to refer to anyone who was not a Christian or a Jew.

herrenvolk **democracy** Concept that emphasized the equality of all who belonged to the master race—not all mankind.

Hessians A term used by Americans to describe the 17,000 mercenary troops hired by Britain from various German states, especially Hesse.

hidalgos The minor nobility of Spain. Many possessed little wealth and were interested in improving their position through the overseas empire.

High Federalists A term used to describe Alexander Hamilton and some of his less-moderate supporters. They wanted the naval war with France to continue and also wanted to severely limit the rights of an opposition party.

Highway Act of 1956 Act that appropriated $25 billion for the construction of more than 40,000 miles of interstate highways over a 10-year period.

hippies People who identified with the 1960s counterculture. They were often depicted as embracing mind-altering drugs, communal living arrangements, and new forms of music.

Hiroshima Japanese city destroyed by an atomic bomb on August 6, 1945.

Hiss, Alger High-level State Department employee who was accused, in a controversial case, of being a communist and Soviet spy.

Hitler, Adolph German fascist dictator whose aggressive policies touched off the Second World War.

HIV-AIDS Acquired immune deficiency syndrome (AIDS) resulting from infection with the human immunodeficiency virus (HIV). It progressively impedes the body's ability to protect itself from disease.

Hmong Ethnically distinct people who inhabited lands extending across the borders of the Indochinese countries of Vietnam, Cambodia, and Laos.

House of Burgesses The assembly of early Virginia that settlers were allowed to elect. Members met with the governor and his council and enacted local laws. It first met in 1619.

House Un-American Activities Committee (HUAC) Congressional committee (1938–1975) that zealously investigated suspected Nazi and Communist sympathizers.

household industry Work such as converting raw materials into finished products done by women and children to provide additional household income.

Howe, William (General) Howe commanded the British army in North America from 1776 to 1778. He won major victories in New York and northern New Jersey in 1776, but Washington regained control of New Jersey after his Trenton-Princeton campaign. Howe took Philadelphia in September 1777 but was recalled in disgrace after Britain's northern army surrendered at Saratoga.

Huguenots French Protestants who followed the beliefs of John Calvin.

Hull House First American settlement house established in Chicago in 1889 by Jane Addams and Ellen Gates Starr.

Human Genome Project Program launched in 1985 to map all genetic material in the 24 human chromosomes. It sparked ongoing debate over the potential consequences of genetic research and manipulation.

Hutchinson, Anne A religious radical who attracted a large following in Massachusetts, especially in Boston. She warned that nearly all of the ministers were preaching a covenant of works instead of the covenant of grace. Convicted of the Antinomian heresy after claiming that she received direct messages from God, she and her most loyal followers were banished to Rhode Island in 1638.

hydraulic mining Use of high-pressure streams of water to wash gold or other minerals from soil.

Immigration Act of 1924 (Johnson-Reed Act) Limited immigration to the United States to 165,000 per year, shrank immigration from southern and eastern Europe to insignificance, and banned immigration from East and South Asia.

Immigration Act of 1965 Law eliminating the national-origins quota system for immigration and substituting preferences for people with certain skills or with relatives in the United States.

Immigration Restriction Act of 1917 Measure that denied any adult immigrant who failed a reading test entry into the United States, and banned immigration from the "Asiatic Barred Zone."

impeach To charge government officeholders with misconduct in office.

impeachment Act of charging a public official with misconduct in office.

imperialists Those who wanted to expand their nation's world power through military prowess, economic strength, and control of foreign territory (often organized into colonies).

impressment Removal of sailors from American ships by British naval officers.

Inca The last and most extensive pre-Columbian empire in the Andes and along the Pacific coast of South America.

indentured servants People who had their passage to America paid by a master or ship captain. They agreed to work for their master for a term of years in exchange for cost of passage, bed and board, and small freedom dues when their terms were up. The number of years served depended on the terms of the contract. Most early settlers in the English colonies outside of New England arrived as indentured servants.

Indian Removal Act (1830) Legislation that offered the native peoples of the lower South the option of removal to federal lands west of the Mississippi. Those who did not take the offer were removed by force in 1838.

indigo A blue dye obtained from plants that was used by the textile industry. The British government subsidized the commercial production of it in South Carolina.

information revolution Acceleration of the speed and availability of information resulting from use of computer and satellite systems.

initiative Reform that gave voters the right to propose and pass a law independently of their state legislature.

Inns of Court England's law schools.

intendant The officer who administered the system of justice in New France.

interchangeable parts Industrial technique using machine tools to cut and shape a large number of similar parts that can be fitted together with other parts to make an entire item such as a gun.

internal improvements 19th-century term for transportation facilities such as roads, canals, and railroads.

internal taxes Taxes that were imposed on land, people, retail items (such as excises), or legal documents and newspapers (such as the Stamp Act). Most colonists thought that only their elective assemblies had the constitutional power to impose internal taxes.

Iran-*contra* affair Reagan administration scandal in which the U.S. secretly sold arms to Iran, a country implicated in holding American hostages, and diverted the money to finance the attempt by the *contras* to overthrow the Sandinista

government of Nicaragua. Both transactions violated acts of Congress, which had prohibited funding the *contras* and selling weapons to Iran.

Iroquois League A confederation of five Indian nations centered around the Mohawk Valley who were very active in the fur trade. They first worked with the Dutch and then the English. They were especially successful in using adoption as a means of remaining strong.

irreconcilables Group of 14 midwestern and western senators who opposed the Treaty of Versailles.

irregular war A type of war using men who were not part of a permanent or professional regular military force. It also can apply to guerilla-type warfare, usually against the civilian population.

itinerant preachers Ministers who lacked their own parishes and who traveled from place to place.

Jackson State (incident) Killing of two students on May 13, 1970, after an escalation in tensions between students at Jackson State University, a historically black institution, and National Guard troops in Mississippi.

Jackson, Andrew President of the United States (1829–1837) who founded the Democratic Party, signed the Indian Removal Act, vetoed the Second Bank, and signed the Force Bill.

Jackson, Thomas J. ("**Stonewall**") A native of Virginia, he emerged as one of the Confederacy's best generals in 1861–1862.

Jamestown Founded in 1607, Jamestown became England's first permanent settlement in North America. It served as the capital of Virginia for most of the 17th century.

Japanese internment Removal of first- and second-generation Japanese Americans into secured camps, a 1942 action then justified as a security measure but since deemed unjustified by evidence.

Jim Crow laws Laws passed by southern states mandating racial segregation in public facilities of all kinds.

Johnson, Lyndon B. President (1963–1969) who undertook an ambitious Great Society program and a major military effort in Vietnam.

joint resolution An act passed by both houses of Congress with a simple majority rather than the two-thirds majority in the Senate.

joint-stock company A form of business organization that resembled a modern corporation. Individuals invested in the company through the purchase of shares. One major difference between then and today was that each stockholder had one vote regardless of how many shares he owned. The first permanent English colonies in North America were established by joint-stock companies.

journeyman Wage-earning craftsman.

judicial review Supreme Court's power to rule on the constitutionality of congressional acts.

Kansas-Nebraska Act Law enacted in 1854 to organize the new territories of Kansas and Nebraska that effectively repealed the provision of the 1820 Missouri Compromise by leaving the question of slavery to the territories' settlers.

Kennan, George (Mr. X) American diplomat and historian who recommended the policy of containment toward Soviet aggression in a famous article published under the pseudonym "X."

Kennedy, John F. President from 1961 to 1963, noted for his youthful charm and vigor and his "New Frontier" vision for America.

Kent State (incident) Killing of four students on May 4, 1970, by the National Guard at a Kent State University protest against the U.S. incursion into neutral Cambodia.

King George's War Popular term in North America for the third of the four Anglo-French wars before the American Revolution (1744–1748). It is sometimes also applied to the War of Jenkins's Ear between Spain and Britain (1739–1748).

King, Martin Luther, Jr. African American clergyman who advocated nonviolent social change and shaped the civil-rights movement of the 1950s and 1960s.

Know-Nothings Adherents of nativist organizations and of the American party who wanted to restrict the political rights of immigrants.

Korean War Conflict lasting from 1950 to 1953 between communist North Korea, aided by China, and South Korea, aided by United Nations forces consisting primarily of U.S. troops.

Ku Klux Klan White terrorist organization in the South originally founded as a fraternal society in 1866. Reborn in 1915, it achieved popularity in the 1920s through its calls for Anglo-Saxon purity, Protestant supremacy, and the subordination of blacks, Catholics, and Jews.

La Raza Unida Mexican American–based movement that scored some political successes in the Southwest in the late 1960s and early 1970s.

lame-duck administration Period of time between an incumbent party's or officeholder's loss of an election and the succession to office of the winning party or candidate.

League of Women Voters Successor to the National American Woman Suffrage Association, it promoted women's role in politics and dedicated itself to educating voters.

Lee, Robert E. U.S. army officer until his resignation to join the Confederacy as general-in-chief.

legal tender Any type of money that the government requires everyone to accept at face value.

Lend-Lease Act A 1941 act by which the United States "loaned" munitions to the Allies, hoping to avoid war by becoming an "arsenal" for the Allied cause.

levee Earthen dike or mound, usually along the banks of rivers, used to prevent flooding.

Lewis and Clark Explorers commissioned in 1804 by President Jefferson to survey the Louisiana Purchase.

liberal Protestants Those who believed that religion had to be adapted to science and that the Bible was to be mined for its ethical values rather than for its literal meaning.

Liberty bonds Thirty-year government bonds with an annual interest rate of 3.5 percent sold to fund the war effort.

liberty tree A term for the gallows on which enemies of the people deserved to be hanged. The best known was in Boston.

limited liability Liability that protected directors and stockholders of corporations from corporate debts by separating those debts from personal liabilities.

Lincoln, Abraham Illinois Whig who became the Republican Party's first successful presidential candidate in 1860 and who led the Union during the Civil War.

Lincoln-Douglas debates Series of seven debates between Abraham Lincoln and Stephen Douglas in their contest for election to the U.S. Senate in 1858.

Lindbergh, Charles A. First individual to fly solo across the Atlantic (1927) and the greatest celebrity of the 1920s.

lintheads Term used by wealthier whites to describe poor whites who labored in southern cotton mills.

living room war Phrase suggesting that television coverage had brought the Vietnam War into the living rooms of Americans and may have led many to question the war.

lockout Act of closing down a business by the owners during a labor dispute.

Lodge, Henry Cabot Republican Senator from Massachusetts who led the campaign to reject the Treaty of Versailles.

logistics Military activity relating to such things as the transporting, supplying, and quartering of troops and their equipment.

long knives The term Indians used to describe Virginians.

Long, Huey Democratic senator and former governor of Louisiana who used the radio to attack the New Deal as too conservative. FDR regarded him as a major rival.

longhorn Breed of cattle introduced into the Southwest by the Spanish that became the main breed of livestock on the cattle frontier.

Lost Generation Term used by Gertrude Stein to describe U.S. writers and artists who fled to Paris in the 1920s after becoming disillusioned with America.

Louisiana Purchase Land purchased from France in 1803 that doubled the size of the United States.

Lowell, Francis Cabot Wealthy Bostonian who, with the help of the Boston Associates, built and operated integrated textile mills in eastern Massachusetts.

loyalists People in the 13 colonies who remained loyal to Britain during the Revolution.

Ludlow massacre Murder of 66 men, women, and children in April 1914 when company police of the Colorado Fuel and Iron Company fired randomly on striking United Mine Workers.

Luftwaffe German air force.

Lusitania British passenger ship sunk by a German U-boat on May 7, 1915, killing more than 1,000 men, women, and children.

MacArthur, Douglas Supreme commander of Allied forces in the southwest Pacific during the Second World War; leader of the occupation forces in the reconstruction of Japan; and head of United Nations forces during the Korean War.

magistrate An official who enforced the law. In colonial America, this person was usually a justice of the peace or a judge in a higher court.

Mahan, Alfred Thayer Influential imperialist who advocated construction of a large navy as crucial to the successful pursuit of world power.

Malcolm X Charismatic African American leader who criticized integration and urged the creation of separate black economic and cultural institutions. He became a hero to members of the Black Power movement.

mandamus A legal writ ordering a person, usually a public official, to carry out a specific act. In Massachusetts in 1774, the new royal councilors were appointed by a writ of mandamus.

manifest destiny The belief that the United States was destined to grow from the Atlantic to the Pacific and from the Arctic to the tropics. Providence supposedly intended for Americans to have this area for a great experiment in liberty.

manumission of slaves The act of freeing a slave, done at the will of the owner.

Marbury v. *Madison* 1803 case involving the disputed appointment of a federal justice of the peace in which Chief Justice John Marshall expanded the Supreme Court's authority to review legislation.

maritime Of, or relating to, the sea.

Marshall Plan Plan of U.S. aid to Europe that aimed to contain communism by fostering postwar economic recovery. Proposed by Secretary of State George C. Marshall in 1947, it was known formally as the European Recovery Program.

Marshall, John Chief Justice of the United States Supreme Court from 1801 to 1835. Appointed by Federalist President John Adams, Marshall's decisions tended to favor the federal government over the states and to clear legal blocks to private business.

martial law Government by military force rather than by citizens.

mass production High-speed and high-volume production.

Massachusetts Bay Company A joint-stock company chartered by Charles I in 1629. It was controlled by Non-Separatists, who took the charter with them to New England and, in effect, converted it into a written constitution for the colony.

massive retaliation Assertion by the Eisenhower administration that the threat of U.S. atomic weaponry would hold Communist powers in check.

matrilineal A society that determines inheritance and roles in life based on the female or maternal line.

Maya A literate, highly urbanized Mesoamerican civilization that flourished for more than a thousand years before its sudden collapse in the ninth century A.D.

McCarthyism Public accusations of disloyalty made with little or no regard to actual evidence. Named after Senator Joseph McCarthy, these accusations and the scandal and harm they caused came to symbolize the most virulent form of anticommunism.

McClellan, George B. One of the most promising young officers in the U.S. army, he became the principal commander of Union armies in 1861–1862.

McKinley, William A seven-term Republican congressman from Ohio whose signature issue was the protective tariff. He was the last Civil War veteran to be elected president.

Menéndez, Francisco An escaped South Carolina slave who fought with the Yamasee Indians against the colony, fled to Florida, was reenslaved by the Spanish, became a militia captain, was freed again, and was put in charge of the free-black town of Mose near St. Augustine in the late 1730s, the first community of its kind in what is now the United States.

merger movement Late-19th and early 20th-century effort to integrate different enterprises into single, giant corporations able to eliminate competition, achieve economic order, and boost profits.

Mesoamerica An area embracing Central America and southern and central Mexico.

Metacom's War (King Philip's War) A war that devastated much of southern New England in 1675–1676. It began as a conflict between Metacom's Wampanoags and Plymouth Colony but soon engulfed all of the New England colonies and most of the region's Indian nations.

Mexican repatriation Secretary of Labor William Doak's plan to deport illegal Mexican aliens to Mexico. By 1935, more than 500,000 Mexicans had left the United States.

microchips Technological improvement that boosted the capability and reduced the size and cost of computer hardware.

middle class Social group that developed in the early 19th century comprised of urban and country merchants, master craftsmen who had turned themselves into manufacturers, and market-oriented farmers—small-scale entrepreneurs who rose within market society.

Middle Ground The area of French and Indian cooperation west of Niagara and south of the Great Lakes. No one exercised sovereign power over this area, but the French used Indian rituals to negotiate treaties with their Algonquian trading partners, first against the Iroquois and later against the British.

midnight judges Federal judicial officials appointed under the Judiciary Act of 1801, in the last days of John Adams's presidency.

militia A community's armed force, made up primarily of ordinary male citizens rather than professional soldiers.

Millennium The period at the end of history when Christ is

expected to return and rule with his saints for a thousand years.

minstrel show Popular form of theater among working men of the northern cities in which white men in blackface portrayed African Americans in song and dance.

missions Outposts established by the Spanish along the northern frontier to aid in Christianizing the native peoples. They also were used to exploit these peoples' labor.

Missouri Compromise Compromise that maintained sectional balance in Congress by admitting Missouri as a slave state and Maine as a free state and by drawing a line west from the 368 309 parallel separating future slave and free states.

modernists Those who believed in science rather than religion and in moving toward equality for men and women and for whites and nonwhites.

Monroe Doctrine Foreign policy doctrine proposed by Secretary of State John Quincy Adams in 1823 that denied the right of European powers to establish new colonies in the Americas while maintaining the United States' right to annex new territory.

Montgomery bus boycott Political protest campaign mounted in 1955 to oppose the city's policy of racial segregation on its public transit system. The Supreme Court soon declared segregation on public transit unconstitutional.

morale The general feeling of the people toward such events as a war. Good morale greatly enhances an ability to fight or sacrifice for a cause.

Mormons Members of the Church of Jesus Christ of Latter-Day Saints, founded by Joseph Smith in 1830; the *Book of Mormon* is their Bible.

Mourning War An Indian war often initiated by a widow or bereaved relative who insisted that her male relatives provide captives to repair the loss.

muckrakers Investigative journalists who propelled Progressivism by exposing corruption, economic monopolies, and moral decay in American society.

napalm Incendiary and toxic chemical contained in bombs used by the United States in Vietnam.

National American Women Suffrage Association Organization established in 1890 to promote woman suffrage; stressed that women's special virtue made them indispensable to politics.

National Association for the Advancement of Colored People (NAACP) Organization launched in 1910 to fight racial discrimination and prejudice and to promote civil rights for blacks.

National Recovery Administration (NRA) 1933 attempt to promote economic recovery by persuading private groups of industrialists to decrease production, limit hours of work per employee, and standardize minimum wages.

National Security Act (1947) Reorganized the U.S. military forces within a new Department of Defense, and established the National Security Council and the Central Intelligence Agency.

National War Labor Board U.S. government agency that brought together representatives of labor, industry, and the public to resolve labor disputes.

nativism Hostility of native-born Americans toward immigrants.

naturalization Process by which people born in a foreign country are granted full citizenship with all of its rights.

Navajo Signal Corp Navajo Indians who conveyed military intelligence in their native language to preserve its secrecy.

naval stores Items such as pitch, resin, and turpentine that were used to manufacture ships. Most of them were obtained from pine trees.

neoconservatives Group of intellectuals, many of whom had been anticommunist Democrats during the 1950s and 1960s, who came to emphasize hard-line foreign policies and conservative social stances.

neo-Federalists Nationalist Republicans who favored many Federalist economic programs, such as protective tariffs and a national bank.

Neolithic The period known also as the late Stone Age. Agriculture developed, and stone, rather than metal, tools were used.

Neutrality Acts of 1935 and 1936 Legislation that restricted loans, trade, and travel with belligerent nations in an attempt to avoid the entanglements that had brought the United States into the First World War.

neutrality U.S. policy toward World War I from 1914 to 1917 that called for staying out of war but maintaining normal economic relations with both sides.

New Freedom Wilson's reform program of 1912 that called for temporarily concentrating government power so as to dismantle the trusts and return America to 19th-century conditions of competitive capitalism.

New Lights Term used to describe prorevival Congregationalists.

New Nationalism Roosevelt's reform program between 1910 and 1912, which called for establishing a strong federal government to regulate corporations, stabilize the economy, protect the weak, and restore social harmony.

New Sides Term used to describe evangelical Presbyterians.

New York's 369th Regiment Black army unit recruited in Harlem that served under French command and was decorated with the *Croix de Guerre* for its valor.

nickelodeons Converted storefronts in working-class neighborhoods that showed early short silent films usually lasting 15 minutes, requiring little comprehension of English, and costing only a nickel to view.

Nixon, Richard President of the United States (1969–1974) during the final years of the Vietnam War. He resigned the presidency when he faced impeachment for the Watergate scandals.

nonimportation agreements
Agreements not to import goods from Great Britain. They were designed to put pressure on the British economy and force the repeal of unpopular parliamentary acts.

Non-Separatists English Puritans who insisted that they were faithful members of the Church of England while demanding that it purge itself of its surviving Catholic rituals and vestments.

normal schools State colleges established to train teachers.

North American Free Trade Agreement (NAFTA) 1994 agreement that aimed to lower or eliminate barriers restricting the trade of goods and services among the United States, Canada, and Mexico.

North Atlantic Treaty Organization (NATO) Established by treaty in 1949 to provide for the collective defense of noncommunist European and North American nations against possible aggression from the Soviet Union and to encourage political, economic, and social cooperation.

Northwest Ordinance Established the Northwest Territory between the Ohio River and the Great Lakes. Adopted by the Confederation Congress in 1787, it abolished slavery in the territory and provided that it be divided into three to five states that would eventually be admitted to the Union as full equals of the original thirteen.

NSC-68 National Security Council Document number 68 (1950) that provided the rationale and comprehensive strategic vision for U.S. policy during the Cold War.

nullification Beginning in the late 1820s, John C. Calhoun and others argued that the Union was a voluntary compact between sovereign states, that states were the ultimate judges of the constitutionality of federal law, that states could nullify federal laws within their borders, and that they had the right to secede from the Union.

Old Lights Antirevival Congregationalists.

Old Northwest The region west of Pennsylvania, north of the Ohio River, and east of the Mississippi River.

Old Sides Antirevival Presbyterians.

oligarchy A society dominated by a few persons or families.

Olmec The oldest pre-Columbian high culture to appear in what is now Mexico.

Onontio An Algonquian word that means "great mountain" and that was used by Indians of the Middle Ground to designate the governor of New France.

Open Door notes (1899–1900) Foreign policy tactic in which the United States asked European powers to respect China's independence and to open their spheres of influence to merchants from other nations.

Open Skies Eisenhower's proposal that U.S. and Soviet disarmament be verified by reconnaissance flights over each other's territory.

open-field agriculture A medieval system of land distribution used only in the New England colonies. Farmers owned scattered strips of land within a common field,

and the town as a whole decided what crops to plant.

pacifist A person opposed to war or violence. The religious group most committed to pacifism is the Quakers.

Panama Canal An engineering marvel completed in 1914 across the new Central American nation of Panama. Connecting the Atlantic and Pacific oceans, it shortened ship travel between New York and San Francisco by 8,000 miles.

parish A term used to describe an area served by one tax-supported church. The term was used primarily in regions settled by members of the Church of England.

Parks, Rosa African American seamstress in Montgomery, Alabama, who, after refusing to give up her bus seat to a white man, was arrested and fined. Her protest sparked a subsequent bus boycott that attracted national sympathy for the civil-rights cause and put Martin Luther King, Jr., in the national spotlight.

parochial schools Schools associated with a church, usually Roman Catholic. The funding of these schools became a major political issue in the 1850s.

passive civil disobedience Nonviolent refusal to obey a law in an attempt to call attention to government policies considered unfair.

patronage The act of appointing people to government jobs or awarding them government contracts, often based on political favoritism rather than on abilities.

patronships Vast estates along the Hudson River that were established by the Dutch.

They had difficulty attracting peasant labor, and most were not successful.

Peace of Paris The 1763 treaty that ended the war between Britain on the one side and France and Spain on the other side. France surrendered New France to Britain. Spain ceded Florida to Britain, and France compensated its ally by ceding all of Louisiana to Spain.

peace without victory Woodrow Wilson's 1917 pledge to work for a peace settlement that did not favor one side over the other but ensured an equality among combatants.

Pearl Harbor Japan's December 7, 1941 attack on a U.S. base in Hawaii that brought the United States into the Second World War.

Penn, William A convert to the Society of Friends in the 1660s, Penn used his friendship with Charles II and James, Duke of York, to acquire a charter for Pennsylvania in 1681, and he then launched a major migration of Friends to the Delaware Valley.

people's capitalism An egalitarian capitalism in which all Americans could participate and enjoy the consumer goods that U.S. industry had made available.

per capita Term used to measure the wealth of a nation by dividing total income by population.

perestroika Russian term describing the economic liberalization that began in the late 1980s.

Perkins, Frances Secretary of Labor under Roosevelt and the first female Cabinet member.

Pershing, John J. Commander of the American Expeditionary Force that began landing in Europe in 1917 and that entered battle in the spring and summer of 1918.

personal liberty laws Laws enacted by nine northern states to prohibit the use of state law facilities such as jails or law officers in the recapture of fugitive slaves.

piedmont A term referring to the land above the fall line but below the Appalachian Mountains.

Pilgrims A pious, sentimental term used by later generations to describe the settlers who sailed on the Mayflower in 1620 and founded Plymouth Colony.

Pitt, William One of the most popular public officials in 18th-century Britain, he was best known as the minister who organized Britain's successful war effort against France in the French and Indian War.

placer mining Mining where minerals, especially gold, were found in glacial or alluvial deposits.

Platt Amendment Clause that the U.S. forced Cuba to insert into its constitution giving the U.S. broad control over Cuba's foreign and domestic policies.

plumbers Nixon's secret intelligence unit designed to stop information leaks to the media.

Plymouth Founded by Separatists in 1620, Plymouth was England's first permanent colony in New England.

political machines Organizations that controlled local political parties and municipal governments through bribery, election fraud, and

support of urban vice while providing some municipal services to the urban poor.

politics of harmony A system in which the governor and the colonial assembly worked together through persuasion rather than through patronage or bullying.

politique A man who believed that the survival of the state took precedence over religious differences.

poll tax A tax based on people or population rather than property. It was usually a fixed amount per adult.

polygamy The act of having more than one wife.

Pontiac An Ottawa chief whose name has been attached to the great Indian uprising against the British in 1763–1764.

pools Technique used by railroads to divide up traffic and fix rates, thereby avoiding ruinous competition.

popular sovereignty The concept that settlers of each territory would decide for themselves whether to allow slavery.

postal campaign Abolitionist tactic to force the nation to confront the slavery question by flooding the mails, both North and South, with antislavery literature. Their hope was to raise controversy within an area that was the province of the federal government.

postmillennialism Belief (held mostly by middle-class evangelists) that Christ's Second Coming would occur when missionary conversion of the world brought about a thousand years of social perfection.

powwow Originally, a word used to identify tribal

prophets or medicine men. Later it was used also to describe the ceremonies held by them.

praying Indians The Christian Indians of New England.

predestination A theory that states that God has decreed, even before he created the world, who will be saved and who will be damned.

Presbytery An intermediate level of organization in the Presbyterian church, above individual congregations but below the synod. One of its primary responsibilities was the ordination and placement of ministers.

presidios Military posts constructed by the Spanish to protect the settlers from hostile Indians. They also were used to keep non-Spanish settlers from the area.

Presley, Elvis Known as "the King" of Rock and Roll, he was the biggest pop star of the 1950s.

private fields Farms of up to five acres on which slaves working under the task system were permitted to produce items for their own use and sale in a nearby market.

privateers A privately owned ship that was authorized by a government to attack enemy ships during times of war. The owner of the ship got to claim a portion of whatever was captured. This practice damaged any enemy country that could not dramatically increase naval protection for its merchant ships.

Proclamation of 1763 Issued by the Privy Council, it tried to prevent the colonists from encroaching upon Indian lands by prohibiting settlement west of the Appalachian watershed unless the

government first purchased those lands by treaty.

Progressive Party Political party formed by Theodore Roosevelt in 1912 when the Republicans refused to nominate him for president. The party adopted a sweeping reform program.

Prohibition Constitutional ban on the manufacture and sale of alcohol in the United States (1920–1933).

proprietary colony A colony owned by an individual(s) who had vast discretionary powers over the colony. Maryland was the first proprietary colony, but others were founded later.

protective tariff Tariff that increases the price of imported goods that compete with American products and thus protects American manufacturers from foreign competition.

Protestant Reformation A religious movement begun by Martin Luther in 1517 that led to the repudiation of the Roman Catholic Church in large parts of northern and central Europe.

provincial congress A type of convention elected by the colonists to organize resistance. They tended to be larger than the legal assemblies they displaced, and they played a major role in politicizing the countryside.

public Friends The men and women who spoke most frequently and effectively for the Society of Friends. They were as close as the Quakers came to having a clergy. They occupied special elevated seats in some meetinghouses.

public virtue Meant, to the revolutionary generation,

patriotism and the willingness of a free and independent people to subordinate their interests to the common good and even to die for their country.

Pueblo Revolt In the most successful Indian uprising in American history, the Pueblo people rose against the Spanish in 1680, killed most Spanish missionaries, devastated Spanish buildings, and forced the surviving Spaniards to retreat down the Rio Grande. The Pueblos maintained their autonomy for about a decade, but Spain reasserted control in the early 1690s.

Puritans An English religious group that followed the teachings of John Calvin. They wanted a fuller reformation of the Church of England and hoped to replace The Book of Common Prayer with sermons. They wanted to purify the Church of England of its surviving Catholic eremonies and vestments.

Quakers A term of abuse used by opponents to describe members of the Society of Friends, who believed that God, in the form of the Inner Light, was present in all humans. Friends were pacifists who rejected oaths, sacraments, and all set forms of religious worship.

quasi-slavery Position that resembled slavery, such as that created by the Black Codes.

quitrent A relic of feudalism, a quitrent was a small required annual fee attached to a piece of land. It differed from other rents in that nonpayment did not lead to ejection from the land but to a suit for debt.

R&D Research and development.

racial profiling Law enforcement practice of using racial appearance to screen for potential wrongdoing.

railhead End of a railroad line, or the farthest point on the track.

railroad gauge Distance between the rails on which wheels of railroad cars fit.

"rainfall follows the plow" Erroneous belief that settlement and cultivation somehow changed the weather. It evolved due to heavier-than-normal precipitation during the 1870s and 1880s.

RAND Think tank developed by the U.S. military to conduct scientific research and development.

Reagan, Ronald Republican president (1981–1989) who steered domestic politics in a conservative direction and sponsored a huge military buildup.

real wages Relationship between wages and the consumer price index.

realism Form of thinking, writing, and art that prized detachment, objectivity, and skepticism.

rebates Practice by the railroads of giving certain big businesses reductions in freight rates or refunds.

recall Reform that gave voters the right to remove from office a public servant who had betrayed their trust.

Red Scare Widespread fear in 1919–1920 that radicals had coalesced to establish a communist government on American soil. In response, U.S. government and private citizens undertook a campaign to identify, silence, and, in some cases, imprison radicals.

redemptioners Servants with an indentured contract that allowed them to find masters after they arrived in the colonies. Many German immigrant families were redemptioners and thus were able to stay together while they served their terms.

redlining Refusal by banks and loan associations to grant loans for home buying and business expansion in neighborhoods that contained aging buildings, dense populations, and growing numbers of nonwhites.

referendum Procedure that allows the electorate to decide an issue through a direct vote.

Refugee Act of 1980 Law allowing refugees fleeing political persecution entry into the United States.

religious bigotry Intolerance based on religious beliefs or practices.

religious right Christians who wedded their religious beliefs to a conservative political agenda and gained growing influence in Republican party politics after the late 1960s.

Republic of Texas Independent nation founded in 1836 when a revolution by residents in the Mexican province of Texas won their independence.

republics Independent Indian villages that were willing to trade with the British and remained outside the French system of Indian alliances.

Restoration era The period that began in 1660 when the Stuart dynasty under Charles II was restored to the throne of England. It ended with the overthrow of James II in 1688–1689.

restorationism Belief that all theological and institutional changes since the end of biblical times were man-made mistakes and that religious organizations must restore themselves to the purity and simplicity of the apostolic church.

restraint of trade Activity that prevented competition in the marketplace or free trade.

revival A series of emotional religious meetings that led to numerous public conversions.

revolving gun turret A low structure, often round, on a ship that moved horizontally and contained mounted guns.

rifling Process of cutting spiral grooves in a gun's barrel to impart a spin to the bullet. Perfected in the 1850s, it produced greater accuracy and longer range.

Robinson, Jackie African American whose addition to the Brooklyn Dodgers in 1947 began the lengthy process of integrating Major League Baseball.

rock 'n' roll Form of popular music that arose in the 1950s from a variety of musical styles, including rhythm and blues, country, and gospel. Its heavily accented beat attracted a large following among devotees of the emerging youth culture.

Rockefeller, John D. Founder of the Standard Oil Company, whose aggressive practices drove many competitors out of business and made him one of the richest men in America.

Roe **v.** *Wade* Supreme Court decision in 1973 that ruled that a blanket prohibition against abortion violated a woman's right to privacy and prompted decades of political controversy.

rolling stock Locomotives, freight cars, and other types of wheeled equipment owned by railroads.

Roosevelt corollary 1904 corollary to the Monroe Doctrine, stating that the United States had the right to intervene in domestic affairs of hemispheric nations to quell disorder and forestall European intervention.

Roosevelt liberalism New reform movement that sought to regulate capitalism but not the morals or behavior of private citizens. This reform liberalism overcame divisions between southern agrarians and northeastern ethnics.

Roosevelt, Eleanor A politically engaged and effective First Lady, and an architect of American liberalism.

Roosevelt, Franklin D. President from 1933 to 1945 and the creator of the New Deal.

Rough Riders Much-decorated volunteer cavalry unit organized by Theodore Roosevelt and Leonard Wood to fight in Cuba in 1898.

royal colony A colony controlled directly by the English monarch. The governor and council were appointed by the Crown.

Russo-Japanese War Territorial conflict between imperial Japan and Russia mediated by Theodore Roosevelt at Portsmouth, New Hampshire. The peace agreement gave Korea and other territories to Japan, ensured Russia's continuing control over Siberia, and protected China's territorial integrity.

Sacco and Vanzetti Case (1920) Controversial conviction of two Italian-born anarchists accused of armed robbery and murder.

sachem An Algonquian word that means "chief."

Safety-Fund Law New York state law that required banks to pool a fraction of their resources to protect both bankers and small stockholders in case of bank failures.

Salem witch trials About 150 people were accused of witchcraft in Massachusetts between March and September 1692. During the summer trials, 19 people were hanged and one was pressed to death after he refused to stand trial. All of those executed insisted they were innocent. Of the 50 who confessed, none was executed.

Saratoga A major turning point in the Revolutionary War. American forces prevented John Burgoyne's army from reaching Albany, cut off its retreat, and forced it to surrender in October 1777. This victory helped bring France into the war.

saturation bombing Intensive bombing designed to destroy everything in a target area.

scabs Strikebreakers who were willing to act as replacements for striking workers, thus undermining the effect of strikes as leverage against company owners.

scalawags Term used by southern Democrats to describe southern whites who worked with the Republicans.

scientific management Attempt to break down each factory job into its smallest components to increase efficiency, eliminate waste, and promote worker satisfaction.

secession The act of a state withdrawing from the Union. South Carolina was the first state to attempt to do this in 1860.

Second Continental Congress The intercolonial body that met in Philadelphia in May 1775 a few weeks after the Battles of Lexington and Concord. It organized the Continental Army, appointed George Washington commander-in-chief, and simultaneously pursued policies of military resistance and conciliation. When conciliation failed, it chose independence in July 1776 and in 1777 drafted the Articles of Confederation, which finally went into force in March 1781.

sedentary Societies that are rooted locally or are nonmigratory. Semisedentary societies are migratory for part of the year.

seditious libel The common-law crime of openly criticizing a public official.

seigneurs The landed gentry who claimed most of the land between Quebec and Montreal. They were never as powerful as aristocrats in France.

Seneca Falls Convention (1848) First national convention of women's rights activists.

separation of powers The theory that a free government, especially in a republic, should have three independent branches capable of checking or balancing one another: the executive, the legislative (usually bicameral), and the judicial.

Separatists One of the most extreme English Protestant groups that were followers of John Calvin. They began to separate from the Church of England and form their own congregations.

September 11, 2001 Day on which U.S. airliners, hijacked by Al Qaeda operatives, were crashed into the World Trade Center and the Pentagon, killing around 3,000 people.

serfdom Early medieval Europe's predominant labor system, which tied peasants to their lords and the land. They were not slaves because they could not be sold from the land.

Seward, William H. Secretary of State under Abraham Lincoln and Andrew Jackson. He was best known for his purchase of Alaska from Russia.

share wages Payment of workers' wages with a share of the crop rather than with cash.

sharecropping Working land in return for a share of the crops produced instead of paying cash rent.

Shays's Rebellion An uprising of farmers in western Massachusetts in the winter of 1786–1787. They objected to high taxes and foreclosures for unpaid debts. Militia from eastern Massachusetts suppressed the rebels.

Sheppard-Towner Act Major social welfare program providing federal funds for prenatal and child health care, 1921–1929.

sickle cell A crescent- or sickle-shaped red blood cell sometimes found in African Americans. It helped protect them from malaria but exposed some children to the dangerous and painful condition of sickle cell anemia.

Sir Walter Raleigh An Elizabethan courtier who, in the 1580s, tried but failed to establish an English colony on Roanoke Island in what is now North Carolina.

sit-down strike Labor strike strategy in which workers occupied their factory but refused to do any work until the employer agreed to recognize the workers' union. This strategy succeeded against General Motors in 1937.

sit-in movement Activity that challenged legal segregation by demanding that blacks have the same access to public facilities as whites. These nonviolent demonstrations were staged at restaurants, bus and train stations, and other public places.

Sitting Bull Hunkapapa Lakota (Sioux) chief and holy man who led warriors against the U.S. Army in Montana Territory in 1876, culminating in the Battle of Little Big Horn.

slash and burn A system of agriculture in which trees were cut down, girdled, or in some way destroyed. The underbrush then was burned, and a crop was planted. Men created the farms, and women did the farming. The system eventually depleted the fertility of the soil, and the entire tribe would move to a new area after 10 or 20 years.

Smith, Alfred E. Irish American, Democratic governor of New York who became in 1928 the first Catholic ever nominated for the presidency by a major party.

Smith, John (Captain) A member of the Virginia Council; his strong leadership from 1607 to 1609 probably saved the colony from collapse.

Smith, Joseph Poor New York farm boy whose visions led him to translate the *Book of Mormon* in late 1820s. He became the founder and the prophet of the Church of Jesus Christ of Latter-day Saints (Mormons).

Social Darwinism Set of beliefs explaining human history as an ongoing evolutionary struggle between different groups of people for survival and supremacy that was used to justify inequalities between races, classes, and nations.

Social Security Act Centerpiece of the welfare state (1935) that instituted the first federal pension system and set up funds to take care of groups (such as the disabled and unmarried mothers with children) that were unable to support themselves.

socialism Political movement that called for the transfer of industry from private to public control, and the transfer of political power from elites to the laboring masses.

sodbuster Small farmer in parts of the West who adapted to the treeless plains and prairies, such as the construction of homes out of sod.

southern yeoman Farmer who owned relatively little land and few or no slaves.

sovereign power A term used to describe supreme or final power.

space shuttle Manned rocket that served as a space laboratory and could be flown back to the earth for reuse.

specie Also called "hard money" as against paper money. In colonial times, it usually meant silver, but it could also include gold coins.

spirituals Term later devised to describe the religious songs of slaves.

Spock, Dr. Benjamin Pediatrician who wrote *Baby and Child Care* (1946), the most widely used child-rearing book during the baby-boom generation.

spoils system System by which the victorious political party rewarded its supporters with government jobs.

Sputnik First Soviet satellite sent into orbit around the earth in 1957.

stagflation Condition of simultaneous economic stagnation and price inflation.

Stalin, Joseph Soviet communist dictator who worked with Allied leaders during Second World War.

Stamp Act Passed by the administration of George Grenville in 1765, the Stamp Act imposed duties on most legal documents in the colonies and on newspapers and other publications. Massive colonial resistance to the act created a major imperial crisis.

staple crop A crop grown for commercial sale. It usually was produced in a colonial area and was sold in Europe. The first staple crops were sugar and tobacco.

Starr, Kenneth Republican lawyer appointed as independent counsel to investigate possible wrongdoing by President Clinton.

States General The legislative assembly of the Netherlands.

stay laws A law that delays or postpones something. During the 1780s, many states passed stay laws to delay the due date on debts because of the serious economic problems of the times.

Strategic Defense Initiative (SDI) Popularly termed "Star Wars," a proposal to develop technology for creation of a space-based defensive missile shield around the United States.

Student Nonviolent Coordinating Committee (SNCC) Interracial civil-rights organization formed by young people involved in the sit-in movement that later adopted a direct-action approach to fighting segregation.

subtreasuries Plan to help farmers escape the ruinous interest rates of the crop lien system by storing their crops in federal warehouses until market prices were more favorable. Farmers could draw low-interest loans against the value of these crops.

subversive Systematic, deliberate attempt to overthrow or undermine a government or society by people working secretly within the country.

Sun Belt Southern rim of the United States running from Florida to California.

Sunday schools Schools that first appeared in the 1790s to teach working-class children to read and write but that by the 1820s and 1830s were becoming moral training grounds.

supply-side economics Economic theory that tax reductions targeted toward investors and businesses would stimulate production and eventually create jobs.

sweated Describes a type of worker, mostly women, who worked in her home producing items for subcontractors, usually in the clothing industry.

synod The governing body of the Presbyterian church. A synod was a meeting of Presbyterian ministers and prominent laymen to set policies for the whole church.

table a petition or bill Act of removing a petition or bill from consideration without debate by placing it at the end of the legislative agenda.

Taft, William Howard Roosevelt's successor as president (1909–1913), who tried but failed to mediate between reformers and conservatives in the Republican Party.

tariff A tax on imports.

task system A system of slave labor under which slaves had to complete specific assignments each day. After these assignments were finished, their time was their own. It was used primarily on rice plantations. Slaves often preferred this system over gang labor because it gave them more autonomy and free time.

Teapot Dome scandal Political scandal by which Secretary of Interior Albert Fall allowed oil tycoons access to government oil reserves in exchange for $400,000 in bribes.

Tecumseh Shawnee leader who assumed political and military leadership of the pan-Indian religious movement began by his brother Tenskwatawa.

tejanos Spanish-speaking settlers of Texas. The term comes from the Spanish word *Tejas* for Texas.

temperance Movement that supported abstaining from alcoholic beverages.

tenancy System under which farmers worked land that they did not own.

Tennessee Valley Authority (TVA) Ambitious and successful use of government resources and power to promote economic development throughout the Tennessee Valley.

Tenochtitlán The huge Aztec capital city destroyed by Cortés.

Tenskwatawa Brother of Tecumseh, whose religious vision of 1805 called for the unification of Indians west of the Appalachians and foretold the defeat and disappearance of the whites.

termination and relocation Policies designed to assimilate American Indians by terminating tribal status and relocating individuals off reservations.

Tet offensive Surprise National Liberation Front (NLF) attack during the lunar new year holiday in early 1968 that brought high casualties to the NLF but fueled pessimism about the war's outcome in the United States.

The Man That Nobody Knows Bruce Barton's best-selling, 1925 book depicting Jesus as a business executive.

think tank Group or agency organized to conduct intensive research or engage in problem solving, especially in developing new technology, military strategy, or social planning.

Third Reich New empire that Adolf Hitler promised the German people would bring glory and unity to the nation.

Third World Less economically developed areas of the world, primarily the Middle East, Asia, Latin America, and Africa.

Tierra del Fuego The region at the southern tip of South America.

tithe A portion of one's income that is owed to the church. In most places, it was one-tenth.

toll roads Roads for which travelers were charged a fee for each use.

tories A term for Irish Catholic peasants who murdered Protestant landlords. It was used to describe the followers of Charles II and became one of the names of the two major political parties in England.

total war New kind of war requiring every combatant to devote virtually all his or her economic and political resources to the fight.

totalitarian movement Movement in which the individual is subordinated to the state and all areas of life are subjected to centralized, total control—usually by force.

Townshend Revenue Act Passed by Parliament in 1767, this act imposed import duties on tea, paper, glass, red and white lead, and painter's colors. It provoked the imperial crisis of 1767–1770. In 1770, Parliament repealed all of the duties except the one on tea.

traditionalists Those who believed that God's word transcended science and that

America should continue to be guided by older hierarchies (men over women, whites over nonwhites, native-born over immigrants).

transcontinental railroad Railroad line that connected with other lines to provide continuous rail transportation from coast to coast.

treasury notes Paper money used by the Union to help finance the Civil War. One type of treasury note was known as a greenback because of its color.

Triangle Shirtwaist Company New York City site of a tragic 1911 industrial fire that killed 146 workers who were unable to find their way to safety.

Triple Alliance One set of combatants in World War I, consisting of Germany, Austria-Hungary, and Italy. When Italy left the alliance, this side became known as the Central Powers.

Triple Entente One set of combatants in World War I, consisting of Britain, France, and Russia. As the war went on, this side came to be known as the Allies or Allied Powers.

Truman, Harry S. Franklin Roosevelt's Vice President who became president when Roosevelt died on April 13, 1945.

trust Large corporations that controlled a substantial share of any given market.

Turner, Nat Baptist lay preacher whose religious visions encouraged him to lead a slave revolt in southern Virginia in 1831 in which 55 whites were killed—more than any other American slave revolt.

Turner's frontier thesis Theory developed by historian Frederick Jackson Turner, who argued that the frontier had been central to the shaping of American character and the success of the U.S. economy and democracy.

Twenty Negro Law Confederate conscription law that exempted from the draft one white man on every plantation owning 20 or more slaves. The law's purpose was to exempt overseers or owners who would ensure discipline over the slaves and keep up production but was regarded as discrimination by nonslaveholding families.

U-2 spy plane Aircraft specializing in high-altitude reconnaissance.

Ulster The northern province of Ireland that provided 70 percent of the Irish immigrants in the colonial period. Nearly all of them were Presbyterians whose forebears had moved to Ireland from Scotland in the previous century. They sometimes are called Scots-Irish today.

Uncle Tom's Cabin Published by Harriet Beecher Stowe in 1852, this sentimental novel told the story of the Christian slave Uncle Tom and became a best seller and the most powerful antislavery tract of the antebellum years.

underconsumptionism Theory that underconsumption, or a chronic weakness in consumer demand, had caused the depression. This theory guided the Second New Deal, leading to the passage of laws designed to stimulate consumer demand.

underground railroad A small group who helped slaves escape bondage in the South. It took on legendary status, and its role was much exaggerated.

UNESCO (United Nations Educational, Scientific, and Cultural Organization) UN organization intended to create peace and security through collaboration among member nations.

unicameral legislature A legislature with only one chamber or house.

Union Leagues Organizations that informed African American voters of, and mobilized them to, support the Republican Party.

Unionists Southerners who remained loyal to the Union during the Civil War.

universal male suffrage System that allowed all adult males to vote without regard to property, religious, or race qualifications or limitations.

urban corridors Metropolitan strips of population running between older cities.

vestry A group of prominent men who managed the lay affairs of the local Anglican church, often including the choice of the minister, especially in Virginia.

vice-admiralty courts These royal courts handled the disposition of enemy ships captured in time of war, adjudicated routine maritime disputes between, for example, a ship's crew and its owner, and occasionally tried to decide cases involving parliamentary regulation of colonial commerce. This last category was the most controversial. These courts did not use juries.

Victorianism Moral code of conduct that advocated modesty, sexual restraint, and separate spheres of activity and influence for men and women.

Vietnam War Conflict lasting from 1946 to 1975, with direct U.S. military involvement from 1964 to 1973. Highly controversial, the war devastated the Vietnam countryside, spilled into all of Indochina, and ended in a victory for communist North Vietnam, which then united the country under its rule.

Vietnamization Policy whereby the South Vietnamese were to assume more of the military burdens of the war and allow the United States to withdraw combat troops.

virtual representation The English concept that Members of Parliament represented the entire empire, not just a local constituency and its voters. According to this theory, settlers were represented in Parliament in the same way that nonvoting subjects in Britain were represented. The colonists accepted virtual representation for nonvoting settlers within their colonies but denied that the term could describe their relationship with Parliament.

VJ Day August 15, 1945, day on which the war in the Pacific was won by the Allies.

Voting Rights Act of 1965 Law that provided new federal mechanisms to help guarantee African Americans the right to vote.

Wagner Act (NLRA) Named after its sponsor Senator Robert Wagner (D-NY), this

1935 act gave every worker the right to join a union and compelled employers to bargain with unions in good faith.

Walker, Madame C. J. Black entrepreneur who built a lucrative business from the hair and skin lotions she devised and sold to black customers throughout the country.

War Hawks Members of the 12th Congress, most of them young nationalists from southern and western areas, who promoted war with Britain.

War Industries Board U.S. government agency responsible for mobilizing American industry for war production.

war on terrorism Global effort, adopted after the attacks of September 11, 2001, by the United States and its allies to neutralize international groups deemed "terrorists," primarily radical Islamic groups such as Al Qaeda.

Washington, George A veteran of the French and Indian War, Washington was named commander-in-chief of the Continental Army by the Second Continental Congress in 1775 and won notable victories at Boston, Trenton, Princeton, and Yorktown, where Lord Cornwallis's army surrendered to him in 1781. His fellow delegates chose him to preside over the deliberations of the Philadelphia Convention in 1787, and after the federal Constitution was ratified, he was unanimously chosen the first president of the United States for two terms.

Watergate Business and residential complex in Washington, D.C., that came to stand for the political espionage and cover-ups directed by the Nixon administration. The complicated web of Watergate scandals brought about Nixon's resignation in 1974.

Western development Disproportionate amount of New Deal funds sent to Rocky Mountain and Pacific Coast areas to provide water and electricity for urban and agricultural development.

wheat blast A plant disease that affected wheat and first appeared in New England in the 1660s. There were no known remedies for the disease, and it gradually spread until wheat production in New England nearly ceased.

Wheatley, Phillis Eight-year-old Phillis Wheatley arrived in Boston from Africa in 1761 and was sold as a slave to wealthy John and Susannah Wheatley. Susannah taught her to read and write, and in 1767 she published her first poem in Boston. In 1773, she visited London to celebrate the publication there of a volume of her poetry, an event that made her a transatlantic sensation. On her return to Boston, the Wheatleys emancipated her.

Whigs The name of an obscure sect of Scottish religious extremists who favored the assassination of Charles and James of England. The term was used to denote one of the two leading political parties of late 17th-century England.

Whiskey Rebellion Revolt in Western Pennsylvania against the federal excise tax on whiskey.

whiskey ring Network of distillers and revenue agents that cheated the government out of millions of tax dollars.

Whitney, Eli The Connecticut-born tutor who invented the cotton gin.

wolfpacks German submarine groups that attacked enemy merchant ships or convoys.

Works Progress Administration Federal relief agency established in 1935 that disbursed billions to pay for infrastructural improvements and funded a vast program of public art.

Wounded Knee Site of a shootout between Indians and Army troops at the Pine Ridge Indian reservation in southwestern South Dakota.

XYZ Affair Incident that precipitated an undeclared war with France when three French officials (identified as X, Y, and Z) demanded that American emissaries pay a bribe before negotiating disputes between the two countries.

Yankee A Dutch word for New Englanders that originally meant something like "land pirate."

yankeephobia Popular term describing strong dislike of the United States, whose citizens were referred to as "yankees," in Latin America.

yellow dog contracts Written pledges by employees promising not to join a union while they were employed.

yellow journalism Newspaper stories embellished with sensational or titillating details when the true reports did not seem dramatic enough.

yeoman A farmer who owned his own farm.

"Young America" movement A group of young members of the Democratic Party who were interested in territorial expansion in the 1840s.

Yorktown The last major engagement of the Revolutionary War. Washington's army, two French armies, and a French fleet trapped Lord Cornwallis at Yorktown and forced his army to surrender in October 1781.

Zenger, John Peter Printer of the *New York Weekly Journal* who was acquitted in 1735 by a jury of the crime of seditious libel after his paper sharply criticized Governor William Cosby.

Zimmerman telegram Telegram from Germany's foreign secretary instructing the German minister in Mexico to ask that country's government to attack the United States in return for German assistance in regaining Mexico's "lost provinces" (Texas, New Mexico, and Arizona).

Zion A term used by the Mormons to describe their "promised land" where they could prosper and live without persecution.

Photo Credits

Chapter 17

p. 629 (left): Library of Congress, Prints and Photographs Division; **p. 629 (right):** Library of Congress, Prints and Photographs Division; **p. 633:** Photographs and Prints Division, Schomburg Center for Research in Black Culture, The New York Public Library, Astor, Lenox and Tilden Foundations.; **p. 637:** Library of Congress, Prints and Photographs Division; **p. 647:** © CORBIS; **p. 649:** © Bettmann/CORBIS; **p. 651:** © Bettmann/CORBIS

Chapter 18

p. 665: © Bettmann/CORBIS; **p. 669:** TM and Copyright © 20th Century Fox Film Corp. All rights reserved. Courtesy: Everett Collection; **p. 674:** Library of Congress, Prints and Photographs Division; **p. 681:** © Bettmann/CORBIS; **p. 687:** © The Granger Collection, New York

Chapter 19

p. 697: Library of Congress, Prints and Photographs Division; **p. 705:** © Bettmann/CORBIS; **p. 712:** Library of Congress, Prints and Photographs Division; **p. 722:** North Wind Picture Archive; **p. 725:** The Kansas State Historical Society Topeka, Kansas

Chapter 20

p. 737: © Lake County Museum/CORBIS; **p. 742:** © Hulton Archive/Getty Images; **p. 751:** © Bettmann/CORBIS; **p. 761:** © Bettmann/CORBIS; **p. 762:** A'Lelia Bundles/Walker Family Collection/www.madamcjwalker.com; **p. 765:** Underwood Photo Archives; **p. 768:** © Bettmann/CORBIS

Chapter 21

p. 774: Culver Pictures; **p. 777:** Brown Brothers; **p. 779:** © CORBIS; **p. 790:** Wisconsin Historical Society; **p. 793:** © Bettmann/CORBIS; **p. 801:** Brown Brothers

Chapter 22

p. 815: © The Granger Collection, New York; **p. 820 (top):** © Bettmann/CORBIS; **p. 820 (bottom):** © The Granger Collection, New York; **p. 825:** "*A Philippine Album: American Era Photographs*" by Jonathan Best. (Bookmark, Manila 1998); **p. 827:** Prints and Photographs Division, Library of Congress; **p. 833:** North Wind Picture Archive

Chapter 23

p. 846: Wisconsin Historical Society; **p. 854:** National Archives; **p. 855:** National Archives; **p. 859:** Imperial War Museum, London; **p. 863:** © Bettmann/CORBIS;

p. 870: © Paramount Pictures/Courtesy: Everett Collection.; **p. 872:** Library of Congress, Prints and Photographs Division

Chapter 24
p. 880: © The Granger Collection, New York; **p. 886:** © Hulton-Deutsch Collection/CORBIS; **p. 889:** © CORBIS; **p. 896:** Brown Brothers; **p. 903:** © John Springer Collection/CORBIS; **p. 910:** © Bettmann/CORBIS; **p. 913:** Security Pacific Collection/Los Angeles Public Library

Chapter 25
p. 922: © Bettmann/CORBIS; **p. 925:** © Bettmann/CORBIS; **p. 930:** © The Granger Collection, New York; **p. 935:** FDR Library; **p. 936:** © Bettmann/CORBIS; **p. 939:** © Lester Lefkowitz/CORBIS; **p. 951:** The Michael Barson Collection

Chapter 26
p. 971: © The Granger Collection, New York; **p. 981:** National Archives #127-N-69559-A; **p. 984 (top):** © Bettmann/CORBIS; **p. 984 (bottom):** © Bettmann/CORBIS; **p. 987:** National Archives; **p. 995:** Everett Collection; **p. 996:** © CORBIS; **p. 1000:** © Universal Pictures/Courtesy: Everett Collection

Chapter 27
p. 1011: © The Granger Collection, New York; **p. 1026:** © Bettmann/CORBIS; **p. 1028:** Library of Congress, Prints and Photographs Division; **p. 1037:** © Margaret Bourke-White/ Time Life Pictures/Getty Images; **p. 1041:** The Michael Barson Collection

Chapter 28
p. 1062 (top): © Bettmann/CORBIS; **p. 1062 (bottom):** © Elliott Erwitt/Magnum Photos, Inc.; **p. 1068:** Library of Congress, Prints and Photographs Division; **p. 1077:** © Bettmann/ CORBIS; **p. 1079:** © Don Cravens/Time Life Pictures/Getty Images

Chapter 29
p. 1116: AP Images/Eddie Adams; **p. 1125:** Everett Collection; **p. 1134:** © UPI-Bettmann/CORBIS; **p. 1142:** AP Images; **p. 1145:** © Bettmann/CORBIS

Chapter 30
p. 1160: © Time & Life Pictures/Getty Images; **p. 1169:** © Eve Arnold/Magnum Photos, Inc.; **p. 1175:** © Bettmann/CORBIS; **p. 1182:** © Owen Franken/CORBIS; **p. 1191:** © Reuters/CORBIS; **p. 1194:** © Andre Jenny/The Image Works; **p. 1197:** © Ralf-Finn Hestoft/ CORBIS

Chapter 31
p. 1207: © Richard Cummins/CORBIS; **p. 1213:** © Keren Su/CORBIS; **p. 1221:** TM and Copyright © 20th Century Fox Film Corp. All rights reserved./The Everett Collection; **p. 1226:** © Rebecca Cook/Reuters/CORBIS

Chapter 32
p. 1237: AP Images/Dennis Paquin; **p. 1243:** AP Images/Gary I. Rothstein; **p. 1245:** AP Images/Pablo Martinez Monsivais; **p. 1249:** AP Images/Khalid Mohammed; **p. 1255:** © Smiley N. Pool/Dallas Morning News/CORBIS

Index

National Defense Education Act
(1958), 1090
National Endowment for the Arts
(NEA), 1200
National Endowment for the
Humanities (NEH),
1200
National Farmers' Alliance and
Industrial Union, 728
National Football League (NFL),
1217
National forests, 798–799
conservation of, 1237–1238
jurisdiction over, 798–799
National Forest Service, 798
Ballinger-Pinchot controversy
and, 800–801
National government.
See Government (U.S.)
National Guard
at Central High School, 1082
in First World War, 844
freedom riders and, 1098
National Hockey League (NHL),
1217
National Industrial Recovery Act
(NIRA, 1933), 931, 942
Nationalism. *See also* Imperialism
distrust of, 1058
jingoism as, 813–814
of Roosevelt, Theodore, 796
Nationalism (socialism form of
Bellamy), 711
Nationalist China, 966
foreign aid to, 1018–1019
Second World War and, 973,
980
Nationalist Party (South Africa),
1024
National Labor Relations Act
(NLRA, 1935), 945, 946, 956
National Labor Relations Board
(NLRB), 946, 1065
National Labor Union, 718–719
National Liberation Front (NLF),
1095–1096
National monuments, 798, 1237
National Organization for Women
(NOW), 1187
National origins system
of immigration, 899
quotas and, 1206
National parks, 798
National Recovery Administration
(NRA), 935–936

National Review (magazine), 1087,
1163
National security
anticommunism and,
1025–1033
in Cold War, 1009–1018
education and, 1089–1090
under Eisenhower, 1053
McCarran Internal Security Act
and, 1031
military offensive and, 1247
payment for, 1061
politics of, 1253–1257
president's power and,
1256–1257
Reagan and, 1176
spying and, 1030–1032
National Security Act (1947),
1014, 1033
National Security Council (NSC),
1014
CIA mandate and, 1056
NSC-68 and, 1019–1020, 1024
National Socialist (Nazi) Party,
965
National Trails Act (1968), 1140
National Union of Social Justice
(NUSJ), 941
National Union Party, 636
National Urban League, 794
National War Labor Board
(NWLB), 853
National Wild and Scenic Rivers
Act (1968), 1140
National Woman's Party (NWP),
767, 789
National Woman Suffrage
Association, 640
National Youth Administration
(NYA), 946
Nation building
as policy, 1239
in Vietnam, 1060
Nation of Islam, 1126, 1225
Native American Graves
Protection and Repatriation
Act (1990), 1195
Native American Rights Fund
(NARF), 1195
Native Americans. *See* American
Indians
Native Son (Wright), 1029
Nativism
Chinese immigrants and, 663
immigration and, 899

NATO. *See* North Atlantic Treaty
Organization (NATO)
Natural History Museum
(New York City), 709
Natural resources, preservation of,
798–799
Natural science, 703
Navajo Indians, 957, 981
Navajo Signal Corps, 981
Naval bases, in Second World
War, 975
Navy (U.S.)
African American dockworkers
killed in, 998
expenditures and battleship size
in (1890–1914), 814
in First World War, 844
Great White Fleet and, 833–834
Guantanamo base for, 824
Mahan and, 812
in Manila, 821
rearmament and, 967
in Second World War, 979
sonar, 849
in Spanish-American War, 817
NAWSA. *See* National American
Woman Suffrage Association
(NAWSA)
Nazi Germany
Austria and, 967
collapse of, 978
defeat of, 978
dismemberment of, 1005–1006
expansion by, 969 (map)
Hitler and, 960
Japanese attack on Pearl Harbor
and, 974
Soviet pact with, 967
war crimes by, 978
"Nazi gold," 978
NBA. *See* National Basketball
Association (NBA)
NBC, 1220. *See also* Television
NCPAC. *See* National
Conservative Political Action
Committee (NCPAC)
NEA. *See* National Endowment for
the Arts (NEA)
Near East
after First World War, 862
immigrants from, 747
Nebraska, 673
Nebraska Territory, Indian "policy
of concentration" and, 676
"Needle trades," 1215